SURVEYS IN
SOCIAL RESEARCH

Social Research Today **edited by Martin Bulmer**

The *Social Research Today* series provides concise and contemporary introductions to significant methodological topics in the social sciences. Covering both quantitative and qualitative methods, this new series features readable and accessible books from some of the leading names in the field and is aimed at students and professional researchers alike. This series also brings together for the first time the best titles from the old *Social Research Today* and *Contemporary Social Research* series edited by Martin Bulmer for UCL Press and Routledge.

Other series titles include:

Principles of Research Design in the Social Sciences Frank Bechhofer and
    Lindsay Paterson
Social Impact Assessment Henk Becker
The Turn to Biographical Methods in Social Science edited by Prue
    Chamberlayne, Joanna Bornat and Tom Wengraf
Quantity and Quality in Social Research Alan Bryman
Research Methods and Organisational Studies Alan Bryman
Field Research: A Sourcebook and Field Manual Robert G Burgess
In the Field: An Introduction to Field Research Robert G Burgess
Research Design second edition Catherine Hakim
Measuring Health and Medical Outcomes edited by Crispin Jenkinson
Methods of Criminological Research Victor Jupp
Information Technology for the Social Scientist edited by Raymond M Lee
An Introduction to the Philosophy of Social Research Tim May and
    Malcolm Williams
*Researching Social and Economic Change: The Uses of Household Panel
    Studies* edited by David Rose
Researching the Powerful in Education edited by Geoffrey Walford

Martin Bulmer is Professor of Sociology and co-director of the Institute of Social Research at the University of Surrey. He is also Academic Director of the Question Bank in the ESRC Centre for Applied Social Surveys, London.

SURVEYS IN SOCIAL RESEARCH

Fifth edition

David de Vaus

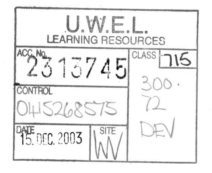

Routledge
Taylor & Francis Group

LONDON AND NEW YORK

First published in 1985
Fifth edition 2002
Reprinted 2004

Published in Australia by:
Allen & Unwin, 83 Alexander Street, Crows Nest NSW 2065
PO Box 8500, St Leonards NSW 1590, Australia

Published elsewhere (excluding North America) by:
Routledge, 11 New Fetter Lane, London EC4P 4EE

Routledge is an imprint of the Taylor & Francis Group

Typeset in Australia by Midland Typesetters, Maryborough, Vic.
Printed and bound in Great Britain by
St Edmundsbury Press Ltd, Bury St Edmunds, Suffolk

British Library Cataloguing in Publication Data
A catalogue record for this book is available from the British Library

ISBN 0-415-26857-5 (hbk)
ISBN 0-415-26858-3 (pbk)

Brief contents

Detailed contents

Boxes, figures, web pointers and tables

FIGURES

WEB POINTERS

TABLES

Preface

This fifth edition of *Surveys in Social Research* is a major revision of the previous editions. Nearly every chapter has been rewritten and includes substantial new sections. The book appears to have met a need among those teaching, studying and undertaking social surveys. I am most grateful for the support and feedback I have received from readers over the years. When I wrote the first edition in 1984 I used a pen and paper: personal computers were not widely available. The internet was a barely accessible resource for specialists in universities, computer-assisted telephone interviewing was still a novelty and the widespread availability of all types of software with easy to use graphical interfaces was unimaginable.

In just one and a half decades the variety and power of the tools and resources available to assist the survey researcher have improved and expanded in ways that have transformed the way in which we go about doing surveys. Most survey researchers have access to very powerful personal computers and software. The software and the hardware are so much easier to use and more powerful and there is so much software to choose from for so many purposes (statistical analysis, graphics, simulations, calculators, spreadsheets, database packages, questionnaire design software, questionnaire administration software etc). Access to wonderful data bases from data archives, downloading of evaluation software from the inter-

net, web-based questionnaires, email surveys, descriptions of analysis methods online and free online textbooks have presented so many new possibilities for the way in which survey research can be taught and practised.

While the resources and possibilities have expanded so dramatically our capacity to learn about them, to find out about them and to make use of them has not kept pace. This is hardly surprising as the volume of new developments is overwhelming.

One of the reasons for revising this book so much is to take advantage of these developments and to guide readers and instructors in their use of these resources. Throughout the text I have provided web pointers which supply web addresses (URLs) for sites you can visit. These point to software sites from which excellent software can be downloaded or used online. You will find sites where you can develop and administer surveys via the internet. Other sites provide online references that expand on the points I make in the book, while some provide simulation software that enable you to experiment and see what happens with statistical results under particular conditions. These web links also take you closer to the real world of research. You will see, online, copies of major questionnaires and codebooks. You can conduct analysis of these data sets online. You can look up the standard coding systems used in major surveys. You can examine results of other research on topics you are studying and find question banks containing excellent sets of questions that other researchers have used. I have tried to make this edition a gateway to discover some of the many online resources that are available.

This edition has also introduced other major revisions. I have paid far more systematic attention to the use of graphs in data analysis. The availability of graphing software has led to an explosion in the use of graphs but graphs are widely misused. Published research too often produces unreadable graphs, graphs with the axes the wrong way around and graphs that are simply inappropriate to the data being displayed. I have focused on the main types of graphs, how to present them and when to use them.

There is a greater emphasis on statistical inference in this edition. In line with current developments more attention has been given to the use of confidence intervals.

The chapter on questionnaire construction has been completely rewritten and expanded. A major addition to the book are the sections on internet samples and new forms of questionnaire administration. Computer-based questionnaire administration is transforming the practice of social research. New methods of administration include web-based questionnaires, email questionnaires, computer-assisted personal interviews, disk by mail questionnaires and other forms of electronic data collection. No book on survey research can afford to ignore these developments which some commentators believe will be the main way in which questionnaires will be conducted in the relatively near future.

There are many other changes throughout the book. I hope that these help readers gain a better appreciation of the art and practice of survey research. I am most grateful to students, readers and other instructors for the positive and most helpful feedback they have provided to me over the years. Many of the changes in this edition result from that feedback. Please continue to provide the feedback.

The heavy use of web links and advice about web-based software raises a problem. The internet is a very dynamic environment. Websites that are available one day either disappear or are restructured so that some of the links I have provided will no longer work by the time you read this book. Furthermore new resources constantly become available. To minimise this problem I have established a website of my own. This website will provide:

■ the links listed in this book (so go to this site and simply click the links rather than (mis)typing them in yourself);
■ any updates for these links;
■ new links I learn of.

Please visit my site and make use of these links. To help make this website useful and up-to-date I invite readers to email me (see website) with:

■ any sites that are not listed which you think might be useful to add;
■ feedback on sites that are no longer working;
■ your comments or questions about the revised edition.

The address of my website is:
www.social-research.org
My email address is:
ddevaus@social-research.org

Finally, I wish to thank those who have enabled me to write this fifth edition. Elizabeth Weiss at Allen & Unwin and Mari Shullaw at Routledge encouraged me to develop this edition and have been patient as I have produced. I thank La Trobe University for providing time away from teaching and administration to make the changes. Finally, I would like to dedicate this book in memory of my friend Gordon Ternowetsky. Gordon was a truly good person whose death has left a big gap in so many lives.

David de Vaus
July 2001

Part I

THE SCOPE OF SURVEY RESEARCH

1

The nature of surveys

The purpose of this chapter is to outline briefly what is meant by the term survey research. Any examination of texts on social research or the popular media shows that the term survey research is used in many different ways. To avoid confusion we must be clear at the beginning about how the term will be used in this book. The way we define what a survey is affects the range of topics for which we can use a survey, the way in which we conduct a survey and our evaluation of the merits and shortcomings of the survey method.

The primary aim of this book is to provide guidance on how to do good surveys. Some critics of the survey method have responded to problems evident in many surveys by urging that we move away from survey research altogether and employ entirely different research methodologies. However, the solution to criticisms of surveys need not be to abandon survey research but to solve the problems that the critics assume are inherent to the survey approach.

Many criticisms of surveys are based on misunderstandings of what surveys can be and are based on examples of poor surveys and the inappropriate use of survey research. This is not the place to review these criticisms or to argue how they are frequently misinformed. The best discussion of these criticisms is available in Catherine Marsh's book titled *The Survey Method: The Contribution of Surveys to Socio-*logical Explanation (1982). The focus of the present book is to show what can be achieved with a good survey and how to achieve this.

WHAT IS A SURVEY?

A survey is *not* just a particular technique of collecting information: questionnaires are widely used but other techniques, such as structured and in-depth interviews, observation, content analysis and so forth, can also be used in survey research. The distinguishing features of surveys are the form of the data and the method of analysis.

Form of data

Surveys are characterised by a structured or systematic set of data which I will call a variable by case data grid. All this means is that we collect information about the same variables or characteristics from at least two (normally far more) cases and end up with a data grid. In Table 1.1 each row represents a case (person) and each column represents a variable or information collected about each case. Since the same information is collected for each case the cases are directly comparable and we end up with a structured or 'rectangular' set of data.

Table 1.1   A variable by case data grid

		Sex	Age	Political orientation	Social class
				Variables	
	Person 1	male	36 years	progressive	working
	Person 2	male	19 years	moderate	lower middle
Cases	Person 3	female	30 years	progressive	upper working
	Person 4	male	55 years	traditionalist	upper middle
	Person 5	female	42 years	traditionalist	middle

The technique by which we generate data about the cases can vary between surveys. We might collect information by giving a questionnaire to each person and then copying answers from each questionnaire into the data grid. Because questionnaires are highly structured they provide a straightforward way of obtaining information for the data grid. However, the data for the grid could be collected by other means such as interviewing or observing each case, by extracting information from records we have on each person or by many other means. There is no *necessary* connection between questionnaires and survey research.

The absence of a necessary connection between the survey method and a particular data collection technique is reinforced by the fact that the cases in the variable by cases data grid need not be people. Technically the case in the data grid is called a *unit of analysis*—it is the 'object' about which we are collecting information. While this frequently is a person it need not be. We could construct a data grid in which the unit of analysis was a country, a year or virtually anything so long as we collect attributes of that case (see section on units of analysis in Chapter 3). If countries were the cases, a list of countries would be listed down the side of the table instead of people, and attributes of countries (e.g. population size, area, density, unemployment rate) would be listed across

the top. If years were the cases, years (e.g. 1970, 1980, 1990, 2000) would be listed down the side with attributes relevant to years across the top (e.g. inflation rate in particular years, divorce rate).

The variable by case data grid is fundamental for survey *analysis* which is based on a comparison of cases. It is this method of analysing data which is the second distinguishing feature of surveys.

Methods of analysis

One function of survey analysis is to describe the characteristics of a set of cases. Thus if we want to describe how a group of people will vote, we need to know how each person in that group intends to vote. A variable by case grid provides this information.

But survey researchers are also interested in causes of phenomena. The survey analyst tries to locate causes by comparing cases. By looking at how cases vary on some characteristics (e.g. some cases will be political progressives and others will be traditionalists), the survey analyst will see if the progressives are systematically different from the traditionalists in some additional way. For example, in Table 1.1 there is variation between cases in how they vote. This is systematically linked to variations in class: the progressives are working class and the traditionalists are middle class. In other words, survey

---

WEB POINTER 1.1   *Units of analysis*

Clear and brief description of the idea of units of analysis.

http://trochim.human.cornell.edu/kb/unitanal.htm

research seeks an understanding of what may cause some phenomenon (e.g. vote) by looking at variation in that variable across cases, and looking for other characteristics which are systematically linked with it. As such it aims to draw causal inferences (e.g. class affects vote) by a careful comparison of the various characteristics of cases. It does not end there. The next step is to ask why class affects vote. Survey researchers need to be very careful, however, to avoid mistaken attribution of causal links (simply to demonstrate that two things go together does not prove a causal link).

This style of research and analysis can be contrasted with other methods. For example, the case study method focuses on particular cases and tries to develop a full and rounded understanding of the cases. The case study method does not fundamentally rely on comparing cases but on fully understanding the 'wholeness' of a particular case and understanding particular attributes of a person (or an organisation or whatever the case is) within the context of the case's other characteristics and history. The experimental method is similar to the survey method in that data are collected in the variable by case grid form, but is fundamentally different in that the variation between the attributes of people is *created by intervention* from an experimenter wanting to see if the intervention creates a difference. For example, the experimenter who wants to know whether a drug cures a disease would take a group of sufferers and divide them into two similar groups. The drug would be administered to only one group and then the recovery rates of the drug and non-drug groups would be compared. Here the variation between the two groups (i.e. drug/non-drug) has been created by the experimenter. A survey approach would not create the variation but would find 'naturally occurring' variation; that is, find a group of sufferers who did not have the drug and compare them with a group of sufferers who did have the drug.

The problem for survey researchers is that they cannot be sure that the two groups are similar in other respects, whereas the experimenter begins with two similar groups and the only difference (in theory) is that only one group receives the treatment. Therefore any difference in recovery rates must be due to the drug. Apart from the potential ethical problems of experimental research (see Chapter 5), these different approaches to obtaining variation between groups lead to quite different methods of analysis.

In any particular study a range of research methods can be used. For example, a study of causes of industrial disputes could involve a survey of attitudes of management and workers, a case study of a particular strike or a particular factory and an experiment where groups of workers work under different conditions to see if this affects the frequency of disputes.

The techniques by which data are collected using any of these methods can vary considerably. In a survey we could observe each case, interview them, give them a questionnaire and so on.

In summary, survey research is one method of collecting, organising and analysing data. The relevant data can be collected by a variety of techniques and in many studies it may be appropriate to use a range of research methods (see Figure 1.1).

QUANTITATIVE AND QUALITATIVE RESEARCH

Survey research is widely regarded as being inherently quantitative and positivistic and is contrasted to qualitative methods that involve participant observation, unstructured interviewing, case studies, focus groups etc. Quantitative survey research is sometimes portrayed as being sterile and unimaginative but well suited to providing certain types of factual, descriptive information—the hard evidence. Qualitative methods are often regarded as providing rich data about real life people and situations and being more able to make sense of behaviour and to understand behaviour within its wider context. However qualitative research is often criticised for lacking generalisability, being too reliant on the subjective interpretations of researchers and being incapable of replication by subsequent researchers.

This distinction between quantitative and qualitative research is frequently unhelpful and misleading. It is more helpful to distinguish between two stages of the research process: collecting data and analysing data.

At the data collection stage it is more useful to distinguish between research methods that yield structured and unstructured data sets than between methods that are quantitative or qualitative. I have already argued that the data grid required for survey research can be filled in using a variety of data collection methods. Furthermore the nature of the data

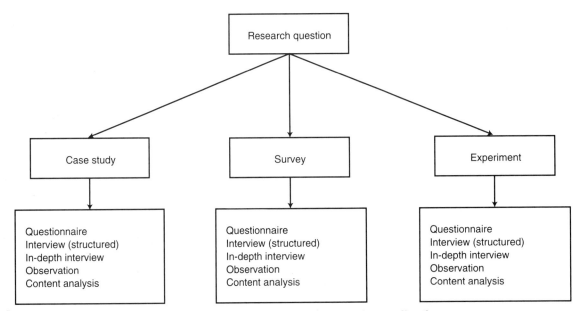

Figure 1.1   A range of methods of research and techniques of data collection

---

WEB POINTER 1.2   *Positivism and survey research*

A brief but useful description of the term positivism.

http://trochim.human.cornell.edu/kb/positvsm.htm

For a more challenging discussion of differences between qualitative and quantitative methods and the assumptions that underlie both approaches you should read two articles by Howard Becker.

www.soc.ucsb.edu/faculty/hbecker/theory.html

www.soc.ucsb.edu/faculty.hbecker/qa.html

---

that are collected for the grid need not be quantitative at all. Each cell in the grid might be filled with numeric or quantitative data (e.g. age, income, years of education, score on an IQ test, number of times assaulted etc) or it may be filled with much more qualitative information. For example the variable (column) about which we are collecting information can be used to indicate the nature of a person's marriage. We could simply ask them to rate the marriage on a scale of 0 to 10 or we could enquire at some depth about the nature of the marriage. In the course of our enquiry we may collect information about equality, conflict, ways of handling conflict, feelings of intimacy and so forth. The clues about equality, conflict, intimacy etc may come from specific interview questions, may be based on obser-

vations or may be based on information gleaned from a number of different topics discussed in a relatively unstructured interview. Whether the data are quantitative or are collected with a questionnaire or some other method does not go hand in hand with a survey. The survey will simply collect *systematic* data that allows for systematic comparison between cases on the same characteristics. Similarly we might collect quantitative data but this does not mean we are conducting a survey. If this is collected from only one case (as in a case study) or is collected only spasmodically from cases we do not have the structured data set that permits survey analysis.

The quantitative/qualitative distinction is also not especially helpful at the data analysis stage. While statistical techniques are typically employed to analyse survey research it is the *logic* of analysis that distinguishes survey research. The logic of survey analysis is that variation in one variable is matched with variations in other variables. The notion of co-variation is not an inherently statistical concept—it is a logical concept that has been systematically formulated by Mill (1879). Statistical methods have been developed as indices of co-variation but this does not mean that the method of analysis is quantitative or statistical. Similarly, causal analysis is a common feature of survey research. That is, survey data are used to evaluate whether one variable affects another (e.g. does religion affect voting preference?). Again, statistical tools are frequently used and are helpful as part of the process of evaluating whether one variable affects another but causal analysis is fundamentally a logical rather than a statistical process.

It is most useful to think of survey research by emphasising that it is a structured approach to data collection and analysis and that it relies on a particular logic of analysis. Typifying survey research using the quantitative/qualitative distinction is misleading and emphasises the use of statistical analysis and quantitative measures at the expense of highlighting the fundamental characteristics of the survey method.

PRACTICE VS IDEAL TYPES

A basic difficulty when trying to describe how to do research is the gap between textbook accounts of how research *should* be done and how it actually *is* done. A number of valuable books have now been published in which some researchers 'come clean' and provide accounts of how they did their research (e.g. Bell and Newby, 1977; Bell and Encel, 1978).

Like my own experience, theirs does not conform to the textbook models.

What ought to be done in a book like this? To describe an 'ideal-typical' model of survey research, in which each step of research is outlined, is not to describe what researchers do. As such it can mislead. When you actually do some research you will find that you are not doing what you 'should'. So should the book describe the reality? Perhaps. But which one? The course that a piece of research actually takes will be peculiar to that piece of research: it is affected by the research topic, the technique of data collection, the experience and personality of the researcher, the 'politics of the research', the types of people or situation being studied, funding and so on. I could describe my experiences but like an ideal-typical model they would not reflect other people's.

I have decided to do a bit of both. I will outline the key steps which a survey researcher must take at some stage and describe the reasoning behind the order in which it is normally suggested they be taken. But, I will also point out that in practice some steps are omitted, things are done out of order and we move backwards and forwards between steps. Guidelines that are provided are not meant to be prescriptive. The guidelines I describe are like signposts or a map to provide some direction and give us clues as to where to go when we get lost. As you become more familiar with the territory you can manage more easily without the map and learn short cuts. What I describe will not always reflect your research experience but will provide guidance. You should not try to follow each step slavishly. The prime goal of research should be to gain accurate understanding and as a researcher use methods and techniques which enhance understanding. Use the method: do not let it use you.

KEY CONCEPTS

Case	Variable
Data collection technique vs research method	Variable by case data grid
Structured data set	Variation
Unit of analysis	

FURTHER READING

Catherine Marsh's book *The Survey Method* (1982) is the best description of the survey method available. Her outline and evaluation of the most substantial criticisms of surveys is direct, clear and stimulating.

Carr-Hill's paper 'Radicalising Survey Methodology' (1984) approaches the criticisms of surveys somewhat differently but suggests ways of overcoming some of the problems from a radical perspective.

Donsbach's paper on 'Survey Research at the End of the Twentieth Century' (1997) provides a critical evaluation of surveys as they are often practised.

The exchange between Greeley (1996) 'In Defense of Surveys' and Lewontin (1996) 'In Defense of Science' in relation to a particular survey (national survey of American sexual behaviour) highlights some of the practical issues involved in evaluating survey research.

Denzin's *The Research Act* (1978) provides a critique of survey research from a symbolic interactionist perspective as do Blumer's papers 'What is Wrong with Sociological Theory?' (1954) and 'Sociological Analysis and the Variable' (1956).

Chapter 3 of the *Sociological Imagination* (1959) by C.W. Mills on abstracted empiricism is a well-known attack on certain forms of survey research. A very useful discussion of positivism is contained in Halfpenny's 1982 book *Positivism and Sociology: Explaining Social Life* clarifies much of the confusion in the way this concept is used in sociology.

Differences between the various types of research designs is discussed fully in de Vaus' book *Research Design in Social Research* (2001). Chapter 4 of Madge's classic text, *The Tools of Social Science* (1965) provides a concise summary of Mill's logic that is relevant to survey analysis. De Vaus (2001) elaborates on the logic of the methods of survey analysis and on concepts of causality.

EXERCISES

1 Draw a variable by case grid for six people and five variables of your choice. Fill in characteristics for each case.

2 Draw three variables by case grids each using a different unit of analysis from the following list: countries, years and people. In each grid use four cases and five variables appropriate to the selected unit of analysis.

3 Different methods of research (survey, experiment and case study) have different characteristics. Next to each characteristic below indicate the method having the particular characteristic.

   a   Can use questionnaires.

   b   Can use unstructured interviews.

   c   Can use observation.

   d   Can use content analysis.

   e   Uses a variable by case grid.

   f   Is based on 'natural' variation between cases.

   g   Researcher creates variation between cases.

   h   Compares the 'treatment' with the 'no treatment' group for analysis.

4 Imagine that you believe being unemployed leads to a loss of self-esteem. Briefly contrast how the case study, the experiment and the survey would differ in their basic procedure for testing this proposition.

2

Theory and social research

This chapter explores the relationship between theorising about society and researching society. I argue that:

- The role of the social scientist is to theorise—not to do social arithmetic.
- Theories must be rigorously tested in the real world they purport to describe.
- Data collection and analysis must be fashioned by theoretical ideas. Social research should not be the endless and unguided collection of bits and pieces of information.
- Theorising and collecting research data should be interdependent components of 'doing social science'.

This chapter provides some guidance on how to begin to combine theoretical questions with empirical research.

THE INTERACTION OF THEORY AND RESEARCH

Observations require explanation but equally explanations need to be tested against the facts. It is not enough simply to collect facts. Nor is it sufficient simply to develop explanations without testing them against facts. Fundamentally sociological research involves a constant interplay between observation and explanation, collection of further facts to test the explanation, a refinement of the explanation and so on.

The development of good explanations involves two related processes: theory construction and theory testing. These two processes are not alternative ways of arriving at good theories but represent two stages with different starting points (see Figure 2.1).

Theory construction is a process which begins with a set of observations (i.e. description) and moves on to develop theories of these observations. It is also called grounded theory (Glaser and Strauss, 1967 and Strauss and Corbin, 1994) because it is based on observation—not simply armchair speculation. Others call it *post factum* theory (Merton, 1968) or *ex post facto* theory since the theory comes after the observation rather than before. The reasoning process that is used in theory building research is called *inductive* reasoning and involves starting with particular observations and drawing out a theory from the observations.

Theory testing differs in that it starts with a theory. Using the theory we predict how things will be in the 'real' world. If our predictions are correct this lends support to our theory. If they are wrong there are three possible explanations:

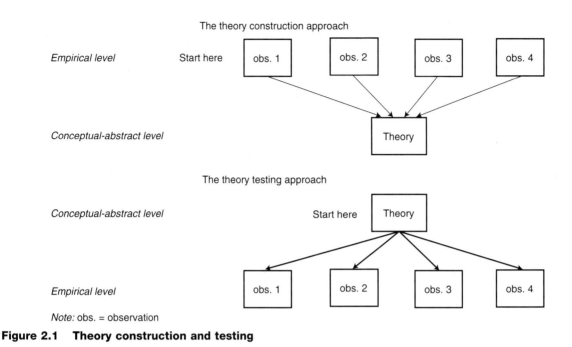

The theory construction approach

Empirical level Start here obs. 1   obs. 2   obs. 3   obs. 4

Conceptual-abstract level Theory

The theory testing approach

Conceptual-abstract level Start here Theory

Empirical level obs. 1   obs. 2   obs. 3   obs. 4

Note: obs. = observation

Figure 2.1 Theory construction and testing

1 The theory is wrong.
2 The prediction has been illogically derived from the theory.
3 The way we have gone about gathering information from the real world was flawed.

The reasoning process employed in theory testing research is called *deductive* reasoning—it involves deducing or predicting that certain things will follow (will be empirically observable) if the theory is true.

Theory building is, in my view, the first stage of developing good explanations, and theory testing follows as an attempt to test rigorously the tentative theory we have arrived at in the theory construction phase. In practice there is a constant interplay between constructing theories and testing them. Rarely are we purely constructing a theory or purely testing a theory.

THE PROCESS OF THEORY CONSTRUCTION

Having made particular observations, the basic question is: *is this observation a particular case of some more general factor?* If it is then we can gain a better understanding of the significance and meaning of the particular observation. For example, Durkheim (1970) observed that the suicide rate was higher among Protestants than among Catholics. But is religious affiliation a particular case of something more general? Of what more general phenomenon might it be an indicator? Similarly, women seem to be more religious than men. Is gender simply a particular case, or an indicator, of some more general concept? Gender might reflect position in the social structure: that women are socially less valued than men and are in this sense deprived. Thus the observation that women are more religious than men might simply indicate a more general pattern that social deprivation leads to increased religiousness.

Establishing the meaning of observations

There is a fundamental difficulty however. How do we know of what more general phenomenon a particular observation might be an indicator? How do we even get ideas of what it might be indicating? It is no simple task to know what particular observations might be indicating at a more general level. There is a real role for creative imagination, a craft which some people seem to be able to master more easily than others. Although there is no ideal way of identifying what the general phenomenon might be there are a number of approaches that can help.

Locating the common factor

If several different factors have a similar outcome we can ask: *what do each of them have in common?* This principle is used in IQ tests where a number of items are listed and you have to pick the odd one out. For example, given the list of pelican, eagle, duck and seagull we work out the odd item by seeing which three items share something in common which the fourth does not. The technique of locating the commonality between particular factors with the same outcome helps us work out the more general concept that the individual observations might represent. An example of this process is provided in Box 2.1.

Existing theories and concepts as a source of ideas

Making a set of observations will not always or even normally lead to the development of new concepts or a new theory. Any attempt to make sense of a set of observations will often use existing concepts and theories. If concepts and theories developed by others seem like reasonable summaries or accounts of what we have observed then we will make use of them. Where our observations are new or different or are not adequately summarised by existing concepts and theories we may need to adapt or modify the existing ideas.

A major problem in using existing theories and concepts is that we may not be open to equally plausible interpretations of the observations. This is especially a problem if we are committed to a perspective. The problem is not so much in using existing

---

BOX 2.1
Durkheim's suicide as an example of inductive reasoning

In his study of suicide Durkheim (1970) developed a social explanation for why people suicide based on inducing a common factor that underlay a set of different facts. He discovered that the suicide statistics indicated that the following groups were the most suicidal:

■ *Protestants* compared with Catholics

■ *older people* compared with younger people

■ *urban dwellers* than rural dwellers

■ *unmarried* than married

■ *childless* than parents

■ *men* than women

■ *wealthy* than poor

Before you read any further see if you can think what the set of suicidal groups (italicised) might have in common. Of what more general factor might they simply be an indicator?

Durkheim believed that he had developed an explanation of suicide by locating such a common factor. He argued that all these types of people were likely to be relatively poorly integrated into society and that it was for this reason that each of these particular types had higher suicide rates. That is, all his particular observations were simply particular cases of the general principle that *the less well integrated people are, the more likely they are to commit suicide.* The likelihood that this induction is correct is increased because he had looked at a number of factors which have the same outcome (higher suicide rate) and he could at least plausibly argue that all the factors shared something in common.

---

concepts but in the level of commitment to them and in failing to examine whether they are the most appropriate ones. When we are committed to a model, whether it be Freudian, Marxist, Weberian, Feminist, Skinnerian or something else, we might ignore equally plausible alternative explanations and simply take every observation as further confirmation of what we already believe. This is very much against the spirit of the theory construction approach where the aim is to let the concepts and ideas emerge from observations. Of course it is never this simple. As we seek to make sense of observations, we bring our commitments, biases and values with us and our attempts to let the concepts emerge are restricted by the limited store of concepts with which we are familiar. The important thing is to realise this and to accept that our interpretations are likely to be clouded by our commitments. We must accept that our interpretations, although plausible or even convincing to ourselves, need to be rigorously tested.

Context

An important way of working out the meaning of an observation is to look at it in context. This is particularly so for the characteristics, behaviour and attitudes of people. For example, take a person who earns $50 000 a year. Do we take this as indicating that they have a reasonable income? Do we classify two people earning $50 000 as being equally well off? The meaning of a $50 000 income depends on many other factors, such as whether it is the only income in the family, the number of dependants, the age of the income earner, other expenses and so on. We have to see this apparently simple observation in the context of other factors to interpret what it indicates.

Ask respondents

In many cases it is wise to ask people why they act or think as they do. This can provide clues about motivations behind actions and assist in interpreting what a particular action or attitude indicates for that person. This is not to say that we accept the stated reasons uncritically, but it can help provide insight into the meaning of behaviour.

Introspection

When we are familiar with a particular type of situation it is worth trying to put ourselves in the role of other people and try to understand their behaviour from their point of view. For example, we might observe that in families where the father or husband loses his job there is more violence than in families where the male is employed. To understand what that

violence indicates and why it occurs it is helpful to try to imagine ourselves in the same situation. Our ability to do so varies according to our familiarity with a situation and also with the ability of particular researchers to put themselves in the position of someone else.

Levels of generality

Regardless of the means by which we move from the particular observations to working out what it might indicate at the more general level we can then go further to even more general levels. For example, using Durkheim's suicide example we developed the generalisation that:

Using the same approach as outlined we can ask: *is this simply a particular example of an even more general pattern?* It could be that it is a particular case of the more general pattern that:

Plausibility and the need for theory testing

The general approach I have been describing is called the inductive approach. It is the process by which we develop explanations by moving from the particular to the general: from the observations to theory. The basic principle is to try to see to what more inclusive set of phenomena our observation might belong.

Theories or explanations arrived at in this way are not the end of the explanation process. These explanations need to be tested rigorously. This is because such *ex post facto* explanations, although consistent with the observed facts, are not necessarily compelling and because a number of quite different explanations might be equally consistent with the facts—we need to have some way of working out which one is best (Merton, 1968: 93). The explanation may be plausible but not convincing.

In Box 2.2 I have provided an example that illustrates the notion of plausibility and the need for rigorous testing of *ex post facto* theories.

BOX 2.2
Gender differences and religion—
plausible explanations

Studies in many countries have consistently found that on all sorts of measures women are more religious than men. A number of 'explanations' have been developed, all of which are consistent with the facts.

1   *Guilt theory:* Women are more religious because religion relieves guilt feelings. Since women have more guilt feelings they are therefore more religious.

2   *Freudian theory:* God is portrayed as a male—a father figure. According to Freud people identify with the opposite sex parent. Therefore women are attracted to a religion with a male god. This also fits with the additional observation that among Catholics men and women are about equally religious. That is because men identify with the Virgin Mary!

3   *Deprivation theory:* In our society women are more deprived than men and since religion fulfils a comforting role it will be the deprived who are most attracted to religion.

4   *Social learning theory:* The socialisation of girls teaches them to be nurturant, obedient, emotional, passive and submissive. Since religion encourages these attributes women find religion more attractive than do men.

5   *Role theory:* Women tend to have primary responsibility for childrearing. Because of the church's emphasis on the family, children's activities associated with the church and the church's role in moral training, mothers get drawn into the church via their children.

(Argyle and Beit-Hallahmi (1975) review the evidence and a range of theories including some of those listed above.)

On the basis of the simple fact (women tend to be more religious than men) all five explanations in Box 2.2 are plausible. The available facts do not allow us to choose between these explanations. We need to obtain further crucial facts to test any explanation. For example, to test the role theory explanation we might collect evidence to see if it is among men and women with young children that the male–female difference in religiousness is greatest. If this is so it would lend additional support for this particular theory above the others. But we would want to test each of the models in additional ways to help see which one had the most convincing empirical backing.

THE PROCESS OF THEORY TESTING

To test a theory we use the theory to guide our observations: we move from the general to the particular. The observations should provide a crucial test of the theory. Thus if we were testing the guilt explanation for the greater religiousness of women, we would at least expect that the greater a woman's feelings of guilt the more religious she would be. Further, we might expect that the preponderance of women over men would be more marked in religions emphasising forgiveness than in religions where forgiveness was not an important theme.

The basic idea then is to derive from the general theory more limited statements which follow logically from the theory. The key is to derive these statements in such a way that if the theory is true so will the derived statement. Having derived these more limited statements we collect data relevant to them and then look at the implications of these data for the initial theory. This process of theory testing is probably best explained with an example. I will outline six ideal-typical stages in this process (Box 2.3).

Six stages in theory testing

Stage 1 Specify the theory to be tested
As an example we will use the theory that industrialisation, because of the need for a mobile and skilled workforce, is a principal cause of the decline of the extended family and the rise of the nuclear family. The need to move because of jobs

---

BOX 2.3 *Stages in testing a theory*

Stage 1: Specify the theory to be tested

Stage 2: Derive a set of conceptual propositions

Stage 3: Restate conceptual propositions as testable propositions

Stage 4: Collect relevant data

Stage 5: Analyse data

Stage 6: Assess the theory

BOX 2.4
Urbanism and extended families— propositions to test a theory

a   *Industrialised countries* will be characterised by *nuclear families* more than will *relatively non-industrialised countries.*

b   Within any country, *rural areas* will be characterised by *extended family structures* more than will *industrialised urban areas.*

c   People who *move for work or education reasons* will have *weaker ties with their extended family* than will people who *do not move.*

d   In industrialised countries there will be little evidence of *nuclear families before industrialisation.*

and training breaks down family ties (Parsons, 1949). That is:

industrialisation → increased mobility → decline of extended family

Stage 2 Derive a set of conceptual propositions

A proposition is a statement which specifies the nature of a relationship between two factors. The previous statements—the greater the guilt the more religious, or the more a church emphasises forgiveness the greater the proportion of women—are both examples of propositions. They are conceptual propositions in that the key terms (guilt, religious, forgiveness) are abstract items that are not directly observable.

Stinchcombe (1968:18–20) argues that the more propositions tested the stronger the test of a theory. Given the theory above, the propositions in Box 2.4 seem to follow logically.

You will notice that the propositions in Box 2.4 are still fairly abstract: the key terms which are italicised are still abstract concepts. Although these conceptual propositions provide us with a better idea of what observations to make, they still do not provide enough clues. What, for example, is an industrialised country? What is an extended family or a nuclear family? The next stage in the process then is to develop testable propositions.

Stage 3 Restatement of conceptual propositions as testable propositions

This stage of theory testing involves a whole set of tasks called *operationalisation*, the process of deciding

how to translate abstract concepts (e.g. industrialisation) into something more concrete and directly observable (see Chapter 4). Having made these decisions we can simply restate each conceptual proposition in testable terms.

The testable proposition has the same *form* as the conceptual proposition. It is, however, more specific—the concepts in the conceptual proposition are replaced with *indicators* of the concepts.

Box 2.5 provides an illustration of a conceptual proposition that has been translated into a testable proposition.

By replacing the concepts with clear and measurable indicators we gain a very clear idea of precisely what data to collect.

Stage 4 Collect relevant data

Having decided what data are relevant to test our theory, we would then collect it (see Chapters 6–8).

Stage 5 Analyse data

Data are then analysed to see:

a   how much support there is for the testable propositions;

b   in turn how much support there is for the conceptual propositions;

BOX 2.5
*Urbanism and extended family ties—
developing a testable proposition*

Conceptual proposition

Rural areas will be characterised by
extended family structures more than will
industrialised urban areas.

Operationalising the key concepts

To test this we need an *operational definition*
of the key concepts: rural, urban, extended
family. Suppose we define urban areas as
areas with a population density of over 60
people per square kilometre and choose a
particular city as an example. Rural areas
might be defined as areas with a population
density of less than eighteen per square
kilometre and we may choose a particular
area as an example. Our indicator of the
extent to which people live in an extended
family might be the proportion of a specified
set of extended kin (e.g. siblings, parents,
cousins, aunts, grandparents) with whom
they have face-to-face contact at least
weekly. These indicators of the concepts are
operational definitions.

Testable proposition

The conceptual proposition can be restated
in its testable form:

*People in [selected rural area] will have
weekly face-to-face contact with a greater
proportion of their extended kin (i.e.
grandparents, parents, aunts, uncles,
cousins, siblings) than will people living in
[selected city]*.

but not in others: some results will be unanticipated
and confusing. This is good since it makes us think
and modify or develop the initial theory and thus
leads to progress. When we try to make sense of our
unanticipated and confusing results we are really
starting on the theory construction phase yet again.
That is, we will modify the initial theory to take
account of the observations we have made. As such
the modified theory will need to be tested rigorously.

***Theory construction and testing:
an ongoing process***

Wallace (1971) has described the process of theory
development as an ongoing interaction between
theory and observation and between theory
construction and testing. This logic of the research
process involving the shuttling back and forth
between theory and observation is summarised in
Figure 2.2.

Even though the terms I have used are not always
applied and the steps not formalised (often not even
recognised), the logic of what I have described is
common in research. People do not always say 'I'm
theory testing now' or 'I'll do a bit of inductive theorising now' or ' my conceptual proposition is . . .', but if
you boil it down this is effectively what a lot of
researchers do. Furthermore, the practice of research
does not by any means always fit neatly into these
systematic approaches. I have outlined them because
they provide a helpful structure to help organise
research and give it some direction. In practice we will
often have to improvise, and compromise. The models
help us organise.

**THE NEED FOR THEORY
AND OBSERVATION**

The emphasis on basing theories on observations and
evaluating them against further observations may
seem to be common sense. However, it is not univer-
sally practised among social scientists. The practice of
some social scientists involves the formulation of
'explanations' which are never systematically tested
empirically. At best examples are used as proof.
Examples, however, are a weak form of evidence, for
regardless of the explanation we can find some
examples to illustrate the argument. The key to
empirical testing is to look for evidence which will

c   in turn how much support there is for the initial
      theory.

Stage 6 Assessing the theory
Rarely is the initial theory completely supported by
the research: results are typically ambiguous and
conflicting. The theory is supported in some respects

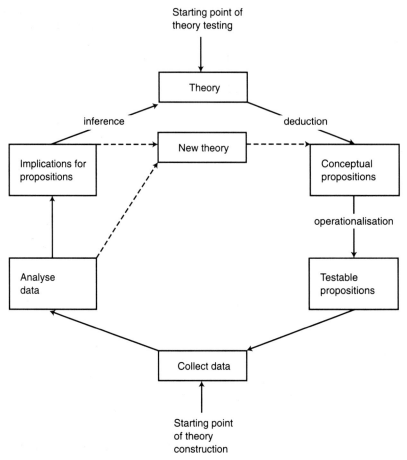

Figure 2.2   The logic of the research process

┌───┐
│   │
│ **WEB POINTER 2.2**   *Links between theory and research*   │
│   │
│ An analogy of the logic of a theory testing   http://trochim.human.cornell.edu/OJtrial/ojhome.htm │
│ approach to research based on a trial   │
│ (the O.J. Simpson trial).   │
│   │
│ Discussion of the link between theory and   http://trochim.human.cornell.edu/kb/strucres.htm │
│ research as an ongoing process.   │
│   │
│ Visit www.social-research.org to use these links and to check for updates and additions. │
│   │
└───┘

disprove the theory, not simply to find supporting illustrations.

Other people, not necessarily social scientists, have accepted theories on other non-empirical criteria. The authority criterion is common: people will accept a theory because of *who* proposed it, not because of the evidence for it. Kuhn (1964) has argued how important this is in many academic disciplines.

Intuition or 'gut feelings' are another common but non-empirical way of assessing the validity of explanations. Values and basic assumptions are also crucial in affecting how convincing and appealing (and thus how popular) a theory is.

Another non-empirical way of assessing or developing a theory is to use the rules of logic rather than of evidence as the main criterion. This approach, which is called a rationalist approach, is illustrated by the classic example of a group of philosophers who, wishing to know how many teeth there were in a horse's mouth, consulted Aristotle (for rules of logic) rather than looking in the horse's mouth.

One response to these non-empirical ways of deriving and evaluating explanations has been the empiricist position which is equally at odds with the approach I have outlined. Advocates of the empiricist approach encourage us simply to collect all the facts and let the facts speak for themselves rather than contaminating the 'true facts' with theory. This approach is untenable: it is not possible to collect all the facts. For example, in 1997 the British Labour Party with Tony Blair as leader achieved a landslide victory in the general election in Britain. Why? To answer this question by collecting all the facts we would have to do precisely that—collect *all* the facts. This would not only be extremely inefficient, it is impossible. So we might decide to collect only the *relevant* facts. But how do we know which facts are relevant and which are irrelevant? The only way is if we have ideas about why Labour and Blair were so popular. These theories which we hold either implicitly or explicitly dictate which observations we make. Theories then are crucial in guiding the observations we make: they provide the foundation for focused observation.

The empiricist position also is unrealistic because the facts do not speak for themselves. Observations take on significance and meaning within a context. Durkheim's (1970) observation that suicide rates were higher among Protestants than Catholics took on much more significance and meaning within the context of his theory about social integration and suicide. Theories help provide a meaning and significance to observations and patterns that might otherwise seem unremarkable. Theories help us 'realise what one finds'.

> Febvre: 'When one does not know what one is looking for, one does not realise what one finds'.
> (in Burke, 1973)

> Pasteur: 'Where observation is concerned chance favours only the prepared mind'.
> (*Oxford Dictionary of Quotations*, 1979: 369)

Further, simply to collect a number of facts gives no idea about how they relate to one another. Theories provide a way of ordering observations and producing plausible accounts of how such observations might interrelate.

SOURCES OF THEORIES

The ideas we use when developing theories and making sense of our data come from a variety of sources.

Sociological perspectives

Within sociology there are a number of distinct perspectives through which the world is interpreted and researched. These include:

- Symbolic interactionist theory
- Social learning theory
- Structural functionalism
- Feminist theory
- Marxism
- Weberian theory
- Conflict theory
- Exchange theory

Different perspectives draw attention to different factors when trying to arrive at explanations. These different perspectives affect which facts we see as relevant and important and how we interpret them. Depending on our perspective(s) we ask different questions and are sensitised to different observations. Box 2.6 illustrates how different perspectives might affect the way we go about researching and explaining the way people vote.

For our current purposes it does not matter which of the perspectives in Box 2.6 best explains voting behaviour. The important thing is to be aware how these perspectives fundamentally affect the types of observations we make.

These perspectives provide clues about what to look for: they are a source of theories about particular aspects of society. All are relevant to a wide range of social phenomena and while no perspective is explicitly about voting, they have implications for voting. They are models of society or of personality rather than theories of a particular phenomenon. They provide ideas about possible explanations and give clues about how to make sense of what we see.

BOX 2.6
Perspectives for explaining voting preference

Why do some people vote for progressive political parties while others prefer more traditional parties? There are a number of sociological and psychological orientations that we might draw on to answer this question. For example:

- A *social learning* perspective will emphasise the way in which a person's socialisation and role modelling behaviour affects voting preferences.

- Some *psychological* perspectives would focus on personality characteristics such as authoritarianism and paranoia.

- A *Freudian* approach might draw attention to unresolved childhood conflicts leading to identification with certain sorts of leaders.

- A *Marxist* perspective might focus on a person's position in the class structure or use the notion of false consciousness or class consciousness.

- A *feminist* might interpret voting behaviour in terms of the roles and responsibilities of women (e.g. child care, poorer workforce position) or in terms of distinctive caring values that women are said to hold.

- A *structural functionalist* who sees society as a system of interdependent parts would explain voting as a result of what is happening in other parts of society. Thus conservative voting patterns may be seen as a response to rapid social change and an attempt to restore some sort of equilibrium.

- An *exchange* perspective emphasises that behaviour is basically motivated by the desire to maximise rewards and minimise costs. Thus it would focus on how people see a particular party as benefiting themselves.

As such they provide a set of glasses through which to view the world.

I do not intend to explore the sources of the various perspectives: that is a task for the history of ideas. However, a good many are illustrated in the classic works of sociology. Thus the works of Marx, Durkheim, Weber, Freud, Skinner, Mead and Parsons are important sources of these perspectives and provide a rich source of ideas when trying to develop theories.

Other sources

Previous research on the topic which you are exploring can provide invaluable leads, articulate theories to test and alert you to possible interpretations of what you observe. Our own imagination and experience can be a useful source of theories. Reflecting on why we behave as we do can provide ideas. Wide reading in sociology, related disciplines, novels, plays and so on can stimulate the imagination. Earlier, the contribution of inductive reasoning and a number of ways of working out what a particular observation might mean were discussed. These same processes can be valuable sources of theories.

THE ROLE OF DESCRIPTIVE RESEARCH

The emphasis on explanation so far does not mean that descriptive research is unimportant. Descriptive research deals with questions of *what* things are like, not *why* they are that way. It includes a wide range of areas such as market research, public opinion polling, media research (ratings surveys), voter intention studies and the like. Governments sponsor a lot of descriptive research: the census and unemployment rate surveys are examples. Sociological studies which describe the social structure of a community, social changes over the past 50 years, or the workings of an organisation are further examples of descriptive research. Descriptive research can be very concrete or more abstract: it depends on what we wish to describe. At the fairly concrete level we might describe the income levels of different types of people or their ethnic background, or we can address more abstract questions such as 'is the modern family isolated?', 'are working-class people characterised by class consciousness?' and 'is society becoming secularised?'

WEB POINTER 2.3   *Sources for social theories and perspectives*

The following websites all provide different ways of learning about social theories and perspectives. Some sites provide original work of a wide range of social theorists, others provide useful overviews of their ideas while others provide summaries of the core ideas of various perspectives (e.g. Marxist, conflict, functionalist etc).

Theories and theorists.	www.mcmaster.ca/socscidocs/w3virtsoclib/theories.htm
	www.geocities.com/CollegePark/Quad/5889/socialth.htm
	http://raven.jmu.edu/~ridenelr/dss/index.html
	www.geocities.com/Athens/Olympus/2147/basesociologists.html
	www.pscw.uva.nl/sociosite/TOPICS/Sociologists.html
Useful summaries of classic articles by important theorists. The summaries include commentaries and place the ideas in a wider context.	www.spc.uchicago.edu/ssr1/PRELIMS/theory.html
Links to numerous other social theory sites.	www.trinity.edu/~mkearl/theory.html
Sociological perspectives and theorists with extracts from their work and summaries from teaching courses.	www.geocities.com/Athens/Olympus/2147/basetheory.html#structure

Visit www.social-research.org to use these links and to check for updates and additions.

Good description is important. It is the basis for sound theory. Unless we have described something accurately and thoroughly, attempts to explain it will be misplaced. As a descriptive statement we might say that families have been getting smaller since the industrial revolution and then try to explain this. But if they have not been getting smaller our explanations will be both wrong and pointless. Furthermore good description can provide a stimulus for explanation and research. Descriptions can highlight puzzles which need to be resolved and as such provide the stimulus for theory construction.

In addition, descriptive research plays a key role in highlighting the existence and extent of social problems, can stimulate social action and provide the basis of well-targeted social policy interventions. Survey research has demonstrated the extent of

poverty in many countries (this was the focus of early survey research—see Marsh, 1982:9–36) and the unemployment surveys can affect public attitudes and government policies. Health surveys are important in the allocation of health resources and the development of effective health promotion programs. Competent description makes it more difficult to deny the existence of problems. Of course there is poor descriptive research just as there is poor explanatory research but this is not inherent in description itself. Some descriptive research seems to be based on empiricist assumptions and ends up as an exercise in mindless fact gathering. But this lack of direction and focus need not characterise good description. Some descriptions seem trivial—no doubt many are—but equally many are important or potentially so.

THE CENTRALITY OF THEORY

The theme of this chapter has been that as soon as we try to answer 'why' questions about society we necessarily start to theorise. I have argued that theories should be empirically based (theory construction) and evaluated against empirical reality (theory testing). I have emphasised that:

1 Theory development is an important goal of social research.
2 Theories which we are testing either implicitly or explicitly guide us to which observations might be relevant to a problem. Theory testing therefore is central to efficient data collection.
3 Theories can help us make sense of a set of observations by helping us see what broader concepts our observations might reflect and by providing a plausible account of how various observations relate to one another.
4 Theories provide guides for analysis: propositions emerge from theories and propositions form a key focus around which data are analysed.

5 Theories provide a context in which to place particular observations which helps us to see the possible significance and meaning of observations. As such they sensitise us to observations we might otherwise ignore.
6 Theories can help us pose challenging questions and to be aware of certain problems. Hopefully they help avoid asking trivial questions and reducing research to social arithmetic.

While theory is central to the research enterprise there is nothing sacred about any particular theory. Theories are always tentative attempts to find a plausible explanation for a set of observations. They ought to be rigorously tested and be subject to modification and revision. In fact the principle of trying to disprove a theory should guide the design of research. Our aim should not simply be to design research to enable us to obtain results favourable to our theory.

KEY CONCEPTS

Concept	*Ex post facto* theories	Operational definition	Theory construction
Conceptual proposition	Grounded theory	Operationalisation	Theory testing
Deductive reasoning	Indicator	Rationalism	
Empiricism	Inductive reasoning	Testable proposition	

FURTHER READING

Merton's *Social Theory and Social Structure* (1968) provides good and well-known introductory discussions of the relation between theory and empirical research in Chapters 2, 3 and 4. Mills provides stinging criticisms of non-empirical theory and non-theoretical enquiry in Chapters 2 and 3 of *The Sociological Imagination* (1959). The whole book is worth reading because of its insistence that sociology is a craft.

Chavetz in *A Primer on the Construction and Testing of Theories in Sociology* (1978) provides a useful and readable book on the nature of theory construction and testing as does Dubin in *Theory Building* (1969).

Two readable papers on theory testing in relation to nursing research are provided by McQuiston and Campbell in 'Theoretical Substruction: A Guide for Theory Testing Research' (1997) and by Acton et al. in 'Theory-Testing Research: Building the Science' (1991). Wallace expands on the circular model of research discussed in this

chapter in *The Logic of Science in Sociology* (1971). But the best analysis of the logic of social research is Rose's *Deciphering Sociological Research* (1982). Glaser and Strauss provide a classic discussion of the nature of theory and the process of theory construction in *The Discovery of Grounded Theory* (1967).

Blumer has provided a excellent demonstration of the importance of theoretical concepts in any research undertaking but especially with inductively based research in his paper entitled 'Science without Concepts' (1934). Denzin also provides an excellent account of one type of theory construction approach in *The Research Act* (1978, pp. 191–6) and de Vaus (2001) illustrates the process of inductive theorising in case study research.

Strauss provides an example of higher level inductive theorising in his book on *Negotiations* (1978) and Glaser provides more insight into the way higher level inductive theorising is best achieved in his book *Theoretical*

Sensibility (1978). Homans provides a brief and readable discussion of the importance of deduced propositions for the development of sociological explanations in his famous, if controversial, book *The Nature of Social Science* (1967).

EXERCISES

1 For each of the following studies say whether it is a descriptive or explanatory study.
   a A study to assess the level of health in society.
   b A study to assess voting intentions.
   c A study to assess whether divorce is linked to the affluence of a family.
   d A study to see whether the age at which people are getting married is increasing.
   e A study to discover people's attitude to the internet.
   f A study to test whether anti-smoking campaigns reduce smoking levels among young people or whether they increase smoking by making smoking appear more attractive by presenting it as a marginalised and forbidden behaviour.

2 In your own words explain the following terms: theory, inductive, deductive, *ex post facto*, operationalisation, empiricist, rationalist.

3 Below are two theories you might hear in everyday conversation. For each of these theories:
   a Translate the theory into a 'box and arrow diagram' as in page 14.
   b Develop at least four conceptual propositions for the theory.

Theory 1
Our affluent society leads to the decline of the self-help ethic which in turn leads young people to expect things to be done for them which creates laziness and this leads to youth unemployment.

Theory 2
Anti-smoking campaigns and rules make smoking appear risky, deviant and marginal. Because young people need to develop a sense of identity that distinguishes them from their parents (and it is their parents' generation that make these rules and run the campaigns), these portrayals of smoking make smoking appear attractive to young people. Therefore anti-smoking campaigns and restrictions will lead to an increase rather than a decrease in smoking among young people.

4 What is the difference between a sociological perspective and a theory?

5 It was argued that the role of theory is central to research. Explain what theory achieves in social research.

3

Formulating and clarifying research questions

Research questions need to be focused. It is not enough to say, for example, 'I'm interested in getting some answers about inequality'. What answers to what questions? Do you want to know the extent of inequality, its distribution, its causes, its effects or what? What sort of inequality are you interested in? Over what period? Where?

The purpose of this chapter is to provide guidelines on how to clarify research questions. It will do this by:

1 outlining the difference between explanatory and descriptive research;
2 providing guidelines on how to focus descriptive research questions;
3 distinguishing between types of explanatory research questions;
4 identifying resources that help in reviewing existing research and thus help focus what research needs to be conducted; and
5 showing how research design is a key element in shaping the way research questions are asked.

The chapter stresses the need to formulate a research question at the beginning of the research—certainly before data are collected. But this emphasis does not mean that the initial research question is the final one. While it is important to know what we are looking for, it is a mistake to let this initial focus blind us from other unanticipated questions which are perhaps more interesting, important or manageable than the initial one. Questions can be refined and new issues emerge while reviewing literature or collecting and analysing data.

TYPES OF RESEARCH QUESTIONS

There is no simple way to refine research questions but I will outline a number of different types of questions and provide some guidelines to help focus research. First, however, it is helpful to define a few terms.

A *variable* is a characteristic that has more than one category (or value). Thus sex is a variable with the categories male and female. Age is a variable with many different categories (one year old, two years old etc). Any case, however, will belong to only one category. A variable then is a characteristic on which cases can differ from one another. In cause-and-effect terms we can distinguish between three types of variables: *dependent, independent* and *intervening* variables (see Box 3.1).

The following diagram illustrates the three types of variables. Education is the independent variable that affects income level (the dependent variable) via its effect on job (the intervening variable).

BOX 3.1 *Dependent, independent and intervening variables*

Type of variable	Description Synonyms	Symbol	Causal diagram
Dependent	Effect Outcome	Y	X → Z → **Y**
Independent	Cause Predictor	X	**X** → Z → Y
Intervening	Mechanism	Z	X → **Z** → Y

WEB POINTER 3.1 *Web reading on types of research and research questions*

Useful explanation of descriptive and explanatory research.	http://trochim.human.cornell.edu/kb/resques.htm
Types of research questions.	http://trochim.human.cornell.edu/kb/resques.htm
Brief discussion of variables.	http://trochim.human.cornell.edu/kb/variable.htm
Brief outline of some ways of defining a research question.	http://trochim.human.cornell.edu/kb/probform.htm

Visit www.social-research.org to use these links and to check for updates and additions.

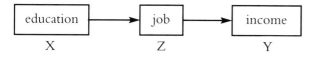

X   Z   Y

Once we have selected a broad topic ask 'what do I want to know about this topic?' Broadly, interests will be descriptive, explanatory or both.

Descriptive research

It is difficult to provide precise rules about how to focus a descriptive research question but five questions can help.

1. What is the *time frame* of our interest?
2. What is the *geographical location* of our interest?
3. Is our interest in broad description or in *comparing* and *specifying* patterns for subgroups?
4. What *aspect* of the topic are we interested in?
5. How *abstract* is our interest?

The way in which these questions help focus a broad research question is illustrated in Box 3.2.

Explanation: searching for causes or consequences

The next three types of research question all involve explanatory research. They only vary their focus and complexity.

Over the last 50 years the divorce rate in most western countries has increased markedly. We may want to know why but have no idea. Diagrammatically then the problem is:

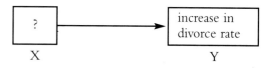

X   Y

Alternatively our interest might be to discover the consequences of the increased divorce rate. Diagrammatically this is:

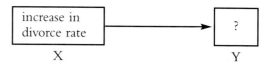

X   Y

Start with a broad topic such as divorce. The following questions can help focus the topic.

1 *Time frame:* Do we want to know about divorce now or in the past, or do we want to look at the trends over, say, the last 50 years?

2 *Geographical location:* Do we want to know about divorce in a part of the country, for the whole nation or for other countries? Or is our interest *comparative*: do we want to compare one country with other countries? If so, which countries?

3 *Comparing and specifying subgroup patterns:* Do we simply want to know, for example, the national divorce rate or do we want to see if it differs according to age of marriage, occupation, length of marriage, educational level and so on?

4 *Aspect:* Does our interest in divorce centre on the divorce rate, divorce laws, problems with property and custody, attitudes to divorce, ways in which people adjust to divorce or something else?

5 *Abstraction:* Are we interested in the raw facts or in what they might indicate at the more abstract level? For example, is our interest in the divorce rate as such or in what it might reveal about, say, level or social conflict? If it is the latter, we will collect other data relevant to measuring conflict (e.g. level of industrial disputes, crime rates, legal actions). If it is in divorce *per se*, we will collect only information on this topic.

The first step in focusing an explanatory research question is to decide whether we are looking for causes or consequences. Second, we must clarify what it is we are seeking the causes or consequences of (e.g. increased divorce rate from 1950 to 2000). The next step is to list possible causes or conse-

quences and then collect relevant data. There are a number of ways of coming up with such a list.

1 *Previous research:* Using a library, the internet or other similar locations, look to see what other researchers have found on the topic (see Web Pointer 3.2). We will often notice gaps in the research, lack of evidence and unresolved debates. These can help focus the research.

2 *The 'facts':* Detailed description of a phenomenon can stimulate ideas about possible causes. For example, if the pattern of divorce over the last 50 years showed a sharp increase in, say, 1976 we could ask what other changes have also occurred at these times and over the 50-year period. These might have something to do with the divorce rate and provide clues about possible causes (e.g. decline of religion except in the mid-1950s, changes in the law in 1976, changed beliefs about personal fulfilment, increased workforce participation for women, changes in welfare provisions).

3 *Our own hunches:* Our own ideas, impressions, beliefs and experiences are valuable sources of ideas so long as we test them against the evidence and are not limited only to them.

4 *Talk to informants:* Often there are people who are particularly well placed to provide ideas and can provide good starting points for research. In this case marriage counsellors, solicitors and social workers may all provide helpful insights.

Once ideas about possible causes have been collected in this exploratory way we might stop there, collect information to test all the ideas or focus on just one or two possible causes.

Explanation: exploring a simple idea

This approach to formulating explanatory research questions is more focused than the previous approach. Instead of asking what has caused the increased divorce rate, we would be more specific and ask: 'has X (e.g. decline in religion) led to the increased divorce rate?' The research then concentrates on this specific question. Diagrammatically we could represent this as:

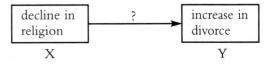

Explanation: exploring more complex ideas

The above idea is relatively simple because it deals with only two concepts. We might find that it is true that the decline of religion has been accompanied by an increase in divorce but what are the mechanisms? Why should religious decline lead to divorce? Can we specify the links? If we can, we should have a better understanding of why divorce has increased. From a variety of sources (see the earlier section on searching for causes and consequences) we might develop the model in Figure 3.1.

In summary there is a variety of types of research questions varying from descriptive to more complex explanatory problems. For descriptive research we must try to be clear and specific about what we want to describe. Box 3.3 lists four key questions to help focus explanatory research questions.

It can be helpful to draw diagrams like those earlier in this section: they can help clarify our thinking. Often these different types of research questions can represent different stages within the one study. Initially we might be interested simply in describing a phenomenon, but then the 'why' questions about causes develop. As we proceed we might focus on one particular cause and then start asking more complex questions about that particular factor. Remember, the task of clarifying research questions is a process rather than a once-and-for-all task which is completed at the beginning of a study.

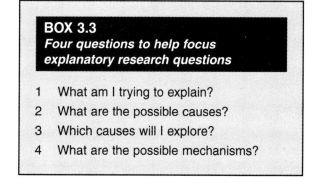

BOX 3.3
Four questions to help focus explanatory research questions

1   What am I trying to explain?
2   What are the possible causes?
3   Which causes will I explore?
4   What are the possible mechanisms?

USING THE INTERNET TO REVIEW EXISTING INFORMATION AND RESEARCH

The process of focusing a research question requires a knowledge of the field, an understanding of previous research, an awareness of research gaps and knowledge of how other research in the area has been conducted. (See the checklist at the end of this chapter for some of the things that your review of the existing literature should examine.) The task of locating previous research on a topic has been made much simpler and faster with widespread access to the internet and the availability of electronic data bases, electronic journals, online journals and sophisticated search engines. The internet is useful in providing access to many types of information (see Web Pointer 3.2).

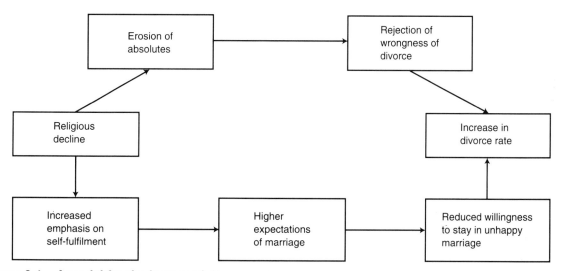

Figure 3.1   A model for the increased divorce rate

Before using this information you need to know how to use the internet effectively. You need to know how and where to look and to evaluate the information obtained. Using the internet there are seven main ways of obtaining information to assist in reviewing a research field.

1 *Information freely available to anyone with access to the internet:* There are three valuable strategies to locate such information.

   a *Use search engines:* Many search engines can locate content on the internet but no one engine searches the whole internet and some are better than others for particular types of material. There are two main types of search engine: the *single search engine* and the *metasearch* engine. Metasearch engines run a number of the single search engines at once and are therefore the best way of locating content.

   b *Follow links:* Many sites have links to other related websites. Clicking on these links will redirect you to that related site. In some ways the process is similar to looking at a bibliography at the end of an article and looking up the references that are listed.

   c *Use gateways:* Gateways are internet sites the purpose of which is to provide many links to other sites on a specified topic. These sites are directories in the same way that the *Yellow Pages* telephone directory lists businesses according to their service or product.

2 *Free access to online catalogues:* Many libraries provide easy, web-based access to their catalogues. Searching these catalogues can indicate the types of material available on given topics. Users with borrowing privileges can borrow these or order them on interlibrary loan. These catalogues usually do not provide indexes of journal articles (see points 5 and 6 below).

3 *Free access to publications and full text articles:* Free access to a large number of online newspapers is available. Many of these only provide access to current news items while some enable searches of older items. Some will notify users of news items on particular topics that appear in specified newspapers (news clipping services).

4 *Restricted access to resources such as online publications:* Many publishers are providing their publications electronically for a fee. Some free online

publications (e.g. many newspapers) are supported by advertisements.

5 *Restricted access to lists of articles in academic journals:* These sites provide notification services of articles from nominated journals as they are published. Most of these services are provided only to registered and paid-up subscribers or libraries.

6 *Restricted access to searchable databases:* These databases contain details of academic articles published in a wide range of journals, from conferences, theses and some books. They provide bibliographic details and abstracts of each article and search engines enable focused searches. These databases are normally accessed through academic libraries. They include papers going back some years and are regularly updated. Databases exist for broad disciplines (e.g. sociology, psychology), for particular topics (e.g. AIDS research) or topics for particular countries (e.g. family research in Australia).

7 *Newsgroups, listservs and chatgroups:* These internet facilities provide a means of obtaining information and ideas more or less interactively. They allow you to ask questions of other people on the internet who visit these interactive sites. There are three main types of sites that are helpful for obtaining this type of information or for testing out ideas.

   a *Newsgroups* are publicly accessible topic areas to which anyone can subscribe without charge and receive and send messages. Some can be useful but many are burdened by junk.

   b *Listservs* are email mailing lists which internet users can join. Each list is dedicated to particular topics. Once a user subscribes to a list they automatically receive 'postings' to the list from other members and can send messages to other members of the list. They are a good way of sharing information and are generally much better than Newsgroups.

   c *Chat groups* enable subscribers to converse in writing with one another in real time. At any one time a number of subscribers of a particular topic-based chat group may be logged onto the internet-based chat group thus enabling those who are logged on to exchange ideas there and then.

WEB POINTER 3.2　*Using the internet to review existing information and research*

Provides a tour of some key internet sites for psychologists, sociologists and many other disciplines. Provides tools and techniques to improve your internet searching. Emphasises critical thinking when using internet resources. This is *the* place to start if you want to become good at using the internet for researching in your discipline area.	www.vts.rdn.ac.uk/
How to locate information on the internet.	http://library.albany.edu/internet/research.html
Excellent tutorial to help evaluate information on the internet.	http://tramss.data-archive.ac.uk/Research Questions/index.asp

Search engines

Describes how to use search engines.	http://library.albany.edu/internet
A brief guide to the effective use of search engines.	www.jisc.ac.uk/subject/socsci/strategy.pdf
Checklist for searching the internet.	www.jisc.ac.uk/subject/socsci/check.pdf
A comprehensive list of general, country-based and topic-based search engines.	www.searchenginecolossus.com/
Valuable list of both single and metasearch search engines.	www2.dynamite.com.au/kiwisunf/Search.htm

Following links

Links to numerous family and social policy sites throughout the world.	www.aifs.org.au
Links to national statistical agencies and online statistics throughout the world.	www.abs.gov.au
	Then select the **Statistics** button and then select **Links to other statistical sites**

Gateways

Social Science Information Gateway (SOSIG).	www.sosig.ac.uk/
Lists of links to social science gateways.	http://odwin.ucsd.edu
Excellent gateway to a wide range of substantive topic areas in sociology.	www.pscw.uva.nl/sociosite/topics/index.html
Extensive list of social science resources on the internet.	www.wcsu.ctstateu.edu/socialsci

WEB POINTER 3.2 *continued*

Subscriber sites to online journals and other publications

Annual reviews of anthropology, sociology, political science, psychology.	http://arjournals.annualreviews.org/socialhome.dtl
Access to electronic versions of a wide range of journals.	http://firstsearch.oclc.org/
Lists online journals of Sage Publications.	www.sagepub.co.uk/journals/details/c001.html
Lists online journals of publisher Taylor and Francis.	www.tandf.co.uk/journals/sublist.html
Fully online, currently free sociology journal.	www.socresonline.org.uk/

Online catalogues

Online catalogues of University Research Libraries in the UK and Ireland.	http://copac.ac.uk/
British Library.	http://blpc.bl.uk/
Canadian websites and catalogues.	www.nlc-bnc.ca/canlib/eindex.htm
European Commission Libraries Catalogues.	http://europa.eu.int/eclas/
Europe's national libraries	www.konbib.nl/gabriel/en/services.html
Yahoo! index of library sites.	http://dir.yahoo.com/Reference/Libraries/
Library web pages and online catalogues.	http://staffweb.library.vanderbilt.edu/breeding/libwebcats.html
Library servers via WWW.	http://sunsite.berkeley.edu/Libweb/
United Kingdom libraries catalogues.	www.bopac2.comp.brad.ac.uk/~bopac2/egwcgi.cgi/egwirtcl/mtargets.egw/1+0
Worldwide list of national library catalogues.	www.library.uq.edu.au/natlibs/
Web-based online catalogues.	www.dex.com

Free online articles

Access to more online newspapers.	http://library.uncg.edu/news/
Access to very large number of online newspapers.	www.onlinenewspapers.com/
Access back issues of newspapers.	www.newstrawler.com/nt/nt_home.html
Provides access to a free web clipping service that notifies re articles on nominated topics from nominated newspapers on publication.	http://nt.excite.com/

WEB POINTER 3.2 *continued*

Lists of restricted access academic journal articles

Free access to Ingenta which enables a free search of articles from a wide range of academic and other journals.	www.ingenta.com
Subscriber access to Blackwell's Electronic Journal Navigator which includes articles and abstracts for papers from a large range of journals.	http://navigator.blackwell.co.uk
Free notification service for articles published in the numerous Taylor and Francis journals.	www.tandf.co.uk/sara/

Restricted access searchable journal databases
(sites for these databases vary from library to library)

Anthropological Index of the Royal Anthropological Institute.	Free online Index to Current Periodicals in the Museum of Mankind Library
EconLit	Includes citations and abstracts from 400+ major journals plus articles in collective volumes books, dissertations, and working papers.
Medline Express	Provides bibliographic citation information and abstracts from 3700+ journals. Includes health topics relating to psychiatry and psychology, social sciences and education, technology, humanities and health care.
PsycInfo	Contains citations and summaries of journal articles, book chapters, books reports and dissertations in psychology and psychological aspects of related disciplines (1984 onwards).
Sociological Abstracts	Provides bibliographic information and abstracts to articles from journals (2500+), sociology conferences, dissertations and selected sociology books (1963 onwards).
Ebsco Megafile	A collection of full text databases covering social and health sciences.

Newsgroups

Topic-based list of newsgroups with search facility.	www.topica.com/dir/?cid=0

Listservs

List of sociology related listservs.	www.pscw.uva.nl/sociosite/mailinglists.html
Social sciences (sociology, anthropology, psychology, law, politics, economics) listservs.	www.mailbase.ac.uk/category/L.html

---

WEB POINTER 3.2 *continued*

List of listserv lists.	http://paml.alastra.com/sources.html
Extensive list of listservs.	http://paml.alastra.com/indexes.html

Visit www.social-research.org to use these links and to check for updates and additions.

SCOPE OF THE RESEARCH

As well as specifying what is to be explained and in what terms it is to be explained, it is helpful to resolve two issues related to the scope of the research before collecting data.

Particular but exhaustive or general but partial?

Will the research focus on a particular case and try to find as many causes as possible or will it seek partial explanations of a class of events? For example, a study of strikes could focus on a particular strike and try to discover all the factors behind that strike (including those peculiar to it alone). Alternatively, it could look at strikes in general and try to locate some factors that tend to be of importance for strikes in general. The first approach that focuses on obtaining thorough accounts of particular cases is called *idiographic* explanation (like idiosyncratic). Finding a partial explanation of a class of cases (e.g. strikes) is called *nomothetic* explanation. If we are committed to doing a survey then we will need to formulate the research question in terms appropriate to nomothetic explanations. If the question is really more suited to an idiographic approach we would be best advised to try another research method.

Units of analysis

A unit of analysis is the unit about which we obtain information: it is the unit whose characteristics we describe. In survey research the unit of analysis often is an individual. In a survey we might ask 2000 people whether they have ever been on strike or what might cause them to go on strike. But other units of analysis are possible. Any region (e.g. country, county, state) could be used so that we look at the strike rate of various regions for example. Time periods can be used. We might compare different years in terms of the strike levels. Events can be used

too. Thus a study could be designed around collecting data about various strikes. A group or organisation (e.g. particular unions) could be the unit of analysis. Many other units of analysis can be used depending on the issue at hand. Poems, paintings, buildings, jokes, newspapers, families and so on could be used.

Working out the unit of analysis is important in two respects. First, being aware of the range of possible units of analysis can help formulate more useful and interesting research questions and highlight a range of types of relevant data. Only to think of collecting data from and about individuals can lead to asking rather restricted research questions. Second, if data cannot be collected using a particular unit of analysis, the general thrust of the question may be retained simply by changing to a unit of analysis about which data are available. For example, we may want to know whether prosperous economic conditions encourage or discourage industrial disputes. Initially we might try to collect data from a country for the last 50 years but if this was unavailable for a particular country we could try another approach by comparing disputation levels in different countries with varying economic conditions. By changing the units of analysis from years to countries we have a different handle on the problem.

Where a number of units of analysis can be used in the one study we can be more confident in the general thrust of the results. It provides a tougher test of a theory. In a study on the effect of economic conditions on strikes it would be best to use both years and countries as units of analysis since this enables us to approach the same question from a variety of angles.

RESEARCH DESIGN

With either descriptive or explanatory research it is necessary to have a frame of reference within which to interpret the results—a frame of reference that enables us to do more than simply report the results.

Descriptive research

When dealing with descriptive questions the need for a frame of reference is fairly obvious. For example, the inflation rate of a country might be 9 per cent. But is this high or low, good or bad, improving or deteriorating? To obtain an appreciation of this figure we need to know how it compares with the inflation rate of other countries or of other years: we need a context to make sense of most data. When collecting data it is necessary therefore to design strategies to ensure that the data needed to provide this context are collected.

Two useful types of information are data about other groups and about the same group of people over time. This information can provide a context in which to view a single piece of data and helps avoid drawing faulty conclusions. Suppose we have collected information about the levels of self-esteem of women who are out of the workforce raising young children, and that we have found that many of these women exhibit low levels of self-esteem. What does this mean? On its own it means very little. It would be much more helpful to be able to compare the findings for these women with those for some other groups. How do they compare with comparable women in the workforce? How do they compare with men who are out of the workforce raising young children? We might be tempted to conclude that being out of the workforce has a detrimental effect on women's self-esteem, but on its own the finding does not justify this conclusion. We need to know whether the self-esteem of women out of the workforce is *different* from that of other comparable groups.

As well as comparing these women with other comparable groups it would be desirable to examine their levels of self-esteem over a period of time and see what their self-esteem was like before they left the workforce, what it was like when they were out of the workforce and what it was like when they returned. Looking at the same group of people over time helps provide a context in which to understand the low self-esteem of mothers out of the workforce.

Explanatory research

When asking research questions that deal with *causal processes* an appropriate research design is absolutely essential. Where the goal is to develop an explanation of the patterns in the data we need to eliminate as many alternative explanations of the patterns as possible. If we develop a causal model that proposes that X produces Y we need to be as sure as we can that it is in fact X and not A, B or C that produces Y. Paying careful attention to research design is an important way of ensuring that possible alternative explanations of the data are eliminated. Good design also gives us more confidence in the conclusions we draw about the causal processes operating.

People use the term 'research design' in different ways. Some use it broadly to include the issues of problem formulation, operationalisation (see Chapter 4), sampling and the selection of data collection techniques. Like Stouffer (1950) I use the term much more narrowly to refer to the *structure of the data* rather than the particular data. The central point of good research design is that it provides a context in which relatively unambiguous statements can be drawn. The aim is to move our conclusions about causal processes from the realm of the plausible and possible to the convincing and compelling.

In the sections that follow I outline a number of

WEB POINTER 3.3 *Illustrations of worked through research questions*

Illustrates the refinement of several research questions and some steps in using the internet for information reviews. These are very helpful examples.

http://tramss.data-archive.ac.uk/ ResearchQuestions/index.asp

Visit www.social-research.org to use these links and to check for updates and additions.

research designs following Stouffer's (1950) discussion. I begin with a description of the *experimental design* and then deal with a number of common variations. These and other designs are discussed in detail in my book *Research Design in Social Research* (de Vaus, 2001). Software provided in the Methodologist's Toolchest can assist in developing useful research designs for your particular project (Box 3.4). Although the experimental design is impractical for most social science research problems, it nevertheless provides a useful benchmark against which to compare other designs and highlight their weaknesses. In so doing it can help us both design and consume research more intelligently and critically. The experimental design also highlights the logic behind many of the statistical techniques covered later in this book.

BOX 3.4
Software to assist with the development of a research design

The *Methodologist's Toolchest* is a set of modules designed to assist with developing and analysing social research. One module, **Research Design**, assists in developing research designs. This module asks for details of your design and forces you to think through elements of the design. It identifies possible problems with the design and makes suggestions for improvements. This module deals with research design in a far more detailed way than is possible in this chapter. This software can be purchased from: www.scolari.co.uk/toolchest/tootlchest.htm.

The classic experimental design

In its simplest form the experimental design has two groups: an experimental group and a control group. It also extends over time so that data are collected at, at least, two points in time (before and after). Between Time 1 (before) and Time 2 (after) the experimental group is exposed to an experimental intervention. The control group is left alone. At both Time 1 and Time 2 the experimental and control groups are measured in relation to the key dependent variable that is of interest in the study. In Figure 3.2 the measure of the dependent variable is indicated by E_1 and E_2, and C_1 and C_2.

Since the experimental group has been exposed to the experimental intervention, we might suppose that differences in the experimental group between Time 1 and Time 2 might be due to the influence of the intervention. To test for an intervention effect we measure the difference between E_1 and E_2 and calculate the change between Time 1 and Time 2 (E_{Change}) for the experimental group.

However, the observed change for the experimental group between Time 1 and Time 2 might be due to factors other than the experimental intervention. A change could occur due to the passing of time, be a result of being measured at Time 1, or be caused by a whole set of other possibilities. For this reason a control, or comparison, group is needed. Ideally this group should be identical to the experimental group at Time 1. However, unlike the experimental group, they are not exposed to any experimental intervention. We can measure them on our dependent variable at both Time 1 and Time 2 and obtain a measure of change over that time (C_{Change}). Since this group was not exposed to the experimental intervention, any change in this group will not be due to this factor.

The crucial thing to look at is *whether the experimental group changed more than the control group*. If the

Method of allocation to groups	Time 1 (T_1) Before	Intervention (X)	Time 2 (T_2) After	
Experimental group (Random allocation)	E_1	Intervention	E_2	$E_{Change} = E_2 - E_1$
Control group (Random allocation)	C_1	No intervention	C_2	$C_{Change} = C_2 - C_1$

Effect = $E_{Change} - C_{Change}$

Figure 3.2   Structure of the classic experimental design

experimental group changed significantly more, we normally would conclude that this is because of the experimental intervention.

Of course, this conclusion is warranted only if both groups were the same to start with and had identical experiences between Time 1 and Time 2. In order to ensure that they are the same to start with, people are *randomly assigned* to the experimental and control groups. So long as the groups are large enough, random assignment should ensure that they are very similar in most respects. Ensuring that they have the same experiences between Time 1 and Time 2 is more difficult and is one reason why experiments are often held in laboratories where this an be controlled to some extent.

An example of an experimental design is illustrated in Figure 3.3. Here the research is designed to test whether an intervention to help smokers stop smoking is effective. We would begin with a pool of people who smoked. We would then randomly allocate these smokers to either an experimental group (those who will do the QUIT smoking program designed to help smokers stop smoking) and the control group (will not do the program). This random allocation should ensure that the two groups would initially smoke to a similar extent and be alike in other ways (age, duration of smoking, gender etc). We would measure the level of smoking in each group before the QUIT program began. Six months after the experimental group had completed their program we would remeasure the percentage in each group who were still smoking. In this example we would observe that in the group that took the program 10 per cent fewer smoke by Time 2. In the control group 3 per cent fewer smoke at Time 2 than at Time 1.

Since there was a reduction of 3 per cent among the control group it is likely that the experimental group would have seen a similar decline in smoking in the same period without the QUIT program. In other words, some of the 10 per cent drop in smoking among the experimental group is likely to be due to factors separate from the program. The effect of the program would be measured by the *difference* in the amount of change between the experimental and control groups (i.e. the program was responsible for a 7 per cent decline in smoking).

By designing the research with the before and after dimension and an experimental and control group, we are in a position to draw much more unequivocal conclusions than we could without that design. We are much more able to draw conclusions about causal processes.

There are a number of problems which make it difficult to use an experimental design for social research. In many situations it is not possible to obtain repeated measures for the same group, thus making it impossible to get measures at both Times 1 and 2. Often it is difficult to obtain a control group. Practical and ethical considerations often make it impossible to introduce experimental interventions. For example, we might be interested in the effect of marital breakdown on the social adjustment of young children. Obviously we cannot allocate people randomly to two groups and somehow cause marital breakdowns in one group and leave the other group alone.

Panel design

This design (see Figure 3.4) uses only the top two cells of the experimental design. It looks at the same

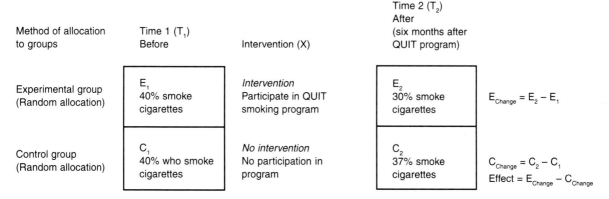

Figure 3.3 Experimental design to ascertain the effect of a QUIT program on smoking

	Time 1 (T_1) Before	Intervention (X)	Time 2 (T_2) After (six months after QUIT program)	
	E_1 40% smoke cigarettes	*Intervention* Participate in QUIT smoking program	E_2 30% smoke cigarettes	Effect = $E_2 - E_1$

Figure 3.4　Panel design to ascertain the effect of a QUIT program on smoking

group of people over a period of time: we would measure smoking levels at both points and the whole group would participate in the QUIT program. The difference in smoking levels between Time 1 and Time 2 provides a measure change over the period.

We might be tempted to conclude that this change is due to the intervention—the QUIT program. However this design does not allow us to draw this conclusion. We need to know the extent to which comparable smokers who did not participate in the QUIT program stopped smoking. There may well have been other events occurring between Time 1 and Time 2 (e.g. increase in price of cigarettes, increased unemployment, new brands released, new marketing strategies of the tobacco companies) that might be responsible for the observed changes in smoking levels.

Quasi-panel design

This is similar to the panel design except that *different* groups of people are studied at the two points of time (see Figure 3.5). This design might be used to avoid the difficulties of keeping track of the same people over time. Using the above example, the

quasi-panel design would involve measuring smoking behaviour of a representative sample of people before implementing a widespread anti-smoking campaign which includes easy access to QUIT programs. After the campaign we would remeasure the smoking behaviour of another representative sample. Any decline in smoking behaviour evident between the two samples might be attributed to the anti-smoking campaign.

However, this design has the same problems of the panel design for drawing causal inferences. It also has the additional problem of being unable to fully match the samples at Time 1 and Time 2. Differences observed between Time 1 and Time 2 might be due to sampling error—differences between the samples. We cannot even be sure that we have measured change—something that the panel design is at least good at.

Retrospective panel design

The panel design has the disadvantage of having to keep track of people over time and of having to wait for a long time on occasions before the results can be collected. Often it is simply not feasible to follow a

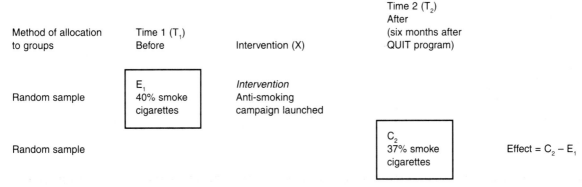

Method of allocation to groups	Time 1 (T_1) Before	Intervention (X)	Time 2 (T_2) After (six months after QUIT program)	
Random sample	E_1 40% smoke cigarettes	*Intervention* Anti-smoking campaign launched		
Random sample			C_2 37% smoke cigarettes	Effect = $C_2 - E_1$

Figure 3.5　Quasi-panel design to ascertain the effect of an anti-smoking campaign on smoking

group of people over time and the drop-out rate in the study can create serious difficulties with comparing Time 1 and Time 2 results.

An alternative approach that can be used to provide a time dimension to the study is to obtain information at one time only but to ask about two or more time points and to find out about events in between these two times (see Figure 3.6). Thus we might ask a sample of people about their current level of smoking and about their level six months earlier (i.e. before an anti-smoking campaign was launched).

Apart from the other shortcomings of the panel design, this design has the difficulty of selective memory and is open to the possibility that people will reinterpret the past in the light of the present. People can mis-remember the past and become confused about time periods. What they remember as six months ago might be two years ago (telescoping) or only two months ago (reverse telescoping) (Menard, 1991). Even if such a study detects 'changes'

we cannot be sure whether the changes are real or perceived.

Retrospective experimental design

The retrospective panel design suffers from the dual problem of the shortcomings of retrospectivity and from having no control group. The first problem means that we cannot be certain about the extent of real change while the absence of a control group means that it is difficult to draw conclusions about causal processes. The retrospective experimental design (see Figure 3.7) is an attempt to deal with the control group problem.

Using this approach we would interview a sample of people and ascertain their level of awareness of the recent anti-smoking campaign (or whether they participated in a QUIT program). We would then ask about their current level of smoking and about their level six months earlier before the campaign. We would then extract from our sample

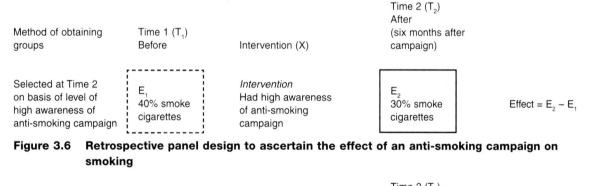

Figure 3.6   Retrospective panel design to ascertain the effect of an anti-smoking campaign on smoking

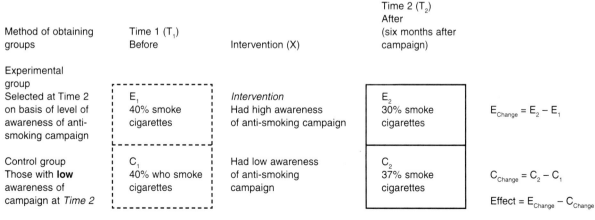

Figure 3.7   Retrospective experimental design to ascertain the effect of an anti-smoking campaign on smoking

those who had a high awareness of the campaign and then extract a group with low awareness. We would try to ensure that the low awareness group were matched in other regards (age, sex, class etc) with the high awareness group. If the level of smoking in the high awareness group declined more than in the low awareness group we might attribute this to the effect of the campaign.

Cross-sectional or correlation design

The most common design used in survey research is the cross-sectional design (see Figure 3.8). Using this approach we collect measures from at least two groups of people at one point of time and compare the extent to which the two groups differ on the dependent variable (e.g. levels of smoking).

For our example we would obtain a random sample of people after an anti-smoking campaign had ended. We would ask these people about their current level of smoking and how aware they were of the anti-smoking campaign. We could then divide people into groups according to how well aware they had been of the campaign. If the campaign was effective we would expect that those with the greatest awareness would also have the lowest levels of smoking. If this turned out to be the case we may be tempted to conclude that the campaign was effective—that it produced a lower level of smoking.

The problem is that the high and low awareness people might differ in other ways apart from their awareness of the campaign. High awareness people might be older, be in poorer health or be distinctive from the low awareness group in some way. *These* differences, rather than high awareness, might have

produced the lower level of smoking. Alternatively, non-smokers may be more conscious than smokers of anti-smoking campaigns. This, rather than the effectiveness of the campaign, would explain the different levels of smoking of the high and low awareness groups. We would need to eliminate these possibilities before we could begin to draw conclusions about the effectiveness of the campaign. Methods of achieving this are discussed in Chapters 16 and 17.

Although the discussion of research designs has been limited to two groups this is not a requirement. Any number of groups can be built into a design. In cross-sectional designs this is particularly common. If we were interested in the effect of campaign awareness on smoking we could have two groups—high and low awareness—and see whether their smoking differed. But we could have, say, six awareness groups ranging from high to low. To the extent that the six groups differ, we might conclude, other things being equal, that campaign awareness is related to smoking levels.

One group post-test only design

The most primitive design—of little use when trying to analyse causal processes—is one that has only one cell of the experimental design (see Figure 3.9). This design involves collecting information from one group at one point in time. For our study of smoking behaviour it would involve asking a sample about their level of smoking some time after an anti-smoking campaign. We might observe that only 30 per cent smoke. Can we tell anything about the effectiveness of the campaign? Not a thing. To use this design for causal analysis requires that we rely on

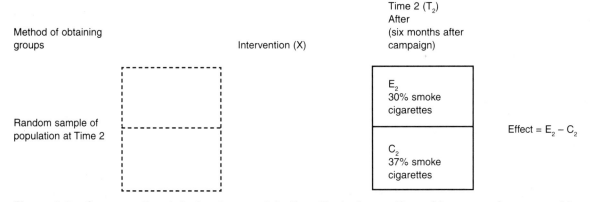

Method of obtaining groups

Intervention (X)

Time 2 (T_2)
After
(six months after campaign)

Random sample of population at Time 2

E_2
30% smoke cigarettes

C_2
37% smoke cigarettes

Effect = $E_2 - C_2$

Figure 3.8   Cross-sectional design to ascertain the effect of an anti-smoking campaign on smoking

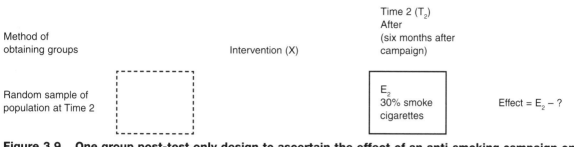

Figure 3.9   One group post-test only design to ascertain the effect of an anti-smoking campaign on smoking

plausible conjecture and our preconceptions and assumptions about the data that *might* be in the 'missing' cells of the design. It requires that we fill in the cells from our imagination rather than from systematic observation. Without an empirical frame of reference against which to compare the 30 per cent figure we can not say anything about causal processes.

Why bother about design?

The aim of this outline of research design has been fourfold. First, rather than suggesting that the experimental design is the only way to proceed, the intention has been to create an awareness of the limitations of designs where cells are missing and to suggest ways of filling in at least some of the cells. The more cells that are filled in with data the better the design will be. In many situations in social research the experimental design will either be impracticable or impossible. Second, the aim has also been to highlight the logic behind the experimental design, for it is in this logic that the rationale of multivariate analysis lies. The use of multivariate analysis with a cross-sectional design is the most common way in which survey researchers attempt to approximate the logic of the classical experiment. Understanding design principles therefore lies at the heart of an understanding of the more sophisticated methods of statistical analysis. Third, an understanding of the principles of research design should help us to be more critical consumers of social research. Finally, an appreciation of design issues highlights the importance of what data to collect (e.g. do we need to ask retrospective questions?) and of thinking through the issues of whom we should collect it from. It is therefore important in questionnaire design and in developing sampling strategies.

REFINING RESEARCH QUESTIONS: A CHECKLIST

To help clarify precisely what your research question is, try to be clear about your answers to the following groups of questions:

1   Aims

   a   What type of study are you doing: Is it descriptive or explanatory?

   b   What will be the main type of contribution of the study? Is it intended to make a practical, theoretical/conceptual or methodological advance?

   c   Is the study testing well-formulated hypotheses or simply asking a set of questions? What are they?

d　How will the study add to what is already known? Are you:

　i　testing a new theory, hypotheses, methods?

　ii　improving on previous methods and theories?

　iii　testing alternative theories?

　iv　trying to resolve conflicting evidence from previous research?

　v　measuring concepts in a new way?

　vi　applying the ideas in a different context and to different types of people and groups than previously?

　vii　seeking to replicate or challenge previous research?

e　Are the ideas you are testing reasonable? Do they make sense in terms of previous research, theory and experience?

f　Are the questions answerable or testable? Is it possible to measure the core concepts (see Chapter 4)? Do you have access to a sample required for doing the study?

2　Context

a　How does the study relate to previous research on the topic? Is it a replication, a test, an extension? What is different about it?

b　How adequate is the previous research? What are the strengths and weaknesses of previous studies? Is there much previous research? Is the previous research consistent or are there conflicting findings and contradictions to be resolved?

c　Have you critically evaluated the previous research? Your review of the research should not simply list what has been done. It should point out the gaps, limitations and other shortcomings. Does your research question emerge out of the shortcomings and gaps (empirical, theoretical or methodological) you have identified in the previous research? If it does not why are you doing the research?

d　Have you examined the most recent research? How up to date is your review? Have you looked at books, reports, work in progress as well as journal articles?

e　How balanced is your review of previous research? Have you simply reported research that confirms your views or have you reported fairly on the full range of available findings?

3　Significance and scope

a　Why is the study worth doing? Of what importance will the results be? If you plan to make a practical, theoretical or methodological contribution of what significance is this likely to be?

b　What are the theories you will be evaluating? What concepts will you be using? Are these important?

c　If you are evaluating theories are you clear what these theories are? Have you drawn a diagram of the theory?

d　What is the scope of the study? Will the findings be widely generalisable?

e　To which wider population or subgroups will the results apply?

f　What will be your unit of analysis? Can you add to previous research by using different units of analysis?

g　To what time period will the results apply?

h　To what region(s) will the results apply?

4　Research design

a　If you are conducting an explanatory study have you specified the type of research design you will be using?

b　What comparison groups will you be using?

c　Will your sample have sufficient diversity so that you can build comparison groups for data analysis? How will you make groups comparable?

d　If you are looking at change do you have a time dimension to your study? Is the time over which you will look at change sufficient? Will you be using a prospective or retrospective approach?

KEY CONCEPTS

Cross-sectional design	Idiographic	Nomothetic	Research design
Dependent variable	Independent variable	Panel design	Unit of analysis
Experimental design	Intervening variable	Quasi-panel design	Variable
Explanation	Intervention	Random allocation	

FURTHER READING

Remarkably few books seriously address how to clarify research problems. The books by Bell and Newby, *Doing Sociological Research* (1977) and Bell and Encel, *Inside the Whale* (1978) are valuable because they show that in actual practice the formulation of research problems is a process.

Babbie, in *The Practice of Social Research* (1995), provides a useful account of options and decisions when designing a research project. Locke et al. *Guide for Planning Dissertations and Grant Proposals* (1999) provides practical advice about focusing research questions. Cooper's book, *Synthesising Research: A Guide for Literature Reviews* (1998), and his earlier article on 'Literature Searching Strategies of Integrative Research Reviewers' (1985) and Fink's book *Conducting Research Literature Reviews: From Paper to the Internet* (1998) provide some useful hints on reviewing the literature as a way of clarifying research questions. Gallagher's recent article on the significant role of the literature review in designing research is also worth looking at.

An advanced book outlining a variety of research designs that is well worth the effort of reading is Campbell and Stanley's *Experimental and Quasi-Experimental Designs for Research* (1963). However it is worth reading Stouffer's paper on 'Some observations on study design' (1950) first. *Research Design in Social Research* (de Vaus, 2001) provides an extensive treatment of a wide range of experimental, panel and cross-sectional designs and examines the strengths and weaknesses of each and the way each design affects the way data are analysed.

EXERCISES

1   For each of the following statements say what unit of analysis is being used.

   a   In the UK for every 1000 women aged 20–24 there were 30.4 who had an abortion in that year of 1998.

   b   In 1998 in the United States the average family in poverty would require an additional US$6620 per year to get on or above the poverty line.

   c   Australia has one of the lowest rates of expenditure on research amongst developed countries.

   d   Within any one year 18 per cent of Australians move.

   e   In the UK the official abortion rate per 1000 women aged 20–24 has changed as follows:

1968 = 3.4	1985 = 20.4
1970 = 10.5	1990 = 28.1
1975 = 15.1	1995 = 25.5
1980 = 18.7	1998 = 30.4

2   You wish to see whether having a secure family income actually makes families function better. Forgetting for the moment how you would measure 'better functioning' or 'secure income', draw design diagrams of a cross-sectional and a panel design to test this idea. Then draw a design that avoids the problems inherent in these two.

3   You wish to do a descriptive study on prejudice. Using the guidelines suggested in Chapter 3, focus this topic into a much more specific research problem.

4   Try putting the theory which is diagrammed in Figure 3.1 into words.

5   For each of the following statements of research findings indicate the type of research design that appears to have been employed and explain what is wrong with the conclusions that are drawn. Concentrate on problems that arise from research design problems.

   a   Sixty-eight per cent of married people scored high on our index of conservatism while only 38 per cent of single people scored high. Marriage makes people more conservative.

b   After observing a sample of childless married couples over a ten-year period we observed that the level of marital happiness declined over this period. Childlessness works against people being happily married.

c   In the early 1970s, before the end of the Vietnam War, surveys showed that tertiary students had strong anti-American attitudes. Recent surveys have shown that these feelings are no longer evident among students. Ending the Vietnam War certainly improved the attitudes of students to the United States.

d   Old people attend church more often than young people. For example, 58 per cent of those over 60 attend church regularly while only 22 per cent of those under 25 do so. From this we can conclude that as people get older they become more religious.

e   The average number of children per family now is 1.8. Families are obviously getting smaller these days.

f   To test the idea that having children makes people happier, a group of parents were asked how happy they felt now compared with before they had children. Eighty-seven per cent said they were happier now than before they had children. From this we can conclude that having children improves people's happiness.

g   A HEADSTART program (a preschool educational program to help disadvantaged children have a head start by the time they commence school) was used to test the effectiveness of HEADSTART. A group of four-year-olds from disadvantaged backgrounds were chosen to enter the program. IQ tests were given at the beginning of the program and again at the end. There was an average gain of ten IQ points over the period of the program. HEADSTART increases children's IQ.

Part II

COLLECTING
SURVEY DATA

4

Developing indicators for concepts

To conduct a survey we must translate any concepts into a form in which they are measurable. This chapter examines three main steps in this process:

1 clarifying the concepts;
2 developing indicators;
3 evaluating the indicators.

Before examining these steps it is helpful to consider an example that illustrates the process and difficulties of developing indicators. Suppose we are interested in the concept *social capital*. This term is being used increasingly in sociological research and the social development literature to characterise something about an important element of societies. The existence or absence of social capital is seen to be critical for understanding social wellbeing, the success or failure of intervention and development programs, crime rates, health profiles of societies, the ability to deal with poverty and so forth. But what is meant by this vague term? When someone argues that increasing crime rates are caused by a lack of social capital what do they mean? How can we tell? We must be able to measure crime rates accurately and define and measure social capital. How do we recognise a society in which the store of social capital is low and one in which it is high?

The first step is to work out what we mean by the concept.

CLARIFYING THE CONCEPTS

Concepts are simply tools which fulfil a useful shorthand function: they are abstract summaries of a whole set of behaviours, attitudes and characteristics which we see as having something in common. Concepts do not have an independent existence 'out there': they do not have any fixed meaning. Concepts are terms which people create for the purpose of communication and efficiency. When developing indicators for concepts the task is not to find indicators which match some concept which has a set definition. It is up to us to first define what we mean by the concept and then develop indicators for the concept *as it has been defined*. By their very nature definitions are neither true nor false; they are only more useful or less useful.

There is a problem here. If concepts have no set meaning then anyone can define a concept any way they wish. The results would be that the concept would become useless; unless people mean the same thing by a word, communication is impossible. In sociology lack of agreement about how words are defined leads to confusion and pointless debates. For example, debates about the extent to which a country is developed, democratic or has low levels of social capital depend substantially on definitions of development, democracy and social capital respectively.

The view that concepts do not have real or set meanings can lead to conceptual anarchy, a problem with no entirely satisfactory solution. The most practical action is to make it very clear how we have defined a concept and to keep this definition clearly in mind when drawing conclusions and comparing the findings with those of other researchers. Although we can define a word any way we wish, there seems to be little value in developing entirely idiosyncratic definitions. Since concepts are used to communicate, it makes most sense to use the word in its most commonly understood sense. If the definition of the concept is idiosyncratic this should be made very clear. Where a concept takes on a number of widely held but different meanings, we will need either to decide on (and justify) one, or to design the research so that we have indicators of each of the different meanings.

How to clarify concepts

Since concepts have no set meanings yet it is crucial that the concepts used in research be defined, how do we go about clarifying them? In practice people use different approaches. I will describe three steps which help in the process.

Obtain a range of definitions of the concept

Before adopting one definition of a concept look for the ways in which others have used the concept. People do not always provide formal definitions so we may need to work out what they mean by the way they have used the term. Their definition may be implicit rather than explicit.

We can get a good idea of the range of definitions by searching textbooks, dictionaries, encyclopaedias and journal articles. The internet assists greatly in this exercise. The internet has online dictionaries, encyclopaedias, articles, web pages and the like that can yield useful information quickly. Online searches of journal databases can speed up the process of identifying the range of ways in which a concept has been defined. Many of the strategies were outlined in the previous chapter. Web Pointer 4.1 illustrates this in relation to social capital and in so doing points to some useful general places to look.

WEB POINTER 4.1   *Discovering definitions of social capital*

Dictionaries

I first went to a website that I knew included dictionaries and reference guides from a range of disciplines such as sociology, economics, psychology, law, literature etc. This is a free site:

>   http://w1.xrefer.com/search.jsp

Using the search facility at this site I found only one definition of social capital. This definition was:

>   The total stock of a society's productive assets, including those that allow the manufacture of the marketable outputs that create private-sector profits, *and* those that create non-marketed outputs, such as defence and education.
>   (*The Penguin Dictionary of Economics*, © Graham Bannock, R.E. Baxter and Evan Davis 1998)

I then looked at more dictionaries. The internet contains many useful specialist dictionaries. I went to the site:

>   www.yourdictionary.com/specialty.html

and searched relevant specialist dictionaries. I searched the *Dictionary of Critical Sociology* and obtained the following definition of social capital:

>   *Social capital:* Generally social capital is the product of people working together to achieve something unattainable to them or individuals. The self, the various forms of material culture as well as society itself

WEB POINTER 4.1 *continued*

cannot be produced by people working as private individuals. Social capital includes material items but is much more than merely the physical base of culture.

(*Dictionary of Critical Sociology*, www.public.iastate.edu/~rmazur/dictionary/s.html)

Search engine

Single search engine

The dictionary site contained a link to a search engine that would search other dictionaries and sites:

http://au.yahoo.com/reference/dictionaries/

A search at this web address turned up a number of useful websites that provided further ideas for definitions of social capital. These sites included:

1   Social Capital Development Corporation at:

www.social-capital.org/

This provided a view of social capital too lengthy to reproduce here.

2   Civic Participation, Social Capital and Leadership at:

www.lajollainstitute.org/LeaderNet/civicpart.html

3   http://muse.jhu.edu/demo/journal_of_democracy/v006/putnam.html

Includes the famous article, *Bowling Alone: America's Declining Social Capital*, by Robert Putnam, a key figure in work on social capital. The site also includes an interview with Putnam.

4   The World Bank site Social Capital and Development at:
www.worldbank.org/poverty/scapital/index.htm

This site had a vast amount of useful material and links to other relevant sites.

Metasearch engine

Using the metasearch engine Copernic 2001 (available for free download from www.copernic.com/), I asked for a search of Australian internet sites containing the term 'social capital'. This identified a large number of sites including:

www.aifs.org.au/institute/pubs/WP21.pdf

www.aifs.org.au/institute/pubs/RP24.pdf

www.act.gov.au/actinfo/futurecommunities/

All three sites provided excellent papers on defining and measuring social capital and links to other sites and references. The papers by Winter and Stone on these sites argue that social capital:

. . . consists of networks of social relations which are characterised by norms of trust and reciprocity. Combined, it is these elements which are argued to sustain civil society and which enable people to act for mutual benefit. (www.aifs.org.au/institute/pubs/RP24.pdf)

and

Social capital exists in the reciprocal relationships between people who know and trust each other, and who have shared interests and beliefs. These relationships operate for the benefit of all involved. They are generated when people come together in families, at work, in neighbourhoods, sporting, social, religious, local organisations and formal as well as informal meeting places.
(www.act.gov.au/actinfo/futurecommunities/)

WEB POINTER 4.1 *continued*

Library catalogue search

By conducting a keyword search for 'social capital' in an online library catalogue, a number of books were identified: Misztral (1996), Putnam (1993) and Fukuyama (1995). These provided further ideas about ways of defining and conceptualising social capital.

Encyclopaedia

I then looked up the *Encyclopaedia Britannica* online at www.britannica.com/. While I found nothing on this site, I was directed to use other search engines such as goto.com and Ask Jeeves. These found a whole set of useful websites. The following definition was provided at www.nhsetrent.gov.uk/newnhs/LanguageAndCulture/SocialCapital/summary.htm:

> Social capital refers to elements such as social trust and networks that people can draw upon to solve common problems. Networks of 'The Public', such as neighbourhood associations, sports clubs and co-operatives, are an essential part of social capital. These assist in:
>
> ■ fostering norms of generalised reciprocity by creating expectations that favours will be returned;
>
> ■ facilitating co-ordination and communication both within and outside the community;
>
> ■ creating a two-way relationship based around the concept of shared/reciprocated favours.

Another site, found in a similar way, included an article that reviewed different types of definitions and measures of social capital:

> http://informel.c3ed.uvsq.fr/soccap1.htm#4

Journal databases

Finally, I searched the Sociological Abstracts online database. This resulted in a list of 507 articles and dissertations that somehow related to this concept. A more careful search would help narrow down this set of articles. Access to Sociological Abstracts is limited to subscribers. Most academic libraries subscribe and provide free access to those with library access.

Visit www.social-research.org to use these links and to check for updates and additions.

Once a number of definitions have been identified we might identify the common elements of these definitions and develop a definition based on these. This approach could produce a definition that incorporates the generally understood meaning of the concept. Many of the definitions of social capital include common elements such as trust, community networks, shared values, a degree of communal responsibility and reciprocity. A definition might be based on these common elements.

An alternative approach to developing a definition is to distinguish between different types of ways in which the concept has been used. For example, the definition obtained from the *Dictionary of Economics* (Web Pointer 4.1) is quite different from the more sociological definitions such as the definition above that refers to social networks, community and the like. Some definitions treat social capital and human capital as the same thing (i.e. the skills, knowledge and cultural know-how that some groups or individuals have that enable them to get ahead or prevent them from doing so). Some definitions include good physical infrastructure (public places to meet, safe places) as a key element of social capital. Others will regard social capital as an attribute of groups rather than of individuals. Where different types of definitions exist you will need to opt for one approach and justify your choice.

Many concepts used in social science research are difficult to conceptualise. Even the more 'factual' demographic concepts such as education, workforce participation and retirement can be difficult to conceptualise and measure. This is not the place to canvass the difficulties with conceptualising these demographic concepts. However, Web Pointer 4.2 directs you to some excellent and sophisticated online articles that review and try to resolve these difficulties.

Decide on a definition

Having listed types of definitions or delineated the most common elements of definitions, we need to decide on which definition to use. We might opt for an existing one, create a new one, choose a classic definition or use a more contemporary one. Regardless of which we do, we need to justify the decision.

In practice, the process of conceptual clarification continues as data are analysed. Clarification is not a once-and-for-all process which precedes research. It is an ongoing process: there is an interaction between analysing data and clarifying concepts. As a result of analysing data we are often in a better position to say what we mean by a concept than before we began. Nevertheless, this process must begin before data collection.

To assign a definition to a concept is to give it a *nominal definition*: it is a working definition which is used in the research. It provides a focus for research and guidance about the type of information to collect. For example, we might define religious beliefs as those with a supernatural element. This helps focus on the range of beliefs to examine but does not specify which beliefs to examine. This is the task of an *operational definition* which will be dealt with shortly.

Delineate the dimensions of the concept

Many concepts have a number of different aspects or dimensions. When clarifying concepts it is often helpful to distinguish between those dimensions. This may result in using only one of the dimensions in the study or it may lead to a more systematic development of indicators for each dimension. Distinguishing between dimensions can lead to more sophisticated theorising and more useful analysis. Box 4.1 illustrates possible dimensions of the concept of social capital.

How do you identify the dimensions of a concept? There is no magical way of doing this. Reading the literature and looking at how other people have used the concept and looking for distinctions they have made can be helpful. For some concepts it is useful to think in terms of social, economic, psychological, political, physical and material dimensions. This can be a useful way of thinking about concepts such as wellbeing and deprivation. Another method is *concept mapping*. This is an approach by which brainstorming with other people helps explore the different ways in which a concept might be unpacked (see Web Pointer 4.3).

We might want to develop measures of all the dimensions of the concept or focus on just one or two. Whichever approach we adopt, delineating the separate dimensions helps in choosing indicators systematically.

DEVELOPING INDICATORS

The process of moving from abstract concepts to the point where we can develop questionnaire items to

---

WEB POINTER 4.2   *Conceptualising common socio-demographic concepts*

You will find discussions of the issues involved in conceptualising

Religion	Ethnicity
Education	Income
Age	Gender
Health	Quality of life
Socio-economic status	Occupation

at: http://qb.soc.surrey.ac.uk/resources/authors/authors.htm

Visit www.social-research.org to use these links and to check for updates and additions.

BOX 4.1 *Dimensions of social capital*

Winter (2000) and Stone (2001) use the following definition:

> [Social capital] consists of networks of social relations which are characterised by norms of trust and reciprocity. Combined, it is these elements which are argued to sustain civil society and which enable people to act for mutual benefit.

Stone calls for measures of social capital that capture all of its dimensions (and sub-dimensions). The two core dimensions are:

1 *Structure* of social relationships—networks
2 *Quality* of social relationships—norms

These two dimensions have various sub-dimensions:

1 *Networks*
　a Type

　b Size and capacity
　c Spacial location
　d Structure (openness, density and homogeneity)
　e Relation
2 *Norms*
　a Trust
　b Reciprocity

Within these various dimensions and sub-dimensions Stone identifies further sub-dimensions (Figure 4.1 identifies *some* of these sub-dimensions). She then reviews ways in which several of these sub-dimensions have been measured and points to the problems of various measures.

WEB POINTER 4.3 *Concept mapping*

An introduction to concept mapping:
　http://trochim.human.cornell.edu/kb/conmap.htm

A fuller and more in-depth description of the technique:
　http://trochim.human.cornell.edu/research/epp1/epp1.htm

The technique applied to mental illness employment program:
　http://trochim.human.cornell.edu/research/ccp/tcands.htm

---

tap the concept is called *descending the ladder of abstraction*. It involves moving from the broad to the specific, from the abstract to the concrete. In clarifying concepts we begin to descend this ladder. A further step is taken when dimensions are specified. Sometimes these dimensions themselves can be further subdivided into some more specific sub-dimensions. The social capital example illustrates this. Initially two dimensions were identified: the *structure* of social relations (networks) and the *quality* of social relations (norms) that promote connection. Within each of these, further sub-dimensions were identified. By identifying sub-dimensions we become a little clearer regarding the particular indicators we might use (see Figure 4.1).

When delineating dimensions and sub-dimensions it is helpful to define the terms as you go. If one aspect of 'norms' is 'trust', what do we mean by trust? Trust in what? Before concepts can be measured we must descend from the lofty and often vague heights of some concepts and deal with these more mundane issues. The process of descending the ladder of abstraction is summarised in Figure 4.1. Web Pointer 4.4 shows the process of descending this ladder through two concepts. Use this Pointer to practise this skill.

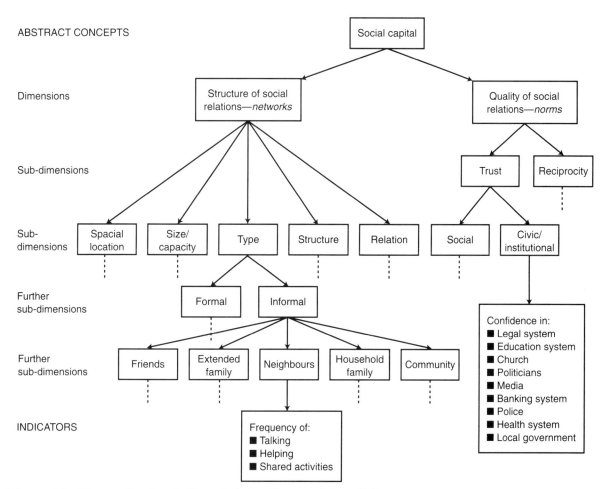

ABSTRACT CONCEPTS

Dimensions

Sub-dimensions

Sub-dimensions

Further sub-dimensions

Further sub-dimensions

INDICATORS

Figure 4.1   Descending the ladder of abstraction: social capital

---

WEB POINTER 4.4   *Poverty and social exclusion*

In September 2000 the Joseph Rowntree Foundation released a report on Social Exclusion and Poverty in Britain. To read this report go to the website:

www.jrf.org.uk/knowledge/findings/socialpolicy/930.asp

Two key concepts are used in this report: *poverty* and *social exclusion*. How has each of these concepts been defined? What dimensions of the concepts have been identified (if more than one)? What indicators have been used for each of the concepts (or dimensions of concepts)?

When we get to the point where we can develop indicators there are three broad problems with which to deal:

1   how many indicators to use;
2   how to develop the indicators;
3   how to form items into a questionnaire (this will be dealt with in Chapter 7).

How many indicators to use

There is no simple answer to this problem but the following guidelines are useful.

1 When there is no agreed way of measuring a concept it may be helpful to develop indicators for a range of definitions and see what difference this makes to the results and interpretations.
2 If the concept is multidimensional, consider whether you are really interested in all dimensions. Are they all relevant to the theory?
3 Ensure that the key concepts are thoroughly measured. The behaviour and attitudes that we are trying to explain and the theorised causes must be carefully measured using several indicators.
4 Typically attitudes and opinions are complex and are best measured with a number of questions to capture the scope of the concept (see Chapter 11).
5 Pilot testing indicators is a way of eliminating unnecessary questions. Initially we might have 50 questions to measure authoritarianism but find that we need only 10 of these items; the additional 40 items might not add anything to our index (see Chapter 11).
6 The number of items is affected by practical considerations such as overall length of the questionnaire and method of administration (see Chapter 8).

How to develop indicators

Where possible it is best to use well-established indicators. Rather than 'reinventing the wheel' why not take advantage of the expert work of other researchers? Many concepts are regularly measured in surveys and measures are readily available. In the UK there has been a deliberate strategy to develop a standard way of asking a question about a broad range of key demographic concepts. The benefit is that it is easy to track change over time and to compare results from different studies when questions have been asked in the same way over time and in different surveys. This strategy in the UK has been called harmonisation and has resulted in a uniformity of definition of concepts, questions and coding classification in a wide range of large-scale national surveys (see Web Pointer 4.5).

Where well-established measures exist they should be used. They may require some modification depending on the nature of the sample (age, education, literacy etc). Some older measures may require updating or adapting for different countries. As well as the harmonised concepts noted above there are many sets of measures available for a range of attitude and related matters (Box 4. 2).

Where proven measures are unavailable you will need to develop your own indicators. Two strategies are helpful in this process. For some research topics, especially those where we are surveying a special

---

WEB POINTER 4.5 *Question Harmonisation Project*

To discover more about harmonising questions and classification categories for a standard range of demographic questions in household surveys go to:

   http://qb.soc.surrey.ac.uk/qb1/resources/harmonisation/booklet96/harmon96_cover.htm

This site also provides the harmonised questions and classifications for the following concepts:

- household composition and relationships between household members
- age and gender of household members
- ethnicity
- marital status of members
- income
- economic status of members
- occupation

- socio-economic status
- level of workforce participation
- industry in which members are employed
- details regarding non-work status
- social security status
- length of residence
- job details
- general health

BOX 4.2   *Sets of indicators of concepts*

A number of collections exist that provide well-established sets of indicators for a wide range of concepts. Some of these are listed below. See also Web Pointer 11.1 for some website resources for sets of questions to measure concepts. To obtain a fuller, regularly updated list of such handbooks and lists of articles that provide indicators for single concepts visit my website at:

www.social-research.org

Refer to the Bibliography for complete publication details of the following list.

Bearden, Netemeyer and Mobley (1993) *Handbook of Marketing Scales: Multi-item Measures for Marketing and Consumer Behavior Research*

Beere (1990) *Gender Roles: A Handbook of Tests and Measures*

Biderman and Drury (1976) *Working Groups on Indicators of the Quality of Employment*

Bowling (1997) *Measuring Health: A Review of Quality of Life Measurement Scales*

Bonjean, Hill and McLemore (1967) *Sociological Measurement: An Inventory of Scales and Indices*

Brodsky, O'Neal and Smitherton (1983) *Handbook of Scales for Research in Crime*

Bruner and Hensel (1993) *Marketing Scales Handbook*

Chun, Cobb and French (1975) *Measures for Psychological Assessment: A guide to 3,000 Original Sources and their Applications*

Comrey, Backer and Glaser (1973) *A Sourcebook for Mental Health Measures*

Coulter (1989) *Measuring Inequality: A Methodological Handbook*

Fabozzi and Greenfield (1984) *The Handbook of Economic and Financial Measures*

Ferneau (1973) *Drug Abuse Research Instrument Inventory*

Fischer and Corcoran (1994) *Measures for Clinical Practice: A Sourcebook. Volume 1—Couples, Families and Children*

Fischer and Corcoran (1994) *Measures for Clinical Practice: A Sourcebook. Volume 2—Adults*

Johnson (1976) *Tests and Measurements in Child Development:* Handbook II

Kane and Kane (1981) *Assessing the Elderly: A Practical Guide to Measurement*

Knapp (1972) *An Omnibus of Measures Related to School-Based Attitudes*

Mangen and Peterson (1984) *Research Instruments in Social Gerontology*

McDowell and Newell (1996) *Measuring Health: A Guide to Rating Scales and Questionnaires*

Meuller (1986) *Measuring Social Attitudes: A Handbook for Researchers and Practitioners*

Miller (1991) *Handbook of Research Design and Social Measurement*

Plake and Impara (eds) (2001) *The Fourteenth Mental Measurements Yearbook*

Robinson, Athanasiou and Head (1969) *Measures of Occupational Attitudes and Occupational Characteristics*

Robinson, Rusk and Head (1968) *Measures of Political Attitudes*

Robinson and Shaver (1976) *Measures of Psychological Attitudes*

Shaw and Wright (1967) *Scales for the Measurement of Attitudes*

Strauss (1969) *Family Measurement Techniques*

Touliatos, Perlmutter and Strauss (1990) *Handbook of Family Measurement Techniques*

---

group (e.g. migrants, Aborigines, young people, childless couples), it is very helpful to use a less structured approach to data collection first (e.g. observation, unstructured interview). This can help us understand matters through the eyes of these people,

learn of their concerns and ways of thinking. This can be extremely helpful in developing relevant and appropriately worded questions for that group.

A second strategy is to use 'informants' from the group to be surveyed. Such people can provide useful clues about meaningful questions. For example, if surveying a trade union it would be helpful to talk to key people in the union to get their ideas and comments on questions.

In the end we have to decide which indicators to use and how to word them. In doing so we need to be as informed as possible about the study population, be clear about what we want to measure, look at other people's efforts and evaluate our own indicators.

EVALUATING INDICATORS

Having developed indicators we have to make sure that they measure the concept we think they are measuring (validity) and ensure that we can rely on the answers people provide. A question is of little use if people answer it one way one day and another the next (this is a question of reliability). Where the indicators lack validity or reliability we have *measurement error*.

It is desirable to assess the reliability and validity of indicators before conducting the study. This involves pilot testing that is done by administering the questions to a similar but smaller sample to that to be used in the actual study (see Chapter 7 on pilot testing). Sometimes people avoid pilot testing by including a large number of indicators in the study and only using those which prove to be valid and reliable. This seems to be the wrong way of doing things since we will end up by defining the concept in terms of the indicators that 'worked'. If this is done then the indicators may not represent the concepts or the theory we set out to test and as such the research can end up having little relevance to the original research question. Do not take the risk. Pilot test first.

Reliability

A reliable measurement is one where we obtain the same result on repeated occasions. If people answer a question the same way on repeated occasions then it is reliable. I will consider three aspects of reliability.

Sources of unreliability
A question may be unreliable due to bad wording: a person may understand the question differently on different occasions. Different interviewers can elicit different answers from the respondent: the gender, ethnic background and dress of the interviewer can influence responses. Another source of error can occur during coding: different coders might code the same response (e.g. occupation) differently. Asking questions on issues about which people have no opinion or have insufficient information can lead to very rough-and-ready answers.

Even well-developed questions will be subject to unreliability problems. For example, studies of the same respondents over time show that they give different answers to questions on different occasions, even though there should have been no change. One study (Schreiber, 1976) shows that for questions about gender, the state where the respondent was born and where they grew up, between 1 per cent and 14 per cent replied differently on the two occasions on which they answered the question (two years apart). Questions asking about the size of the place where they grew up, the respondent's education level and their father's occupation had even higher levels of unreliability, ranging from 22 per cent to 34 per cent error.

Testing reliability
There are a number of well-established methods of testing the reliability of indicators. The best methods, however, only apply to measuring the reliability of scales where we have a set of questions to measure the one concept rather than single-item indicators (see pages 180–6).

Where we have a single question to measure a concept or characteristic it is particularly important to make sure it is reliable. Basically the *test-retest method* is the only way to check the reliability of single questions: ask the same people the same questions at intervals of two to four weeks and calculate the correlation between the answers on both occasions. If the correlation is high (a rule of thumb is 0.8 or above) then we assume that the question is reliable. Unfortunately the test-retest method is a poor one. It is often difficult to give the same test to the same sample twice. A way to alleviate this problem is to trial the question on a smaller but similar practice sample to that to be used in the study—here it may be possible to test-retest. Another problem is memory: people may remember their answers from the first occasion and answer the same way the second time to be consistent. This can artificially inflate the apparent reliability of the questionnaires. Furthermore, when people answer a question differently at the retest stage it is not always clear what this means. It may mean that the measure is unreliable or unstable but the inconsistency of responses could reflect the fact that people's attitudes have changed or that the attitude really is unstable.

Increasing reliability

The best way to create reliable indicators is to use multiple-item indicators: they are more reliable and we have easier methods of assessing their reliability (see Likert scales in Chapter 11). But for many issues it is appropriate only to ask a single question. There is little point in asking how old someone is, or asking about their gender in six different ways. The best course is to use well-tested questions from reputable questionnaires (see Web Pointers 4.1 and 4.6 and Box 4.2).

Other methods of improving reliability involve careful question wording, interviewer training and working out methods of coding. It is wise to avoid questions about which people are unlikely to have an opinion or knowledge, or to provide 'do not know' or 'cannot decide' responses.

Validity

A valid measure is one which measures what it is intended to measure. In fact, it is not the measure that is valid or invalid but the use to which the measure is put. We might use educational level to measure social status. The issue is not whether we have measured education properly but whether this is a suitable measure of social status. The validity of a measure then depends on how we have defined the concept it is designed to measure. There are three basic ways in which to assess validity. Ultimately none of them is entirely satisfactory but they are the best we have.

Criterion validity

Using this approach we compare how people answered our new measure of a concept, with existing, well-accepted measures of the concept. If their answers on both the new and the established measure are highly correlated this is taken to mean that the new measure is valid.

There are two problems with this approach. First, we must assume the validity of the established

---

WEB POINTER 4.6   *Questions and questionnaires on the web*

A number of internet sites provide copies of questionnaires from major surveys. These questionnaires can be invaluable in helping develop questions. Many of these sites enable you to search a set of questionnaires for all questions used to tap a particular concept.

The Question Bank: This is a free UK site with full questionnaires from a wide range of major national surveys.	http://qb.soc.surrey.ac.uk
The Roper Centre: This US site provides access to 350 000 questions asked on national public opinion surveys since 1935. It is a free site but you will have to register first.	http://roperweb.ropercenter.uconn.edu/iPOLL/login/ipoll_login.html
General Social Survey: A free US site with the full question wording, searchable by topic, for questions asked in this major national survey since 1972. Use the subject index option to locate questions.	www.icpsr.umich.edu/GSS99/subject/s-index.htm
The ZEUS database at the University of Mannheim: This is an excellent, free site from which to obtain the wording of a large number of questions for social surveys.	http://zeus.mzes.uni-mannheim.de/ab_data.html

measure. A low correlation between the new and existing measure is interpreted as meaning that the new measure is invalid. But it could be the old one that is invalid. Often we will be developing a new measure because we are unhappy with the existing measure. So to validate the new test by using the old one seems self-defeating. Second, for many concepts in the social sciences there are no well-established measures against which to check our new measure.

A related approach is to give our measure to *criterion groups*. Thus a new measure of political conservatism might be given to members of conservative and radical political groups. If the members of the conservative group come out as conservative on the measure and the radical group members come out as radical, this provides good evidence for the measure's validity. Unfortunately, for many concepts criterion groups are not available.

Content validity

This approach to evaluating validity emphasises the extent to which the indicators measure the different aspects of the concept. A test of arithmetic skills that deals only with subtraction and does not measure ability at multiplication, addition or division lacks content validity. The test may be a fine test of abilities at subtraction and would be a valid measure of this but would not be a valid test of arithmetical skills. The validity of a test depends on the use to which it is put and not on the test *per se*. Whether we agree that a measure has content validity depends ultimately on how we define the concept it is designed to test. Given the disagreement about the 'content' of many social science concepts it is difficult to develop measures which have agreed on validity.

Construct validity

This approach evaluates a measure by how well the measure conforms with theoretical expectations. Suppose we have developed a new measure of alienation and we wish to evaluate it. First we might say, on the basis of theory, that social class will be related to alienation: the lower the class the higher the alienation. We administer the alienation questions as well as measuring the social class of our respondents. If our results show that the lower the class the higher the alienation we might say the new measure has construct validity. This approach may be all right if the theory we use is well established but it is open to

two dangers. First, if when using the new measure the theoretical proposition is *not* supported, how do we know whether it is our new measure that is invalid—the theory may be wrong or the measure of the other concept (class) may be invalid. Second, we must avoid developing a test so that it supports the theory. If we use a theory to validate our measure and then use the (valid!) measure to test the theory we have established nothing.

In the end there is no ideal way of determining the validity of a measure. The method chosen will depend on the situation. If a good criterion exists use it; if the definition of the concept is well defined or well accepted use this approach; if there are well-established theories which use the concept which we wish to validate, use this approach. If all else fails we have to say this is how the concept is defined and these measures, on the face of it, seem to cover the concept, and to give the measure to other people (referred to as a panel of judges) to see what they think. This approach will indicate the *face validity* of the concept.

The problem of meaning

One of the problems in developing valid indicators is interpreting the meaning of people's responses. The same behaviour may mean different things or indicate different things for different people. Whilst it is difficult to eliminate this problem with any research technique, there are steps that can be taken to help alleviate it. For an excellent discussion of this issue see Marsh (1982).

One approach is to use a variety of methods of data collection. In particular, observation and in-depth interviewing can give the researcher insight into the meaning of behaviour and attitudes expressed in questionnaires. This can help make more intelligent interpretations of the patterns discovered in the analysis of questionnaire data.

The *pattern* of people's responses can also help us understand the meaning of particular responses. For example, we will interpret the meaning of regular church attendance differently for the person who also prays regularly and expresses agreement with religious doctrines than for the regular attender who does neither of these things. In other words we can use other information to help put the response to a particular question in context.

We can also be more direct and ask people why

they behave in a particular way or why they express a particular attitude. While people are not always aware of the reasons, answers to these 'why' questions can provide valuable insights (see Marsh, 1982: 104–11).

None of these approaches resolves the problem of accurately finding the meaning particular behaviours and attitudes have for particular people. It is important to be aware of the problem and to take what steps are available to minimise it. An awareness of the problem should encourage survey researchers to be more thorough in the way data are analysed and be more sensitive in the way results are interpreted. It also should cause survey researchers to supplement their questionnaire studies with more in-depth data collection techniques.

DEVELOPING INDICATORS: A CHECKLIST

To assist with the task of developing indicators use the following checklist.
1   Identify the concepts for which indicators are required.
   a List the concepts required to measure the:
      i independent variable(s)
      ii dependent variable(s)
      iii intervening variable(s)
      iv grouping variables
      v socio-demographic concepts.
2   Develop nominal definitions.
   a Search the literature and develop a list of ways each concept is defined.
   b Select a particular type of definition or develop a new one.
3   Unpack the concepts.
   a For each concept:
      i identify relevant dimensions
      ii identify relevant sub-dimensions.

   b Decide which dimensions to focus on:
      i all dimensions?
      ii selected dimensions/sub-dimensions only?
   c Justify the selection of particular dimensions.
4   Develop indicators.
   a Work out the number of indicators required for each concept:
      i single
      ii multiple.
   b Determine whether there are existing and proven indicators.
   c Evaluate the existing indicators:
      i appropriate for the method of data collection to be used?
      ii need updating?
      iii appropriate for the particular country in which they are to be used?
      iv appropriate for the particular sample (given age, gender, education etc)?
   d What evidence is there for the:
      i reliability of the existing indicators?
      ii validity of these indicators?
   e Develop new indicators (if required).
      i use informants, unstructured exploratory interviews, brainstorming sessions
      ii develop indicators appropriate to method of data collection
      iii develop indicators appropriate to proposed sample.
   f Develop initial measures.
5   Pilot test questions (new and existing).
   a Use sample comparable to final sample.
   b Evaluate question for:
      i reliability
      ii validity
      iii quality of questions (see Chapter 7).

KEY CONCEPTS

Construct validity	Dimensions of a	Measurement error	Reliability
Content validity	concept	Nominal definition	Validity
Criterion validity	Face validity	Operational definition	
Descending the ladder	Harmonisation	Operationalisation	
of abstraction	Indicator	Pilot test	

FURTHER READING

Often the problems of developing indicators for concepts are reduced to discussions of reliability and validity. For a thorough and clear discussion of issues involved in assessing reliability and validity see Carmines and Zeller's paper 'Reliability and Validity Assessment' (1979). They provide a more advanced and statistical treatment of these measurement issues in Zeller and Carmines, *Measurement in the Social Sciences* (1980). For a less statistical approach to issues of measurement, Bateson's *Data Construction in Social Surveys* (1984) provides an excellent and sophisticated discussion of data construction and develops a theory of this process.

Classic papers on the translation of concepts into indicators are in the edited collection by Lazarsfeld and Rosenberg, *The Language of Social Research* (1955) and Lazarsfeld, Pasenella and Rosenberg's *Continuities in the Language of Social Research* (1972). Some useful examples are provided by Hirschi and Selvin in *Delinquency Research: An Appraisal of Analytic Methods* (1967) Chapter 2. Berger provides a useful discussion on the nature of definitions of religion (1974) while Chapter 11 in Glock and Stark's *Religion and Society in Tension* (1965) provides an example of unpacking this concept into its various dimensions. Babbie's discussion on the nature of concepts in *The Practice of Social Research* (1995) Chapter 5 is of interest. Burgess has produced a useful guide to issues in defining and measuring a range of social variables in *Key Variables in Social Investigation* (1986).

A critical evaluation of a number of concepts and their indicators is provided in journals such as *Social Indicators Research*. These include Diener and Suh (1997) 'Measuring Quality of Life'; Larsen, Diener and Emmons (1985) 'An Evaluation of Subjective Well-Being Measures'; Larson (1996) 'The World Health Organization's Definition of Health: Social Versus Spiritual Health; Lester (1997) 'Operationalizing "Modernization"'; Pandey and Nathwani (1996) 'Measurement of Socio-Economic Inequality Using the Life-Quality Index'; Parmenter (1994) 'Quality of Life as a Concept and Measurable Entity'; Raphael, Renwick and Brown (1996) 'Quality of Life Indicators and Health: Current Status and Emerging Conceptions'.

EXERCISES

1 Explain why indicators must be developed for concepts.
2 Why might different people develop quite different indicators for the same concept?
3 Why is developing a nominal definition both problematic and important?
4 a Using the *Question Bank* website (http://qb.soc.surrey.ac.uk/nav/fr_home.htm) use the search facility within the question bank home page (click the search button) to locate a good question or questions for each of the following concepts:
   ■ attitudes towards homosexuality;
   ■ religiousness;
   ■ attitudes towards contraception and actual contraception practices.
  b Use the *The Roper Centre* site (http://roperweb.ropercenter.uconn.edu/iPOLL/login/ipoll_login.html) to locate questions to ascertain attitudes towards:
   ■ trust in government;
   ■ tax cuts.
  c Using the *General Social Survey* site (www.icpsr.umich.edu/GSS99/subject/s-index.htm) locate a good question to measure each of the following:

   ■ attitude to capital punishment;
   ■ work satisfaction;
   ■ experience of sexual harassment in the workplace.
5 List three variables or concepts for which single item indicators would be adequate and three for which multiple indicators would be more appropriate. For the multiple-item concepts explain why you would use multiple items.
6 Develop a set of questions to measure conservatism. Explain the steps you have taken to move from the concept to your set of questions.
7 Use the web search strategies listed in Web Pointer 4.1 to develop a definition of *domestic violence*. As well as identifying a definition also identify dimensions or types of domestic violence. Then, see if you can find questions on the internet or elsewhere that you could ask to ascertain whether a person had been a victim of domestic violence.
8 In exercise 3 for Chapter 2 you developed a diagram and conceptual propositions for a theory. Using the same theory and propositions:
  a clarify the concepts in your propositions;
  b develop indicators for each concept;
  c develop testable propositions.

9   The United Nations has been developing a measure of Human Development. It has established the *Human Development Index* as a means of reflecting the level of human development in each nation in the world. Go to the website www.undp.org/hdro/anatools.htm and read the document on that page. Then clarify what the concept 'human development' is. How does the UN use of the term human development differ from other ways in which development is conceived? What dimensions of this concept are identified? What indicators are used for those dimensions?

5

Ethics and data collection

Any survey will be shaped by three broad sets of considerations: technical, practical and ethical. Technical considerations involve ensuring that matters such as sample design, questionnaire construction, scale development and the like are as rigorous as possible. Practical considerations mean that the survey design must take account of realities such as budgets, deadlines and the purpose of the research (e.g. student project, PhD thesis, government report). Ethical considerations must also shape the final design of a survey. This chapter:

■ outlines some of the ethical issues that arise during survey data collection;
■ distinguishes between responsibilities to survey respondents and those to colleagues, sponsors and the public.

Ideally a survey will be technically correct, practically efficient and ethically sound. In reality these matters frequently conflict and require careful balancing. We can design a technically sophisticated and feasible project but it may need to be changed so that it is ethically sound. For example, we could devise ways of obtaining close to 100 per cent response rates by compelling people to participate or by giving the impression that participation was compulsory. But such compulsion would encounter ethical problems regarding voluntary participation. Participation in surveys might be higher if we lied about the purposes of the research but this compromises the principle of informed consent.

There are two broad approaches to making ethical decisions about research. One is to establish a *set of rules* and follow these regardless of the consequences for the research (Kimmel, 1988: 46). For example, you might adopt the rule that you should tell the truth regardless of the consequences or that you will only collect information from or about people with their fully informed consent. However, following such rules rigidly will mean that you cannot conduct a lot of research or, if you do, the results will be so contaminated that they would be of little value. Suppose, for example, that you adopt the rule that people should be fully informed about the purpose of research before they participate. This sounds fine but a detailed explanation of these purposes can distort the way people answer questions. If you explain that you are examining the level of sexual harassment in the workplace it is highly probable that this will affect the way people behave or answer questions and thus undermine the study. Furthermore, rigidly keeping to the rule that we should not collect information without a person's informed consent may prevent us from asking a person for any information about, say, other family members (a common occurrence in surveys) without the consent of those other family members.

Another way of making ethical decisions in research is to follow ethical guidelines but to use judgment far more than the rule-based approach would allow. Using this approach we take account of the *consequences* of a particular course of action and judge whether the potential benefits of the research outweighed the risks to the participants.

While using judgment might be more realistic than the rule-based approach it does have its problems. As a researcher we are an interested party who has an interest in seeing the research completed. It is easy to develop justifications whereby we believe that any short-term harm to study participants is outweighed by possible long-term benefit to society at large. No doubt some of the more outrageous misuse of human subjects in medical research has been justified in these terms. We can always justify all sorts of dubious research by anticipating *potential* long-term benefits which in reality are never realised.

Another problem with a judgment-based approach to making ethical decisions in research is that the assessment of costs to the participants and the benefits to society are subjective decisions based on the researcher's own moral position of what is good or bad and what is important and unimportant. Our own beliefs or prejudices about the relative importance of some people can also unintentionally influence the way we judge the harm to certain people. Medical and social research is full of examples where people from disadvantaged groups (e.g. black Americans, homosexuals, working-class gang members) have been afforded a lower level of privacy or care than would have been acceptable had the participants been more socially advantaged.

It is neither helpful nor possible to prescribe a set of ethical rules to be followed when conducting surveys. Research is conducted in different settings and with different methods and samples and requires judgments based on the context. The discussion that follows raises some ethical matters that can arise when collecting survey data. The purpose is to ensure that these matters are anticipated and dealt with as the survey is developed.

Our ethical responsibilities in research extend to various types of people—all of whom might be affected by the research itself or by the research results. Among these are:

- the research participants;
- the profession and professional colleagues;
- the wider public;
- sponsors and funders of the research.

Given the different interests of these different research stakeholders we can find ourselves having to meet conflicting ethical principles and balancing these with technical and practical considerations (Crespi, 1998).

RESEARCH PARTICIPANTS

Most professional codes of ethics stress the importance of five ethical responsibilities towards survey participants:

1 voluntary participation
2 informed consent
3 no harm
4 confidentiality anonymity, and
5 privacy.

Voluntary participation

This principle means that people should not be required to participate in a survey. Even though surveys do not involve physical risks to people that participation in medical experiments might, we are nevertheless invading their privacy and will normally seek personal information and private views. At the very least we are taking up their time.

Voluntary participation, however, conflicts with the methodological principle of representative sampling. Given the choice, certain types of people (e.g. those with lower levels of education, from non-English-speaking backgrounds) are more likely than others to decline to participate in surveys and can result in biased samples. However, compulsory participation is not the solution. Although compulsion might minimise bias it will undermine the quality of the responses. Since there are ways of statistically adjusting for known sample biases (see Chapter 6 on weighting and Chapters 16 and 17 on statistical controls) it is best to maximise the quality of responses and do all we reasonably can to encourage voluntary participation.

One way of ensuring that participants understand that participation is voluntary is to tell them explicitly. For example, at the beginning of a questionnaire respondents can be told:

> Although your participation in this survey will be greatly valued, you are not required to participate. You can stop at any point or choose not to answer any particular question. Just let the interviewer know.

Within this context of voluntary participation it is worth thinking about the following types of practices:

■ Governments that can *require by law* that citizens participate in certain surveys and census collections.

■ Institutions that require clients, students, patients, benefit recipients etc to complete forms. Although not called surveys these data collections have all the characteristics of a survey (see Chapter 1 on the form of data). While these data collections can be useful for monitoring, planning and reporting, participation is typically required.

■ Students who, as part of class requirements, are required to participate in a survey or experiment.

Researchers cannot always ensure that participation by all people is voluntary. Some questionnaires involve the 'indirect participation' of people. For example, a questionnaire that asks about the income, education and occupation of a person's parents or partner can be an invasion of the privacy of those people and means that these people are 'participating' involuntarily. A survey in which children are asked about parental behaviour is clearly one in which the parents are 'involuntary participants'.

Informed consent

Informed consent is a close cousin of voluntary participation. Voluntary participation implies that participants make a choice, and true choice requires accurate information if it is to be truly voluntary.

Typically the requirement of informed consent in a questionnaire or interview survey means that participants are informed about a range of matters relating to the survey (see Box 5.1).

While the issue of informed consent seems entirely reasonable and desirable it is not completely straightforward. *How much* information should we

---

> **BOX 5.1**
> **Guidelines for providing informed consent**
>
> ■ The purpose of the study and its basic procedures.
>
> ■ An outline of any reasonably foreseeable risks, embarrassment or discomfort (e.g. some questions may deal with very private or sensitive matters).
>
> ■ A description of the likely benefits of the study.
>
> ■ A description of how the respondent was selected for the study.
>
> ■ An offer to answer any questions.
>
> ■ A statement that participation is voluntary and that the respondent is free to withdraw at any time or to decline to answer any particular question.
>
> ■ The identity of the researcher and the sponsor.
>
> ■ Some information about the way in which the data and conclusions might be put.

---

provide before a participant can be considered informed? How *fully* informed should participants be? What does it mean to be informed? Providing more information does not mean that people will be any better informed. Simply providing detailed descriptions of the study does not mean that respondents will be any more enlightened as a result. Indeed, detailed technical information may confuse, distract and overwhelm rather than inform. Too much detail may discourage participation—not because people are better informed but because they are bored to distraction.

Furthermore, providing details about the study—especially detailed information about the study design, the hypotheses and theories being tested—can distort responses and undermine the validity of the findings.

One solution to this problem is to provide basic information and to offer to answer further questions. While few people might ask questions, we should be prepared to answer them. If the information might distort responses we can explain tactfully that this is a concern and offer to deal with the questions *after* the interview or questionnaire has been completed. In some psychological research in particular, participants are deliberately deceived since accurate knowledge would invalidate the study. Where this is warranted it is crucial that participants be fully debriefed after the study.

This raises the question of *when* consent should be obtained. Most ethics committees require that consent is obtained *before* participation.[1] However, in the case of surveys at least, participants have little idea of what they are really agreeing to until they have seen the actual questions. There is a good case for arguing that people can only provide *informed* consent *after* they have completed the questionnaire or interview.

How should informed consent be demonstrated? A common way is to ask participants to sign a written informed consent form. However, a signed informed consent form is not always necessary nor possible. For example, it would be extremely difficult to obtain a signed informed consent form for a telephone interview. A postal survey could ask that a signed consent form be returned with the questionnaire but it seems rather unnecessary. In the case of telephone, internet, mail and email surveys (see Chapter 8) it is important that a record is kept of the information provided to participants, but it seems reasonable to assume that continuing with the telephone interview or completing and returning the questionnaire demonstrates consent.

There are problems with asking people to sign consent forms. Not only does it formalise the interview unduly and lead to a loss of rapport, it can also make some people more suspicious about the research. I recall one survey of refugees from a country racked by civil war where there was a great deal of fear for the fate of relatives back home. When they were asked to sign a form in writing they were terrified and simply refused to participate further. Similarly, in a study of older workers which dealt with feelings about work and retirement many participants would not sign forms for fear that their employers would somehow identify them and that this could affect decisions about compulsory redundancy. This reluctance to sign a form was not because of the study itself but because of the *form*. They feared signing the form—any form. The same problem can be anticipated for many minority groups or for surveys involving sensitive issues.

Research sheds some light on the effect of informed consent on participation in social surveys. Singer (1993) found that detailed, truthful information provided before completing questionnaires or telephone surveys had little effect on the response rate overall or to particular questions. However, she found that when participants were asked for *signed* consent the response rate dropped by 7 per cent regardless of whether signatures were requested before or after interviews.

Other issues complicate the matter of informed consent. Should consent include an agreement regarding the uses to which the data might be put? Some people would prefer not to participate in a study if they were aware of the conclusions that might be drawn or the purposes to which it might be put. For example, welfare recipients might prefer to avoid participating in surveys that could lead to the reduction of welfare payments.

Finally, *who* should give consent? In research of young children, intellectually disabled and others who may not be in a position to fully understand the implications of participating in a survey, who should give permission? Participation still ought to be voluntary but consent may need to be obtained from other people (e.g. parents, guardians, school authorities etc) as well as from the participant.

No harm

In some experimental studies participants are potentially exposed to harm because of the intervention of researchers. For example, in medical experiments in which new drugs are trialled, participants may be exposed to potential danger. In psychological experiments participants might be exposed to stimuli or be induced to behave in ways that they later regret and find distressing.[2]

These dangers are less evident in surveys. Since survey researchers rely on natural variation in samples rather than induced variation (see Chapter 3 on research design), and rely on natural change over time rather than deliberately creating change, there is little danger that surveys will create the harm that experimental studies can. This is not to say that surveys are without their dangers. The questions that survey researchers ask—such as those about family relationships, sexual behaviour, unpopular attitudes—can distress and embarrass respondents and may create psychological harm.

Simply selecting a person for a survey can be harmful. I recall one study of domestic violence victims in which the researcher wanted to know why women who issued complaints to the police about a violent husband later withdrew their complaint. The study was well intentioned and was designed to help women facing domestic violence. Names of women who withdrew complaints against their partners were obtained properly through the courts where such complaints are lodged as public documents. Questionnaires were then sent to these women. A number of women were extremely distressed by the simple fact that they had been selected for the survey. They had mistakenly believed that their complaint was secret and they were hurt and humiliated by the fact that the researcher knew their name.

Where surveys are administered through third parties (e.g. to students via their teacher; to employees through their supervisor) these third parties must not see the responses before the questionnaires are returned to the researcher. In one study I conducted on religious attitudes among school students the questionnaires were returned in sealed envelopes to the school office. When I collected the questionnaires from one Catholic school I discovered that the sealed envelopes had been opened. I never knew who opened them or whether the individuals who completed particular questionnaires were identifiable, but the potential of this breach of confidentiality is clear.

Anonymity and confidentiality

The most obvious way in which participants can be harmed in survey research is if the confidentiality of responses is not honoured. Typically, survey participants are assured that their answers will be either anonymous or confidential. As part of the process of obtaining informed consent it should be clear to respondents how their responses will be treated.

Sometimes researchers fail to distinguish between anonymity and confidentiality and can thus inadvertently mislead respondents. Anonymity means that the researcher will not and cannot identify the respondent. Confidentiality simply means that the researcher can match names with responses but ensures that no-one else will have access to them.

Postal surveys that use identification numbers are not anonymous. Face to face interviews rarely are anonymous. Telephone surveys may or may not be anonymous—it depends on the method of obtaining telephone numbers. If the researcher contacts a person using random digit dialling the interview is probably anonymous.

The *perception* and the *fact* of anonymity are important. If respondents are likely to suspect your assurances of anonymity it is better to assure them of the confidentiality rather than the anonymity. This must be a matter of judgment. On sensitive matters such as drug use and sexual behaviour people are more likely to respond if they are given strong assurances of confidentiality (Singer et al., 1995). On more innocuous topics, assurances of anonymity rather than confidentiality probably make little difference.

There are three main reasons for assuring confidentiality.

1 to improve the quality and honesty of responses, especially on sensitive issues;
2 to encourage participation in the study and thus to improve the representativeness of the sample;
3 to protect a person's privacy.

Do not promise confidentiality unless you can keep the promise. It is inappropriate to promise confidentiality when you know that other people outside the study will have access to the information and can identify the respondents. Very difficult ethical dilemmas can arise. Sometimes, after a promise of confidentiality is given, you might discover information that you feel requires action but which would betray the promise of confidentiality. For example, in a study of school children you might learn the identity of a drug pusher or a teacher who is sexually molesting students. In a study of prisoners you might learn of plans for an escape or the identity of a person who murdered an inmate. In such cases you face the problem of your promise of confidentiality against the harm caused to others by respecting that promise. Make sure that you do not make unrealistic promises of confidentiality.

If you are conducting the research under contract for another person or organisation you will need to establish who owns the data and who will have access to it. You will need to ensure that, should you not own the data, procedures are in place to maintain the confidentiality of respondents.

When promising confidentiality make sure that you are aware of the legal situation. You may be legally obliged to report suspicions of child abuse.

Depending on the context in which data are collected it may be subject to freedom of information legislation. In many countries research data collected with the guarantee of confidentiality do not enjoy legal privilege and can be subpoenaed by courts. In this context it is important to clarify your rights to maintain the confidentiality of data when working in government agencies or under contract. Contracts frequently make explicit statements about the ownership of data and it is important to ensure that these provisions do not compromise your undertakings regarding confidentiality.

There are a number of steps that can be taken to protect the confidentiality of data. As mentioned earlier, it is imperative to guard against 'third party data collectors' (e.g. teachers, supervisors etc) who might have access to the completed questionnaires before they are returned to you. Other people working in a research team, including those who code and enter the data, must be made aware of their ethical responsibilities in this regard.

Once data are collected there are two broad strategies to ensure that confidentiality is maintained. The first is to separate identifying information from a respondent's answers. This can be done by providing cases with ID numbers and having a separate file in which these ID numbers are linked with the person's name. In many cases you will not need to keep any record of the person's name at all. If you do not need to follow up respondents after they have returned their questionnaire you can simply give each person an ID and destroy any identifying personal data (name and address). If follow up is required then a separate file can be created in which the ID number is attached to personal data. Access to this file can be tightly restricted so as to avoid its misuse. Standard procedures for limiting access to computer files (passwords on files, encryption etc) should make these data extremely secure.

Another danger to confidentiality arises when data come from a particular locality, group or organisation. For example, a census of a small township could be used in such a way as to breach confidentiality. If unit record data (i.e. data with a separate record for each case) such as a census were made available and the particular town was identified it would be a simple matter to identify particular people and learn how they answered questions in the census. If the town had one doctor and the census data indicated people's occupations it would be easy to locate the doctor and identify that person's responses. Other people in small subgroups in known localities can be identified by a set of cross-tabulations (Chapter 13). For example, there may be twenty teachers in the town but because we also know the age, gender, marital status and educational qualifications of people it would not be difficult to identify individuals who had a unique set of these characteristics (e.g. female teacher, aged 35, married, with two children and holding a Bachelor of Science degree).

If survey data are to be made publicly available they must first be confidentialised. There are a number of ways of confidentialising data before releasing it.

1   Restrict the release of unit record data and ensure that where these data are released people sign undertakings to respect the confidentiality of individuals.
2   Remove information that could help with such identification. For example, when census authorities release any unit record data, detailed locality identifiers are removed so that it is not possible to identify where any individual comes from.
3   Collapse categories of variables from highly specific (e.g. exact occupation, precise age, exact country of birth, precise education qualification) and place individuals into broad groups thus making it almost impossible to obtain highly specific information about any case.

WEB POINTER 5.1 *US Census confidentiality guidelines*

An excellent review of issues and solutions to confidentiality concerns in public release data sets from the US Census Bureau.

www.ipums.org/~census2000/2000pums_bureau.pdf

Visit www.social-research.org to use these links and to check for updates and additions.

Privacy

While the principles of voluntary participation and confidentiality are partly based on the principle of a person's right to privacy, the right to privacy extends beyond these matters. Privacy can also mean that people can expect to be free from *intrusion*; that is, they do not want companies or survey researchers contacting them unless permission for such contacts has been given.

The expectation that you will not be contacted without permission is a lively issue on the internet where 'spamming' is deeply frowned on. Spamming is the practice of broadcasting uninvited emails to lists of people who have not indicated that they want to receive such mail. The issue has become heated because of the ease of distributing email to vast lists of people at virtually no cost. Marketers and others could clog up email inboxes with junk email.

The codes of ethics of many e-marketing organisations forbid spamming. Those who use e-surveys should avoid the invasion of privacy that the unsolicited distribution of electronic questionnaires involves (see Chapter 8 on internet surveys). Distributing e-surveys in this way will create resentment and hostility both to yourself and to survey researchers in general.

Telephone survey requests also can be intrusive. Such surveys are routinely conducted on weekends and evenings when survey companies have learned people are most likely to be home. As more and more market research companies and survey researchers have adopted telephone survey methodology the intrusiveness of this method has become a sensitive issue for some people.

It is difficult to know how to deal with this problem since there is no way to know beforehand whether or not a *request* to participate in a survey will be regarded as an invasion of privacy. It is not possible to obtain good random samples (see Chapter 6 on sampling concepts and types) if we have to rely on existing lists of people who have volunteered to participate. The only way to obtain good random samples is to give everyone an equal chance of being selected. Perhaps a reasonable compromise is to contact people *inviting* but not in any way pressuring them to participate.

There are many other considerations that should govern the way in which survey researchers should go about collecting data. These include matters such as discrimination, harassment, respect for others, conflict of interest and many others. These issues are dealt with to varying extents in the codes of ethics of the professional organisations in Web Pointer 5.2.

COLLEAGUES, THE PROFESSION, SPONSORS AND THE PUBLIC

Colleagues and the profession

The way we collect data and observe our responsibilities to respondents has an impact on other researchers. We should avoid treating respondents and others in such a way as to discredit the research enterprise, making it impossible for future researchers to research the same population.

In addition we should present sufficient details of the research, the sampling, instruments and other aspects of methodology that would enable other professionals to properly evaluate and replicate the research. Increasingly, publicly funded researchers are expected to deposit their data in public archives to be made available to others for further analysis. Not only does this practice guard against scientific fraud and the fabrication of results or sloppy data analysis, it also means that the data can be more effectively and widely used.

A further ethical responsibility to colleagues, especially those closely involved in the research, is to properly acknowledge the contributions of colleagues. This may include authorship rights or some other form of acknowledgment. Sometimes senior researchers take for granted the contributions of more junior research workers (e.g. research assistants). To do so can mean that the senior investigators are misrepresenting their own role in the collection and analysis of data.

Sponsors

In seeking funding support for research there are also ethical responsibilities to sponsors regarding the way we collect data. These responsibilities include:

■ Avoiding overstating our expertise with a particular methodology.[3]

■ Not over-claiming what can be learned and applied from the research or the particular methodology.

WEB POINTER 5.2 *Codes of ethics of professional organisations*

Organisation	URL
Council of American Survey Research Organizations (CASRO)	www.casro.org/casro.htm
American Association of Public Opinion Research	www.aapor.org/ethics/
Social Sciences and Humanities Research Council of Canada	www.sshrc.ca/english/programinfo/policies/ ethics.htm
American Sociological Association Code of Ethics	www.asanet.org/members/ecoderev.html
American Psychological Association	www.apa.org/ethics/code.html
British Sociological Association	www.britsoc.org.uk/about/ethic.htm
ESOMAR: The World Association of Research Professionals	www.esomar.nl/codes_and_guidelines.html
The Australian Sociological Association	www.newcastle.edu.au/department/so/tasa/ tasa6.htm#Section1
ESOMAR Guide to Opinion Polls	www.esomar.nl/guidelines/opolls.htm
ESOMAR Ethical Guidelines for Internet Surveys	www.esomar.nl/guidelines/internet_guidelines.htm
Survey Research Section of the American Statistical Association	www.tcnj.edu/nethcstat/start.html

Visit www.social-research.org to use these links and to check for updates and additions.

- Making the sponsor aware of the limitations of the study.
- Respecting the confidentiality of privileged information regarding the sponsor gained in the course of the study. Failure to do so would certainly undermine research access by future researchers.

The public

When reporting study findings we should ensure that we provide sufficient information so that the results are not misleading. As a matter of course we should provide readers with methodological details about data collection, sampling, and the ways in which data were prepared for analysis. The principle should be to provide readers with sufficient information so that

they can evaluate the results in the light of the methodological quality of the research.

We should also make any sponsorship arrangements clear to the public and other consumers of the research. Although most researchers will try to collect, analyse and report data without fear or favour, we would be mistaken to pretend that the political context in which data are collected, the source of funds, contractual obligations and sponsorship of the research have no impact on what data are collected and the way they are interpreted. If you were reading research on the effects of smoking on health you undoubtedly would want to know if the research was sponsored and funded by the tobacco industry. If crime research highlighted an increasing crime rate and the need for more police we should know if the research was sponsored by the Police Union.

DATA COLLECTION ETHICS CHECKLIST

1 How will the sample be selected? Will this affect:
  a the privacy of potential respondents;
  b the perception that participation really is voluntary?
2 How will the voluntary nature of participation be:
  a · communicated;
  b demonstrated?
3 How will you deal with reluctant potential participants?
4 What data will you collect?
  a Is there any danger that this will:
    i compromise the respondent's feelings of privacy;
    ii harm the participant in any way?
  b How will any potential problems with privacy or harm be dealt with?
5 What undertakings will you give regarding confidentiality?
  a Will you promise:
    i anonymity;
    ii confidentiality?
  b What qualifications will be given to any such undertakings?
  c Can you deliver on your undertaking given:
    i the law;
    ii contractual obligations;
    iii ethical responsibilities to others?
6 How will you implement the principle of informed consent?
  a What information will be provided about the study?

b Will there be any deception involved? Is this justified?
  c How and from whom will you seek consent?
  d When will consent be sought:
    i before collecting data;
    ii after collecting data?
  e How will consent be demonstrated?
7 Will respondents require debriefing at the completion of the interview/study?
8 Does the research require approval from an institutional ethics committee?
9 What information will you provide regarding funding/sponsorship of the research to:
  a respondents;
  b colleagues;
  c other readers of any research findings?
10 Have you fairly informed sponsors of:
  a the limitations of the methodology;
  b the capacity of the study to deliver the expected benefits;
  c your own level of competence to conduct the study?
11 Have you provided sufficient information to readers of the research to enable the informed reader to fairly evaluate the results and to be aware of the limitations of the data?
12 Have other people contributed to the research? How will you acknowledge their contribution?
13 Will you make the data set available to others for further analysis? If so what steps will you take to confidentialise the data?

KEY CONCEPTS

Confidentialising data	Privacy
Confidentiality	Responsibility to colleagues
Informed consent	Spamming
No harm to participants	Voluntary participation

ENDNOTES

[1] Most research institutes, government departments, universities and hospitals have an ethics committee, the purpose of which is to ascertain whether a research proposal meets ethical guidelines. Typically, funding and approval is not available until the approval of an ethics committee has been given.

[2] The Milgram experiments on obedience are classic examples of this. See Baumrind (1964) and Milgram (1964).

[3] It is worthwhile distinguishing between misrepresentation and diffidence or lack of confidence at this point. Many people will lack confidence about their capacity to undertake some analysis. Sometimes this is well based but in others it stems from undue modesty.

FURTHER READING

An excellent overview of the ethical issues involved in social science research is Kimmel's books *Ethics and Values in Applied Social Research* (1988) and *Ethical Issues in Behavioural Research: A Survey* (1996) and in Homan's *The Ethics of Social Research* (1991). Seiber's collection of papers in her book *The Ethics of Social Research: Surveys and Experiments* (1982) and Reynolds' book *Ethical Dilemmas and Social Science Research* (1979) both provide thorough discussions of a wide range of issues.

Ritzer's 1974 edited collection *Social Realities: Dynamic Perspectives* presents a series of views and lively excerpts that highlight some of the ethical issues involved in real life research. Seiber's book *Planning Ethically*

Responsible Research (1992) provides very useful guidelines to students for conducting ethically responsible research.

Issues of informed consent are thoroughly dealt with in *A History And Theory Of Informed Consent* by Fadden and Beauchamp (1986) while Singer's 1993 paper and 1995 paper (with Thurn and Miller) provide a thorough analysis of the effects of informed consent and confidentiality assurances on survey responses.

Although they are now getting somewhat old, the books by Barnes *Who Should Know What? Social Science, Privacy and Ethics* (1979) and by Boruch and Cecil *Assuring the Confidentiality of Social Research Data* (1979) both provide useful overviews of confidentiality issues.

EXERCISES

1   As part of a survey on the way parents raise their children you ask about discipline. In the process you discover that a parent is using discipline techniques that you believe constitute child abuse. However, you have guaranteed confidentiality. What should you do?

2   In this study, as part of the informed consent procedures, you outline to respondents the areas about which questions will be asked. You are aware that you are obliged by the law to report any instance where you suspect that child abuse may be taking place. The law adopts a definition of child abuse that is much stricter than many parents would accept (e.g. hitting a child with an object) and it is likely that some parents will disclose behaviour that they see as innocent but which falls under the definition of child abuse. You fear that if you tell them of your obligation to report and explain the types of behaviour that are reportable many people will either refuse to participate or will not report their actual methods of discipline thus invalidating the findings. What should you do?

3   After carefully informing a person of the purpose and content of a project the person agrees to participate in an interview for the project and signs an informed consent form to indicate this. Some time later the person indicates that on reflection they do not want to be part of the study and they want their information to be destroyed. However, you have spent both time and money on this case and are well

advanced with your data analysis. What should you do? Why?

4   A team of interviewers has collected data for your survey of 2000 adults. After publishing your results in a journal you discover that one interviewer did not administer the questionnaires but fabricated answers. What should you do? You decide to reanalyse the data and find that no patterns are changed significantly. What should you do?

5   In the course of interviews among marijuana users to whom you have promised confidentiality you learn of the identity of a person who is distributing hard drugs. What should you do?

6   You obtain the membership list of a secretive religious sect and wish to obtain their views on a number of political, ethical and religious matters. You believe that they would be unwilling to participate in a study of the views of members of that sect so you send them a survey questionnaire telling them that they have been selected at random as part of a nationwide survey of opinions? Is this a justifiable way of obtaining data that would otherwise be inaccessible? Why, or why not?

7   A researcher wants to obtain information about the way university affects the attitudes of students about the roles of males and females. The first step is to measure their attitudes when they come to university and to this end the researcher obtains permission to include a set of questions in the questionnaire that the university

requires all new students to complete when they enrol. The university questionnaire includes questions about the student's background, their parents' background, their educational aspirations and their reasons for attending this particular university. Do you see any ethical problems with their research exercise?

8   A university requires that all lecturers administer a student evaluation questionnaire at the end of each subject to measure the level of satisfaction of students with the particular subject. What ethical issues arise in this exercise and what measures would you take to ensure that ethical guidelines were adhered to?

6

Finding a sample

This chapter outlines the principles and procedures for obtaining accurate samples that enable us to generalise from a sample to a wider population. It outlines how to:

- obtain different types of samples;
- develop and use internet-based samples;
- determine how large a sample needs to be;
- deal with non-response;
- improve sample quality by weighting;
- use samples obtained by other people by conducting secondary analysis.

SOME SAMPLING CONCEPTS

A fundamental goal of research is to be able to generalise—to say something reliably about a wider population on the basis of the findings in a particular study. There are two basic types of generalisation.

1   *Statistical generalisation:* statistical generalisations are those where we use probability theory to estimate the likelihood that the patterns observed in the smaller group—the *sample*—will hold in the larger group—the *population*. Probability theory enables us to say, with a specific degree of confidence, how likely the patterns in a sample are to reflect those in a wider popu-

lation. Statistical generalisation relies on having randomly drawn representative samples and is the mode of generalisation used in sample survey research.

2   *Replication*: this is the method used in experimental research. Most experiments in which people participate are not based on statistically representative samples. Thus we cannot use statistical generalisation as a basis for generalising from experimental results. Instead we test the generalisability of the experimental findings by repeating or replicating the experiment in different circumstances and with different sorts of participants. If the findings are replicated regardless of the context, methods and participant characteristics we will become more confident that the results apply widely. How widely they apply will be subject to ongoing replications.

Before outlining sampling techniques it is worth introducing a few technical terms. A *census* is obtained by collecting information about every member of a group; that is, the *population*. In sampling, population has a technical meaning and should not be confused with the population of a country or a region. A population is the set of units that the sample is meant to represent. The units that make up the population will depend on the units of analysis (see Chapter 3). In national surveys the population is usually defined as all adults (18+) who are non-institutionalised (i.e. live in households). For another study the population might be all employed people or all families with children under five years old.

A *sample* is obtained by collecting information about only some members of the population. Before selecting the sample it is critical that the population is properly defined. Once we have established the scope of the population we then obtain a *sampling frame*—a list of the population elements. From this list we select a sample.

For example, if we wanted to obtain a sample of university students we would need to define the population of university students. Do we mean students from all universities or just one? Are we interested in universities in one country or a number of countries? Does it consist of current students only? What about those who have suspended their enrolment but will return to study? Do we mean full-time students only? What about postgraduate students? Do we include staff who are also post-graduate students? Once we had specified the population we would obtain a list of all population members. From this list we would use one of a number of sampling methods to select a representative sample of students.

When selecting a sample from a sampling frame the goal is to do so in such a way that it is representative of the population. A *representative sample* is one in which the profile of the sample is the same as that of the population (e.g. gender, class, age, race etc).

To ensure that a sample is representative of the population it is crucial that certain types of people in the population are not systematically excluded or under-represented. If we tried to obtain a sample of a suburb by going around during the day and knocking on every twentieth door we would systematically under-represent those types of people who are not at home during the day (e.g. men, dual worker families). Such a sample is *biased*. Similarly, an incomplete sampling frame that omitted certain types of population members (e.g. a list of university students that excluded part-time enrolments) would be biased if our population definition included part-time students. A biased sample cannot be used to generalise the population without making statistical adjustments, called *weighting*, during the analysis stage of the survey.

The best way of ensuring that the sample is representative is to make sure that all people in the population have an equal (or at least known) chance of being included. There are two broad types of samples: *probability* and *non-probability*. Probability samples are the surest way of obtaining samples that are representative of the population.

In summary, the goal of sampling is to obtain a sample that properly mirrors the population it is designed to represent. This involves defining the population, obtaining an unbiased sampling frame, and selecting a sample using probability sampling methods. This should result in a final sample that is smaller than the population but has a similar 'shape' (see Figure 6.1).

Even with probability sampling it is unlikely that the sample will be perfectly representative. By chance alone there will be differences between the sample and the population. These differences are due partly to *sampling error*. The important thing is that the characteristics of most randomly selected samples will be close to those of the population. For example, if just before the next general election 53 per cent of the voting population intend to vote for the Labor Party then most samples will produce estimates close to this figure. Since most random samples produce estimates close to the true population figure we can use probability theory to help estimate how close the

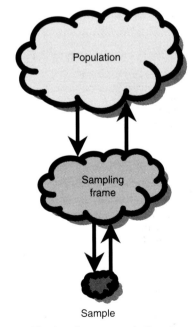

Figure 6.1 Moving from population to sample

true population figure is likely to be to the figure obtained in any particular sample (called a sample estimate). A statistic called *standard error* is used for this purpose (see the discussion on sample size in this chapter and Chapter 13). Probability samples are preferable because they are the more likely to produce representative samples and enable estimates of the sample's accuracy. Most of this chapter will deal with probability sampling: types, required size, minimising cost and dealing with non-response.

TYPES OF PROBABILITY SAMPLES

There are four main types of probability samples. The choice between these depends on the nature of the research problem, the availability of good sampling frames, money, the desired level of accuracy in the sample and the method by which data are to be collected.

Simple random sampling (SRS)

There are five steps in selecting a SRS.

1 Obtain a complete sampling frame.
2 Give each case a unique number starting at one.
3 Decide on the required sample size.
4 Select numbers for the sample size from a table of random numbers (see Box 6.1).

5 Select the cases that correspond to the randomly chosen numbers.

The process can be illustrated with a detailed example. Figure 6.2 provides a complete sampling frame for a population of 50 people and each person has been given a number between 1 and 50.

Box 6.1 illustrates the steps involved in using a table of random numbers to select a sample of ten cases from the sampling frame in Figure 6.2. Box 6.2 illustrates the sample selected using these methods.

One of the problems of SRS is that it requires a good sampling frame. While these may be available for some populations (e.g. organisations such as schools, churches, unions), adequate lists are often not available for larger population surveys of a city, region or country. In addition, where a population comes from a large area, as in national surveys, and where data are to be collected by personal interviews the cost of SRS is prohibitive. It would probably involve interviewers travelling long distances just for one interview. To survey a large area it is best to use either another sampling strategy (see the outline of multistage cluster sampling), or another method of collecting the data such as mail questionnaires, telephone surveys or internet-based surveys. In other words SRS is most appropriate when a good sampling frame exists and when the population is geographically concentrated or the data collection technique does not involve travelling.

Number	Name	Number	Name	Number	Name
01	Adams, H.	18	Iulianetti, G.	35	Quinn, J.
02	Anderson, J.	19	Ivono, V.	36	Reddan, R.
03	Baker, E.	**20**	**Jabornik, T.**	**37**	**Risteski, B.**
04	Bradsley, W.	**21**	**Jacobs, B.**	**38**	**Sawers, R.**
05	Bradley, P.	22	Kennedy, G.	39	Saunders, M.
06	Carra, A.	23	Kassem, S.	40	Tarrant, A.
07	Cidoni, G.	24	Ladd, F.	41	Thomas, G.
08	Daperis, D.	**25**	**Lamb, A.**	42	Uttay, E.
09	Devlin, B.	26	Mand, R.	43	Usher, V.
10	Eastside, R.	**27**	**McIlraith, W.**	44	Varley, E.
11	Einhorn, B.	28	Natoli, P.	45	Van Rooy, P.
12	Falconer, T.	29	Newman, L.	**46**	**Walters, J.**
13	Felton, B.	30	Ooi, W.	47	West, W.
14	Garratt, S.	31	Oppenheim, F.	48	Yates, R.
15	Gelder, H.	**32**	**Peters, P.**	49	Wyatt, R.
16	Hamilton, I.	33	Palmer, T.	**50**	**Zappulla, T.**
17	Hartnell, W.	**34**	**Quick, B.**		

Figure 6.2   Selecting a simple random sample from a sampling frame

BOX 6.1 *Using a table of random numbers*

1 Determine how many digits the selected number should contain. This will be the same number of digits as the largest number assigned in the sampling frame (e.g. largest number is 50, therefore we require two-digit numbers).

2 Select which digits in each set you will use to select your two-digit number. For example, if the sets of numbers each contain five digits, which two will you use? The first two digits?

3 Select a random starting point in the table

of random numbers (e.g. first column, second row).

4 Determine a method of moving through the table in a consistent pattern (e.g. across the table, using every second column and every row).

5 If the selected number is out of range, that is, higher than the highest number in the sampling frame, skip the number and proceed to the next eligible number.

6 If the number has already been selected go to the next eligible number.

Table 6.1 A table of random numbers

74605	60866	92941	77422	78308	08274	62099
20749	78470	94157	83266	37570	64827	94067
88790	79927	48135	46293	05045	70393	80915
64819	73967	78907	50940	98146	80637	50917
55938	78790	04999	32561	92128	83403	79930
66853	39017	82843	26227	25992	69154	38341
46795	21210	43252	51451	47196	27978	49499
95601	36457	34237	98554	46178	44991	43672
98721	44506	37586	67256	88094	51860	43008
61307	12947	43383	34450	62108	05047	15614
37788	01097	15010	97811	27372	81994	60457
36186	66118	90122	45603	94045	66611	69202
96730	13663	14383	51162	50110	16597	62122
98831	31066	21529	01102	28209	07621	56004
35450	24410	88935	84471	46076	60416	10007
92031	42334	27224	09790	59181	66958	91967
02863	16678	45335	72783	50096	52581	15214
80360	89628	47863	21217	62797	11285	42938
58193	16045	72021	93498	99120	36542	41087
66048	95648	94960	58294	07984	87321	23919

Systematic sampling

Systematic sampling is similar to SRS and has the same limitations except that it is simpler. To obtain a systematic sample follow these steps:

1 Obtain a sampling frame.
2 Determine the population size (e.g. 100).
3 Determine the sample size required (e.g. 20).
4 Calculate a sampling fraction by dividing the population size by the required sample size (100 ÷ 20 = 5).

5 Select a starting point by randomly selecting a number between 1 and 5 (or whatever the sampling fraction is; e.g. select number 3).

6 The selected number is the starting point so case 3 is selected.

7 Use the sampling fraction to select every nth case. With a sampling fraction of 5 select every 5th case and obtain a sample of 20 cases.

Apart from the problems systematic samples share with SRS they can encounter an additional one:

BOX 6.2 *Selecting a SRS of ten cases*

■ Using the sampling frame in Figure 6.2, the table of random numbers in Table 6.1 and the steps in Box 6.1 results in the following selections.

■ We require ten two-digit numbers.

■ We will use the first two digits in each set.

■ We will begin in the first column of row 2. This gives the number 20749. We will use the first two digits which results in the number 20. We would select case 20 (Jabornik) from the sampling frame.

■ We will move across the table selecting every second column and every row. This

results in the selection of the following sets of numbers of which only some (those in bold) result in an in range number (between 1 and 50).

20749	94157	**37**570	94067
79927	**46**293	70393	
64819	78907	98146	**50**917
78790	**32**561	83403	
66853	82843	**25**992	**38**341
21210	51451	**27**978	
95601	**34**237		

Step 1: Determine population size	01	21	41	61	81
100	02	22	42	62	82
	03	**23**	**43**	**63**	**83**
	04	24	44	64	84
Step 2: Determine sample size required	05	25	45	65	85
20	06	26	46	66	86
	07	27	47	67	87
	08	**28**	**48**	**68**	**88**
Step 3: Calculate sampling fraction (population ÷ sample)	09	29	49	69	89
= 100 ÷ 20	10	30	50	70	90
	11	31	51	71	91
= 5	12	32	52	72	92
	13	**33**	**53**	**73**	**93**
	14	34	54	74	94
Step 4: Select random starting point within first 5 cases	15	35	55	75	95
e.g. 03	16	36	56	76	96
	17	37	57	77	97
	18	**38**	**58**	**78**	**98**
Step 5: Select every 5th case	19	39	59	79	99
= sample of 20	20	40	60	80	100

Adapted from http://trochim.human.cornell.edu/kb/sampprob.htm

Figure 6.3 Drawing a systematic sample

periodicity of sampling frames. That is, a certain *type* of person may reoccur at regular intervals within the sampling frame. If the sampling fraction is such that it matches this interval, the sample will include only certain types of people and systematically exclude others. We might have a list of married couples arranged so that every husband's name is followed by his wife's name. If a sampling fraction of four was used (or any even number in this case) the sample would be all of the same sex (see Figure 6.4). If there is periodicity in the sampling frame then either mix up the cases or use SRS.

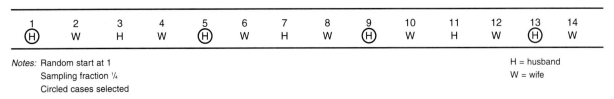

Notes: Random start at 1   H = husband
       Sampling fraction ¼   W = wife
       Circled cases selected

Figure 6.4   The effect of periodicity

Stratified sampling

Stratified sampling is a modification of SRS and is designed to produce more representative and thus more accurate samples. But this greater accuracy comes at the cost of a more complicated procedure. On the whole stratified sampling has similar limitations to SRS. For a sample to be representative the proportions of various groups in the sample should be the same as in the population. Because of chance (sampling error) this will not always occur. For example, we might conduct a study in which the ethnic background of respondents is expected to affect the way people answer questions. To avoid distortions due to the chance under- or over-representation of particular ethnic groups in the final sample we would stratify the sample by ethnic backgound to guarantee that each ethnic group will be represented in the sample in its correct proportion.

To stratify a sample:

1   select the stratifying variable (e.g. ethnic background);
2   divide the sampling frame into separate lists—one for each category of the stratifying variable (i.e. one for each ethnic group);
3   draw a systematic or SRS of each list.

This procedure will guarantee that in the final sample each ethnic group will be represented in its correct proportion.

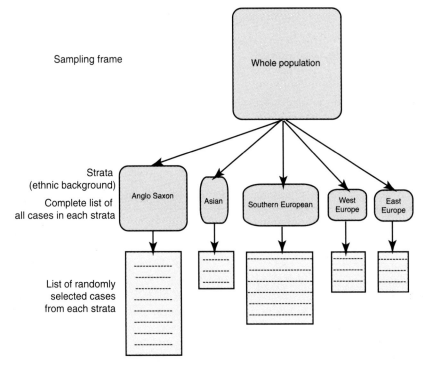

Sample of each ethnic group is proportionate to size of group in whole populations

Figure 6.5   Stratified random sampling

Stratifying samples requires that the sampling frame contains information regarding the stratifying variable so that the frame can be divided up. Since stratified sampling also involves SRS or systematic sampling it requires unbiased sampling frames.

The problem with all the sampling techniques considered so far is that they are of limited use on their own when sampling a geographically dispersed population with whom we want to conduct face-to-face interviews. They are also of no direct help with drawing a sample in which no sampling frame is available. When conducting large area surveys (e.g. national or even city wide) both these problems exist. Multistage cluster sampling is an attempt to overcome these difficulties.

Multistage cluster sampling

This technique of obtaining a final sample involves drawing several different samples (hence its name) and does so in such a way that the cost of final inter-viewing is minimised.

The basic procedure of sampling the population of a city for which there was no sampling frame of residents involves the following steps (see Figure 6.6).

1   Divide the city into *areas* (e.g. electorates, census districts). These areas are called *clusters*.
2   Select a SRS of these clusters.
3   Obtain a list of *smaller areas* (e.g. blocks) within the selected clusters.
4   Select a SRS of smaller areas (e.g. blocks) within each of the clusters selected at stage 2.
5   For each selected block obtain a list of *addresses* of households (enumeration).
6   Select a SRS of addresses within the selected blocks.
7   At each selected address select an *individual* to participate in the sample.

How are individuals selected from the chosen households? One method designed to avoid bias is to use a procedure developed by Kish (1949). Once households have been selected they are numbered systematically from 1 to 12. When interviewers arrive at a particular house they make a list of all people in the household who fit the requirements of the sample. The list is arranged so that all males are listed first from eldest to youngest, then females in the same way. Then using the grid (see Table 6.2) they select a particular person based on the number

assigned to that household (between 1 and 12) and the number of eligible people in the household. Thus in a household assigned number 9 in which there were four eligible people the fourth listed person would be interviewed. A less cumbersome method is to select the household member whose birthday is closest to the interview date.

An important issue in multistage sampling is how many clusters (whether they be districts, blocks or households) to sample at each stage. The general principle is to maximise the number of initial clusters chosen and consequently select only relatively few individuals or units within each cluster. The reason for this is that it is important that different districts are included initially. If only one or two were selected (e.g. two upper-middle-class suburbs) we could end up with a very unrepresentative sample. By maximising the chance for variety initially, we increase the chance of maintaining representativeness at later stages. The problem is that as the number of clusters chosen initially increases so do the travelling costs later on. In the end a compromise between cost and sampling error has to be made.

One way of minimising the effect on representa-tiveness of reducing clusters is to use stratification techniques. Thus, when selecting districts, put them into various strata (e.g. status, prices, density, age composition etc) and then randomly select districts within the strata. The same principle can apply when selecting blocks.

Another problem with sampling areas is that the number of households in various districts or blocks will differ. This could easily lead to missing blocks in which there is a large number of a particular type of household. For example, we might survey a city and miss out on all the blocks with high-rise government housing. This would clearly lead to an unrepresenta-tive sample. This danger is reduced by maximising the number of districts sampled and by using strati-fying procedures. Another approach is to use a modi-fied version of multistage cluster sampling known as *probability proportionate to size* (PPS) sampling (Kish, 1965: 217–45). It is unnecessary to describe this in detail here but it operates so that the probability of a block being chosen depends on the number of households it contains. Thus a block with four times as many households as another has a four times greater chance of being selected. To avoid biasing the final sample the same number of people are chosen from each block regardless of its size. Thus the block

Stage one

1	2	3	4	5	6	7	8	9	10
11	12	13	14	15	16	17	18	19	20
21	22	23	24	25	26	27	28	29	30
31	32	33	34	35	36	37	38	39	40
							41	42	43
							44	45	46

Divide city up into districts and select a sample (shaded areas selected)

Stage two

1	2	3	4	5	6
7	8	9	10	11	12
13	14	15	16	17	18
19	20	21	22	23	24

High Street

North Road

Deep Street

New Road

Old Street

Ruda Street
Penlyne Avenue
Trinian Street
Bachus Road
Moss Avenue
Sainsbury Avenue
Box Road

Divide district into blocks and select a sample within each selected district (shaded blocks selected)

Stage three

1.	1 Box Road	(13.)	67 Sainsbury Avenue
(2.)	3 Box Road	14.	65 Sainsbury Avenue
3.	5 Box Road	15.	63 Sainsbury Avenue
4.	7 Box Road	16.	61 Sainsbury Avenue
5.	9 Box Road	(17.)	59 Sainsbury Avenue
6.	11 Box Road	18.	57 Sainsbury Avenue
7.	52 Old Street	19.	12 New Road
8.	50 Old Street	20.	10 New Road
(9.)	48 Old Street	(21.)	8 New Road
10.	46 Old Street	(22.)	6 New Road
11.	44 Old Street	23.	4 New Road
12.	42 Old Street	24.	2 New Road

In each selected block list each household and randomly selected households (circled)

Stage four
List names in each selected household and use selection grid to select a person

Figure 6.6 Steps in multistage cluster sampling

Table 6.2 Grid for selecting individuals in multistage sampling

Assigned number of address	Total number of eligible persons					
	1	2	3	4	5	6 or more
1 or 2	1	1	2	2	3	3
3	1	2	3	3	3	5
4 or 5	1	2	3	4	5	6
6	1	1	1	1	2	2
7 or 8	1	1	1	1	1	1
9	1	2	3	4	5	5
10 or 11	1	2	2	3	4	4
12	1	1	1	2	2	2

Source: Hoinville et al., 1977: 82

with 100 households has four times the chance of being chosen than a block with only 25 households. But since, say, only five households are chosen in each block, regardless of size, the higher probability of a large block being chosen is compensated for by the lower probability of a particular household on that block being chosen. The point of PPS sampling is simply to ensure proper representation of densely populated blocks.

The principles of multistage cluster sampling can be applied to other contexts where there are no easily available sampling frames. For example, a survey of members of a national organisation such as a church or union might start by sampling areas of the country, then districts within each area. Within each district a list of branches (comparable to blocks) could be compiled and sampled. For each selected branch, membership lists could be obtained and a sample drawn from these.

INTERNET SAMPLES

Chapter 8 examines ways in which survey questionnaires are administered to samples. Some methods of administration necessarily introduce problems with obtaining representative samples. Telephone surveys encounter some sampling problems in that some people do not have telephones or can avoid telephone surveys because of unlisted numbers or by using answering machines to screen calls. However the increasing use of the internet to administer surveys introduces new sampling problems. Internet surveying will be discussed in Chapter 8 but it is appropriate to consider the sampling implications of internet surveys here.

Types of internet surveys

There are two broad ways in which internet surveys are conducted:

1. email surveys;
2. web page based surveys.

Email surveys

There are different of ways of conducting email surveys but from the sampling perspective these do not matter. These surveys are restricted to people who have access to an email account on the internet and involve sending an email (with a questionnaire included) to a list of email addresses. The quality and usefulness of such a sample will depend on the quality of the email list, the response rate and the population to which you want to generalise.

Great care must be taken in emailing questionnaires to email lists. Unsolicited email is called *spamming* and is regarded by net users as a breach of 'netiquette'. Not only will sending unsolicited emails generate considerable hostility, it is also ineffective. Spamming results in very low response rates and may result in very poor quality data.

Web page based surveys

These surveys require that the respondent visit a web page (URL). From this page they will be given a questionnaire. Typically respondents are recruited to web page questionnaires in one of the following ways.

Pop-up questionnaires. When a person happens to visit the page a questionnaire will pop up or the respondent will be asked if they want to go to a URL (web address) to answer a questionnaire. This method of sample recruitment depends entirely on people happening to visit your site and then agreeing to answer the questionnaire. Such samples cannot be generalised to any particular population.

Advertising on other sites. Other sites might advertise your survey. This method can attract people from a wide range of sites and result in a large number of responses but it is difficult to think what population such a sample represents.

Listserv, newsgroup and chatgroup advertising. You might advertise your questionnaire or invite participation from people on internet-based lists. For example, you may invite members of particular listservs, newsgroups or chatgroups (see Chapter 8 for description and addresses). The value of this recruitment method and the sample quality will depend on the characteristics of these lists and groups.

Email invitations. These may be sent to people whose email addresses you have. Email lists can be purchased on the internet. Those who agree to participate would then be given a URL to visit to answer the questionnaire. This recruitment method is affected by the quality of the lists you have and the people who respond and agree to participate.

Commercial internet panels. Agencies recruit 'panels' of questionnaire respondents. These respondents are normally volunteers who receive rewards of one sort or another for their participation. Companies with large panels will, for a fee, contact members of their panel that fit your sample requirements (e.g. young women with children under ten; retired men etc) and obtain completed questionnaires. In some cases the lists of some companies will contain people who provided their names and details on the internet for other purposes but those names have been made available to the research companies. The more reputable companies do not work this way since the ethics of obtaining a sample this way are questionable. If you are interested you can register for some panels by going to the following site and selecting one of many companies that give rewards to panel members. You can go to:

   http://members.home.net/webrewards/
   newsites.htm

Commercially recruited representative samples. A few companies have recruited a nationally representative sample that can be contacted on the internet (see Box 6.3). These companies will administer your survey to this representative panel for a fee. These representative panels are rare and expensive because of the cost to the company of recruiting them.

   The common criticism of internet-based samples is that they are unrepresentative and that we

---

BOX 6.3
A representative internet sample

A commercial company, Knowledge Networks, has overcome the bias of internet access by recruiting a sample and then connecting them to the internet. They say:

> We enrol selected households by means of a combination of special delivery mail, and telephone contacts. Starting with a random sample of phone numbers, we use multiple reverse directories to find the associated addresses. If an address is available we send an advance letter of introduction, alerting household members to expect a phone call within a week. Any US household with a telephone has the potential to be selected for the Knowledge Networks Panel, which includes computer users and non-computer users.

> In exchange for free Internet hardware and connectivity, participants agree to complete a maximum of one survey per week per household member, each about five minutes long. During the first phone contact, the interviewer collects basic demographic information. Knowledge Networks maintains profile data on every respondent.

> Recruited households receive free hardware, such as a set-top box, which is shipped to the home, and free Internet connection paid for by Knowledge Networks on a monthly basis. Follow-up assistance is available both online and via a toll-free 'customer care' line. If necessary, we'll even provide on-site installation and set up.

www.knowledgenetworks.com/science/difference.html

---

cannot generalise from them. This criticism is well founded if we want to use the internet for general population samples. Figure 6.7 illustrates the way in which an internet sample of the general population would be biased. The first bias is introduced by having to own or have access to a computer. This introduces age, class and gender bias. From this already biased population we would be restricted to

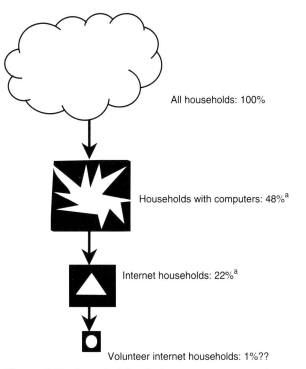

All households: 100%

Households with computers: 48%[a]

Internet households: 22%[a]

Volunteer internet households: 1%??

Figure 6.7   Sample bias in internet surveys of households

[a] ABS, 2000

Note: Australian household computer ownership and internet access are high by international standards. The 1 per cent figure for volunteers is my guesswork.

those with internet access which would not be a typical representation of computer owners. The biases this introduces are outlined in Box 6.4. Then, from among those who can access the internet we may end up relying on the subset that would volunteer for a survey. At the outset we have no idea what this subset is representative of. It would be safe to assume that they will not be typical internet users.

Internet samples and representativeness

Given the limited and biased penetration of internet access there are only three main ways of using the internet to gain representative general population samples:

1   *Connect a random sample to the internet.* Obtain a random population sample through non-internet-based means and then connect those without internet access to the internet. This is The Knowledge Network solution.

2   *Use multi-mode methods of questionnaire administration.* This involves using the internet for those in a sample that have access to the internet and using telephone, face-to-face or postal questionnaires to sample those without internet access. Apart from being complex this method encounters problems due to 'mode effects'. Mode effects are the effects on responses of the particular method by which a questionnaire is administered. If different methods are used for different types of people this may distort the survey results.

3   *Using quota internet samples.* While both methods above could be used to produce probability samples and thus should result in samples that are representative (with a known margin of error), internet-based quota samples are used to make the sample representative of a population *in specific respects.* Commercial companies may, from a large pool of names, be able to select people who meet particular quota requirements that will make the sample representative of the population in those respects (e.g. correct proportion of males under 25, females under 25 etc). Alternatively, researchers who recruit the sample may screen the sample by asking questions at the beginning and only select those who meet the quota requirements. However, this sample will remain biased in other respects (e.g. limited to those who use the internet).

The use of internet samples

The fact that internet samples are unlikely, at the present stage, to be representative of the general population does not mean that they have no value or future. At present the internet can be a very useful means of obtaining representative samples of specific populations. Organisations in which all staff are online can provide excellent internet samples of the organisation. High access to the internet among certain sectors of the population (e.g. young middle-class males; professionals etc) means that the internet may be a viable means of obtaining quite good samples of these groups. Many associations collect email information from members. For members who are on the internet web surveys can be used while other modes may be viable for those who are not 'wired'.

BOX 6.4 *Characteristics of internet users*

The characteristics of internet users are carefully monitored by a number of companies and are of special interest to market research companies. The following sites provide details from studies of the characteristics of internet users:

www.cc.gatech.edu/gvu/user_surveys/
User_Survey_Home.html

www.nielsenmedia.com/

www.nua.ie/surveys/ [good for international figures].

These surveys have some methodological limitations but indicate that internet users are typically young (48 per cent under 35), male (66 per cent), white (87 per cent), highly educated (60 per cent have a tertiary degree), professionals (45 per cent are middle/upper management or professionals) who live in the city (86 per cent). These users are also predominantly from western countries. In 1998 57 per cent of internet users were from North America; 22 per cent from Europe; 17 per cent from Asia; 3 per cent from South America, 0.75 per cent from Africa and 0.5 per cent from the Middle East.

Sources: www.gvu.gatech.edu/user_surveys/survey-1998-10/graphs/graphs.html#general [Accessed 1/10/2000] www.nua.ie/surveys/analysis/graphs_charts/1998graphs/location.html [Accessed 1/10/2000]

The Australian Bureau of Statistics (ABS, 2000) conducted a survey of a representative sample of the adult Australian population (users and non-users of the internet) and found the biases regarding internet access. The figures in the table below represent the percentage of people in each grouping (e.g. age grouping, occupational grouping etc) who have access to the internet.

Age	%	Occupation	%	Highest qualifications	%
18–24	72	Manager/professional	69	Secondary	28
25–34	56	Clerical, sales, service	55	Trade	31
35–44	46	Trade, labourer	38	Certificate	41
45–54	36	**Gender**		Diploma	59
55–64	22	Male	45	Degree	80
65+	6	Female	37		
Location		**Employment status**			
Urban	45	Employed	54		
Rural	33	Non-employed	19		

Source: ABS, 2000

While internet samples are by no means adequate yet for general population surveys we must not ignore the deficiencies of samples obtained with other methods of questionnaire administration (Chapter 8). Response rates to face-to-face surveys are declining. Telephone samples are confronting problems due to technological developments such as mobile phones, pagers, faxes, modems, the internet, call forwarding, voicemail and other services that make it increasingly difficult and expensive to even speak to potential respondents.

SAMPLE SIZE

The required sample size depends on two key factors:

1 the degree of accuracy we require for the sample;
2 the extent to which there is variation in the population in regard to the key characteristics of the study.

We need to decide how much error we are prepared to tolerate and how certain we want to be about our generalisations from the sample. Two statistical concepts, sampling error and confidence intervals, help us specify the degree of accuracy we achieve and the concept of confidence level specifies the level of confidence we can have in our generalisations. These concepts are explained in Chapter 13 (pp. 231–4) and it may be helpful to read this section now.

In Table 6.3 the sample sizes required to obtain samples of varying degrees of accuracy are listed. The figures in this table are calculated so that we can be 95 per cent confident that the results in the population will be the same as in the sample plus or minus the sampling error. Thus, if in a sample of 2500 cases we found that 53 per cent intended to vote for the Labor Party, we can be 95 per cent confident that 53 per cent plus or minus 2 per cent (i.e. between 51 and 55 per cent) of the population intends to vote Labor.

There are several things to note about the relationship between sample size and accuracy. First, when dealing with small samples a small increase in sample size can lead to a substantial increase in accuracy. Thus increasing the sample from 100 to 156 reduces sampling error from 10 per cent to 8 per cent. With larger samples increasing the sample size does not have the same payoff. To reduce sampling error from 2.5 per cent to 2 per cent we need to increase the sample by 900 cases. The rule is that to halve the sampling error we have to quadruple the sample size. Beyond a certain point the cost of

increasing the sample size is not worth it in terms of the extra precision. Many survey companies limit their samples to 2000 since beyond this point the extra cost has insufficient payoff in terms of accuracy.

Second, the *size of the population* from which we draw the sample is largely irrelevant for the accuracy of the sample. It is the absolute size of the sample that is important. The only exception to this is when the sample size represents a sizeable proportion of the population (e.g. 10 per cent). In such cases a slightly smaller sample is equally accurate. The calculation of sample size in this situation requires the application of a *finite population correction* (see Moser and Kalton, 1971: 147 for the formula to make the adjustments).

The third point is that the figures in Table 6.3 assume a heterogeneous population. For a population in which most people will answer a question in the same way, a smaller sample will do. Thus for a study on voting, a population where 50 per cent intend voting Labor and 50 per cent for other parties (a 50/50 split) would require a larger sample than one where 80 per cent intended to vote Labor. Table 6.4 lists the required sample sizes depending on the degree of accuracy required and the estimated population variation for the key study variables.

In the end the sample size must take into account the degree of diversity in the population on key variables, the level of sampling error that is tolerable and the reliability required of the sample. Decisions about one factor have implications for other factors as Figure 6. 8 illustrates.

There are difficulties in determining sample size. Apart from requiring that we specify the degree of precision needed, we must also have a rough idea how people are going to answer the question; that is, we must have an idea of the variation (split). The problems with this are twofold—we often do *not* have this information, and surveys often have more than one purpose. On one key variable of interest there may be an anticipated split of 80/20 but on another it may be closer to 50/50. For such multipurpose surveys it seems best to play safe and determine size on the basis of the important variables on which there is likely to be greatest diversity within the sample.

Another matter in working out the sample size occurs when we need to break the sample into subgroups (e.g. males and females). How large do these subgroups need to be? The strict answer is that the sample size and variation *within each group* should

Table 6.3 Sample sizes required for various sampling errors at 95% confidence level (simple random sampling)

Sampling error[a] %	Sample size[b]	Sampling error	Sample Size
1.0	10 000	5.5	330
1.5	4 500	6.0	277
2.0	2 500	6.5	237
2.5	1 600	7.0	204
3.0	1 100	7.5	178
3.5	816	8.0	156
4.0	625	8.5	138
4.5	494	9.0	123
5.0	400	9.5	110
		10	100

Notes: [a] This is in fact two standard errors.
  [b] This assumes a 50/50 split on the variable. These sample sizes would be smaller for more homogeneous samples (see Table 6.4).

Table 6.4 Required sample sizes depending on population homogeneity and desired accuracy

Acceptable sampling error[a]	Per cent of population expected to give particular answer					
	5 or 95	10 or 90	20 or 80	30 or 70	40 or 60	50/50
1% 1 900	3 600	6 400	8 400	9 600	10 000	
2%	479	900	1 600	2 100	2 400	2 500
3%	211	400	711	933	1 066	1 100
4%	119	225	400	525	600	625
5%	76	144	226	336	370	400
6%	—[b]	100	178	233	267	277
7%	—	73	131	171	192	204
8%	—	—	100	131	150	156
9%	—	—	79	104	117	123
10%	—	—	—	84	96	100

Notes: [a] At the 95 per cent level of confidence

[b] Samples smaller than this would normally be too small to allow meaningful analysis

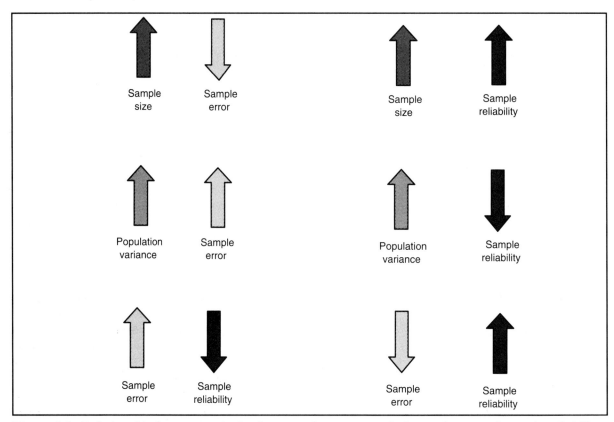

Figure 6.8 Relationship between sample size, sample error, population variance and sample reliability

determine the sample size required for each group. If there are 500 males then the sampling error for the males will be a function of this sample size. Even though the whole sample has 1000 cases (and thus a confidence interval of 6.1 per cent at the 95 per cent confidence level in a population of ten million) the confidence interval for males would be 8.8 per cent. The same would apply to females. This means

---

WEB POINTER 6.1 *Sample size calculators*

There are a number of sample size calculators available on the internet to calculate the required sample size with different levels of sampling error (different width confidence intervals) at different confidence levels and for samples with varying degrees of heterogeneity.

Sample size and confidence interval for different confidence levels.	www.surveysystem.com/sscalc.htm
Calculates sample sizes required for different confidence levels and intervals.	www.azplansite.com/samplesize.htm www.au.af.mil/au/hq/selc/samplsiz.htm http://assessments.ncs.com/ncscorp/research/ calc.htm
Calculating sample error.	www.dssresearch.com/SampleSize/ sampling_error.asp
Ex-Sample—a module in the methodologist's toolchest	www.scolari.co.uk/frame.html?
Power and precision: a powerful but expensive calculator for ascertaining sample size taking into account a large number of different conditions and for different types of analysis. Also marketed by SPSS as SamplePower. An evaluation download is available.	www.power-analysis.com/
NCSS: another powerful, flexible and expensive calculator for ascertaining sample sizes for different circumstances and for a wide variety of analyses. An evaluation download is available.	www.ncss.com/download.html

Visit www.social-research.org to use these links and to check for updates and additions.

---

that your estimates for males and females separately would be less precise than for the sample overall.

This might be acceptable but you need to be conscious of this—especially for the main ways in which you divide your sample. If you are breaking the sample up into a number of relatively small groups the sampling error (and thus the confidence interval) for those groups will be relatively high.

This brings us to a final point. Despite all the figures in the tables we should think ahead to how we intend to analyse the results. In practice a key determinant of sample size is the need to look separately at different subgroups. Make sure that the sample is sufficiently large so that when it is broken down into separate subgroups (e.g. age, class, sex) there will be

sufficient numbers in each. As a rule of thumb try to ensure that the smallest subgroup has at least 50 to 100 cases (Hoinville et al., 1977: 61).

Of course desired accuracy is not the only factor in working out the sample size: cost, time and access to respondents are also key factors. The final sample size will be a compromise between cost, accuracy and ensuring sufficient numbers for meaningful subgroup analysis.

NON-RESPONSE

For a variety of reasons people selected in a sample may not finally be included. Some will refuse, others will be uncontactable and others will be uninterviewable. Non-response can create two main problems:

1   unacceptable reduction of sample size;
2   bias.

The problem of sample size can be tackled in two ways. First, employ techniques designed to reduce non-response. These include paying attention to methods of collecting data, careful training of interviewers (Hoinville et al., 1977), use of interpreters, and calling back at several different times of the day and week (see Chapter 8). Second, we can draw an initial sample that is larger than needed. Assuming good techniques we will still get about 20 per cent non-response, so we might draw an initial sample that is 20 per cent larger than we expect to end up with.

This, however, does nothing to avoid the problem of bias. Often non-responders are different in crucial respects from responders (e.g. older, lower education, migrant background) and increasing the sample size does nothing to produce the correct proportions of various groups if some types systematically do not respond. The difficulty is not so much the bias itself, since there are statistical techniques for minimising its influence in the analysis (see pp. 5–6, 175), but in working out what the bias is and the extent to which it occurs. Once this is known, suitable allowances can be made (Smith, 1989). There are three main ways of obtaining information to enable adjustments for bias.

First, use what observable information can be picked up about non-responders. Where contact is made but people refuse to participate, information about gender, age and ethnic background can be gleaned. A person's house, car and suburb can provide additional clues.

Second, some sampling frames can provide useful information. For example, if official records provided the sampling frame for members of an organisation, we could identify characteristics of the non-responders by using information in the records such as gender and age; and depending on the organisation we might learn about income, education and so forth.

Third, if characteristics of the population from which the sample is drawn are known we can simply compare the characteristics obtained in the sample with those of the population. Any differences between the sample and the population indicate the areas of bias and the extent of the differences indicates the degree of bias. With this information adjustments can be made during analysis to neutralise the effect of non-response bias.

WEIGHTING SAMPLES

Non-response, deliberate oversampling of some small but important categories of people and inadequate sampling frames can result in samples that do not represent the population in important respects even though probability sampling techniques are used. In such cases weighting the sample may be worthwhile. The purpose of weighting is to adjust the sample for oversampling, non-response and so on so that the sample profile on key variables reflects that of the population. In effect weighting involves statistically increasing or decreasing the 'numbers' of cases with particular characteristics so that the proportion of cases in the sample is adjusted to the population proportion.

How to weight a sample on a single characteristic

Weighting a sample for a single variable involves four steps which are also illustrated in Box 6.6.

First, select the variable on which to weight. For example, if you want to ensure that the sample percentages for gender are the same as for the population you will weight by gender. If you plan to adjust (weight) for several characteristics in the sample you should first select the variable with the greatest discrepancy between the population and the sample.

Second, for each category of the weighting variable obtain the *population* and *sample* percentages for each category of the weighting variable (i.e. percentage of males and females in the population and sample respectively). If population figures are unavailable you cannot weight by this variable.

Third, calculate weights for each category of the weighting variable. These weights are calculated by dividing the population percentage by the sample percentage (see Box 6.6).

$$weight = \frac{population\%}{sample\%}$$

Finally, create a new variable called the WEIGHT variable. This variable will be created by you within a data processing program (e.g. SPSS) and when you run the program this variable will be applied to adjust the sample according to the weights.

How to weight a sample on two or more characteristics

There are several methods of weighting for several variables but I will focus on just one method. This method involves simultaneously re-weighting for

---

> **BOX 6.6**
> *Calculating sampling weights for gender*
>
> *Step 1:* Select the variable—gender
>
> *Step 2:* Obtain population and sample percentages:
>
> | | Sample | Population |
> |--------|--------|------------|
> | Male | 35% | 50% |
> | Female | 65% | 50% |
>
> *Step 3:* Calculate weights for each category of the variable:
>
> Male weight = 50 ÷ 35 = 1.43
> Female weight = 50 ÷ 65 = 0.77
>
> *Step 4:* Create a weight variable. In SPSS this would be achieved with the following instructions:
>
> COMPUTE WEIGHT1=0.
> IF (SEX=*male*) WEIGHT1=1.43.
> IF (SEX=*female*) WEIGHT1=0.77.
>
> To apply these weights in SPSS you would include the following instruction in your program before conducting the analysis:
>
> WEIGHT   WEIGHT1.

---

several variables but requires a large sample to be feasible.

If you wanted to weight for, say, three variables at once you would need to follow steps similar to weighting for just one variable. The main difference is that instead of obtaining the population and sample percentages for the categories of just one variable you would obtain the percentage of the whole sample that has each *combination* of characteristics of the three variables. For example, if we wanted to weight for gender (male/female), occupation (blue/white) and education (low/high) we would find the percentage of blue collar females with low education, the percentage of blue collar females with high education and so on.[1] There are five steps in weighting for multiple variables at once. These steps are illustrated in Box 6.7.

BOX 6.7 *Weighting for three variables at once*

Sample percentages for the combination of characteristics on three variables:

	Male		Female	
	Blue	White	Blue	White
Lo educ	10	20	10	15
Hi educ	15	10	10	10

Population percentages for the combination of characteristics on three variables:

	Male		Female	
	Blue	White	Blue	White
Lo educ	15	10	15	10
Hi educ	15	10	15	10

Weights:

	Male		Female	
	Blue	White	Blue	White
Lo educ	15 ÷ 10 = 1.5	10 ÷ 20 = 0.5	15 ÷ 10 = 1.5	10 ÷ 15 = 0.67
Hi educ	15 ÷ 15 = 1	10 ÷ 10 = 1	15 ÷ 10 = 1.5	10 ÷ 10 = 1

Computing the weight variable in SPSS for the three variables involves applying the weights calculated above to particular combinations of characteristics of the three variables.

Compute WT = 0.

IF (sex = *male*) and (occ = *blue*) and (educ = *lo*) WEIGHT = 1.5.

IF (sex = *male*) and (occ = *blue*) and (educ = *hi*) WEIGHT = 1.

IF (sex = *male*) and (occ = *white*) and (educ = *lo*) WEIGHT = 0.5.

IF (sex = *male*) and (occ = *white*) and (educ = *hi*) WEIGHT = 1.

IF (sex = *female*) and (occ = *blue*) and (educ = *lo*) WEIGHT = 1.5.

IF (sex = *female*) and (occ = *blue*) and (educ = *hi*) WEIGHT = 1.5.

IF (sex = *female*) and (occ = *white*) and (educ = *lo*) WEIGHT = 0.67.

IF (sex = *female*) and (occ = *white*) and (educ = *hi*) WEIGHT = 1.

Note: In SPSS the italicised values would be replaced with the relevant codes—see Chapters 9 and 10.

Step 1: Select weighting variables.

Step 2: Obtain population and sample percentages of each possible combination of the categories of the three variables.

Step 3: Calculate weights in the same way as described for a single variable.

Step 4: Compute a WEIGHT variable using the weights.

Step 5: Apply this weight variable in SPSS.

SECONDARY ANALYSIS

For many of us it is extremely difficult to obtain samples that are sufficiently large and representative for adequate analysis: we do not have the time, money or expertise to obtain a really good sample. This problem is compounded when we need data for a whole nation rather than a local area, when we need to collect data over a period of time for a longitudinal study or when data are required from different countries to allow comparative analysis. All too often the 'solution' is either to abandon the project or to collect a very inadequate sample (too small and unrepresentative).

But in many cases there is an alternative: data collected by other people or agencies can often be appropriately used to address the research question at hand. This is called *secondary analysis*. Major research is conducted by government agencies (e.g. census offices), large research organisations and well-established research teams that have excellent samples and often include data about a wide range of attitudes, behaviours and personal attributes which make them suitable for research projects well beyond the purposes envisaged in the initial survey. It is becoming conventional (and is often a requirement of publicly funded projects) that, with appropriate safeguards to guarantee anonymity, (see Chapter 5) data are deposited in a publicly accessible data archive once the primary researchers have completed their analyses. The resultant data sets are available for purchase at extremely low prices.

Web Pointer 6.2 provides the internet links to a large number of data sets that are available. These contain some excellent sets of data that allow for the analysis of change over time where the same questions are asked in repeated surveys. They also allow for comparative analysis where the same questions are asked in surveys in different countries. A few sites enable you to undertake limited online analysis of these national data sets at no cost.

Even where data sets are not available from data archives they can sometimes be constructed by the researcher from published data (see Web Pointer 6.3). Government year books and other publications provide an ideal source of over-time and possibly comparative data. Each year statistics are published on a wide range of matters including social welfare, crime, income, education, migration and the like. The data are provided in aggregate form for a state or country for that year and are not appropriate for analyses in which the individual is the unit of analysis. But where a country, year or region can appropriately be used as the unit of analysis (see p. 30) data sets can be constructed where the aggregate figures provided become the value for the variable for that unit.

For example, crime statistics, social welfare expenditure, unemployment levels and so on are published each year. Using year as the unit of analysis, a number of variables can be created from these figures. Variables for a number of different types of crime could be created and the values for those

---

WEB POINTER 6.2
Sources of data sets using probability samples for secondary analysis

Archive sites from which data sets can be downloaded (normally after registration, undertakings regarding use and privacy and payment of a fee)

The main UK site for social science survey data sets.	www.data-archive.ac.uk/
Provides a search facility and access to a listing of 851 internet sites of numeric social science statistical data, data libraries, social science gateways, addresses and more.	http://odwin.ucsd.edu/idata/
This site provides links to data throughout the world.	http://research.ed.asu.edu/siip/webdata/
A UK site for major British longitudinal studies.	www.cls.ioe.ac.uk/
The British Household Panel Survey with data sets form at least seven waves.	www.iser.essex.ac.uk/bhps/index.php
The Interuniversity Consortium for Political and Social Research (ICPSR) site is the main US archive for social science survey data sets.	www.icpsr.umich.edu/archive1.html
International Social Science Survey Program which provides comparable data from national surveys throughout the world.	www.issp.org/
Links to social science data archives throughout Europe, North America and elsewhere.	www.nsd.uib.no/cessda/europe.html

In such situations the much cheaper non-probability techniques are used. These techniques are appropriate when sampling frames are unavailable or the population is so widely dispersed that cluster sampling would be too inefficient. For example, it would be very difficult to obtain a random sample of homosexuals or marijuana users. Any attempt to do so would either be so expensive that we would end up with a sample too small for meaningful analysis or the rate of dishonesty and refusal would produce such a bias that the sample would not be representative despite probability sampling methods.

In the preliminary stages of research, such as testing questionnaires, non-random samples are satisfactory. On occasions researchers are not concerned with generalising from a sample to the population and in such cases representativeness of the sample is less important. Instead they may be interested in developing scales (see Chapter 11) or in a tentative, hypothesis-generating and exploratory look at data patterns. Some research is not all that interested in working out what proportion of the population gives a particular response but rather in obtaining an idea of the range of responses or ideas that people have. In such cases we would simply try to get a wide variety of people in the sample without being too concerned about whether each type was represented in its correct proportion.

Purposive sampling is a form of non-probability sampling where cases are judged as typical of some category of cases of interest to the researcher. They are not selected randomly. Thus a study of leaders of the conservation movement might, in the absence of a clearly defined sampling frame or population, select some typical leaders from a number of typical conservation groups. While not ensuring representativeness, such a method of selection can provide useful information.

Quota sampling is another common non-probability technique aimed at producing representative samples without a random selection of cases. Interviewers are required to find cases with particular characteristics: they are given quotas of particular types of people to fill. The quotas are organised so that in terms of the quota characteristics the final sample will be representative. To develop quotas we decide on which characteristic we want to ensure the final sample is representative of (e.g. age), find out the distribution of this variable in the population and set quotas accordingly. Thus if 20 per cent of the popu-lation is between 20 and 30 years old and the sample is to be 1000, then 200 of the sample (20 per cent) will be in this age group. If twenty people were doing the interviewing and each had identical quotas of 50, each interviewer would find ten people in this age group (20 per cent of 50). Quite complex quotas can be developed so that several characteristics (e.g. gender, age, marital status) are dealt with simultaneously. Thus an interviewer would be assigned a quota for unmarried females between 20 and 30 years, married females between 20 and 30 years and for each other combination of the three quota variables (see Moser and Kalton, 1971: 129).

Quota techniques are non-random because interviewers can select any cases that fit certain criteria. This can lead to bias as interviewers will tend to select those who are easiest to interview and with whom they feel most comfortable (e.g. friends). Another difficulty with quota sampling is that accurate population proportions may be unavailable. Finally, since random sampling is not used, it is impossible to ascertain the accuracy of any estimates from a quota sample.

Availability samples are also common but must be used with caution and only for specific purposes. These samples are the least likely of any technique to produce representative samples. Using this approach anyone who will respond will do. Surveys where newspapers ask readers to complete and return questionnaires printed in the paper, pop-up web surveys, or TV station 'phone-in' polls are examples of such samples. While these techniques can produce quite large samples cheaply their size does not compensate for their unrepresentativeness. This type of sample can be useful for pilot testing questionnaires or exploratory research but must not be used to make any claim to representing anything but the sample itself.

SAMPLING CHECKLIST

When making sampling decisions in a survey the following checklist should be helpful.

1 What is the population to which you want to generalise?
2 Is an adequate, unbiased sampling frame available?
   a Will you have access to this sampling frame?

b   If not, can a sampling frame be generated via a multistage sampling procedure?

3   What method of questionnaire administration will be used?

  a   What implications does this method have for the adequacy of the sampling frame?

  b   What methods will be used to minimise biases introduced by the sampling frame and method of administration?

4   What method of sampling will be employed?

  a   Probability or non-probability?

  b   If probability, which method?

    i   If systematic, is the sampling frame likely to be subject to periodicity?

    ii   If stratified sampling, what variables will be used to stratify? Why?

    iii   Will the sampling frame contain information by which to stratify?

    iv   If multistage cluster sampling—what are the stages? How many clusters will be used?

  c   If non-probability, which method will you use?

    i   What is your justification for non-probability?

    ii   What strategies are being used to test/enhance representativeness?

5   How large a sample is required?

  a   What is the variability of the sample on key characteristics?

b   What is the population size? Is a finite population correction required?

c   Will the analysis require separate analysis of subgroups?

  i   If so what is the likely size of the subgroups?

  ii   Will some subgroups need to be over-sampled to ensure adequate numbers for meaningful analysis?

d   What is the estimated sampling error/confidence interval for the sample and the main subgroups?

e   What is the estimated non-response? Does the initial sample selection take account of the level of non-response?

f   How do practicalities affect the sample size?

  i   What is the estimated cost per sample unit?

  ii   How long will it take to collect information from each unit?

6   Will the sample require weighting?

  a   If so, on what characteristics is it likely to require weighting?

  b   Will you have the information by which to weight?

    i   Population parameter?

    ii   Sample information?

KEY CONCEPTS

Bias	Non-probability	Random sample	Sampling frame
Census	sampling	Replication	Simple random sample
Clusters	Non-response bias	Representative sample	Statistical generalisation
Cluster sample	Periodicity	Sample	Stratification
Confidence intervals	Population	Sample error	Systematic sampling
Confidence level	Probability sampling	Sample heterogeneity	Weighting
Multistage sampling	Quota sample	Sampling fraction	

ENDNOTE

[1]   This would be achieved in SPSS with a cross-tabulation of gender by occupation by education using total per cent—see Chapter 14.

FURTHER READING

Good general and easy to read introductions to sampling are provided by Fink (1995), Henry (1990) and Maisel and Hodges-Persell (1996). Moser and Kalton provide a first rate introduction to the main issues of sampling in Chapters 4–7 of *Survey Methods in Social Investigation* (1971) and in Kalton (1983). A particularly good illustration of multistage sampling is given in Chapter 5 by Warwick and Lininger (1975). Lavrakas (1993) provides a clear discussion of the special issues involved in obtaining samples for telephone surveys. The definitive reference is Kish's *Survey Sampling* (1965). This provides a comprehensive discussion which ranges from the simple to complex mathematical issues. For a book that is a little more accessible read Sudman's *Applied Sampling* (1976) which deals with many practical problems, provides examples and is realistic. An excellent and more concise account is provided by Sudman in a chapter in the *Handbook of Survey Research* (1983).

Issues in obtaining samples from 'rare' populations are tackled in Kalton (1983, 1993) while valuable discussions of quota sampling are available in Marsh and Scarbrough's paper 'Testing Nine Hypotheses About Quota Sampling' (1990) and in Curtice and Sparrow (1997) 'How Accurate Are Traditional Quota Opinion Polls?'. Frankel and Frankel provide an instructive account of the development of sampling techniques in their article 'Fifty Years of Survey Sampling in the United States' (1987) as does Kalton (2000) for the last 25 years while Sudman and Blair (1999) anticipate future developments in 'Sampling in the Twenty-First Century'.

Hyman's book *Secondary Analysis of Sample Surveys* (1972) remains an excellent introduction to secondary analysis. Kiecolt and Nathan's 'Secondary Analysis of Survey Data' (1985) and Dale, Arber and Proctor (1988) offer thorough discussions of the benefits and costs of secondary data and provide many practical pointers about how to evaluate and effectively use secondary data in *Doing Secondary Analysis*.

EXERCISES

1 Find a page of your telephone directory with relatively few businesses and draw a simple random of twenty people from the first column. Use the table of random numbers (Table 6.1). List *all* your workings used to draw this SRS.

2 Using the same page of the directory select a systematic sample of 40 people using the whole page. Show all your workings.

3 Turn to Figure 6.2. Assume that cases 11, 5, 20, 38, 17, 18, 40, 49, 12, 1, 20, 21, 44, 46, 14, 23, 48, 14, 22 are female. Draw a stratified sample of fourteen people using gender as the stratifying variable. Show all your workings.

4 Using a street directory of your city, select a multistage cluster sample. For the first stage use the directory's key map in which you can see the whole city, divided up by map number. Select fifteen areas and list them showing your workings. Then randomly select only *one* of these areas. Divide it into sixteen equally sized units (use a 4 × 4 grid) and randomly select a sample of four of these units. For this exercise select only *one* unit and then proceed to draw a sample of individuals from this unit. Assume for this exercise that each residential block has exactly the same number of households (e.g. 50). Show all your workings and list the problems you have encountered.

5 For the above exercise describe two ways in which you could have increased the likely accuracy of the sample without increasing the final sample size.

6 How would you go about obtaining a probability sample of members of Rotary in your country? Assume there is no access to a national list of members and you want to personally interview people but wish to minimise costs.

7 Outline the difference between:
   a bias and sampling error;
   b probability and non-probability samples;
   c quota and systematic samples;
   d a representative sample and a random sample;
   e a sample and census.

8 You want to draw a simple random sample of voters in your electorate to see how they intend to vote. Assume there are about 70 000 voters in your electorate. How large a sample would you need? Explain the assumptions you have made in determining your sample size.

9 Think of two research topics in which you would need to use non-probability sampling techniques and explain why a probability sample would not be feasible.

10 What does it mean to have a sampling error of 4 per cent at the 95 per cent confidence level?

11 Go to sample size calculator at the following website:

www.surveysystem.com/sscalc.htm

Using the 'Determine Sample Size' calculator calculate the required sample size for each of the sampling scenarios in the grid below (i.e. different population sizes and different required confidence intervals).

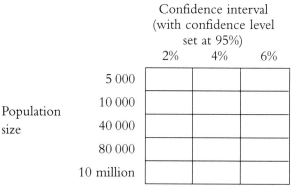

	Confidence interval (with confidence level set at 95%)		
Population size	2%	4%	6%
5 000			
10 000			
40 000			
80 000			
10 million			

Summarise what the resulting sample sizes tell you about:

a the relationship between population size and the required sample size;

b the impact of a smaller confidence interval (i.e. greater precision of estimates from the sample) and required sample size.

12 Using the 'Find Confidence Interval' calculator calculate the confidence interval for each of the sampling scenarios in the grid below (i.e. different sample sizes and different variation (split) in the population). In all calculations use a 95 per cent confidence level and set the population at 500 000.

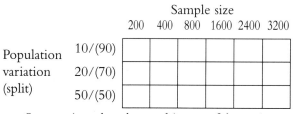

	Sample size					
Population variation (split)	200	400	800	1600	2400	3200
10/(90)						
20/(70)						
50/(50)						

Summarise what the resulting confidence intervals tell you about:

a The relationship between population variation and the confidence interval.

b The impact of increasing the sample size (i.e. greater precision of estimates from the sample).

c The impact on confidence interval of increasing sample size and increasing population variation.

d The impact on confidence interval of decreasing population variation and increasing the sample size.

13 Examine the grid below. Each cell is meant to indicate a particular sampling scenario. Thus cell (a) represents a sampling situation where the population has 100 000 units, the sample size will be 500 units and the variation in the population is low (10/90 split on a two category variable).

Without using the sample size calculator indicate:

a the sample with the *lowest* confidence interval;

b the sample with the *highest* confidence interval.

		Population size			
		100 000		1 million	
	Sample size	500	1000	500	1000
Population variation (split)	10/90	a	b	c	d
	50/50	e	f	g	h

14 Below is the marital status of a national sample and the marital status for the same country as recorded by the census.

a Calculate the weights required for each marital status category.

b Use these weights to recalculate the number of people in each marital status category after the weights are applied (multiply N by weight).

	Sample	Population (Census)
Never married	44.8% (1003)	30.6%
Married	44.6% (998)	57.0%
Divorced/separated	5.6% (126)	6.3%
Widowed	5.0% (113)	6.1%
Total	(2240)	

7

Constructing questionnaires

Questionnaires are the most common method of collecting survey data. This chapter outlines how to:

- construct individual survey questions that work;
- get the wording of questions right;
- use a variety of question formats;
- test whether your questions satisfy the principles of good question design;
- structure and design questionnaires from individual questions;
- modify questionnaires depending on the way in which they are to be administered;
- pilot test a questionnaire to see if it works.

SELECTING AREAS

Typically, when using questionnaires, it is difficult to go back to people to collect additional information. Therefore it is crucial to think ahead and anticipate what information will be needed to ensure that the relevant questions are asked.

There are a number of ways of working out which questions to ask. First, the research problem will affect which concepts need to be measured (see Chapter 3). Second, the indicators we devise for these concepts are crucial in determining which questions to ask (see Chapter 4). Third, our hunches about the mechanisms by which variables are linked or about factors which might explain relationships will require that certain questions be included (see Chapter 16). Fourth, the way data are to be analysed affects what information is needed: it is pointless collecting information which cannot be analysed and frustrating to discover that you do not have the necessary data for certain analysis. It is not possible to develop a questionnaire that can be analysed properly unless you first understand methods of analysis (see Chapters 12 to 17). Finally, the method by which the questionnaire is to be administered affects the type of questions that can be asked. If the questionnaire is administered by a trained interviewer more complex questions can be used since there is opportunity for clarification. In addition, follow-up questions which draw on answers to earlier questions can be used. With self-administered questionnaires such as those sent out by post you need to concentrate on clarity and simplicity.

In summary, the art of questionnaire design involves thinking ahead about the research problem, what the concepts mean and how we will analyse the data. The questionnaire should reflect both theoretical thinking and an understanding of data analysis.

QUESTION CONTENT

It is helpful to distinguish between five distinct types of question content: behaviour, beliefs, knowledge, attitudes and attributes (Dillman, 1978: 80). Imagine that you are conducting a study on the topic of workforce participation of mothers of preschool age children and you had a sample of mothers—some with young children, others with older children. Before you could formulate any questionnaire items you would need to be very clear about the issues in which you are interested.

If you were interested in *behaviour* you would formulate questions to establish what people *do*. For example, you would ask whether the respondent is working or did work with a preschool age child. Depending on the precise research question this can provide useful information. It can provide a map of which types of mothers work and which types do not and may help locate factors which facilitate or hinder workforce participation. But too often researchers try to use behavioural measures to extrapolate to beliefs and attitudes. This is open to real dangers of misinterpretation. Since people are neither very consistent nor rational and may not have the luxury of behaving as they might like, any conclusions we can draw about beliefs or attitudes from behaviour are very limited.

If you are interested in *beliefs*—in what people believe is *true or false*—you need to ask quite different types of question. For example, you might ask people for their estimate of the percentage of mothers with preschool-age children who are in the paid labour force or ask about what they believe to be the effects of day care centres on the emotional

development of preschool-age children. The focus of belief questions is on establishing what people think is true rather than on the accuracy of their beliefs.

Knowledge questions have some similarities to belief questions. They seek to discover respondents' knowledge of particular facts, such as the percentage of children in child-care, the government programs designed to assist parents with pre-schoolers to work part-time, and the tax implications of working part-time. However, while belief questions are designed to discover *what* people believe, knowledge questions are formulated to establish the *accuracy* of their beliefs. The difference between knowledge and belief questions lies less in the construction of the question than in the way the answers are interpreted and used.

Belief questions can be distinguished from those that aim to establish the respondent's *attitudes*. Whereas belief questions ascertain what the respondent thinks is true, attitude questions try to establish what they think is *desirable*. An attitudinal focus might ask about attitudes regarding whether or not mothers with preschool-age children ought to participate in the workforce.

Finally, *attribute* questions are designed to obtain information about the respondents' characteristics. Such questions would normally include information about their age, education, occupation, gender, ethnicity, marital status and so forth. For the study of workforce participation of mothers with preschool-age children you might ask about attributes such as the number of children, the age of the child, income, type of job, whether the job was full-time or part-time and other related information.

It is important to be clear about the precise type of information required for a number of reasons. First, the failure to adequately distinguish between these five types of information arises from a lack of clarity about the research question and inadequate conceptualisation. This can lead to the collection of quite the wrong type of information. If we are interested in exploring people's actual behaviour, a set of questions that in fact taps beliefs or attitudes will be of little use. Second, we might be interested in all five types of information. An awareness of the five types of information that can be collected should lead to the systematic development of questions for each type rather than a haphazard set of questions on the broad topic which may or may not tap all types of topic. Third, when it comes to analysis and the development of scales (see Chapter 11), it is important to develop composite measures; however, these normally need to be composite measures of the same type of information. Attitude questions can be combined with other attitude questions to form an index of some sort or another but it would normally be quite inappropriate to combine the four types of information into a single measure: they tap quite different things.

Direction, extremity and intensity of attitudes

It is important to distinguish the *direction* of a person's attitude from both the *extremity* of their position and the *intensity* with which they hold that position. Each of these three aspects of an attitude requires a different sort of question.

We may wish to know people's views about whether government economic policy ought to be directed more at reducing inflation and the government deficit or at reducing unemployment. We could discover the *direction* of a person's attitude by simply asking them which of the two policy directions they think is the more desirable. But we could learn more by asking how *extreme* their view is. There are two ways in which this is commonly done. The first is to provide a statement that expresses a *position* (e.g. the government's first priority ought to be to reduce unemployment even if this leads to increased inflation and problems with the deficit) and asking them to say how strongly they agree or disagree with it. Alternatively, a seven-point scale might be used in which 'reduce inflation' is placed at one end and 'reduce unemployment' at the other. Respondents can be asked to indicate where they would place themselves between these two positions.

This approach does not necessarily detect the *intensity* with which a position is held. Although extremity and intensity of an attitude may often go together, they are not the same thing. A person can hold extreme positions but do so with little passion. People may vote for extreme left- or right-wing political parties without having a fervent commitment to that party. Questions that measure a person's attitude *position* can usefully be followed up with questions to detect the attitude *intensity*.

PRINCIPLES OF QUESTION DESIGN

Before dealing with the specifics of question wording and answer formats it is important to highlight six broad principles that must be built into question design.

Reliability

The question should be answered in the same way on different occasions if given to the same person (assuming that the person has not changed in the meantime). A question that fails to achieve consistent responses is unreliable. Ambiguous or vague question wording may produce unreliable responses as respondents 'read' the question differently on different occasions.

Validity

A valid question is one that measures what we think it does. Thus if we use self-rated health (i.e. how healthy are you?) as a measure of health we need to be confident that it measures health rather than something else such as optimism and pessimism. If we use an IQ test to measure intelligence we want to be sure that it does in fact measure intelligence, rather than social class background.

Discrimination

Explanatory survey analysis requires that there is variation in the sample on the key variables. If we wanted to see if there was a link between gender and income we would have to have a sample in which there were men and women and in which there was a good variety of income levels. Low variance may reflect real homogeneity (or sameness) within the sample (e.g. gender and income level). But it can also stem from poor question design—a limited range of response alternatives can produce low variance. If our questions do not pick up actual variation in the sample then the information obtained by the question will be of no use at the data analysis stage. For example, if we asked about income and simply had two response categories of 'Less than $100 000 a year' and 'Over $100 000 a year' we would not identify much variation in the sample. Most people would be in the 'Less than $100 000 a year' category. For analytic purposes all these people would be treated as though they were the same despite what might be considerable income differences. A question with finer grained response categories would identify greater variation across the sample. Good questions will be sensitive to measuring real and meaningful differences in a sample.

When measuring attitudes low variance can also stem from using extreme attitude statements. For example, an extreme statement such as 'In a country such as this, assassination of political leaders is acceptable in order to bring about political change' will probably yield low variance. The solution is to provide sufficient response alternatives to detect meaningful variation and to avoid using extreme or absolute statements.

Response rate

Ideally all respondents will answer every question that applies to them but experience tells us that some questions can elicit relatively high non-response. Non-response needs to be minimised both because of the loss of information and the data analysis difficulties it introduces. Non-response is affected by question content, question construction, method of administration and questionnaire length. Intrusive, sensitive, irrelevant or repetitive questions as well as those that are poorly worded, difficult to understand, difficult to answer or have insufficient response categories can frustrate respondents and produce non-response.

Same meaning for all respondents

When analysing questionnaires we assume that all respondents have answered the same questions. However if respondents interpret the questions in different ways they are effectively answering different questions. If I use the term 'old people' or 'elderly people' in a question respondents will use different definitions for the terms 'old' or 'elderly' and in effect be answering different questions. Careful question design is needed to minimise this problem.

Relevance

Each question must earn its place in your survey. For each question ask yourself whether it really is necessary.

WORDING QUESTIONS

Considerable attention must be given to developing clear, unambiguous and useful questions. To do this the wording of the questions is fundamental. The checklist of seventeen questions in Box 7.2 will help you to avoid the most obvious problems with question wording.

1 Is the language simple?

Avoid jargon and technical terms. Look for simple words without making questions sound condescending. Use simple writing guides or a thesaurus to help (see Gowers, 1962; Strunk and White, 1972). A question such as 'Is your household run on matriarchal or patriarchal lines?' will not do!

2 Can the question be shortened?

The shorter the question the less confusing and ambiguous it will be. Avoid questions such as: 'Has it

---

BOX 7.2 *Question wording checklist*

1 Is the language simple?
2 Can the question be shortened?
3 Is the question double-barrelled?
4 Is the question leading?
5 Is the question negative?
6 Is the respondent likely to have the necessary knowledge?
7 Will the words have the same meaning for everyone?
8 Is there a prestige bias?
9 Is the question ambiguous?
10 Is the question too precise?
11 Is the frame of reference for the question sufficiently clear?
12 Does the question artificially create opinions?
13 Is personal or impersonal wording preferable?
14 Is the question wording unnecessarily detailed or objectionable?
15 Does the question have dangling alternatives?
16 Does the question contain gratuitous qualifiers?
17 Is the question a 'dead giveaway'?

happened to you that over a long period of time, when you neither practised abstinence nor used birth control, you did not conceive?'.

3 Is the question double-barrelled?

Double-barrelled questions are those which ask more than one question. The question 'how often do you visit your parents?' is double-barrelled. Separate questions about a person's mother and father should be asked.

4 Is the question leading?

A leading question is one where either the question structure or wording pushes people to provide a response that they would not have given had the question been asked in a more neutral way (Payne, 1951; Bradburn and Sudman, 1979; Belson, 1981). Questions such as 'Do you oppose or favour cutting defence spending even if cuts turn the country over to communists?' are obviously leading. Leading questions give respondents the impression that there is a 'correct' response. Avoid linking an attitude position, policy or whatever with a prestigious person. Avoid phrases such as 'Do you agree that . . .?' or 'Does this seem like a good idea to you?'. The particular terminology you use can be leading. Think of the different impact of the choice of words 'abortion', 'killing unborn babies' or 'ending a pregnancy'.

5 Is the question negative?

Questions which use 'not' can be difficult to understand—especially when asking someone to indicate whether they agree or disagree. The following question could be confusing:

> Marijuana should not be decriminalised
> –Agree
> –Disagree

Rewording the question to 'Marijuana use should remain illegal' avoids the confusion caused by using 'not'.

6 Is the respondent likely to have the necessary knowledge?

When asking about certain issues it is important that respondents are likely to have knowledge about the issue. A question which asks 'Do you agree or disagree with the government's policy on legalising drug injecting rooms?' would be unsatisfactory. For

issues where there is doubt, we might first ask a filter question to see if people are aware of the government's policy on drug injecting rooms and then ask the substantive question only if people answered 'yes' to the filter question. Alternatively, we should offer the respondent the opportunity to say that they are not sure what the government's policy is.

7 Will the words have the same meaning for everyone?

Depending on factors such as age group, subcultural group and region, the meaning of some words will vary, so care must be taken either to avoid such words or to make your meaning clear. People also vary in how they define certain terms. For example, the answers people give to a question that asks them if they have been a victim of a crime in the last five years will depend on what they include in their definition of crime. For example, despite its illegality, some people may exclude domestic violence from their definitions of crime, thus leading to its underreporting.

8 Is there a prestige bias?

When an opinion is attached to the name of a prestigious person and the respondent is then asked to express their own view on the same matter, the question can suffer from prestige bias. That is, the prestige of the person who holds the view may influence the way respondents answer the question. For example, 'What is your view about the Pope's policy on birth control?' could suffer from prestige bias. Effectively the question is double-barrelled: the answer may reflect an attitude about the Pope or about birth control—we cannot be sure which.

9 Is the question ambiguous?

Ambiguity can arise from poor sentence structure, using words with several different meanings, use of negatives and double negatives, and using double-barrelled questions. The best way to avoid ambiguity is to use short, crisp, simple questions.

10 Is the question too precise?

While we need to avoid questions which invite vague and highly imprecise responses we also need to avoid requiring answers that need more precision than people are likely to be able to provide reliably. Precise answers are not necessarily accurate answers. Asking for too precise an answer can produce unreliable responses and add nothing useful to the study (Foddy, 1993). For example, asking people 'How many times in the last year did any member of your household visit a doctor?' may yield precise figures but they are likely to be both inaccurate and unreliable.

11 Is the frame of reference for the question sufficiently clear?

If you ask 'How often do you see your mother?', establish within what time frame—within the last year? the last month? If you mean the frequency within the last year, ask 'Within the last year how often would you have seen your mother on average?' and then provide alternatives such as 'daily' through to 'never' to help further specify the meaning of the question.

12 Does the question artificially create opinions?

On certain issues people will have no opinion. You should therefore offer people the option of responding 'don't know', or 'no opinion'. This can lead to some people giving these responses to most questions which can create its own problems, but not including these alternatives will produce highly unreliable, and therefore useless, responses (see p. 106 for further discussion).

13 Is personal or impersonal wording preferable?

Personal wording asks respondents to indicate how 'they' feel about something, whereas the impersonal approach asks respondents to indicate how 'people' feel about something. The approach you use depends on what you want to do with the answers. The impersonal approach does not provide a measure of someone's attitudes but rather the respondent's perception of other people's attitudes.

14 Is the question wording unnecessarily detailed or objectionable?

Questions about precise age or income can create problems. Since we normally do not need precise data on these issues we can diffuse this problem by asking people to put themselves in categories such as age or income groups.

15 Does the question have dangling alternatives?

A question such as 'Would you say that it is frequently, sometimes, rarely or never that . . .?' is an awkward construction. The alternative answers are provided before the respondent has any subject matter to anchor them to. The subject matter should come *before* alternative answers are listed.

16 Does the question contain gratuitous qualifiers?

The italicised qualifiers in the following examples would clearly affect the way people answer the question—they effectively present an argument for a particular response. 'Do you oppose or favour cutting defence expenditure *even if it endangers our national security?*' and 'Do you favour or oppose increasing the number of university places for students *even if it leads to a decline in standards?*'

17 Is the question a 'dead giveaway'?

Absolute, all-inclusive or exclusive words are normally best avoided. Examples of such 'dead give-away' words (Payne, 1951) are: all, always, each, every, everybody, never, nobody, none, nothing. Since these words allow no exceptions few people will agree with the statement that includes them and this in turn will result in low variance and poor question discrimination.

SELECTING QUESTION TYPE

The other aspect of question construction is to decide on the response format. Should it be open or closed? If a closed format is used then a number of alternative types are available.

Open and closed formats

A closed or forced-choice question is one in which a number of alternative answers are provided from which respondents are to select one or more of the answers. An open-ended question is one for which respondents formulate their own answers.

There is disagreement about which style is preferable. A major problem of forced-choice questions is that on some issues they can create false opinions either by giving an insufficient range of alternatives from which to choose or by prompting people with 'acceptable' answers. Further, the forced-choice approach is not very good at taking into account people's qualifiers to the answers they select.

There are, however, a number of advantages to *well-developed* forced-choice questions. Where the questionnaire is long or people's motivation to answer is not high, forced-choice questions are useful since they are quick to answer. This is particularly so if the questionnaire is self-administered rather than administered by a skilled interviewer who can establish rapport and increase motivation.

From a researcher's point of view, forced-choice questions are easier to code (see Chapter 9). Answers to both closed and open questions need to be grouped into categories at some stage. The difficulties of doing this with open-ended questions often mean that they never get used. Even if they are grouped, researchers normally interpret answers and put them in categories. Researchers can misinterpret the answers and thus misclassify responses. Forced-choice questions allow respondents to classify themselves, thus avoiding coders misclassifying what people meant.

A further advantage of closed questions is that they do not discriminate against the less talkative and less articulate respondents. Asking people to formulate their own responses is fine for those who can do it but the danger is that researchers will be overly influenced by these responses and ignore the opinions of the less articulate and less fluent.

A set of alternative responses can serve as useful prompts for respondents. For example, a question asking about the newspapers and magazines a person has read in the last week will detect a higher readership level if the names of newspapers and magazines are listed in a checklist than if the open-ended question is simply asked without the list of responses.

If forced-choice questions are used, it is necessary to put a lot of thought into developing alternative responses. The range must be exhaustive: a thorough range of responses must be listed to avoid biasing responses. This can be done by careful pilot testing using less structured approaches to locate the range of likely responses and by using the category called 'other (please specify)' to allow for unanticipated responses.

The choice of open or closed questions depends on many factors such as the question content, respondent motivation, method of administration, type of respondents, access to skilled coders to code open-ended responses and the amount of time available to develop a good set of unbiased responses. There is no right or wrong approach.

RESPONSE FORMATS AND LEVEL OF MEASUREMENT

In Chapter 12 the concept of level of measurement will be discussed. Go to pp. 203–6 and read the section on levels of measurement. In that section you will see that the level of measurement of a variable is based on the response categories of a variable and the relation of one response category to another.

The level of measurement of a variable is fundamental in the choice of statistical methods when we come to analyse the data. The way we frame many questions will influence the level of measurement of a variable and thus the way we analyse data later on.

From a data analysis perspective it is generally best to have data that are measured at the interval level. This enables us to use a wider range of statistical methods and allows us to use the more powerful techniques should we need them. From this perspective it is desirable to design questions so that they result in interval-level variables. However, the principles of good questionnaire design are not always consistent with this and we may have to settle for less precise question formats that collect ordinal-level data. We will then be restricted to methods of analysis that only require this sort of data.

We have some control over the level of measurement of a variable. The way we ask the question, or more precisely, the sort of response alternatives provided will yield data at a nominal, ordinal or interval level (see Figure 7.1).

DEVELOPING QUESTION RESPONSES

There are three guiding principles when developing question responses.

Exhaustiveness (or inclusiveness)

Ensure that the response alternatives provide a sufficient range of responses to cover all respondents. A question that asks about marital status and includes only 'married' and 'divorced' as alternatives is not providing an exhaustive set of options.

Numeric rating scales (see below) are a good way of providing an exhaustive set of responses for many questions. Attitude questions should generally include a 'don't know' or 'no opinion' option (see p. 106) so that those with no opinion are provided for. For some

> **Interval level**
> *How many years of formal education have you completed since you left secondary school? (circle the number that applies to you)*
>
> 0   1   2   3   4   5   6   7   8   9   9+
>
> **Ordinal**
> *What is the highest level of qualification you have completed since leaving secondary school?*
>
> ☐ Certificate
> ☐ Diploma
> ☐ Bachelor's degree
> ☐ Graduate diploma
> ☐ Masters degree
> ☐ PhD
>
> **Nominal**
> *Since leaving secondary school which of the following best describes what you have been doing?*
>
> ☐ Further study
> ☐ Working full-time (for an income)
> ☐ Working and studying
> ☐ Home duties
> ☐ Travelling
> ☐ None of the above

Figure 7.1   Question format and level of measurement

questions it is appropriate to add an open category where respondents can create their own answer if the set provided has not been exhaustive. For example, a question asking about the respondents' country of birth might provide a list of the most common countries but add a final, catch-all category of 'Other (please specify)' to cover those respondents not covered by the preset responses.

Exclusiveness

This principle means that for each 'question' a person can provide one and *only one* answer to the 'question'. That is, the alternate responses should be mutually exclusive. This is not a problem with rating scales and questions where the response alternatives are graded along a single continuum. Respondents may have difficulty identifying where on the continuum they lie but in principle they lie at a particular point.

Exclusiveness is a problem where a person might quite legitimately select more than one of the alternative responses, as illustrated in Figure 7.2.

There are several ways of dealing with this problem. The first would be to add additional cat-

> In your workplace would you say that getting ahead is based on merit or gender?
>
> ☐   Merit
> ☐   Gender

Figure 7. 2   Non-exclusive responses

egories such as 'Both' or 'Neither'. Another solution is to reduce the choices to a single choice by asking people to nominate which of the alternatives is *most* important. In this case the question could be rephrased to read 'In your workplace which would you say is the more important for getting ahead: merit or gender?'

Another solution is to treat each response as a separate question or variable. For example, instead of asking whether gender or merit is the more important we could ask respondents to show how important each factor is (e.g. 'Important', 'Not important', and 'No opinion'). Similarly, in checklist questions each item can be thought of as a separate variable for data analysis with the categories of 'selected' and 'not selected' (see the section on multiple response coding in Chapter 9). In this way the principle of exclusiveness is preserved.

Balancing categories

An imbalance of responses in one direction can produce bias (Payne, 1951). Where response categories can be ordered from high to low there should be the same number of response alternatives either side of what might be considered the neutral position. For example, the alternatives in Figure 7.3 will introduce bias and underestimate the level of disapproval.

DEVELOPING RESPONSE ALTERNATIVES FOR CLOSED-CHOICE QUESTIONS

A range of ways of responding to closed-choice questions are available. The type of response

> ☐   Completely approve
> ☐   Strongly approve
> ☐   Approve
> ☐   Neither approve nor disapprove
> ☐   Disapprove

Figure 7.3   Unbalanced response alternatives

alternative has major implications for response rates to questions, coding and the way data are analysed. The particular formatting of these response alternatives will differ depending on the mode of questionnaire administration (see Chapter 8).

Numerical rating scales

Rating scales involve a set of responses where the alternative answers are ordered from low to high. Respondents need to indicate where between the low and high extremes lies their attitude. There are a variety of ways in which rating scales are structured.

Likert scales

This approach to measuring attitudes involves providing a statement that reflects a particular attitude or opinion. Respondents indicate their level of agreement or disagreement with the statement. Usually respondents are given the alternatives of strongly agree, agree, neither agree nor disagree, disagree and strongly disagree. This style of question may be presented as a single item question or as a set of questions arranged in a grid format. The grid format, apart from saving space, is easy to answer and is used for sets of items that form scales (see Chapter 11). For the purpose of data analysis each statement to which an answer is sought is a separate variable (see Figure 7.4).

Horizontal rating scales

These scales provide respondents with opposite attitude positions and asks them to indicate with a number where, between the positions, their own view falls (see Figure 7.5).

Semantic differential

This method provides *opposite adjectives*, rather than attitude positions, to describe someone or something. These adjectives are placed at the opposite ends of the numeric scale. Each pair of adjectives provides a separate variable for data analysis (see Figure 7.6).

Vertical rating ladder

You might want to ask people to rate the status of particular universities such as Harvard, Oxford, Princeton, Cambridge and Melbourne. You might provide respondents with a rating ladder like that below and ask them to indicate where on this ladder they would place the status of each university. Different universities could share the same rating and each university would be treated as a separate variable for analysis purposes (see Figure 7.7).

Scores

Rather than using graphical rating scales we might simply ask the respondent to write in a score to

To what extent do you agree or disagree with each of the statements as far as your immediate supervisor is concerned?	Strongly agree	Agree	Neither agree nor disagree	Disagree	Strongly disagree
1 Criticises people in a manner which builds their motivation	☐	☐	☐	☐	☐
2 Admits to their mistakes	☐	☐	☐	☐	☐
3 Takes action without waiting to be asked to	☐	☐	☐	☐	☐
4 Praises others' ideas and contributions	☐	☐	☐	☐	☐
5 Takes personal responsibility when things go wrong	☐	☐	☐	☐	☐

Figure 7.4   Likert-style questions in a grid format

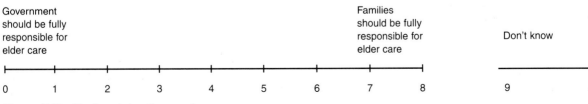

Some people think that the government should provide for proper care of the elderly while others think that it is the responsibility of families.

Government should be fully responsible for elder care

Families should be fully responsible for elder care

Don't know

0   1   2   3   4   5   6   7   8   9

Figure 7.5   Horizontal rating scale

I would like you to describe your workplace using the following set of descriptions. For each description circle the number below the line to indicate where your workplace falls.

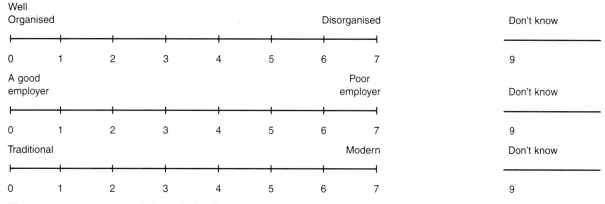

Figure 7.6   Semantic differential rating scales

	Rank	University
High	10	
	9	Oxford; Cambridge
	8	Harvard
	7	
	6	Princeton
	5	
	4	
	3	Melbourne
	2	
Low	1	

Figure 7.7   Vertical rating ladder

indicate their rating. There are a number of formats for doing this.

Out of 10
Instead of providing the diagram you could simply ask respondents to indicate their rating of something by giving it a score out of 10. For example, the question in Figure 7.8 might be used to study job satisfaction.

Feeling thermometer
With the feeling thermometer (Figure 7.9) each group becomes a variable during the analysis.

The list below describes various features of jobs. For each feature think of your current job and say how satisfied you are with that aspect of your job by giving a score out of 10. If you are completely satisfied you should give this feature a score of 10. If you are completely dissatisfied give it a score of 0. If you are neither satisfied nor dissatisfied give it a score of 5. You can give any score between 0 and 10. How would you rate your current job in relation to:

☐ ☐ the feeling of accomplishment it gives you
☐ ☐ the level of enjoyment and interest it gives
☐ ☐ the security and predictability it gives you
☐ ☐ the people you get to meet at work
☐ ☐ the amount of money you earn

Figure 7.8   Score out of 10 rating scale

Despite the differences between these various rating scales they have important characteristics in common.

■ They all require that respondents give one and only one response to each item.
■ They all produce variables where the responses can be ordered from high to low.
■ The way in which each item is answered is not constrained by the way in which other items in a set are answered. This is distinctly different from questions that require the ranking of responses.

Ranking

The ranking format requires respondents to rate the importance or strength of agreement *relative to the way other items in the set have been rated*. This format

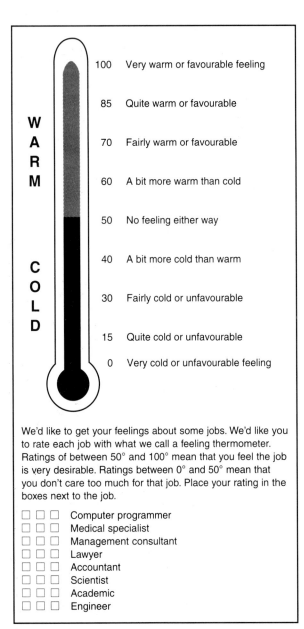

We'd like to get your feelings about some jobs. We'd like you to rate each job with what we call a feeling thermometer. Ratings of between 50° and 100° mean that you feel the job is very desirable. Ratings between 0° and 50° mean that you don't care too much for that job. Place your rating in the boxes next to the job.

☐ ☐ ☐ Computer programmer
☐ ☐ ☐ Medical specialist
☐ ☐ ☐ Management consultant
☐ ☐ ☐ Lawyer
☐ ☐ ☐ Accountant
☐ ☐ ☐ Scientist
☐ ☐ ☐ Academic
☐ ☐ ☐ Engineer

Figure 7.9   Feeling thermometer

provides answers that indicate the *relative* rather than the *absolute* importance of items. Figure 7.10 provides an example.

Depending on how many items are listed we might just ask that the top two and bottom two items be ranked. Where there are relatively few items (e.g. four or five) we might ask that they all be ranked. With this format there are two ways of creating variables for analysis (see Chapter 14).

Listed below is a set of issues that can influence the way in which people decide to vote in general elections. Please rank each of these issues to indicate how important they are to *you* when you decide to vote. Place 1 in the box next to the most important issue, 2 next to the second most important issue and so on. Do not place the same number in more than one box.

☐ Policies to reduce unemployment
☐ Improving the environment
☐ Spending more money on education
☐ Getting tough on crime
☐ Reducing taxation
☐ Improving social welfare support
☐ Improving health services
☐ Reducing immigration

Figure 7.10   Ranking response format

Checklists

This format involves listing a set of items and asking that the respondent simply select those that apply (see Figure 7.11).

Binary choice formats

These formats require the respondent to choose between one of two fixed alternatives.

Dichotomous questions

These questions ask the respondent to select between one of two alternatives. Checklists are effectively binary choice questions (select or do not select). Other examples are illustrated in Figure 7.12.

Paired comparisons

Another form of the binary choice is a set of paired comparisons where the respondent is given a set of

---

Listed below are some adjectives, some of which are 'favourable', some of which are 'unfavourable', some of which are neither. Please tick the boxes beside the characteristics that best describe you as a person. Most people choose three or four, but you may choose more or fewer if you want.

☐ Ambitious   ☐ Happy
☐ Athletic   ☐ Obliging
☐ Cautious   ☐ Highly strung
☐ Good looking   ☐ Poised
☐ Moody

Figure 7.11   Checklist response format

What is your sex?

☐ Male
☐ Female

Do you smoke cigarettes?

☐ Yes
☐ No

Figure 7.12   Dichotomous response format

overlapping pairs of items and asked to select one response from each pair (see Figure 7.13).

Multiple choice formats

This format requires respondents to choose just *one* response from a list of three or more alternatives. Many of the numeric rating scales are actually a form of multiple choice format. Additional types of multiple choice formats are described below.

Choice between multiple nominal categories
Respondents are asked to select one alternative from a list of responses. These responses have no set order and cannot be ranked in any sense from high to low. An example is a question on marital status (see Figure 7.14).

Choice between ordinal categories
Other multiple choice questions will have a set of responses that should be ordered from low to high (see Figure 7.15).

Choice between ordered attitude statements
While the Likert format asks respondents for the extent of agreement with a particular attitude statement this format provides alternative attitude positions and asks which is closest to the respondents' own view (see Figure 7.16).

Numerical answers
Some questions can be answered by a numerical response. This might be a precise numeric answer as required in example (a) in Figure 7.17 or it may group a set of numeric answers (e.g. income in dollars) into broader numeric bands as illustrated in example (b) in Figure 7.17.

NON-COMMITTAL RESPONSES

No opinion and don't know responses

Generally you should allow for a 'don't know' or 'no opinion' response. There are many issues to which people will have given no thought and hold no

Governments have to make choices between the areas to which they give priority when allocating government expenditure. For each pair of expenditure areas below tick the one you think ought to be given priority.

☐ Education	☐ Education	☐ Health
☐ Social welfare	☐ Health	☐ Social welfare
☐ Defence	☐ Defence	☐ Environment
☐ Health	☐ Industry support	☐ Health
☐ Environment	☐ Family support	☐ Law and order
☐ Recreation	☐ Law and order	☐ Defence

Figure 7.13   Paired comparison response format

What is your current marital status?

☐ Married/de facto
☐ Never married
☐ Widowed
☐ Separated
☐ Divorced
☐ Other

Figure 7.14   Multiple nominal responses

How often do you attend church or a place of worship?

☐ At least weekly
☐ Two or three times a month
☐ About once a month
☐ Once every three months
☐ Almost never
☐ Never

Figure 7.15   Multiple ordinal responses

Which of the following statements comes closest to your belief about God (tick one box only):

☐ I know God really exists and have no doubts about it.
☐ While I have doubts, I feel that I do believe in God.
☐ I find myself believing in God some of the time but not at others.
☐ I don't believe in a personal God, but I do believe in a higher power of some kind.
☐ I don't know whether there is a God and I don't believe there is a way to find out.
☐ I don't believe in God.

Figure 7.16   Multiple attitude statements

---

a   How many people under the age of eighteen live in your household on a regular basis?

☐ ☐

b   Questions with numerical answers can require precise numeric answers or may place numeric answers into groups. Instead of asking for precise income we might ask respondents to nominate to which income band they belong. For example:

What was your own income from your salary or wage, before tax, in the year 2001?

☐ None
☐ $1–$4999
☐ $5000–$9999
☐ $10 000–$14 999
☐ $15 000–$19 999
☐ $20 000–$29 999
☐ $30 000–$39 999
☐ $40 000–$49 999
☐ $50 000–$64 999
☐ $65 000–$79 999
☐ $80 000–$99 999
☐ $100 000 or more

Figure 7.17   Numeric response format

---

opinion. To force them to express an opinion where they really do not have one is to create false and unreliable answers (Converse and Presser, 1986).

The danger with using 'don't know' and 'no opinion' alternatives is that some respondents select them out of *laziness*. We can discourage respondents routinely selecting these responses by making them less conspicuous in the questionnaire (Schuman and Presser, 1981; Converse and Presser, 1986). In written self-administered questionnaires there is little alternative but to include 'don't know' or 'no opinion' along with other alternatives. However with telephone and face-to-face interviews we can rely on respondent-initiated non-response rather than offering it as an

up-front alternative. That is, we will accept 'don't know' without *offering* it as an alternative (see Figure 7.18).

Inclusion of the middle alternative

Another sort of non-committal answer is the 'sitting on the fence' answer. That is, where there is an ordered set of responses (e.g. for and against something) should we provide a middle alternative (neither for nor against)? There is some disagreement about what to do in this situation. Some people argue that the middle alternative should *not* be included since omitting it forces people to indicate the direction of their opinion and stops people sitting on the fence. On the other hand, including the middle position avoids artificially creating a directional opinion (see Converse and Presser, 1986; Sudman and Bradburn, 1982; Presser and Schuman, 1980).

One way of proceeding is not to *offer* the middle alternative when the questionnaire is administered by an interviewer but to record a middle position response if it is *volunteered*. In self-administered questionnaires it is desirable to offer the middle position to avoid forcing people to indicate a level of commitment that they do not have.

NUMBER OF RESPONSE CATEGORIES

Experts do not agree about the number of response categories that should be provided (Schwarz et al., 1985).

Dichotomies: One approach is to ask the respondent to select between one of two alternatives (Payne, 1951). For example, we might ask customers if they are satisfied or dissatisfied with the level of service they received. The problem with dichotomous

---

Do you agree or disagree that all people ought to have free access to government funded health care?

☐ Agree
☐ Disagree
☐ Don't know *(instruction to interviewer—do not offer this response; code only if respondent will not offer an agree or disagree response)*

Figure 7.18   Respondent-initiated 'don't know' response

responses is that they often provide a poor response distribution because people's real position lies somewhere between the two extremes (e.g. somewhat satisfied).

Five point scales: The Likert format (see Figure 7.4) provides five response alternatives which gives more flexibility. It provides a measure of intensity, extremity and direction. If needed you can later collapse five categories down to two or three.

Longer scales: The use of longer scales can have some advantages in that they allow for greater discrimination. For example, a ten-point scale allows for the detection of finer differences between people than would be possible with a five-point scale (see Alwin, 1997). This can be useful for attitudes where people tend to only use the top end of the scale— a common problem with questions that measure satisfaction. For example, questions that ask about life satisfaction typically indicate high levels of satisfaction. This partly reflects the social desirability of certain responses but a ten-point scale allows people to give a 'satisfied' response while still indicating some qualification to this.

However too many fine distinctions can be baffling and there is the danger that fine distinctions confuse greater precision with greater accuracy. In deciding on the number of response categories it is helpful if you have some sense of the spread of the variable when fewer categories are used. The main justification for using a larger number of response categories is that fewer categories are insensitive to real differences. The other consideration is sample size and the way data will be analysed. There is probably little point in using nine response categories when in the final analysis the categories will be collapsed down to three for analysis purposes.

RESPONSE SETS

Some respondents are liable to provide a certain type of answer regardless of the content of the question. There is the problem of *acquiescence*—the tendency to *agree* with a statement regardless of its content—and the problem of *social desirability*—the tendency to provide the respectable rather than the true response.

Social desirability

Many people answer survey questions so that they look good in their own eyes and in the eyes of interviewers. Consequently socially 'desirable' behaviours (e.g. amount of exercise) are over-reported while socially 'undesirable' behaviours and attitudes (e.g. alcohol consumption, sexist and racist attitudes) are under-reported (Bradburn and Sudman, 1978; Sudman and Bradburn, 1982; Foddy, 1993).

The techniques listed in Box 7.3 can help reduce social desirability as a factor in question responses.

Acquiescent response sets

Acquiescence (Foddy, 1993) is greatest among respondents with low education, in face-to-face interviews, where general rather than specific questions are used and where respondents have not really formed an opinion. It is more likely in attitude questions that use the agree–disagree format than in rating scales or the selection between different attitude statements.

Where acquiescence is likely to be a problem adopt a response format that minimises the problem and make sparing use of the agree–disagree format. Where the agree–disagree format is needed ensure

---

WEB POINTER 7.1 *Sets of response alternatives*

The sites below provide a very useful set of response wordings with a varying number of response categories for questions where the response categories can be ranked from high to low in some respect.

Sample Sets of Response Alternatives	www.au.af.mil/au/hq/selc/smpl-h.htm
The intensity of words	www.au.af.mil/au/hq/selc/smpl-g.htm

Visit www.social-research.org to use these links and to check for updates and additions.

BOX 7.3
Reducing social desirability response sets

There are four main techniques of asking questions to reduce social desirability problems:

1 everybody does it (question a);

2 use an authority (question b);

3 build in an excuse (question c);

4 ask a less specific question (question d).

   a Even the calmest of parents get angry at their children some of the time. Did your children do anything in the last seven days to make you feel angry?

   b Many doctors now think that drinking wine reduces heart attacks and aids digestion. Have you drunk any wine in the last seven days?

   c We know that people are often very busy and can find it difficult to find time to engage in regular exercise. How often have you engaged in exercise designed to improve your fitness in the last seven days?

   d Have you ever, *even once*, hit your partner in anger?

---

non-conservative statements). In this way if people are inclined to agree with any statement the acquiescence effect should cancel out.

QUESTIONNAIRE LAYOUT

There are six areas to which attention needs to be given when combining questions into a questionnaire.

Answering procedures

With open-ended questions ensure that you leave sufficient space for answers to avoid having to cram in responses. But do not leave so much space as to discourage completing the questionnaire because the task appears too daunting.

With closed questions respondents can be asked to either tick appropriate boxes or brackets or circle a number next to responses (see Figure 7.19).

When using any of these procedures, the area for answering can be on the left or right of the response but make sure you justify your typing on the answer side as below.

1 [ ] Agree		Agree [ ] 1
2 [ ] Disagree	OR	Disagree [ ] 2
3 [ ] Can't decide		Can't decide [ ] 3

Electronic means of administering questionnaires (see Chapter 8) have enabled an additional range of ways of respondents answering questions (see Web Pointer 7.3).

Contingency questions

Since you do not want respondents to waste time reading questions which are not relevant to them we

---

that the 'pro' attitude statements are matched by a similar number of 'anti' statements (e.g. a set of attitude questions designed to measure conservatism should aim for a similar number of conservative and

---

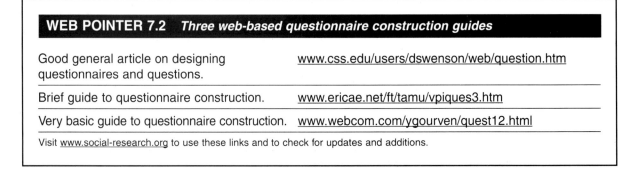

WEB POINTER 7.2 *Three web-based questionnaire construction guides*

Good general article on designing questionnaires and questions.	www.css.edu/users/dswenson/web/question.htm
Brief guide to questionnaire construction.	www.ericae.net/ft/tamu/vpiques3.htm
Very basic guide to questionnaire construction.	www.webcom.com/ygourven/quest12.html

Visit www.social-research.org to use these links and to check for updates and additions.

Square brackets, parentheses or boxes (tick the box)
1 [ ] Agree   1 ( ) Agree   1 □ Agree
2 [ ] Disagree   OR   2 ( ) Disagree   OR   2 □ Disagree
3 [ ] Can't decide   3 ( ) Can't decide   3 □ Can't decide

Precoding (circle the number)
1 Agree
2 Disagree
3 Can't decide

Figure 7.19   Different answering formats for closed-choice questions

---

WEB POINTER 7.3   *Computer-based answering formats*

Computer-based surveys have introduced new ways of formatting questions that can be illustrated online. Go to the following internet address and select the 'respondent's view' for each of the question types provided:

www.surveysaid.com/marketing_masters/
ssdocs/screens.htm

Visit www.social-research.org to use these links and to check for updates and additions.

---

can use filter or contingency questions (Figure 7.20) to direct respondents to questions that, given previous responses, are applicable to them.

The use of arrows and inset boxes to highlight follow-up questions is a useful way of avoiding confusion when using contingency questions. Computer-based surveys automatically take respondents or interviewers to the next applicable question (see Chapter 8).

Instructions

To help the questionnaire flow, use the following types of instructions where appropriate.

■ *General instructions:* These should include an introduction to the purpose of the questionnaire, assurance of confidentiality, how the respondent was chosen, how and when to return the questionnaire (where relevant).

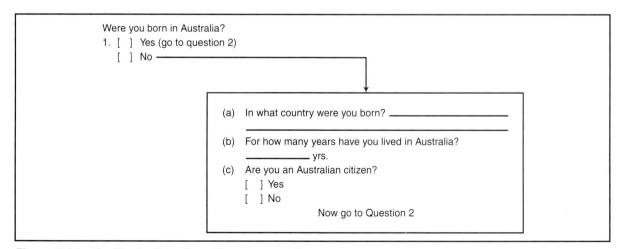

Were you born in Australia?
1. [ ] Yes (go to question 2)
   [ ] No ─────────────────

(a) In what country were you born? _____
    _____
(b) For how many years have you lived in Australia?
    _____ yrs.
(c) Are you an Australian citizen?
    [ ] Yes
    [ ] No
           Now go to Question 2

Figure 7.20   An illustration of contingency questions

■ *Section introductions:* When the questionnaire can be divided into subsections provide a brief introduction to each section such as 'Finally we would like to know just a little about your background so we can see how different people feel about the topics about which you've answered questions'.

■ *Question instructions:* Indicate how many responses the respondents can tick (e.g. the most appropriate, as many as apply, one only).

■ *'Go to' instructions:* Ensure you make use of these when using contingency questions that require respondents to skip some questions. In electronic questionnaires these skips are automated.

Use of space

To encourage people to complete a questionnaire avoid cluttering it. The following hints may help:

■ Unless you are using a booklet format print questions on one side of the page only. It is too easy for people to miss questions printed on the backs of pages. The blank backs of pages are also useful for respondents to write additional comments.

■ Provide a column about 2.5 centimetres wide on the right-hand side for computer coding for paper questionnaires (see Chapter 9).

■ Leave sufficient space for open-ended questions. In electronic questionnaires the space for open questions can automatically expand to accommodate any length open response.

■ List alternative responses *down* rather than across the page.

■ In electronic questionnaires you should consider placing just one or two questions on a screen. Even if this means you use many screens it does not make the questionnaire look 'thicker' or longer and therefore does not make the questionnaire appear more onerous.

The task of questionnaire layout has been made easier with software specially designed for producing questionnaires (Web Pointer 7.4).

Order of questions

A good questionnaire is one in which there is a logical flow to questions. The following nine points provide some guidelines.

1 Commence with questions that respondents will enjoy answering.
   a These should be easily answered questions.
   b Factual questions should be used initially.
   c Do not start with demographic questions such as age, marital status, etc.

WEB POINTER 7.4 *Software for producing questionnaires*

The task of questionnaire layout has been made easier by the power of widely available word processors. Specialised software that has been developed for electronic surveys has made the process even simpler. This software can produce both electronic and professional looking paper questionnaires. Demonstration versions of the software are available for download from the internet.

SphinxSurvey	www.scolari.co.uk/sphinx/sphinx.htm
SurveyWriter	www.surveywriter.com/HomePage.html
SurveyTracker	www.surveytracker.com/
SurveyWin	www.raosoft.com/products/interform/index.html
Survey Said	www.surveysaid.com/
Infopoll Designer	www.infopoll.com/
More	My website www.social-research.org provides additional software links and advice for questionnaire design.

d Ensure that the initial questions are obviously relevant to the stated purpose of the survey.

2 Go from easy to more difficult questions.

3 Go from concrete to abstract questions.

4 Open-ended questions should be kept to a minimum and, where possible, placed towards the end of the questionnaire.

5 Group questions into sections. This helps structure the questionnaire and provides a better flow.

6 Make use of filter questions to ensure that questions are relevant to respondents.

7 When using a series of positive and negative items to form a scale, mix up the positive and negative items to help avoid an acquiescent response set.

8 Electronic questionnaires can randomise the order of questions within sections for each respondent to help minimise the effect of question order within sections.

9 Where possible try to introduce a variety of question formats so that the questionnaire remains interesting.

Setting up for coding

If the data are to be analysed by computer and you are using a paper questionnaire (rather than an electronic questionnaire—see Chapter 8) it is useful to prepare for this by allocating codes to responses in the questionnaires so that a number is printed in the questionnaire next to responses. This precoding is possible only for forced-choice questions (see Figure 7.19). Depending on the way in which data are to be entered for computer analysis, computer column numbers may need to be allocated to each variable in the right-hand margins (see Chapter 9).

WEB POINTER 7.5 *Questionnaire examples on the internet*

A valuable way to learn about questionnaire layout and the differences that follow from different modes of questionnaire administration is to look at actual examples of questionnaires. The following sites provide some examples.

Postal questionnaires	http://ssda.anu.edu.au/SSDA/CODEBOOKS/AES98/aes98cbk.rtf (the actual questionnaire is on pp. 156–81 of this file)
	http://ssda.anu.edu.au/SSDA/CODEBOOKS/ACRS99/d1018pub.pdf (the questionnaire is on pp. 112–32 of the file)
Face-to-face questionnaires:	
Social capital questionnaire	www.worldbank.org/poverty/scapital/library/ugquest.pdf This questionnaire was used in a face-to-face survey on social capital in Uganda.
Healthy retirement questionnaires	www.umich.edu/~hrswww/center/qnaires/download.html This site enables you to download and view a large number of questionnaire modules from the US-based longitudinal study on health and retirement. It provides many examples of questionnaire layout and instructions appropriate to a face-to-face survey.

WEB POINTER 7.5 *continued*

British household panel survey	www.iser.essex.ac.uk/bhps/doc.pdf_versions/index.html Questionnaires from each phase of this important longitudinal study plus questionnaire show cards and other devices are available for downloading.

Web-based questionnaires	www.surveyspot.com/
	(join site and complete online surveys)
	www.raosoft.com/products/interform/tour/csaf.html
	www.accesscable.net/~infopoll/Library.htm
	www.raosoft.com/products/interform/index.html
	www.surveysaid.com/marketing_masters/ssdocs/
	    javademo.htm
	www.perseusdevelopment.com/surveytips/
	    samplesurveys.html
	www.hostedsurvey.com/
	www.elisten.com/
	www.surveywriter.com/survey/survey1/Demo_1.asp?
	www.webintel.net/websurvey4/
	http://members.aol.com/andersontl/surveys/
	    dissertation.htm

Visit www.social-research.org to use these links and to check for updates and additions and addition links to online questionnaires.

Questionnaire length

There is a widespread view that long questionnaires or interviews should be avoided. The reasoning is that long questionnaires increase the burden on respondents and this leads to increased reluctance to participate and thus leads to non-response.

However a thorough review of the available evidence shows that there is little research that supports this commonsense assumption (Bogen, 1996). While the common advice is to keep mail questionnaires as short as possible, and there is a belief that people will not participate in long telephone interviews, the evidence to support these issues is mixed. Some evidence shows a very slight tendency for long questionnaires to yield a slightly lower response rate while other studies show either no effect or indeed the opposite trend—better response rates are higher in longer questionnaires.

Unfortunately it is difficult to disentangle the effect of questionnaire length from other factors such as topic, sample type, mode of administration, survey sponsorship, format and so forth. It becomes difficult to identify how much effect length has on its own. Where an effect of length is detectable it usually only holds in the initial phase of a study and disappears at the follow-up phase.

No doubt there will be a point at which length will affect response rates. A questionnaire that is too short may make the survey seem too insignificant to bother about while a questionnaire or interview that took several hours to complete would probably be too demanding. However we simply do not know the thresholds at which length on its own affects response rates.

The simplest advice regarding questionnaire length is not to make the questionnaire longer than is really necessary but not to be obsessed with length. As a general rule the experience of participating in the survey should be made as pleasant and rewarding as possible (Dillman, 1978). However there is no automatic link between brevity and finding a survey rewarding. Pay attention to the other aspects of survey design, and ensure that they minimise respondents' burden, and length will probably become a relatively unimportant factor in determining response rates.

TELEPHONE QUESTIONNAIRES: ADDITIONAL CONSIDERATIONS

In general, the principles outlined in this chapter apply to questionnaires administered by mail, face-to-face, telephone and via the internet. But because telephone interviews rely totally on verbal communication, they have some special requirements.

Question wording

Relying on respondents retaining all the spoken information in the question places real limits on how much information can be packed into one question. If *too many response categories* are included in the question, there is a danger that the respondent will arbitrarily select one. There are three main approaches to help alleviate this problem.

First, the number of response categories can be reduced. This is the most obvious approach when questions have a large number of response categories that are ordered on a continuum. Figure 7.21 shows how a question on job satisfaction could be modified by reducing the number of response categories (part (a) of Figure 7.21). Because this can lead to an undesirable loss of detail, an alternative is to adopt the format in part (b) of Figure 7.21 where the response categories are converted to a numerical scale and people are asked to say where on the scale they would lie. Because of its numerical character, it is more readily retained when described verbally.

A second approach is to use a two-step procedure and divide the question into two parts with the first part designed to find out the respondent's direction of feeling while the second asks about the intensity or specifics of their feeling (see Figure 7.22).

A third way of dealing with the retention problem is to repeat the alternatives by building the responses into the question as well as listing them as a set of alternative responses (see Figure 7.23).

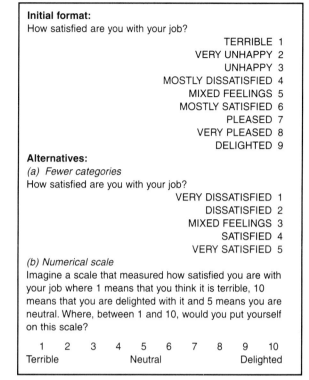

Figure 7.21   **Simplifying response categories for telephone surveys**

Layout

Since it is the interviewer rather than the respondent who sees the telephone questionnaire, the primary concern with questionnaire layout for a telephone survey must be to assist the interviewer to administer it accurately and to code the answers as the interview proceeds. The following guidelines should be helpful.

1   Provide detailed guides to interviewers *on the questionnaire* or on the computer screen if a Computer Assisted Telephone Interview (CATI) is being conducted.

2   Make it very clear to the interviewer whether the alternative responses are to be read out. This can be achieved by giving specific instructions and by highlighting responses to be read out by using upper-case characters (see Figure 7.24). Precoded responses that are not to be read out should be clearly distinguished from those that are. Using lower-case characters in brackets is helpful in this respect.

3   Clearly distinguish between instructions (use upper-case italics) and the question.

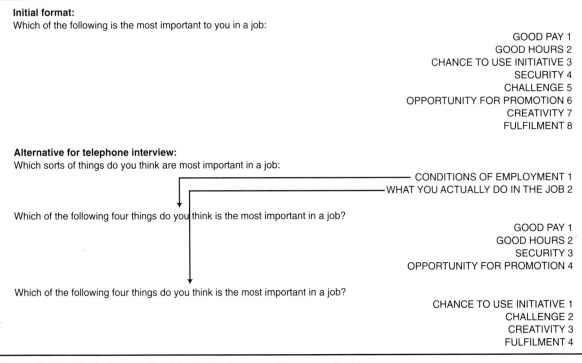

Figure 7.22 Two-step method for reducing question complexity

Among the things that people look for in a job are good pay, flexible hours, security and opportunities for promotion. Which of these four do you think is the most important?

GOOD PAY 1
GOOD HOURS 2
SECURITY 3
OPPORTUNITY FOR PROMOTION 4

Figure 7.23 Incorporating responses into the question

4 State how many responses can be coded.
5 Where filter questions are used, make it as clear as possible where the interviewer is to go next. The format described earlier may be used but the one used in Figure 7.24 may be more effective in telephone interviews where big jumps in the questionnaire are required. Where CATI is being used these skips are automated.
6 In paper versions of a telephone interview place the codes to the right of the question, as close to the coding column as possible. Right justify the responses (see Figure 7.24). In CATI, coding is automated and need not concern the interviewer.

PILOT TESTING: EVALUATING QUESTIONS AND QUESTIONNAIRES

Once a questionnaire has been developed, each question and the questionnaire as a whole must be evaluated rigorously before final administration. Evaluating the questionnaire is called *pilot testing* or *pretesting*. Converse and Presser (1986) provide a brief discussion of pilot testing. Box 7.4 summarises the steps in full pilot testing.

Three stages of pilot testing questions

Stage 1—Question development
The purpose of testing at this stage is to establish how to phrase each question, to evaluate how respondents interpret the question's meaning and to check whether the range of response alternatives is sufficient. While new questions will need to be intensively pretested, previously used (and tested) questions should also be evaluated. Questions that 'worked' in one context may be inappropriate for the particular sample you are using. Questions that worked in the 1950s for a general population sample

(a) **If a federal election was held tomorrow how likely is it that you would vote?**
     . . . (READ OUT)

GO TO

WOULD NOT VOTE	1	(c)
(CODE ONE ONLY) UNLIKELY TO VOTE	2	
WOULD PROBABLY VOTE	3	
WOULD DEFINITELY VOTE	4	
(Undecided)	5	(c)

(b) **What types of issues would be important in deciding the way you voted?**
     (PROBE BUT DO NOT *READ OUT PROMPTS)*

(Environmental issues)	1
(Economic)	2
(Unemployment)	3
(Social welfare)	4
(CODE AS MANY AS APPLY) (Defence)	5
(Education)	6
(Nuclear)	7
(Crime/law and order)	8
(Transport)	9
(Corruption)	10
(Interest rates)	11
(Other) *(RECORD DETAILS)*	12

(c) *(ASK ALL)*
     Which of the following statements best describes the way you feel about the current government?
     . . .
     . . .

Figure 7.24   **Use of typefaces to distinguish between parts of the question**

BOX 7.4   *Stages in pilot testing questionnaires*

Stage 1:	*Question* **development**	**Stage 2:**	*Questionnaire* **development**
Type:	Declared pre-test	Type:	Undeclared
Check for:	1 Sufficient variation in responses	Check for:	1 Does the questionnaire flow?
	2 How the question is understood		2 Do the skips work?
	3 Whether all items are necessary		3 Is it too long?
	4 Whether scale items scale (see pp. 184–6)		4 Do respondents sustain their interest?
	5 Item non-response	**Stage 3:**	**Polishing pilot test**
	6 Evidence of acquiescence	Type:	Undeclared
		Check for:	Effectiveness of changes after stages 1 and 2

in the United States may no longer be appropriate in a study of eighteen-year-old students in Australia or Britain half a century later.

In this testing phase, respondents are told that the questions are being developed and they are being asked to help improve them. It is called a *declared* or *participating pretest*. The respondent is quizzed intensively about a set of individual questions. They might be asked how they would phrase the question, what they had in mind when they gave a particular answer and whether there were unavailable alternative answers they would have preferred to have given. We might present a respondent with different wordings for the same question and ask them if they would give the same answer now or ask which they found clearest and so forth. Because of its intensive nature, only a limited number of questions can be tested in this stage of pilot testing.

Stage 2—Questionnaire development

By administering a complete questionnaire (usually considerably longer than the final questionnaire), this stage enables the further evaluation of individual items and the questionnaire as a whole. Rather than relying on respondents' comments about the questions, this stage analyses their answers and uses the interviewer's comments to improve the questionnaire.

More often than not, this stage is *undeclared*. That is, in order to simulate the final questionnaire administration, respondents are not told that the questionnaire is still under development.

Stage 3—Polishing pilot test

We use the information gained in Stage 2 to revise questions where necessary, shorten the questionnaire, reorder questions and finalise the skip patterns. Attention should also be given to the final *layout* of the questionnaire to ensure that it is clear for interviewers and respondents.

Pilot testing items

The evaluation of individual questionnaire items should examine at least six points.

1 *Variation:* If most people give similar answers to a question, it will be of little use in later analysis (p. 96).
2 *Meaning:* Check to ensure that respondents understand the intended meaning of the ques-

tion and that you understand the respondent's answer.
3 *Redundancy:* If two questions measure virtually the same thing, only one is needed in the final questionnaire. If two items are designed to tap the same concept and correlate over, say, 0.8, then you can drop one of the items (see Chapter 11).
4 *Scalability:* If a set of questions is designed to form a scale or index (see Chapter 11), check to ensure that they do so. There is no point including items in the final questionnaire which do not belong to the scale for which they were designed.
5 *Non-response:* The refusal of a large number of people to answer a particular question produces difficulties at the data analysis stage (see pp. 84, 175–6, 194–5) and can lead to serious reductions in sample size. Questions which, in Stage 1, produce respondent hesitation, reluctance or refusal to answer are likely to produce a high level of non-response later.

Non-response can arise for a variety of reasons. The question might be unclear, too intrusive, provide insufficient responses or appear to be too similar to previously answered questions. Questions that appear to have nothing to do with the stated purpose of the survey can also result in high non-response, as can open-ended questions that appear to require considerable effort to answer. Questionnaire layout, including cramming and confusing skip instructions, can lead to accidental non-response.
6 *Acquiescent response set:* One way of detecting an acquiescent response (pp. 107–8) set is to take questions that seem completely contradictory and see how many people agree with both of them. If there is evidence of a response set, it is best to replace the agree–disagree format with another type of question.

Pilot testing questionnaires

As well as testing individual questions, the questionnaire as a whole needs evaluating. At least four things should be carefully checked:

1 flow
2 question skips
3 timing
4 respondent interest and attention.

Flow

Do questions seem to fit together? Are the transitions from one section to another smooth? Does the interviewer find the skips difficult to follow, resulting in awkward pauses? Do the transitions sound long-winded? Does the questionnaire move too quickly or jump from topic to topic too quickly to allow respondents to gather their thoughts? *Listening* to an interviewer rather than reading the questionnaire helps detect problems in its flow.

Question skips

Where filter questions are used, it is important to ensure that the skip patterns do not lead to skipping more questions than was intended or lead to dead ends in the schedule. To help check that the skip patterns are correct, draw a flow chart based on the question instructions to ensure that the instructions direct respondents through the questionnaire as intended.

Timing

The Stage 2 questionnaire will be much longer than the final one, but it is helpful to time each section (or even subsection) so that you can gain some idea of how much needs to be cut for the final stage. The final phase should also be carefully tested to ensure that it takes approximately the estimated time both so that respondents can be told how long the questionnaire will take and so that accurate survey budgeting can be completed. If the questionnaire is too long, then fewer questionnaires can be administered (assuming telephone or face-to-face administration methods). This can lead to an unacceptable reduction of sample size.

Respondent interest and attention

If respondents seem to be getting bored, the questionnaire may be too long. A greater variety of types of question may help avoid monotony. Particular sections or questions might lead to a particular loss of attention. These should be noted and either restructured, removed or placed at the end of the questionnaire, where they will do less damage. Bored respondents will provide unconsidered and unreliable answers and produce high non-response to questions.

How to pilot test

Phase 1: Who to pretest?

As far as possible, pretesting should be conducted with people who resemble those to whom the ques-tionnaire will finally be given. Depending on the questionnaire content, it will be important to match particular characteristics of the pilot and final samples. Age, gender, educational and ethnic characteristics should normally be matched. The importance of other features such as employment status, religion, family life stage and the like may depend on the purpose of the survey. Naturally, the closer the match between the pilot sample and the final sample, the better.

When the survey is of a particular subgroup (e.g. organisation, ethnic group) it is helpful to obtain feedback from key insiders who have a good knowledge of the group. They can help avoid offensive questions, highlight questions that could be particularly useful in tapping the desired concepts and highlight problems with language (e.g. too complex, ambiguous meaning, special meaning for the group etc), as well as alerting the researcher to misunderstandings about the group. This is particularly valuable in Phase 1.

Phase 2: How many to pretest?

Because of the intensive nature of Phase 1, it is often not possible to test a large number of people. Since the evaluation of the questionnaire in Phases 2 and 3 involves the quantitative analysis of respondents' answers, it is important to give the questionnaire to as many people as possible. Too few respondents may well mean that problems such as non-response, variation, response sets and the like remain undetected. Somewhere between 75 and 100 respondents provides a useful pilot test.

Phase 3: Who should conduct the interviews?

A selection of interviewers who represent the range of experience of those who will finally administer the questionnaire will provide the most realistic simulation of the administration of the survey. There is value in the questionnaire designer also administering, or at least sitting in on, some pilot interviews to help keep in touch with the realities of the interview situation.

Phase 4: Code responses

Try coding responses to the Phase 2 questionnaire—especially the open questions and 'other (please specify)' responses to closed questions. Difficulties in coding these questions can highlight problems with the question wording (e.g. frame of reference not clear, ambiguity etc), or even indicate that the investigator is unclear what the question is really about. It can also be useful to ask interviewers to code some of the questionnaires as this can help make them aware of the coding problems produced by poor interviewing and help them interview more precisely (e.g. it can help sharpen up the precision with which interviewers obtain occupational data).

Phase 5: Interviewer debriefing

Since the interviewer has the hands-on experience with the questionnaire, it is essential to learn from their experience as well as from the respondents' answers to questions. It is useful to give the interviewer a brief questionnaire to complete after each pilot interview. A variety of evaluation questions are possible, but Converse and Presser (1986: 72) suggest asking the interviewer at least to indicate:

- any questions that made the respondent uncomfortable;
- questions that had to be repeated;
- questions that appeared to be misinterpreted;
- questions that were difficult to read or questions the interviewer came to particularly dislike;
- sections that dragged;
- sections where the respondent seemed to want to say more.

In addition interviewers should be encouraged to provide marginal comments on the main questionnaire itself, and the questionnaire designer should talk with the interviewers about the questionnaire.

The advice to pilot test questionnaires is probably one of the most ignored suggestions regarding questionnaire design. The pressure to get things done, over-confidence combined with inexperience and practical difficulties all too often cause people to take the chance and skip this whole stage. It is a risk that is not worth taking.

QUESTIONNAIRE DESIGN CHECKLIST

1 Is the research question(s) clear? (See Chapter 3 checklist.)
2 What content is each question designed to measure? Is the question to measure:
   a An attitude?
   b An attribute?
   c A belief?
   d A behaviour?
   e Knowledge?
3 If the question is designed to tap attitudes or beliefs what do you want to know about the attitude/belief:
   a Direction?
   b Extremity?
   c Intensity?
4 Is each question:
   a Reliable?
   b Valid?
   c Sufficiently sensitive to variation?
   d Likely to achieve a good response rate?
   e Have the same meaning for all respondents?
   f Relevant to the research question?
5 Is the specific wording of each question suitable? (See Box 7.2 for a detailed checklist.)
6 What type of response format does the questionnaire item require:
   a Open?
   b Closed?
7 What level of measurement do you want the item to achieve:
   a Nominal?
   b Ordinal?
   c Interval?
8 For closed questions which type of closed format is required:
   a Rating?
   b Scores?
   c Ranking?
   d Checklist?
9 How will non-committal responses be handled?
   a Will a 'middle response' be included?
   b Will a 'don't know' option be available?
10 Are the response categories:
   a Exhaustive/inclusive?
   b Exclusive?
   c Balanced?
11 Are clear instructions provided throughout the questionnaire?
12 How will respondents indicate their responses?
13 Is there sufficient space?
14 Are any skips clear and simple to follow?
15 Does the order of questions conform to the principles of question order?
16 How will coding be handled?
   a Will questions be precoded?
   b How will open-ended questions be coded?
   c How will data be entered into the computer?

d Is the coding layout in the questionnaire sufficiently clear as to minimise data entry errors?

17 Will pilot testing be used? If not why not?

18 Which types of pilot testing will be employed:

a Declared?

b Undeclared?

c Both?

19 Do the questions work? (See Box 7.4 for a detailed checklist.)

KEY CONCEPTS

Acquiescent response set	Contingency question	Level of measurement	Question frame of reference
Attitudes	Dead giveaway question	Likert format	Ranking format
Balanced response categories	Declared pretest	Multiple choice	Rating scale
Beliefs	Double-barrelled question	Multiple response question	Response set
Binary choice	Exclusiveness	Numerical rating scale	Semantic differential format
Checklist format	Exhaustiveness	Open-ended question	Social desirability response set
Closed question/ forced-choice question	Extremity of attitudes	Personal/impersonal question wording	Undeclared pretest
Closed response question	Filter question	Prestige bias	
	Gratuitous qualifier	Pretest/pilot test	
	Inclusiveness	Question discrimination	
	Intensity of attitudes		
	Leading question		

FURTHER READING

A useful and readable introduction to question working is *The Art of Asking Questions* (1951) by Payne. Warwick and Lininger provide a useful introduction to questionnaire design in Chapter 6 of *The Sample Survey* (1975) but Oppenheim's *Questionnaire Design and Attitude Measurement* (1968) and Converse and Presser (1986) provide more comprehensive treatments of questionnaire construction.

In recent years a number of more advanced specialist books containing research about the best way of wording questions and constructing questionnaires have become available. The best of these are Bradburn and Sudman, *Improving Interview Method and Questionnaire Design* (1979), Schuman and Presser, *Questions and Answers in Attitude Surveys* (1981) and Sudman and Bradburn, *Asking Questions: A Practical Guide to Questionnaire Design* (1982) and Foddy's *Constructing Questions for Interviews and Questionnaires* (1992). All these are well worth careful reading as they provide evidence about question format and help confront a lot of the folklore about questionnaires. Two books that examine how questionnaire design must take account of the method of administration are Dillman, *Mail*

and Telephone Surveys: The Total Design Method (1978) and Groves and Kahn's *Surveys by Telephone: A National Comparison with Personal Interviews* (1979). Belson provides detailed guidance on technical matters of wording in *The Design and Understanding of Survey Questions* (1981) and Singer and Presser (1989) and Turner and Martin (1984) contain sets of excellent specialised papers on question construction.

Books that provide sets of questions to tap various concepts and provide useful questions and ideas were provided in Box 4.2. For further references and references to particular journal articles for measures see my web page at www.social-research.org. Further reading on pretesting is available in several useful articles. Ornstein (1998) in 'Pretesting and Data Collection', Presser and Blair (1994) in 'Survey Pretesting: Do Different Methods Produce Different Results?' and Reynolds et al. in 'Pretesting in Questionnaire Design: A Review of Literature and Suggestions For Further Research' (1993) all provide relatively recent accounts of pretesting practice. Foddy's (1996) paper 'The In-depth Testing of Survey Questions' provides a useful overview of one particular aspect of pilot testing.

EXERCISES

1 Design five questions on the topic of smoking tobacco products. One question should tap beliefs about smoking tobacco products, the others should be designed to measure attitudes, attributes, knowledge and behaviour respectively in relation to this topic.

2 Examine the questions in Figures 7.1 to 7.18 and indicate whether the question is tapping attributes, attitudes, knowledge, beliefs or behaviour.

3 Describe what is wrong with each of the following questions.

a How often do you have contact with your mother? (tick one box for each type of contact)

	See	Phone	Write
Daily			
Weekly			
Monthly			
Yearly			
Never			

b Do you feel that the contact you have with your mother is:
[ ] Too much
[ ] About right
[ ] Too little
[ ] Not important

c Do you feel that your relationship with your mother is affected by her desire to obtain vicarious gratification from your achievements?
[ ] Yes
[ ] No
[ ] Cannot tell

d Do you agree or disagree that your mother does not treat you as an adult?
[ ] Agree
[ ] Disagree
[ ] Undecided

e Overall how do you get on with your parents?
[ ] Very well
[ ] OK
[ ] Not so well
[ ] Badly

f What is your present income?

g Most people in this country say they are opposed to Asian migration. How do you feel about Asian migration to this country? (mark on the scale between 0 and 10)

Opposed _____ Agree
0 1 2 3 4 5 6 7 8 9 10

h [Ask married women only]
Many women who stay at home full-time looking after young children say they feel frustrated. What frustrations did/do you feel at this stage?

i Why did you drop out of your course at university?
[ ] Lecturer was hopeless
[ ] I was too lazy to put in a reasonable amount of work
[ ] I got sick and got too far behind

4 Develop a brief questionnaire designed to test the proposition that conservatism is a product of four factors: stage in the life cycle, social class, level of conservatism of one's parents and level of religiousness. Take care with both your questionnaire wording and layout. Try administering it to two or three people to see how it works.

5 Set out your version of the above questionnaire using the principles of layout for a telephone survey.

6 Using the web addresses in Web Pointer 4.6 locate questions on the topics listed below from the specified question databases and 'cut and paste' these into a word processing document. Note: you may require Adobe Acrobat Reader to access some documents on some databases. If this is not installed on your computer it can be downloaded and installed for free from the following site:

www.adobe.com/products/acrobat/
readstep2.html

a Using the Question Bank website obtain the questions relating to attitudes to abortion from three different studies (e.g. British Attitudes Survey, British Election Study etc).

b Using the ZEUS website obtain the questions about homosexuality.

c   Using the General Social Survey obtain questions on Respondent's education (EDUC), Respondent's occupation (OCC), religious preference (RELIG) and subjective social class (CLASS).

8

Administering questionnaires

This chapter focuses on four main matters:

1 the main methods of administering survey questionnaires;
2 a comparison of these methods in terms of (a) response rates, (b) sampling quality, (c) the implications for questionnaire structure, (d) the quality of answers, and (e) practicalities of administering the questionnaires;
3 the role of computers in administering questionnaires;
4 practicalities of administering questionnaires using each of the main administration methods.

While face-to-face interviews have had a good reputation, alternatives should be considered. Mail and telephone techniques have improved in recent years and internet-based surveys provide an entirely new administration option. The conventional wisdom is that response rates have been steadily declining in recent years and will continue to do so (Steeh, 1981; Bradburn, 1992). However, this belief has been challenged by Smith (1995). Regardless of which view is correct it is essential to achieve high response rates at an economical cost. The range of methods for collecting survey data have implications both for response rates and the cost of obtaining good samples.

MAIN METHODS OF ADMINISTRATION

Face-to-face interviews

Using this method, trained interviewers administer the questionnaire personally to a respondent. The interviewer records and codes answers as the interview proceeds. With trained interviewers relatively complex questionnaires with complex branching patterns (see Chapter 7 on contingency questions) and special modules can be administered. Since the interviewer is on the spot they can answer respondent questions, clarify misunderstandings and probe answers to open-ended questions.

Most face-to-face interviews are Paper and Pencil Interviews (PAPI) in which the interviewer records answers on paper questionnaires. In some interviews computer technology is used to assist interviewers who use a laptop computer to administer an electronic questionnaire. These electronic questionnaires automatically code responses and automatically apply skips and filters based on earlier answers. These electronic face-to-face interviews are called Computer-Assisted Personal Interviews (CAPI).

Telephone interviews

The expense and time that face-to-face interviews require and the development of computer technol-

> **BOX 8.1**
> *The technology of administering questionnaires*
>
> | | |
> |---|---|
> | PAPI | Paper and Pencil Interview |
> | CAPI | Computer-Assisted Personal Interview |
> | CATI | Computer-Assisted Telephone Interview |
> | CASI | Computer-Assisted Self Interview |
> | DBM | Disk By Mail interview |
> | Email | Plain text in body of email |
> | HTML email | Questionnaire in body of email or as attachment formatted in Hypertext Markup Language (HTML— the formatting language of the web) |
> | Email with executable questionnaire | CASI/DBM style questionnaire distributed by email |
> | Web-based HTML survey | Questionnaire written wholly in HTML and distributed via a web-based site |
> | Dynamic web survey | Questionnaire written with a survey writing software package that has similar interactive features to a CAPI, CATI or CASI questionnaire. Also includes additional scripts written in a particular programming language (e.g. Perl, ActiveX). |

ogy (discussed later in this chapter) have encouraged the growth of telephone interviewing. Telephone interviews involve making telephone contact with selected sample members (see below) and asking the questions over the telephone. These interviews are usually conducted using Computer-Assisted Telephone Interviewing (CATI) equipment and software (see below). These CATI surveys are normally administered from a central interviewing centre. This centralised location helps avoid the safety problems of personal interviews and enables greater supervision and quality control.

Telephone interview methods allow skilled interviewers to build rapport yet maintain considerable respondent anonymity. It is also relatively easy to follow up respondents who are not at home and telephone interviews are much cheaper to conduct than personal interviews since no travelling is involved.

Postal self-administered questionnaires

While telephone and face-to-face interviews are administered by a trained interviewer, postal surveys are self-administered. Since postal surveys rely on respondents understanding and answering the questionnaire, it must be easy to follow and the meaning of questions should be self-explanatory.

These surveys are much cheaper to administer but typically achieve poorer response rates than telephone or personal interviews. To improve response rates great care must be taken with the survey questionnaire and the follow up of non-responders. These self-administered surveys are mainly PAPI surveys. Coding responses of PAPI surveys can be expensive and some survey organisations are now using optical scanning to reduce both cost and coding errors (Dillman, 2000; see Chapter 9 on methods of data entry).

Some postal questionnaires are distributed on floppy disk as electronic questionnaires. This method is variously called the Disk By Mail (DBM) interview or the Computer-Assisted Self Interview (CASI). These questionnaires resemble CATI and CAPI questionnaires: they are self coding, include automatic skips, control the order in which questions are answered and help reduce item non-response (see computer-assisted interviewing later in this chapter). In addition, these CASI questionnaires enable the use of visually engaging question formats, colour, graphics and even audio. Respondents do not need any special software and the questionnaire is simple to answer and return by mail or email. The obvious limitation with the DBM and CASI methods is they are restricted to respondents with computer access.

Internet surveys

Since the mid-1990s the internet has become a viable and popular means of administering questionnaires.

There are three main ways in which the internet has been used for surveys: with emails, via web pages and a combination of email and the web.

Email

Email questionnaires come in three different forms.

1 Plain text questions inserted as part of an email. This is the most basic method of email survey in which respondents simply edit the email message to indicate their responses.
2 A formatted questionnaire sent as an email attachment. The questionnaire might be formatted with a word processor or with the web formatting language—Hypertext Markup Language (HTML).
3 An interactive questionnaire, similar to the DBM/CASI questionnaires described earlier, can be sent as an email attachment, answered and returned by email.

Web pages

Questionnaires which have all the dynamic, interactive features of CAPI and CATI questionnaires plus impressive visual enhancements (see the discussion of computer-assisted questionnaire administration) can be made available on the internet. This involves placing the questionnaire on a web server and getting respondents to visit the relevant web page to answer the questionnaire. These questionnaires are constructed with specialised and easy to use internet survey software (see Web Pointer 8.1). Some software is available to construct the questionnaire interactively on the web but the best software packages require you to create the questionnaire on your own computer and then 'upload' it to the internet. When respondents complete and submit their answers to the web server their responses are automatically coded. Limited analysis can be conducted automatically and be made immediately available to provide feedback to respondents. When the web survey closes the data are normally placed in a database for further statistical analysis by the researcher.

Combined web page and email

This method involves making an electronic version of the questionnaire available on the internet. Respondents download the questionnaire to their

---

WEB POINTER 8.1 *Web survey software and links*

Internet surveys resource site This site provides links to survey software and survey administration sites. Free evaluation software is often available. This site contains useful links to discussions of internet surveys.	http://surveys.over.net/method/topics.html
Tim Macer Services Strong list of internet survey software with excellent search engine and reviews of many products.	www.macer.co.uk/
Association of Survey Computing Listing of web survey software.	www.asc.org.uk/Register/index.htm
Fully online surveys You produce questionnaires on these sites and make them available for others to complete. No special software is required. The sites listed provide limited free survey facilities. Other companies charge for these services.	http://webintel.net/websurvey4/ www.createsurvey.com/ www.isurveys.com/default.html www.custominsight.com/ www.zoomerang.com/

WEB POINTER 8.1 *continued*

Software for building, conducting and analysing surveys with downloadable evaluation versions
These software packages require the researcher to install the package on their computer, to produce the questionnaire. The questionnaire is then uploaded to a web server for administration. The sites below contain free evaluation copies of these packages.

Infopoll	www.infopoli.com/products/survey/
Survey Said	www.surveysaid.com/index.html
Perseus Survey Solutions	www.perseus.com/
Raosoft products	www.raosoft.com/info/pricing/purchaseinfo.html
Sumquest	www.sumquest.com/index.htm
PinPoint	www.logo.com/pinpoint/index.html
Survey Gold 6	http://surveygold.com/
Survey Tracker	www.surveytracker.com/
Sawtooth Survey System	www.sawtooth.com/products/
Survey System	www.surveysystem.com/
SNAP Survey	www.mercatorcorp.com/index.htm
Inquisite	www.inquisite.com/Products/default.asp

Visit www.social-research.org to use these links and to check for updates and additions.

---

own computer and then email the responses directly to the researcher. Web pages are simply used as a means to distribute the survey but responses are returned directly to the researcher via email.

COMPUTER-ASSISTED QUESTIONNAIRE ADMINISTRATION

All four modes of questionnaire administration outlined above can use computers to create and administer questionnaires (see Box 8.1).

These computer-assisted methods have many advantages. These include:

1 *Complex branching:* Branching (or filtering) directs respondents to particular parts of the questionnaire depending on the way they have answered previous questions (see Chapter 7). While trained interviewers can do this in face-to-face PAPI surveys, computers simplify this process.

2 *Piping:* Piping feeds answers to earlier questions into later questions. For example, a respondent might nominate pizza, chocolate and hamburgers as their three favourite foods from a list of twenty food products. For each selected product we want to know when they last ate it, how often they eat it and their knowledge of its fat content. Rather than having each of these focused questions prewritten for each of the initial twenty products, piping technology simply takes the names of the three selected products and inserts this product name (e.g. pizza) into one question template such as 'When did you last eat *<piped product name>*?' The same question is then rebuilt but *<chocolate>* will be placed into the *<product name>* section. This results in a dynamic questionnaire in which questions are constructed 'on the fly' based on earlier answers.

Piping is useful in longitudinal surveys where responses in earlier stages can be used to modify questions in subsequent stages. Piping can also remind people of answers provided at an earlier stage. Suppose that in a longitudinal survey of retirees we ask pre-retirees to say how much they expect to enjoy being retired. Twelve months later their answers can be 'piped' into a follow-up questionnaire. For example we might say 'Just before you retired you said that you expected that you would <*piped information from answers in pre-retirement survey*> your retirement. How have you actually found it? Has it been better or worse than you expected or about the same?'

3 *Feedback:* The dynamic capacity of computer-administered questionnaires enables us to provide immediate feedback to respondents based on answers or mistakes. For example, if the respondent fails to answer a question they can be reminded that they have missed the question. This can reduce unintentional non-response.

4 *Error checking:* Computer-based questionnaires can detect some response errors. Respondents can be automatically prompted when they provide an *invalid* type of response. Where numeric responses are required the computer can check that the response is within an allowable numeric range. If a question asked what percentage of a person's leisure time is spent on particular activities, error checking could automatically check that the percentages add up to 100 per cent.

5 *Consistency checks:* These can be built into the questionnaire. For example, if a person indicates that they are eighteen years old and in response to a later question indicate that they have four children they might be asked to check their answers since such a combination is unlikely.

6 *Enforce question answering requirements:* Some respondents to PAPI questionnaires do not follow question answering instructions. For example, they might be asked to select only one of a set of five alternatives. Too often they select more than one. Computer-based questionnaires can prevent answers that do not conform to the instructions.

7 *More engaging interface:* Computer-assisted questionnaires can produce attractive and interesting questionnaires. A limited use of colour, different fonts, graphics and audio can make the experience of answering the questionnaire more enjoyable which should improve response rates.

8 *Range of response types:* Computer-based software can present responses in a greater variety of ways including graphical sliding scales, dropdown lists, menus and the like (see Chapter 7).

9 *Random question order:* One way of reducing response sets (see Chapter 7) is to randomise question order. By randomising question order for each respondent within a block of questions (e.g. a set of attitude statements) question order effects can be controlled.

10 *Order of answering:* Since the order in which questions are asked can influence answers it is desirable to control the order in which respondents answer questions. This can be achieved with computer-based questionnaires.

11 *Automatic coding and data file creation:* Computer-assisted questionnaires can automatically code closed responses and enter open responses into a database ready for data analysis. This saves money and time and eliminates coding errors.

12 *Sample controls:* Computer-based questionnaire administration can control the sorts of people that are accepted as respondents. For example, if a quota sample is sought the software can determine whether the potential respondent fits quota requirements. The software can also prevent the same person responding to the survey more than once (see discussion of quality in internet surveys later in this chapter).

The advantages of computer-administered surveys must be balanced against the requirement that respondents must have access to a suitable computer and feel sufficiently comfortable with computers. This requirement may produce such substantial sampling problems (see Chapter 6 on internet samples) as to outweigh the potential advantages. Equipment set up costs of CATI and CAPI surveys can be high and may require that these surveys are contracted to commercial survey companies. Internet-based surveys have fewer set up costs but administration costs may be high depending on access to servers and samples. Nevertheless internet samples are typically a cost efficient form of surveying.

FOUR METHODS COMPARED: STRENGTHS AND WEAKNESSES

The choice between survey methods will depend on the nature of the survey, the sample, time and cost

---

WEB POINTER 8.2   *The impact of cyberspace on research*

An article that is worth having a look at is by Cornick at the site:

www.csaf.org/cyber.htm

The article is entitled 'Cyberspace: Its Impact on the Conventional Way of Doing and Thinking About Research'. This paper raises issues about how the internet will impact on social science research methodology. It examines the potential impact of cyberspace on five areas of research methodology:

1   framing the research question

2   sampling

3   statistics

4   research design

5   writing the report.

---

constraints, the importance of response rates and the types of questions (van der Zouwen and de Leeuw, 1990). Drawing partly on Dillman (1978), this section outlines the relative merits of the four approaches by focusing on five broad considerations:

1   response rates;
2   obtaining representative samples;
3   effects on questionnaire design;
4   quality of answers; and
5   implementing the survey.

Response rates

One of the most common criteria by which a method is judged is the response rate it achieves. Face-to-face interviews have traditionally been seen as the most effective in this respect while telephone and particular mail surveys and internet surveys have developed the reputation for low response rates. But this is misleading. The response rate obtained in a particular study will be due to the combined effect of the topic, the nature of the sample, the length of the questionnaire, the care taken in implementing the particular survey and other related factors. There will be situations where a well-administered mail or internet survey will yield response rates at least equal to both personal and telephone interviews and at a much lower cost. The important thing is to identify the situations in which different approaches should and should not be used.

Personal and telephone surveys tend to achieve higher response rates than mail and internet surveys

in *general population* samples, but even here it partly depends on the topic of the survey. Hox and de Leeuw (1994) and de Leeuw and Collins (1997) review the response rates to 45 studies using face-to-face, telephone and postal administration methods. They conclude that face-to-face interviews have the highest average response rate (70 per cent), followed by telephone surveys (67 per cent) and postal surveys (61 per cent). In surveys of *specific, more homogeneous groups* (e.g. members of an organisation, teachers, nurses), mail surveys seem to be about as good as other techniques—especially when the topic under investigation is of particular relevance to the group (Dillman, 1978, 2000). We can anticipate that web-based surveys will yield good response rates when used in particular contexts—for example, in surveying members of a company in which all staff are networked. Furthermore, the more anonymous internet and postal methods may achieve better response rates for sensitive topics where anonymity is important (de Leeuw and Collins, 1997).

One problem in comparing the different methods is that the method of calculating response rates is likely to overestimate the non-response for mail questionnaires. In many internet surveys it is impossible to calculate a response rate—depending on the method by which the sample is obtained (refer to Chapter 6). A common way of calculating the response rate is with the formula:

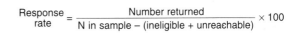

$$\text{Response rate} = \frac{\text{Number returned}}{\text{N in sample} - (\text{ineligible} + \text{unreachable})} \times 100$$

In face-to-face interviews and in telephone interviews it is easier to work out how many were ineligible or unreachable. In mail surveys, however, we have to assume that a non-response is a refusal unless informed otherwise. This relies on ineligible people contacting the researcher or the post office returning questionnaires of unreachable respondents—neither of which can be relied on. In internet surveys in which the sample is based on volunteers who are attracted to the survey site there is no way of calculating the number in the sample who choose not to respond.

Obtaining representative samples

Since non-responders tend to be different from those who respond (older, less educated, non-English-speaking background), low response rates can *bias* the sample. Since mail surveys require reading and writing rather than listening and internet surveys require internet access, they are more prone to this type of bias.

Other factors also introduce bias, or at least make it difficult to estimate and thus correct for any bias. A random sample is one where there is an equal or at least known probability of all members of the population being selected. Where a complete list of all members of the population is available then all members have an equal chance of selection regardless of the method by which the questionnaire is administered. For mail and especially telephone surveys, lists from which to draw the sample are normally used. These lists are often out of date and incomplete (e.g. not all people have telephones or are in directories), some categories of people will be systematically under-represented. Internet surveys face the most serious problems in obtaining representative samples of the general population. Indeed, given the biased nature of access to the internet (refer to Chapter 6) the internet, at this stage, cannot be used to obtain representative general population samples.

The same biases may affect surveys of more specific populations. Where accurate and complete sampling frames exist all four of the questionnaire administration methods can achieve relatively unbiased samples. The extent to which this occurs will depend more on follow-up procedures, population characteristics and survey implementation details (e.g. language difficulty, topic etc).

To obtain a random sample it is necessary to have some *control over who completes the questionnaire*. With personal and telephone interviews it is possible to obtain a listing of household members and then ask for the person who meets the selection requirements (see Table 6.2). But with mail questionnaires it is much more difficult to control who fills out the questionnaire. Although we can ask the person who receives the mail questionnaire to pass it on to the appropriate person, we cannot be sure that this happens. Internet surveys are open to the same problem. Where volunteer samples are used there is no control over who completes the survey. With targeted samples particular individuals can be invited to participate (via emails) but we cannot be sure that the targeted person is the person who finally replies. A further potential problem with internet surveys is that the same person can respond many times (ballot box stuffing).

Gaining access to the selected person can be a problem with personal interviews. Where respondents are widely scattered, the cost and time involved in locating respondents can be prohibitive. Simply gaining access to some respondents can be difficult—especially where people have dogs or other protection devices. In contrast, mail and telephone methods avoid this problem but encounter a problem in ensuring that the mail is sent to the correct address—a significant problem in samples with high levels of geographical mobility. Telephone surveys now face the problem of unlisted numbers, answering machines, mobile phones and phones connected to the internet. Access using internet surveys is, of

---

WEB POINTER 8.3 *Response rate calculators*

Response rate calculator using different methods of calculating response rates   http://home.clara.net/sisa/casro.htm

Visit www.social-research.org to use these links and to check for updates and additions.

course, limited to people on the internet and is made more problematic by out-of-date email lists, difficulties obtaining email addresses and infrequent checking of email.

Survey method effects on questionnaire design

Because of the varying input of the interviewer and the capacity to make use of complex questionnaire structures, the different methods impose different constraints on the type, format and number of questions that can be asked.

While personal interviews once provided the greatest flexibility in terms of question design and enabled the use of complex sets of skips and special modules, computer-assisted interviewing has allowed other methods of administration to provide these advantages (see computer-assisted questionnaire administration earlier in this chapter).

The method of administration is often seen to dictate the *length of the questionnaires* with the common view being that mail and internet questionnaires must be very brief while face-to-face questionnaires can be much longer. But it is not quite as simple as this (see Chapter 7). The optimal length of a questionnaire will depend on the nature of the sample and the topic under investigation: the more specialised the population and the more relevant the topic, the longer the questionnaire can be. Indeed, for some topics a short questionnaire will produce low response rates because people will consider it too trivial or superficial (Dillman, 2000: 305).

Because of the personal contact, face-to-face interviews can last longer than the other methods. However, the ability to extend personal interviews has its disadvantages. In long interviews either tiredness or impatience can affect the quality of answers as the interview progresses. Telephone surveys seem to be relatively unaffected by their length and can feasibly last up to 30 minutes. Once people start an interview on the phone they are unlikely to hang up. Dillman's research with mail questionnaires shows that general public surveys have an optimal length of about twelve pages or 125 items (Dillman, 1978, 2000). Length seems to be less important in postal surveys of relevant topics in specialised populations. We know less about the effect of the length of internet surveys.

The method of administration also affects the type of question that can be asked. Computer-assisted methods allow us to ask relatively *complex questions* with any of the administration methods. Without computer-assisted methods, face-to-face surveys with trained interviewers are the best suited for complex questionnaires and for questions that require visual aids. In mail and internet questionnaires respondents may simply give up if they find the questionnaire difficult. Because telephone interviews have no visual or written material, care must be taken to avoid questions with a large number of options (see pp. 113–14).

Mail questionnaires have difficulty with *boring questions*. Because of the personal contact involved, both telephone and particularly face-to-face interviews encounter fewer difficulties with boring questions. However, computer-assisted interview methods can use visual aids and other 'gimmicks' to help combat question boredom. A related problem is the problem of *item non-response*. In telephone and personal interviews, interviewers can check for missed questions and try to coax answers from reluctant respondents. PAPI-based mail surveys can encounter greater item non-response problems. Computer-assisted mail surveys and internet surveys can reduce item non-response by having the program detect missed questions and prompting the respondent before proceeding to the next set of questions.

Open-ended questions are best used when people can answer verbally rather than in writing: many people experience difficulties putting their ideas in writing. Mail and internet questionnaires are therefore not as well suited to open-ended questions.

With PAPI-administered questionnaires personal interviews using a trained interviewer are best suited to complex questionnaires with skips and *filter questions*. Mail questionnaires can only use very limited skips as respondents can quickly become confused. Computer-assisted administration methods are the best way of implementing complex sets of questions requiring filters and skips.

The *sequence* in which people read questions can affect answers. For example, in a series of questions about attitudes to tax reductions and attitudes about government programs to assist the unemployed, the order in which people read the questions could easily influence their answers. PAPI-based mail questionnaires provide no control over the order in which people answer questions, thus obscuring the extent to which answers might be affected by later questions. Since face-to-face and telephone interviews are administered by interviewers question order is controlled. Internet questionnaires also can control the order in which questions are presented to respondents. Computer-assisted administration methods can also randomise the order of sets of questions so that the effect of question order and acquiescence is minimised.

Quality of answers

It is one thing to obtain answers but quite another to obtain accurate answers. In this respect, face-to-face interviews can perform less well than the more anonymous mail and internet-based questionnaires. Responses to sensitive or controversial questions can be affected by *social desirability* considerations—giving acceptable rather than true answers. While this danger exists regardless of the administration method, it will be greater with the more personalised methods of questionnaire administration.

Another problem that is especially evident in face-to-face interviews is that the *observable characteristics* (e.g. gender, race, class) of even the best-trained interviewer can affect responses (Hox, 1991). For example, the gender of the interviewer relative to the respondent is likely to produce quite different responses on questions such as abortion and attitudes to sexual mores. Telephone surveys can be affected in a similar way while mail and internet surveys avoid the direct impact of interviewer characteristics.

Some interviewers contaminate results: they may place their own interpretation on questions, reveal their opinions or even fabricate results. Supervised telephone interviews should avoid this problem while mail and internet surveys avoid interviewer *subversion*.

The *opinions of other people* can also distort responses. Postal and internet surveys are open to this problem—in fact we can never be sure who actually completes the questionnaire. In face-to-face interviews the presence of another person can affect responses while telephone interviews are the least affected by this problem.

If questions require respondents to *consult with other people*, or look up information, postal and internet surveys are most suitable since these can be stopped and restarted at a later time. Since face-to-face and telephone surveys are normally completed in one sitting it is more difficult to consult with others to obtain accurate information.

Implementing the survey

The most serious problems of face-to-face questionnaires relate to their implementation. Despite their other problems, mail, telephone and internet surveys come into their own in this regard.

Nowhere is this clearer than in relation to *obtaining suitable staff*. Personal interviewers require careful training, need to be available for night and weekend work, must be willing to face potentially unpleasant and unsafe situations alone, be able to approach strangers, and need to have the personal skills to conduct an objective interview. The difficulties in obtaining such interviewers means that less than well-trained staff may be employed which in turn can undermine many of the potential advantages of the face-to-face interview.

Telephone surveys are less demanding in this respect. They do not require night and weekend travel and avoid the dangers of working alone with strangers. It is therefore easier to find interviewers. Furthermore, because time is not spent in travelling, fewer interviewers are required to conduct a telephone survey. If conducted from a central location, closer supervision and on-the-job training mean that interviewers do not have to be as experienced as the face-to-face interviewer. Internet surveys do not require interviewers and can be conducted by a single person. The construction and distribution of an internet survey has been simplified by survey software packages (see Web Pointer 8.1) but still requires a person with good computer skills. Mail surveys are the least demanding in terms of staffing requirements. Rather than finding people with interviewing skills, they require a well-organised person with good clerical skills. A large mail survey can be conducted readily by one or two staff.

Where *speed* is important, telephone surveys can be conducted in a matter of days provided sufficient interviewers are available. Similarly, internet surveys can produce large samples very quickly if they are linked to high volume sites. An internet survey sent to lists of frequently checked email addresses can produce quick responses. In contrast, mail surveys are slow. The time needed for questionnaires to reach people, to allow time to complete the questionnaire and to allow for two or three follow-up periods requires an administration period of six to eight weeks.

Cost is another crucial factor that affects the choice of questionnaire administration method.

The relative advantages of the four methods depend very much on what type of survey is being conducted. For national probability surveys face-to-face interviews would cost, on average, about five times as much as telephone surveys and up to twenty times more than a mail survey (Dillman, 1978: 71), but for a small local community survey the relative costs of the various methods can be very similar. The cost advantages of any method depend on how geographically dispersed the sample is: the greater the dispersion, the more expensive the face-to-face survey. Mail and internet surveys are barely affected by greater distance while telephone charges can be affected to some extent. The costs of printing will be greater for mail questionnaires where considerable attention has to be given to presentation but the cost of this per interview declines as the sample size increases. Internet surveys may involve the cost of software purchase and costs of placing the questionnaire on a 'host server'.[1] The cost of software per respondent declines as the sample size increases but the cost of hosting generally increases with sample size and the duration of the survey. Costs of face-to-face and telephone interviews will vary depending on the number of callbacks made—with face-to-face interviews being the most dramatically affected by this. Postal surveys will be similarly affected but the cost of follow-up reminders is negligible in internet surveys.

Taken overall, face-to-face surveys are normally better at obtaining representative samples and produce the fewest constraints in terms of questionnaire construction and question design, while PAPI-based mail questionnaires are generally the least satisfactory in these respects. But the reverse is true as far as the quality of answers is concerned; mail and internet questionnaires are likely to be best in this regard while face-to-face interviews encounter more problems than either mail or telephone methods. In general, face-to-face interviews are the least satisfactory when it comes to the practicalities of administration while mail, internet and telephone methods have considerable, though different, advantages. In the end it is impossible to decide which method is best: the relative strengths and weaknesses vary according to the characteristics of the survey. Decisions about sample size and distribution, the number of callbacks, types of questions, nature of the population, survey topic, amount of money available, availability of skilled personnel and time constraints must all be taken into account when selecting a method of administration. Table 8.1 summarises the advantages and disadvantages of the various methods of administering questionnaires.

MULTI-MODE METHODS OF ADMINISTRATION

The problem of recruiting suitable samples with some administration methods (e.g. the internet) has led some survey researchers to implement multi-mode administration methods (Dillman, 2000). This involves using the internet for those with internet access but using telephone, postal or personal interviews for those without internet access. Alternatively, to contain the cost of face-to-face interviews, telephone or postal surveys might be used for respondents who are widely scattered, thus saving on travel costs.

While this multi-mode strategy may recruit more representative samples it introduces a new problem. Questionnaire responses are subject to *mode effects*. That is, the mode of administration can affect the way people respond (see earlier discussion of the four methods). If certain types of people are surveyed with one method (e.g. internet) while other types are surveyed with a different method (e.g. face-to-face) these two modes may distort group differences. For example, we know that internet users are predominantly middle class. If an internet survey was used for those with internet access and face-to-face interviews were used for the rest we may find differences in the survey between the reported attitudes and behaviour of middle-class and working-class respondents. However, we do not know whether these apparent class differences are due to the mode of administration or real class differences.

Mixed mode methods are more defensible if different methods are used for different *variables* rather than for different *respondents*. For example, we could collect all income data using a self-administered postal questionnaire and attitudinal and behavioural data via a telephone survey. We could then match data from the two modes for each individual and analyse the data to see if income was related to attitudes and behaviour. While the mode of collection might affect the way people answer a question, using different modes for different questions should not affect the way two variables are related to each other. For example, the different modes of collecting income and attitudinal data

Table 8.1 Advantages and disadvantages of mail, face-to-face, telephone and web-based questionnaire surveys[a]

Scoring 1 = poor; 2 = satisfactory; 3 = good **Mode of delivery**	**Face-to-face** PAPI	**Phone** CAI[b]	**Mail** PAPI	**Web** CAI[b]
Response rates				
General samples	3	3	3	1
Specialised samples	3	3	3	3[a]
Representative samples				
Avoidance of refusal bias	3	3	1	2
Control over who completes questionnaire	3	2	2	2
Gaining access to selected person	2	3	3	3[a]
Locating selected person	2	3	3	3[a]
Effects on questionnaire design				
Ability to handle:				
Long questionnaires	3	2	2	2
Complex questionnaires	2	3	1	3
Boring questions	3	2	1	2
Item non-response	3	3	1	3
Filter questions	3	3	2	3
Question sequence control	3	3	1	3
Open-ended questions	3	3	1	2
Quality of answers				
Minimise social desirability	1	2	3	3
Make question order random	1	3	1	3
Ability to minimise distortion due to:				
Interviewer characteristics	1	2	3	3
Interviewer opinions	1	2	3	3
Influence of other people	2	3	1	2
Allows opportunities to consult	2	1	3	3
Avoids interviewer subversion	1	3	3	3
Implementing the survey				
Ease of obtaining suitable staff	1	2	3	3
Speed	1	3	1	3
Cost	1	2	3	3

Source: adapted in part from Dillman (1978)

Note: [a] Assuming respondent has regular internet access

[b] Computer Assisted Interviews

should *not* be responsible for any *links* we observe between people's income and their attitudes.

MAXIMISING RESPONSE RATES IN PERSONAL INTERVIEWS

A number of techniques can increase the response rate in face-to-face interviews.

1 If a respondent is not at home, call back up to four times. Call twice on different weekdays, once during the evening and once at the weekend.

2 The timing of the visits should take into account the characteristics of respondents: daytime will be most difficult for locating men and evenings will be less appropriate for those who may feel vulnerable to night visitors.

3 An advance letter or phone call may help allay suspicion of visits by interviewers.

4 A confident approach which assumes cooperation but avoids argumentativeness and belligerence will improve cooperation.

5 Avoid looking like a salesperson: use a clipboard rather than a briefcase.

6 Dress in a neat but neutral manner.

7 When introducing yourself give your and the organisation's name, explain the purpose of the survey and emphasise its confidentiality. Be ready to explain how the person came to be selected and to meet possible objections to participating.

8 Provide a written sheet from the survey organiser in which these things are explained and a contact number is provided (see Web Pointer 8.4).

9 Use an identity card with your photograph and the name of the survey organisation attached to your clothing.

10 Do not imply that the respondent is required to participate: the voluntary nature of the survey should be made clear (refer to Chapter 5).

11 If the respondent is too busy, try to make a specific time to return.

12 Try to avoid people refusing on behalf of others. If the required person is unavailable, try to find out when you might call back and talk with them.

13 Addresses where an interview is refused might be given to another, more experienced interviewer, perhaps with different characteristics (gender, age, class) from the initial interviewer.

ENSURING QUALITY IN PERSONAL INTERVIEWS

Some general factors that can improve the frankness and care with which questions are answered are set out below.

Training and supervision

1 A well-constructed field manual can anticipate many problems and answer questions. For complex surveys these can be very detailed (see Web Pointer 8.5).

2 To give new interviewers learning experience and confidence they should be accompanied by a supervisor on their first few interviews. The supervisor should largely conduct the initial interview, progressively playing a smaller role.

3 Supervisors should provide immediate feedback on interviews and completed schedules. This provides the opportunity to maximise the quality of later interviews by giving positive feedback and identifying problems with coding, probing, legibility or completion.

4 Selection and training should focus on the interviewer's ability to read fluently, speak clearly and be able to ad lib answers to interviewee's questions.

5 Random checks by supervisors on completed interviews should ensure that the interview has actually been conducted.

Techniques for personal interviewing

A wide range of techniques to improve rapport and assist in the interview process are available, including those listed below.

1 Promote a relaxed atmosphere in which the respondent can concentrate (avoid doorstep interviews).

2 Try to discourage the presence of third parties.

3 Discourage a third party from offering opinions by politely suggesting that their opinions would be of interest at the end of the interview.

4 Sit opposite the respondent.

5 Use eye contact to establish rapport.

6 Never leave the questionnaire behind for the

WEB POINTER 8.4 *Introductory information for survey respondents*

A useful template for designing a survey introduction is provided by the Office for National Statistics in the UK at the following web address:

www.statistics.gov.uk/nsbase/other_activities/surveys_taking_part.asp

A pamphlet prepared by the same organisation can be viewed at:

www.statistics.gov.uk/nsbase/other_activities/downloads/ask_the_people.pdf

---

WEB POINTER 8.5 *Field manual for National Health Survey*

Field manual used in the US National Health Survey—an excellent example of the types of matters that a good field manual for a major survey must attend to:

ftp://ftp.cdc.gov/pub/Health_Statistics/NCHS/Survey_Questionnaires/NHIS/1998/

Visit www.social-research.org to use these links and to check for updates and additions.

respondent (or someone else in the household) to complete at their leisure.

7 An interview is not an equal exchange of information. Try to keep the respondent on the track but avoid making the interview sound like a test. Avoid trying to educate or convert the respondent.

8 To discourage respondents giving answers that they think the interviewer might want, it is important to avoid giving the interviewee any idea of your opinions. Avoid showing anger or surprise. If they ask for your views, deflect the question at least until the end of the interview, saying that it is best to wait until then.

9 When a person seems to provide an answer to a later question in response to an earlier question, still ask them the later question. Since question order can affect responses it is desirable for all interviewees to answer the questions in the same order. In such situations the apparently redundant question might be prefaced by saying 'I'd just like to check . . .'.

10 Open-ended questions often require probing to encourage full answers. This can be accomplished by the use of an expectant glance, or phrases such as 'mmm', 'and?', 'Can you tell me more?', 'I'm not quite clear what you mean by that', 'What other reasons?', 'What else?', 'Exactly why do you think that's important?', 'Could you be a little more specific?'.

11 Because uniformity is desirable, questions should be read exactly as they appear on the interview schedule.

12 Rather than relying on memory, answers should be recorded as they are given.

13 The schedule should be checked at the completion of the interview to ensure that no question has been missed.

SMOOTH IMPLEMENTATION OF PERSONAL INTERVIEWS

A variety of steps can help surveys using face-to-face interviews to run smoothly. These steps include those listed below.

1 Careful route planning by the interviewer is required to minimise the time and expense of travelling.

2 Notification to the police will help alleviate anxiety about strangers visiting houses in the neighbourhood.

3 A field controller will normally be required to allocate addresses to interviewers, arrange payment, keep time sheets, answer queries from both interviewers and respondents, ensure a supply of questionnaires, check completed questionnaires and ensure that interviews are being completed at a satisfactory rate.

4 A system by which interviewers record details of interviews, travel, callbacks and times of visits needs to be carefully organised before the interviews commence.

MAXIMISING RESPONSE RATES IN POSTAL SURVEYS

The discussion below relates to PAPI-based postal surveys since these are the most common form of mail survey. DBM (Disk By Mail) postal surveys would require additional instructions regarding how to install the questionnaire, assurances about viruses, how to save and return responses and perhaps a special Frequently Asked Questions (FAQs) set of information.

The cover letter

The cover letter provides the main chance to motivate the respondent to complete the questionnaire. This letter should be simple, businesslike, written on official letterhead and no more than one page in length. It should include the following (Figure 8.1):

1 official letterhead;
2 date on which the questionnaire is mailed;
3 full name and address of the respondent (where available);
4 an explanation of the study's purpose and usefulness;
5 an explanation of how the respondent was selected and the importance of their response;
6 an assurance of confidentiality and a brief explanation of the purpose of any identifying number on the questionnaire;
7 an indication of what will be done with the results and an offer to make the results available;
8 an offer to answer any questions that might arise and a free contact telephone number to call;

School of Social Sciences

La Trobe University
Bundoora Campus
Victoria 3086
Australia
Telephone (03) 9479 1111

25 May 2001

Ian Hamilton
617 Mountain View Ave
Mount Paradise
Victoria 3093

Twelve months ago the government introduced laws restricting the places in which people are permitted to smoke tobacco products. Restrictions now apply to smoking in any enclosed public place, including restaurants, hotels and casinos.

Now that these laws have been in place for twelve months we want to know how people feel about these restrictions. We believe it is important that people who are affected by these laws have the opportunity to be heard. We want to hear your views on whether or not you support or oppose these new restrictions on smoking.

Your household is one of a small number in which people are being asked to give their opinion on this matter. Your address was drawn in a random sample of the entire state and, to be truly representative, it is crucial that you and no-one else completes the questionnaire and that each questionnaire is returned.

Your answers will be completely confidential. The identification number on the first page is simply to check whether we have received your questionnaire. This will save us contacting you again after you have returned your questionnaire. Your name will never be placed on the questionnaire.

You can be sure that no-one will ever know how you responded to the questions. The survey results will be made available in statistical form to government departments, politicians and the media. If you would like a summary of the results for yourself, simply write 'copy of results' and your name and address on the back of the envelope when returning the questionnaire. Alternatively, the statistical results will be made available on the internet at the address: www.smokingsurvey.com.

I would be happy to answer any questions you might have. Please write or call. The special tollfree telephone number is (013) 222 2222.

Thank you for your assistance.

Yours sincerely

David de Vaus
Project Director

Figure 8.1 Initial cover letter for a mail survey

9 a handwritten signature in blue ink that stands out as being personalised;
10 official position of the researcher.

Preparing the envelopes

Since the first task is to get the respondent to open the envelope, it is important to personalise it and avoid making it look like advertising. Use stamps rather than bulk postage and include a stamped, self-addressed envelope to minimise the effort involved in returning the questionnaire. Use stamps rather than a business reply system to produce a greater sense of personalisation.

Using incentives

Small incentives such as a felt pen or postage stamp can be sent with the first mail-out to induce a feeling of obligation in the respondents. Incentives included with the initial questionnaire are more effective than those promised if the questionnaire is returned (Church, 1993).

Material incentives can help increase response rates, but can add considerably to the cost of a study. More important than material incentives is the necessity of maximising non-material rewards (feeling of doing something useful, being treated as important) and minimising costs (time, frustration) (Dillman, 1978: 12–18).

Selecting the mail-out date

Most recent evidence suggests that the day of the week on which the questionnaire is posted has virtually no effect on response rates. Furthermore, the time of the year when the survey is conducted seems to make no difference to response rates. It makes sense to avoid mailing in the main holiday periods when many respondents will not be at home. However, the use of a systematic follow-up procedure will reduce even the impact of holiday period postal surveys (Dillman, 2000).

Follow-ups

Two or three follow-ups are needed to achieve response rates similar to those obtained with either telephone or personal questionnaires. Each follow-up provides an opportunity to persuade the respondent

to complete the questionnaire and will take a slightly different approach.

Pre-survey contact

Contacting respondents by mail or telephone a few days before sending out the questionnaire, advising them to expect a questionnaire, can increase response rates.

The first follow-up

One week after the first mail-out, the first follow-up should be sent to all respondents. This can even be prepared at the same time as the initial questionnaires are sent out. It takes the form of a postcard with the respondent's address typed on one side and a brief reminder on the other. It is designed to thank early responders and to remind rather than persuade non-responders. Figure 8.2 provides an example of the content of this first reminder.

The second follow-up

This follow-up should be sent only to people who have not responded after three weeks and will contain a new letter, a replacement questionnaire and a new stamped return envelope. The cover letter will tie the letter to the previous ones and be similar in content to the first one but more insistent in tone.

The third follow-up

If funds and time allow, or the level of response requires, a third follow-up may be used. The effectiveness of this follow-up will come not from a more strongly worded letter but from the persistence of the researcher: this will be the fifth letter the respondent will have received. To emphasise the importance of the survey, certified mail has been used to induce a sense of urgency and importance. Certified mail has proven to be very effective in increasing response rates from reluctant responders (Dillman, 2000). The cover letter will deal with similar areas to the initial letter using slightly different words, but place more emphasis on the importance of completing the survey, provide an explanation of why certified mail is being used (to ensure delivery) and be accompanied by a further copy of the questionnaire. Another return envelope should be included.

Since certified mail may inconvenience respondents who are not at home when the postal service attempts to deliver it, other special ways of

Last week we mailed you a questionnaire asking for your views about the government laws restricting smoking in public places.

If you have completed and returned the questionnaire please accept our sincere thanks. If not, could you please complete it today? As it was sent to a small representative sample it is most important that your views are included in the study if we are to represent people's views adequately. Remember, we are not trying to push our own views or arguments about the government's laws. We simply want to find out and report what people like you think.

If by some chance you did not receive the questionnaire, or if you have mislaid it, please call me today on our tollfree line (013) 222 2222 and I will send you another copy right away.

Yours sincerely

David de Vaus
Project Director

Figure 8.2 First follow-up postcard

making the final follow-up contact may be preferable. Priority paid postage, courier delivery and telephone calls have all been used and, especially telephone calls, are as effective as certified mail in achieving improved response rates (Dillman, 2000).

Undelivered questionnaires

A proportion of questionnaires will be returned either because the address is unknown or the respondent had moved. The addresses should be checked against the original list from which the sample was drawn and corrected where possible. Where the respondent has moved it might be possible to obtain a more recent address by using another list (e.g. check electoral roll, telephone book, employer). If the respondent has died they should be dropped from the sample. It is important to record the reasons why questionnaires were not delivered as this is important when calculating the response rate (see p. 127).

Answering respondents' questions

Since some respondents will have questions, someone should be readily available to help. They may need to clarify how the respondent was selected, explain the importance of the study, or advise the caller what to do in the case of the respondent being away, too ill or unable to read.

SMOOTH IMPLEMENTATION OF POSTAL QUESTIONNAIRES

It is important to develop a thorough timetable of the steps of the survey, indicating on what dates various tasks are to be performed and listing the supplies that will be needed.

Supplies

As far as possible, *all* supplies and printing should be completed before sending out the first questionnaire. The dates printed on the letters should reflect the actual dates on which the questionnaires or letters are sent.

Failure to ensure that all supplies are available when required can lead to major problems with follow-up procedures. The supplies required will depend on response rates at each stage and decisions about the number and type of follow-ups. Table 8.2 provides an estimate of the supplies needed per 100 initial sample members with three follow-ups and assuming a response rate of 35 per cent to the initial mailing, 60 per cent after the first reminder and 70 per cent after the second reminder.

Identification numbers

To avoid duplicating or missing identity numbers on questionnaires and ensuring that the identity numbers on your records correspond with those on

Table 8.2 Supplies per 100 sample members in a mail survey

	Initial mail-out	Follow-up			
		1st	2nd	3rd	Total
Envelopes (mail and return)	200	00	80	60	340
Stamps (mail and return)	200	100	140	60	500
Letters	100	100	40	30	270
Questionnaires	100	00	40	30	170

the questionnaires, it is important to put the identity numbers on questionnaires just prior to mailing and to check that the name on both the envelope and the cover letter match with each other and with the identification number on your files.

Staffing

Someone needs to be available to answer queries from respondents and to maintain records of respondents and of ineligible sample members. Although there probably will not be many of these, provision still needs to be made. Careful records need to be kept indicating which questionnaires have been returned so that unnecessary reminders will not be sent and to enable the calculation of the current response rate.

MAXIMISING RESPONSE RATES IN TELEPHONE SURVEYS

Obtaining good response rates with telephone interviews depends on two main factors: locating the respondent and getting them to agree to take part in the interview. Once a person begins an interview they nearly always complete it.

Locating the respondent

Once a sample of names or households has been selected (see below) the interviewer first has to make contact through that telephone number and then with an appropriate person within the household. Timing of calls is therefore important. While the most appropriate time to call people will depend on

the nature of the sample, it is possible to provide some guidelines for general population surveys. Dillman (1978) recommends that the initial call commences early in the week. For numbers that do not answer, the next call should be at the weekend, either in the afternoon or evening. For those still not contacted, weekday afternoons are tried next followed by weekday mornings. If time permits, the remaining non-contacts can be put aside for a week or so before trying one last call. Care should be taken to call at socially acceptable times and if contact is made at an inappropriate time apologise and try to arrange a more suitable time. Locating respondents in telephone surveys is becoming increasingly problematic because of changing telephone technology (see 'gaining cooperation' in this chapter).

Once a number is located we need to ensure that it is the type of number that is appropriate to the study (e.g. a household rather than a business) and then select the appropriate member of the household to interview. Methods of selection are outlined in Table 6.2.

Gaining cooperation

The interviewer needs to state concisely the purpose of the call. Respondents will normally listen to this introduction before they decide to cooperate or refuse. But it must be brief: it will cover similar areas to those dealt with by the cover letter in a mail survey. After ascertaining that you have the correct number and that it is a household residence, an introduction similar to the following could be used:

This is _____ from _____ university. We are doing a statewide research study to find out people's views about government restrictions on smoking in public places. Your telephone number was drawn from a random sample of the entire state. The questions I need to ask will take about __ minutes. If you have any queries I'd be happy to answer them. Could I ask you these questions now?

If specific household members were to be interviewed, a respondent selection procedure would need to be inserted into the introduction.

One way of increasing acceptance rates and providing more information about the study is to send an advance letter three to five days before phoning. The format and content of the letter would be similar to that for the initial mail questionnaire. When contact is made the respondent may have questions or raise reasons why they cannot participate in the study. It is important to be prepared for these. Dillman (1978: 260–3) provides a set of likely problems and useful responses.

ENSURING QUALITY IN TELEPHONE SURVEYS

The quality of the questionnaire, interviewers and sample quality affect the quality of a telephone survey. Questionnaire design and the principles of interviewing have already been discussed (see Chapter 6) but sample considerations deserve further attention. There are two methods of obtaining a list of telephone numbers to call: obtaining a systematic sample from telephone directories (directory listing) or obtaining a randomly generated set of telephone numbers for the exchange areas covered by the survey (random digit dialling).

For the *directory listing* method to be effective, up-to-date directories of the whole sample area are needed. Where this is not possible the sample will be biased and will add to bias caused by people with unlisted numbers. Mobile cell phones further complicate the issue of obtaining a full directory listing of an area since these phone numbers are not tied to an area. From a sampling frame of eligible numbers we estimate the number of relevant phone numbers (e.g. residences) in each directory, decide on the sample size and draw a systematic sample. This task is simplified by electronic telephone directories and software that can electronically draw samples from these electronic lists.

Random digit dialling involves obtaining a list of exchanges (indicated by the first three or four numbers in a telephone number)[2] and using a table of random numbers to generate the remaining four or so numbers that will be attached to the exchange number to make up a telephone number. This method avoids the need to obtain directories and should enable contact with unlisted numbers. Unfortunately it does not enable us to select between business and residential addresses and can produce a lot of unnecessary calls. Further, not all possible telephone numbers in an exchange are allocated, thus leading to a lot of time spent trying to contact non-existent numbers. These problems make it difficult to deter-mine the reasons for unanswered calls, thus creating complications when calculating response rates.

SMOOTH IMPLEMENTATION OF TELEPHONE SURVEYS

A central telephone interviewing facility with CATI software will greatly assist the implementation of a telephone survey. Not only does a CATI facility help with interview quality and integrity by enabling good supervision, it also assists in ensuring that calls are made in the most systematic and efficient manner.

Once a sample of telephone numbers is generated, a number, address and name (if appropriate) needs to be attached to each interview schedule— a task that can be accomplished as each call is made. Each interview schedule should have a cover page to which this information is attached and which allows the interviewer (or the CATI software) to easily make a record of calls to that number. The cover sheet should make provision to record which call it is, the date and time, the interviewer, the outcome of the call and space to note down specific times at which a call-back has been arranged. Space should be provided to record the final outcome of the number—was an interview refused, contact never made, number disconnected and so forth.

A system for making call-backs needs to be implemented. The survey manager or the CATI software should sort interview schedules according to their status: weekday call-back, evening call-back, weekend call-back, specific time call-back, refusal, complete interview, wrong number and so forth. This enables a systematic scheduling of call-backs.

CATI software ensures the smooth flow of questions and automatic coding of responses. However it is obviously crucial that the programming of the software is properly done, carefully checked and piloted. Before using the software in real interviews the interviewers need to be properly trained in its operation. Care needs to be given to employing sufficient interviewers for the various stages of the interview program. Telephone interviewing can be exhausting and breaks are required. It is helpful initially to have up to 50 per cent more interviewers on duty than are actually interviewing at any one time. As the interviewing proceeds and mainly requires call-backs, fewer interviewers will be needed.

MAXIMISING RESPONSE RATES IN INTERNET SURVEYS

It is not possible to calculate response rates for internet surveys in which a questionnaire is placed on a website and anyone who comes across it can answer it. However where the survey is given to a defined sample via the internet it is meaningful to talk about response rates and thus of ways of increasing them.

The first step is to get the survey to the selected sample in a way that makes people want to respond. One way of doing this is to email respondents an invitation to participate and an explanation of the survey together with the URL where the questionnaire can be completed. Explain how their email was selected and avoid 'spamming' (see Chapter 5 on privacy). An alternative is to pay an internet survey company to distribute the survey to their established respondent panels. Another approach is to rely on site visitors but to require potential respondents first to complete a brief eligibility questionnaire so that you select a sample with the characteristics in which you are interested.

Gaining cooperation in an internet survey involves similar principles to any other sort of survey. Assurances of *confidentiality or anonymity* should be provided. Many people are justifiably suspicious about anonymity on the internet so do not promise more than you can confidently deliver. Ensure that the experience (and especially the initial experience) of the site/questionnaire is *interesting* and *inviting*. The attractive interface options on the internet mean that colour, different fonts, graphics and a variety of attractive response formats can easily make the site inviting and easy to read. Highlighting the *public value* of the survey will encourage participation as will *incentives* and *sponsorship* from reputable institutions.

If the survey involves downloading and opening files you will need to be able to assure respondents that the file is *virus free*. Response rates should be improved by providing feedback while answering the questionnaire and by making results available to the respondent. Many survey software packages enable live data analysis—providing the respondent with up-to-date survey results immediately upon completion of the questionnaire.

Another important way of achieving reasonable response rates is to *follow up non-responders*. Where the sample is recruited through email lists the task of follow-up is fairly straightforward. You have the choice of reminding all sample members to complete the survey or, if you can identify them, simply email reminders to non-responders. One way to maintain the anonymity of respondents yet track non-responders is to ask responders to send an email when they submit their anonymous questionnaire. This enables you to identify non-responders and follow them up cheaply and simply.

ENSURING QUALITY IN INTERNET SURVEYS

Good samples are fundamental to good quality internet surveys. The sampling problems encountered in internet surveys have already been discussed (in this chapter and Chapter 6). A central consideration in *sample quality* is the method by which the questionnaire is distributed. You will recruit a more useful sample if you know the characteristics of the population the sample is meant to represent and the sample has been recruited using probability methods. Relying on volunteer visitors to a website will simply produce a collection of responses rather than a quality sample.

Try to prevent *unauthorised access* to the questionnaire. If the questionnaire is provided for selected respondents ensure that not just any visitor to your site can answer it. This can be done by not providing a link to the questionnaire on a web page but rather providing a specific URL to selected participants. Alternatively usernames and passwords can be given to your selected respondents via email. Procedures can also be implemented to prevent 'ballot stuffing'—the practice of the same person responding on many occasions.

The quality of responses should be improved if respondents are confident that their responses are *anonymous* (or at least *confidential*) *and secure*. The methods by which security and anonymity mechanisms can be built into an internet survey depend on the particular form of internet survey and cannot be detailed here.

Earlier I encouraged the use of graphics features available on internet surveys. However these features must be used judiciously. Too many gimmicks can dominate the questionnaire design. Too many flashing graphics, changing features, rotating pictures, gaudy colours and the like simply divert attention from the main purpose of the questionnaire page.

Careful use of skips and piping can greatly simplify

and personalise the task of answering complex questionnaires and thus improve the quality of answers. Item non-response can be minimised by design features that remind respondents that they have missed a question. This reminder can simply *remind* respondents about the missed question or can *require* an answer before proceeding. In general it is better to remind than require. A powerful feature of computer-based questionnaires is the capacity to *validate responses* 'on the fly' (p. 125) and this feature should be used wherever possible to improve data quality.

Finally, since internet questionnaires are self-administered it can be helpful to provide online explanations, definitions and examples to assist respondents if they require help. Some respondents may require technical help and some of this can be provided in a 'frequently asked questions' part of the questionnaire.

SMOOTH IMPLEMENTATION OF INTERNET SURVEYS

The simplest way to ensure that an internet survey proceeds smoothly is to use a specially designed *internet survey software package*. These packages simplify the process of writing the questionnaire, making it web compatible, placing it on the internet and receiving responses. The right package will avoid the need to learn programming languages such as HTML, ActiveX, Java and Perl (see Web Pointer 8.1 for links to some of these packages).

The second most important factor in implementing an internet survey is to be conscious of the *type of equipment respondents are likely to have*. Do not assume that respondents will have the latest computer with loads of memory, fast graphics and audio and superfast internet connections. Do not expect that they will have the latest browser or operating system and do not expect them to download software to upgrade their system for your survey. This means that you should avoid using the latest resource-hungry features of the internet survey software packages. Furthermore, do not assume a high level of *computer literacy*. Provide clear and simple instructions and have ways in which respondents can obtain help.

When planning the internet survey check that your ISP or your institution (e.g. university, government department) allows you to place the survey on their internet server. For security reasons not all ISPs allow users to post interactive surveys on their server and not all will allow respondents to return their responses via the server.[3]

You will need to decide on the *method by which responses are to be returned*. Different software allows different methods. If your ISP permits, responses can be sent to the server where they are compiled into a database and forwarded to the researcher. Alternatively the software may allow responses to be sent automatically to you via email (e.g. Keypoint and Perseus do this) and compiled into a database. Ensure that your software can handle the selected return method and that the method provides the security and confidentiality you have promised.

Finally you should check what *other software* is required. Do you need a database package? Do you need a statistical package to conduct more sophisticated analysis? If additional packages are to be used make sure that you can export data generated by your survey software to the database or statistical analysis software.

QUESTIONNAIRE ADMINISTRATION CHECKLIST

The selection of a questionnaire administration method will never be straightforward. In selecting your method you will need to address the following questions.

1 How will the sample requirements affect the selection of administration method?
   a To which population do you want to generalise?
   b What sampling frames are available?
   c How large a sample do you require?
   d Is a representative sample required?
   e How geographically dispersed is the sample?
   f How much control do you need to exercise over the final selection of sample members?
   g Does your proposed sample have good internet access?
   h Do you have access to the sample via the telephone?
   i How much is the safety of researchers/ interviewers a concern given the sample?
   j What is the likely literacy level (computer and reading/writing) of sample members?

k   What do you anticipate would be the level of cooperation of the sample using the various methods of administration?
2   How does the content of the survey affect choice of administration method?
  a   How sensitive are the questions?
  b   How desirable is anonymity for this sample/topic?
  c   Is there a danger that, given the topic, that interviewer characteristics will affect answers?
  d   What do you anticipate will be the level of interest of the questions?
  e   Would the questions benefit from being able to use audio, graphic and other prompts and stimuli?
3   How do funding considerations affect the choice of administration methods?
  a   Can you afford commercial agencies to collect your data?
  b   Do you need to maximise your sample size but at little additional cost per unit?
4   What other resources do you have access to?
  a   Do you have the computer equipment for a computer-based method?

b   What internet access do you have?
c   What are the rules of your internet service provider regarding distribution of questionnaires, receiving replies and placing scripts on the server?
d   How much time do you have for the study?
e   What skills are available (e.g. telephone interviewers, programmers etc)?
f   Do you have the required skills and knowledge for the chosen method?
g   Do you have the required software if you are using a computer-assisted method?
5   What method best suits the nature of your questionnaire?
  a   How complex is the questionnaire structure?
  b   How important is it that respondents answer questions in a set order?
  c   Will respondents need to be able to go and find information to answer the questionnaire?
  d   What do you estimate to be the danger of item non-response?
  e   Do you have many open-ended questions?

KEY CONCEPTS

Ballot box stuffing	Data validation	HTML	Response rate
Branching	DBM	Internet server	URL
CAPI	Directory listing	ISP	Web page survey
CASI	sampling	Mode effect	
CATI	Dynamic questionnaire	PAPI	
Computer-assisted	Email survey	Piping	
interviewing	Follow-ups	RDD sampling	

ENDNOTES

[1]   To make a questionnaire available on the internet it must be placed on a web server (a computer to which all people on the internet have access). This requires 'uploading' the questionnaire to the server of your internet service provider (ISP). The ISP may or may not charge for this service. Alternatively there are commercial survey companies that will allow you to upload your questionnaire onto their server and they will host it. Normally these commercial sites charge for this service.

[2]   Again mobile cell phones complicate the selection of phone numbers because they are not based on particular telephone exchanges.

[3]   In particular many ISPs will not allow you to install CGI scripts on their server. These CGI scripts are produced by some of the survey packages and facilitate the interactive and dynamic aspects of the questionnaire.

FURTHER READING

Dillman's *Mail and Telephone Surveys* (1978) provides an excellent and detailed description of these techniques. His more recent (2000) *Mail and Internet Surveys: Tailored Design Method* provides an updated and somewhat revised approach. The journal *Public Opinion Quarterly* contains many articles on all four methods. Hoinville, Jowell and associates provide good introductions and a good bibliography to personal and postal surveys in *Survey Research Practice* (1978). Lavrakas (1993) provides a thorough practical guide for conducting telephone surveys.

A splendid set of papers on modes of administration and interviewer effects is provided in Singer and Presser (1989). Arleck and Settle (1995) provide concise and useful summaries of the practical issues in conducting mail and interview surveys as do Rossi et al. in the *Handbook of Survey Research* (1983). Craig et al. (2000) are some of the few authors who tackle the issue of safety in social research but this must be an important consideration in choosing research methods. Three recent articles deal with different types of e-surveys. Cho and LaRose (1999) and Kaye and Johnstone (1999) describe their experiences of conducting an e-survey while Schaeffer and Dillman (1998) examine ways of improving email response rates and discuss the value of multi-mode strategies. Couper (2000) reviews the issues, approaches and current state of knowledge regarding web surveys. Dillman has provided a range of his papers on e-surveys on his website http:// survey.sesrc.wsu.edu/dillman/papers.htm.

EXERCISES

1 Which method of questionnaire would you select to best deal with the following:
  a some topic likely to be of only marginal interest to most respondents;
  b highly personal or controversial questions;
  c a survey that needs to be completed quickly;
  d boring questions;
  e it will be difficult to find the respondent at home;
  f a survey of a particular organisation;
  g respondents are unlikely to have the required information at hand;
  h finances are very limited;
  i the questionnaire is difficult to follow;
  j the researcher is the only person conducting the survey—trained interviewers are either unavailable or too expensive;
  k the questionnaire is relatively long;
  l no satisfactory sampling frame exists;
  m a high response rate is particularly important;
  n the sequence in which questions are answered is important;
  o responses are likely to be affected by social desirability factors.

2 Explain the reasons for your choice in each of the above situations.

3 Imagine that you had to obtain people's views about reducing taxation and about their attitude to the government cutting, maintaining or increasing social welfare and environment programs. Produce an introduction that you would use to convince people to participate in the survey. Prepare a different introduction for each of the methods of questionnaire administration.

4 Go to the website http://webintel.net/ websurvey4 (Active Survey) and register. This will enable you to create an online internet survey. Think of a simple survey topic and use Active Survey to build and administer your questionnaire. Build the survey and then make it available online. This free survey facility allows you to build questions that make use of many internet survey features (e.g. skips, required response, varying response formats, preventing ballot stuffing when you first set up the survey). You can also employ some pre-written questions by using the survey wizard, specifying reports of the progressive survey results (select the reports tab). You can have the survey automatically sent to a panel of volunteers registered with this site. You can specify the characteristics of the respondents you want (click the 'registered' tab) and they will be alerted that your questionnaire awaits.

5 Go to the site www.dssresearch.com/mainsite/ surveys.htm and complete the health assessment survey. This simple survey illustrates the live analysis feature of internet surveys.

6   Go to the website www.greenfieldonline.com/
and click on the members area icon (you may
have to join but it's free) and then look at some
of the online surveys. Fill out a survey and then
evaluate the survey using the criteria covered in
Chapters 7 and 8 of this book.

7   What are the main advantages and disadvantages
of each of the following questionnaire administration methods?
a   postal
b   internet (web page)
c   face-to-face
d   telephone.

Part III

SETTING
UP THE DATA
FOR ANALYSIS

9

Coding

The quantitative analysis of survey data requires that answers to questions are converted into numbers. Many variables also require that answers be classified into categories. This process of converting answers to numbers and classifying answers is called *coding*. This chapter examines the six main steps in coding and classifying questionnaire data. These steps are:

1   classifying responses
2   allocating codes to each variable
3   allocating column numbers to each variable
4   producing a codebook
5   checking for coding errors
6   entering data.

Each of these is considered in turn and the chapter concludes with a discussion of some of the complexities of coding.

CLASSIFYING RESPONSES

Coding is more than the allocation of numbers to responses. It also involves the creation of a classification system that imposes a particular order on the data. This in turn affects the way data are analysed. These classification systems are not objective systems but are created by people and reflect the historical and cultural ways in which we make sense of the world around us. As creators and consumers of research we need to be aware that classification systems shape what we find.

The cultural and political character of classification systems is obvious in the racial classification system of apartheid South Africa where race was classified as white, black and coloured. Why did race have to be classified in this way? Why did race need to be classified at all? Who decides what divisions are important?

Classification systems are human constructions and the system that is used can reflect particular social and political arrangements. Classifications are historically and culturally relative and change over time and differ between countries. The classification system for occupations used at the beginning of the twentieth century will be very different from that used in the beginning of the twenty-first century. The way in which religious affiliation is coded in the United States will be somewhat different from the way it is classified in Australia and very different from that in which it would be coded in the Middle East.

None of this, however, means that we escape the need to classify. It simply means that we need to be aware that the classification systems we use need not be set in concrete and that the schemes we use can affect the way we see our data and the world around us.

Once classification schemes have been developed our task is to allocate codes to each of the categories in the classification. These classification schemes can be developed either before a questionnaire is administered or afterwards.

Precoding

Much of the work in classifying responses is undertaken at the questionnaire design stage where a set of fixed responses is provided to respondents. Codes are allocated to these responses and these codes are normally visible in printed questionnaires to assist with data entry at a later stage (see Figures 9.1 and 9.3). In electronic questionnaires these codes are not visible but are programmed into the questionnaire program and responses are automatically coded.

Postcoding

Open-ended questions will be coded after the data have been collected. Postcoding is done either by:

■ using systematic, pre-existing standard coding schemes; or
■ developing a coding scheme based on the responses provided by respondents.

For standard questions such as occupation, religion, country, offences etc where there can literally be thousands of possible responses it makes sense to use existing standardised coding schemes. There are a number of reasons for favouring these coding schemes.

1 They are systematic and have been developed by people with considerable expertise with the particular variables and after considerable consultation.
2 These coding schemes are publicly available and make the coding schema more transparent.
3 They reduce coder error.
4 They enable other researchers and the consumers of research to see how the data were constructed and to take this into account when evaluating the findings.

5 Repeated surveys are used to track changes over time (e.g. crime surveys are used to track changes in crime and offence rates). To properly track change it is critical that the same classification rules are followed over time.
6 International comparisons are an increasingly important part of social research. Transparent and systematic classification schemes are fundamental to such comparisons.

The need for systematic classification schemes has resulted in major national and international agencies developing comprehensive classification standards for some of the core demographic variables such as country of birth, ethnicity, health, education, religion, causes of death etc. Links to some of these schemes are provided in Web Pointer 9.1.

ALLOCATING CODES TO EACH VARIABLE

Each variable has at least two categories and any person must belong to one and only one category. The essence of coding is to give a distinctive code to each category of a variable.

Multilevel classification schemes

Most standard classification schemes allow for coding at different levels of detail. Many of these have three levels ranging from level one that has broad classifications, level two that breaks these broad classifications into sub-categories and a third, finer level that breaks these sub-categories into finer levels. Table 9.1 provides extracts from three levels of the Australian Standard (criminal) Offence Classification.

When coding you will need to decide what level of detail you need to reflect in your coding. Often all you will need is the top level of general coding but the level used will depend on particular circumstances (see Box 9.1).

Are you: (tick box)	1 [ ] Married	Are you: (circle number)	1 Married
	2 [ ] Never married		2 Never married
	3 [ ] Separated		3 Separated
	4 [ ] Divorced		4 Divorced
	5 [ ] Widowed		5 Widowed
	6 [ ] Other		6 Other

Figure 9.1 Two methods of precoding questions

WEB POINTER 9.1 *Coding and classification schemes for core demographic variables*

Occupation

US Standard Occupational Classification (SOC) http://stats.bls.gov/soc/soc_home.htm

Australian Standard Classification of Occupations (ASCO) www.abs.gov.au/ausstats/abs@.nsf/ StatsLibrary?OpenView then select link to ABS classifications and select catalogue 1220.0

Canadian Standard Classifications (SOC91) www.statcan.ca/english/Subjects/Standard/ standard_classifications.htm

United Nations (ISCO) www.ilo.org/public/english/bureau/stat/class/ isco.htm

---

Employment status

United Nations www.ilo.org/public/english/bureau/stat/class/ icse.htm

---

Industry

Australia www.abs.gov.au/ausstats/abs@.nsf/ StatsLibrary?OpenView then select link to ABS classifications and select catalogue 1292.0

UK www.statistics.gov.uk/nsbase/themes/ compendia_reference/Articles/downloads/ structur.pdf

Canada (NAICS) www.statcan.ca/english/Subjects/Standard/ standard_classifications.htm

US Standard Industry Classification (SIC) www.instantaccess.co.uk/pga/sic.htm

Health and disability

United Nations: International Classification of Functioning, Disability and Health (ICIDH-2) www.who.int/icdh

United Nations: International Statistical Classification of Diseases and Related Health Problems (10th Revision) (ICD-10) www.who.int/msa/mnh/ems/icd10/icd10.htm

Australia: Major diagnostic categories www.prometheus.com.au/healthwiz/ majrdiag.htm

---

Education

United Nations: International Standard Classification of Education (ISCE) http://unescostat.unesco.org/en/pub/pub0.htm

Australia www.abs.gov.au/ausstats/abs@.nsf/ StatsLibrary?OpenView then select link to ABS classifications and select catalogue 1271.0

WEB POINTER 9.1 *continued*

Ethnicity and ancestry

USA: Standards for the Classification of Federal Data on Race and Ethnicity (US Office of Management and Budget)

http://clinton4.nara.gov/textonly/OMB/fedreg/directive_15.html

USA

http://wonder.cdc.gov/wonder/prevguid/p0000330/p0000330.htm

Use of Race and Ethnicity in Public Health Surveillance (critique of the standards specified in the above link). This article demonstrates the problematic and political nature of classification and coding schemes.

Ancestry

www.ipums.org/~census2000/2000pums_bureau.pdf

Appendix B

Country

Australia

www.abs.gov.au/ausstats/abs@.nsf/StatsLibrary?OpenView then select link to ABS classifications and select catalogue 1269.0

Language

Australia

www.abs.gov.au/ausstats/abs@.nsf/StatsLibrary?OpenView then select link to ABS classifications and select catalogue 1267.0

Religion

Australian Standard Classification of Religious Groups (ASCRG)

www.abs.gov.au/ausstats/abs@.nsf/StatsLibrary?OpenView then select link to ABS classifications and select catalogue 1266.0

USA: A list of US Protestant denominations used in the General Social Survey

www.icpsr.umich.edu/GSS99/index.html Click on Appendix. Select appendix k.

Crime/Offences

Australia

http://www.abs.gov.au/ausstats/abs@.nsf/StatsLibrary?OpenView then select link to ABS classifications and select catalogue 1234.0

Causes of death

Australia

142 causes
www.prometheus.com.au/healthwiz/142death.htm

85 causes
www.prometheus.com.au/healthwiz/85death.htm

WEB POINTER 9.1 *continued*

	22 causes
	www.prometheus.com.au/healthwiz/22death.htm
Time use	
United Nations	www.un.org/depts/unsd/timeuse/tuaclass.htm
Other countries	Links from the United Nations site
Other sites	
United Nations	Other sites with useful information regarding classification systems:
	Statistical classifications registry
	http://esa.un.org/unsd/cr/registry/regrt.asp
	Lists and links to sets of international classifications (economic, health, products etc)
	www.un.org/depts/unsd/class/famlist1.htm
University of Surrey UK	Very useful article with links and comments and refs on a number of UK classifications
	http://qb.soc.surrey.ac.uk/resources/ classification/socintro.htm

Developing a set of codes from the answers given

Often we will need to develop our own set of codes based on the responses obtained in the survey. For example, we might ask people to indicate what they think will be the major problem facing the country in ten years time. We might be able to anticipate some answers and develop a partial coding scheme beforehand, but there will be many responses that we probably could not predict.

The first step in developing these codes is to be clear about the purpose of the question. This is followed by the examination of between 50 to 100 questionnaires and seeing if responses can be classified into broad groupings. Once this is done, the more specific responses should be placed under the broad headings and assigned specific codes. For example, we might be able to group responses about major problems in ten years time under headings such as social, economic, moral, military, environmental, political, religious and so on. Having done this, we can develop specific codes for responses

under each heading. Under the environmental heading, we might have responses that fall into categories such as overcrowding, air quality, water quality, scarcity of resources, extinction of species, greenhouse problems, ozone problems etc.

When developing these codes, try to make the categories and codes flexible so that additional codes can be added later as more questionnaires are examined. Use multiple-digit codes so that there are plenty of spare codes if they are needed. A system something like that in Table 9.1, where a range of codes are allocated initially to a broad category (e.g. environmental problems) and more specific codes are allocated to specific answers under this broad heading, is desirable.

Multiple answers

An essential part of coding for survey analysis is to ensure that each respondent has one and only one code for each variable. Therefore each answer to a question (or more precisely each category of a variable) must have a distinctive code. When coding

Table 9.1   Multilevel coding scheme of criminal offences

Level 1
01 Homicide and related offences
02 Acts intended to cause injury
03 Sexual assault and related offences
04 Dangerous or negligent acts endangering persons
05 Abduction and related offences
06 Robbery, extortion and related offences
07 Unlawful entry with intent/burglary, break and enter
08 Theft and related offences
09 Deception and related offences
10 Illicit drug offences
11 Weapons and explosives offences
12 Property damage and environmental pollution
13 *Public order offences*
14 Road traffic and motor vehicle regulatory offences
15 Offences against justice procedures, government security and government operations
16 Miscellaneous offences

Level 2
13 **Public order offences**
131 Disorderly Conduct
132 Regulated Public Order Offences

Level 3
13 **Public order offences**
131 *Disorderly Conduct*
    1311   Trespass
    1312   Offensive Language
    1313   Offensive Behaviour
    1314   Criminal Intent
    1315   Conspiracy
    1319   Disorderly Conduct, nec
132 *Regulated Public Order Offences*
    1321   Betting and Gambling Offences
    1322   Liquor and Tobacco Offences
    1323   Censorship Offences
    1324   Prostitution Offences
    1325   Offences Against Public Order Sexual Standards
    1329   Regulated Public Order Offences, nec

Source: ABS, 1997, Australian Standard Offence Classification, catalogue no. 1234.0
Note: nec = not elsewhere classified

some types of open-ended questions, one problem is that people often provide several answers to the one question or the same answer could be coded under two different headings. For example, even though we might have asked only about what people think the major problem will be in ten years' time, a person might nevertheless give three problems. How do you decide which answer to code? One method is to select only the first answer and ignore the rest. But this seems rather arbitrary, and means that valuable information is lost. Another approach is to use a multiple response coding strategy.

The other problem is that the same answer can be coded under several different codes. For example, someone might say that the biggest problem will be 'overpopulation that will lead to greater air pollution and increase the problems of poverty'. This could be coded using a code for overcrowding, a code for air pollution or under a social problems code that relates to poverty. If only one code is allocated, the coder will have to make a decision. This needs to be done in consultation with other coders. Sometimes codes can be allocated according to a preset order of priorities. You might decide that in cases where a response could be allocated both an environmental and some

---

BOX 9.1 *Considerations in level of detail when coding*

1 *What categories make sense?* The theories with which you are working or your reporting needs will suggest sensible and necessary levels of coding.

2 *Comparison with other research:* With what other data will your results be compared? It may be necessary to code to the same level as the other results to enable comparisons.

3 *Sample size:* Does the sample size justify the detailed coding? Will there be so few people in most categories as to make the fine detail of little use?

4 *Data analysis:* How are the data to be analysed? Will analysis require the fine

graded categories to be combined during analysis? If so why code so finely in the first place?

5 *Resources:* How much time and money do you have? Fine coding will normally take longer and cost more than general coding?

6 *Coding error:* The finer the coding scheme the greater the likelihood of coding error.

7 *Computer-assisted coding:* Computer-based coding software exists for some variables (e.g. occupation and industry). Where this is available it may be feasible to code to a fine level quickly, efficiently and accurately.

---

other code, the environmental code will take priority. Clearly this sort of decision can produce distortions in the data and any such policy will depend on the purposes of the survey and needs to be made very clear to readers.

Coding multiple responses to closed questions

Where respondents provide several responses, the best method of coding is to create a set of variables to 'hold' those responses. There are two approaches for developing these variables. Either the multiple dichotomy method or the multiple response method

can be used. The difference between these two methods can be illustrated using a question about the qualities people think are important in children. These qualities are listed in Table 9.2.

We might provide 500 respondents with a list of these qualities and ask them to indicate which two of twelve qualities they felt were most desirable in children. This would provide us with 1000 responses (500 people each giving two responses).

We could develop two sets of variables from this. The first approach is called the *multiple dichotomy method*. This involves creating a separate variable for each of the twelve categories of the question.

Table 9.2   Multiple codes using the multiple dichotomy method

Variable number	Is this quality important?	Yes (code = 1)	No (code = 2)	Total N
1	Good manners	60	440	500
2	Tries hard to succeed	103	397	500
3	Honesty	89	411	500
4	Neatness and cleanliness	213	287	500
5	Good sense and sound judgment	30	470	500
6	Self-control	54	446	500
7	Gets along well with other children	69	431	500
8	Obeys parents	149	351	500
9	Responsibility	21	479	500
10	Considerate	70	430	500
11	Interested in why and how things happen	40	460	500
12	Is a good student	102	398	500

A person will be given a 'yes' code for the two variables (answers) they selected and a 'no' code for the ten variables they did not select. Thus we would develop a variable for 'manners' which would have two categories to indicate whether or not it was selected. Another dichotomous variable would be created for 'tries hard', another for 'honesty' and so forth until we had twelve dichotomous variables. We could then obtain frequency distributions for each variable to see how often it was selected.

The alternative approach is to use the *multiple response method*. Instead of creating a separate variable for each category of the question, we would create only two variables into which we would place a respondent's two choices. Each of these two variables would have twelve categories to reflect each of the possible choices. Thus the variables might be called 'choice 1' and 'choice 2' (see Table 9.3).

Regardless of which way we code the answers, we record the same number of people giving each response. The difference is in the way we break the answers up into variables and in the codes we give each of these variables.

Multiple responses to open questions

Open questions can often produce multiple responses that require the creation of several variables to capture the responses. A survey of recently divorced people might ask respondents what they feel were the main factors that contributed to their marital breakdown. No doubt many people will list a variety of factors.

When coding responses it will normally be best to construct a number of variables into which to code responses. We still have to choose between the multiple dichotomy approach and the multiple response method. Which approach is chosen will depend on the number of different answers that are given and on the particular focus of the study. If there are a large number of factors given, this could lead to a very large and cumbersome number of dichotomous variables.

In such cases it might be best to use the multiple response method. This would involve finding the case with the largest number of factors listed and creating that many variables. Each of these variables will have the same number of identical codes. Each person will then be given a code on each of the variables.

For example, the largest number of factors that any respondent listed might be five. Accordingly we would create five variables that we might call factor 1, factor 2, factor 3, factor 4 and factor 5. We would then develop an exhaustive list of factors given and give each of those factors a unique code. We might find 25 different factors listed over all the respondents. Thus we might give alcohol a code of 1, unfaithfulness a code of 2, financial pressures a code of 3, violence a code of 4 and so forth (see Figure 9.2). The same set of codes would be used for each of the five variables (factor 1 to factor 5). The first case we come across might list only one factor—alcohol—so that case would receive a code of 1 on the factor 1 variable and a missing value code on the remaining four variables. The second case might list three factors—violence, alcohol and unfaithfulness. They would be given a code of 4 on factor 1, 1 on factor 2, 2 on factor 3 and a missing value code on factor 4 and factor 5. The third case might only mention parental interference and financial pressures, and would thus be coded as 25 on factor 1, 3 on factor 2 and 99 on the remaining variables (see Figure 9.2).

Using the multiple response approach can lead to some difficulties with analysis. If we wanted to find out how many people gave a particular response (e.g. violence), we would have to look at the information contained in five variables. For any

Table 9.3 Multiple codes using the multiple response method

Code		Variable 1 (Choice 1)	Variable 2 (Choice 2)
1	Good manners	40	20
2	Tries hard to succeed	65	38
3	Honesty	32	57
4	Neatness and cleanliness	108	105
5	Good sense and sound judgment	4	26
6	Self-control	30	24
7	Gets along well with other children	20	49
8	Obeys parents	60	89
9	Responsibility	3	18
10	Considerate	42	28
11	Interested in why and how things happen	8	32
12	Is a good student	88	14
	Total N	500	500

List of codes

Code	Response
1	Alcohol
2	Unfaithfulness
3	Financial pressures
4	Violence
. . .	. . .
25	Parental interference
99	No answer

Case 1:
Alcohol

Case 2:
Violence
Alcohol
Unfaithfulness

Case 3:
Parental interference
Financial pressures

Coded cases

	Factor 1	Factor 2	Factor 3	Factor 4	Factor 5
Case 1	01	99	99	99	99
Case 2	04	01	02	99	99
Case 3	25	03	99	99	99
. . .	. . .	. . .	. . .	. . .	. . .

Figure 9.2   Coding multiple responses to an open question

given person, this cause could have been coded into any of the five variables. One way of analysing data coded in this way is to use a *multiple response analysis* from statistical analysis programs such as SPSS, Statistica or Simstat (see Web Pointer 9.2). This provides a way of analysing responses to all five multiple response variables at the same time. (It counts across all the variables and adds up how many times a given response is given over all the variables.) This method is useful for relatively simple analysis such as frequencies and cross-tabulations (see Chapter 14), but is of no use for the more advanced multivariate techniques and makes the calculation of summary statistics such as correlations impossible. If a particular factor (e.g. violence) is to be the focus of the analysis and multivariate analysis and summary statistics (e.g. correlations) are required, multiple dichotomies would be used rather than multiple responses.

Coding numerical data

For some variables such as age, income, number of children and so on, people's answers are already in numerical form so it is not necessary to convert these answers into codes. We can simply code the exact answers. Thus if someone is 39 years old we would simply give them the code 39. Often people are asked to tick a particular income or age category (e.g. 25–35; 36–45). In these cases it is best to give people a code which represents the midpoint of the category. Thus for someone in the category 36–45 we could code them as 40.

Coding missing data

Each variable for each case should have a code even if a person does not answer a question. These codes are called missing data codes and are coded in the same way as normal, valid responses. The main thing

---

WEB POINTER 9.2   *Multiple response analysis*

Discussion and explanation

Go to the statsoft site at:

   www.statsoftinc.com/textbook/stbasic.html#Multiple responses-dichotomies

and select the last entry in the table of contents 'Multiple response/dichotomies'.

This section shows how multiple responses and multiple dichotomies are analysed.

Software

STATISTICA software also performs multiresponse analysis. A demonstration version of statistica can be downloaded from the statsoft site at:

   www.statsoft.com/download.html

SIMSTAT is a very versatile package that can be downloaded for evaluation and purchased for a reasonable price (also special priced student edition):

   www.simstat.com/

---

to ensure when working out how to code missing data is to allocate a distinctive code for missing data. That is, make sure that the code you allocate is different from a valid code (i.e. one which represents an actual answer to the question).

Since there are different reasons why people do not answer questions, different codes are often given to different types of missing data. There are four main types of non-response to questions.

1   The respondent was not required to answer the question (e.g. a question asking about the ages of someone's children would not be appropriate to someone who had already indicated that they have no children).
2   Not ascertained: maybe the interviewer missed the question, or the respondent missed it, or it was not clear what someone's answer was.
3   The respondent refused to answer.
4   The respondent did not know the answer or did not have an opinion. Sometimes this response is treated as a valid response while on other occasions the researcher will want to treat it as missing data.

It may be desirable to give a different missing data code to each of these different types of non-response. There are no set rules about what particular codes should be allocated to missing data as long as the missing data code will not be confused with a

valid code. Which codes are 'available' for missing data depends on how many valid codes there are for the question. If 'available', −1, 0 or 9 are often used. It is desirable (but not always possible) to give the same missing data code to as many variables as possible to avoid confusion and make computer programming simpler.

ALLOCATING COLUMN NUMBERS TO EACH VARIABLE

To enter codes onto a computer they must be put on a *record*. In the early days of computing a record was a computer card that could contain up to 80 digits. If more than 80 digits were required for all the respondent's answers a second card or record would be used for that *case*. These days with electronic recording of data a record can be much longer than 80 columns. The records for each case are then placed together in a *data file* in which the first record represents the first respondent, the next record represents the second respondent and so forth.

It is still useful to think of how many columns a variable will need to be allocated on a record. To work out how many columns need to be allocated for coding a variable simply identify the highest possible code for the variable and count the number of digits that this code contains. If the highest code has only one digit (i.e. any number from 0–9) only one column is required. A two-digit code (10–99) requires two columns; a three-digit number (100–999) requires three columns, and so forth.

If unsure how many columns will be needed (e.g. with an open-ended question), play safe and allocate more columns than needed—empty columns do not matter. Make sure that you anticipate your missing data codes when working out what the highest code will be. If we have allocated, say, two columns for a variable but a particular code only needs one column we must ensure that we right justify the codes. Thus if we have two columns (e.g. columns 6–7) in which to place a code of 4 we should code this as 04 not as 4 blank (i.e. 04 not 4).

When entering codes from a questionnaire onto a person's computer record it is best to place the code for a particular record in the same place (columns) for each case. For example, we might put the code for 'paid job' in column 5 for each case, 'type of work' in columns 6–7 and so forth (see Figures 9.3 and 9.4). To avoid confusion, and to assist data entry operators, columns are allocated for each variable before questionnaires are printed. This enables the printing of the columns in which a variable is to be coded on the questionnaire (see Figure 9.3) and means that data entry operators can enter data onto the computer straight from the questionnaire. Normally, the right-hand margin of the questionnaire is reserved for this purpose: next to the question the columns allocated to that variable are printed and beside that are spots in which the code for that question can be written by a coder. The data entry operator can then just look down this margin, enter the codes into the computer and keep a constant check that they are entering the codes in the correct columns. In electronic questionnaires these columns are not visible but will be programmed into the questionnaire and used by the program when automatically building a database for the responses.

When allocating codes in a questionnaire allocate columns to variables sequentially. Thus allocate the first column(s) to the first variable (question) in the questionnaire, the next columns to the next question and so on. In the example in Figure 9.3, four columns have been allocated for identification numbers thus allowing up to 9999 different identity codes to be used. For a sample of more than 9999 people, more columns would be allocated for identification numbers.

IDENT	1–4
Do you currently have a paid job? Yes □ 1 No □ 2	5
What kind of work do you do?	6–7
How old are you?	8–9
Generally speaking how would you describe your political views? Traditional □ 1 Middle of the road □ 2 Progressive □ 3 Other □ 4	10
How do you feel about the government's current immigration policy?	11–12
Are you: Male □ 1 Female □ 2	13
Are you currently: Married □ 1 Never married □ 2 Divorced □ 3 Separated □ 4 Widowed □ 5 Other □ 6	14

Figure 9.3 Example of allocating codes and coding columns in a questionnaire

Columns	1	2	3	4	5	6	7	8	9	10	11	12	13	14
Case 1	0	0	0	1	1	0	1	3	9	1	0	4	1	3
Case 2	0	0	0	2	2	9	9	2	5	3	0	9	1	2
Case 3	0	0	0	3	1	1	5	5	4	1	0	6	2	5

Figure 9.4 Three records of a data file for questions in Figure 9.3

Figure 9.4 illustrates records for the first three cases in a data file for the variables from the questions in Figure 9.3. For each case the same information is coded in the same columns of a given record. Thus on each record 1 we have an identification number in columns 1–4, one (0001,0002); age is in columns 8–9 and so forth. Thus for each case we know that the codes in particular columns represent a person's response to a particular question. This data file has the same structure as the variable by case grid described in Chapter 1.

PRODUCING A CODEBOOK

Having decided how to code each response to each question, it is important to make a systematic record of all the decisions made. This record is called a *codebook* and the following information is normally included (see Figure 9.5).

1 The exact wording of the question.
2 A name by which the variable is referred to in the program. In the codebook list the name given to each variable.
3 The type of data that is used for that variable. Is it numeric, alphanumeric (often called *string variables* and consisting of letters rather than numbers), currency, a date or some other format?
4 The first and last column numbers in which the variable is located.
5 The valid codes for each question.
6 The missing data codes for each question.
7 Any special coding instructions used for coding particular questions.

CHECKING FOR CODING ERRORS

Coding errors can create serious problems during data analysis. The most serious error is if data are entered in the wrong columns for some cases. But miscodes are a more common problem. These can occur during the data collection phase, during manual coding of answers or during the data entry phase. It is probably impossible to eliminate all coding errors but the problem can be reduced by locating and correcting as many errors as possible.

The task of locating and correcting incorrect

codes can be both tedious and time consuming but must be done. Three main checks should be made.

Valid range checks

For any variable there are only certain codes which are legitimate either as valid codes or as missing data codes. Any code outside this range indicates a wrong code and needs to be corrected. For example, if a code of 6 was found for the question in Figure 9.5 this would be a wrong code. This problem can be identified at the data entry stage if a computer-based data entry program that will only accept answers within a pre-specified range is used. Computer-based questionnaires can also prevent this problem at the data collection stage by the same method. A final check can be made by obtaining frequency distributions of all variables and checking that all codes are within the expected range.

Filter checks

If contingency questions are used, some questions should only be answered by certain people depending on how they answered a previous question. For example, someone who said they had no paid job should not answer questions about their job satisfaction. Invalid responses can be detected by cross-tabulating the paid job answers with the job satisfaction answers (see Chapter 14). Checks also can be built into computer-based data collection and be used with smart data entry programs.

Logical checks

Certain sets of responses will be illogical. The above is one sort but others can occur. For example, if someone's age is coded as 50 it seems illogical if the age of their eldest child is coded at 48. Detecting these sorts of illogical codes takes a lot of time and requires careful thinking about illogical combinations of codes.

It is tempting to avoid a lot of this checking: it is time consuming and often finds relatively few mistakes. In my view it is still worth doing. Certainly the most important stages are in initial coding when it is best to draw up a codebook carefully and know beforehand how answers are to be coded, but it is also important to use experienced data entry operators who use data-checking procedures. Many researchers require *double entry data entry* that requires that once all the data have been entered they are entered again. During the second entry the codes are

Q1:	Do you currently have a paid job?
Variable name:	PJOB
Column:	5
Data type:	Numeric
Valid codes:	1 Yes
	2 No
Missing values:	0 Inappropriate
	9 Not ascertained
Coding instructions:	If respondent helps spouse in jobs (e.g. on a farm, bookkeeping etc but is not specifically paid, code as having paid work).

Figure 9.5   An example of a codebook entry for a single question

---

WEB POINTER 9.3　*Online codebooks and manuals*

Australian Election Survey	http://ssda.anu.edu.au/SSDA/CODEBOOKS/ AES98/contents.html
General Social Survey: The GSS codebook provides an alternative format to that of the Election Survey	www.icpsr.umich.edu/GSS99/subject/ s-index.htm
US National Health Interview Survey	ftp://ftp.cdc.gov/pub/Health_Statistics/NCHS/ Dataset_Documentation/NHIS/1998/
An excellent manual on codebook construction and data file construction	www.icpsr.umich.edu/ACCESS/dpm.html

Visit www.social-research.org to use these links and to check for updates and additions.

---

automatically matched with those entered the first time. Inconsistencies can then be resolved on the spot.

ENTERING DATA

In the past data were always coded manually and entered into the computer by keypunch operators. However advances in computer technology have radically changed the whole process of data entry. There are now three main data entry methods.

Manual data entry
This remains a common method. Three common methods of manual data entry are:

1 Spreadsheet packages such as EXCEL—each column can be defined as a variable and each row as a case. Columns can be set to accept only certain types of data (e.g. numeric).
2 Database packages such as ACCESS—data entry forms can be set up that simulate the questionnaire and accept only preset types of data and a preset range of values for each variable.
3 Specialised data entry programs such as SPSS Data Entry.

Scanning
This method requires that a printed questionnaire be set up in such a way that the completed question-

naire can be optically scanned using optical mark recognition (OMR) technology. OMR methods require that respondents or interviewers indicate their answers by shading boxes with a pencil. The OMR scanner reads the questionnaire and is set up so that shaded boxes in particular locations on the page are automatically coded and placed in a database.

This method of data entry can work well so long as respondents or interviewers carefully follow the somewhat fiddly instructions. Incorrect completion of questionnaires can require a lot of corrective and data cleaning work. This method can enter data quickly if all goes well but should still be adopted only after careful consideration and pilot testing work.

More recent developments in imaging and optical character recognition (OCR) hold more promise than OMR. Dillman (2000) reviews these developments and assesses their viability and implications for the way questionnaires are designed.

Automatic data entry
CAPI, CATI, email and web-based questionnaires eliminate the data entry stage altogether. Coding is done automatically and answers are automatically entered into a database. By eliminating the manual data coding and data entry steps this process can reduce coding error but error can still occur at the data collection stage and during questionnaire programming.

In the table below please put the age and sex of each of your brothers and sisters in the order in which they come in your family. Put yourself in the table too and indicate which person you are by an asterisk (*).

Position	1st	2nd	3rd	4th	5th	6th	7th	8th	9th
Sex									
Age									

Figure 9.6   A multivariable question

ISSUES THAT COMPLICATE CODING

While a single question in a questionnaire is often a single variable this need not be so. Depending on the structure of the question and the number of responses that can be given to the question a single question might contain information for a number of different variables. With each question we need to carefully consider whether it is a single or multivariable question. If it is a multivariable question we need to delineate what each variable is, work out how each will be coded and allocate computer columns for each of the variables.

Figure 9.6 provides a question in which respondents are asked to record information about their brothers and sisters. In this question there are a large number of possible variables: the number of siblings someone has, the number of brothers, the number of sisters, the respondent's position in the family, the age gaps between siblings, the number of same sex siblings and so on. Depending on which of these variables are of interest, codes and columns will need to be allocated accordingly.

There are other questions which are in fact multivariable questions. For example, where someone is allowed to tick more than one response to a question, each possible response becomes a variable to which people are effectively answering yes (by ticking) or no (by not ticking). In the question in Figure 9.7 each possible response would be a separate variable and would have to be allocated a separate column (see earlier discussion of multiple dichotomies).

Another complexity when coding is the opposite of the above: instead of extracting several variables from the one question several questions can be used to establish the code on one variable. Scaling is one example (see Chapter 11) of this but there are others. For instance, when trying to code someone's social status we will not rely on just one

Within the last year have you helped your mother in any of the following ways? (tick all that are appropriate)

Loaned or given money (over $200)	[ ]
Helped during illness	[ ]
Provided comfort in difficult times	[ ]
Given valuable gifts (over $200)	[ ]
Given a hand when needed	[ ]

Figure 9.7   Another type of multivariable question

characteristic of a person but a particular mix. If we were using only occupation to establish social status how would we code this for a married woman since in our society a married woman tends to take on the status of her husband? It would be misleading to code the status of a woman who did some part-time clerical work but was married to a doctor as having clerical status. We could give married women their husband's occupation status score. But is this accurate? What if a woman had a higher status job than her husband—how would we code this? The aim here is not to resolve these problems but to point out that often a code can involve a mix of information contained in various questions. Often we can just code each question individually and use the computer to create a new variable out of all the pieces of information (refer to Chapter 10). But where *judgment* is involved it is often not possible or it is very difficult to do this by computer. Therefore judgment coding is best done before data entry.

CODING CHECKLIST

1   Can variables be precoded?
2   Which precoding schemes will be used?

3 How will open-ended questions be coded? Will you:
  a develop your own classifications;
  b use a standard classification?
4 How will the coding be done?
  a manually?
  b automatically?
5 Has the questionnaire been formatted to facilitate this coding? Does it contain:
  a actual codes next to responses;
  b space in which to write codes;
  c column numbers for codes?
6 Who will code? What arrangements have been made for
  a coder training;
  b establishing inter-coder consistency;
  c a coding manual and record of coding decisions?

7 How will the coded data be entered into a data file?
  a Manually? If so by whom? By specialist data entry personnel?
  b Scanning? Has the questionnaire been set up properly for this and piloted?
  c Automatic? If so how will this programming be done and checked?
8 What checks have you put in place to reduce coding error?
  a Coder training and manuals?
  b Automatic checks in data entry templates or electronic questionnaires?
  c Will double data entry be used?
  d At the preliminary data analysis stage?

KEY CONCEPTS

Codebook	Multilevel classification scheme	Multiple response coding	Standardised classification scheme
Coding			
Computer column	Multiple dichotomy response coding	Postcoding	Valid range check
Filter check		Precoding	
Logic checking		Record	

FURTHER READING

There are few comprehensive treatments of coding. Each of the following references provides useful chapters which are very readable. Perhaps the best are Warwick and Lininger, *The Sample Survey: Theory and Practice* (1975), Chapter 9 and Moser and Kalton's *Survey Methods in Social Investigation* (1971), Chapter 16. Babbie's discussion in Chapter 13 of *The Practice of Social Research* (1995) is very down to earth and Hoinville and Jowell's *Survey Research Practice* (1977), Chapter 8 covers similar material. Bateson's *Data Construction in Social Surveys* (1984) approaches the issue of coding from a more theoretical perspective and highlights the theoretical rather than technical issues involved.

'The Guide to Good Coding Practice' of the UK Market Research Society (1983) provides practical advice for coders. Orwin's 1994 chapter 'Evaluating Coding Decisions' provides a very useful discussion of sources and types of coding error and provides sensible strategies for minimising coding errors. Fielding (1995) provides advice for coding both open and closed questions while Montgomery and Crittenden (1977) deals with the issues in reliably coding open-ended questions. Hak (1997) considers problems with open coding in comparative international research and stresses the need for consistent coder training.

Lyberg et al. (1997) provide a collection of very good but more technical papers, many of which deal with coding issues in their edited collection *Survey Measurement and Process Quality.*

EXERCISES

1 For an earlier exercise on questionnaire design you will have developed a short questionnaire. Develop a full codebook for this questionnaire.

2 Ask a wide range of people an open-ended question (e.g. what do you think of university?) and develop a coding scheme from the answers given.

3   Formulate one closed-choice multivariable questionnaire item. Then identify the variables that you would create to represent the answers to this question. Construct these variables using both the multiple dichotomy method and the multiple response method.

4   Under what circumstances would you precode questions?

5   What are the advantages and disadvantages of precoding?

6   Explain, with examples, how you would check that data have been coded and entered onto the computer correctly.

7   You have used an open-ended question in a survey asking people about the conditions under which they believe that capital punishment is justifiable. Imagine that no-one listed more than four different conditions, but overall there were ten different situations mentioned by various respondents. For the purpose of this exercise you will need to imagine what these ten conditions might be (it does not matter what conditions you come up with). Show how you would go about coding the responses to this question using both the multiple dichotomies method and the multiple response method of coding.

8   a   Use the occupational coding scheme located at:
www.abs.gov.au/ausstats/abs@.nsf/
        StatsLibrary?OpenView
then select link to <u>ABS classifications</u> and select catalogue 1220.0.
        Using this coding scheme what codes would you give to the following occupations?
    ■   youth worker (6 digit code) Look in the Associate professionals classification
    ■   process worker (3 digits)
    ■   psychiatrist (6 digits)
    ■   personal assistant.

    b   Go to the site
www.abs.gov.au/ausstats/abs@.nsf/
        StatsLibrary?OpenView
then select the link to <u>ABS classifications</u> and select catalogue 1234.0 and provide first, second and third level codes for the following offences:
    ■   manslaughter
    ■   dangerous or negligent driving
    ■   cheque or credit card fraud.

10

Preparing variables for analysis

This chapter outlines four main steps in preparing data for analysis. These are:

1 changing, collapsing and reordering the categories of variables;
2 creating new variables from existing ones;
3 standardising variables to enable better comparisons; and
4 dealing with missing data.

Preparing variables for analysis is one of the most time-consuming parts of data analysis. Once variables have been modified in the ways outlined below, the main data analysis in which propositions are tested can be remarkably simple and quick. However, in reality, not all the processes outlined in this chapter will be completed before the main data analysis is conducted. As initial results are examined, further ideas about how we can refine our analysis by better recoding and creating new variables will emerge.

Before modifying variables using the approaches described below be sure to do two things. First, return to the original concepts, research questions and theoretical models you have developed. To use the concepts implied by the research questions and models the data must be organised in such a way that these concepts are appropriately measured for the final analysis.

Second, familiarise yourself with the data before modifying it. It is best, at this point, to obtain a frequency table for each variable (see Chapter 13 on frequency tables). Not only does this provide a final check to ensure that all the codes are within the valid range, it also provides a first look at some of the characteristics of the sample and the sorts of responses that have been given. We can get an idea of the shape of the distributions on key variables and note which variables have very little variation, which categories have almost no cases and so forth. Being familiar with the data is helpful in guiding the subsequent data preparation steps.

Before reading the next section stop and turn to pp. 203–6 and read about *levels of measurement* of variables. The discussion that follows relies on an understanding of levels of measurement.

CHANGING CATEGORIES

Initial decisions about the number of categories are made when constructing the questionnaire and when postcoding open-ended data (see Chapter 9). However you will frequently need to refine these codes subsequently. Computer programs make it very easy to collapse and change codes.

There are a variety of ways in which the categories of variables may need changing.

Collapsing categories

Frequently the initial coding of a variable results in more categories than we require or can accommodate for data analysis. For example, when coding a question about country of birth we might have allocated a separate code for each country but for analysis purposes need only to distinguish between industrialised and non-industrialised countries or between broad categories of countries (e.g. North America, Central and South America, Australasia, South-East Asia, Middle East, Northern Europe, Southern Europe etc). Many of the detailed standard coding schemes (refer to Chapter 9) contain more detail than most of us are likely to require. The advantage of the initial detail is that it provides the flexibility to enable us to collapse the categories in a variety of different ways.

There are a number of reasons why it is often desirable to collapse categories of variables.

1   The detailed coding may not reflect the form of the variable which is relevant to the research problem. As such recoding can be used to create a new version of the variable. For example, we might recode detailed occupational codes into simply blue-collar and white-collar categories. Or we might have asked people how they feel about the gun control and initially have coded responses as 1 = strongly favour controls; 2 = moderately favour; 3 = mildly against; 4 = strongly against controls. If we wanted to use this question to measure not whether people were for or against gun control but to measure *strength* of feeling on gun control we would combine codes 1 and 4 (strong opinion) and combine codes 2 and 3 (more ambivalent).

2   For analysis in which cross-tabulations or frequency tables (see Chapters 13 and 14) are used it is extremely helpful to avoid using variables with a lot of categories. The more categories, the more difficult a table is to read; I try to keep to a maximum of six or seven categories for cross-tabulations. However, the enthusiasm to enhance readability by 'compressing' a variable must be tempered by commonsense. Avoid collapsing a variable so much that it becomes too crude for the research question being addressed.

3   If there are very few people in a category it can be worth combining the category with another suitable category. Very low frequencies can produce misleading tables and statistics.

4   Elaborating bivariate relationships (refer to Chapter 16) involves selecting a variable and dividing the sample into separate subgroups—one for each category of the selected variable. If this variable has a lot of categories it becomes extremely difficult to undertake reliable and interpretable analysis.

5   Collapsing categories can highlight patterns in the data that might otherwise not stand out. However, you should not collapse categories simply to create the appearance of a relationship. There should always be a sound justification for the way categories are combined. Table 10.1 provides an illustration of recoding a variable in a justifiable way to highlight but not create a relationship between two variables.

On the other hand we need to be careful not to recode in such a way as to mask a relationship as is illustrated in Table 10.2.

Of course collapsing categories is not always necessary. Many methods of analysis do not benefit from this—especially those methods designed for numeric, interval-level variables (see Chapters 15 and 17).

Approaches to collapsing categories

There are two main approaches to working out which categories should be combined.

The substantive approach

This approach involves combining categories that seem to fit together: the categories have something in common. Working out which categories go together is normally a matter of commonsense: if you cannot give a sensible name to the combined category then it is probably a meaningless category. Which categories go together depends in part on the purposes for which you are using the variable. For example, occupations could be collapsed into industry-based categories so that all jobs associated with a particular industry are grouped together into broad categories (e.g. health, natural science, transport, agriculture, construction etc). Alternatively, occupations could be collapsed into prestige groupings so that those with highest prestige are

Table 10.1 Relationship between education and gender (uncollapsed and collapsed form)

	Uncollapsed					Collapsed	
	Male	Female				Male	Female
Completed university	13	7					
Other tertiary	7	6		At least some tertiary		40	27
Some university	20	14					
Trade	16	21		Trade		16	21
Completed secondary	22	5		Completed secondary		22	5
Some secondary	17	39		Some secondary or less			
Primary only	5	8				22	47
N	244	243				244	243

Table 10.2 An illustration of how recoding can mask a relationship

	Unrecoded version				Recoded version	
	Male	Female			Male	Female
Strongly agree	50%	15%		Agree	60%	60%
Agree	10	45				
Disagree	30	5				
Strongly disagree	10	35		Disagree	40	40
N	500	500	N		500	500
Gamma = 0.37				Gamma = 0.00		

combined in one group, those with moderately high prestige in another group and so forth. Or occupations could be classified according to the amount of training involved so that those which require a degree are put in one category, those requiring a diploma in another and so on. When collapsing categories make sure that you do not collapse them in such a way that nearly everyone ends up in the same category.

With ordinal and interval variables which have ranked categories, collapsing is mainly a matter of establishing cutting points along a continuum. Using the substantive approach we might divide an eleven-point scale (0–10) into three groups so that approximately the same number of *codes* are collapsed into each category (see Table 10.3).

The distributional approach

This approach is restricted to recoding variables where the categories or values have a natural order from low to high—that is, ordinal and interval-level variables (see 'levels of measurement' section in Chapter 12).

Often the meaning of a particular response to a question is best interpreted in *relative* than in *absolute* terms. For example, how are we to regard the income level of a person who earns $30 000 a year: is this low, medium or high? It depends on the other incomes with which it is compared. If most people earn less then it is *relatively* high; if most earn more it may be *relatively* low. We can classify a particular value of a variable as high or low depending on the values of other people in the sample. This approach to collapsing categories has the advantage of letting the data define what is low, medium or high rather than us imposing some external, unrealistic definition.

Recoding according to the distribution of the variable involves dividing the sample up into roughly equal sized groups of *cases*. This involves selecting *cutting points* on the variable that achieve the subdivision into equal sized groups of cases. Dividing the sample into two equal sized groups is called

Table 10.3 Illustration of collapsing a variable into three groups using substantive and distributional recoding methods

Question: On a scale of 0 to 10 how would you rate your marriage where 0 is terrible and 10 is excellent?

	Substantive recoding	Score	%	Cumulative %	Distributional recoding
Terrible	The bottom third of codes	0	3	3	Bottom third of cases. Relatively most unhappy.
		1	5	8 (3 + 5)	
		2	3	11 (8 + 3)	
		3	4	15 (11 + 4)	
	Middle third of codes	4	7	22 (15 + 7)	
		5	10	32 (22 + 10)	
		6	9	41 (32 + 9)	The relatively 'in between' cases.
	Top third of codes	7	10	51 (41 + 10)	
		8	15	66 (51 + 15)	
		9	15	81 (66 + 15)	Top third of cases. Relatively
Excellent		10	19	100 (81 + 19)	the most happy third.

dichotomising. Dividing it into three equal sized groups is called *trichotomising.* Box 10.1 lists the steps required to trichotomise a variable.

To divide the variable into a different number of groups we would simply select different cutting points using the cumulative per cent column. To dichotomise (two groups) simply select the code that is closest to the 50 cumulative percentage. To divide into four groups use the codes that correspond to the 25, 50 and 75 cumulative percentage figures.

Notice that in Table 10.3 the *sample* has been divided into approximately three equal groups as opposed to dividing the *categories of the variable* into three equal lots (0–3, 4–6 and 7–10). Dividing the sample rather than the categories into three equal-sized groups avoids ending up with categories that include very few people.

Rearranging categories

Rather than collapsing the number of categories we may simply want to rearrange them into a more logical order. Arranging categories in a logical order can have the effect of:

■ creating an order more appropriate to the focus of the analysis;
■ making tables easier to read;
■ changing the level of measurement of a variable and thus affecting the methods of analysis that can be applied to the variable.

We may have a variable indicating the industry in which a person works. Table 10.4 lists the initial order of industry categories. There is no obvious order to these categories. However we might be undertaking analysis that is focusing on unionisation in the workplace and its impact on job satisfaction. For this analysis it might make sense to organise the industry categories according to the level of unionisation of the industry. This would provide a logical order to the categories and probably make it easier to read tables later on. Table 10.4 indicates the way in which the variable might be recoded to reflect the unionisation of the industry.

Table 10.5a provides an example of a variable in which the placement of the 'No qualifications' category is inappropriate. Since all the other categories are ordered from highest to lowest qualifications the placement of no qualifications next to postgraduate qualifications is incongruous. Table 10.5b presents a reordered version of the same variable.

Reordering in this way changes the level of measurement of the variable from nominal to ordinal. A nominal variable is one where the categories are not ranked in any sense while an ordinal variable has categories that are rank ordered (see Chapter 12 on levels of measurement). By changing the position of the 'No qualifications' category we have changed the level of measurement of this variable. In so doing we have increased

---

BOX 10.1
Steps in trichotomising a variable using the distributional approach to recoding

1 Ensure that the variable is either ordinal or interval-level.

2 Decide on the number of categories into which the sample (and variable) is to be subdivided.

3 If three categories are required (e.g. low, medium and high) divide the sample into the third with the lowest scores, the middle third, and the top third with the highest scores.

4 Obtain a frequency table of the variable.

5 Examine the cumulative percentage column (see Table 10.3 and Chapter 13 on frequency tables).

6 Locate the cumulative percentage closest to 33 per cent (this gives the bottom third of cases).

7 Then look across to the code or value that corresponds to this cumulative percentage. All people who obtained this code or lower will be placed in one category of the recoded variable. This group will represent the 'low' group.

8 Locate the cumulative percentage closest to 67 per cent to select the middle third. The code or value that corresponds to the 67th per cent figure in the cumulative percentage column provides the cutting point between the 'middle' and 'high' groups.

9 The remaining cases (those above the 67 per cent mark) will constitute the top third of cases—the 'high' group (see Table 10.3).

10 In the example in Table 10.3 we would recode the variable so that codes

 ◼ 0 to 5 = low (poor)

 ◼ 6 to 8 = middle (moderate)

 ◼ 9,10 = high (excellent).

11 Use a computer program to apply the recode. In SPSS the instruction would be:

RECODE   varname (0 thru 5=1)
(6 thru 8=2)(9,10=3).

VALUE LABELS   varname 1 'Poor';
2 'Moderate'; 3 'Good'.

Table 10.4   Rearranging categories into a logical order appropriate to project

(a) Original version			(b) Revised version		
Code	Industry	% in unions	New code	Industry	% in unions
1	Agriculture, forestry and fishing	15	1	Agriculture, forestry and fishing	15
2	Mining	54	2	Wholesale and retail	18
3	Manufacturing	40	3	Construction	37
4	Electricity, gas and water	59	4	Manufacturing	40
5	Construction	37	5	Mining	54
6	Wholesale and retail	18	6	Electricity, gas and water	59

the range and power of the statistical methods that can be applied to this variable. Chapters 12–17 show how the level of measurement of variables fundamentally affects the choice of methods of analysis.

Reverse coding

Sometimes even though the categories of a variable are rank ordered they are ordered in the *opposite* way to that which is required. For example, we may prefer to order the categories of the qualifications variable in Table 10.5b from lowest qualification to highest

Table 10.5 Reordering categories of a variable

(a) Original version

Highest qualification obtained since leaving school

	Frequency	Valid per cent	Cumulative per cent
1 No qualification	*588*	*33*	*33*
2 Postgraduate degree	132	7	41
3 Bachelor degree	193	11	52
4 Undergraduate diploma	68	4	56
5 Associate diploma	132	7	63
6 Trade qualification	403	23	86
7 Non-trade qualification	247	14	100
Total	1763	100	
System missing	134		
Total	1897		

(b) Reordered version

Highest qualification obtained since leaving school

	Frequency	Valid per cent	Cumulative per cent
1 Postgraduate	132	7	7
2 Bachelor degree	193	11	18
3 Undergraduate diploma	68	4	22
4 Associate diploma	132	7	30
5 Trade qualification	403	23	53
6 Non-trade qualification	247	14	67
7 No qualification	*588*	*33*	*100*
Total	1763	100	
System missing	134		
Total	1897		

BOX 10.2
Maximising the level of measurement of variables

■ The higher the level of measurement of variables the greater the range and power of the statistical methods that can be used.

■ In general it is preferable to maximise the level of measurement of a variable.

■ Nominal level variables have the lowest level of measurement followed by ordinal and then interval-level variables.

■ See Chapter 12 for a fuller discussion.

---

qualifications. A more common reason for reversing the order of categories is when constructing a scale (see Chapter 11). A scale is a composite measure of a concept that is created by examining a person's responses to a set of questions and then combining answers into a single composite measure of the underlying concept. For example, we might ask a number of questions about a person's political attitudes and use these to construct a single summary measure of how right wing or left wing the person is.

Before such a measure can be created each of the variables that contribute to the composite measure should be scored in the same direction. That is, a high score on each variable must mean the same thing. However, when constructing questionnaire items for

a scale it is normal to mix up the direction of the statements to which people respond: some will be positive while others will be negative (see Chapters 7 and 11). Thus in a political orientation scale agreement with some statements might indicate a left-wing outlook while agreement with others will reflect a right-wing outlook.

Where we want to combine variables that are coded in different directions we need to reverse code some variables so that they are all coded in the same direction. This involves:

■ deciding what you want a high code on each variable to mean (e.g. high code = left wing);
■ selecting items where the coding is opposite to that which you require;
■ reverse code these variables.

The logic of reverse coding is illustrated in Table 10.6. In this example the item has 5 values (1, 2, 3, 4, 5) that require reversing to the values indicated in the new code column.

This reverse coding can be achieved with the following SPSS syntax but similar syntax would be used with many other programs.

Table 10.6 Reverse coding

Original code	New code
1	5
2	4
3	3
4	2
5	1

> *General form of the recode command*
> Recode   *varname to be reverse coded* (initial value=new value) (*initial value=new value*) etc.
>
> *Example*
> Recode   POL1 (1=5)(2=4)(3=3)(4=2)(5=1).

Alternatively the following syntax is easier, especially when the variable to be reverse coded has a lot of values (e.g. 10 or 100) where 'Highvalue' is the maximum possible valid code of the initial variable. In this case the highvalue is 5.

> *General form of the recode*
> Compute   *NEWVAR = (Highvalue of OLDVAR + 1) − OLDVAR.*
>
> *Example*
> Compute   NEWPOL1 = (5 + 1) − POLVIEW1.

This transformation produces a new variable (NEWPOL1) and a new value on this variable for each person. The value for each person would be computed by subtracting their code on the initial variable from 6 (i.e. highvalue + 1). Thus all people with an initial code of 5 would obtain a new code of 1 (i.e. (5 + 1) − 5 = 1); those with an initial score of 4 would be recoded to a score of 2 (i.e. 6 − 4 = 2) and so on. If the initial variable was scored on a scale of 1 to 100 the transformation would be:

Compute   NEWVAR=101−OLDVAR.

In one simple step this would reverse code all 100 values of the original variable.

CREATING NEW VARIABLES

As well as recoding variables, new variables can be created from existing ones by using information from a set of questions. In this way some very useful and sophisticated variables can be developed. Normally this is done in one of three ways:

1   developing scales (techniques of scaling and the purpose of scales will be discussed in Chapter 11);

2   using conditional transformations;
3   using arithmetic transformations.

Conditional transformations

This approach to creating variables involves specifying a new variable and its categories and then specifying the conditions a person must meet to be placed in a given category. This is best explained with an example.

Suppose that in a study of marriages we want to create a variable that reflects the marital history of both husband and wife. The survey has asked about the marital history of the husband and the wife separately but we want to create a new variable that combines this information into a single variable.

The new variable is created by classifying people according to the conditions they meet on the two base variables. Creating variables in this way is achieved by examining the *codes* (1 or 2) on each of the constituent variables (HMAR and WMAR) and creating a new variable (MTYPE) with categories based on various combinations of the codes. In this case we would create three categories for MTYPE: (1) first-timer marriage; (2) mixture; (3) both previously married (refer to Table 10.7).

The creation of variables that relies on cases meeting a set of specific conditions is achieved in most computer packages by using IF statements. These work by pinpointing cases that meet the specific conditions. If a case meets the condition then the case is assigned to the specified category of the new variable. The logic of these IF statements is illustrated below (the particular format will vary between computer packages).

> IF (HMAR=1 AND WMAR=1) then MTYPE=1. (i.e. both first timers)
> IF (HMAR=1 AND WMAR=2) then MTYPE=2. (i.e. mixed)
> IF (HMAR=2 AND WMAR=1) then MTYPE=2. (i.e. mixed)
> IF (HMAR=2 AND WMAR=2) then MTYPE=3. (i.e. both previously married)

We could create other variables to indicate whether the marriage was interracial, interethnic or inter-religious using much the same logic. From two pieces of information we can create a new piece.

Table 10.7 Creating a new variable based on meeting specific conditions of other variables

Variable definitions

Original variable	Variable name	Codes
Husband's marital history	HMAR	1 First marriage 2 Previously married
Wife's marital history	WMAR	1 First marriage 2 Previously married

New variable
Marital type — MTYPE — Based on previous marital history of both husband and wife

Defining types
MTYPE

			HMAR	
			1 First marriage	2 Previously married
WMAR	1 First marriage		Type 1	Type 2
	2 Previously married		Type 2	Type 3

MTYPE
1 Both first timers
2 Mix of first timer and remarriage
3 Both remarrying

Creating new variables with arithmetic transformations

The strategy previously described involves specifying particular values of each variable and allocating cases to categories of a new variable if, and only if, they meet all the particular specified conditions.

When working with interval-level variables where the codes have a real numeric meaning (e.g. age, income, year of birth, size of household etc) we can create new variables by various arithmetic computations. The process of creating variables in this way is really no different from what we do in everyday life.

For example, suppose we want to see if the age difference between a husband and a wife affected the degree of equality in their marriage. If we know the age of the husband (HUSBAGE) and of the wife (WIFEAGE) we can readily construct a third piece of information—age difference (AGEDIFF)—by simply subtracting the wife's age from the husband's age to indicate the age difference. This simple arithmetic operation can be performed very easily in most statistical analysis packages. In SPSS the general form of the syntax for this operation is:

COMPUTE *nevarname = arithmetic expression.*

For the previous example the syntax becomes:

COMPUTE AGEDIFF = HUSBAGE – WIFEAGE.

We may have collected information about a person's annual income but for our particular analysis we need to know their fortnightly income. This can be obtained by creating a new variable simply by dividing annual income (ANNINC) by 26 (number of fortnights in the year) to construct a new variable indicating fortnightly income (FORTINC). In SPSS the syntax for this operation is:

COMPUTE FORTINC=ANNINC/26.

If we want to adjust a person's annual income in 1995 into year 2000 dollars we can use an arithmetic operation to adjust for inflation. Suppose inflation over the 1995–2000 period was 15 per cent in total. We could create our new variable (ADJ95INC) by multiplying 1995 income (INC95) by 1.15. In SPSS the syntax for this operation is:

COMPUTE ADJ95INC=INC95 * 1.15.

If we need to know a person's total income (TOTINC) but have only asked about individual income sources (salary, government benefits, interest, dividends etc) we can create a new variable that simply adds together the individual sources of income to produce TOTINC. In SPSS the syntax for this operation is:

COMPUTE TOTINC=SALINC +
    BENINC + INTINC + DIVINC etc.

In summary, new variables can be produced by adding, subtracting, multiplying or dividing (or any combination) of variables and values. To learn about particular ways of performing these operations you will need to consult the particular syntax requirements of your data analysis program. The key thing to remember is that the logic of creating these variables is nothing more than a formalisation of the process we engage in every day to process and create information.

STANDARDISING VARIABLES

Often it is not the exact scores people have on a variable that are of most interest but their scores *relative* to other people in the sample. We are sometimes required to compare apples with oranges as we analyse and contrast quite different variables. Often we have to convert scores into a 'common currency' before they can be usefully analysed. One way of doing this is to *standardise* the variables.

There are many situations in which standardisation may be required but I will mention only three:

1 comparing and combining scores on variables with very different distributions;
2 comparative studies where units of measurement (e.g. income) are incomparable;
3 change over time where the value of units changes over time (e.g. income changes with inflation) so adjustments need to be made to express income in some common unit that removes the effect of inflation.

Standardising using z-scores

When dealing with interval-level variables we can convert a person's score on the variable to *standardised scores* or *z-scores*. A z-score is a person's score expressed as the number of standard deviation units that a person's score is from the mean of the variable (see pp. 225–6 for a discussion of the mean and the standard deviation).

To anticipate this discussion the mean is the arithmetic average on a variable. When we talk of the average age of a group or the average mark in a class we are really talking of the mean. The mean provides a summary of all cases in a group. Most individuals will have actual scores that differ somewhat from the mean—some will have lower scores and others will have higher scores. The standard deviation is a measure of how much the cases in the group deviate from the mean and from one another. The higher the standard deviation figure (relative to the mean) the greater the cases in the group differ from one another and from the mean.

The z-score for any individual tells us two things:

1 how far the individual's score is from the mean;
2 the individual's *position* in the group.

A person with a z-score of 0 is average on that variable. If the score is negative they are below the average and if positive they are above the average. The larger the score the further they are from the average. A score of 1.0 means the person is 1 standard deviation above the mean. A score of 1.1 means the person is 1.1 standard deviations above the mean. By examining standard deviations we can judge a person's ranking or relative standing on any variable. People with positive z-scores rank above those with negative z-scores. The higher the positive z-score the higher the position: the higher the negative z-score the lower the person's position.

Because of the way z-scores are calculated we can compare z-scores on entirely different variables. For example, we can compare a person's 1995 income with their 2005 income. Even though the actual income will be different due to inflation we can see how their income compares to the mean and to other people on both occasions and thus see whether their relative income and income position has changed.

The z-score for any interval-level variable is calculated with the formula:

$$z_i = \frac{x_i - \overline{X}}{s}$$

where

z_i = z score of an individual on the standardised variable;

x_i = the score of the individual on the variable before standardisation;

$\overline{X}$ = the mean of the variable before standardisation;

s = the standard deviation of the variable before standardisation.

Table 10.8 illustrates the calculation of individual z-scores in different contexts. In panel a the 1995 income (US dollars) is converted to z-scores for four individuals. The income for the same four individuals is calculated for 2005 incomes. Not surprisingly 2005 incomes are higher than 1995 incomes in dollar values since there has been 50 per cent inflation over the ten-year period. Despite the different dollar incomes the z-scores indicate that individuals A and B have not changed their *relative* income position. They remain 1.0 and 1.1 units below the average. However the relative positions of individuals C and D have changed. Individual C is relatively better off in 2005 (2.2 units above the average compared with 1.67 in 1995) and individual C is relatively worse off in 2005 (1.1 units above the mean in 2005 compared with 1.8 units above in 1995). Despite the difficulties caused by the change in the meaning of units (dollars) over time the z-scores provide a way of adjusting so that we can make meaningful comparisons.

Panel c of Table 10.8 provides the 2005 income of four different cases in UK pounds. How do cases A, B, C and D compare with cases W, X, Y and Z? We cannot meaningfully compare the actual

Table 10.8 Conversion of income into z-scores: over time and between countries comparisons

(a) 1995 dollars

Case	A	B	C	D
$\bar{X}$	$40\,000	$40\,000	$40\,000	$40\,000
Std devn	$3000	$3000	$3000	$3000
x_i	$37\,000	$36\,000	$45\,000	$45\,500
	$\dfrac{37\,000 - 40\,000}{3000}$	$\dfrac{36\,000 - 40\,000}{3000}$	$\dfrac{45\,000 - 40\,000}{3000}$	$\dfrac{45\,500 - 40\,000}{3000}$
	$= \dfrac{-3000}{3000}$	$= \dfrac{-4000}{3000}$	$= \dfrac{5000}{3000}$	$= \dfrac{5500}{3000}$
z_i	$= -1.0$	$= -1.33$	$= +1.67$	$= +1.8$

(b) 2005 dollars (inflation = 50%)

Case	A	B	C	D
$\bar{X}$	$60\,000	$60\,000	$60\,000	$60\,000
s	$4500	$4500	$4500	$4500
x_i	$55\,500	$54\,000	$70\,000	$65\,000
	$\dfrac{55\,500 - 60\,000}{4500}$	$\dfrac{54\,000 - 60\,000}{4500}$	$\dfrac{70\,000 - 60\,000}{4500}$	$\dfrac{65\,000 - 60\,000}{4500}$
	$= \dfrac{-4500}{4500}$	$= \dfrac{-6000}{4500}$	$= \dfrac{10\,000}{4500}$	$= \dfrac{5000}{4500}$
z_i	$= -1.0$	$= -1.33$	$= +2.2$	$= +1.1$

(c) Pounds 2005

Case	W	X	Y	Z
$\bar{X}$	£32\,400	£32\,400	£32\,400	£32\,400
s	£2400	£2400	£2400	£2400
x_i	£30\,000	£29\,200	£37\,700	£35\,120
	$\dfrac{30\,000 - 32\,400}{2400}$	$\dfrac{29\,200 - 32\,400}{2400}$	$\dfrac{37\,700 - 32\,400}{2400}$	$\dfrac{35\,120 - 32\,400}{2400}$
	$= \dfrac{-2400}{2400}$	$= \dfrac{-3200}{2400}$	$= \dfrac{6800}{2400}$	$= \dfrac{2720}{2400}$
z_i	$= -1.0$	$= -1.33$	$= +2.2$	$= +1.1$

incomes of the UK and US cases. However the conversion into standardised units (z-scores) enables such comparisons. In this case, we see that the four cases are in exactly the same *relative* position in the two countries.

Standardising for different distributions

As well as standardising to enable comparisons over time or between variables measured in different units, standardising also helps when comparing variables that are measured in the same units but that have very different distributions.

When two variables have very different distributions it is very difficult to compare their scores meaningfully. Even though a person may obtain the same score on two variables the *meaning* of the score may be very different. For example, the meaning of a mark of 75 per cent in an easy examination in which everyone obtained a score of at least 75 per cent will mean something very different from a mark of 75 per cent on a difficult examination where most people failed and virtually no-one achieved a score of 75 per cent.

If the scores on two variables are meant to be regarded as equivalent then the scores need to be adjusted when the variables have very different distributions. Suppose we want to develop an index of life satisfaction based on five items, each of which is designed to measure feelings of satisfaction with various aspects of life—with their job, marriage, education, standard of living and social life. For each question people are required to indicate, within a range of 1 to 10, how satisfied they are with that particular aspect of their life. The higher the score,

the more satisfied they are with that part of their life. For the sake of the example, imagine that on the marriage satisfaction question most people were satisfied, with everyone indicating a satisfaction level somewhere between 5 and 10 with the average being 7.5. However, on the standard of living question most people indicated that they were dissatisfied, with everyone giving a score of 5 or less with the average being 2.5 and a standard deviation of 1.5 (see Figure 10.1).

Should a score of 5 on the marriage question be regarded as equivalent to a score of 5 on the standard of living question? Should it carry the same weight in indicating general life satisfaction? Although we are dealing with the same response (5) the response takes on quite a different meaning when viewed in the context of the rest of the people who answered the question. In the case of marriage a score of 5 indicates relative dissatisfaction, while it reflects relative satisfaction in relation to the standard of living. The point is that scores that people obtain have no *absolute* meaning but are *relative* to the distribution in which they occur.

By standardising variables we adjust them for their different distributions and the variables can then contribute equally to any final composite index.

Adjustments with ordinal level variables

The method of standardising described above assumes that the variables are interval-level variables. With ordinal variables (i.e. scores are ranked but the differences between scores cannot be quantified) a person's score on the variable can be converted to a *rank*.

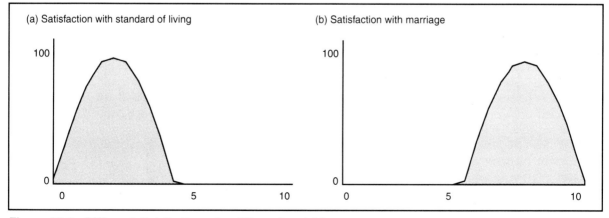

Figure 10.1 Different distributions for different variables

BOX 10.3 *Standardising item scores*

1 Subtract the average score from each individual's score on the variable.

2 Divide the answer by the measure of spread for that variable.

3 For interval variables the standardised score = (individual's score – mean) / standard deviation.

4 For ordinal variables the standardised score = (individual's score – median) / range.

5 Standardising an interval variable in this way re-expresses the raw score as standard deviation units (or z-scores) that the person is from the mean. A person scoring 5 on marital satisfaction (mean = 7.5; standard deviation = 1.5) will receive a standardised score of –1.67. The same score of 5 on satisfaction with standard of living (mean = 2.5; standard deviation = 1.5) would be re-expressed as +1.67.

A rank is obtained by deciding on the number of categories into which cases are to be ranked. Cases are then placed into one of those categories. Comparisons across variables are made on the basis of whether a case is in the same ranked category on both variables. Change over time is measured in terms of whether a person's rank order changes over time.

The number of categories used can be anything from two to the number of cases in the sample. For example, we could decide to create ten ranked categories for a variable. The first category would be the 10 per cent of cases with the lowest score, the second category would be for the next lot of 10 per cent of cases and so on until the tenth category was for the 10 per cent of cases with the highest scores on the original variable. These ten groups are called *deciles*. If we divided the cases into just four groups, with the bottom category for the bottom 25 per cent of cases etc, the groups are called *quartiles*. If five groups are used the groups are called *quintiles*. If 100 groups are used the categories are called *percentiles*. Converting a variable into a set of ranked

---

BOX 10.4
Standardising variables with SPSS

The mechanics of standardising will vary according to the syntax rules and built-in functions of different computer packages. In SPSS there are two ways in which to standardise a variable:

Use the COMPUTE command

1 obtain the mean and standard deviation of the variable to be standardised

2 use the COMPUTE command to create a new version of the variable. The general format of the compute command will be:

COMPUTE *Name for standardized variable*=(original variable–mean)/ standard deviation.

Where the actual mean and standard deviation values are substituted in the formula

Example: variable name: SATMAR; Mean=7.5; Standard deviation=1.5

COMPUTE NEWSAT=(SATMAR–7.5)/1.5

Use the DESCRIPTIVES command

Syntax:

DESCRIPTIVES *name of variable to be standardized*

/SAVE.

This instruction will automatically create a new standardised version of the specified variable. The name of the standardised variable will be the same as the original variable but will commence with the letter Z.

Menus:

Analyze ▼

  Descriptive statistics ▶

    Descriptives . . .

      Variables *insert name of variable to be standardized*

        ☑ save standardized values as variables

      ☐OK

categories can be called the 'ntile method' of converting variables. The larger the number of *n*tiles the more finely we can differentiate between cases. The finer the differentiation the more sensitive the variable is to changes in rank or differences in ranks on different variables.

Converting variables into a set of ranked categories achieves similar outcomes that converting scores into z-scores achieves. It assists in comparing variables with different distributions, variables measured in different units of measurement or for adjusting for change in the meaning of the values (e.g. actual income). By comparing rank order we remove the impact of these differences and simply focus on a person's *relative* position on different variables.

THE PROBLEM OF MISSING DATA

Almost always survey data have missing values: answers to some questions will be missing. This raises several issues:

1 How can questions be improved to minimise missing values?
2 How are missing values coded?
3 Do missing values introduce a bias in the analysis?
4 How are missing values to be taken into account during analysis? Are there ways of substituting valid values for missing values?

Since the first two issues have been dealt with elsewhere in this book (Chapter 7, p. 116, and Chapter 9, pp. 155–6) this section focuses on handling missing values at the data analysis stage.

Checking for missing data bias

Are people for whom we have missing values on a variable different from those with valid values? For example, do those who refuse to answer questions about income tend to have other characteristics such as ethnic background or education level in common? If certain types of people produce missing data for particular variables then the results of the analysis could be biased because some types of people are under-represented in the analysis of that variable.

We need to assess whether missing data do introduce bias. The simplest way of doing this is to divide the sample into two groups: those with missing values and those with valid values on a particular

---

BOX 10.5
Converting variables to ntile ranks

The method of converting scores to *n*tiles varies between computer packages. With SPSS scores can be converted into any number of ranks. Where the number of ranks is fewer than the sample size there will be tied ranks.

In SPSS the simplest way of converting a variable into *n*tiles is:

Syntax:

RANK   *Varname*(s)

/ntiles=*n*.

You will insert the actual variable names to be converted and the number of ranks you require on the *n*tiles subcommand.

Menus:

Transform ▼

Categorize variables . . .

Create variables for: *insert variable names to be converted into* ntiles

Number of categories: *insert number of categories e.g. 4 for quartiles, 5 for quintiles, 100 for percentiles etc.*

OK

This creates a new variable. It will have the same variable name as the selected variable except that it will be preceded with the letter 'n' to indicate that the categories represent *n*tile ranks.

---

variable. (Care must be taken to exclude cases who were *not required* to answer the question from the analysis.) Having divided the sample into these two groups, examine how the two groups answered other questions. Cross-tabulations or comparison of means (see Chapter 15) can be useful ways of conducting this analysis.

For example, if we have missing data on the income variable, we would divide the sample into those who did and those who did not reveal their income. This results in a dichotomous variable (a variable with two categories). We can then cross-tabulate this variable with other variables (e.g. other key variables that will be examined in the analysis, or with variables that we suspect might reveal a bias, such as ethnicity). If there is a link between these other variables (e.g. ethnic group) and not answering the income question then any income analysis may be affected by the under-representation of some ethnic groups in the income data.

Minimising the effect of missing values

There are a variety of methods for dealing with missing data at the data analysis stage. When deciding which method to use:

- try to minimise the loss of cases and data;
- avoid distorting sample variance and correlations;
- strive for simplicity.

Missing values are a problem because they reduce the number of cases available for analysis. In scale construction, bivariate and multivariate analysis, this can lead to an unacceptable loss of cases.

Hertel (1976) has outlined a number of alternative ways of dealing with missing values. The first three of these methods involve deleting either cases or variables from the analysis. The remaining methods involve substituting the missing value with a valid code. This substitution that requires using a new, best guess value is called *imputation*. Some of these methods use statistical techniques that will be covered in Chapters 13 to 17. You may choose to look at these sections first or reread this section when you have read the analysis section of this book.

Delete cases

Using this approach, any case that has missing data on any one of the *set* of variables being analysed is eliminated from further analysis. This method, called *listwise* deletion of missing data, can lead to the loss of a lot of data: valid answers on many questions are disregarded simply because of a non-answer on one question. Because many people will have failed to answer one question in a set, this approach can lead to an unacceptable reduction in sample size. Hertel (1976) advises against this method if it leads to a loss of more than 15 per cent of cases. However, if the missing data are clustered in a small number of cases, then you might wish to eliminate those cases as the quality of the data from those cases may be suspect.

Delete variables

If a particular variable is responsible for a large number of the missing values, that variable can be dropped from the analysis. The advantage of this is that we do not lose any cases and, at the same time, we eliminate an unreliable item. The advisability of this approach depends on how important that particular variable is for the analysis.

Pairwise deletion

This frequently used approach can be used in multivariate analysis (e.g. factor analysis, regression, reliability etc) that is based on a zero-order correlation matrix (see Chapter 15 and Table 15.13). Using pairwise deletion when calculating the correlation between any two variables, all cases that have nonmissing values for those two variables are used to calculate the correlation even if those cases have missing values on other variables being used in the analysis. Using the pairwise approach we get a correlation matrix in which each coefficient may be based on a different number of cases. The disadvantage of the pairwise approach is that it leads to some loss of cases, but this is not nearly as marked as with the listwise approach.

Sample mean approach

If we do not know the value on a variable for any given person, then the best guess for that person is the same as the measure of central tendency for that variable (see Chapter 13 on descriptive statistics). With interval-level variables we can replace missing values with the value of the mean of that variable for the sample (see Chapter 13 on interval variables). The problem with this approach is that it reduces the variability of the sample on the variable and thus reduces the correlation between this and other variables (see Chapter 14 on using summary statistics).

The group means approach

One way of overcoming the problem of reducing variablility on the variable is to use *group* means rather than the overall sample mean. To do this we divide the sample into groups on a background variable (e.g. ethnicity, gender, education) that is well correlated with the variable for which we want to replace missing values. We then obtain the mean for the 'missing data variable' within each category of the selected background variable. For example, when estimating income for people who refused to answer the income question, we might divide the sample into groups according to their education level and then subdivide each education level group into male and female subgroups. We then obtain the mean income for the non-missing cases within each subgroup. Thus we might find that the mean income for tertiary educated females is $37 000 and the mean for tertiary educated males is $42 000 and so forth. Using the group means approach we simply substitute these mean values for missing values for people according to the subgroup to which they belong.

The disadvantage of this approach is that it exaggerates the extent to which people in a group are similar to one another. This can inflate the correlations between variables when using the variable for which the missing data have been estimated.

Random assignment within groups
This approach is similar to the group means approach in that it relies on dividing the sample into subgroups on the basis of background variables that are likely to be correlated with the variable for which missing values are being imputed. But this approach differs in that it does not involve substituting the group mean for any missing data. Instead, when we locate a case with missing data on a particular variable we simply look at the value on the same variable of the nearest preceding case with a valid code and substitute this value for the missing value. This method means that missing values are replaced by a variety of different values and thus does not affect sample or group variability. It therefore has no effect on the strength of correlations and avoids any loss of cases. Despite being somewhat more complex to execute, it is a desirable way of handling missing data.

Regression analysis
This is a more complex method that involves the use of regression to predict the value of a person on the missing data variable (see Chapters 15 and 17).[1] Since the regression will be based on a matrix in which the pairwise method will be used, this approach leads to some loss of cases (see Chapter 17).

Which method should be used to handle missing data? Of the methods that involve estimating valid values for missing values, the random assignment of numbers is the least likely to lead to data distortions but it is more complex. Of the approaches that involve losing data or cases, the pairwise solution is generally best and is easily accomplished with most computer packages. On occasions, however, other approaches are more appropriate. If most missing data are due to a few cases or a particular variable we might question the quality of responses from those cases or for that variable and decide that it is better to eliminate what may be unreliable data.

DATA PREPARATION CHECKLIST

1 Are the categories of the variable the most meaningful for the problem being addressed? If not, recode to better categories.
2 Are there too many categories to allow data to be clearly presented in tables or graphs? If so, reduce the number of categories by recoding.
3 Are there categories with too few cases to allow meaningful analysis? If so, combine small categories with other appropriate categories.
4 Which method of collapsing categories makes most sense for the variable? Is the method selected suitable for the level of measurement of the variable?
5 If you select the substantive method of collapsing, how many categories will you collapse to? Have you put too many people in one category so that the variable has very little variation?
6 If selecting the distributional method of recoding is the variable ordinal or interval (it should be)? How many categories are you going to collapse to? Why?
7 Is the order of the categories of the variables suitable for the way in which the variable will be used? Is the order logical? Is it easy to read?
8 Can the level of measurement of the variable be increased by reordering some of the categories?
9 If the variable is ordinal or interval does the variable need to be reverse coded? If the variable is to be combined with other variables in a scale is it coded in the right direction?
10 Do you require variables not in the data set but that can be constructed from existing variables?
11 If so, what is the level of measurement of the variables you will use to build another variable?
    a If at least one of the variables is nominal you will need to use conditional transformations of variable creation.

b   If all the 'building block' variables are ordinal or interval will you use conditional transformations or the arithmetic transformations to create the new variable?

12 Do you need to compare people on different variables?

a   Are these variables measured using different units of measurement?

b   Are the distributions of the variables to be compared quite different?

c   If so you will need a method of adjusting variables to convert them to a 'common currency'.

13 If the variables require converting to a common currency:

a   What is the level of measurement of the variables?

b   If ordinal, convert the variables using the 'ntiles approach' and rank cases. How many ntiles do you require?

c   If interval, will you use the 'ntiles' or 'z-score' method of adjusting the variables?

14 Do the variables have missing data?

15 Does the missing data create bias?

16 How will you handle missing data? Will you:

a   Ignore it?

b   Delete cases or variables that produce a lot of missing data? If you delete cases or variables will you use the listwise or pairwise method of deletion?

c   Impute valid values to substitute for missing data? If so which method of imputation will you use?

KEY CONCEPTS

Arithmetic transformation	Group means substitution	Nominal level	Reverse coding
Conditional transformation	Imputation	ntile ranking	Standardisation
Decile	Interval level	Ordinal level	Substantive recoding
Dichotomise	Level of measurement	Pairwise deletion	Trichotomisation
Distribution-based recoding	Listwise deletion	Percentile	z-score
	Means substitution	Quartile	
	Missing data bias	Quintile	
		Recoding	

ENDNOTE

[1] Imputing using regression estimates can be complex but has been simplified enormously in SPSS using the Missing Values Analysis optional module. This enables data to be updated with imputed values using a specified set of predictor variables.

FURTHER READING

Marsh (1988) provides some excellent and readable chapters on a variety of ways of standardising and adjusting variables in *Exploring Data*. She also illustrates some imaginative ways of using standardised and adjusted data. Chapter 9 of Hoinville, Jowell and associates' *Survey Research Practice* (1978) deals with some issues on how to classify values of variables. Warwick and Lininger outline some things to do when preparing for analysis in Chapter 10 of *The Sample Survey* (1975). Further aspects of variable preparation for more advanced analysis are discussed in Chapter 4 of Tabachnick and Fidell (1983).

EXERCISES

1 List the steps you would normally take to prepare your data for analysis.

2 a Turn to Table 13.1a and collapse it into four categories on the basis of the variable's distribution.

   b Collapse Table 13.1a using the substantive approach. Justify your classification.

   c Compare the advantages and disadvantages of the two approaches.

3 Dichotomise the variable in Table 13.5.

4 How might you recode religious affiliation in Table 13.1c? Give reasons for your answer.

5 a Explain why reverse coding may be necessary.

   b Write the SPSS syntax to reverse code the variable in Table 13.5.

6 a What is the purpose of standardising the scores on some variables?

   b Order the following z-scores from lowest to highest: -1.5; 1.4; 0.1; -1.96; 1.1.

7 Here is the list of religious groupings and in brackets following each is an approximation of the percentage of people in each grouping (Australian figures). Arrange these categories in a sensible order. List alternative ways in which they could also have been ordered.

   Anglican (11%); Baptist (2%); Brethren (0.2%); Catholic (28%); Churches of Christ (1.2%); Church of England (17%); Congregational (0.5%); Greek Orthodox (2.6%); Indefinite (0.4%); Jehovah's Witness (0.3%); Hebrew (0.6%); Lutheran (1.7%); Muslim (0.4%); No religion (2.6%); Not stated (9.8%); Presbyterian (3%); Salvation Army (0.50%); Seventh Day Adventist (0.3%); Uniting (12%)★; Other Christian (2.7%); Protestant (undefined) (3.2%).

   ★ a combination of Methodist, Presbyterian and Congregational churches.

8 The table below shows a set of data for ten people for seven variables. In each cell of the table the numbers represent codes for each variable. The ★ symbol indicates missing data. The seventh variable is gender where M = male and F = female. All the other variables are interval-level variables.

   a If you correlated var 3 with var 4, how many missing cases would you have if you used the pairwise method of handling missing data? How many missing cases would the listwise method result in?

   b Without imputing new values for missing values, what steps would you take to minimise the influence of missing values for this set of data?

   c Using the sample means approach, develop substitute scores for the missing values scores for var 1.

   d Using the group means approach (use gender as the grouping variable), develop substitute scores for missing values for var 3.

   e Use the random assignment of values within groups approach (use gender as the grouping variable) to develop substitute values for missing values for var 1.

CASE	Var 1	Var 2	Var 3	Var 4	Var 5	Var 6	Gender
1	7	*	2	2	4	4	M
2	4	9	*	1	1	2	M
3	6	2	2	2	*	7	F
4	*	9	7	1	6	4	F
5	0	4	8	4	6	3	F
6	5	1	7	3	*	8	M
7	6	7	*	5	3	9	M
8	5	*	4	2	*	6	F
9	*	7	*	7	*	1	M
10	6	4	6	*	8	5	F

11

Building scales

We use the basic principle of scaling every day. When we meet people for the first time we try to build a picture of them: we develop impressions of their friendliness, intelligence, trustworthiness and so forth. These impressions rarely rely on one piece of information but are a composite picture based on a number of clues.

In survey research a scale is simply a more formalised and systematic version of this everyday activity. A scale is a composite measure of a concept, a measure composed of information derived from several questions or indicators. To create a scale we simply convert the information contained in several relatively specific indicators into one new and more abstract variable. Thus, instead of measuring conservatism simply by asking what political party someone votes for, we would ask about a range of issues which we think tap conservatism. These questions are then combined into a single index of conservatism.

This chapter outlines:

■ reasons why and when it is desirable to use scales rather than single indicators;
■ the logic of summated scales and provides a detailed discussion of how to construct one type of summated scale—a Likert scale;
■ the way in which factor analysis is used to identify and construct scales;

■ some issues that complicate the construction and interpretation of scales and some solutions to these problems.

WHY BOTHER BUILDING SCALES?

There are several reasons why it is desirable to measure a concept by using multiple indicators rather than one. First, it helps get at the complexity of the concept. Unless we have defined a concept very narrowly we need multiple indicators to tap the complexity of most concepts (see Chapter 4). To measure religiousness we could ask how often someone attends church, but if we see religiousness as more complex than this we would also ask about beliefs or ritual observance, and work out how important religion is in a person's life. Taken together these questions provide a better measure of religiousness than a rather barren and partial single measure.

Second, multiple indicators assist in developing more valid measures. Often one observation on its own can be misleading and we need to see it in the context of other observations to avoid misinterpretation. For example, if we only look at how someone votes we might consider those who vote for the more conservative political parties to be conservative and those voting for progressive parties as less conservative. But many of those who vote for progressive parties may be politically conservative in many respects so we need to interpret a person's vote within the context of other political attitudes. Multiple-item scales can help us avoid some of the distortions and misclassification which can arise by using only single-item measures of complex concepts.

Third, multiple indicators increase reliability. The way in which a question is worded can affect substantially the way people answer it. If we rely on only one question, people's answers could be largely a function of the wording of the question. Using a number of questions should minimise the effect of one which is poorly worded.

Fourth, multiple indicators enable greater precision. A single question does not allow us to differentiate between people with much precision. For example, using suburb of residence as a measure of a person's social status leads to a very crude classification. We would classify residents from wealthier suburbs as higher status than those residents from poorer suburbs but we are treating a lot of people whose status varies (e.g. those in wealthier suburbs) as though they were the same status. Additional questions about, say, occupation, education and income would help differentiate between the status levels of those whom we had treated as of equal status. Thus we get a better ranking of people according to their status and can distinguish between small status variations. With a single indicator this precision is not possible.

Fifth, by summarising the information conveyed by a number of questions into one variable the analysis is simplified considerably. Instead of analysing each question separately we can analyse many variables simply and in the one attempt.

SUMMATED SCALING: THE LOGIC

A scale consists of answers to a number of questions. For each question people receive a score depending on their answer. The score is allocated to particular answers depending on how favourable the answer is to the attitude being measured. The scores for each question are then added together to provide each person with an overall score for that set of questions (scale score). This scale score is taken to indicate a person's 'position' on the abstract dimension which the individual questions are intended to tap. An analogy for a scale score is a student's marks in a subject. The student will complete a number of pieces of work (e.g. an essay, a report, an examination and a tutorial discussion) and receive a final mark. The final mark is meant to reflect the student's grasp of the subject. This is measured by summing the scores for each component into one overall score.

The questions shown in the table below designed to measure traditionalism illustrate the process of constructing a summated scale.

Depending on how an individual answers the set of questions the scale score for that person will vary (see Figure 11.1). Since strong agreement with traditionalist statements receives high scores then high scale scores indicate high traditionalism.

The format of the questions above is a common format but is not the only format that can be used. Summated scales simply require that we measure the strength of some opinion using a numerical value to indicate a person's 'position' on a number of questions. There are many means by which we measure strength of opinion on particular items and these have been discussed in some detail in Chapter 7.

There are a variety of types of summated scales including Thurstone scales, Guttman scales and Likert scales—all of which are named after their

		Strongly agree	Agree	Undecided	Disagree	Strongly disagree
a	If you start trying to change things very much you usually make them worse.	[ ] 4	[ ] 3	[ ] 2	[ ] 1	[ ] 0
b	If something grows up over a long time period, there will always be much wisdom in it.	[ ]	[ ]	[ ]	[ ]	[ ]
c	It is better to stick by what you have, than to try new things you do not really know about.	[ ]	[ ]	[ ]	[ ]	[ ]
d	We must respect the work of our forebears and not think that we know better than they did.	[ ]	[ ]	[ ]	[ ]	[ ]
e	A person does not really have much wisdom until they are well along in years.	[ ]	[ ]	[ ]	[ ]	[ ]

Person				Item								Scale score	Interpretation
	a		b		c		d		e				
1	4	+	4	+	4	+	4	+	4	=		20	Very highly traditionlist
2	4		2		1		0		3	=		10	Moderate
3	2		1		2		1		1	=		7	Moderate
4	0		0		0		0		0	=		0	Very non-traditionlist

Figure 11.1 An illustration of scale scores

developers. In this chapter I will focus on the most common type—Likert scales. Thurstone and Guttman scales have become less common in recent years (see Web Pointer 11.2).

LIKERT SCALES

The problem common to all scaling techniques is how do we know which questions to include in the scale? We cannot simply add together the scores from any set of questions: we must be confident that they all tap the same underlying concept. To work out which items legitimately belong to the scale there are three main stages.

1 constructing a rough scale;
2 selecting the best items;
3 creating the final scale variable.

Construct a rough scale

There are six steps to constructing a rough scale.

1 *Identify the concept that the scale is designed to measure.* It is often said the current generation of young people are preoccupied with the present and do not think enough about or plan sufficiently for the future. To test this belief we would need to measure the concept *present–future orientation*. Since it would be difficult to do this with a single measure a composite scale is appropriate.

2 *Develop a set of questions which, on the face of it, seem to measure the relevant concept.* These questions usually consist of a mixture of favourable and unfavourable statements to which people are asked to express the extent of their agreement and disagreement. The statements are selected to reflect an orientation to the attitude of interest.

Since one aim of scaling is to be able to distinguish between people who fall at differ-

ent points along an attitude continuum (e.g. present–future orientation), there is no point in developing extreme items with which everyone will agree (or everyone disagree). For example, the following item would not be very good:

'I never think about the future at all.'

It would be better to develop a less extreme question such as:

'It's all very well to develop plans for the future but the first priority should be the here and now.'

The process of constructing the rough, initial scales is illustrated in Box 11.1.

3 *Ask a group of people, who are similar to those to whom we finally want to give the questions, to answer these draft questions.*

4 *Score each person's response to each question.*

5 *Reverse code items as required.* It is important that a score on each item has the same meaning. Thus if we want a high score on the final scale to reflect a future orientation we will need to ensure that every item is scored to reflect this. Since some items may not be coded in the desired direction some reverse coding may be required (see Chapter 10).

6 *Add up each person's score on each item to obtain their scale score.* In this case the highest score could be 65 (five on each of thirteen items) and indicates high future orientation. The minimum score of thirteen (one on each of the thirteen items) equals a very low future orientation.

When doing secondary data analysis (see Chapter 6 on secondary analysis) we will often want to construct scales for which the initial investigators did not specifically design questions. Nevertheless there may be questions in the data set that enable us to produce satisfactory scales. When constructing scales from an existing data set we still have to select a set of items from which to construct a rough scale.

BOX 11.1 *Set of positive and negative questions for a future orientation scale*

	Strongly agree	Agree	Undecided	Disagree	Strongly disagree
1 Eat, drink and be merry for tomorrow we die.	1	2	3	4	5
2 I am a fairly ambitious person. (+)	1	2	3	4	5
3 If people thought ahead more we would not be facing many of today's problems. (+)	1	2	3	4	5
4 I tend not to think about the future very much.	1	2	3	4	5
5 Conserving our resources for the future is one of the most important issues facing the world today. (+)	1	2	3	4	5
6 I try to save money for a rainy day rather than spend it as soon as I get it.	1	2	3	4	5
7 I prefer to enjoy the present rather than to plan ahead.	1	2	3	4	5
8 The trouble with many people is that they are not prepared to wait for things. (+)	1	2	3	4	5
9 It's all very well to plan for the future but the first priority should be to deal with present problems.	1	2	3	4	5
10 I mainly take life as it comes rather than always planning ahead.	1	2	3	4	5
11 Zero population growth is an important goal given the likely overpopulation in the future. (+)	1	2	3	4	5
12 There is so much to worry about in the present that I do not give the future that much thought.	1	2	3	4	5
13 It is important to make plans for the future and not just accept what comes. (+)	1	2	3	4	5

There are two complementary approaches that help identify possible scale items. One approach is conceptual, the other is empirical.

First, we can get an idea of which items might go together by looking at their content. For example, we might be interested in developing a scale of conservatism. By examining the questions in a survey we will identify a number which, on the face of it, would

---

> ## BOX 11.2
> ### Direction of coding of scale items
>
> 1. Decide what a high score on the scale will mean.
> 2. Check whether all individual items are scored so that a high score on the item means the same as a high score on the scale.
> 3. Reverse code items if necessary (see Chapter 10 on reverse coding).
> 4. If item-scale coefficients are negative it is probably because the item with the negative correlation has not been reverse coded.

---

probably tap this concept as we understand it. The second part of selecting the initial scale items is to obtain a correlation matrix (pp. 290–1) of the items that might conceivably belong together. This correlation matrix will provide correlations of each item with each other item. Items that belong together in a scale will normally have at least modest correlations with each other item in the scale.

When selecting items from a matrix it is important not to rely only on the correlations. The items must also belong together conceptually. A correlation between gender and measures of self-esteem does not mean that gender should be part of our measure of self-esteem. By examining which items seem to be correlated and which conceptually belong together we will obtain an initial set of items from which to construct an initial scale using the techniques described above. We will then need to refine the scale and select only the best of these initial items.

Selecting the best items

We need to look at each item to see if it really belongs to the scale. This process of assessing each item is called *item analysis* of which there are two aspects—unidimensionality and reliability.

Test for unidimensionality

A unidimensional scale is one in which each item measures the same underlying concept. We need to eliminate items which do not measure the concept. To do this, check to see if the responses to a particular item reflect the pattern of responses on other items. If it does not we can assume it is because the item is measuring something different from the other items and we can drop it from the scale. For example, if people who tend to be future oriented on most questions do not seem to be future oriented on a particular question we would drop that particular question. The way to work out whether the responses on a particular item reflect the responses on other items is to calculate a correlation coefficient between response on the item with their responses on the set of items that make up the rest of the scale. Correlation coefficients range between 0 and 1. The coefficient that tests the fit between an item and the rest of the scale is called the *item-to-scale coefficient*. The higher it is the more clearly an item belongs to the scale. *As a rule of thumb, if it is less than 0.3 then the item is dropped from the scale.* Calculating an item-to-scale coefficient for each of the initial items and dropping the inappropriate ones should result in a unidimensional scale. A further test for unidimensionality can be done with factor analysis where a unidimensional scale should result in a factor solution with only one factor (see discussion below).

Test for reliability

A reliable scale is one on which individuals obtain much the same scale score on two different occasions. An unreliable scale is the result of unreliable items, so we need to test each item for its reliability. Since it is often not possible to get people to answer the same questions on two occasions to assess reliability (see Chapter 4), an alternative approach is to look at the consistency of a person's response on an item compared to each other scale item (item–item correlations). This provides a measure of the overall reliability of the scale. The index of this is given by a statistic *Cronbach's alpha coefficient*. This ranges between 0 and 1. The higher the figure the more reliable the scale. As a rule of thumb *alpha should be at least 0.7* before we say that the scale is reliable. The size of alpha is affected by the reliability of individual items. To increase the alpha of the scale, and thus the scale's reliability, drop all unreliable items. To identify which items are unreliable we need to calculate what the alpha would be if a particular item was dropped. Fortunately most statistical packages that calculate Cronbach's alpha also calculate alpha estimates if any

---

WEB POINTER 11.1   *Sources for established scales*

Rather than inventing scales from scratch it makes sense to see if there are existing scales that you can use or adapt. There are many handbooks and websites that assist with this.

Description	URL
My website provides lists of articles in which scales are available.	www.social-research.org
Online reference library.	http://ericae.net/ftlib.htm
The Buros Institute for Mental Measurements has an excellent test locator.	www.unl.edu/buros/
Mental Measurements Yearbook. This reviews many scales and tests each year. Bibliographic and database access details.	www.unl.edu/buros/catalog.html#mmy
Large number of online tests you can take and from which you can obtain ideas. No information is available regarding the validation of these tests. Well worth visiting and can be fun.	www.queendom.com/tests.html
Tests in Print (TIP) serves as a comprehensive bibliography to all known commercially available tests which are currently in print	Murphy, L.L., Impara, J.C. and Plake, B.S. (eds) (1999) *Tests in Print V*, Lincoln, Nebraska: Buros Institute of Mental Measurements.
List of handbooks	Box 4.1 of this book.

---

given item was to be dropped from the scale. This helps identify items that should be dropped.

The figures in Table 11.1 illustrate how items are selected for a final scale. These figures would be generated by statistical programs that perform reliability analysis (see Web Pointers 11.1 and 11.2). The item-total correlations indicate that items 1, 5 and 11 do not form part of a unidimensional scale since the item-total correlations are below 0.30. These items should be deleted.

The other part of evaluating the scale is to examine the alpha. With all the items included the alpha is 0.65. This is lower than desirable. If item 7 is deleted the scale alpha would rise to 0.77. This means that item 7 is unreliable and therefore would be dropped.

Having decided which items are worth including in the final scale we would recalculate people's scale score and recheck the scale using the statistics outlined above. Assuming these are satisfactory we

Table 11.1   An illustration of scale testing coefficients

Item	Item-total correlations	Alpha if item deleted
1	0.27*	0.72
2	0.48	0.62
3	0.61	0.60
4	0.40	0.65
5	0.21*	0.68
6	0.52	0.58
7	0.34	0.77*
8	0.60`	0.64
9	0.49	0.68
10	0.33	0.60
11	0.23*	0.72
12	0.49	0.66
13	0.57	0.59

Alpha for scale = 0.65

can now use these items in the main data collection phase of the study.

Creating the final scale

The final step in producing a Likert scale is to create a new variable that contains a scale score for each respondent. The discussion so far has examined how to identify which items belong to the scale. Creating the final scale is a simple matter of creating a new variable using an arithmetic transformation (see Chapter 10 on arithmetic transformations).

In the case of simple Likert scales the scale is created by adding together the scores of each of the items selected. In the example in Table 11.1 items 1, 2, 3, 4, 6, 8, 9, 10, 12 and 13 belong to the scale. The SPSS syntax to create the scale is:

```
COMPUTE  scalename = item1 + item2 +
    item3 + item4 + item6 + item8 + item9 +
    item10 + item12 + item13.
```

Using the method discussed we *began* with a *concept* and developed questions to tap that concept. An alternative approach is to ask a wide range of questions and see if there is a pattern to the way people answer sets of questions, then look at what sets of items people answer in a consistent way. By looking at which items 'go together' we can try to see what more general concept they might reflect. The statistical technique used in this more inductive approach to scaling is called *exploratory factor analysis* (see Kim and Mueller, 1978a, 1978b).

FACTOR ANALYSIS

Factor analysis is an appropriate method for scale development when analysing a set of interval-level, non-dichotomous variables. It is a mathematically complex method of reducing a large set of variables to a smaller set of underlying variables referred to as factors. Fortunately computer packages can handle the complex computations, so this section focuses on the logic and steps of factor analysis.

> Since this section deals with some statistical concepts that have not yet been covered in the book you might decide to leave this section until you have become familiar with the material in Chapters 12–17.

The basic aim of factor analysis is to examine whether, on the basis of people's answers to questions, we can identify a smaller number of more general factors that underlie answers to individual questions. For example, we might ask people what attributes they consider to be important for children to have (e.g. good manners, obedience, neatness, imagination, independence and self-control). By examining the pattern of answers, we might see that some people emphasised good manners, obedience and neatness and placed little weight on imagination, independence and self-control and vice versa. In other words, some variables tended to cluster together.

Factor analysis helps us identify this sort of patterning in the responses to a set of questions. For example, despite having answers for six attributes in

---

WEB POINTER 11.2 *Scaling statistics*	
Full discussion of Cronbach's alpha.	http://ubmail.ubalt.edu/~harsham/stat-data/ opre330Surveys.htm#rCronbachs
Discussion of a range of scaling techniques and the range of statistics used to evaluate scales. A very useful guide.	www2.chass.ncsu.edu/garson/pa765/ standard.htm
A very useful general description of the Likert, Thurstone and Guttman scaling techniques.	http://trochim.human.cornell.edu/kb/ scalgen.htm

Visit www.social-research.org to use these links and to check for updates and additions.

children, the answers to these six items might reflect just two more general, underlying attitude dimensions or factors. We might say that the first set of variables represents an attitude dimension about *conformity*, while the second set reflects the dimension of *autonomy*. If our aim is to reduce data to make analysis simpler, it is useful to be able to identify which variables belong together and to have a method of combining these variables into scales.

There are four main steps in forming scales using factor analysis. At each of these stages there are a variety of ways of doing the factor analysis, but only one main method will be discussed here. The four steps are:

1   selecting the variables to be analysed;
2   extracting an initial set of factors;
3   extracting a final set of factors by 'rotation';
4   constructing scales based on the results at step 3 and using these in further analysis.

To illustrate these steps I will use eight variables that relate to the job characteristics that people value (see Table 11.2).

Selecting variables for analysis

A problem with factor analysis is that, regardless of the variables used, a set of 'underlying' factors will be produced—whether they make sense or not. Indeed, factor analysis is particularly prone to the GIGO (garbage in, garbage out) problem. Since the 'solution' (i.e. extraction of factors) is based on correlations between variables, we can produce factors from variables that have nothing in common conceptually. We might find that the variables education, age and income are empirically correlated and they might

therefore be identified as a factor in factor analysis. But this does not mean that they are really measuring the same underlying dimension. The variables might be causally related rather than reflecting some underlying factor.

When selecting variables to be factor analysed, *it is important to be able to assume that correlations between the variables will not be causal.* Instead, correlations between the variables are assumed to be produced by some third, common factor (see Figure 11.2). In practical terms, this means that when selecting variables to be analysed we should avoid including variables that are likely to be causes of other variables in the analysis.

We should also ensure that the variables to be analysed have at least reasonable correlations with some other variables in the analysis. At the variable selection stage it is helpful to obtain a correlation matrix of potential variables, inspect it and exclude those variables that do not correlate with any others in the analysis. (If you are not familiar with a correlation matrix or how to read a matrix stop reading and turn to pp. 290–1 before proceeding.)

As Table 11.3 shows, some variables correlate well with some, but not all, other variables. For example, INIT is correlated with RESPONS and ACHIEVE but not with PAY, HOURS, HOLIDAYS, PRESSURE or SEXBOSS. A close examination of the pattern of correlations shows that certain clusters of variables correlate with each other but not with other clusters of variables. It is this clustering that factor analysis detects.

There are a number of ways of assessing whether a set of variables in a correlation matrix is suitable for factor analysis (see Norusis, 1985: 128–9). Among

Table 11.2 Variables used in the factor analysis example

Variable name	Extent to which each characteristic is considered important for a job
PAY	Income from job
INIT	Opportunities to use initiative
RESPONS	Having responsibility
ACHIEVE	The feeling of achieving something
PRESSURE	Not too much pressure
HOLIDAY	Generous holidays
HOURS	Good hours
SEXBOSS	Having a boss of the same sex

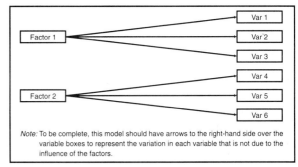

Note: To be complete, this model should have arrows to the right-hand side over the variable boxes to represent the variation in each variable that is not due to the influence of the factors.

Figure 11.2 Graphic representation of the causal assumptions underlying a two-factor factor analysis

Table 11.3 Correlation matrix of variables in the factor analysis

Variable	Pay	Init	Respons	Achieve	Pressure	Holiday	Hours	Sexboss
PAY	1.00							
INIT	0.17	1.00						
RESPONS	0.20	0.40	1.00					
ACHIEVE	0.16	0.40	0.33	1.00				
PRESSURE	0.18	0.08	0.12	0.07	1.00			
HOLIDAY	0.31	0.14	0.21	0.07	0.32	1.00		
HOURS	0.38	0.14	0.17	0.10	0.32	0.39	1.00	
SEXBOSS	0.12	0.06	0.07	0.00	0.04	0.14	0.06	1.00

KMO = 0.75

these is a statistic called KMO which ranges from 0 to 1. If this statistic yields high values above 0.7, then the correlations, on the whole, are sufficiently high to make factor analysis suitable. More care should be taken if these KMO values lie between 0.5 and 0.69, and KMO values below 0.5 mean that factor analysis would be inappropriate for that set of variables. Dropping some variables that do not correlate well with any others (e.g. SEXBOSS) should help. Measures similar to the KMO value can also be obtained for each variable to give some indication of which variables might be dropped from further analysis (see Norusis, 1985: 129–30).

Extracting an initial set of factors

The main aim of exploratory factor analysis is to see whether a smaller number of common factors can account for the pattern of correlations between a larger number of variables. Do the individual variables co-vary because they have underlying factors in common? To extract factors, two decisions are necessary. The first is to decide on which of a number of methods of extracting the factors is to be used. Kim and Mueller (1978a, 1978b) discuss these alternatives.

The second decision is to work out *how many* factors to extract. Since the aim of factor analysis is to represent a set of variables as simply as possible, the best factor analysis will have as few factors as necessary. A factor analysis can extract as many factors as there are variables, but a lot of these factors will be meaningless and of no value. We should retain only the best factors. But what are the best factors?

One common way of determining which factors to keep is to use a statistic called the *eigenvalue*. In factor analysis we are testing a causal model in which unknown factors are the independent variables and

the individual variables are dependent (see Figure 11.2 for a representation of this). Since we do not know, initially, how many factors 'exist', then any number of models could be used. The problem is to work out which one is best. The best model will be the simplest (i.e. with the fewest factors) and explain the most variance in the original set of variables. If we are to work out which factors to keep, we should keep those that explain most variance in the set of individual variables. (If you are unfamiliar with the concept of variance, stop reading and read the section on variance on p. 226 before reading further.)

The eigenvalue is a measure that attaches to factors and indicates the amount of variance in the pool of original variables that the factor explains. The higher this value, the more variance the factor explains. To be retained, factors must have an eigenvalue greater than 1. In the initial phase of extracting factors, a number of tables are produced. One of these tables provides various figures, including eigenvalues for each factor (see Table 11.4).

In this example, only two factors have an eigenvalue greater than 1. This means that we will use only two factors to summarise the eight variables. Once the number of factors has been determined, a factor matrix is produced for the factors that qualify for further analysis (see Table 11.5). In this matrix, each column represents a factor and the figures in the column represent the correlation (factor loading) between that factor and the particular variable (in the row).

The eigenvalue of a factor is the amount of variance in all the variables that is explained by that factor. This figure is obtained by squaring the correlations in the factor matrix (to obtain the proportion of explained variance for each variable) and then adding each of these squared figures in the column.

Table 11.4 Communalities, eigenvalues and per cent of explained variance in the unrotated solution

Variable	Communality	Factor	Eigenvalue	% of variance	Cum pct
PAY	0.43	1	2.39	29.9	29.9
INIT	0.62	2	1.38	17.3	47.2
RESPONS	0.54	3	0.99	12.6	59.6
ACHIEVE	0.59	4	0.80	10.0	69.6
PRESSURE	0.40	5	0.68	8.5	78.1
HOLIDAY	0.55	6	0.61	7.6	85.7
HOURS	0.57	7	0.58	7.3	93.0
SEXBOSS	0.07	8	0.56	7.0	100.0

Note: The initial extraction has two parts: initial and final. In the final stage, the figures for the selected factors (e.g. those with an eigenvalue above 1.0) are listed. I have listed all the figures here for the sake of completeness.

Table 11.5 Unrotated factor matrix for variables and factors in Table 11.4

Variable	Factor 1	Factor 2
PAY	0.63	−0.20
INIT	0.56	0.56
RESPONS	0.60	0.43
ACHIEVE	0.48	0.60
PRESSURE	0.49	−0.40
HOLIDAY	0.63	−0.40
HOURS	0.64	−0.39
SEXBOSS	0.22	−0.15

Thus, for factor 1 the total variance explained by factor 1 is $(0.63)^2 + (0.56)^2 + (0.60)^2 + (0.48)^2 + (0.49)^2 + (0.63)^2 + (0.64)^2 + (0.22)^2 = 2.39$. This is the same figure as the eigenvalue for factor 1 in Table 11.4. The factor that explains most variance will be factor 1, with factor 2 explaining the second most variance and so on.

One measure of a good factor analysis is the amount of the total variance in the original set of variables that is explained by the factors. The greater the explained variance, the better the solution. But to increase the total variance explained we have to increase the number of factors. This is one reason why the rule of only using factors with an eigenvalue of 1 or higher is used.

Sometimes we may have a large number of factors with eigenvalues greater than 1, but for the sake of simplicity we do not wish to retain all the factors. How do we decide which of the factors with eigenvalues greater than 1 to retain? One way is to look at the total amount of variance explained in the whole set of variables by various numbers of factors. This information is provided in the Cum pct column

in Table 11.4. As the number of factors increases, the total amount of variance explained increases. But it increases by smaller amounts with each additional factor. You have to make a decision when the additional factors do not lead to sufficient increases in the explained variance and only use the factors up to this point. Other methods for deciding how many factors to keep are discussed in Kim and Mueller (1978b: 41–5).

Clearly we can maximise the amount of variance explained overall by increasing the number of factors used. But since this is often undesirable, we can try to maximise explained variance by *eliminating the odd variable whose variance the main factors do not account for.* We can detect which variables are problems in this respect by calculating a statistic for each variable, called its *communality.*

In our example, two main factors have been extracted. The communality figure for each variable is obtained by using the correlation between each of these two factors and the variable and calculating the proportion of variance in that variable that is explained by the combination of the two extracted factors. This is obtained by squaring each of the coefficients for a particular variable in the factor matrix (Table 11.5) and adding them together. The answer is called the *communality of the variable.* Communalities range from 0 to 1. The higher the figure the better the set of selected factors explain the variance for that variable. The communality for PAY is calculated by $(0.63)^2 + (-0.20)^2 = 0.44$.

If the communality figure is low, it means that the variance for that variable is not explained by the selected factors. Normally it is best to drop variables with low communalities and thus increase the total variance explained by the two factors. In this example, dropping SEXBOSS with a low communality of 0.07 increases the total variance explained by the factors from 47 per cent to 54 per cent. The rest of this analysis is based on the exclusion of the SEXBOSS variable.

In summary, the initial extraction stage enables us to work out how many factors we will need for our final solution. The number of factors selected will be affected by the eigenvalues and the amount of total variance accounted for. There is a tradeoff between the desirable goals of maximising total explained variance and minimising the number of factors needed. One way of both maximising explained variance and minimising the number of factors required is to drop variables with very low communality figures.

Extracting the final factors—rotation

Once we know how many factors to use, we need to clarify which variables most 'belong' to each factor. Except when we have a single-factor solution (i.e. only one factor emerges) we expect that some variables will 'belong' to one factor and others will 'belong' to another.

The initial extraction of factors does not make it clear which variables belong most clearly to which factors. Often, as in the unrotated example in Table 11.4, many variables will 'load' on several factors and some factors will have almost every variable loading on them. To clarify which variables belong to which factors, and to make the factors more interpretable, we proceed to a third stage called *factor rotation*. Ideally rotation will result in factors on which only some variables load and in variables that load on only one factor.

There are a number of methods of 'rotating' variables, but these will not be discussed here. (See Kim and Mueller, 1978b for a discussion of the concept of rotation and the differences between the various methods.) One of the most widely used methods of rotation is *varimax* rotation. The following example is based on this.

Table 11.6 provides a rotated factor matrix. This matrix is crucial to interpreting the results of the factor analysis.

High loading variables 'belong' to the factor on which they load. The pattern of high and lower coefficients in the rotated matrix makes it much easier to see which variables belong to which factor.

Table 11.6   Rotated factor matrix

Variable	Factor 1	Factor 2
HOURS	0.76	0.09
HOLIDAY	0.74	0.08
PRESSURE	0.65	–0.01
PAY	0.61	0.22
INIT	0.09	0.78
ACHIEVE	0.01	0.76
RESPONS	0.20	0.71

Although there is no absolute rule as to how high a coefficient should be before a variable is said to load on a factor, it would be unusual to use variables with coefficients below 0.3.

Before interpreting the pattern of coefficients in Table 11.6 it is worth mentioning a few problems that you might come across at this point:

■ *Variable loads on more than one factor:* If a variable loads relatively highly on two or more factors, there are several options. A different method of rotation might resolve the problem. Alternatively, you might leave things as they are but when creating factor-based scales from the analysis (see below), only include the variable in the factor for which it loads most highly. Finally, you might decide that the variable that loads on several factors contaminates the analysis too much and drop it from the factor analysis.

■ *Variable loads only weakly on all factors:* If this is the case, then the communality of the variable will be low and the variable should be dropped from the analysis.

■ *Negative loadings:* The sign on a factor loading does not mean anything about the strength of the relationship between the variable and the factor. A negative sign only has meaning relative to the signs on the other variables: different signs simply mean that the variables are related to the factor in opposite directions. For this reason you should consider coding the variables in the same direction (reverse coding some variables) before the analysis.

At this stage the main statistical work of a factor analysis has been done and the researcher needs to interpret the results. Having located variables that go together empirically, you need to try to infer some conceptual commonality from the empirical commonality of the variables that load on a given factor.

In our example, the factors make some sense. The variables that load on the first factor seem to have something in common. They relate to *conditions* of work—pay, generous holidays, no pressure and good hours. By contrast, the variables that load on factor 2—sense of achievement, responsibility and initiative—emphasise the *content* rather than the conditions of the job. The first factor might be called *extrinsic* work orientation and the second might be called *intrinsic* work orientation.

Reducing the initial eight variables to two meaningful factors has two benefits. It may alert us to groupings of variables that we would not otherwise have thought of and thus enables us to work at a more sophisticated conceptual level. It also greatly simplifies subsequent analysis. For example, we might be interested in gender differences in job orientation. Rather than examining gender differences on each of the eight variables we can look at gender differences on just the two factors. As a result of the factor analysis, we might rephrase our original question and ask questions such as whether men look for intrinsic rewards in jobs while women look for extrinsic rewards.

To use the identified factors in subsequent analysis, we can construct scales based on the information provided by the factor analysis.

Factor scores and scales

There are at least three different ways of forming scales using the information gained from a factor analysis. We can create:

1 unweighted factor-*based* scales;
2 weighted factor-*based* scales; and
3 factor scales.

Unweighted factor-based scales are the easiest and are very similar to the summated scales discussed earlier in this chapter. They are based on only some of the information gained from the factor analysis and can be illustrated in relation to the extrinsic work orientation factor. To construct a scale in this way, we simply select the variables that will form the scale by choosing those with a reasonable loading on that scale (e.g. variables with loadings above 0.3) and then adding up people's raw scores on each of the selected variables to obtain their scale score. For the extrinsic work orientation score we could construct an additive scale from the variables HOURS, HOLIDAY, PRESSURE and PAY.

Alternatively we can construct a *weighted factor-based scale* using some or all of the variables and taking their *factor loadings* into account. Using this approach we can include all the variables or only the variables above a certain value. Instead of simply adding up people's scores on each of these variables, we weight their score by the loading. Table 11.7 provides an example of this for one person. You should note that including the variables that load weakly on the scale does not make much difference one way or another. Because the weights on these variables are so low, they contribute very little to the final scale score.

The SPSS syntax required to create a weighted factor-based scale is:

> General format:
>
> COMPUTE scalename = (varname1 * factor loading) + (varname2 * factor loading) + (varname3 * factor loading) + (varname4 * factor loading) etc.
>
> For factor 1 variables in Table 11.6:
>
> COMPUTE EXTRINS = (HOURS * 0.76) + (HOLIDAY * 0.74) + (PRESSURE * 0.65) + (PAY * 0.61).

The third type of scale is the most complex and is called a *factor scale*. The two types described above are factor-*based* scales (i.e. they used information supplied by the factor analysis). Factor scales are normally created by computer programs as part of the factor analysis routines.

The factor scale approach uses respondent's standardised scores on each variable rather than their raw

Table 11.7 Weighted factor-based scores for one person

Variable	Weight	Individual's original score	Weighted score (weight × raw score)
HOURS	0.76	3	2.28
HOLIDAY	0.74	4	2.96
PRESSURE	0.65	5	3.25
PAY	0.61	3	1.83
INIT	0.09	2	0.18
ACHIEVE	0.01	2	0.02
RESPONS	0.20	1	0.20
Scale score		20	10.72

scores (see pp. 171–3). Instead of multiplying these standardised individual scores by factor loadings (as in weighted factor-based scales), the standardised scores are multiplied by (weighted) *factor scores*. Factor scores are computed by factor analysis programs and supplied in the output. Factor analysis programs create factor scales by producing a score for each person on the factor by multiplying a person's standardised score for each variable with the factor score for the same variable. The factor scale that is produced in this way has a mean of 0. An example of the creation of scores on a factor scale is provided in Table 11.8.

ISSUES THAT COMPLICATE SCALING

There are four important problems which can complicate the construction and use of scales:

1 interpreting scale scores;
2 equivalence of items;
3 forcing scales to have meaningful upper and lower limits;
4 the problem of missing data.

Interpreting scale scores

Since a scale score is a summary of a person's responses to a number of questions, there is some loss

of detail when using scale scores. This leads to a number of difficulties. First, we do not know how a person has responded to any particular question. Second, even though two people have the same scale scores it does not mean that they have answered particular questions identically. The same scale scores can be achieved with quite different sets of answers. Although two people might be similar in their overall attitude they might differ markedly on particular questions.

Third, scale scores must be interpreted in relative rather than absolute terms. This is so in two senses. Someone with a score of 30 on a conservatism scale with a range of 0–40 cannot be described as 75 per cent conservative or twice as conservative as someone with a score of 15. Since scale scores do not have a precise interpretation, all we can say is that the higher someone's scale score is, the more conservative they are likely to be.

There is another sense in which scale scores are relative. We often want to know whether someone's score is 'high' or 'low'. This can be best worked out relative to the distribution of scale scores for other people in the sample. For example, on a scale with a 0–40 range, how do we interpret a score of 30? If nearly everyone else got between 30 and 40 then a score of 30 is *relatively* low. If nearly everyone got below 30 then 30 is a *relatively* high score. Often researchers say that the scores of the third of the sample with the highest scores will be called high and the scores of the third with the lowest scores will be called low. The scores of the middle third will be called moderate (see Figure 11.3). This technique was discussed in more detail in Chapter 10.

Equivalence of items

In the discussion of Likert scales so far, each item in a scale contributes equally to the final scale score. In the examples used, each item has had a score range of one to five. Sometimes researchers feel a particular item is more important than others and want strong agreement with it to contribute more than five points to the final scale. To do this the item can be *weighted*. To make an item twice as important as other items, we might score strong agreement as ten, agreement as eight and so forth. Apart from difficulties in working out how much extra weighting a particular item should have, researchers normally find little merit in this procedure and treat all items in a

Table 11.8 **Producing an individual's score on a factor scale**

Variable	Factor score for variable	Individual's standardised score	Weighted score (factor score × std score)
HOURS	0.40	0.22	0.09
HOLIDAY	0.39	0.74	0.29
PRESSURE	0.36	1.11	0.40
PAY	0.30	0.17	0.05
INIT	−0.07	−0.25	0.02
ACHIEVE	−0.11	−0.30	0.03
RESPONS	0.003	−0.61	0.002
Factor scale score			0.882

Note: The standard scores and factor scores are automatically calculated by programs such as SPSSX, as are the final factor scales and individual factor scale values. In this example the standard scores are the standard scores for the raw values in Table 11.7

Individual scale scores

Sample 1:	5	9	12	15	20	23	29	32	38
		low			moderate			high	
Sample 2:	5	9	10	11	13	15	17	18	20
		low			moderate			high	
Sample 3:	27	29	32	34	35	36	37	39	40
		low			moderate			high	

Figure 11.3   Relative classification of scale scores as low, moderate and high in three samples

Likert scale as being equally important and develop what are called *equal weight scales*.

Two main problems emerge when developing equal weight scales. These are caused by variables that have very different distributions and by variables that have a different number of response categories.

Combining items that have quite different *distributions* into a scale will mean that different items, in effect, will be weighted differently in the final scale score. The problem here revolves around the *meaning* of particular scores or answers on the various items used to build the scale. The need to standardise variables with very different distributions was discussed in Chapter 10.

The second problem with constructing equally weighted scales arises when we wish to combine items with different numbers of response categories. Unless adjustments are made, the different 'length' of the items will mean that some items are automatically more important. For example, one item may have two categories (agree/disagree) with codes 1 and 2, another may have five categories (strongly agree to strongly disagree) with codes 1, 2, 3, 4 and 5, while another might have ten categories with finer gradations of agreement and disagreement and be scored 1–10. In this case strong disagreement with the ten-category item would give someone a score of 10, strong disagreement with the five-category item a score of 5, and disagreement with the two-category item a score of 2. Clearly disagreement with the ten-category item contributes much more to a final scale score than it does with the other items.

A way of adjusting for different-length items is to use a form of standardisation as described in Chapter 10. If people's scores on each of a set of different-length items are converted into a standard score of one sort or another the problem is solved. If the scores are expressed in standard deviation units

(z-scores) then all the items on the scale will have the same potential length, thus ensuring that each item has an equal potential weight in the final scale score. Alternatively, if we wished all item scores to be positive,[1] we could produce a new variable that adjusts for the different number of categories of the variable by dividing the raw scores on the original variable by the variable's standard deviation (Newvar = oldvar / standard deviation). This method provides equally weighted items but does not adjust for different distributions of each variable in the way that z-scores do.

Forcing scales to have meaningful upper and lower limits

A difficulty when dealing with scales made up from either standardised items or from raw scores is in knowing what the lower and upper limits of the scale are. Depending on the number of items in a scale, their distribution, the number of categories in each item and the minimum and maximum scores of each item, the lower and upper values of a scale can vary between any two values. Thus a score of, say, 56 or minus 12 has no immediate meaning without first looking at the minimum and maximum values of that scale, its distribution and so forth. The problem is compounded when, in the same piece of analysis, we are dealing with several scales, each with different minimum and maximum values.

In order to overcome these problems and to make the meaning of scale scores a little more intuitive, it is desirable to convert the scales so that they have a specified minimum and maximum value.

One way of achieving this is to use the following transformation. The instructions here are those used in SPSS. Other comparable programs will enable similar transformations.

COMPUTE newscale = ((oldscale − minimum scale value) / range) * n

where:

Newscale = score for new scale with defined upper and lower values

Oldscale = score on old scale

Minimum scale value = lowest *observed* value on old scale

Range = range of observed scores on old scale (highest score − lowest score)

n = upper limit for new scale

Using this formula the scale scores will be forced between 0 and the number indicated by n. The following examples show how this is done for a scale where:

Minimum observed score on the old scale = 5

Maximum observed score on the old scale = 20

Range = 15

Old scale name = OLD

New scale name = NEW

COMPUTE NEW = ((OLD − 5) / 15) * 10.

Example 1

Individual score on old scale = 20 (i.e. highest observed score)

Desired upper limit for the scale = 10

$$Score on new scale = ((20 - 5) / 15) * 10$$
$$= (15/15) * 10$$
$$= 1 * 10$$
$$= 10$$

Example 2

This individual's score is 5 (lowest observed score).

$$Score on new scale = ((5 - 5) / 15) * 10$$
$$= (0/15) * 10$$
$$= 0 * 10$$
$$= 0$$

Example 3

This individual's score is 7.5 on the old scale.

$$Score on new scale = ((7.5 - 5) / 15) * 10$$
$$= (2.5/15) * 10$$
$$= 0.17 * 10$$
$$= 1.7$$

If we wanted the scores to be on a 0 to 100 scale we would simply multiply by 100 rather than 10. If we wanted all scores to be between 0 and 1 we would multiply by one.

The problem of missing data

A scale score is arrived at by adding up a person's score on each item. However, if a person has not answered all the questions how is a score obtained for each item for that person? When coding answers for survey analysis a person must receive a code or score for every question—even if they have not answered it. When they have not answered it they are given a missing data code (see Chapter 9). This missing data code can be any code except the code for a legitimate answer (a valid code). However, these codes create problems when trying to form scale scores.

The problem of missing data is illustrated in Table 11.9. In this example, missing data have been coded as 9. When this score is included in the addition to arrive at a scale score it distorts the scale score by inflating it. Had 0 been used it would have deflated the scale score. On the basis of questions answered, persons A and B are identical but the missing data in the scale score hides this.

There are a number of ways of dealing with this problem.

The first is to *exclude cases* with missing data on any of the scale items from the analysis. This is the obvious solution where missing data is due to cases being required to skip particular questions. It is also a reasonable solution with large samples where there are very few cases with missing values and these missing values are randomly distributed across cases.

Table 11.9 Problems of missing data for scaling

Person	Item										Scale
	1	2	3	4	5	6	7	8	9	10	score
A	1	1	1	9	9	9	1	1	1	1	34
B	1	1	1	1	1	1	1	1	1	1	10

A second solution is to *substitute valid values* for missing values. There is a variety of ways of doing this and these methods have already been discussed in Chapter 10 (see also Downey and King, 1998).

The third solution is to *adjust for the number of items* with valid codes. This approach is only appropriate for summated scales. The simplest way of achieving this is to simply *calculate the mean score on the variables that have valid codes*. This will automatically adjust for the number of questions a person has answered. This can be illustrated with some examples of answers to five questions each of which has a range of codes of 1–5. In each case individuals have given the same type of answer to each question they have answered (5 on a 5 point scale) but have answered a different number of items. The unadjusted scores differ because of the different number of questions answered. By dividing this score by the number of items the final score for each respondent is 5—indicating the 'extreme' way in which they have answered individual questions (see Table 11.10).

This adjustment is easily made with programs such as SPSS with the simple instruction:

> COMPUTE *adjusted varname* = MEAN
> *(variable list of items for scale)*

The score obtained in this way can then be subjected to the same transformations described earlier to standardise for the distribution of the variable.

SCALING CHECKLIST

1 What variables do you want to scale?
2 Do you have a concept for which you want to scale a set of items (Likert approach) or do you have a set of items and want to see what scales emerge from the set of items (factor analysis approach)?
3 What do you want a high score on the final scale to indicate?
4 Are items scored in a consistent direction?
5 Is reverse coding required?
6 Is there missing data on any of the variables to be scaled?
7 What method of handling missing data will you implement?

For Likert scales
8 Do you want an equal weight Likert scale?
9 Do any of the variables need to be standardised? If yes, is it because:
  a You want an equal weight scale but the items to be scaled have an unequal number of categories?
  b The distribution of the items differs markedly?
10 When you conduct the reliability analysis of your scale items what are the analysis statistics?
  a Are all item-scale coefficients above 0.3? (If not drop the items below 0.3.)
  b Are all item-total coefficients positive? (They should be. If they are not then an item probably requires reverse coding.)
  c Is Cronbach's alpha above 0.7?
  d Can alpha be improved by dropping any items?
11 When poor items are dropped do the scale statistics meet normal requirements?
12 What upper and lower limits do you want your final scale to have? Is a transformation required to achieve this?

Factor analysis
13 Are your selected variables suitable for factor analysis?
  a What are the KMO values of the variables?
  b Are any of the variables likely to be related in cause and effect terms? (If so, they should not be in the factor analysis together.)

Table 11.10   Illustration of the effect of adjusting scale scores for a number of items with valid codes

Scores on questions

	Q1	Q2	Q3	Q4	Q5	Unadjusted total	N of items answered	Adjusted score (Unadj. total/N of items)
Case A	5	5	5	5	5	25	5	5
Case B	5	5	5	5	–	20	4	5
Case C	5	5	5	–	–	15	3	5

14 After the initial extraction of factors (using principle components analysis method) how many factors are worth keeping?
   a   What are the eigenvalues of the best factors?
   b   How much variance in particular variables do the factors with an eigenvalue >1 explain?
15 Are there problem variables that should be dropped from the analysis?
   a   Do any variables have a very low communality?

16 After rotating the factors (normally using the varimax method) which variables load on the main factors?
17 Do the factors make sense (look at the nature of the variables that load on the factor)? If so, name the factor.
18 What method will you employ to construct scales from the factor analysis?
   a   Factor scales?
   b   Unweighted factor-based scales?
   c   Weighted factor-based scales?

KEY CONCEPTS

Adjusting for missing items	Factor	Reliability	Unweighted factor-based scale
Adjusting scale length	Factor analysis	Rotation	Weighted factor-based scale
Communality	Factor loading	Scale	
Cronbach's alpha	Factor scale	Standardised scale	
Eigenvalue	Factor score	Standardised variable	
Equal-weight scale	Item-scale (item-total) correlation	Summated scale	
Explained variance	Likert scale	Unidimensionality	

ENDNOTE

1   z-scores represent the number of standard deviations a person lies below or above the mean and take on negative and positive values which, when added, sum to zero.

FURTHER READING

An old but still useful introduction to scaling is Bert Green's paper 'Attitude Measurement' (1954). *Techniques of Attitude Scale Construction* (1957) by Edwards is also an old but useful book. Some of the issues of scaling are addressed in section one in Lazarsfeld, Pasanella and Rosenberg's collection of papers in *Continuities in the Language of Social Research* (1972). The Sage University Paper series on Quantitative Applications in the Social Sciences has published a number of technical papers on a wide range of scaling techniques. Of these the two most accessible and most wide ranging are McIver and Carmines' 'Unidimensional Scaling' (1981) and Spector's 'Summated Rating Scale Construction' (1992).

Papers on a range of other scaling techniques are provided in these two publications. Downey and King (1998) compare different ways of handling missing data in Likert scales. Proctor (1995) provides a good basic introduction while Dunn-Rankin offers a more comprehensive but more difficult treatment in *Scaling Methods* (1983). Very good treatments of factor analysis are provided in Kim and Mueller (1978a and 1978b) and in the *SPSSX Advanced Statistics Guide* by Norusis (1985).

EXERCISES

1 In your own words explain why it is desirable to build scales.
2 What is the difference between reliability and unidimensionality?

3 Use the questions in Box 11.1 designed to test future orientation and administer them to some people (if done as a class, obtain about 100 cases). Using the steps described, test to see

which items belong to the scale. You will need to use a statistical package such as SPSS or SIMSTAT that includes reliability analysis for this. Make sure that you work out what to do with missing data.

4 From the correlation matrix (Table 1) below decide which items you would select to include in a scale (or scales).

5 Imagine a set of ten questions designed to measure conservatism. Each item is scored from 1 to 5 with 5 being given to the most conservative response to each question. Non-answers were coded as 9.
   a What would be the scale score of someone who was most conservative on every question?
   b What is the minimum scale score possible?
   c What would a scale score of 54 suggest?
   d If two people both obtained a scale score of 25 what conclusions can you draw about how they answered each question?
   e If one person obtained a scale score of 15 and another a score of 30, what conclusions would you draw from this?

6 Imagine you obtained the coefficients in Table 2 when testing the ten items for the previous scale. What would you do on the basis of these? Why?

7 Explain, using an example, why missing data cause problems when scaling.

8 Outline the three main ways in which missing data are dealt with when building scales.

9 Explain, using an example, why items with a different number of response categories can cause problems when building scales.

10 Table 3 shows some details about a set of questions we want to form into an equal weight scale. As they are, would they form an equal weight scale? Why or why not? If they would not form an equal weight scale as they are, how would you go about ensuring that each of the items had an equal weight in the final scale?

11 Table 4 shows some details about three composite scales, each of different lengths, in which the items have been equally weighted. Each of the scales had the following characteristics:
   a A person obtained the following scores on the three untransformed scales: Scale A = 6.0; Scale B = 2.2; Scale C = 9.0. Using the formula on p. 194 convert these scores to scores on transformed scales that would have a minimum value of 0 and a maximum value of 10. What do the transformed scores tell you when you compare this person's score on the three transformed scales?
   b A person obtained the following scores on each of the untransformed scales: Scale A = 7.0; Scale B = 7.2; Scale C = 7.3. Convert these scores to scores on scales that would

Table 2

Item	Item-total correlations	Alpha if item deleted
1	0.56	0.59
2	0.20	0.68
3	0.33	0.67
4	0.47	0.62
5	0.21	0.71
6	0.51	0.62
7	0.72	0.60
8	0.43	0.73
9	0.50	0.64
10	−0.57	0.61

Overall alpha 0.62

Table 1

			Variables				
	A	**B**	**C**	**D**	**E**	**F**	**G**
A	1.00	0.05	0.00	0.21	−0.03	0.09*	0.32*
B	0.05	1.00	0.21*	0.10	0.44*	0.17*	0.01
C	0.00	0.21*	1.00	0.03	0.26*	0.11	0.09
D	0.21*	0.10	0.03	1.00	−0.04	0.00	0.18*
E	−0.03	0.44*	0.26*	−0.04	1.00	0.30*	−0.02
F	0.09	0.17*	0.11	0.00	0.30*	1.00	0.04
G	0.32*	0.01	0.09	0.18*	−0.02	0.04	1.00

* = significant at the 0.01 level

Table 3

Item	N of categories	Minimum possible value	Maximum possible value	Mean	Standard deviation
A	2	0	1	0.59	0.13
B	10	1	10	3.51	2.04
C	4	1	4	3.13	0.78
D	5	0	4	3.03	0.86
E	7	1	7	3.49	1.99
F	10	0	9	7.56	3.24
G	5	0	4	1.98	1.12

Table 4

Scale	Lowest observed score	Highest observed score	Lowest possible score	Highest possible score
A	5.5	8.9	2.5	11.6
B	0.7	10.5	0.6	11.5
C	6.5	0.5	5.5	23.0

have a minimum value of 0 and a maximum value of 10. What does a comparison of the transformed scores tell you?

12 Tables 5a–e show statistics produced for a factor analysis of eight variables. Your task is to inspect the statistics and answer the questions that follow.

People were asked how justifiable they felt certain behaviours were. Each variable is scored on a scale from 1 to 5 with 1 meaning that the action was never justifiable and 5 indicating that it was always justifiable. The eight variables are: AFFAIR = Married person having an affair; UNSAFE = Accepting unsafe work conditions even if for higher wages; HOT = Buying something you knew was stolen; DIVORCE = Divorce justifiable; ABORT = Abortion justifiable; BENEFITS = Claiming government benefits to which you are not entitled; LIE = Lying in your own interest; HOMO = Justifiability of homosexuality.

a If you were redoing this factor analysis, are there any variables that you would omit? Give reasons for your decision.

b On the basis of the figures in Table 5a, what variables would you anticipate will cluster together into factors? Explain your answer.

c Examine Table 5b. On the basis of these figures, what is the optimal number of factors needed to represent this set of variables? Explain in your own words the meaning of the following figures in the second table: 0.55 (communality); 3.14 (eigenvalue); 39.3 (% of variance); 56.7 (cum pct). Show how the figures of 0.55 and 3.14 would have been calculated.

d Examine Table 5d. What name would you give each factor? What do the high figures mean? What do the low figures mean?

e On the basis of the information in Table 5e, calculate:
    i   the unweighted factor-based scale score for the individual whose scores are provided;
    ii the weighted factor-based scale score;
    iii the factor scale score.

13 Using the test locator program at the BUROS website www.unl.edu/buros/ obtain a bibliographic reference for a scale for each of the following concepts:
■ abortion attitudes
■ attitude to homosexuality
■ optimism
■ marital adjustment
■ efficacy.

Table 5a   Zero-order correlation mix

	AFFAIR	UNSAFE	HOT	DIVORCE	ABORT	BENEFITS	LIE	HOMO
AFFAIR	1.00							
UNSAFE	0.28	1.00						
HOT	0.35	0.29	1.00					
DIVORCE	0.38	0.16	0.17	1.00				
ABORT	0.38	0.18	0.21	0.55	1.00			
BENEFITS	0.31	0.28	0.50	0.12	0.14	1.00		
LIE	0.49	0.30	0.41	0.25	0.30	0.36	1.00	
HOMO	0.40	0.14	0.20	0.44	0.45	0.14	0.26	1.00

KMO = 0.81

Table 5b   Communality, eigenvalues and variance figures before rotation

Variable	Communality	Factor	Eigenvalue	% of variance	Cum pct
AFFAIR	0.55	1	3.14	39.3	39.3
UNSAFE	0.35	2	1.39	17.4	56.7
HOT	0.61	3	0.78	9.7	66.4
DIVORCE	0.65	4	0.68	8.5	74.9
ABORT	0.65	5	0.58	7.3	82.2
BENEFITS	0.61	6	0.51	6.4	88.6
LIE	0.53	7	0.47	5.9	94.5
HOMO	0.57	8	0.44	5.5	100.0

Table 5c   Unrotated factor loadings

Variable	Factor 1	Factor 2
AFFAIR	0.74	−0.02
LIE	0.69	0.23
ABORT	0.65	−0.48
DIVORCE	0.62	−0.51
HOT	0.62	0.48
HOMO	0.61	−0.44
UNSAFE	0.49	0.33
BENEFITS	0.55	0.55

Table 5d   Rotated factor matrix

Variable	Factor 1	Factor 2
BENEFITS	0.78	−0.00
HOT	0.77	0.09
LIE	0.65	0.32
UNSAFE	0.58	0.11
DIVORCE	0.07	0.80
ABORT	0.12	0.80
HOMO	0.12	0.75
AFFAIR	0.50	0.54

Table 5e   Factor scores for variables on factor 1*

Variable	Factor score	Raw score	Standard score
AFFAIR	0.15	2	0.30
UNSAFE	0.28	4	0.85
HOT	0.38	4	0.68
DIVORCE	−0.12	3	0.15
ABORT	−0.10	5	1.10
BENEFITS	0.40	4	0.40
LIE	0.27	5	0.90
HOMO	−0.09	1	−0.20

* includes the raw and standardised scores for a particular individual for each of the variables for a given individual

Part IV

ANALYSING
SURVEY DATA

12

Overview of analysis

Once data have been collected they have to be analysed. This chapter outlines four broad factors which affect how they are analysed. Subsequent chapters examine the particular methods of analysis and related statistics in more detail. Four factors which affect how the data are analysed are:

1 the number of variables being examined;
2 the level of measurement of the variables;
3 whether we want to use our data for descriptive or inferential purposes;
4 ethical responsibilities.

THE NUMBER OF VARIABLES

How we analyse data depends on what we want to know. If we simply wish to describe one characteristic of the sample at a time (e.g. sex, vote, income level) we will use a *univariate* (one variable) method of analysis. If we are interested in two variables simultaneously we will use a *bivariate* (two variable) method. For example, if we wanted to see if gender and voting preference were related (i.e. do women vote differently from men?) we would use a bivariate method. If our research question makes use of three or more variables we would use a *multivariate* technique. We might be interested in income: why do some people earn more than

others? We might say it is due to two factors: education level and gender. Since we are using three variables (income, gender and education) here, we would use a multivariate technique.

Before analysing data we must be clear about the question we are trying to answer. This will dictate the broad type of analysis we choose. Once we have decided, for example, that we need to use a bivariate technique, we will then need to choose between a range of such techniques. In practice we develop and refine our research questions in the process of analysis so we move between univariate, bivariate and multivariate techniques. Initially, for example, we might formulate a question: do people's incomes vary because of different levels of education (bivariate—education and income)? Initial bivariate analysis might show that income does vary to some extent according to education level but that we also need to look at other variables. We then reformulate the question and include additional variables such as gender. This question might then require the use of a multivariate technique.

LEVELS OF MEASUREMENT

Having decided to use univariate, bivariate or multivariate techniques we have to decide which particular technique to use within these broad categories. A key factor in this choice is the level of measurement of the variables being used.

Any variable is composed of two or more categories or attributes. Thus gender is a variable with the categories male and female, country of birth is a variable with the categories being particular countries. The level of measurement of variables refers to how the categories of the variable relate to one another. There are three main levels of measurement: interval[1] (also called continuous), ordinal and nominal (also called categorical or qualitative). Three characteristics of the categories of a variable determine its level of measurement (see Figure 12.1):

1 whether there are different categories;
2 whether the categories can be rank ordered;
3 whether the differences or intervals between each category can be specified in a meaningful numerical sense.

Interval level

An interval variable is one in which the categories can be ranked from *low to high* in some meaningful way. In addition to ordering the categories from low to high it is possible to specify the *amount of difference* between the categories or values. Age, when measured in years, is an example of an interval variable. We can rank–order the categories of age (years) from youngest (lowest) to oldest (highest). Furthermore, we can specify the amount of difference between the categories. The difference between the category '20 years old' and the category '25 years old' is five years. Variables such as the weekly number of hours of paid work, IQ, height, weight and income (in dollars) are all variables where the categories are numeric and where the *intervals* between the categories can be specified precisely.

Ordinal level

An ordinal variable is one where we can rank–order categories from low to high. However, we cannot specify in numeric terms *how much* difference there is between the categories. For example, when the variable age has categories such as 'child', 'adolescent', 'young adult', 'middle aged' and 'elderly' the variable is measured at the ordinal level. The categories can be ordered from youngest to eldest but we cannot specify precisely the age gap between people in different categories. Measuring the level of

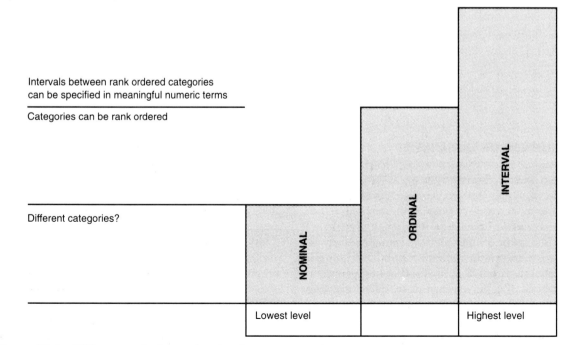

Figure 12.1   Differences between levels of measurement

workforce participation as full-time, part-time and not in the labour force would produce an ordinal variable.

Nominal level

A nominal variable is one where the different categories have no set rank–order. With a nominal variable it makes no sense to say that the categories can be ordered from low to high in some sense. Religious affiliation is a nominal variable where we can distinguish between categories of affiliation (e.g. Jewish, no religion, Roman Catholic, Orthodox, Protestant, Islamic). These categories have no natural rank–*order*.

Influencing the level of measurement

The level of measurement of a variable can be thought of as ranging from low to high. Nominal-level variables are the lowest level followed by ordinal and then interval level which is the highest level. The higher the level of measurement the more information the variable contains. The categories of the interval-level variable provide three types of information compared to an ordinal variable that contains two types of information and nominal that contains only one type of information.

As a general rule it is better to construct variables so that they are measured at a higher level. Not only do such variables provide more information but they also open up a wider range of methods of statistical analysis. The higher the level of measurement the more powerful are the methods of analysis that can be used.

The level of measurement of a variable is not a fixed or inherent characteristic of a variable. It is a product of the way in which we conceptualise and measure the variable. The way the variable is measured is a consequence of the way a questionnaire item is framed and the nature of the response categories provided. This means that as researchers we need to think about the level of measurement we want to achieve. Our decisions about this will influence the way we frame and code questions (see Chapters 7 and 9). This in turn will affect the way we can analyse the data we collect.

The format of the question and response categories

If we ask people how much paid work they have and provide 'none', 'part-time' and 'full-time' as response categories, the variable will be ordinal. If we ask them how many hours per week they work it will be interval. If we ask how many hours per week and provide the responses of 'none', '1–10', '11–20', '21–30', '31–40' and '40 plus' it is an ordinal variable. This is because the difference between people in the various grouped categories cannot be specified precisely. One person may be in the 11–20 category and another in the 21–30 category. Since we do not know the precise number of hours they each work we cannot tell how much difference there is in the hours each works. The difference could be as little as one and as much as nineteen hours.

The application

In some situations it is legitimate to rank the categories of a variable, thus treating it as ordinal, and for other applications it is not meaningful to rank them. For example, a list of religious affiliations would not be ranked if we simply wished to classify the group to which a person belonged (e.g. Methodist, Presbyterian, Baptist, Catholic, Anglican, Jehovah's Witness, Jewish, Moslem etc), but if we wanted to use religious affiliation as a proxy measure to reflect something about level of integration into mainstream groups in society it could be meaningful to rank religious groups for this purpose.

Which level of measurement to aim for

Since the level of measurement of a variable can be affected by a researcher's decisions, which is the best level to aim for? There are at least seven things to consider.

1   A wider range of methods of analysis is appropriate as the level of measurement of variable increases.

2   More powerful and sophisticated techniques of analysis are only appropriate for interval-level variables.

3   Higher levels of measurement provide more information—but is this really necessary?

4   Questions that require a lot of precision and detail can be unreliable since people often do not have accurate, detailed information.

5   People may be reluctant to provide precise information but may provide it in more general terms (e.g. income bracket, age cohort).

6 Numerical data collected in grouped form (e.g. age, income categories) can be converted to interval data if we make particular assumptions.

7 If a variable is measured at an interval level it is simple to reduce it to ordinal or nominal levels. With the exception already noted, data collected at low levels of measurement cannot be converted to higher levels.

In summary, it is generally advisable to measure variables at the highest level appropriate to that variable, but considerations of reliability, response rate and need will mean that measurement at lower levels often makes most sense.

METHODS OF ANALYSIS

The method of analysis adopted depends on the complexity of the research question. If the research question involves only one variable, select a method of analysis appropriate for univariate analysis. If the question involves two variables use a method designed for bivariate analysis and so on (see Figure 12.2). Within each level of analysis (univariate, bivariate, multivariate) there is a range of methods of analysis (Table 12.1). The choice between methods is determined in part by the level of measurement of the variables involved: some methods of analysis are appropriate only for variables measured at certain levels (e.g. interval). Having chosen an appropriate method of analysis, the choice of statistics to be used with that particular method is affected both by the method of analysis itself and the level of measurement of the particular values. These points are discussed in detail in Chapters 13 to 17.

DESCRIPTIVE AND INFERENTIAL STATISTICS

Only two points need to be made about statistics at the moment. The choice of statistics is determined by many previous decisions such as the method of analysis, level of measurement of the variables and complexity of the research question (univariate, bivariate or multivariate). The analyst's task is to work out, given these decisions, which statistics to use.

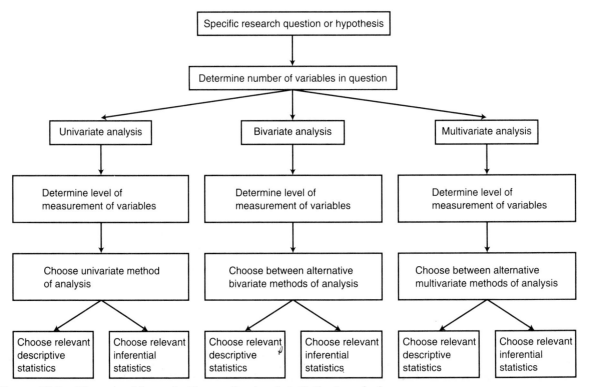

Figure 12.2   Flow chart for selecting methods of statistical analysis

Table 12.1   Some methods of survey analysis

Univariate methods		Bivariate methods		Multivariate methods
1 Frequency distributions	1	Crosstabulations	1	Conditional tables
	2	Scattergrams	2	Partial rank–order correlation
	3	Regression	3	Multiple and partial correlation
	4	Rank–order correlation	4	Multiple and partial regression
	5	Comparison of means	5	Path analysis

Statistics are only a tool for analysis: we need to choose the appropriate tool for the job in hand.

There are two basic types of statistics: descriptive and inferential.

Descriptive statistics

Descriptive statistics are those that summarise patterns in the responses of cases in a sample. They provide information about, say, the 'average' income of respondents or indicate whether education level affects the voting patterns of people in the sample.

There are three broad ways in which descriptive analysis is conducted and presented: tabular, graphical and statistical.

1   *Tabular:* Tabular analysis involves presenting the results of analysis in tables. This might be in the simple form of a frequency table (see Figure 12.3), a cross-tabulation (see Chapter 14) or some other type of table.
2   *Graphical:* Frequently the information contained in a table can be presented as a graph. For simple analysis a graph might display patterns more readily than a table might (see Figure 12.3).

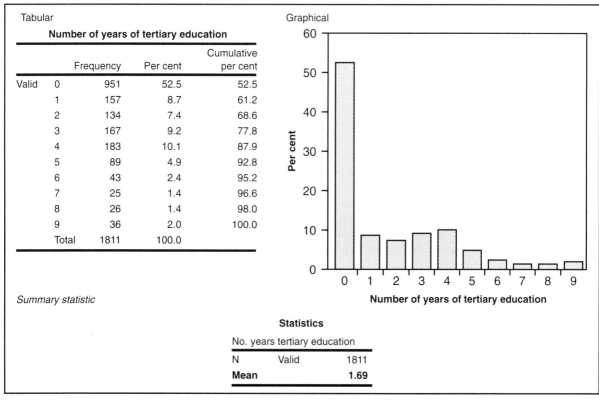

Figure 12.3   Three ways of presenting descriptive analysis of a single variable

3 *Statistical:* Statistics provide summary measures of information contained in a set of cases. These descriptive statistics are frequently a single number and do not contain as much information as a table or graph but they can provide an easily understood snapshot of a set of cases. In Figure 12.3 the summary statistic is an average (mean) which tells us that the average number of years of tertiary education of all people in a sample of 1811 people is 1.69 years.

Inferential statistics

Typically, we are not interested simply in describing the attitudes and characteristics of just the people in a sample. Rather, we want to generalise the results from the sample to a wider population. The function of inferential statistics is to provide an idea about whether the patterns described in the sample are likely to apply in the population from which the sample is drawn. When we have a sample that is obtained by probability sampling methods (see Chapter 6) we can use inferential statistics for this purpose.

There are two main types of inferential statistics:

1 interval estimates;
2 tests of statistical significance.

Interval estimates

Since a sample is not a whole population there will always be a margin of error. The real patterns in the population are unlikely to be exactly the same as those in the sample. The larger the sample and the less variation in the population the smaller this margin of error. Interval estimates provide an estimate of the margin of error—the range around the sample figures where the true population figures are likely to lie. For example, before any election, samples of about 2000 people are asked how they will vote. Suppose 52 per cent say they will vote Labor and 48 per cent say other parties. We do not want to know how these 2000 people would vote but how the whole electorate is likely to vote. Inferential statistics help estimate how close to the sample's voting preferences the population's vote will be: inferential statistics enable us to infer from the sample to the population. Similarly, the average income in a sample might be $40 000. We can use inferential statistics to calculate within what range of $40 000 the real average in the population is likely to be.

Tests of statistical significance

An alternative way of working out whether we can generalise from a sample to a population is to ask how likely is it that the patterns found in the sample will exist in the population. While interval estimates tell us about the margin of error between sample figures and population figures, tests of significance tell us how likely it is that the sample findings would exist within the population as a whole. To be precise, tests of significance tell us how likely it is (with a given sample size) that we would find the particular pattern observed in a sample if such a pattern did not really exist in the population. That is, how likely is it that the sample figures do not reflect population figures.

Thus, we might find in a sample that women are more likely than men to vote for a conservative political party. This is a descriptive finding for the sample. Is this pattern simply likely to hold in the sample but not in the population? If the sample consisted of ten people we would have no confidence that this gender difference would hold in the population. If it was a much larger sample and there was a considerable gender difference in the sample we might have more confidence that the pattern in the sample reflects something that is 'out there' in the population rather than simply reflecting a poor sample—or sampling error. Tests of statistical significance provide a systematic way of estimating whether sample figures will hold up in the population.

The following chapters focus more on descriptive statistics than inferential statistics. The use of descriptive statistics requires the most imagination and skill and is the most productive in terms of understanding any phenomenon. Once we have analysed data using descriptive techniques we should use inferential statistics to see the likely match between the sample patterns and those in the population. But the first and key task is to discover these patterns and processes. This is the task of descriptive statistics.

ETHICS AND ANALYSIS

Data analysis is not just a technical matter. Social scientists have ethical responsibilities to analyse data properly and report it fairly.

It is not difficult to analyse and report results in ways that distort the underlying patterns. It is easy to use selectively 'juicy' quotes from in-depth interviews to support almost any proposition you might want to suggest. It is barely more difficult to report statistical data in such a way as to mislead readers. Selective reporting and selective, distorted analysis can readily paint a highly misleading picture. Huff's book *How to Lie with Statistics* (1954) provides plenty of lighthearted examples of how this can be done.

Although it should go without saying that falsification of results is unacceptable, there are plenty of examples in scientific literature where people have either fabricated results entirely or changed figures to make them appear more impressive. The pressure to publish, to complete work quickly, to save money or to be politically correct can tempt people to fabricate results. Those who do fabricate results no doubt expect that the chances of detection are slight. They are probably correct.

Replication of results has been one of the key safeguards against falsification. Replication requires that another researcher can collect comparable data in the same way and thus check the veracity and reliability of any set of results. This is an important safeguard in experimental research where it is possible to reproduce the conditions under which another researcher has conducted an experiment. Unfortunately, true replication is less achievable in survey research. This is because social surveys rely on samples in a particular place and time, and to the extent that the time and place of two surveys (and thus the sample) are different, then any variation between results might be defended in terms of sample differences. This makes true replication difficult. An unscrupulous person could fabricate or at least modify results and claim that any differences between these and those of other researchers are due to sample differences or sampling error.

Results can be misrepresented without fabricating them. You can distort results by inappropriately analysing data. It is really quite easy. It will become evident as you read the following chapters that variables can be recoded to produce the desired results. Analysis can be restricted to particular variables that produce the desired results while ignoring analysis that is not so supportive. Inappropriate techniques might be used for the data, multivariate analysis neglected (see Chapters 16 and 17), poor quality scales produced (see Chapter 11) and graphs might be distorted to give the impression we are looking for (see Chapter 13). It is not difficult to conduct

analysis in such a way that it will mislead readers and other consumers of social research. In the end we must rely on honesty rather than the fear of detection to produce good research.

Inappropriate analysis may not be deliberate but may mislead nonetheless. It is therefore important that researchers ensure that they have the necessary skills to analyse data thoroughly and appropriately. To do otherwise is hardly different from the surgeon who may be able to perform an appendectomy undertaking brain surgery. The pretence of greater expertise than one possesses is misrepresentation and therefore unethical behaviour. Ignorance of appropriate methodology—or at least the representation of greater expertise than one possesses—is just as unethical as falsification of results. Inappropriate analysis can be just as misleading as deliberate falsification of data.

Perhaps the most common way in which researchers mislead is by only reporting convenient or 'positive' results. Rather than fabricating results or manipulating data to achieve the desired results, a misleading impression can be achieved easily by simply not reporting inconvenient results. Data are usually complex and some results will support a particular hypothesis while others may contradict it. The appropriate course of action when one comes up with 'negative' results is to modify the theory to accommodate these awkward results and thus reflect the complexity of social life. However, the temptation is to have one's simple theory supported and to report only the data that do this. In science and social science few people achieve fame by finding that two variables are unrelated or by having their ideas disproven. It is the discovery of patterns and relationships rather than the discovery of chaos and complexity that wins attention. No doubt some results are misreported or flawed for this reason.

An important safeguard against misreporting or misanalysis of results is to make data sets publicly available through data archives in which researchers deposit their data sets and make them available to other researchers for secondary analysis. In Australia this is done via the Social Science Data Archives at the Australian National University; in Britain it is done via the ESRC data archives at the University of Essex and in the USA via the ICPSR archives at the University of Michigan. Making data available for analysis by others is perhaps the survey researcher's closest approximation to replication. While it does not prevent falsification of the original data set, it does act as a check on misanalysis.

There are those who argue that this plea for full and fair analysis and presentation of results is impossible. They argue that all research is necessarily subjective and that our values and assumptions inevitably affect the questions we ask and the way we analyse and interpret data. Instead of allowing the facts to speak for themselves, they argue, we make the facts speak for us. There is some merit to this view. However, it is an abrogation of responsibility to argue that because our judgments are clouded by our values and background we can give up trying to be thorough and demanding in our analysis. The best antidote to this sort of subjective analysis is to acknowledge our own position and to deliberately look for evidence that might *disprove* our own theory.

Some of those who are more idealistic might argue that full and thorough analysis does not really matter. Some will assert that values are all important and that the primary role of the researcher is to bring about worthwhile change in the society we study. That is, we should be social activists rather than social researchers.

We should acknowledge that data collection and analysis are affected by our values and that this may cause us to fall short of the ideal of full and thorough analysis. But this is not to say that we should give up our attempts to stand back from our values and assumptions and to test them against the data. We should look at all the data we collect rather than that which suits our purposes. We should rigorously test our scales and evaluate the validity and reliability of our variables. We should look for 'negative' results and do all we can to report inconvenient results. It is only by doing this that we can extend our knowledge beyond that which our beliefs and prejudices dictate. If there is one lesson to be learned from history it is that those who believe that they have the final truth and that they know what is good and right for the rest of us are almost certain to be mistaken.

It is therefore important that the social scientist be involved in *testing* the beliefs of ourselves and of others as to what the 'real' world is like.

OVERVIEW OF ANALYSIS: A CHECKLIST

Before analysing data we have to be clear about the broad type of analysis we require. There are four broad considerations when selecting methods of analysis.

1   What is the level of measurement of each of the variables being used in any particular piece of analysis? In determining this ask:
    a   Can the categories of the variable be rank–ordered?
    b   Can the differences between the categories be specified in meaningful numeric terms?
    c   What level of measurement is required/ preferable?
    d   Can the level of measurement of the variable be altered by reordering or collapsing the categories of the variable (refer to Chapter 10)?
2   How many variables will any particular piece of analysis require?
3   What type of analysis is required?
    a   Is descriptive analysis required?
        i   What form will the description take? Will it be tabular, graphical or in summary statistical form?
    b   Is inferential analysis required?
        i   Is inferential analysis justified? Is the sample a probability sample?
        ii What type of inferential analysis is required: interval estimates or tests of significance?
4   Have the ethical principles of full, fair, appropriate and challenging analysis been applied to the selection of data to be analysed and reported?

KEY CONCEPTS

Bivariate	Interval-level variable	Nominal-level variable	Rank order
Descriptive statistics	Level of measurement	Numeric difference	Summary statistic
Inferential statistics	Multivariate	between categories	Test of significance
Interval estimates		Ordinal-level variable	Univariate

ENDNOTE

1   There is another level of measurement called ratio level. For the purpose of this book there is no need to distinguish between interval and ratio levels of measurement. In this book the term interval level of measurement is taken to mean both interval and ratio levels of measurement.

FURTHER READING

Useful discussions of the distinctions made in this chapter are made in most introductory statistics books. Brief outlines are available in section A of Freeman's *Elementary Applied Statistics* (1965) and Johnson's *Social Statistics* *Without Tears* (1977). Very thorough discussions are available in Loether and McTavish, *Descriptive Statistics for Sociologists* (1974), Chapters 1 and 2 and in their *Inferential Statistics for Sociologists* (1974), Chapters 1 and 10.

EXERCISES

1   List ten nominal, ten ordinal and ten interval-level variables. Try to select variables that are sociological. If the level of measurement of the variable could differ depending on response categories, make it clear why you are treating it at the level you are.

2   What level of measurement are the variables in the traditionalism scale in Chapter 11?

3   What level of measurement is each variable in Figure 9.3?

4   Develop three questions that tell us something about a person's religiousness. One question should yield nominal data, another will yield ordinal data and the third will produce interval data.

5   For each of the following problems which analysis technique would you use: univariate, bivariate or multivariate?

   a   To determine the proportion of males and of females in your sample.

   b   To determine the income distribution in the sample.

   c   To see if sons get on better with their fathers than do daughters.

   d   To see if ethnic background is related to frequency of contact with siblings.

   e   To see if education level affects income differently for males and females.

   f   To see if the income levels of older people differ from those of younger people.

6   In your own words describe the different functions of inferential and descriptive statistics.

7   List the advantages and disadvantages of obtaining interval-level data.

8   For each of the three variables below three sets of responses have been provided. In each case one set of responses would produce a nominal level variable, an ordinal and an interval-level variable. Indicate which sets of responses will produce a nominal variable, an ordinal variable and an interval variable.

   a   Age

      i   Answer format: How old are you? ___ years ___ months

      ii   □ Younger than 20   □ 20–24 □ 25–29   □ 30–34 □ 35–39   □ 40–49 □ 50–59   □ 60+

      iii   □ Young □ middle aged □ elderly

   b   Intelligence

      i   IQ category: □ imbecile, □ idiot, □ moron … □ genius

      ii   My IQ score is: ___ points

      iii   Which of the following best describes the way you think? □ Creative thinker □ Intuitive thinker □ Logical thinker □ I don't think much at all

   c   Children

      i   Are you a parent? □ Yes   □ No

      ii   How many children do you have? □ 0   □ 1–2   □ 3+

      iii   How many children do you have? ___

9   List methods by which you can minimise the chances of researchers misrepresenting their data through misanalysis or fabrication.

13

Univariate analysis

This chapter is divided into two main sections. The first deals with descriptive analysis and outlines three main ways of doing descriptive analysis using tables, graphs and summary statistics. The second section explains the use of two types of inferential statistics—significance tests and interval estimates. The outline of both descriptive and inferential analysis distinguishes between the use of these methods for nominal, ordinal and interval-level variables.

DESCRIPTIVE STATISTICS

A core part of univariate analysis is describing the distribution of variables. Since all variables have two or more categories or values we can examine the way in which cases are distributed across these categories. There are a number of aspects of such distributions to consider.

1   *Simple description:* how many people belong to particular categories? Which categories have a lot of cases and which have few cases?
2   *Typicality/central tendency:* do cases tend to belong to particular categories? What is the typical category(ies) to which people belong?
3   *Variation:* are cases concentrated in a few categories or are they spread fairly evenly across the categories? How similar (homogeneous) or dissimilar (heterogeneous) is the sample?
4   *Symmetry/skewness:* for variables where categories are rank-ordered from low to high, do cases tend to cluster towards the low or the high end? Or do they cluster towards the middle of the variable?

Tabular analysis

Frequency tables are the normal tabular method of presenting distributions of a single variable.

The frequency tables in Table 13.1 illustrate the elements of a frequency table.

■   *Column 1:* The values or categories of the variable.
■   *Frequency column:* The number of people in each category.
■   *Per cent column:* The per cent of the *whole sample* in each category.
■   *Valid per cent column:* The percentage *of those who gave a valid response to the question* that belongs to each category. This is normally the percentage that is used when reporting results.
■   *Cumulative per cent column:* The *rolling addition of* percentages from the first category to the last valid category. For example, in Table 13.1b,

Table 13.1 Frequency distributions

(a) Left–right political position

		Frequency	Per cent	Valid per cent	Cumulative per cent
	0 Left	41	2.2	2.6	2.6
	1	13	0.7	0.8	3.4
	2	36	1.9	2.3	5.6
	3	121	6.4	7.6	13.2
	4	171	9.0	10.7	23.9
	5	635	33.5	39.7	63.6
	6	182	9.6	11.4	75.0
	7	173	9.1	10.8	85.9
	8	137	7.2	8.6	94.4
	9	25	1.3	1.6	96.0
	10 Right	64	3.4	4.0	100.0
	Total	1598	84.2	100.0	
Missing	−1 Missing	299	15.8		
Total		1897	100.0		

(b) Number of years of tertiary education

		Frequency	Per cent	Valid per cent	Cumulative per cent
	0	951	50.1	52.5	52.5
	1	157	8.3	8.7	61.2
	2	134	7.1	7.4	68.6
	3	167	8.8	9.2	77.8
	4	183	9.6	10.1	87.9
	5	89	4.7	4.9	92.8
	6	43	2.3	2.4	95.2
	7	25	1.3	1.4	96.6
	8	26	1.4	1.4	98.0
	9	36	1.9	2.0	100.0
	Total	1811	95.5	100.0	
Missing	−1 Missing	86	4.5		
Total		1897	100.0		

(c) Religious affiliation

		Frequency	Per cent	Valid per cent	Cumulative per cent
Valid	1 Roman Catholic	493	26.0	26.9	26.9
	2 Anglican/C of E	474	25.0	25.8	52.7
	3 Uniting/Methodist	196	10.3	10.7	63.4
	4 Orthodox Church	62	3.3	3.4	66.8
	5 Presbyterian	104	5.5	5.7	72.4
	6 Other	189	10.0	10.3	82.7
	9 No religion	317	16.7	17.3	100.0
	Total	1835	96.7	100.0	
Missing	−1 Missing	62	3.3		
Total		1897	100.0		

52.5 per cent have no tertiary education; 61.2 per cent have one year *or less* of tertiary education (52.5% + 8.7%); 77.8 per cent have three years or less of tertiary education.

■ *Third last row:* The total number of respondents who gave *valid* answers to this question. This is the base for calculating the valid per cents (e.g. in Table 13.1c there are 493 Roman Catholics,

1835 people answered the religion question, [493 ÷ 1835] × 100 = 26.9%).

■ *Second last row:* The number of cases that did *not* have a valid response for this variable. These are called 'missing' cases.

■ *Bottom row:* The total sample size (including 'missing' cases).

Box 13.1 summarises the information necessary for a frequency table.

There are different ways of reading frequency tables. One approach involves examining the particular percentages in specific categories. The other approach involves looking at the table *as a whole*— examining the *shape* of the distribution.

A scan of the valid percentages can quickly give a sense of the heterogeneity (diversity) and homogeneity (similarity) in the sample. If there are reasonable percentage figures across the different categories (as in Table 13.1c) then the sample is fairly heterogeneous. If just a few categories account for the bulk of the cases (as in Table 13.1a where 62 per cent of cases fall into the middle three categories) then the sample is fairly homogeneous.

A table can also show whether the distribution

of ordinal and interval variables is symmetrical or skewed. Examining the centre point of the variable and then examining the distribution either side of the centre point can reveal a symmetrical distribution. In a symmetrical distribution the distribution of cases on one side of centre will be mirrored on the other side. In Table 13.1a the distribution is fairly symmetrical. The midpoint is five on the left–right political position scale. On both sides of this centre point the percentage numbers closely mirror each other. This can be seen more clearly in the graph of this same table (Figure 13.1).

Table 13.1b is not symmetrical. Where cases are clustered at one end of a distribution of an ordinal or interval variable the distribution is *skewed*. When cases are clustered at the low end the distribution is *positively skewed*; when clustered at the high end it is *negatively skewed*. The distribution in Table 13.1b is

---

BOX 13.1
Required information in a frequency table

When presenting a frequency table, avoid unnecessary clutter. Normally the following information should be provided (see also Table 13.2):

1 table number and title;

2 labels for the categories of the variable;

3 column headings to indicate what the numbers in the column represent;

4 the total number on which the percentages are based;

5 the number of missing cases;

6 the source of the data.

It may also be necessary to provide footnotes to the table in which the actual question or working definition on which the table is based is provided.

Table 13.2 Frequency tables (stripped down)

(a) Left–right political orientation (stripped down table)

	Valid per cent	Cumulative per cent
0 Left	3	3
1	1	4
2	2	6
3	8	13
4	11	24
5	40	64
6	11	75
7	11	86
8	9	94
9	2	96
10 Right	4	100
Total	1598	

Missing cases = 299

(b) Religious preference (stripped down table)

	Valid per cent
Roman Catholic	27
Anglican/C of E	26
Uniting/Methodist	11
Orthodox Church	3
Presbyterian	6
Other	10
No religion	17
	100
Total	1835

Missing cases = 62

positively skewed—the higher percentage numbers are at the low end of the scale. This is represented visually in Figure 13.6.

Graphical analysis

Univariate distributions can often be displayed effectively with graphs. There is a range of graphs that can be used to display these distributions. Most graphs have some common elements but within many of these elements choices are made which produce quite different graphs (see Box 13.2).

The choice between graph types largely depends on the number of categories and level of measurement of the variable. The characteristics of the main types of univariate graphs are described below.

Bar charts

Axes	Has both X-axis (bottom) and Y-axis (side).
Level of measurement	Nominal, ordinal or interval.
Number of categories of the variable	Relatively few (no more than 10) since each category is represented by a separate bar. Too many bars

makes the graph very difficult to read. Consider combining categories with tiny numbers, unless representing them separately is important.

Position of X-axis	Can be either across the bottom (results in a vertical bar chart—Figure 13.1) or on the side (horizontal bar chart—Figure 13.2).
Scale of the Y-axis	Can be either numbers (frequency/count—Figure 13.2) or per cent (Figure 13.3). Per cent is preferable as it is easier to interpret. However when dealing with small overall numbers (less than 100) the numbers may be preferable.
Representation of bars	Being a single variable each bar will be represented by the same colour and pattern (e.g. Figure 13.3).
Labels	Normal labels will indicate the variable description, its categories and the way in which amount is represented (count/per cent).

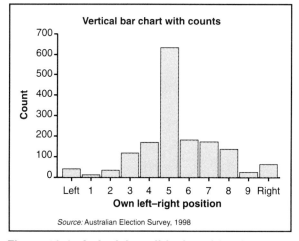

Figure 13.1 Left–right political position (vertical bar chart)

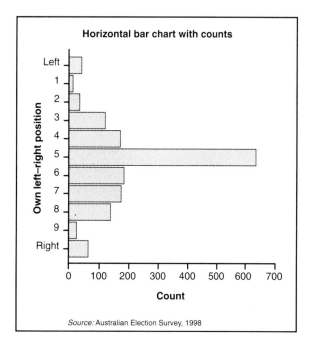

Figure 13.2 Left–right political position (horizontal bar chart)

BOX 13.2 *Elements of univariate graphs*

X-axis	All graphs (except the pie graph) will have an X-axis. The X-axis represents the *categories* of the variable being displayed.
Placement of X-axis	The X-axis can be placed ■ horizontally (on the bottom of the graph); or ■ vertically (on the side of the graph).
Scales/units of X-axis	The X-axis will be divided into units. These units will reflect the: ■ categories of the variable; ■ level of measurement of the variable.
Y-axis	All graphs (except the pie graph) will have a Y-axis. The Y-axis represents the *quantity* of each category of the variable.
Placement of Y-axis	The Y-axis can be vertical or horizontal. This will depend on the placement of the X-axis.
Scale/units of Y-axis	The Y-axis will be divided into units to represent the frequency of each category of the variable (except for boxplot). This will be expressed as either: ■ numbers ■ percentages.
How variable categories are represented	The number or per cent of each category can be represented by: ■ bars ■ points on a line ■ an area ■ pie slices.
Enhancements	To make graphs easier to read we can add: ■ grid lines ■ numbers on bars.
Labels	All graphs should include labelling to make the contents of the graph clear. These should include: ■ figure number and title ■ axis labels ■ scale values ■ legend ■ notes.

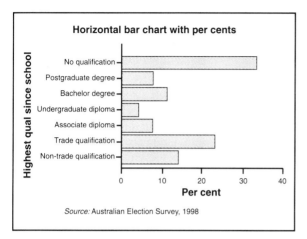

Figure 13.3   Highest level of tertiary education

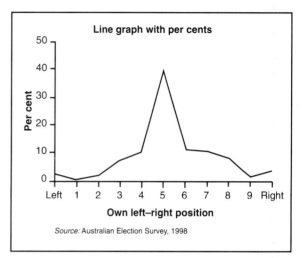

Figure 13.4   Left–right political position (line graph)

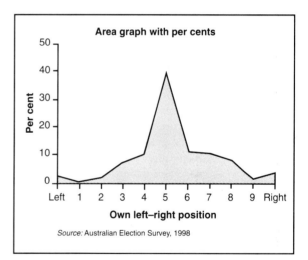

Figure 13.5   Left–right political orientation (area graph)

Line graphs and area graphs

Axes	Has both X-axis and Y-axis.
Level of measurement	Mainly interval or continuous variables but may be used for ordinal variables.
Number of categories of the variable	More than two. Can handle variables with a large number of values.
Position of X-axis	Normally on the bottom of the graph.
Scale of the Y-axis	Can be either numbers (frequency/count) or per cent. Per cent is preferable.
Representation of line (area)	Can change thickness, colour and style of line and place markers on it for each category of the variable (line).
Labels	Normal labels indicate the variable description, its categories and the way in which amount is represented (Figures 13.4, 13.5).

Histogram

Axes	Has both X-axis and Y-axis.
Level of measurement	Interval (continuous).
Number of categories of the variable	More than two. Can handle variables with a large number of values. Each bar represents a range of values of the variable.
Position of X-axis	Normally on bottom of graph.

Scale of the Y-axis	Can be either numbers (frequency/count) or per cent. Per cent is preferable as it is easier to interpret.
Representation of bars	Being a single variable each bar will be represented by the same colour and pattern.
Labels	Normal labels indicate the variable description, its categories and the way in which amount is represented.

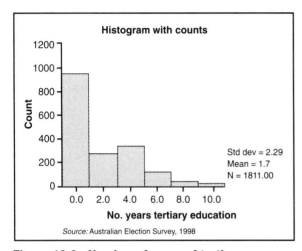

Figure 13.6 Number of years of tertiary education (histogram)

Other

Unlike the bar chart there are no gaps between the bars in the histogram. The X-axis does not display every individual value of the variable since this is assumed to be a continuous variable.

Since the variable is interval-level, a normal curve is sometimes placed on the graph to indicate how the distribution of the variable matches a normal distribution (see Figure 13.7).

Pie chart

Axes   Has no axes.

Level of measurement   Any level.

Number of categories of the X-variable   Relatively few (no more than 10) since each category is represented by a separate slice. Too many slices make the graph very difficult to read. Consider combining categories with tiny numbers unless representing them separately is important.

Position of categories of the variable   Rather than each category of the variable being represented by a bar or point on a line, a pie chart represents each category with a 'pie slice'.

Units of slices   The size of each pie slice is indicated by the size of the slice relative to others (see Figure 13.8). The number of cases or the percentage of cases can also be indicated.

Representation of slices   Each slice is represented by a unique colour or pattern. Particular slices can be 'exploded'.

Labels   Normal labels indicate the variable description, its categories and the way in which amount is represented.

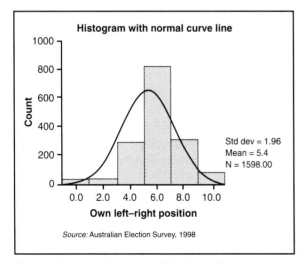

Figure 13.7 Left–right political position (histogram with normal curve)

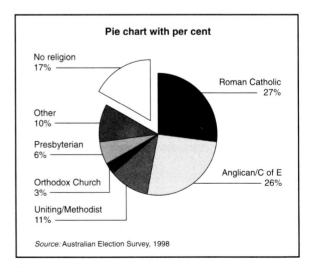

Figure 13.8 Religious preference (pie chart)

Boxplot

Axes   In univariate analysis the boxplot has only one axis.

Level of measurement   Ordinal or interval.

Number of categories of the X-variable   The more the better.

Position of X-axis   Can be either across the bottom (results in a vertical boxplot) or on the side (horizontal boxplot).

Type of information provided   Rather than representing the number of people giving particular answers, the boxplot represents the distribution of the variable based on summary measures of the distribution. In particular it displays the median, the interquartile range (see measures of central tendency later in this chapter) and the minimum and maximum values in the distribution. In Figure 13.9 the minimum score for males on the left–right scale was 0 (extreme left wing) and the maximum was 10 (extreme right wing). The median was 5 (centre) and the middle 50 per cent of males (i.e. excluding the 25 per cent most left and 25 per cent most right) had left–right scores between 4 and 7.

Labels   Normal labels indicate the variable description, its categories and the way in which quantity is represented.

One of the factors that influences selection of graph type is the level of measurement of the variable. Table 13.3 summarises which graphs can be used for variables according to the variable's level of measurement.

Distortions with graphs

Graphs can be a powerful way of illustrating patterns in data but they can also distort patterns. The most common way this is done is by altering the scales on the X- and Y-axes. Since there are no established ways in which the scales on the X-axis and Y-axis are set it is easy to 'stretch' one scale and 'shrink' the other (called altering the 'aspect ratio'). These changes can radically alter the visual impression provided by a graph.

Figure 13.10 illustrates how a visual image can be dramatically altered by stretching or shrinking the scales on the X- and Y-axes. The figures reflect the level of workforce participation among men aged 55–59 from 1975–2000 and projected forward to 2010. Figure 13.10a shows a downward trend from 83 per cent male workforce participation rate in 1975 down to a projected 66 per cent rate in 2010. This represents a decline of 17 percentage points—not a trivial change. However, this might not be the sort of change to which we want to draw attention. Figure 13.10b presents a much 'better' picture—virtually no decline. It would be even 'better' if we omitted to put the percentage labels on

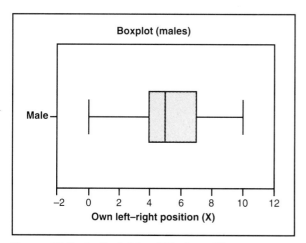

Figure 13.9   **Left–right political position (horizontal boxplot of males)**

Table 13.3   **Graph type by level of measurement**

	Level of measurement		
	Nominal	**Ordinal**	**Interval**
Bar charts	✔	✔	?
Line graphs	✗	?	✔
Area graph	✗	?	✔
Histogram	✗	✗	✔
Boxplot	✗	✔	✔
Pie chart	✔	✔	?

Key   ✔ = appropriate
       ? = OK but normally not the best choice
       ✗ = inappropriate

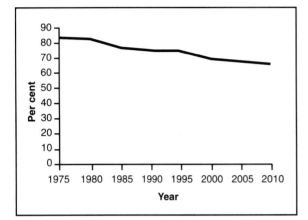

(a) Initial graph showing modest downward trend

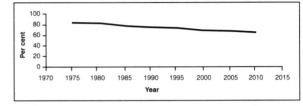

(b) Minimising downward trend by shortening Y-axis and lengthening X-axis

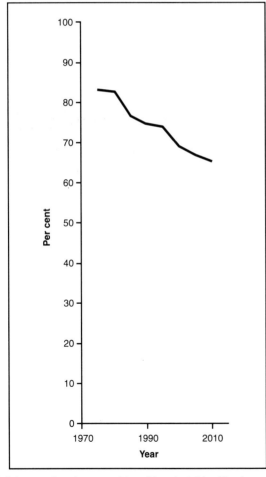

(c) Increasing downward trend by stretching Y-axis and shrinking X-axis

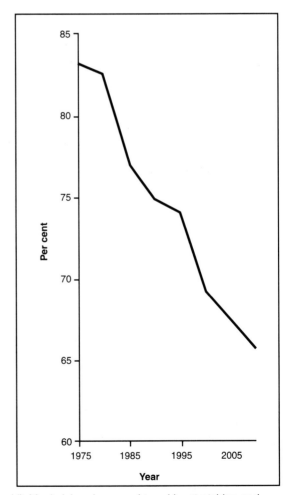

(d) Maximising downward trend by stretching and abbreviating Y-axis and shrinking X-axis

Figure 13.10   Distorting graphs by changing scales

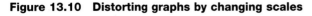

the Y-axis so that the degree of change is even less obvious! Although Figure 13.10b shows a slight change in the labour force participation of older men it is clearly so trivial that there is nothing to worry about!

But suppose we wanted to draw attention to the 'alarming decline' in labour force participation of older men. We could produce Figure 13.10c. Simply by stretching the Y-axis and shrinking the X-axis we can produce the appearance of a sharper decline. If this does not convey the disturbing decline sufficiently we can simply change the Y-axis further. Why have all that wasted space in the bottom half of the graph? By starting the Y-axis at 60 per cent we can produce a much sharper decline in older men's workforce participation, as Figure 13.10d shows. This is a truly dramatic decline about which something must be done!

Web Pointer 13.1 provides online sources of software for graph production.

Summary of descriptive statistics

As well as displaying distributions we can summarise them. I have already outlined some of the characteristics of distributions that can be seen either in graphs or tables. These same characteristics can be summarised with simple and concise statistical measures. There is a range of univariate statistics designed for this purpose. The choice of statistic depends on the level of measurement of the variable and the aspect of the distribution to be summarised (e.g. averages, variability, normality, skewness etc).

Web Pointer 13.2 provides some online reading resources regarding tables, graphs etc.

Nominal variables

Since a nominal variable is one for which there is no necessary ranking of categories, it does not matter in what order the categories are arranged. However,

---

WEB POINTER 13.1   *Software for producing graphs*

There is an ample supply of software for producing professional graphs. Commercial software such as Microsoft Word, Excel and SPSS can produce excellent graphs that can be easily imported into word processing documents and reports. All the main spreadsheet programs such as Lotus, Quattro etc include excellent graphing software.

Graph paper Download a shareware program to print a variety of types of graph paper for hand drawing your own graphs.	http://perso.easynet.fr/~philimar/graphpa peng.htm
Deltagraph 4 A powerful graphing package that can create some stunning pictorial graphs. A download trial package is available.	www.spss.com/deltagraph/
Prism Graphpad A powerful program with a trial download. Probably much more than users of this book would require.	www.graphpad.com/prism/Prism.htm
Shareware to create graphs ChartTamer v.3 1.1	www.sebd.com
Clickit Graph 2.5	www.clickitgraph.com

```
┌─────────────────────────────────────────────────────────────────────────────┐
│ ███████████████████████████████████████████████████████████████████████████ │
│ WEB POINTER 13.2   Reading resources on the web                              │
│ ███████████████████████████████████████████████████████████████████████████ │
│                                                                              │
│ How to use frequency tables, graphs,                                         │
│ central tendency, variation and skew          http://glass.ed.asu.edu/stats/lesson1/ │
│ ─────────────────────────────────────────────────────────────────────────── │
│ Distributions                                 http://faculty.vassar.edu/~lowry/webtext.html │
│                                               www.psychstat.smsu.edu/introbook/sbk13.htm │
│ ─────────────────────────────────────────────────────────────────────────── │
│ Another thorough outline of frequency         www.psychstat.smsu.edu/introbook/sbk07.htm │
│ distributions and the use of grouped data in  www.psychstat.smsu.edu/introbook/sbk09.htm │
│ frequency distributions                                                      │
│ ─────────────────────────────────────────────────────────────────────────── │
│ Visit www.social-research.org to use these links and to check for updates and additions. │
└─────────────────────────────────────────────────────────────────────────────┘
```

there may be a logical order. Thus a list of countries could be arranged according to their region (e.g. Australasia, Western Europe, Africa), by size or a number of other criteria depending on the use of the data.

Often it is helpful to combine different categories. This avoids having very large and unreadable tables with many categories that are very similar or have very few people in them. By combining categories in these ways tables become more readable and patterns become more obvious. However, the way in which categories are combined will affect the statistics used to summarise the variable's distribution.

Two main types of summarising statistics are used for nominal variables: those used to indicate typical values (central tendency), and those used to indicate group variation.

Central tendency: the mode

Measures of central tendency are averages: they indicate typical responses. There are several different types of averages and the choice between these averages is largely determined by the level of measurement of the variable for which we want to indicate the typical value or response. With nominal variables the only way to indicate the typical response is to identify the single most common response. The most common response, the one with the largest number of cases, is called the *mode*. In Table 13.2b the single most common response is 'Roman Catholic', thus 'Roman Catholic' is the mode.

There are problems with using the mode to measure the typical response.

1 Picking the most common response does not tell us *how typical* it is. For example, in Table 13.2b the modal religious preference is Roman Catholic (27 per cent) but this is not very typical of the sample as a whole. We need to know how typical the mode is (see variation: the variation ratio).

2 Some distributions have more than one mode so it is not possible to use one figure to summarise these bimodal or multi-modal distributions. Table 13.2b has two modal groups: Roman Catholic (27 per cent) and Church of England (27 per cent).

3 The mode is very dependent on how the categories of a variable have been collapsed. If we combine some categories, we can get a lot of people in some categories and thus this combined category could become the mode. Had we not combined them or combined them differently we could have obtained a different mode. In this sense the mode is unstable and open to manipulation. Nevertheless, with nominal data it is the best we have.

Variation: the variation ratio

Variation statistics, or measures of dispersion as they are often called, provide a way of summarising how diverse a group is. While measures of central tendency provide a snapshot of what is typical in a sample, measures of dispersion provide a snapshot of the degree of difference or variation in a sample. There are a number of different measures of variation and the choice is largely dependent on the level of measurement of the particular variable we are trying to summarise.

For nominal variables the appropriate measure of variation is the *variation ratio* (symbolised as v). It is easily calculated by seeing what percentage of people are *not* in the modal category. The variation ratio is normally expressed as a proportion. This is simply done by moving the decimal place on the percentage figure (per cent not in modal category) two places to the left. Thus in Table 13.2b the mode is Catholic which contains 27 per cent of the sample. The percentage not in the modal category is therefore 73 per cent. The variation ratio therefore is 0.73.

It is desirable to use a measure of variation alongside a measure of central tendency. The measure of central tendency gives us an idea of what is typical while the measure of variation gives a sense of how typical typical is. The more variation there is in a sample the less well the average summarises the sample. In the case of the variation ratio—the higher the variation ratio the more poorly the mode summarises the overall distribution.

Ordinal variables

Since the categories of ordinal variables can be ranked these categories should be put in their correct rank order in a frequency table. Failure to do so will distort both patterns in the data and statistics used to summarise them.

Central tendency: the median

While the mode can be used for ordinal data the *median* is preferred because it takes account of the fact that people can be ranked on ordinal variables. The median is worked out by ranking each *case* in a distribution from low to high on the variable and finding the middle person. Whatever category the middle person belongs to is the median category (see Figure 13.11).

Whenever there is an even number of people in a group there is no actual middle person. In such cases, the median is the point between the two cases that lie each side of the imaginary middle person (Figure 13.12).

When dealing with a large number of people, as is normally the case in survey research, it is quite easy to work out the median category (i.e. the category to which the middle person belongs). This is done by obtaining a frequency table for the variable and examining the cumulative percentage column. To locate the median simply look down this column until the cumulative percentage nudges over 50 per cent and then look at the category of the variable that corresponds to this. The middle person is this 50th per cent person in the cumulative percentage column (see Table 13.4). In the income distribution in Table 13.4, 49 per cent have an income of $35 000 or less (cumulative percentage column). The person who will tip

Case						middle case ↓					
	1	2	3	4	5	6	7	8	9	10	11
Social class	LWC	LWC	UW	UW	LM	MM ↑ median = MM	MM	MM	UM	UM	UC

Notes: LWC = lower working class; UW = upper working; LM = lower middle; MM = Middle middle; UM = upper middle; UC = upper class

Figure 13.11   Working out the median with an odd number of cases

Case						middle case ↓				
	1	2	3	4	5	6	7	8	9	10
Social class	LWC	UW	UW	MM	MM	MM ↑ median = MM	MM	UM	UM	UC

Figure 13.12   Working out the median with an even number of cases

Table 13.4 Working out the median using the cumulative per cent

	Annual income		
	Frequency	**Valid per cent**	**Cumulative per cent**
Less than $5 000	51	3	3
$5 001 to $10 000	168	10	13
$10 001 to $15 000	113	7	19
$15 001 to $20 000	131	8	27
$20 001 to $25 000	125	7	35
$25 001 to $30 000	116	7	41
$30 001 to $35 000	128	8	49
$35 001 to $40 000	**116**	**7**	**56**
$40 001 to $45 000	97	6	61
$45 001 to $50 000	110	6	68
$50 001 to $60 000	139	8	76
$60 001 to $70 000	108	6	82
$70 001 to $80 000	100	6	88
$80 001 to $90 000	42	2	91
$90 001 to $100 000	43	3	93
More than $100 000	117	7	100
Total	1 704	100	
−1 Missing	193		
Total	1 897		

the cumulative per cent over the 50 per cent mark will be in the next income group ($35 001–$40 000). Therefore the median income category is $35 001–$40 000.

Variation: the interquartile range

If most cases in an ordinal distribution are in categories close to the median category, the median will be a good summary of the group as a whole. If many cases have values that are very different from the median it is not such a good summary of the group. One way to assess the summarising value of the median is to look at the entire *range* of scores in a distribution. The wider the range the less adequate the median is. While this can be useful in some distributions (Figures 13.13b and c) the range can be badly distorted by a few extreme cases, thus under-estimating the summarising value of the median (see Figure 13.13a).

To avoid this distorting effect of extreme cases we can drop the bottom 25 per cent of cases and the top 25 per cent. This enables us to look at the variability of the middle 50 per cent of the sample without being unduly influenced by extreme cases. The cut-off points for dropping the bottom and top 25 per cents are called the *first* and *third quartiles* respectively. The cut-off point for the first quartile is expressed in

terms of the value (code) of the category of the 25th percentile—that is, the '25th per cent person'. This can be worked out in the same way as the median. Simply examine the cumulative per cent column of a frequency table and look for the category in which the cumulative per cent nudges over the 25 per cent mark. The value of the corresponding category is the first quartile cut-off. In Table 13.5 the first quartile cut-off is the 'very pleased' category with the code of 2. The cut-off point for the top 25 per cent (the third quartile) is determined by looking for the category in which the cumulative per cent nudges over 75 per cent. In Table 13.5 this is 'mostly satisfied' with the code of 4. This means that the *interquartile range* is 2 (i.e. 4 − 2)—the middle 50 per cent of cases range between being very pleased and mostly satisfied with their job. The narrower the interquartile range the better the median represents the distribution as a whole.

Interval variables

Interval-level variables are those in which categories can be ranked and the differences between categories can be quantified in precise numerical amounts. These are normally continuous variables. Examples of such variables might be income (measured in

Case		1	2	3	4	5	6	7	8	9	10	11	12
(a) Number of children		0	0	1	1	2	2	2	2	2	2	3	11
							Median						

Median = 2 (value between case 6 and 7)
Range = 11   Because of extreme score (value of 11 for case 12) high range value
Interquartile range = 1 (first quartile cut-off   underestimates usefulness of median
is value between case 3 and 4; third quartile)

(b) Number of children		0	0	1	1	1	2	2	2	2	2	3	3
							Median						

Median = 2
Range = 3   Low range reflects adequacy of median
Interquartile range = 1

(c) Number of children		0	0	0	1	2	2	2	2	6	6	9	12
							Median						

Median = 2
Range = 12   High range reflects inadequacy of median
Interquartile range = 5

Figure 13.13   Attributes of the range and interquartile range

Table 13.5   Satisfaction with your job

		Frequency	Per cent	Valid per cent	Cumulative per cent
	1 Delighted	123	7.3	8.7	8.7
	2 Very pleased	286	16.9	20.2	28.9
	3 Pleased	368	21.7	26.0	54.8
	4 Mostly satisfied	335	19.8	23.6	78.5
	5 Mixed feelings	180	10.6	12.7	91.2
	6 Mostly dissatisfied	55	3.2	3.9	95.1
	7 Unhappy	38	2.2	2.7	97.7
	8 Terrible	32	1.9	2.3	100.0
	Total	1417	83.5	100.0	
Missing		279	16.5		
Total		1696	100.0		

dollars), age (in years and months), and height (in centimetres). When these variables are placed in *groups* they should be treated as ordinal rather than interval variables (see Table 13.4).

Central tendency: the mean
The mean (expressed as $\overline{X}$) is the most common measure of central tendency for interval variables. It is calculated simply by adding the scores for each case in the sample and dividing the result by the number of cases in the sample (see Table 13.6).

There are two important problems when using the mean.

1   It can be distorted by extreme cases. If a person who earned $1 million was added to Table 13.6

the mean would be $108 091. In this case the mean does not adequately reflect the bulk of the group.

Table 13.6   Calculating the mean

	$ income			$ income
Case 1	12 000	Case	6	20 000
2	13 000		7	21 000
3	15 000		8	22 000
4	16 000		9	25 000
5	18 000		10	27 000

Total income = $189 000
Total cases = 10
$\overline{X}$ = $18 900

Table 13.7   The same mean for two different distributions

Group A		Group B	
Age	N	Age	N
30	0	30	40
35	10	35	10
40	20	40	0
45	40	45	0
50	20	50	0
55	10	55	10
60	0	60	40

Total N = 100   Total N = 100
$\overline{X}$ = 45 years $\overline{X}$ = 45 years

Note: In these tables the $\overline{X}$ has been obtained by multiplying the relevant age categories by the number of people (N) in that category

2   We can obtain the same mean for two quite different distributions (see Table 13.7). For these reasons it is necessary to have some way of knowing how well the mean summarises the distribution. To do this the appropriate measure of dispersion is used.

Variation: variance and standard deviation

One purpose of a measure of dispersion is to evaluate how well a mean summarises a distribution. The greater the variation in a group the less well the mean represents what is typical.

The normal measures of variation for interval level variables are two closely related statistics—variance and standard deviation. The logic of these statistics is best illustrated by an example. Suppose we have two groups of people as in Table 13.7.

Despite the same mean the *distribution* of the ages in the two groups is vastly different, the mean being a more adequate summary in group A than in group B. The standard deviation would tell us this without us having to look at the frequency table.

The logic of calculating the variance or standard deviation statistics is to see how 'far' each case is from the mean, to add up all these 'deviations' and to obtain an overall average of these deviations to indicate the level of dispersion. The actual procedure is a little more complex but is worth going through as it illustrates the logic. We will do this for group A.

The formula for variance s^2 is:

$$s^2 = \frac{\Sigma(X_i - \overline{X})}{N}$$

and the standard deviation (s) is simply the square root of s^2,

$$s = \sqrt{s^2}$$

where

X_i = an individual's score on the variable e.g. age),
$\overline{X}$ = the mean (e.g. 45 years old),
Σ = the sum of,
N = total number of people in the sample.

To calculate the variance:

1   Subtract the mean from each individual's score to see how much each person differs from it. That is:

$$(X_i - \overline{X})$$

2   Square each of these numbers. We have to do this because the amount of variation of cases below the mean will be the same as that above the mean. Since all these differences have to be added later, the negative and positive differences would add to zero, we square each number:

$$(X_i - \overline{X})^2$$

3   Add up all these 'squared deviations':

$$\Sigma(X_i - \overline{X})^2$$

4   Divide this answer by the number of cases in the sample to get the 'average of the squared deviations' or variance. That is:

$$s^2 = \frac{\Sigma(X_i - \overline{X})}{N}$$

For our example this would work out as in Table 13.8.

Since variance is not easily interpretable we can calculate the standard deviation (symbolised s) which is the square root of the variance. (Obtaining the square root of variance simply 'undoes' the squaring of numbers during the calculation of variance.) In Table 13.7 the standard deviation is about 5.5.

The lower s is, the better the mean is as a summary measure. This can be seen in relative terms. In group B where the mean is obviously a less satisfactory measure, s is 14—it shows that the mean is a more accurate summary for group A than for group B.

Table 13.8 Working out the standard deviation

1 Age	2 N	3[a] $(X_i - \bar{X})$	4 $(X_i - \bar{X})^2$	5[b] col. 2 × col. 4 $(X_i - \bar{X})$
30	0	—	—	—
35	10	−10	100	1000
40	20	−5	25	500
45	40	0	0	0
50	20	5	25	500
55	10	10	100	1000
60	0	0	—	—

Total N = 100
$\bar{X}$ = 45

Total 3000

Given the variance formula this means that

$$s^2 = \frac{3000}{100} = 30$$

Notes: [a] This would be the deviation for each person in this age category.
 [b] Since there are a number of people in this category we can get the total squared variation for all those in that category by multiplying column 4 by column 2.

Symmetry and skewness

The distributions of interval (and ordinal) level variables can be either symmetrical or skewed as we have already seen in the discussion of graphs. Rather than using a graph to indicate symmetry/skewness we can use the skewness statistic to measure symmetry.

If a distribution is perfectly symmetrical the skewness statistic will have a value of 0. If the distribution is positively skewed (i.e. clustered to the low end of the distribution) the skewness measure will have a positive value. If it clustered to the high end it will have a negative value.

It is a little difficult to interpret how skewed a distribution is by simply looking at the skewness statistic since it has no upper or lower limits. One guide is to look at the standard error of skewness (this will be computed together with skewness by most computer packages). A rule of thumb is that if the skewness statistic is twice as large as the standard error of skewness then the distribution is skewed. The greater the ratio between the standard error of skewness and skewness the more skewed the distribution is.

Table 13.1a illustrates a fairly symmetrical distribution while Table 13.1b provides an example of a skewed distribution. Table 13.9 provides the skewness figures for these same variables distributions. For Table 13.1a the symmetry of the distribution is reflected in the skewness figure of 0.005. In contrast, Table 13.1b is positively skewed. This is summarised by the skewness statistic of 1.328 (which is over 20 times as large as its standard error).

Kurtosis

Distributions can also be described in terms of how high or how flat the 'peak' is. Table 13.1a has a relatively high peak. Distributions with a high peak are distributions that are highly clustered and are said to have positive kurtosis (leptokurtic). Those with a flat profile are less clustered and have negative kurtosis (platykurtic).

A normal distribution is neither flat nor highly peaked and will have a kurtosis score of 0 (and a skewness of 0). Positive kurtosis (peaked distributions) is indicated by a positive value for the kurtosis statistic while negative kurtosis (flat distributions) is indicated by a negative value for the kurtosis statistic. Tables 13.1 a and b both are relatively peaked as indicated by their positive kurtosis score (Table 13.9).

Other shapes

Of course distributions might not approximate any of the shapes discussed so far. Ordinal and interval variables can take on other shapes to those discussed. For example, the distribution might be more like a J-curve or may be U-shaped (Figure 13.14).

Table 13.9   Skewness and kurtosis figures for Tables 13.1(a) and (b)

	N	Skewness		Kurtosis
	Statistic	Statistic	Std error	Statistic
Left–right political position	1598	0.005	0.061	0.839
Number of years of tertiary education	1811	1.328	0.058	1.065

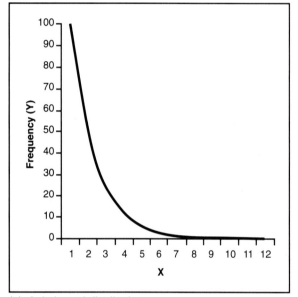

(a) A J-shaped distribution

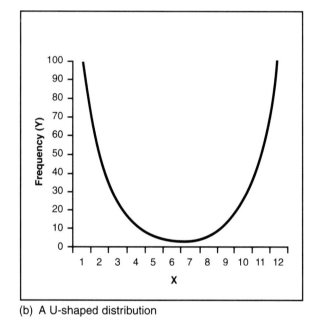

(b) A U-shaped distribution

Figure 13.14   A J-shaped and a U-shaped distribution

INFERENTIAL STATISTICS

Once we have examined the way in which cases are distributed across the categories of a variable the next question to ask is whether the pattern in the sample is likely to reflect the pattern in the population from which the sample was drawn. Answering this type of question is the purpose of inferential analysis. There are two main approaches to inferential analysis: significance testing and making interval estimates. The particular methods of doing inferential analysis depends on the level of measurement of the variables.

Significance tests for nominal and ordinal variables

Before outlining specific techniques it is helpful to explain the logic of significance testing.

It is standard to begin analysis by assuming a particular pattern in the population. For example, we may assume that the distribution of cases is even across the categories of the variable (e.g. 50 per cent in both categories of a two-category variable). This *assumption* about the population is called a *null hypothesis*. We then examine the *actual* pattern in the *sample*. Is there the same percentage of cases in each category in the sample?

It is unlikely that the distribution of cases in the sample will exactly match the assumption we have made about the population. In Table 13.10 the sample observation of 54/46 deviates from the 50/50 assumption for the population. There are two ways of interpreting the discrepancy between our *assumption* and the sample *observation*.

1   The sample is unrepresentative. Despite random sampling techniques we can still obtain poor

Table 13.10 Illustration of population assumption and sample observation

Should marijuana be legalised for personal use?	Agree	Disagree
Population assumption of no difference	50%	50%
Sample observation	54%	46%

Does the sample observation mean that people in general are more likely to agree than disagree with legalisation?
Or could the deviation from the 50/50 distribution simply be due to sampling error?

samples. This is called *sampling error*. Thus the discrepancy between the pattern observed in the sample and the population assumption of equal percentages in both categories could be because our sample is not a fair representation of the population.

2 The assumption of equal percentages in the population is incorrect. The difference between the pattern in the sample and the assumption for the population is much greater than can be accounted for by sampling error. If this is so then we would *reject the null hypothesis* of equal percentages in both categories in the population.

If we accept the first interpretation that the sample result (uneven distribution across categories of the variable) is due to sampling error, we would continue to say that in the population there will be the same percentage of cases in each category (i.e. we maintain our assumption of equal percentages across the categories). We would therefore treat the sample results as effectively indicating a pattern of no difference between the categories (i.e. treat the 54/46 split as though it is really a 50/50 split).

If we accept the second interpretation—that the initial assumption of a 50/50 split in the population was wrong—we would regard the sample finding of a 54/46 split as reflecting the type of split that exists in the population. Thus, we would accept that the sample result of 54/46 reflects the actual population pattern—people in general are more likely to agree than disagree with the legalisation of marijuana.

When we have two alternative ways of interpreting results (sampling error vs real differences) we have to have a way of working out which interpretation is correct. We do this with tests of statistical significance.

The logic of these tests is simple. *If there is no difference in the percentage* of people in each category of the variable in the population, *how likely is it that we would obtain a random sample in which sampling error produced a difference between categories as big as we have observed* (e.g. 54/46)? For example, if we drew 100 random samples how likely is it that we will get a faulty one, one in which we observe a 54/46 split when the population split is 50/50? It is conventional to say that if there is a chance that more than five out of 100 samples would produce such differences due simply to sampling error, this is too great a risk. Our particular sample could have been one of those five! Accordingly, we would say that the chance of our result being produced by sampling error is too high and thus continue to assume that the cases are evenly distributed across the categories of the variable. Some people are tougher and say that if more than one out of 100 samples could produce, by chance alone, category differences as great as we have observed, this is too great a risk.

If, on the other hand, we find that only very few samples could produce, by chance (sampling error), our observed category differences, we will accept that our sample observation is 'real' and reflects real differences in the population.

Since we never take 100 samples of the same population we have to estimate *if 100 samples were taken* how many by chance alone would give category differences as strong as we have observed in our sample. Probability theory provides us with an estimate of the likelihood that the percentage differences in our sample are due simply to sampling error. (We will not go into this theory but we should be aware that it assumes we use simple random samples.) A test of statistical significance is the estimate of this likelihood.

The figures obtained in these tests range from 0.00 to 1.00 and are called *significance levels*. What do they mean? Let us take a figure in between, 0.50. This means that in 50 out of 100 samples (simply multiply the figure by 100) we would get percentage differences between categories as large as we have observed purely because of sampling error (chance). Being cautious people we feel this is too great a chance that the differences are not 'real'; we would not reject the assumption of no differences between the categories in the population. We would continue to treat the actual differences as inconsequential.

If we obtain a significance level of 0.05 this

out of 100 samples would come ↓ the percentage differences we ur sample. A result of 0.01 means ... means one in 1000. Obviously *the lower the signy... e level, the more confident we are that our observed percentage differences reflect real differences in the population.*

I do not intend to go through how to calculate tests of significance. Again these are easily available in computer packages, and formulas are available in any statistics book, but there is one problem computer packages do not solve. Most packages will print out a significance level between zero and one. At what point do we reject the original assumption of no difference in the population? Conventionally 0.05 or 0.01 are used as the critical cut-off point. These levels are, however, conventional and arbitrary.

The trouble with using the 0.05 level is that this can be too easy a test of the null hypothesis of no difference: we might reject the assumption of no difference between the categories (i.e. 50/50 split) in the population when there really is no difference (the split really is 50/50). Making this mistake is called a *Type I Error* and is most likely with large samples. Thus with large samples it is advisable to use the 0.01 level as the cut-off point. The trouble with using

0.01 consistently is that it can lead to Type II Errors—being too tough; that is, accepting the null hypothesis when we should reject it. That is, we might continue to say that the population split is 50/50 when in fact it is not. This is particularly likely with small samples. As a rule of thumb use 0.05 for small samples and 0.01 or lower for larger samples.

There is a variety of ways to test statistical significance for nominal and ordinal variables. Different tests are used for variables with just two categories (dichotomous variables) and those with three or more categories. Tables 13.11 to 13.15 summarise the characteristics of the most common tests.

For dichotomous variables the binomial test is a useful significance test. The example in Table 13.11 illustrates that the sample finding of a 51/49 split in conservative and labor voting intention is consistent with the assumption of a 50/50 split between conservative and labor voting intention in the population.

The binomial test is not restricted to testing samples against a null hypothesis of 50/50. Nor is it restricted to comparisons with a hypothetical population. It can be used for other splits against *known population proportions.* This can be useful in evaluating how representative a sample is or for testing the idea that a particular sample differs from the general

Table 13.11 Interpreting binomial test results

Test	Binomial test
Number of categories	2
Level of measurement of variables	Nominal or ordinal
Null hypothesis	That 50 per cent of the population will belong to each category. That is, there are no differences between the categories.

Example 1		**Conservative**	**Labor**
	Sample	51%	49%
	Null hypothesis	Population distribution is really 50/50	
	Sample size = 1509	Binomial test significance level 0.22	
	Interpretation	There is a 22 per cent chance that the 51/49 deviation from a 50/50 split is due to sampling error. We will continue to assume that the real distribution is 50/50. People in the population are just as likely to vote labor as conservative.	

Example 2		**Conservative**	**Labor + like-minded parties**
	Sample	47%	53%
	Null hypothesis	Population distribution is really 50/50	
	Sample size = 1644	Binomial test significance level 0.02	
	Interpretation	In a sample of this size there is only a 2 per cent chance that the 47/53 deviation from a 50/50 split is due to sampling error. People in the population are more likely to vote for labor (and like-minded parties) than for conservatives.	

population. For example, we may have a random sample of families in which there is a child with a serious disability. We may want to know whether marital breakdown is more common among such families than in the population overall. Table 13.12 illustrates how to interpret this type of situation.

One sample chi-square test

Where we have a variable with *three or more categories* we can test whether the differences between the percentages across the categories is due to chance or is likely to reflect real percentage differences in the population. We normally begin by assuming that the percentages in the population will be the same in all categories of the variable. We then test to see if the sample fits this assumption. The one sample chi-square test is used to assess whether any misfit

between the sample patterns and population assumptions is likely to be due to sampling error.

Interval estimates for nominal and ordinal variables

A second form of inferential statistic is the interval estimate (see Chapter 12 on inferential statistics). For nominal and ordinal variables with two categories we can calculate an interval estimate. Interval estimates provide a different type of information than tests of significance. Rather than estimating how likely the sample pattern will hold in the population interval estimate procedures calculate the likely margin or error in the sample figures (see Chapter 6 on sample error and Chapter 12). Suppose for example that a sample of voters found that 48 per cent planned to

Table 13.12 Binomial test with a known population percentage

Example	Null hypothesis	Child disability has no impact on marital breakdown. The breakdown rate will be the same in disability families as in the population at large.	
		Intact marriages	**Broken marriages**
	Population (national statistics collection)	69%	31%
	Sample observations (disability families)	65%	35%
	Sample size = 1522	Significance of binomial test	0.000
	Interpretation	Families in which there is a child with a disability are more likely than families in general to suffer marital breakdown. There is almost no chance that the higher rate of breakdown observed among the sample of disability families is simply due to sampling error.	

Table 13.13 Using and interpreting the one sample chi-square test

Level of measurement	Nominal but can be used for ordinal and interval with relatively few categories.		
Number of categories	Three or more.		
Null hypothesis	The cases are distributed *evenly* across all the categories of the variable.		
Example			
Null hypothesis	The three forms of discrimination are equally prevalent (i.e. no difference in per cent experiencing particular forms of discrimination).		

Form of discrimination experienced	Racial/ethnic	Gender	Age
Expected percentages	33.3	33.3	33.3
Observed in sample	33.1%	37%	29.8%
Sample size = 332	Chi square	2.6	Significance = 0.27
Interpretation	There is a 27 per cent chance that the differences between the *observed distribution* and the *expected distribution* (same percentage for each form of discrimination) are due to sampling error. Therefore continue with null hypothesis that each form of discrimination is equally prevalent.		

vote for the main conservative political party at a forthcoming election. What is the likely margin of error of this estimate? How close is the true population figure likely to be to 48 per cent?

If we have a random sample then probability theory again provides the answer. If we took a large number of random samples most will come up with percentage estimates close to that which actually exists in the population. In only a few samples will the sample estimates be way off the mark. In fact the sample estimates would approximate a 'normal' distribution (Figure 13.15).

The problem is that if we have just one sample how do we know how close *our* sample percentage is to the true population percentage? Our sample could be one of those which is way out but it is more probable that it will be one of those close to the true population percentage (since most samples will be close). But even so, *how close* is it likely to be?

To estimate this we can use a statistic called the *standard error* of the binomial using the formula:

$$S_B = \sqrt{\frac{PQ}{N}}$$

where
  S_B = standard error for the binomial distribution
  P = per cent in the category of interest of the variable
  Q = per cent in the remaining category(ies) of the variable
  N = number of cases in the sample.

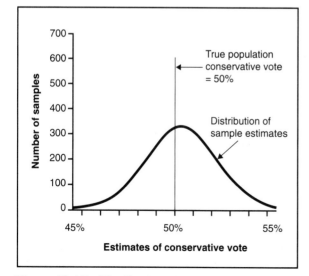

Figure 13.15   Distribution of sample estimates

Our sample estimate is that 48 per cent will vote conservative. This will be the value of P (the per cent of the category we are focusing on). Therefore 52 per cent will vote for other parties (Q). The sample size is 1644. We can substitute these numbers in the formula and estimate within what range of the sample estimate of 48 per cent the conservative vote really will be.

We calculate the standard error using the formula above. In this case it is:

$$S_B = \sqrt{\frac{(48)(52)}{1644}}$$

$$= \sqrt{\frac{2496}{1644}}$$

$$= \sqrt{1.52}$$

$$= 1.23$$

Having calculated the standard error (1.23), we can take advantage of probability theory to estimate the range within which the population percentage is likely to be. Probability theory tells us that, *in 95 per cent of samples, the population percentage will be within ± two standard error units of the sample percentage.* Put differently, there is a 95 per cent chance that the population percentage will be within ± two standard error units of the sample percentage. We can therefore use the sample percentage to estimate within what range the population percentage is likely to be. This range is called the *confidence interval* and our degree of certainty that the population percentage will fall within that range (95 per cent) is called the *confidence level*. The figure we get from calculating S_B is a percentage.

In this case the standard error is 1.23 per cent (two standard errors = 2.46 per cent) and the sample percentage indicates that 48 per cent say they will vote conservative. Therefore, there is a 95 per cent chance that the population percentage intending to vote conservative is 48 per cent ± 2.46 per cent. That is, the true population percentage intending to vote conservative is likely to be somewhere between 45.54 per cent and 50.46 per cent.

The size of the standard error is a function of sample size. To estimate the population percentage with a smaller margin of error (i.e. a small confidence interval) we need to reduce the standard error. To do this the sample size must be increased. However, we must increase the sample size substantially to reduce the sampling error: quadrupling the sample size halves the standard error.

For variables that have more than two categories we can calculate the same statistics by focussing on one category of the variable (P) and combining the rest (Q). You can then work out the standard error and calculate the confidence interval at the 95 per cent level (i.e. ±2 standard error units).

Significance tests for interval variables

The binomial and chi-square tests of significance discussed earlier can be used for interval data. But with interval data we do not need to limit ourselves to examining percentages. Instead we can calculate the *mean* of the whole distribution and ask whether the mean for the sample differs from an assumed or known population mean.

This can be illustrated using a known population mean. Suppose we had a sample of 590 divorced people for which the average age of marriage was 22.6 years. We want to know whether the average age of first marriage is any different for people who divorce than for couples in general. Do people who divorce seem to be those who marry at a younger age? Suppose that we know from national statistics that the average age of first marriage is 23.5 years. Is the average age in our sample of divorced people (22.6 years) likely to reflect that divorced people on

average marry at a younger age than couples in general? Or could the difference between divorced and other couples (22.6 cf. 23.5) simply be due to sampling error? The *one sample T-test* can help answer this question (see Table 13.14).

There are other ways of looking at interval-level distributions apart from focusing on the mean. We can examine whether the sample distribution of the variable forms a normal distribution.[1] The one sample Kolmogorov-Smirnov test is used for this purpose (Table 13.15).[2]

Interval estimates for interval variables

With nominal and ordinal variables we estimated the margin of error of sample percentages. With interval-level data we can estimate the margin of error of our sample means using the same general logic.

If, in a sample, the mean income is \$30 000 we might want to know what the mean for the population is. Because of sampling error the sample mean is unlikely to exactly mirror the population mean. Consequently, we cannot simply use the sample mean as indicating the precise mean income for the population.

Using the same logic that we used in calculating the interval estimates for percentages we can estimate the range within which the population mean is likely

---

Table 13.14   Applying the one sample T-test

Test	One sample T-test
Level of variable	Interval
Number of categories	More than two
Null hypothesis	The mean in the sample is the same as the known population mean.
Example	Do people who divorce marry at a younger age than those who do not divorce?
Sample size	560
Sample mean (divorcees)	22.6 years at first marriage
Known population mean	23.5 years at first marriage
Null hypothesis	The difference between the average age of marriage of divorced people and that of couples in general is so small as to be likely to be due to sampling error.
T-test significance level	0.000
Interpretation	The difference in age of first marriage of our divorced sample and the general population is sufficiently large for a sample of this size that it almost certainly reflects a real population difference rather than being due to sampling error.

Table 13.15 Applying and interpreting the one sample Kolmogorov-Smirnov test

Test	One sample Kolmogorov-Smirnov test
Level of variable	Interval
Number of categories	More than two
Assumption	The variable is normally distributed in the population from which the sample is drawn.
Null hypothesis	That the variable has a normal distribution.

Example	Is income normally distributed?	
	Sample results	One sample Kolmogorov-Smirnov test = 4.06
		Significance = 0.000
	Interpretation	Since the significance is 0.000 we can reject the null hypothesis. The income distribution is different from the assumed distribution (a normal distribution) and there is virtually no chance that this difference is due to sampling error. It is highly probable that income is not normally distributed in the population.

to lie. To do this we calculate a statistic called the *standard error of the mean* using the formula:

$$S_m = \frac{s}{\sqrt{N}}$$

where

S_m = standard error of the mean
s = standard deviation
N = number of cases in the sample

Having calculated the standard error we can use the rule that for 95 per cent of samples the population mean will be within ± two standard error units of the sample mean. Put differently, there is a 95 per cent chance that the population mean will be within ± two standard error units of the sample mean.

In this example, let us suppose that the S_m = $1000 (2 S_m = $2000). Since the mean income is $30 000 we can conclude that there is a 95 per cent chance that the population mean will be somewhere within the range of $28 000 – $32 000 (i.e. $30 000 ± $2000).

SELECTING THE APPROPRIATE STATISTIC

The statistical analysis outlined in this chapter can be performed easily with a wide range of statistics packages. A small selection of these are outlined in Web Pointer 13.3. Other packages are listed on my website at www.social-research.org.

Table 13.16 summarises the statistics mentioned in this chapter. It indicates which descriptive and inferential statistics are used for variables at each of the three levels of measurement.

There is an enormous variety of statistics from which you may choose for univariate, bivariate and multivariate analyses. The choice of statistic depends on a range of considerations, a few of which have been discussed in this chapter. To assist with this choice a number of statistics selection programs are available. These programs ask about what you are wanting to do and the nature of your variables. They then suggest a suitable statistic for your needs. Some useful selection programs are listed in Web Pointer 13.4.

Table 13.16 Choosing summary descriptive statistics for different levels of measurement

	Nominal	Ordinal	Interval
Averages			
Mode	✔	?	?
Median	✗	✔	?
Mean	✗	✗	✔
Dispersion/variation			
Variation ratio	✔	?	?
Interquartile range	✗	✔	?
Variance/standard deviation	✗	✗	✔
Symmetry			
Graph/visual	✗	✔	✔
Skewness statistic	✗	✗	✔
Kurtosis			
Graph/visual	✗	✔	✔
Kurtosis statistic	✗	✗	✔

Key ✔ = appropriate
? = OK but not best
✗ = not appropriate

WEB POINTER 13.3 *Links to software suitable for univariate d*

Listing of statistics software
Good up-to-date site of commercially available software for statistical and social survey analysis.

www.asc.org.uk/Register/

The site is a little out of date but provides links to many social science stats software sites.

www.stir.ac.uk/Departments/HumanSciences/ SocInfo/

Commercial statistics packages
SPSS
An excellent, comprehensive and user-friendly statistical package which originated as a survey analysis package. A wide range of statistics, tables and graphs.

www.spss.com
See my website www.social-research.org for the SPSS commands/menu selections required to access the statistics discussed in this chapter.

EXCEL: Spreadsheet

Most spreadsheet software enables you to simply calculate univariate statistics and produce professional tables and graphs. They also calculate statistics via statistics functions. This requires that you have the raw data in the spreadsheet. You can then apply the *function* facility to calculate means, standard deviation, skewness etc. With Excel simply select INSERT (top menu) FUNCTION / STATISTICAL and then select from the many different statistical functions.

STATISTICA
DEMO 1: The Interactive *STATISTICA* Application with the *Electronic Manual* provides access to a basic statistics module. It also includes a comprehensive *Electronic Manual* and many example data files on which you can perform various analyses (using a large selection of provided data sets) and create different kinds of graphs. Downloadable demo version is available.

www.statsoft.com/download.html#demo

STATGRAPHICS
Downloadable evaluation version of Statgraphics 5. Includes wide range of statistical and graphics options. In addition a number of statistics modules ('Statlets') are available for download evaluation. These same statlets are also available for online analysis.

www.sgcorp.com/standard_edition.htm

SIMSTAT
Excellent and easy to use program with a wide range of statistics for univariate, bivariate and multivariate analysis. Available for download and evaluation.

www.simstat.com

nline analysis
Glass's online data analysis site.
Online analysis software for most stats
discussed in this chapter.

http://glass.ed.asu.edu/stats/online.htm

WEBSTAT (free online data analysis routines).

www.stat.sc.edu/webstat/version2.0/

STATLETS
Excellent online software—free for academic
uses.

www.sgcorp.com/on-line_computing.htm

Shareware
STATCALC 3
A reasonable and cheap package with
downloadable trialware.

www.acastat.com/prod01.htm

MODSTAT
This program performs over 250 statistical tests
including all those discussed in this chapter. It is
a DOS or Windows program, runs easily with
limited RAM and costs only US$22. The learning
curve is practically nonexistent.

http://members.aol.com/rcknodt/pubpage.htm

Available at ZDNET download site
Type in software name in the search engine on
this page.

www.zdnet.com/downloads/powertools/

Get a full-featured spreadsheet for free.

Sphygmic Software Spreadsheet

As-Easy-As–use a powerful, versatile
spreadsheet.

www.triusinc.com

Doing statistical data analysis, WINKS is a
novel Windows statistical data analysis and
graphing application based on the KWIKSTAT
program. It greatly simplifies statistical data
analysis and offers an understandable and
easy-to-use method of creating a wide range of
charts and graphs.

WINKS v4.62

XLSTAT
An excellent Microsoft Excel add-on that offers
a wide variety of statistical analysis tools and
greatly simplifies the process of statistical
analysis with Excel.

www.xlstat.com

UNIVARIATE ANALYSIS CHECKLIST

When deciding what univariate analysis to do ask yourself the following questions.

1 What type of analysis is required?
   a Descriptive?   b Inferential?
2 If descriptive, how will the analysis be presented?
   a In tabular form?   c As summary
   b Graphical form?   statistics?
3 What is the level of measurement of the variable being analysed?
   a Nominal?   c Interval?
   b Ordinal?
4 If tabular analysis is to be used:
   a Which data will you use in the table: Per cents or valid per cents?
   b Will cumulative percentages be reported?
   c How will missing data be handled?
   d Does the table have too many categories? Do values need grouping?
   e Are the categories in the required order?
   f Is the table sufficiently uncluttered?
   g Does the table present the required information?
5 If graphical analysis is to be used:
   a Have you selected the right graph given the level of measurement of the variable?
   b Is the graph suited to the number of categories of the variable?
   c How will the axes be placed?
   d Will you use counts (frequency) or per cents for the Y-axis?
   e Is the aspect ratio of the axes appropriate?

f Is the graph properly labelled?
6 If summary statistics are used for descriptive analysis which aspect of the distribution are you describing?
   a Central tendency?
   b Variation?
   c Symmetry/skewness?
   d Kurtosis?
   e Other aspects of shape?
   f Does the particular method of analysis match the level of measurement of the variable?
   g Have you used a measure of dispersion along with a measure of central tendency?
7 If inferential analysis is to be undertaken:
   a Do you have a random sample?
   b Are you requiring:
      i a significance test;
      ii an interval estimate?
   c If a significance test is required:
      i does the variable have two or more than two categories;
      ii is the significance test suitable given the number of categories of your variable;
      iii are you comparing your sample with a hypothetical population or a known population parameter;
      iv what is your null hypothesis?
   d If interval estimates are required:
      i what is the level of measurement of your variable;
      ii are you testing for the interval around a percentage or around the mean?

WEB POINTER 13.4   *Statistical selection software*

There is a number of useful computer-based programs that assist in the selection of the appropriate form of statistical analysis. These prompt you with simple questions. When you have answered each question you are advised of a likely method. Five such useful programs are:

Statistics coach   Part of SPSS. Click the Help button in SPSS to access the Coach.

Statistical Advisor   www.statsoft.com/textbook/advisor.html

Selecting Statistics   http://trochim.human.cornell.edu/selstat/ssstart.htm

Knodt's Help with Statistical Analysis   http://members.aol.com/statware/pubpage.htm#A2SSYY

Methodologist's Toolchest   Although neither online nor free this excellent set of packages designed to assist methodologists, has a statistics selection module. It also has an excellent set of hyperlinks that explain various statistics.

KEY CONCEPTS

Average	Missing cases	Positive skewness	Symmetrical
Binomial test	Mode	Sample heterogeneity	distribution
Central tendency	Negative kurtosis	Sample homogeneity	Type I error
Cumulative per cent	Negative skewness	Scale of axis	Type II error
Frequency distribution	95 per cent confidence	Skewness	Valid per cent
Frequency table	level	Standard deviation	Variance
Interquartile range	Null hypothesis	Standard error of the	Variation ratio
Interval estimate	One sample	binomial	X–axis
Kurtosis	Kolmogorov–	Standard error of the	Y–axis
Mean	Smirnov test	mean	
Measure of dispersion	One sample T-test	Statistical significance	
Median	Positive kurtosis		

ENDNOTES

[1] This can be important to know for a number of reasons including the fact that many bivariate and multivariate statistics assume that variables are normally distributed.

[2] More precisely the one sample Kolmogorov–Smirnov test indicates whether the distribution of the variable *in the population from which the sample is drawn* forms a normal distribution.

FURTHER READING

For a very clear, well organised and simple account of descriptive summary statistics see section B of Freeman's *Elementary Applied Statistics* (1965) or Johnson's *Social Statistics Without Tears* (1977). Both provide gentle introductions and show how to calculate these statistics. Mueller, Schuessler and Costner also do this in *Statistical Reasoning in Sociology* (1977), Chapters 3–7 as well as providing more detail on graphic presentation. A very comprehensive outline is provided by Loether and McTavish in Part II of *Descriptive Statistics for Sociologists* (1974). Chapters 3 and 4 of *SPSSX: Introductory Statistical Guide* (1983) by Norusis also provide a very accessible account of these statistics.

Loether and McTavish (1974) provide an excellent outline of graphing techniques in Chapter 4 of *Descriptive Statistics*. Tufte provides a classic account of graphs in *The visual display of quantitative information* (1983) as does Schmid in *Statistical Graphics* (1983) but Henry's *Graphing Data* (1995) is probably the most useful for social science data. Huff provides excellent tips about distortions with graphs in *How to Lie with Statistics* (1954) and the website www.math.yorku.ca/SCS/Gallery/ provides a useful discussion and examples of principles of graphic design.

Inferential statistics for univariate analysis are discussed fully in Loether and McTavish, *Inferential Statistics for Sociologists* (1974), Chapter 5 and in Mueller et al. (1977), Chapter 13.

EXERCISES

1 From the data below construct two properly labelled frequency tables. The first will be a frequency table for marital status and the second will be of age grouped in five-year categories (15–19; 20–24; 25–29; 30–34 etc). Calculate percentages by excluding missing data. Where appropriate calculate cumulative percentages. In this data the age and marital status are presented next to each other on a case-by-case basis. Age is given in years. Marital status is coded as: M = married; W = widowed; N = never married; S = separated; D = divorced. Thus the first case is 32 years old and married. A dash means missing data.

32M, 48W, 68M, 83N, 60M, 29M, –N, 68M, 56M, 54M, 22M, 72M, 25M, 58M, 48M, 43M, 23M, 43M, 52M, 32M, 76W, 33M, 43M, 30M, 27M, 86S, 49–, 44M, 42M, 50M, 30M, 44M, 64–, 28M, 44M, 26M, –D, 19M, 51M, 40D, 36M, 38M, 66M, 56M, 71W, 34M, 59M, 27M, 29M, 30M, 45M, 36M, 64M, 39M, 36–, 66S, 43M, 56W, 58M, 35S, –M, 63M, 41M, 82W, 45M, 43M, 23M, 27S, 42M, 36M, 24M, 33M, 37M, 57M, 38M, 39D, 29M, 53M, 58M, 50M, 41M, 45M, 38M.

2 Explain briefly in words the pattern contained in each frequency table you have produced.

a Age distribution

i Is the age distribution skewed? If so, what sort of skew does it have?

ii What statistic would you use to summarise the average age in this distribution?

iii Calculate the appropriate average age.

iv Is the age distribution homogeneous or heterogeneous?

v What statistic would you use to summarise the degree of variation in this age distribution?

vi What would be an appropriate graph to display the frequency table data? Draw the graph.

vii Assuming these data are from a random sample, what inferential analysis would be appropriate for the age data?

viii The variance for age (not grouped in five-year categories) is 240.52. What would be the standard deviation for this table? Explain what this standard deviation figure tells us.

b Marital status

i Is the marital status distribution skewed?

ii What statistic would you use to summarise the average marital status in this distribution?

iii Calculate the appropriate average marital status.

iv Is the distribution of marital status homogeneous or heterogeneous?

v What statistic would you use to summarise the degree of variation in this distribution?

vi What would be an appropriate graph to display the frequency table data? Draw the graph.

vii Assuming these data are from a random sample, what inferential analysis would be appropriate for the marital status data?

viii 81 per cent are married. In the population from which the sample is drawn within what percentage range would you estimate are married (estimate at the 95 per cent confidence level)?

3 Explain why it is normally desirable to use a measure of dispersion in conjunction with a measure of central tendency.

4 Explain in your own words some potential advantages and disadvantages of using summary statistics in univariate analysis.

5 What measure of central tendency and variation would be most appropriate for each of the following variables: number of siblings; country of birth; crime rate (crimes per 100 000 of population); marital status; age (young, middle-aged and old).

6 Examine Table 13.5 and answer the following questions.

a What is the level of measurement of this variable?

b Reproduce Table 13.5 but include only the information necessary.

c What is the median for this distribution?

d Why are the percentages in the per cent and valid per cent columns different?

e   In this random sample 8.7 per cent say that they are delighted with their job. What would be your estimate of the percentage in the population that would feel this way (at the 95 per cent confidence level)?

7

	Valid Missing	Your hours paid work past
N		281.00
Mean		23.35
Std. Error of the mean		0.58
Median		24.00
Mode		0
Std. Deviation		21.67
Variance		469.48
Skewness		0.302
Std. Error of skewness		0.065
Kurtosis		–1.070
Percentile	25	0.00
	50	24.00
	75	40.00

The statistics above are for a variable indicating the respondents' number of hours of paid work in the last week. Answers are recorded as actual hours. Those with no paid work are recorded as having zero hours of paid work. Examine these statistics and answer the following questions.

a   What do the specific figures for mean, median and mode indicate?

b   Is this distribution a normal distribution?

c   Is the distribution skewed? If so, in what direction? What does your answer mean?

d   Would you think that this sample is homogeneous or heterogeneous in relation to hours of paid work? What evidence is there for your answer?

e   Is the distribution flat or peaked?

f   What is the interquartile range for this distribution? What does your answer mean?

g   What is the interval estimate for the mean (at the 95 per cent confidence level)?

8   The statistics below were obtained when testing for statistical significance. For each variable briefly explain what:

a   the null hypothesis is;

b   the significance tells you about the null hypothesis and the likely patterns in the population.

Test	Variable	Population	Sample	Test	Sig. level
One sample T-test	Years of education	Known population figure Mean = 11.0	Mean = 11.47	6.4	0.000
One sample T-test	Number of siblings	Known population figure = 3	Mean = 2.9	1.9	0.09
One sample chi-square test	Approval of euthanasia	Assumed 33 approve 33 undecided 33 disapprove	57% 31% 12%	547	0.000
Binomial test	Gender	Assumed 50% male 50% female	51% 49%		0.61
Binomial test	Trade union membership	Known in population Member = 33% Not member = 67%	24% 74%		0.000

14

Bivariate analysis: nominal and ordinal variables

Bivariate analysis includes a large number of different methods. This chapter concentrates on the main approaches to bivariate analysis of nominal and ordinal variables. This chapter:

■ focuses on variables with relatively few categories;
■ explores tabular, graphical and statistical techniques;
■ distinguishes between techniques designed for descriptive analysis and those used for inferential purposes;
■ aims to provide an overview of the range of methods of bivariate analysis and a framework for selecting the most appropriate method;
■ concentrates on the logic of various approaches and on interpretation of statistical results rather than on computation;
■ leaves the analysis of interval-level variables to the next chapter.

The heart of bivariate analysis is to see whether two variables are related (associated). The various methods of analysis and statistics simply differ in the way they represent such relationships. Two variables are associated or related when the distribution of values on one variable differs for different values of the other. Thus, if the way people vote differs according to their social class then vote and class are associated. If the pattern of voting is much the same despite class differences then the two variables are not associated, but are independent of one another. In other words, when subgroups (defined by belonging to one category or another of a given variable) differ systematically on another variable the variables are associated. When subgroups do not differ they are independent of one another.

When two variables are related then knowing a person's characteristic on just one variable improves our predictions about other characteristics of that person. For example, if education and income are related then knowing someone's education gives us a better idea of their income level. If social class and voting preference are related then knowing a person's social class will improve our guesses about their voting preference.

While knowing one thing about a person will improve our guesses about their other characteristics our guesses will not be infallible. Knowing that education and income are associated means that we will guess that if a person has a high education they may have a high income. A person with low education will be expected to have a low income. While this may be true, as a general rule, it will not always be the case. Bivariate analysis provides a systematic way of measuring whether two variables are related and if so how strongly they are related.

The main purpose of trying to detect a

relationship between two variables is to help in the task of explanation. For example, it is one thing to show, using univariate analysis, that people vary in how conservative they are. It is quite another to explain *why* some people are more conservative than others. Is it because of their gender, their social class, their age, their race or something else? If we find that women are more conservative than men we say we have partly explained conservatism (i.e. why some people are more conservative than others): it is because of their gender. We would then go further and ask *why* are women more conservative than men. Our answer may be speculative or may be based on further analysis (multivariate analysis). Looking for relationships between two variables is only a first step in achieving explanations but it is fundamental. There are a variety of ways of establishing whether two variables are related. Which methods are used depends on the level of measurement of the variables, the number of categories of each variable and the audience to which the analysis is directed.

TABLES

Cross-tabulations are the main tabular method for displaying data for detecting an association between two variables.

The structure of cross-tabulations

One way of thinking of a cross-tabulation is to think of it as a set of frequency tables set side by side in one table. For example, suppose we obtained a frequency table about attitudes towards homosexuality (see Table 14.1a). If we wanted to look at the attitudes of males only we could construct a frequency table consisting of males only (see Table 14.1b). We could also construct a frequency table of females only (see Table 14.1c). Having separate frequency tables for males and females then allows us to compare the responses of males and females. Tables 14.1a, b and c can be presented more efficiently as a cross-tabulation (see Table 14.2).

Table 14.1   Attitude to homosexuality broken down by gender

(a) Attitude to homosexuality: all respondents			(b) Attitude to homosexuality: MALES			(c) Attitude to homosexuality: FEMALES		
	ALL			MALES			FEMALES	
		Valid per cent			Valid per cent			Valid per cent
Homosexuality	Always wrong	64.7	Homosexuality	Always wrong	73.8	Homosexuality	Always wrong	56.0
	Often wrong	24.5		Often wrong	17.1		Often wrong	31.6
	Mainly or always right	10.7		Mainly or always right	9.0		Mainly or always right	12.4
	N	1631		N	799		N	832

Table 14.2   Attitude to homosexuality by gender

		Gender		
		1 Male	2 Female	Total
Attitude to homosexuality	1 Always wrong	73.8%	56.0%	64.7%
	2 Often wrong	17.1	31.6	24.5
	3 Mainly or always right	9.0	12.4	10.7
	N	799	832	1631
		100.0%	100.0%	100.0%

A careful examination of Table 14.2 will show that column 1 is the same as frequency Table 14.1b; column 2 is the same as frequency Table 14.1c and column 3 is the same as frequency Table 14.1a. In fact, each column in a cross-tabulation is a frequency table for a different subgroup while the final column (called column marginals) is the frequency table for the whole group.

A cross-tabulation consists of two variables and contains a number of elements. These are summarised in Box 14.1. A fundamental part of constructing and reading cross-tabulations are independent and dependent variables. If you are at all unclear about these go back to pp. 22–3 and refresh your memory before proceeding.

Table 14.3 provides a simple cross-tabulation of two variables: attitude to homosexuality and gender. When constructing a cross-tabulation, the *independent variable* (gender) is usually placed across the *top* of the table and a *column* is created for each category of that variable (male, female). The *dependent* variable is usually placed on the *side* of the table and a *row* is allocated for each category of that variable (always wrong, often wrong, mainly or always right).

Tables can be described by their size, which is based on the number of rows and columns. Table 14.3 is a three (rows)-by-two (columns) table. Each column and row should be labelled so that it is clear which category of the variable the column or row represents. The name of the variable that is across the top should be clearly labelled, as should the name of the side variable.

The intersection of a row and column is called a *cell*. The cell is used to represent cases which have the characteristic of *both* that column and that row. Thus the top left-hand cell represents people who are male (column) and think that homosexuality is always wrong (row). Each cell indicates how many people

are in that cell. In Table 14.3 these are actual numbers of cases and are referred to as the *count* or *cell frequency*.

> **BOX 14.1**
> **_Elements of a cross-tabulation_**
>
> A cross-tabulation consists of:
>
> 1 *Labels and title:* the title indicates the two variables being cross-tabulated (dependent variable by independent variable), labels are provided for variables and for each category of both variables.
>
> 2 *Rows and columns:* one *column* is allocated for each category of the independent variable and one *row* for each category of the dependent variable.
>
> 3 *Cells and cell contents:* cells represent cases who have *both* the characteristic indicated by the column *and* the characteristic indicated by the row. The contents of each cell may be the number of cases that have the two characteristics or the percentage with those characteristics.
>
> 4 *Marginals:* these represent the total number or percentage of cases in a particular category of a variable. These numbers will be very similar to the numbers in a frequency table for the same variable.
>
> 5 *Notes.*

Table 14.3 Attitude to homosexuality by gender (cell frequencies)

Count

		Gender		
		Male	**Female**	**Total**
Attitude to homosexuality	Always wrong	590	466	1056
	Often wrong	137	263	400
	Mainly or always right	72	103	175
	N	799	832	1631

Marginals represent totals of one sort or another. The *column marginals* (799, 832) indicate the total number of cases in that column. *Row marginals* (1056, 400, 175) indicate the total number of cases in that row. The *grand total* (1631) indicates the total number of people in the sample. The sum of the row totals or the sum of the column totals should be the same as the grand total. In Table 14.3 these marginals are actual numbers of people, but in Table 14.4 these are converted into percentages of the total in the particular row or column.

Percentaging a cross-tabulation

It is normally easier to interpret percentages than raw numbers when trying to detect association in a table. This involves converting cell frequencies into percentages. Here we confront a difficulty because we can convert each cell frequency into three different percentages (as in Table 14.4), each having an entirely different meaning.

A percentage is calculated by working out what proportion of the total a particular number represents. In the top left-hand cell (male, always wrong) there are 590 cases. To convert this number to a percentage we perform the calculation $\frac{590}{total} \times \frac{100}{1}$. But which of the three totals do we use—the

column total (799), the row total for the cell (1056) or the grand total (1631)? Depending on which total is used we get a different percentage with a different interpretation.

Using the *column total* will produce a *column percentage*. Thus, for the top, left-hand cell we have a frequency of 590 and a column total of 799 males. To convert this cell frequency to a *column* per cent we get $\frac{590}{799} \times \frac{100}{1} = 73.8\%$. This means 73.8 per cent *of the 799 males* (i.e. of people in that column) think that homosexuality is always wrong. It does **not** mean that 73.8 per cent of those who think that homosexuality is always wrong are males. Column per cents are the percentages that normally are used in cross-tabulations—especially when the independent variable is on the top of the table.

Using the *row total* will produce a *row percentage*. This gives $\frac{590}{1056} \times \frac{100}{1} = 55.9\%$. This means that 55.9 per cent *of those who think homosexuality is always wrong* are males.

Using the *grand total* will produce a *total percentage* which in this case gives $\frac{590}{1631} \times \frac{100}{1} = 36.2\%$. This means 36.2 per cent *of the whole sample* were males who think homosexuality is always wrong.

Table 14.4 includes all three percentages as well as the cell frequency in each cell. Which figures you use and include in the table depends on the purpose

Table 14.4 Attitude to homosexuality by gender (frequencies, row per cent, column per cent and total per cent)

			Gender		Total
			Male	Female	
	Always wrong	Count	590	466	1056
		Row %	55.9%	44.1%	100.0%
		Column %	73.8%	56.0%	
		% of total	36.2%	28.6%	64.7%
	Often wrong	Count	137	263	400
		Row %	34.3%	65.8%	100.0%
Homosexuality		Column %	17.1%	31.6%	
		% of total	8.4%	16.1%	24.5%
	Mainly or always right	Count	72	103	175
		Row %	41.1%	58.9%	100.0%
		Column %	9.0%	12.4%	
		% of total	4.4%	6.3%	10.7%
		Count	799	832	1631
	Totals	Column %	100.0%	100.0%	
		% of total	49.0%	51.0%	100.0%

BOX 14.2
Steps in detecting relationships in cross-tabulations

When trying to detect association in a table the steps are to:

1   Determine which variable is to be treated as independent.

2   Choose appropriate cell percentages:

   a   **column percentages** if the independent variable is across the **top**;

   b   **row percentages** if the independent variable is on the **side**.

3   Compare the percentages for each subgroup of the independent variable *within* one category of the dependent variable at a time.

4   *If the independent variable* is across the **top**, use **column** percentages and compare these **across** the table. Any difference between these reflects some association.

5   If the independent variable is on the **side** use **row** percentages and compare these **down** the table. Any difference between these reflects some association.

---

for which you are using the table. These issues are discussed more fully below.

Some important points should be noted about column, row and total percentages:

■   column percentages should always add to 100 per cent down a column;

■   row percentages should add to 100 per cent across the row;

■   total percentages should add to 100 per cent over the whole table.

If you are not sure which percentages are being used in a table, look to see which way they add to 100 per cent. Often the figure of 100 per cent is placed at the bottom of a column or end of a row to indicate the direction in which percentages are calculated.

In addition to the cell percentages, I have included some additional marginal figures in Table 14.4. The row marginal per cents (64.7%, 24.5%, 10.7%) reflect the percentage of the total sample in each row. The column marginal per cents of 49.0% and 51.0% represent the percentage of the sample that is male and female respectively.

Reading a cross-tabulation

Having seen the elements of a table, how do we read it to see if the two variables in it are associated? What we are doing when trying to detect association between two variables is comparing subgroups in terms of their characteristics on the dependent variable. Since gender in our example is the independent variable, we have male and female groups. We will look at the attitudes of each subgroup (i.e. males and females) towards homosexuality.

If these subgroups (or categories) of the independent variable differ in terms of their characteristics on the dependent variable (i.e. if they have different attitudes), we would say gender and attitudes towards homosexuality are associated; if there is no difference between the groups, the two variables are not associated. In this case, men and women do differ, so there is an association (see Table 14.2). Box 14.2 outlines the main steps in reading a cross-tabulation to detect if two variables are associated.

The character of relationships

Once we have determined from a table whether or not there is a relationship we can describe its character. There are three aspects to look at:

1   strength
2   direction
3   nature.

Strength

A strong relationship is one where the category of the independent variable to which a person belongs makes a very substantial difference to their characteristics on the dependent variable. Thus, if there are large differences between subgroups (as defined by the categories of the independent variable) there is a strong relationship. If the differences are small, the relationship is weak. The question of what constitutes large and small differences will be discussed later.

Direction

When dealing with either ordinal or interval variables we can also describe the direction of the relationship: it can be positive or negative. *A positive relationship is one in which people who score high on one variable are more likely than others to score high on the other variable*; those who score low on one variable are more likely than others to score low on the other variable. There is a consistency in their 'position' on the two variables. A simple example of a positive relationship is that between education level and income level: the higher the education the higher the income. The lower the education the lower the income.

The concept of being low and high on variables is sometimes confusing. You need to think in terms of the way variables have been *numerically coded*. It is in terms of these numerical codes that we can describe the direction of relationships.

In Table 14.2 I have inserted the numerical codes for each category of both variables. The codes for male and female are 1 and 2 respectively. For the homosexuality variable the code of 1 represents strong disapproval while 3 represents approval. In this table those who have a *low code* on the gender variable (males) are more likely (than those with a high code on the gender variable—females) to also have a *low code* on the homosexuality variable (i.e. disapprove). That is, of those with a low gender code (i.e. males) almost 74 per cent have 'low approval' of homosexuality compared to only 56 per cent of those with a 'high' gender score. This relationship is therefore positive.

The simplest way of detecting a positive relationship between variables is to examine the first *row* of the cross-tabulation (assuming the side variable is the dependent variable and is at least measured at the ordinal level). Simply compare the column percentages across this first row. If the percentages

become smaller as you move left to right across the row the relationship is probably positive. Also check the bottom row. If the percentages *increase* as you move left to right across the bottom row the relationship probably is positive.

A negative relationship is one in which people who are high on one variable tend to be low on the other and vice versa. For example, the relationship between approval of legalising marijuana and age is negative: the older (*higher*) the age the *less* they approve of legalising marijuana (see Table 14.5).

Nature

Association of ordinal or interval variables can be linear, curvilinear or non-linear. The statistics to be described later mainly measure linear association so we need to be able to detect curvilinear association by looking at a table. A linear relationship means a 'straight line' relationship. Table 14.5 reflects linear relationships. We can tell this because as we compare across the subgroups (categories of the independent variable) the percentages *change in a consistent direction*: as we move across the disagree row (i.e. seeing whether the percentage who disagree with legalising marijuana change as age increases) the percentages steadily increase. Had the percentages consistently decreased this would also indicate a linear relationship. Sometimes in tables where there are many categories, there may be small 'bumps' as we move across but if there is a basic trend in one direction the relationship most probably is linear.

A curvilinear relationship shows a different pattern (see Table 14.6). Comparing across the categories of age, we see in the first row (income under $35 000) that the percentages are high, low, and then high again on the low-income category. That is, the two ends of the age continuum have the highest concentrations of low-income earners while those in

Table 14.5   Approval of legislation of marijuana by age (a negative relationship)

		Age group				
		(1) 18–29	(2) 30–39	(3) 40–49	(4) 50–59	(5) 60+
Should legalise marijuana	(1) Disagree	30%	37%	42%	50%	59%
	(2) Can't decide	21%	20%	20%	20%	20%
	(3) Agree	49%	43%	38%	31%	21%
	Total N	263	344	392	318	407
		100%	100%	100%	100%	100%

the middle age groups have fewer low-income earners. In the high-income row we see the opposite pattern—few young people are high-income earners and likewise for older people. High-income earning peaks in middle age and then declines. A curvilinear relationship can be detected when both extremes of the scale are similar, while those in the middle are different.

Tables without a clear pattern

On occasions tables display no clear pattern in terms or direction or linearity but there will still be some sort of association. That is, there will be percentage differences between the column per cents as we compare these within a row but the percentage changes show no discernable pattern. They neither increase nor decrease in a consistent direction as they would if the relationship was linear. These relationships are best described as *non-linear* relationships.

Presenting cross-tabulations

The basic principle in presenting readable tables is to provide only the information necessary for accurate interpretation: avoid cluttering tables. It is becoming conventional to put the independent variable across the top. When presenting a table we can include a lot of information, but normally a skeleton of basic information is all that is necessary since we can reconstruct the full table from the skeleton should the need arise (see Davis, 1968). Box 14.4 lists the type of information you should always include in a cross-tabulation and the information you should normally exclude. Table 14.7 is a reconstruction of Table 14.4 using these principles. Clearly Table 14.7 is both easier to read, takes less space and is less liable to be misread.

When to use tables

Although tables provide maximum information they are often inappropriate, especially when dealing with variables with a large number of categories. If one variable (say age) had 30 categories and the other had just five we would have a table with 150 cells. Such tables are almost impossible to read. Depending on the sample size such tables can lead to many cells with few or no cases, which, in turn, complicates meaningful interpretation. As a rule of thumb do not use tables when variables have more than six or seven categories and even then only do so with relatively large samples so that there are sufficient numbers in the categories. With small samples you will often need to restrict analysis to variables with just two or three categories each. If your variables have too many categories you have two options:

1 collapse the categories (see Chapters 9 and 10);
2 do not use tables at all—simply use an appropriate summary statistic.

GRAPHS

Producing graphs to display relationships between two nominal or ordinal variables is similar to that for univariate analysis. Rather than repeating information covered in Chapter 13, this chapter will focus on the differences between univariate and bivariate graphs. The software for producing univariate graphs is normally also designed for producing bivariate graphs (see Web Pointer 13.1).

We have seen that a cross-tabulation can be thought of as a set of frequency tables placed side by side. Each column in a cross-tabulation contains the same information as the valid percentage column in

Table 14.6   Income by age group (a curvilinear relationship)

		Age group				
		(1) 1–25	**(2) 26–39**	**(3) 40–55**	**(4) 56–65**	**(5) 66+**
Income category	(1) Less than $35k	49%	37%	34%	60%	89%
	(2) $36k to $50k	20	24	22	17	6
	(3) $51k+	31	39	44	22	5
	N	152	417	575	242	235
		100%	100%	100%	100%	100%

BOX 14.3 *Detecting the character of relationships in cross-tabulations*

Note: These guidelines only apply if both variables are at least ordinal level.

Strength

- Compare column percentages within rows.
- The greater the percentage differences (on average) between these column percentages the stronger the relationship.
- Where there are a number of rows focus on comparing column percentages in those rows towards the top and bottom of the table rather than those towards the middle.

Direction

Assuming ordinal variables and dependent variable on the side of the table:

Positive relationships

- Compare column percentages in **first** row. These should **decrease** as you move from left to right across the row (40%, 30%, 15%).
- Compare the column percentages in the **last** row (not bottom marginals). These should **increase** as you move from left to right across the row (20%, 35%, 45%).
- Where there are a number of rows focus on those rows towards the top and bottom of the table rather than those towards the middle.

Negative relationships

- Compare column percentages in **first** row. These should **increase** as you move from left to right across the row (20%, 35%, 45%).
- Compare the column percentages in the **last** row. These should **decrease** as you move from left to right across the row (40%, 30%, 15%).
- Where there are a number of rows focus on those rows towards the top and bottom of the table rather than those towards the middle.

Nature

Assuming ordinal variables and dependent variable on the side of the table and at least three columns:

Linear

- Compare column percentages in **first** row. These should **change in a consistent direction** as you move from left to right across the row (e.g. 20%, 35%, 45%, or 45%, 35%, 20%).
- Compare the column percentages in the **last** row. These should **change in a consistent direction** as you move from left to right across the row.
- Where there are a number of rows, focus on those rows towards the top and bottom of table rather than those towards the middle.

Curvilinear: U-shaped

- Compare column percentages in **first** row. The percentages will **decrease** as you begin to scan from left to right across the row and then **increase** again. The percentages will **dip** and then rise again (e.g. 40%, 20%, 45%).
- Compare the column percentages in the **last** row. These should **increase** as you move from left to right across the row and then **decrease**. The percentages will **peak**, then decrease (e.g. 25%, 50%, 25%).
- Where there are a number of rows, focus on those rows towards the top and bottom of table rather than those towards the middle.

Inverted U-shaped

- Compare column percentages in **first** row. The percentages will **increase** as you begin to scan from left to right across the row and then **decrease** again. The percentages will **peak** and then decline (e.g. 25%, 50%, 25%).
- Compare the column percentages in the **last** row. These should **decrease** as you move from left to right across the row and then **increase**. The percentages will **dip**, then increase (e.g. 40%, 20%, 45%).
- Where there are a number of rows, focus on those rows towards the top and bottom of table rather than those towards the middle.

BOX 14.4 *Information to include in a cross-tabluation*

Include

1 A *table number and title.* The title should read: dependent variable BY independent variable (e.g. Table 14.1: Vote by occupation).

2 Labels clearly identifying both variables and each category of both variables.

3 Percentage signs after the first percentage in each column. This indicates that the numbers are % (see Table 14.4).

4 Footnotes to provide necessary information and to avoid long titles and labels.

5 Excluded cases should be indicated in a footnote (e.g. 'don't know' and 'no answer' responses).

6 Column % should be placed in each cell (assuming the independent variable is across the top of the table).

7 Column marginal total beneath each column. This shows the number of cases on which the percentages are based and enables the re-calculation of cell frequencies and the grand total, should this be necessary.

Exclude

1 *All marginals* except column frequencies.

2 *Code* numbers associated with variable categories.

3 *Decimal points:* round off percentages in larger samples (e.g. 200+).

4 *Grand total* (this can be reconstructed by adding column frequencies).

5 *Cell frequencies* (these can be reconstructed by dividing column percentages by 100 and multiplying this by the column total frequency).

6 *Total and row %* (as these do not illustrate association when the independent variable is across the top).

Table 14.7 A 'skeleton' cross-tabulation

		Gender	
		Male	**Female**
	Always wrong	74%	56%
Homosexuality	Often wrong	17	32
	Mainly or always right	9	12
	N	799	832

a frequency table except that it relates just to those people who belong to a particular category of the independent variable. In the same way a bivariate graph can be thought of as several univariate graphs combined into one graph.

In effect, a bivariate graph will represent the distribution on the dependent variable separately for each category of the independent variable. A legend will indicate the particular categories of the independent variable being examined at any point. We can then see whether the category of the independent variable to which people belong makes a difference to how they respond on the dependent variable. In other respects bivariate graphs for nominal and most ordinal variables will be much the same as most univariate graphs.

Four main types of bivariate graph are widely used:

1 clustered bar chart
2 stacked bar chart
3 line graph
4 boxplots.

Clustered bar chart

Figure 14.1 provides a bar chart of two variables: interest in politics and age group. The bottom axis has separate clusters of bars for each category of the dependent variable: one cluster for those who have a great deal of interest in politics, one cluster for those with some interest and one for those with no interest. If we had a univariate bar chart for this variable we would simply have three individual bars representing the percentage of the whole sample with each level of interest in politics.

In a bivariate bar chart we examine each category of the dependent variable according to a person's value on the independent variable. In this case we want to see if age is linked to the level of interest in politics. We take one category of the dependent variable at a time (as we took one row at a time in a cross-tabulation) and break the distribution down according to age group. We can immediately see that age is linked to the level of interest in politics. Just looking at those with a great deal of interest only 23 per cent of 18–29-year-olds have a great deal of interest. A greater percentage of 30–39-year-olds have a great deal of interest (27 per cent) while 53 per cent of those aged 60 or more have a great deal of interest in politics.

The opposite picture emerges when we look at those with no interest. Here a relatively large percentage of 18–29-year-olds have no interest (37 per cent). As the age group increases there are

fewer people with no interest with only 9 per cent of the 60-plus group having no interest.

Figure 14.1 also visually shows the linear nature of the relationship between age and interest in politics. Examining the 'extreme' categories of the dependent variables (a great deal of interest and no interest) the bars within each cluster show a clear upward or downward trend.

Figure 14.2 illustrates a curvilinear relationship. Examining the 'extreme' categories of the dependent variable—those earning less than $35 000 and those earning more than $51 000—we can readily see the shape of the relationship. The shape of the bars in the first cluster shows the U-shaped pattern and the shape of the bars in the higher income cluster illustrates an inverted U shape. Overall this graph illustrates the curvilinear nature of the relationship we had observed in the table.

Vertical bar charts can be rotated to produce a horizontal bar chart (see Figure 14.3).

Stacked bar chart

Stacked bar charts provide another way of representing bivariate patterns. The horizontal axis has a separate bar for each category of the dependent variable. Thus, in Figure 14.4 the first bar represents those with a great deal of interest in politics. This bar is broken into sections according to age group (the independent variable). The sections represent the

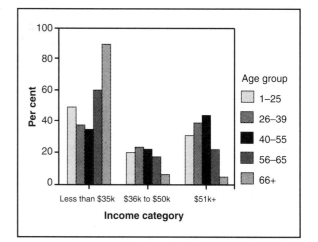

Figure 14.1   Clustered vertical bar chart of interest in politics by age group indicating a linear relationship

Figure 14.2   Clustered bar chart of age by income indicating a curvilinear relationship

percentage of particular age groups that belong to that bar or column. The first section of the first bar is the percentage of 18–29-year-olds who had a great deal of interest in politics; the next section of the bar is the percentage of 30–39-year-olds who had a great deal of interest in politics and so forth. Each section is comparable to the equivalent bars in Figure 14.1.

The way to read the stacked bar chart to detect any relationship is to compare the size of the sections *within a bar*. This is the same as comparing column per cents across the columns of a cross-tabulation. We can see the age effect on interest in politics by observing the increasing size of the blocks in the 'great deal' column as age increases. Similarly, the size

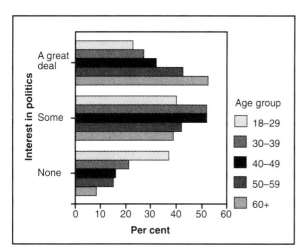

Figure 14.3 Horizontal clustered bar chart indicating a linear relationship

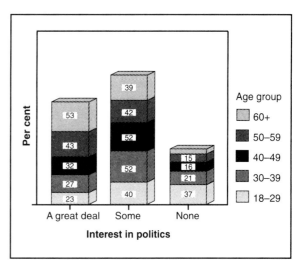

Figure 14.4 Stacked bar chart of interest in politics by age

Table 14.8 Summary characteristics of a clustered bar chart

Axes	Has both horizontal axis (bottom) and vertical axis (side)
Level of measurement of independent variable	Nominal, ordinal or interval
Level of measurement of dependent variable	Nominal, ordinal or interval
Number of categories of the independent variable	Relatively few (no more than 5 or 6) since each category is represented by a separate bar and if this is repeated for each category of the dependent variable you will have a very confusing set of bars and a cluttered graph. Too many bars make the graph very difficult to read. Consider combining categories.
Number of categories of dependent variable	Very limited number (2 to 4) since a separate cluster of bars is produced for each category of the dependent variable.
Position of axis for dependent variables	Can be either across the bottom (results in a vertical bar chart—Figure 14.1) or on the side (horizontal bar chart—Figure 14.3).
Scale of the vertical axis	You will usually use percentages. Since you will compare groups in which there are different numbers of people you will be unable to make meaningful comparisons without using percentages.
Scale of the horizontal axis (vertical bar chart)	Units of the dependent variable.
Representation of bars	A different colour/patterned bar will be used for each category of the independent variable.
Labels	Normal labels will indicate the variable description, its categories and the way in which amount is represented (count/per cent). The labels for the independent variable are provided in the legend.
Reading the percentages	The percentages are column per cents. They are the percentage of the given category of the independent variable that belong to the specific category of the dependent variable. In Figure 14.1 the first bar is 23 per cent of 18–29-year-olds have a great deal of interest in politics (<u>not</u> 23 per cent of those with a great deal of interest in politics are 18–29 years old).

of the blocks in the 'none' column gets smaller as age increases.

Line graph

The line graph that is used to display relationship between two variables has a separate line for each category of the independent variable. The horizontal axis indicates the categories of the dependent variable. Thus in Figure 14.5 the line for females indicates that 43 per cent score 5 on the left–right political continuum and 37 per cent of males score 5.

The best way to read such a graph to detect a relationship between the two variables is to compare the shape of the two lines and evaluate how different the lines are. The greater the difference between the lines the stronger the relationship. As well as comparing the two lines as a whole they can be compared at any particular point along the line (e.g. compare percentage of males and females who score 5). This comparison is the same as comparing the column per cents across columns (within a row) in a cross-tabulation.

Line graphs are best used when the independent variable has very few categories. Figure 14.5 is relatively easy to read. However, Figure 14.6 is quite difficult to read let alone interpret. The number of

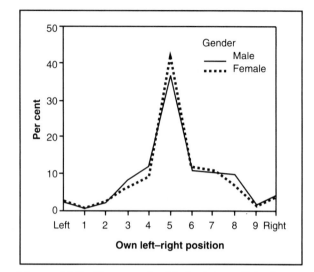

Figure 14.5 Line graph of left–right political position by gender

lines in Figure 14.6 results from the independent variable (age group) having five categories. One way of reducing the clutter of this graph would be to combine some age groups or to focus on just particular age groups. Alternatively a different type of graph (e.g. clustered bar) might be used instead.

Table 14.9 Characteristics of a stacked bar chart

Axes	Has both horizontal axis (bottom) and vertical axis (side).
Level of measurement of independent variable	Nominal, ordinal or interval.
Level of measurement of dependent variable	Nominal, ordinal or interval.
Number of categories of the independent variable	Relatively few (no more than 5 or 6) since each bar is divided into blocks with each block representing a category of the independent variable.
Number of categories of dependent variable	Each bar represents one category of the dependent variable. Therefore using variables with more than 5 or 6 categories make the graph very difficult to read.
Position of axis for dependent variable	Can be either across the bottom (results in a vertical stacked bar chart—Figure 14.4) or on the side (horizontal stacked bar chart).
Scale of the vertical axis	Percentages. Since you will compare groups in which there are different numbers of people you will be unable to make meaningful comparisons without using percentages.
Scale of the horizontal axis (for vertical stacked bar)	Units of the dependent variable.
Representation of bars	Within each block a different colour/patterned block will be used for each category of the independent variable.
Labels	Normal labels will indicate the variable description, its categories and the way in which amount is represented (per cent). The labels for the independent variable are provided in the legend.
Reading the percentages	The percentages are column per cents. They are the percentage of the given category of the independent variable who belong to the specific category of the dependent variable. In Figure 14.4 in the first section of the 'great deal of interest' bar 23 per cent of 18–29-year-olds have a great deal of interest in politics.

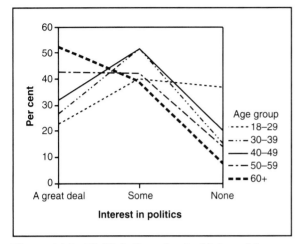

Figure 14.6 **Multiple line chart of interest in politics by age**

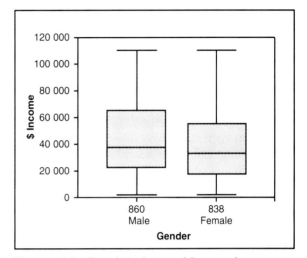

Figure 14.7 **Boxplot of annual income by gender**

Boxplots

Boxplots provide another way of examining the distribution of a dependent variable separately for each category of an independent variable. Figure 14.7 shows the differences in gross annual income by gender.

The solid boxed section indicates the income range of the middle 50 per cent of the distribution of males and of females. The line in the middle of each solid section indicates the median income for males and females. The bottom section indicates the income range of the 25 per cent of lowest-income-earning males and females (see Figure 14.7).

The comparison of the two groups indicates that the median income of females is lower than that of males. Furthermore, the poorest 25 per cent of females have a lower income than the poorest 25 per cent of males—to be among the bottom 25 per cent of male income earners is not the same as being among the bottom 25 per cent of female income earners. Conversely being among the top 25 per cent of female income earners does not mean that you will be as well off as if you were in the top 25 per cent of male income earners.

Table 14.10 **Characteristics of a multiple line chart**

Axes	Has both horizontal axis (bottom) and vertical axis (side).
Level of measurement of independent variable	Nominal, ordinal or interval.
Level of measurement of dependent variable	At least ordinal, preferably interval.
Number of categories of the independent variable	Only a small number since a separate line is generated for each category of the independent variable. Too many lines are confusing.
Number of categories of dependent variable	At least three but is better when there are plenty of categories or values.
Position of axis for dependent variable	Normally on bottom.
Scale of the vertical axis	Usually use percentages.
Scale of horizontal axis	Units of the dependent variable.
Representation of lines	Each line needs to be differentiated by characteristics such as line colour, thickness and pattern (solid, dashed etc).
Labels	Normal labels will indicate the variable description, its categories and the way in which amount is represented (per cent). The labels for the independent variable (lines) are provided in the legend.
Reading the percentages	The percentages represented by the lines are column per cents. The percentages represent the percentage of the subgroup who obtained particular scores on the dependent variable.

USING SUMMARY STATISTICS

While tables and graphs can provide detailed information about the way in which two variables are associated, summary statistics can provide a very concise index of the extent to which two variables are related. The main way in which to summarise the extent to which two variables are related is to use correlation coefficients (also called measures of association). Correlation coefficients are a class descriptive statistics.

There are many different types of correlation coefficients, different ones being appropriate to particular situations. In essence a correlation coefficient is simply an index that provides a succinct description of the extent and character of the relationship between two variables. This section will outline the logic of coefficients designed for nominal and ordinal variables and clarify how to select from among the range of such statistics.

There are two broad types of correlation coefficient (or measures of association) that can be used: chi-square based and proportional reduction of error (PRE) measures. I will outline the *logic* rather than the precise computation of each of these approaches.

Chi-square based correlations

To calculate the chi-square based correlation coefficients we first calculate a statistic called chi square and then convert this to a correlation coefficient. The logic of chi square is best explained with an example.

We begin with what is called a set of *observed frequencies*. These reflect the relationship between two variables as *observed* in a survey (Table 14.13). In this table we can see that males and females differ slightly from one another. How strong a relationship does this male–female difference reflect?

To answer this question we work out what the table would look like *if there was no association* between the variables (these are called *expected frequencies*). Since 53 per cent of the sample think that a woman should be able to have an abortion whenever she wants one (see row marginal in Table 14.13) we would expect, if there was no association between gender and abortion attitudes, that the same percentage of males, and females (i.e. 53 per cent each) would approve of readily available abortion. Table 14.14 presents the *expected* frequencies and percentages for this hypothetical situation of no male–female difference.

Next we check to see the extent to which the *observed* frequencies differ from what we would expect on the assumption of no association. If the observed frequencies differ 'sufficiently' from the expected frequencies we can say there is an association. Chi square is a statistic that is calculated by examining the differences between the observed and expected frequency for each cell. Using the information from Tables 14.13 and 14.14 the chi-square figure is 2.65 (see Web Pointer 14.2 for web-based chi-square calculators if you want to compute this yourself).

Table 14.11   Characteristics of boxplots

Axes	Has both horizontal axis (bottom) and vertical axis (side).
Level of measurement of independent variable	Nominal, ordinal or interval.
Level of measurement of dependent variable	Ordinal or interval.
Number of categories of the independent variable	Only a small number since a separate boxplot is generated for each category of the independent variable. Too many plots become difficult to read.
Number of categories of dependent variable	The more the better.
Position of axis for independent variable	Normally on bottom.
Scale of the vertical axis (in a vertical boxplot)	The units of the dependent variable. If the dependent variable is income measured in dollars the vertical axis will be scaled in dollars.
Scale of the horizontal axis (vertical boxplot)	Units of the independent variable.
Labels	Normal labels will indicate the variable description, its categories and the way in which amount is represented (per cent).

BOX 14.5 *Characteristics of correlation coefficients*

1 *Strength:* The coefficient will always be between 0 and 1: the higher the figure the stronger the association. Zero means no association; 1.00 means perfect association (see Table 14.12).

2 *Direction:* Coefficients for ordinal (and interval) variables can include a minus sign. This simply indicates that the association is negative (no sign means it is positive). The sign indicates nothing about the strength of the relationship.

3 *Character:* Some coefficients only detect whether there is a linear relationship while others can detect non-linear relationships.

4 *Symmetric coefficients:* Some coefficients are unaffected by which of the two variables is the independent variable (called symmetric coefficients). Asymmetric coefficients yield different results depending on which variable is treated as independent.

5 *Causality:* An association between two variables does not prove that they are causally related.

6 *Level of measurement:* Different measures of association are appropriate depending on the level of measurement of the variables being considered.

Table 14.12 Three tables indicating different strengths of association

	No association		Moderate association		Perfect association	
	Male	**Female**	**Male**	**Female**	**Male**	**Female**
Yes	65%	65%	30%	75%	0%	100%
No	35	35	70	25	100	0
Totals	225	175	225	175	225	175
	Correlation = 0.000		Correlation = 0.50		Correlation = 1.00	

Table 14.13 Abortion attitude by gender (observed distribution)

		Gender		
		Male	**Female**	**Total**
	Whenever they want one	466 55%	448 51%	914 **53%**
Feelings about abortion	Only in special circumstances	345 41%	383 44%	728 **42%**
	Should not be allowed	38 4%	46 5%	84 **5%**
Total		849 **49%**	877 **51%**	1726 100%

One problem with the chi-square figure is that the result has no upper limit. The size of the chi-square figure is affected by the sample size and the table size. It is therefore difficult to make much sense of the chi-square figure on its own. To deal with this problem a number of statistics have been developed which convert the raw chi-square figure into a correlation coefficient between 0 and 1 (see below).

PRE-based correlations

The other main type of correlation coefficient is the PRE (proportional reduction of error) measure. Since this type of coefficient uses a different logic to the chi-square measures it is worth explaining their general logic.

If we wanted to predict a person's attitude to abortion without knowing anything about the person our best guess would be to predict the most common response in the sample. For example, since the most common attitude to abortion is 'whenever they want one' (see total column in Table 14.15) this would be our safest guess for any given person.

However we would guess incorrectly in a fair number of cases.

If two variables are related then knowing a person's characteristics on one of these variables should help us guess their characteristics on the other variable better. For example, if church attendance is related to abortion attitudes then knowing a person's frequency of church attendance should help us better guess their attitudes to abortion. In Table 14.15 we see that regular church attenders most often approve of abortion only in special circumstances (63 per cent). If we knew that a person was a regular church attender we would guess that they would approve of abortion only in special circumstances. For those that never attend church we would guess 'whenever they want one' since this is the most common response of the non-attenders. We would still make some wrong guesses.

If two variables are related the total number of wrong guesses (error) we make when we know a person's characteristics on a related variable will be less than if we guessed without this knowledge. If two variables are not related then knowing some-

Table 14.14 Abortion attitude by gender (expected distribution)

		Gender		
		Male	Female	Total
Feelings about abortion	Whenever they want one	450 53%	464 53%	914 **53%**
	Only in special circumstances	358 42%	370 42%	728 **42%**
	Should not be allowed	41 5%	43 5%	84 **5%**
Total		849 **49%**	877 **51%**	1726 100%

Table 14.15 Attitude to abortion by frequency of church attendance

		Church attendance			
		Regular	Sometimes	Rarely/Never	Total
Feelings about abortion	Whenever they want one	20%	48%	63%	53%
	Only in special circumstances	63	47	36	42
	Should not be allowed	17	5	1	5
	N	327	201	1176	1704

thing about the person will not improve our guessing.

These PRE-based correlation coefficients indicate how much better we can predict a person's score on a variable given knowledge of another variable. This type of coefficient is calculated in such a way that it always yields a figure between 0 and 1. The specific interpretation of a PRE-based coefficient is the percentage improvement in predicting correct values of one variable on the basis of another variable. A coefficient of 0.8 would indicate a very strong relationship and means that a variable improves the accuracy of our predictions on the dependent variable by 80 per cent. A correlation of 0.10 is a weak relationship in which the improvement in predictions is only increased by 10 per cent. Different PRE-based coefficients are available depending on the level of measurement of the variables being considered (see below).

Interpreting correlation coefficients: direction

While the size and sign of a coefficient provide important information they are not sufficient to properly interpret a coefficient. To make sense of a correlation coefficient we also need to know the *direction of coding of the variables*. For example, in Table 14.16 what does the correlation of 0.35 between approval of homosexuality and church attendance mean? Without examining the cross-

tabulation we can only interpret the coefficient by examining the direction of coding of both variables. Since the relationship is *positive* the correlation of 0.35 means the *higher* the code on church attendance the *higher* the code on homosexuality tolerance. The way church attendance is coded is that a high code means *rare* (low) attendance while a high code on homosexuality means tolerance of homosexuality. Therefore a positive relationship means that non-church attenders (high code) are more tolerant (high code) than church attenders of homosexuality.

Similarly, the negative correlation of −0.21 between attitude to the reintroduction of the death penalty and educational qualification must be interpreted by reference to the direction of coding of both variables. Qualifications are coded so that the higher qualifications have a low code while lower qualifications have a high code. Attitude to the death penalty has been coded so that a low code indicates approval of the death penalty and a high code indicates disapproval. A negative relationship means that people who have a *low* code on one variable tend to have a *high* code on the other. In this case this means a low code on qualifications (i.e. highly qualified) tend to score high (disapprove) on the capital punishment. In other words the highly qualified disapprove of capital punishment more than the unqualified.

Even the relationship between gender and income must be interpreted bearing in mind the direction of coding. The relationship is negative but

Table 14.16 Effect of coding direction on correlation coefficients

Coding direction for variables

Denomination	1=Catholic; 2=Protestant; 3=Other religious group; 4=None
Church attendance	1=Regularly; 2=Sometimes; 3=Rarely/Never
Age group	1=18–29; ... 6=60 or over
Gender	1=male; 2=female
Post school qualifications	1=postgraduate; ... 8=no qualifications
Income	17 categories 1=lowest income category; ... 17=highest income category
Tolerance of homosexuality	1=intolerant; ... 3=tolerant
Approval of reintroduction of death penalty	1=strongly approve; ... 5=strongly disapprove

Correlations

a	Church attendance by denomination	Cramer's V=0.28
b	Income by denomination	Cramer's V=0.10
c	Homosexuality by church attendance	Gamma=0.35
d	Death penalty by age group	Gamma=−0.03
e	Income by gender	Gamma=−0.11
f	Death penalty by qualifications	Gamma=−0.21
g	Income by qualifications	Spearman's=−0.28

what does this mean? It means that the higher the gender the lower the income. In this case what does 'higher gender' mean? Look at the coding: male=1 and female=2. Therefore the higher the gender (females) the lower the income—females earn less income than males.

Examine the other coefficients in Table 14.16 and try to interpret them. The key point is that correlation coefficients are summaries. You need tools to unpack the meaning of these summary measures and the absolutely essential tool is knowing how each variable is coded.

Interpreting correlation coefficients: strength

As an index of the strength of a relationship, the higher the correlation coefficient the stronger the relationship. But what level constitutes a strong relationship? If the correlation is weak what will the coefficient be? Is a coefficient of 0.5 weak, moderate or strong?

There are two factors that make it difficult to answer these sorts of questions:

1 Some types of correlation statistics tend to yield higher coefficients than others for the same set of data.
2 The size of the coefficient is affected by the sample size. It is much easier to obtain a high coefficient with small samples than with large samples. (For a discussion of this see the site: www.statsoftinc.com/textbook/esc.html#Why_significance_of_a_relation_between_variables_depends)

The meaning of weak, moderate and strong is to some extent relative. In social science data where most outcomes have many causes no two variables are likely to be very strongly related. However, in the physical sciences the correlation between two variables might be extremely high because of the influence of natural laws. In social sciences a correlation of 0.30 might be regarded as *relatively* strong. Often for theoretical purposes it is the relative importance of factors that matters more than the absolute importance.

Having said this it is nevertheless useful to provide some rule of thumb descriptors for different sized correlation coefficients. Those in Box 14.6 are similar to those provided by Davis (1971) and Cohen (1988). The website www.sportsci.org/resource/stats/effectmag.html provides a fuller discussion of what constitutes a strong relationship.

Correlation coefficients when both variables are nominal

The chi-square based correlation coefficients are appropriate when both variables are measured at the nominal level. The two most useful chi-square based correlation coefficients are *phi* and *Cramer's V*. Phi is used for 2-by-2 tables (both variables have just two categories and Cramer's V is used when at least one of the two nominal variables has three or more categories). Both these coefficients range between 0 and 1.0 and that makes them interpretable as a measure of the strength of the relationship. A figure near 0 indicates a very weak relationship while a figure nearer 1 indicates a very strong relationship. Other characteristics of these two coefficients are outlined in Table 14.17 (p. 261). Unfortunately these coefficients do not have the same precise interpretation as a PRE-based correlation where the coefficient can be interpreted as a percentage improvement in prediction. Furthermore, Cramer's V coefficients cannot be reliably compared between tables of different sizes (Agresti, 1986: 219).

The main PRE-type coefficients for two nominal variables are *Yule's Q*, *lambda*, and *Goodman and Kruskal's tau*. Of these, Yule's Q is only appropriate for 2-by-2 tables. Lambda is not very useful as it detects only certain types of relationships. Goodman and Kruskal's tau is appropriate for a pair of nominal variables for any size table (2-by-2 or larger) and is probably the most useful of the PRE-based coefficients for nominal variables. Other characteristics of these coefficients are summarised in Table 14.17.

Web Pointer 14.2 provides links to online calculators that compute many of these statistics.

Statistics when both variables are ordinal

The most common statistics when both the variables in a cross-tabulation are ordinal level is gamma. Alternatives are Somer's d, and Kendall's tau$_c$. These three statistics all measure only linear association.

Gamma is a PRE measure of association, the characteristics of which are summarised in Table 14.17. There are other statistics that can be used to measure association between two ordinal variables but gamma is preferred when variables have relatively few categories.

BOX 14.6 *Interpreting strength of relationship coefficients*

Coefficient	Strength	Alternate descriptors
0.00	No (linear) association	
0.01–0.09	Trivial (linear) relationship	Very small, insubstantial, tiny, practically zero
0.10–0.29	Low to moderate (linear) relationship	Small, low, minor
0.30–0.49	Moderate to substantial (linear) relationship	Medium
0.50–0.69	Substantial to very strong (linear) relationship	Large, high, major
0.70–0.89	Very strong (linear) relationship	Very large, very high, huge
0.90+	Near perfect	

These interpretations apply equally to positive and negative relationships.

WEB POINTER 14.1 *Statistical selection guides*

There are a number of useful computer-based programs that assist in the selection of the appropriate form of statistical analysis. Four useful such programs are:

Statistics coach	Part of SPSS. Click the Help button in SPSS to access the Coach.
Statistical Advisor	www.statsoft.com/textbook/advisor.html
Selecting statistics	http://trochim.human.cornell.edu/selstat/ssstart.htm
Knodt's Help with statistical analysis	http://members.aol.com/statware/pubpage.htm#A2SSYY

Statistics for two ordinal variables with many categories

When a variable has a large number of categories we have the option of reducing the number of categories and thus using tables, graphs, gamma and so forth. But collapsing variables can be undesirable and lead to an important loss of information that is provided by the more detailed coding of a variable with many categories. Where we want to retain the full detail of such variables we will be unable to use tables and many graphs will not be appropriate.

However there are summary statistics that can be used in such situations. The two most common statistics are Kendall's tau_c and Spearman's rho. *Kendall's*

tau_c is best to use when one variable has a large number of categories and the other has relatively few categories. *Spearman's rho* is the preferred correlation coefficient for ordinal variables with a lot of categories. The characteristics of Spearman's rho are summarised in Table 14.17.

Statistics for mixed levels of measurement

When examining relationships between variables with mixed levels of measurement (e.g. nominal and ordinal, nominal and interval or ordinal and interval) specially designed statistics may be available for particular situations. More often than not, however,

---

WEB POINTER 14.2
Online calculators for bivariate statistics and further discussion of bivariate statistics

Content	URL
A variety of calculators for calculating chi square and related statistics (gamma, Kendall's tau$_c$, Somer's d etc) from cross-tabulation input.	http://members.aol.com/johnp71/javastat. html#CrossTabs
Online chi-square calculators.	www.stat.sc.edu/webstat/version2.0/ www.physics.csbsju.edu/stats/contingency.html http://davidmlane.com/hyperstat/chi_square.html http://ebook.stat.ucla.edu/~jbond/TABLES/
Explains and calculates Spearman's correlation.	http://nimitz.mcs.kent.edu/~blewis/stat/scon.html
Modstat: Calculates a wide range of statistics.	http://members.aol.com/rcknodt/pubpage.htm
A good discussion of cross-tabulation analysis, bivariate graphs and correlation coefficients. *Beware:* This discussion places the independent variable on the *side* rather than the top of the table and incorrectly asserts that cross-tabulations are only for nominal variables.	www.statsoftinc.com/textbook/stbasic. html#Cross-tabulation Go to the section on *Cross-tabulations & stub-and-banner tables*
Nominal measures of association: A first-rate and accessible discussion of a wide range of statistics used to detect correlation between nominal variables.	www2.chass.ncsu.edu/garson/pa765/ assocnominal.htm
First-rate discussion of ordinal measures of association.	www2.chass.ncsu.edu/garson/pa765/ assocordinal.htm

---

we will need to make do with statistics designed for two nominal variables or two interval variables.

Box 14.7 provides the general principles involved in selecting statistical measures based on the level of measurement of the variables. The points listed under number 4 are particularly relevant to examining relationships between variables with mixed levels of measurement.

Correlation coefficients for non-linear relationships

When analysing ordinal variables relationships will not necessarily be linear. However, the correlation coefficients for ordinal data that have been discussed so far only detect linear relationships. To

check whether there is a non-linear relationship a coefficient that is sensitive to non-linear relationships is required. Unfortunately there is no co-efficient designed specifically for this purpose with ordinal variables. One solution is to use a measure of association designed for nominal variables. These coefficients (e.g. Cramer's V, Goodman and Kruskal's tau) will detect non-linear relationships but are insensitive to any information provided by the order of categories in ordinal variables.

A useful approach is to obtain both a linear measure of association (e.g. Gamma, Kendall's tau$_c$) and a non-linear measure (e.g. Goodman and Kruskal's tau). As a general rule, if Goodman and Kruskal's tau is higher than gamma it probably indicates a non-linear relationship. Such a pattern certainly warrants a closer

Table 14.17 Characteristics of various measures of nominal and ordinal association

	Appropriate table size	PRE interpretation?	Range	Directional?	Symmetric?	Linear only?	Other characteristics
Nominal measures							
Phi	2 × 2	No	0–1[a]	No	Yes	No	Lower coefficients than Yule's Q.
Cramer's V	Larger than 2 × 2	No	0–1	No	Yes	No	More sensitive to a wider range of relationships than lambda but cannot reliably be compared for different sized tables.
Yule's Q	2 × 2	Yes	0–1	No	Yes	No	Higher coefficients than phi. Same as gamma in 2 × 2 table. Always 1.0 if an empty cell.
Lambda	Any size[d]	Yes	0–1	No	Yes[c]	No	Insensitive and not recommended.
Goodman and Kruskal's tau	Any size[d]	Yes	0–1[b]	No	No	No	Preferred measure for nominal variables. Obtained in SPSS by requesting lambda statistic.
Ordinal measures							
Gamma	Any size[d]	Yes	0–1	Yes	Yes	Yes	Gives higher coefficients than other ordinal coefficients.
Somer's d	Any size[d]	Yes	0–1	Yes	Yes[c]	Yes	
Spearman's rho	Any size	Yes	0–1	Yes	Yes	Yes	Good for variables with large number of categories.
Kendall's tau_b	Any size but must/should be 'square'	Yes	0–1	Yes	Yes	Yes	Will only achieve value of 1.0 if both independent and dependent variables have the same number of categories.
Kendall's tau_c	Any size		0–1		Yes	Yes	Can achieve value of 1.0 if both independent and dependent variables do not have the same number of categories.

a   Under certain conditions the maximum may be less than 1.0 (Guildford, 1965: 336).

b   Will only achieve a value of 1.0 if there is perfect association and the independent and dependent variables have the same number of categories.

c   There is an asymmetric and symmetric version of these statistics.

d   If these statistics are being used in conjunction with a table rather than simply summarising a relationship the table size should be limited.

BOX 14.7
Guidelines in selecting correlation coefficients appropriate to the level of measurement of variables

1 Statistics designed for use with low levels of measurement can be used for analysis where the variables have been measured at a higher level. (Thus Cramer's V or Goodman and Kruskal's tau can be used for ordinal data.) In general this is not advisable since we lose information.

2 Statistics designed for higher levels of measurement (e.g. ordinal variables) should not be used when analysing data measured at a lower level (e.g. nominal level).

3 Dichotomous variables (i.e. two categories) can be regarded as being at any level of measurement. Therefore treat dichotomous variables as being at the same level of measurement of the other variable being examined.

4 When one variable is nominal and the other is ordinal we can use one of three approaches to select the appropriate correlation coefficient.

   a *Dichotomous variables:* If one variable is dichotomous let the other variable

determine the choice of the coefficient. For example, if a dichotomous nominal level variable (e.g. gender) is cross-tabulated with an ordinal level variable, we can treat them both as ordinal and select the appropriate statistic (gamma).

   b *Use a 'weaker' statistic:* We can always treat a higher level of measurement as though it is a lower level (we cannot do the opposite). When neither variable is dichotomous, treat both variables as though they both are at the same level of measurement of the variable measured at the *lowest* level. Thus if one variable is nominal and the other is ordinal, treat both as though they are both nominal.

   c *Use a specially designed statistic:* There are specifically developed statistics designed for various combinations of levels of measurement. These are not widely used but are listed in Table 15.14.

---

inspection of the cross-tabulation to see if the relationship is non-linear.

Weaker than expected relationships

Researchers new to data analysis are frequently disappointed at how low their correlation coefficients are. Many new researchers anticipate clear and strong patterns when examining relationships between two variables. In social science research the reality frequently is that expected relationships are either non-existent or weak. There are many possible reasons for finding weaker than expected relationships (see Box 14.8).

One important reason is that our expectations are unrealistic. Relationships between social science variables—particularly those involving attitudes—are normally weaker than social science and popular

stereotypes would have us believe. Social behaviour and attitudes are highly complex and influenced by many factors, so we should not expect any one variable to be strongly related to another. A weak relationship between age and conservatism, for example, should not be surprising, since many factors other than age affect conservatism. If, as social scientists, we accept the notion of multiple causation and understand something of the complexity of human social behaviour, we should mainly anticipate fairly weak correlations. It is better to accept that most relationships are weak than to overinterpret results.

INFERENTIAL STATISTICS

The logic of inferential statistics and the distinction between tests of significance and interval estimates

BOX 14.8
A checklist when obtaining weaker than expected relationships

1 Are the indicators you've used appropriate? What results do you obtain with substitute measures of the same concept?

2 Do either of the variables require recoding? Is the coding masking a relationship?

3 Does the relationship hold in some subgroups and not others? This could deflate the overall relationship (see Chapter 15).

4 Do the characteristics of the sample deflate the relationship? Perhaps there is an over-representation of groups where the relationship could be expected to be weak.

5 Is the relationship weak because either or both of the variables has low variance? (see Chapter 5).

6 What method has been used for dealing with missing values? Some imputation methods can deflate correlations (see Chapter 10).

7 Have you checked for a non-linear relationship? You may have used a linear measure for a non-linear relationship.

8 Are there outliers that have affected the relationship?

9 Could a suppressor variable be affecting results? (see http://ericae.net/ft/tamu/supres.htm).

10 Are your expectations realistic?

combination with descriptive statistics. Both types of statistics provide different information but each set of information is most useful when seen in the context of the other. Thus a correlation coefficient describes the extent of association between two variables. The significance test tells us whether that relationship is likely to be due simply to chance (sampling error) or whether it is likely to hold in the population from which the sample was drawn. Since we are not normally interested just in the sample, the test of significance provides very useful information. Even if we get a moderate or strong correlation in the sample, but the test of significance suggests that it could be due to sampling error, we are not going to spend much time developing explanations for the relationship or putting much weight on it. In other words, it is important to look at both the correlation coefficient *and* the test of significance to avoid misinterpreting the correlation coefficient. Equally there is little value in just using the test of significance, since all this tells us is that a relationship in the sample exists (or does not exist) in the population. But it tells us nothing about the character of the association: its strength, direction or linearity. It is important to remember that a test of statistical significance does not say anything about the strength of a relationship. It simply tells us whether any relationship that does exist (be it weak or strong) is likely to occur in the population from which the sample is drawn. The links between measures of association and tests of significance are illustrated in Table 14.18.

Significance tests

When using tests of significance in conjunction with correlation coefficients we will test a null hypothesis using the same logic as in Chapter 13. In bivariate analysis the null hypothesis is that there is no relationship between the two variables; that is, the correlation is 0. However the *actual* correlation will rarely be exactly 0. We therefore encounter the problem:

1 Is the observed correlation greater than zero because of sampling error (i.e. the correlation in the population really is zero but sampling error has produced by chance a correlation greater than zero)?

2 Is the observed correlation greater than zero because the assumption of zero correlation in the population is wrong (i.e. we can reject the null

were outlined in Chapters 12 and 13. There is no need to repeat the discussion but three points must be emphasised:

First, statistical inference is only appropriate when the description is based on a random sample.

Second, each correlation coefficient will have its own linked measure of statistical inference.

Third, inferential statistics should be used in

Table 14.18   The links between correlations and tests of significance

Correlation	Significance	N	Interpretation
0.35	0.27	100	Moderate association in sample but too likely to be due to sampling error. Continue to assume correlation of 0 in the population.
0.15	0.001	1500	Weak association but is very likely to hold in the population.
0.64	0.01	450	Strong relationship that is likely to hold in the population.
0.04	0.77	600	Negligible association. Highly probable that the correlation differs from zero due only to sampling error. Continue to assume correlation of 0 in the population.

hypothesis and accept that sample correlation reflects a real correlation in the population)?

The test of significance (often referred to as a p-value) helps resolve these questions by providing an answer to the question 'If there really is no correlation between the two variables in the population, what is the chance that random sampling would produce a correlation coefficient as far from zero (or further) as observed in the sample?'

Tests of significance produce a p-value (probability value) between 0 and 1. The lower the p-value the less the chance that the correlation was produced by sampling error. That is, a *low* p-value means that the sample correlation probably reflects a *real* correlation in the sample.

Table 14.19 provides the correlation coefficients and significance levels for earlier cross-tabulations. The relationship between gender and attitudes to homosexuality that we have seen earlier can by summarised with gamma which indicates a moderate relationship between these variables. An examination of the earlier cross-tabulation (Table 14.2) indicates the content of this relationship—that women are more tolerant than men. The significance level of 0.000 means that a relationship this strong is extremely unlikely to have occurred due to sampling error. It therefore is most likely that it reflects a relationship this strong in the population.

The correlation between gender and approval of abortion is 0.05 (gamma). This gamma means that the relationship between these two variables is very weak—it is very close to 0, the level assumed by the null hypothesis. The significance level of 0.22 means that there is a very good chance that this correlation is higher than zero simply because of sampling error.

Accordingly we would continue to assume that, despite a correlation of 0.05, the real correlation is 0.00.

An examination of the significance levels in each row of Table 14.19 indicates that two of the correlations are statistically non-significant with significance levels of 0.22 and 0.74. In these cases there is a considerable chance (22 per cent and 74 per cent respectively) that the correlation deviates from zero simply due to sampling error.

Six of the relationships are statistically significant at the 0.000 level. That is, in each case the correlation is 'significantly' greater than zero—the size of the correlation cannot be attributed to sampling error. However in these six rows the actual strength of the correlation varies substantially from 0.11 (income by gender) to 0.57 (abortion approval by church attendance). This illustrates that the significance level does *not* indicate anything about the strength of a relationship. Only the correlation coefficient can provide this information.

We cannot assume that because there is a strong correlation in the sample that the correlation will necessarily hold in the population. It is true that given a similar sample size a strong association is more likely to hold in the population than a weaker one. However, the size of the sample is important. We can obtain a strong relationship in a small sample that will not be statistically significant: it is unlikely to occur in the population. This is because with a small sample the likelihood of sampling error is much higher than in a large sample. With small samples it is often difficult to achieve statistical significance. On the other hand, with large samples the probability of sampling error is much less. Any relationship we observe is less likely to be due to sample error. Thus

Table 14.19 Correlations and significance levels for selected tables and figures in Chapter 14

Table	Variables	X			Y		Coefficient	Correlation	Significance level
		N of categories	Level of measurement		N of categories	Level of measurement			
14.2	Homosexuality (Y) by gender (X)	2	Nominal (dichotomous)		3	Ordinal	Gamma	0.33	0.000
14.5	Legalise marijuana (Y) by age group (X)	5	Ordinal		3	Ordinal	Gamma	−0.25	0.000
14.6	Income category (Y) by age group (X)	3	Ordinal		3	Ordinal	Gamma	−0.31	0.000
14.13	Approval of abortion (Y) by gender (X)	2	Nominal (dichotomous)		3	Ordinal	Gamma	0.05	0.22
14.15	Approval of abortion (Y) by church attendance (X)	3	Ordinal		3	Ordinal	Gamma	0.57	0.000
Fig. 14.5	Left–right (Y) by gender (X)	2	Nominal (dichotomous)		11	Ordinal	Gamma	0.01	0.74
Fig. 14.6	Left–right (Y) by age (X)	5	Ordinal		11	Ordinal	Spearman's rho	0.20	0.000
Fig. 14.7	Income (Y) by gender (X)	2	Nominal (dichotomous)		17	Ordinal	Gamma	0.11	0.000

with large samples it is easier to obtain statistical significance—even for quite weak relationships (see Table 14.18).

A number of critics have argued that far too much weight has been placed on tests of significance in data analysis (Selvin, 1957) and have suggested that such tests should be abandoned (Labovitz, 1970) or used only under very strict conditions. For example, tests of significance are only appropriate when we have a simple random sample. Some tests assume that the variables are normally distributed. There is certainly merit in these criticisms and they highlight that the most important part of data analysis is that which takes place at the sample level where we try to detect relationships and search for explanations (see Chapters 14 to 17). The American Psychological Association task force into the use of statistical significance testing stresses this same point. Its report, which is available on the web at:

www.apa.org/journals/amp/amp548594.html

discourages the simple reliance on significance tests and encourages the use of interval estimates and reporting information about the nature and extent of any relationships between variables. This use of such descriptive measures is the realm of descriptive statistics on which this and subsequent chapters concentrate. Descriptive statistics help us to make sense of our data and in social research this is crucial. Knowing that our sample results will hold in the population is useful additional information but is sterile unless we have first thoroughly and imaginatively analysed our sample data using descriptive statistics.

Interval estimates

In Chapter 13 the logic and use of interval estimates was outlined in relation to univariate analysis. Interval estimates can also be used with many bivariate statistics.

When correlation coefficients are calculated we can obtain approximate standard error statistics and calculate confidence intervals of the correlation coefficient. Although using confidence intervals with ordinal level correlations is less common than with many other statistics it is nevertheless appropriate to outline the logic of this form of statistical inference.

Confidence intervals for correlation coefficients enable us to estimate how close the actual population correlation is likely to be to the sample correlation.

With PRE-based correlations (Goodman and Kruskal's Tau, gamma, Kendall's Tau_b and Tau_c, Somer's d) approximations of the standard error can be computed for these statistics. Although not all statistical analysis programs provide standard error statistics for correlation coefficients, SPSS calculates the asymptotic standard error for these correlations. Although these calculations assume an infinite sample they can be used to approximate the standard error in reasonable sized samples (e.g. certainly for samples of 1000 or more). The standard error for these correlations can be computed using the standard rule that at the 95 per cent confidence level the population correlation will be ±2 standard errors of the sample correlation. (Agresti, 1986: 229). For Spearman's correlation the standard error that is calculated for Pearson's correlation can be used (Gardiner and Altman, 1989) (see Chapter 15).

> **Rule:** If the confidence interval includes zero then the null hypothesis (of no association) cannot be rejected at the stated level of confidence. If the interval does not include zero then the null hypothesis can be rejected.

Using standard error figures we can calculate the confidence interval—the range within which the correlation in the population is likely to lie. If this range includes zero we cannot be confident that the population correlation is *not* zero. We would therefore adopt the conservative position and assume that the population correlation is zero. If the confidence interval does not include zero we can be confident that the population correlation is not zero and thus reject the null hypothesis of zero correlation. For example, the gamma correlation for the relationship between age group and approval of marijuana (see Table 14.5) is −0.25. The standard error is 0.027. Thus there is a 95 per cent chance that the population gamma is between −0.25 ± 2(0.027) or −0.25 ± 0.054. That is, the true correlation will be between −0.314 and −0.206.

BIVARIATE ANALYSIS FOR NOMINAL AND ORDINAL VARIABLES CHECKLIST

When undertaking bivariate analysis of nominal or ordinal variables you should ask the following questions:

WEB POINTER 14.3 *Bivariate inferential analysis*	
Content	**URL**
A good brief discussion of significance levels.	www.statsoftinc.com/textbook/esc.html# What _is "statistical_significance"_(p-level)
Clear discussion of the logic of hypothesis testing and significance levels.	http://davidmlane.com/hyperstat/ logic_hypothesis.html
Good discussion of relationship between sample size, strength of correlations and statistical significance.	www.statsoftinc.com/textbook/esc.html# Why_stronger_relations_between_ variables_are_more
An explanation of why only large samples will produce weak relationships that are statistically significant.	www.statsoftinc.com/textbook/esc.html# Why_small_relations_can_be_proven_ significant_only_in_large
A very good discussion of confidence intervals, sample size, significance levels and confidence intervals.	www.sportsci.org/resource/stats/generalize. html#effect
Calculators for confidence intervals of some ordinal measures of association (but only for very limited range of table sizes).	Download the program SISA tables from the following website: http://home.clara.net/sisa/pasprog.htm#SPRT This program can calculate statistics for 2×2, 2×7 and 3×3 tables. It calculates confidence intervals for Kendall's tau, gamma and lambda. Alternatively the site http://home.clara.net/sisa/index.htm enables the same online analysis but is restricted to 2×2 and 2×5 tables
A calculator for confidence interval for a Pearson's or Spearman's correlation.	http://glass.ed.asu.edu/stats/analysis/rci.html
A spreadsheet calculator for (among other things) calculating confidence limits for Pearson's r and other normally distributed statistics.	www.sportsci.org/resource/stats/xcl.xls
A series of quotes from statisticians who object to the slavish (and often inappropriate) use of significance tests—especially when used on their own.	www.indiana.edu/~stigtsts/quotsagn.html

1 What type of analysis is required?
   a Descriptive?
   b Inferential?
2 If descriptive, how will the analysis be presented?
   a In tabular form?
   b Graphical form?
   c As correlation coefficients?
3 What is the level of measurement of the variables being analysed?
   a Nominal?
   b Ordinal?
4 If cross-tabulations are being used:
   a Do the variables have too many categories? Do categories need combining?
   b Is the independent variable at the top of the table?
   c Have you used column per cents? Do percentages add up to 100 in each column?
   d Is the table uncluttered? Does the table provide the required information?
   e How will missing data be handled?
5 If graphs are used:
   a Does the form of graph suit the level of analysis of the variables?

   b Do the number of categories of the variables need reducing?
   c Have you got the placement of the independent and dependent variables in the correct positions?
   d Will you use counts or percentages on the vertical axis?
   e Is the graph properly labelled?
   f Is the aspect ratio of the graph appropriate?
6 If correlation coefficients are being used:
   a Does the correlation coefficient match the level of measurement of the variables?
   b Is the correlation coefficient suited to the number of categories of the variable?
   c How have you checked for non-linear relationships?
7 If inferential analysis is to be undertaken:
   a Do you have a probability sample?
   b Are you requiring:
      i A significance test?
      ii An interval estimate?
   c Does the inferential statistic match the descriptive statistic you have used?

KEY CONCEPTS

Association	Curvilinear relationship	Marginals	PRE measure
Asymmetric coefficient	Dichotomous variable	Measure of association	Row percentage
Column percentage	Goodman and Kruskal's	Negative relationship	Somer's d
Correlation coefficient	tau	Non-linear relationship	Statistical independence
Cramer's V	Kendall's tau$_c$	Phi	Symmetric coefficient
Cross-tabulation	Linear relationship	Positive relationship	Yule's Q

FURTHER READING

An exceptionally well organised and clear account of the main measures of association depending on the level of measurement of variables is provided by Freeman in *Elementary Applied Statistics* (1965) in section C. Another helpful outline is in Chapter 6 of Johnson's *Social Statistics Without Tears* (1977). A brief but excellent overview of the range of statistics available is provided in Nie et al. in *SPSS: Statistical Package for the Social Sciences* (1975) pp. 218–30 and by Norusis in *SPSSX: Introductory Statistics Guide* (1983) Chapter 5. Clear but slightly more technical discussions are given by Loether and McTavish in Chapters 6 and 7 of *Descriptive Statistics for Sociologists* (1974) and in Mueller, Schuessler and Costner in Chapter 8 of *Statistical Reasoning in Sociology* (1977). The readings provided

on the websites referred to in Web Pointers 14.2 and 14.3 provide excellent discussions of bivariate descriptive and inferential statistics that extend beyond that provided in this book.

Schmid and Schmid in their *Handbook of Graphic Presentation* (1979) and Henry's *Graphing Data* (1995) provide useful information about the use of graphs for bivariate data. The site www.statsoft.com/textbook/stgraph.html describes a wide range of graphs that can be used for bivariate analysis. In its graphics gallery function SPSS also provides a very useful summary of the types of graphs and the requirements for using the graph appropriately.

Two helpful outlines of how to use cross-tabulations

are available. Appendix A of Rosenberg's *The Logic of Survey Analysis* (1968) gives a guide to reading tables and Davis provides excellent guidelines about the presentation of both simple and complex tables in 'Tabular Presentation' (1968). Marsh (1988: 139–42) provides very useful guidelines about what to include in cross-tabulations. Ehrenberg (1975) provides worthwhile ideas about effective ways of presenting tables.

For more complex treatments of measures of association used with cross-tabulations see Chapters 1–3 of Davis's *Elementary Survey Analysis* (1971) in which the logic of these measures is clearly explained. More technical papers are by Reynolds in his paper 'Analysis of Nominal Data' (1977), Chapters 1 and 2, Hilderbrand, Laing and Rosenthal in 'Analysis of Ordinal Data' (1977), and by Liebetrau in 'Measures of Association' (1983) Chapters 1–4.

EXERCISES

1 Construct a cross-tabulation from the following 50 people. In these data there are two variables: gender (M=male; F=female) and vote (O=Other; L=Labor). When constructing this table include the count, row, column and total percentages in each cell and include column and row marginals.

M–L F–L F–O M–L M–O F–L F–O F–O M–L
M–O M–O F–O M–L M–O F–O F–L M–L
M–L F–L F–O M–L F–O M–L M–O F–O F–O
M–L M–L F–O M–L F–O M–L M–O F–O F–L
F–O M–O F–O M–L M–L F–O F–O M–L F–L
M–L F–O M–L F–O F–O M–L

2 Explain what the following figures in your table mean:
75%; 12%; 76%; 26.

3 Reconstruct your table showing only the necessary information to detect whether the two variables are related.

4 Describe the character of the relationship in the table you have produced.

5 For each of the following statements indicate whether it is true or false.
a Statistics which can be used for nominal level variables also can be used for interval level variables. [T] [F]
b Statistics designed for use with low levels of measurement can also be used for higher levels of measurement but not vice versa. [T] [F]
c Statistics designed for use with ordinal data can be used for nominal data. [T] [F]

6 Describe the nature of the association in the following table.

		Social class		
		Low	**Medium**	**High**
Number	None	11%	28%	45%
of	Few	23	18	35
arrests	Many	66	54	20
	N	129	260	73

7 Which measure(s) of association would you use for each of the following pairs of variables?
a Highest level of education (primary, secondary, tertiary/age group (less than 30, 30–50; 51–69; 70+).
b Gender/self-esteem (high, low).
c Approval of abortion (approve, no opinion, disapprove)/religion (Protestant, Catholic, Jewish, none, other).
d Gender/marital status (married, widowed, divorced).
e Quality of relationship with mother (good, neutral, poor)/social class (upper, middle, lower).

8 Draw cross-tabulations to illustrate the following types of relationships. (Use only percentages for this exercise and be sure to label your tables properly.) Select whatever variables seem appropriate.
a A 2 × 2 table reflecting a strong negative relationship.
b A 2 × 2 table reflecting a very weak positive relationship.
c A 3 × 2 table reflecting a moderate, linear, positive relationship.

d   A 3 × 2 table reflecting a moderate, linear, negative relationship.

e   A 3 × 2 table reflecting a curvilinear relationship.

9   If a table reflects a clear curvilinear relationship, linear measures of association will be (circle one):

high   moderate   low   can't tell

10 If there is a non-linear relationship between two ordinal variables which measure of association would you use?

11 What does it mean to say two variables are independent of one another?

12 Explain in your own words why it is worth using correlation coefficients rather than simply looking at cross-tabulations.

13 a   What do the following coefficients mean? 0.05; 0.25; 0.5; −0.85; 0.8.

    b   Which of the above coefficients reflect the strongest relationship?

14 What is the difference between a measure of association and a test of significance?

15 Why is it desirable to use tests of significance?

16 If in a random sample we obtain a correlation of 0.30 between two variables, what does this tell us about their correlation in the population?

17 What does it mean to say that a relationship is significant at the 0.05 level?

18 Interpret each of the following sets of results

	Correlation	Significance
a	−0.45	0.001
b	0.15	0.001
c	0.64	0.37
d	0.24	0.05
e	0.05	0.66

19 In the above question why might the correlation of 0.64 be non-significant but the much weaker correlation of 0.15 be significant?

20 What is wrong with the following statements?

    a   There was a significant relationship between gender and income (correlation = 0.60).

    b   Age is strongly related to prejudice (significance = 0.001).

15

Bivariate analysis for interval-level variables

Interval-level variables are generally not suited to the types of analysis covered in Chapter 14. The techniques in Chapter 14 largely rely on variables having only a small number of categories. Interval-level variables frequently have a large number of different values. This chapter:

- explores techniques suitable to analysing interval variables *without* having to collapse these variables into a small number of categories;
- describes methods of analysis when the dependent variable is interval-level and the independent variable is categorical (comparison of means);
- describes the use of correlation coefficients when both the independent and dependent variables are interval-level (Pearson's correlation and rank–order correlation);
- introduces the analysis technique called regression analysis;
- outlines graphing methods and descriptive statistics suitable for interval-level variables;
- shows how to compare means to establish the existence of relationships;
- describes the use of tests of significance and interval estimates suitable for interval-level variables;

- provides a guide sheet to assist in selecting correlation coefficients discussed in Chapters 14 and 15.

INTERVAL-LEVEL DEPENDENT VARIABLES WITH CATEGORICAL INDEPENDENT VARIABLES

Frequently in social science research we need to analyse data in which we have an interval-level dependent variable such as income level, education level and nominal or ordinal independent variables such as gender, social class or age group.

Since interval-level dependent variables frequently have a large number of possible values (think of the different income levels in a sample of 2000 people) we cannot rely on the same tabular and graphical methods discussed in previous chapters. We need a way of handling the detail that these interval-level statistics provide. There are two main ways in which this is done:

1 collapse the categories of the interval-level variables (e.g. into income groups, age groups etc) and use the tabular or graphical methods discussed in Chapter 14;

2 use techniques that can handle a large number of numeric values.

The second approach is generally preferable. Not only does it allow more powerful statistical methods to be used, it retains the information provided by the finer grained measurement of interval-level variables. The first part of this chapter focuses on the use of techniques that do not require collapsing the values of interval-level variables.

Where we have an interval-level dependent variable and a categorical independent variable the analysis involves comparing groups of people in terms of how they 'score' on an interval-level dependent variable. The 'groups' are defined by the categories of the independent variable to which people belong. For example, we might compare men and women (gender being the independent variable) in terms of their 'score' on income (dependent variable). The approach uses summary measures of the dependent variable and compares these summary measures across groups (men and women).

The most common summary measure used in this context is the mean of the dependent variable. The mean of the dependent variable is calculated for people in each group. In this example we would compare the mean income of males with that of females. If there is a difference between these income means we might conclude that gender is associated with income.

However we are not limited to just using means for these comparisons. Rather than looking at the average income of males and females we might be more interested in seeing whether the variation in incomes is greater among males than among females. Or perhaps we might want to know whether the male income distribution is more skewed than that of females. Although this chapter will focus more on comparisons of means you should not feel that your analysis must be limited to this.

Tabular analysis

There are a number of ways of presenting this type of comparative summary information in tabular form. The most common way is to use a simple table such as that in Table 15.1.

In the example in Table 15.1 age groups are the categories of the independent variable. The means are the mean scores of each age group on the

Table 15.1 Means on left–right scale by age group

	Own left–right position		
Age group	**Mean[a]**	**N**	**Std deviation**
18–29	5.01	212	1.73
30–39	4.88	296	1.78
40–49	5.38	345	1.78
50–59	5.46	293	2.02
60+	5.89	353	2.09
Total	5.37	1499	1.93

[a] Left–right position has scores ranging from 0 to 10 with 0 = most left wing and 10 = most right wing.

dependent variable—political position. Given the way political position is scored, the higher the mean for an age group the more right wing that group is. In this case the oldest groups are the most right wing with a mean of 5.89. With the exception of the 18–29-year-olds the trend is that the older the group the more right wing they are. The relationship tends to be linear (as age increases so does the level of right wing orientation).

The table also indicates the standard deviation for each age group. This measures how alike people are in each age group regarding their left–right orientation. The higher the standard deviation the more varied the group is. Here the youngest group are the most alike with a standard deviation of 1.73. The older the group is, the more diverse the group is. Why this is so is an interesting question that could lead to some interesting theorising about the way in which political positions are formed and evolve.

The final piece of information that should be included in such a table is the number of people in each group. This is important information since it indicates the number of people on which the means and standard deviations are based. When these numbers are very small it can lead to quite unreliable means and standard deviations which require very careful interpretation.

Tree diagrams

Another way in which the information in Table 15.1 can be presented is with a tree diagram. Although this approach does not seem particularly startling with just two variables it can be very helpful when more than two variables are being used.

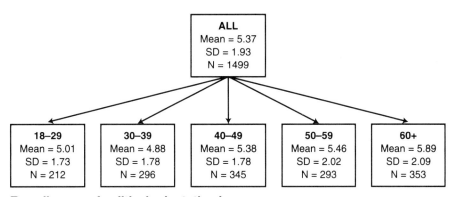

Figure 15.1 **Tree diagram of political orientation by age**

Graphical

As with tables, the graphs for interval-level dependent variables and categorical (groups) independent variables use summary measures of the dependent variables. Instead of using percentages or frequencies, as in the graphs in Chapter 14, these graphs will use means, standard deviations etc on the vertical axis. The horizontal axis will indicate the groups or the categories of the independent variable.

The graphs in Figure 15.2 represent the summary data in Table 15.1 in seven different ways.

Figure 15.2a graphs the means in Table 15.1 as a vertical bar chart and Figure 15.2c plots the same values as a horizontal bar chart while Figure 15.2f uses a line chart for the same values. The line chart should only be used if the independent variable is ordinal.

You will observe in these three graphs that age group appears to make a considerable difference to the mean left–right orientation. However, this effect is exaggerated by the scale of the vertical axis (horizontal in Figure 15.2c). These graphs were produced by SPSS which, by default, truncates the values on this axis. The full range of values for left–right orientation should range from 0–10 but SPSS focuses on the values where the groups *differ*. This may be desirable but you should be aware of the way this can exaggerate differences. Figure 15.2b is the same as Figure 15.2a except that it includes the full range of values on the vertical axis. Including the full range of values gives a different impression of the importance of age differences.

Figure 15.2d uses a different summary

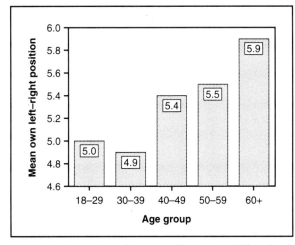

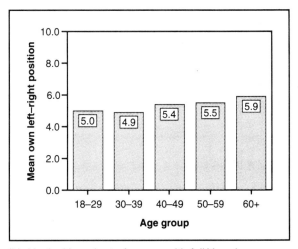

(a) Vertical bar chart of means with truncated Y scale

(b) Vertical bar chart of means with full Y scale

Figure 15.2 **Different graphic representations of the information in Table 15.1**

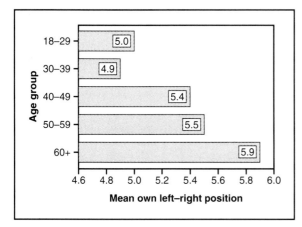

(c) Horizontal bar chart of means with truncated Y scale

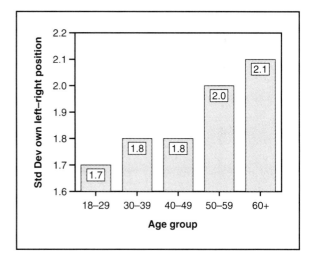

(d) Vertical bar chart of standard deviations with truncated Y scale

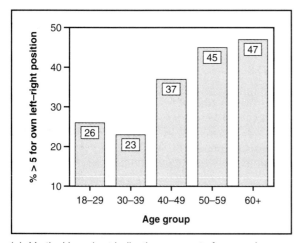

(e) Vertical bar chart indicating per cent of cases above a score of 5 on left–right orientation

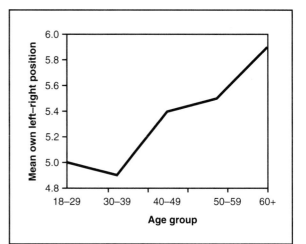

(f) Line graph of means with truncated Y scale

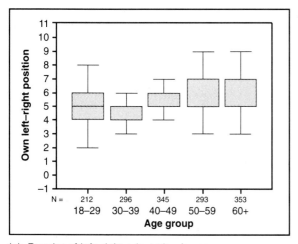

(g) Boxplot of left–right orientation by age group

Figure 15.2 *continued*

measure—standard deviation. This indicates the same picture as the figures in Table 15.1 where the older age groups are more heterogeneous than the younger groups. Figure 15.2e uses a different summary measure—in this case the percentage of people above the midpoint of the scale. That is, it displays the per cent in each age group that are to the right of centre on the political spectrum.

Finally Figure 15.2g displays the relationship between age group and political leaning with a boxplot. This indicates that the median orientation is the same for each age group but that there are still important differences in other aspects of the distribution. The smaller boxes for those in their thirties and forties suggests relative similarity within these age groups while the other groups are more varied within. Again, the boxes (which represent the middle 50 per cent of the distribution of each age group) indicates how the older age groups are more right leaning than the younger groups (except for those aged 18–29).

Summary statistics: descriptive analysis

The two main ways in which descriptive analysis will proceed when dealing with an interval dependent variable and a categorical independent variable are by examining the:

1   actual differences between groups;
2   the correlation between the two variables.

Actual differences

Using this approach requires that we describe how much the groups differ on the dependent variable. This will be reported in terms of the actual differences between the groups.

Most often these descriptions will report differences between the means of the groups but equally we could report differences in the variation, the skew and so forth. Where the independent variable has just two categories this reporting is straightforward.

Table 15.2 provides income data from males and females. From this we can easily calculate the differential for males and females: males, on average, earn $5299 more than females. Furthermore the income distribution is a little more varied among males than females as indicated by the differences in the standard deviation figures.

These descriptions become a little more complex when the independent variable has more categories. Take for example the income by age group figures in Table 15.3.

There are many different sets of income differences here. There are two main ways of expressing these differences.

1   a grid of differences;
2   baseline comparisons.

Grid of differences   In the grid (Table 15.4) the income difference between each possible age group pairs has been calculated. This grid can be read by comparing the difference in the row as indicating how much difference there is between the age group in the row compared to that in the selected column. A positive figure means the row age group earns that much more, on average, than the column group while a negative figure means they earn less.

Differences against a specified baseline   An alternative approach is to select a baseline against which to compare all the other groups. This approach is simpler but provides less information. In the baseline table (Table 15.5) the average income of each group is compared to that of the '66+' age group and clearly shows how much better off each age group is than this older group. Alternatively the comparison income differences could be between each age group and the overall average.

Correlation coefficient: ETA

These comparisons of actual income differences between groups can be useful but are also cumbersome.

Table 15.2   Mean income by gender

Gender	Mean	N	Std deviation
Male	$44 640	860	$30 288
Female	$39 341	838	$28 248
Total	$42 024	1 698	$29 410

Table 15.3   Income by age group

Age group	Mean	N	Std deviation
18–25	$42 516	152	$30 429
26–39	$48 189	417	$28 026
40–55	$50 243	575	$29 720
56–65	$34 628	242	$27 173
66+	$19 777	235	$17 518
Total	$42 242	1 621	$29 476

Table 15.4   Grid of average income differences by age group: comparison of differences between pairs of age groups

	18–25	26–39	40–55	56–65	66+
26–39	$5 673				
40–55	$7 727	$2 056			
56–65	–$7 888	–$13 559	–$15 615		
66+	–$23 274	–$28 410	–$30 466	–$14 851	
ALL	–$274	–$5 945	–$28 410	$7 614	$22 465

Note: This is read by comparing the difference in the row as indicating how much difference there is between the age group in the row compared to that in the column. A positive figure means the row age group earns that much more, on average, than the column group while a negative figure means they earn less.

Table 15.5   Average income differences of age groups with baselines

	66+ baseline	ALL
18–25	+$23 274	+$274
26–39	+$28 410	+$5 945
40–55	+$30 466	+$28 410
56–65	+$14 851	–$7 614
66+		–$22 465

Note: A positive figure means the row age group earns more than the column baseline. A negative number indicates that the row group earns less than the column baseline.

A simpler way of expressing the link between age group and income is to use a correlation coefficient (see Chapter 14). The coefficient that is designed for an interval-dependent variable and a categorical-independent variable is *eta*.

Like other coefficients eta ranges from 0 to 1. However it is not restricted to detecting just linear relationships—it can also detect non-linear relationships. Because of this, eta does not have a positive or negative value. Furthermore, eta is not a symmetric measure—a different coefficient is generated depending on which of two variables is treated as the dependent variable. Table 15.12 summarises these characteristics.

For the relationship between age group and income, eta is 0.36. The earlier relationship between gender and income (Table 15.2) results in a weaker eta of 0.09.

Summary statistics: inferential analysis

If your data are based on a random sample it is appropriate to use inferential analysis on the statistics generated by the descriptive analysis. Once again we can think in terms of statistical significance and interval estimates.

Comparing means

When comparing the means of groups we compute income differences between groups (Table 15.4). The question we must then ask is: 'Are these differences between the means sufficiently large as to reflect real population differences?' Or could the difference between the means simply be the result of sampling error? If the difference is small and the sample is small there is a good chance that the differences between the group means can be attributed to sampling error. If there are large differences between group means in a large sample the differences are probably not due to sampling error.

We can be more systematic than simply guessing whether the differences in means are real or due to chance. To do this we begin with the null hypothesis that any differences between the means of the groups is due to sampling error—that the real difference between the group means is effectively zero.

There are two tests that are used to evaluate whether or not to reject the 'no difference' assumption: the T-test and the F-test. Both these statistics have a similar interpretation but the selection between them depends in part on the number of 'groups' being compared.

Dichotomous independent variable

When the independent variable has just two categories (e.g. male/female; under 40/over 40) we are comparing the means on the dependent variable for the two groups. We begin by assuming that the means of the two groups are identical and that any differences are due to sampling error. For samples where both groups have at least twenty cases we can use the T-test. (There are various forms of the T-test. In most survey research it is appropriate to use the independent samples T-test.)

Significance testing

Table 15.6 provides the type of output that is generated by statistical programs such as SPSS. In this case the T-test is used to test whether the difference between the mean incomes of men and women (a difference of $5299) is likely to be due to sampling error. The first table in Table 15.6 indicates the means for both men and women. The second section provides T-test results for two scenarios: one where the income variation among women is the same as for men and one where it is different. The calculation of the T-test is a little different depending on whether the two groups have similar variance or not. The Levine test tells us which of the two T-tests to use. If the 'sig' level for the Levine test is above 0.05 use the T-test where equality of variance is assumed (first line). If the Levine 'sig' is less than 0.05 use the T-test where equality of variance is not assumed (second line).

In this case we can assume equality of variance among males and females and use the top T-test. This yields a t value of 3.726 with a significance of 0.000.

This significance level can be interpreted in the same way as earlier significance tests. If it is less than 0.05 we will accept that the differences between the male and female mean incomes is unlikely to be due to sampling error. That is, we reject the notion of no difference.

Interval estimate

The output in Table 15.6 also produces a standard error. Like standard error figures we have encountered earlier, this allows us to estimate the income difference between males and females in the populations—at least within a range. Using the rule that there is a 95 per cent chance that the population mean will lie within ±2 standard errors of the sample mean a confidence interval or interval estimate can be calculated. In this case the confidence interval is $2509 to $8088. In other words we can be confident that there is a male–female income difference that it is somewhere between $2509 to $8088 in the population (see last two columns of second part of Table 15.6).

Independent variables with three or more categories

Where the independent variable has three or more categories the T-test is not appropriate for testing

Table 15.6 Independent samples T-test: income by gender

	Gender	N	Mean	Std deviation	Std error mean
Income	Male	860	$44 640	$30 288	$1033
	Female	838	$39 341	$28 248	$976

Independent samples test

		Levene's test for equality of variances		T-test for equality of means					95% confidence interval of the difference	
		F	Sig.	t	df	Sig. (2-tailed)	Mean difference	Std error difference	Lower	Upper
Income	Equal variances assumed	3.013	0.083	3.726	1696	0.000	**$5299**	**$1422**	**$2509**	**$8088**
	Equal variances not assumed			3.729	1692.763	0.000	$5299	$1421	$2512	$8086

mean differences. Instead we use the F-test. In many respects this appears similar to the T-test. The typical output for this is provided in Table 15.7 for the relationship between age group and income.

Earlier in Table 15.3 we saw the mean income for each of the five age groups. Are the differences between these means likely to be due to sampling error or reflect a real difference in the population? The F-test statistics in Table 15.7 help answer this question.

Without detailing the calculations involved this output indicates a F-test figure of 60.834 with a significance level of 0.000. This significance level means that there is almost no chance that the differences between the mean income of the five age groups is due to sampling error. There are real differences. We can safely reject the null hypothesis of no difference between the age group means.

However there is one problem. Since there are five age groups we do not know which particular age groups have significantly different means. In Table 15.4 we saw that there were ten unique pairs of age group comparisons. The differences between some age groups might be due to sampling error while others might not be.

We therefore require one further step in this analysis and conduct what is called a *post hoc comparison*. This is simply an examination of income differences between each of the ten pairs of age groups. It enables us to identify which *pairs* of groups have sufficiently large differences that are unlikely to be due to sampling error. To do this we can use one of a number of tests. I will illustrate just one of these: the Scheffé test (see Table 15.8).

To read Table 15.8 look at the first two columns. Combinations based on these two columns create pairs of age groups. The first row represents the pair of age groups 18–25 and 26–39. The average income difference between them is −$5673 (18–25-year-olds earn on average this much *less* than 26–39-year-olds).

Could this difference be due to sampling error? The 'sig' column indicates that there is a 31.6 per cent chance that a difference this size could be due to sampling error. The next two columns provide the confidence interval for the income differences between these two age groups. This confidence interval ranges from −$13712 to $2366. That is, the real difference could be anywhere from 18–25-year-olds earning $13712 *less* than the 26–39-year-olds to $2366 *more* than the 26–39-year-olds. Since this range includes zero we cannot be sure that there is any real difference between these two age groups.

Scanning down the column headed 'mean difference', the differences marked with an asterisk (★) indicate age group pairs that do have real differences in their income levels (as indicated by the 'sig' column). In each case we can examine the confidence intervals to arrive at an estimate of the likely real income differences between these age groups. One thing that's obvious in these post hoc comparisons in Table 15.8 is that the older groups stand out as being different from the other groups and that the difference is in the direction of the older group earning significantly less than other age groups.

Significance of eta

Like the correlations discussed in Chapter 14, eta can be tested for statistical significance. We can test to see if eta is significantly greater than 0. The simplest way of doing this is to examine the significance of the F-test (or T-test). If this is statistically significant you can be confident that eta is significantly greater than zero. If this test is not significant neither will eta be.

Earlier I reported an eta of 0.36 for the relationship between age group and income. The F-test for this pair of variables was significant at the 0.000 level so we can be confident that an eta at least this high would be found in the population. Similarly the eta of 0.09 between gender and income, while much

Table 15.7   F-test of income by age group

			ANOVA		
	Sum of squares	**df**	**Mean square**	**F**	**Sig.**
Between groups	184207514226	4	46051878556	60.834	0.000
Within groups	1223328705700	1616	757010338		
Total	1407536219926	1620			

Table 15.8 The results of a Scheffé test for age group and income

Multiple comparisons

Dependent variable: Income
Scheffé

Age group	Age group	Mean difference (I–J)	Std error	Sig.	95% confidence interval	
					Lower bound	Upper bound
18–25	26–39	–$5 673	$2 607	0.316	–$13 712	$2 366
	40–55	–$7 727	$2 509	0.051	–$15 465	$11
	56–65	$7 888	$2 848	0.105	–$893	$16 670
	66+	$22 740*	$2 864	0.000	$13 908	$31 571
26–39	18–25	$5 673	$2 607	0.316	–$2 366	$13 712
	40–55	–$2 054	$1 770	0.853	–$7 511	$3 403
	56–65	$13 561*	$2 223	0.000	$6 705	$20 418
	66+	$28 413*	$2 244	0.000	$21 492	$35 334
40–55	18–25	$7 727	$2 509	0.051	–$11	$15 465
	26–39	$2 054	$1 770	0.853	–$3 403	$7 511
	56–65	$15 615*	$2 108	0.000	$9 114	$22 117
	66+	$30 467*	$2 130	0.000	$23 898	$37 036
56–65	18–25	–$7 888	$2 848	0.105	–$16 670	$893
	26–39	–$13 561*	$2 223	0.000	–$20 418	–$6 705
	40–55	–$15 615*	$2 108	0.000	–$22 117	–$9 114
	66+	$14 852*	$2 520	0.000	$7 081	$22 622
66+	18–25	–$22 740*	$2 864	0.000	–$31 571	–$13 908
	26–39	–$28 413*	$2 244	0.000	–$35 334	–$21 492
	40–55	–$30 467*	$2 130	0.000	–$37 036	–$23 898
	56–65	–$14 852*	$2 520	0.000	–$22 622	–$7 081

* The mean difference is significant at the 0.05 level.

weaker, is nevertheless significant at the 0.000 level (F = 13.88; P < 0.000).

TWO INTERVAL-LEVEL VARIABLES

When both the independent and dependent variables are interval-level a different set of analysis tools are available. Since these variables typically have a large number of categories tables such as cross-tabulations are hardly feasible. Graphs can be used but much of the analysis of two interval variables relies on summary statistics. These include correlation coefficients, regression coefficients, tests of significance and interval estimates.

Graphs

The main graphical way of displaying a relationship between two interval-level variables is to use a scatter-plot.

A scatterplot is a graph consisting of a horizontal and vertical axis and data points. The horizontal axis (called the X-axis) represents the values of the independent variable and the vertical axis (the Y-axis) represents the values of the dependent variable. The values of the two variables for any given case serve as the co-ordinates of the point representing that case (see Figure 15.3). In Figure 15.3 each dot represents a person and indicates the number of years of tertiary education they have and the income they report.

The way the points are scattered on a scatterplot reflects the strength, direction and nature of the relationship between the two variables. In Figure 15.3 there is a general pattern that the more years of tertiary education a person has completed the higher their income. The line in the graph is called a *regression line* or the line of best fit. This line is analogous to the mean in univariate analysis. The mean summarises a single distribution. A regression line

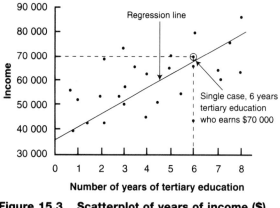

Figure 15.3   Scatterplot of years of income ($) by years of tertiary education

summarises a *relationship*: it is like an average of the intersecting points between education and income. The direction of this line indicates something of the nature of the relationship: it trends upwards which in this case means that as education increases income tends to increase.

A scatterplot can provide visual information about a relationship. Figure 15.4 illustrates six scatterplots which reflect different aspects of relationships.

1   *Strength:* the more concentrated the points the stronger the relationship (scatterplots a and e).
2   *Direction:* when the slope of the points is upwards moving from left to right (scatterplots a and b) the relationship is positive. A downward slope reflects a negative relationship (scatterplots d and e).
3   *Nature:* when the points roughly form a straight line the relationship is linear. Where they form a curved line (f) it is curvilinear. Where there is no pattern (c) there is no relationship.

Summary statistics: Pearson's correlation

Even though the character of a relationship can be visually obvious, scatterplots can become very difficult to decipher in large samples. To better summarise the relationship in the scatterplot and to enable more advanced analysis it is desirable to summarise the relationship with a correlation coefficient. Pearson's correlation (Pearson's r) is used for two interval-level variables.

In Figure 15.3 the dots are reasonably scattered.

Let us suppose that the Pearson's r for this relationship is 0.36. When Pearson's r is squared (i.e. r^2) it is a PRE measure of association which is based on the same logic of PRE measures as outlined in the previous chapter. It differs from other PRE measures simply in terms of how error is defined. This PRE measure of association is indicated by the symbol r^2 which in this case is 0.13. See Box 15.1 for the meanings of r^2.

The problem with r^2 is that the method of calculating r^2 means that there are no negative signs: r^2 is always positive. It is very useful in telling us how *strong* the relationship is but not its *direction*. Pearson's r tells us the direction. In the first five scatterplots in Figure 15.4a I have included a Pearson's r coefficient beneath. This provides a single figure index of the strength and direction of any *linear* relationship between the two variables. You will notice that the more concentrated the points, the higher the coefficient. In scatterplot f the correlation is zero because Pearson's r only detects linear relationships. Web Pointer 15.1 provides an interactive demonstration of the way in which the scatter of cases is reflected in the size of the r coefficient.

Frequently people report only r since this provides information about the direction. To obtain a meaningful measure of the strength of the relationship we should square this figure: often this is left up to us (to do this simply multiply r by r). This convention of reporting only r can be misleading since the r coefficient is always larger than r^2 and if you forget to square r the strength of association can be exaggerated (e.g. if r = 0.36, r^2 = 0.13; if r = 0.40, r^2 = 0.16).

Web Pointer 15.2 provides further interactive simulations and reading on Pearson's r. It also provides simulations of regression statistics—a different method of looking at relationships between interval-level variables.

Regression analysis

The methods of analysis discussed so far allow us to work out whether two variables are associated: whether people who vary on one variable also vary systematically on the other. We can also determine how strongly these variables are associated. But we may want more information. For example, we may want to know *how much* someone with a given amount of education is likely to earn: in particular

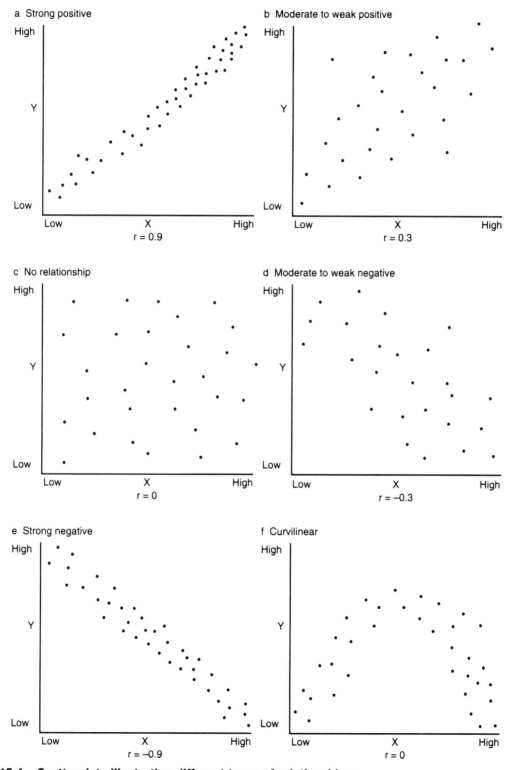

Figure 15.4 **Scatterplots illustrating different types of relationships**

BOX 15.1
Expressing the meaning of r²

There are a variety of ways of expressing the meaning of r^2. They all mean much the same thing but the different ways of talking about r^2 can highlight the type of information provided by a correlation. The r^2 of 0.13 for the relationship between years of tertiary education and income can be expressed as:

■ Differences in years of tertiary education accounts for (explains) 13 per cent of the variance in income (explained variance).

■ 13 per cent of the variation in income is due to the different tertiary education levels of people in the sample.

■ There is a 13 per cent improvement in predicting Y from X over Y alone.

■ If everyone in the sample had the same level of tertiary education then there would be 13 per cent less inequality in income.

■ Conversely, 87 per cent of the variation in income is not due to tertiary education (unexplained variance).

how much difference will staying on at university for another year make to someone's income level? Correlation will tell us how likely more tertiary education is to affect income (the higher the correlation coefficient the more likely), but regression analysis tells us *how much* difference it is likely to make. It enables us to make predictions about people's scores on the dependent variable (e.g. dollars earned) if we know their score on the independent variable (years of tertiary education). It enables us to

say how much *impact* each additional unit of the independent variable will have on the dependent variable.

Regression analysis is linked closely to Pearson's correlation and scatterplots. In the scatterplot in Figure 15.3 all the points were summarised with a single line: the regression line or line of best fit. This line had two functions: to predict Y scores, and to help calculate r^2. The first function is the most relevant for regression and it is on this we shall concentrate.

Regression coefficients

Figure 15.3 is a scatterplot showing a relationship between years of tertiary education and income. This scatterplot is reproduced in Figure 15.5 without the data points. The regression line is used to summarise these data points and is used for predictions and to assess the impact of tertiary education on income. To predict how much someone with five years tertiary education would earn, we simply follow the vertical

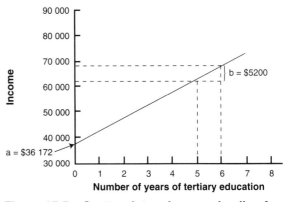

Figure 15.5 **Scatterplot and regression line for relationship between income and years of tertiary education**

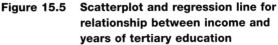

WEB POINTER 15.1 *Pearson's correlation and the scatter of data points*

An interactive demonstration of the relationship between the scatter of data points and the size of Pearson's correlation coefficient

www.stat.berkeley.edu/users/stark/Java/Correlation.htm

Visit www.social-research.org to use these links and to check for updates and additions.

WEB POINTER 15.2
Correlation and regression: interactive simulations and further information

Provides a detailed but understandable description of the purpose and computation of correlation and regression statistics.	http://faculty.vassar.edu/~lowry/webtext.html
An excellent and easy to use online calculator to compute correlation and regression statistics. Requires import or direct entry of data. Useful to experiment with.	http://faculty.vassar.edu/~lowry/corr_stats.html
An excellent regression simulator. You place the points on a scatterplot and see the effect on the slope of the regression line and the B coefficient. Experiment with 'outliers'.	www.math.csusb.edu/faculty/stanton/m262/ regress/regress.html
Another excellent interactive regression and correlation simulator. Place data points on a scatterplot and examine the effect on the regression line (slope) and the correlation coefficient. Can also set a correlation coefficient and generate points and line for that coefficient.	www.stat.uiuc.edu/~stat100/java/guess/ PPApplet.html
A simple interactive regression simulator designed to illustrate the effect of outliers on a regression line.	www.stat.sc.edu/~west/javahtml/Regression. html
Provides animated demonstrations of relationships between data points, slope correlation, standard error etc.	www.ruf.rice.edu/~lane/stat_sim/comp_r/index. html
Clear discussion and explanation of Pearson's r and its computation. Explains confidence interval for r and other useful information.	http://davidmlane.com/hyperstat/A34739.html
Using real data sets this interactive program enables you to see the effect of adding data points, outliers etc.	www.stat.berkeley.edu/users/stark/Java/ ScatterPlot.htm
Probably the best simulator for showing the relationship between correlation and regression. Shows relationship between scatter and correlation.	www.stat.berkeley.edu/users/stark/Java/ Correlation.htm
A good exercise that asks you to say which correlation fits which scatterplot. Tests understanding of relationship between nature of scatter and correlation.	www.stat.uiuc.edu/~stat100/java/guess/ GCApplet.html

---

WEB POINTER 15.2 *continued*

Creates a scatterplot and regression line and computes basic correlation and regression statistics. Data may be entered from the keyboard, mouse or using pre-loaded datasets.	www.ctc.edu/~tkaupe/211/java/correlate/correlate.htm
Explores correlation in a simple question and answer format and goes beyond what is possible in this book. Accessible, shows how to use SPSS for correlations and discusses the assumptions that should be met for doing correlation and regression.	www2.chass.ncsu.edu/garson/pa765/correl.htm
Simple and useful discussion of statistical significance in relation to correlations. Discusses links between sample size, correlation strength and statistical significance. Select Elementary Concepts button.	www.statsoftinc.com/textbook/stathome.html
Very good discussion of correlation and regression that includes a series of interactive, online applications for demonstrating and simulating points being made in the discussion.	http://espse.ed.psu.edu/statistics/Chapters/Chapter13/Chap13.htm

Visit www.social-research.org to use these links and to check for updates and additions.

---

grid line for five years until we reach the regression line. Then we go horizontally until we reach the income axis. This provides our prediction of the income of someone with five years tertiary education. In this case it is $62 172. If we do the same for someone with six years tertiary education the prediction would be $67 372. If you look carefully, for every extra year of education the predicted income is $5200 higher. In other words for every extra 'unit' of the X variable (a year of education), we get an average increase of 5200 units of Y (i.e. $5200). That is, *on average* a year of tertiary education has a 'payoff' of $5200.

The impact of X on Y (education on income) is 5200. This is variously called the regression co-efficient, the *slope* or the *b coefficient*. The b coefficient is always expressed in the units of measurement of the Y variable (the dependent variable). In this case b is 5200, which means $5200. It reflects the gradient of the regression line: here the gradient is 1 in 5200.

Figure 15.5 indicates how to work out the slope and shows why b is 5200. If you examine the two vertical dotted lines, the distance between these represents one unit difference in X. The dotted line for five years meets the regression line at $62 172 (follow horizontal dotted line to Y-axis) and the six-year dotted line meets the regression line at $67 372. The difference between the two points at which the regression line is intersected is $5200—the slope or regression coefficient.

The other point to note is the point at which the regression line passes through the Y-axis. This point is variously call the Y–intercept or the constant and is symbolised by the letter 'a'. It represents the predicted income of someone with a value of zero on the X variable (i.e. no tertiary education).

Using this scatterplot with the regression line we could make predictions of income for people with varying levels of tertiary education. A more efficient way of presenting the same information and making the same predictions is to use the algebraic equation for the straight line. This is an important equation and is worth memorising. The equation is $\hat{Y} = a + bX$.

There are four parts to this.

1 Ŷ means the value we would predict on the Y variable (e.g. income);
2 a is the point at which the regression line crosses the Y-axis;
3 b is the slope of the line or the regression coefficient;
4 X is any value of the X variable.

If we know the values of a and b we can predict Y values for any value of X. I am not going into how to calculate a and b without a scatterplot. This is easily done by computer packages. We know that in this case a = 36 172 and b = 5200. Let us predict the Y value for someone who is six on the X variable (i.e. six of education). We simply substitute these values in the above equation.

$$\hat{Y} = a + bX$$
$$= 36\,172 + 5200(6)$$
$$= 36\,172 + 31\,200$$
$$= \$67\,372$$

Notice that this is the same prediction as would be made from the scatterplot. To make a prediction for someone with five years of tertiary education (i.e. value of five on X), simply substitute five for six in the equation and thus multiply the b figure by five.

Knowing the equation, all we ever need then are the a and b coefficients and we can make predictions. This is quicker and more efficient than using scatterplots. In most research reports only the a and b coefficients are provided.

As well as enabling us to make predictions on Y for individuals, the regression coefficient b provides a general measure of how much *impact* X has on Y. Even if we do not want to make specific predictions about how much we might earn if we take a three-year tertiary degree, we might want to know how much difference such a degree might make to our earning power. To do this we simply look at the regression coefficient. Alternatively, we might want to compare the b coefficients for various subgroups. For example, we might want to see if tertiary education has the same impact or payoff for males and females or for people in government employment compared with those in private enterprise. In Table 15.9 we can simply compare the b coefficients to see which types of people benefit most financially from tertiary education.

Table 15.9 Regression coefficients of years of tertiary education on income for various subgroups

	a	b
Male	15 000	4500
Female	13 500	3200
Public service	14 000	800
Private enterprise	12 000	1600

Box 15.2 summarises the key characteristics of regression coefficients that help interpret their meaning.

Regression with non-interval variables: dichotomous variables

Although designed for interval-level variables, regression can be used for nominal or ordinal *independent* variables. A dichotomous (two-category) variable meets the requirements of interval-level measurement. Even where the categories have no natural order they nevertheless satisfy the mathematical requirements of order: the categories cannot get out of order. The requirement of equal intervals between categories is also satisfied, since with only two categories there can only be one interval which is, by definition, equal to itself. For this reason we can

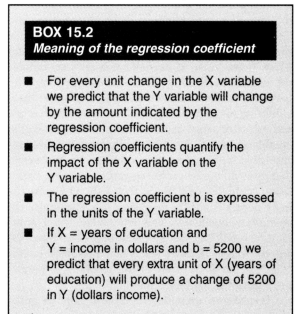

BOX 15.2
Meaning of the regression coefficient

■ For every unit change in the X variable we predict that the Y variable will change by the amount indicated by the regression coefficient.

■ Regression coefficients quantify the impact of the X variable on the Y variable.

■ The regression coefficient b is expressed in the units of the Y variable.

■ If X = years of education and Y = income in dollars and b = 5200 we predict that every extra unit of X (years of education) will produce a change of 5200 in Y (dollars income).

use any dichotomous variable, coded 0 and 1, in regression analysis (e.g. gender, native born/overseas born).

For example, we may use regression to predict income on the basis of gender. To do this we would use the formula:

$$\hat{Y} = a + bX$$

where

$\hat{Y}$ = predicted income
a = $36 172
b = $4000
X = gender where female is coded 0 and male is coded 1.

Substituting these values we get

$$\hat{Y} = 36\,172 + 4000X$$

Since females are coded as 0 their predicted income is $36 172. Since males are coded as 1 their predicted income would be $36 172 + $4000(1) = $40 172. When using dichotomous variables the value of b represents the difference between the average income of females and males—in this case, $4000.

The difference between correlation and regression

Although linked, regression and correlation provide quite different but complementary information. If all the cases in a scatterplot actually lay on the regression line there would be a perfect relationship between the two variables (check the website in Web Pointer 15.1). If we knew someone's score on one variable we could use the regression line to predict with perfect accuracy scores on the other variable: there would be no discrepancy between the predicted and real values of actual cases. In this case the correlation coefficient would be 1.00, indicating a strong relationship between the two variables. To the extent that cases do not lie on the regression line, the correlation coefficient will be less than 1.00. The more the cases depart from the regression line, the lower the correlation coefficient. This reflects the lower accuracy of predicting the scores of real cases from the regression line. In other words the correlation coefficient can act as an index of the accuracy of predictions from the regression line.

Regression uses the regression line to make predictions. It provides estimates of how much

impact one variable has on another. Correlation coefficients provide a way of assessing the accuracy of those estimates. Thus it makes sense to use a regression coefficient and a correlation coefficient together. Both coefficients provide different information: the r^2 helps us work out how much reliance to place on our regression estimates. If we used regression to estimate that another year of tertiary education would add $5200 to someone's earning power, we could use r^2 to provide an idea of how likely our estimate is to accord with reality. If r^2 is low we should not be too surprised if the extra $5200 does not eventuate. If r^2 is high we would have considerable confidence in the regression estimates.

A strong relationship (reflected in a high r^2) does not tell us anything about how much impact one variable has on another. For example, the b coefficient of years of education on income might be only $300, which is a slight impact, but the relationship may still be strong in that most cases lie close to the regression line. This is illustrated in graph c in Figure 15.6. To say that the relationship is strong simply means that if we predict an extra $300 for each year of education we can be fairly certain that this prediction will hold up in reality. Alternatively, there can be a high b coefficient but this does not imply a strong relationship (see Figure 15.6, graph a). Our best estimate might be that b is $5200 but if cases are widely scattered (i.e. a weak relationship) predictions will not be very close to reality. Figure 15.6 illustrates that there is no necessary link between the size of the regression coefficient and the strength of the relationship.

When can regression be used?

In general, regression can only be used:

■ when both the variables are interval-level—dummy regression analysis (see pp. 328–30) can be used in certain situations with a nominal or ordinal independent variable;
■ when we wish to make predictions about the scores of individual cases or groups;
■ to measure the impact or amount of change one variable produces in another. It cannot be used to measure the strength of a relationship.

Finally, a word of caution about regression coefficients. They are asymmetrical: they will be different according to which variable is independent.

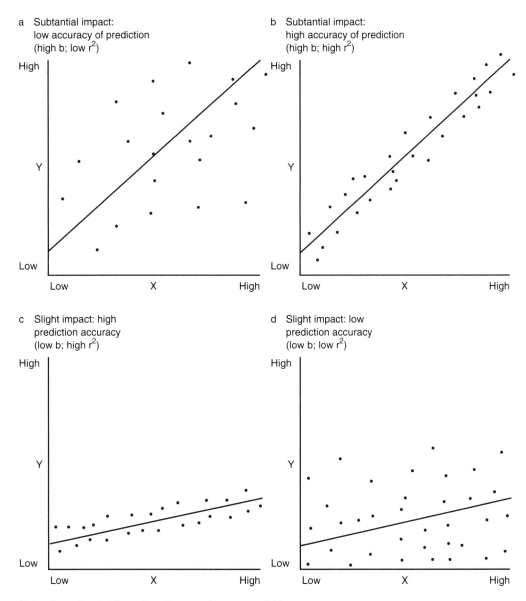

a Subtantial impact:
   low accuracy of prediction
   (high b; low r^2)

b Subtantial impact:
   high accuracy of prediction
   (high b; high r^2)

c Slight impact: high
   prediction accuracy
   (low b; high r^2)

d Slight impact: low
   prediction accuracy
   (low b; low r^2)

Note: Assuming that in each scattergram the same variables
      and scales of measurement are being used

Figure 15.6   Scatterplots displaying the relationship between correlation and regression

When using them, make it very clear which variable is dependent and which is independent.

Summary statistics: inference

Tests of significance

We can apply tests of significance to Pearson's correlation and to regression coefficients. In each case we begin with the null hypotheses that r=0 and that b=0. Statistical packages will routinely provide tests of significance for both these coefficients. These tests have the same interpretation as those outlined earlier.

Table 15.10a reports the r coefficient for the correlation between tertiary education and income. This coefficient of 0.36 is statistically significant at the

Table 15.10 Correlation and regression output for tertiary education on income (small sample)

(a) Pearson's r

Correlations

		Income	No. years tertiary education
Income	Pearson correlation	1.000	0.36**
	Sig. (2-tailed)		0.000
	N	94	94
No. years tertiary education	Pearson correlation	0.360**	1.000
	Sig. (2-tailed)	0.000	
	N	94	94

** Correlation is significant at the 0.01 level (2-tailed)

(b) Regression

Coefficients[a]

	Unstandardised coefficients		Standardised coefficients			95% confidence interval for B	
	B	Std error	Beta	t	Sig.	Lower bound	Upper bound
(Constant)	$36 172	$3 933		9.197	0.000	$28 362	$43 983
No. years tertiary education	$5 175	$1 404	0.357	3.687	0.000	$2 387	$7 962

[a] Dependent variable: Income.

0.000 level. In other words a correlation at least this strong can reasonably be expected to exist in the population. Table 15.10b provides the regression statistics for the same variables. The column headed B provides the regression coefficient ($5175) which indicates the predicted impact of each year of tertiary education on income. The significance level of 0.000 on the same row indicates that this amount is significantly different from zero. That is, there is virtually no chance that a b coefficient this large could be due simply to sampling error.

Interval estimates for regression coefficient
The same table also provides a standard error for b and a confidence interval. The confidence interval for the b coefficient is $2387 to $7962. This means that the real impact of each additional year of tertiary education is likely to be somewhere within this range.

This is a rather wide range. This is largely because this analysis is based on a small sample of only 94 cases. If we conducted the same analysis on a larger sample of 1657 we obtain different coefficients and a much narrower confidence interval (see Table 15.11). In this case, with a larger sample, the predicted impact of education on income is $3365 with a confidence interval between $2772 and $3957. The larger sample enables us to narrow down the band within which the true impact of education on income is likely to lie.

Interval estimates for Pearson's correlation
As with other correlation coefficients, confidence intervals can be calculated for Pearson's correlation. The computations for this are quite complex but are not computed by programs such as SPSS. Furthermore, we cannot simply apply the ±2 standard errors rule to compute the confidence interval. However a simple calculator is available online on the internet for calculating the confidence interval for Pearson's correlation (see Web Pointer 15.3).

Table 15.11 Regression output for tertiary education on income (large sample)

	Coefficients[a]							
	Unstandardised coefficients		Standardised coefficients				95% confidence interval for B	
	B	Std error	Beta	t	Sig.	Lower bound	Upper bound
(Constant)	$36 609	$874		41.886	0.000	$34 895	$38 324
No. years tertiary education	$3 365	$302	0.264	11.132	0.000	$2 772	$3 957

[a] Dependent variable: RINCREAL.

WEB POINTER 15.3 *Confidence interval calculators for Pearson's r*

Simple online confidence interval calculator for Pearson's correlation.	http://glass.ed.asu.edu/stats/analysis/rci.html OR http://ebook.stat.ucla.edu/textbook/bivariables/correlation/rci.html
Simcalc (part of simstat)	www.simstat.com/simstw.htm
A spreadsheet-based calculator for calculating confidence intervals for Pearson's r and for a range of other statistics.	www.sportsci.org/resource/stats/xcl.xls

Visit www.social-research.org to use these links and to check for updates and additions.

RANK–ORDER CORRELATION

When we have two ordinal level variables with a large number of categories and wish to see if they are correlated, we have two options. We can combine categories and use the cross-tabulation approach or we can use rank–order correlation. Combining categories can lead to a loss of detail and distort patterns, so rank–order correlation is normally a preferable technique.

Rank–order correlation involves ranking all cases on both variables and then treating the *ranks* as though they are values of interval-level variables. That is, the categories of the variable are in effect converted from the actual categories to ranks which are assumed to be numerically meaningful and equidistant. People's relative position on the two variables is then used to help compute the correlation between the two variables. This effectively means that the variables are treated as interval-level variables. However, these variables will not have a normal distribution so Pearson's correlation cannot be used. Instead, Spearman's rho (a variation of Pearson's r) or Kendall's tau are used instead. (For a discussion of the procedures see Nie et al., 1975: 2888ff.)

Both Kendall's tau and Spearman's rho are normal correlation coefficients. They range between 0 and 1, can have a negative sign, only measure linear relationships, and are symmetrical. The main differences between the two is their method of dealing with tied ranks (i.e. when two or more people are on the same rank or category of a variable). It is suggested (Nie et al., 1975: 289) that this difference makes Kendall's tau more appropriate when there are likely to be a lot of tied ranks (i.e. when there are a lot of cases and relatively few categories in either variable). Where the ratio of cases to categories is smaller (i.e. fewer people and 'larger' variables), Spearman's rho may be more appropriate. In general, Spearman's rho produces coefficients higher than Kendall's tau but close to Pearson's r.

Table 15.12 Characteristics of interval-level coefficients

Statistic	Appropriate table size and level of measurement	PRE interpretation?	Range	Directional?	Symmetric?	Linear only?	Other
Eta	Any size but X variable must be categorical and Y variable must be interval.	Yes (when squared)	0–1	No	No	No	
Pearson's r	Any size. Both variables interval.	r^2 has PRE interpretation	0–1	Yes	Yes	Yes	Assumes normal distribution.
Spearman's rho	Best for variables with large range of values where there will be few tied ranks. Used for ordinal variables.	No	0–1	Yes	Yes	Yes	Does not assume normal distribution.
Kendall's tau	Best for variables with large range of values where there will be few tied ranks but can be used where one variable has fewer categories thus producing tied ranks. Used for ordinal variables.	No	0–1	Yes	Yes	Yes	Does not assume normal distribution. Normally lower coefficients than rho.
Regression coefficient (b)	Interval dependent and interval (or dichotomous) independent. Number of categories—unimportant.	No	0–no upper limit	Yes	No	Yes	Measures impact of X on Y. Measured in units of dependent variable.

CORRELATION MATRICES

A whole set of bivariate correlations can be presented in a very efficient fashion by using correlation matrices as exemplified in Table 15.13.

The variables across the top of this matrix are the same as those down the side. The way to read the matrix is to map the coordinates. Thus the correlation between occupational prestige and income is –0.412. To obtain this figure locate the occupational prestige variable across the top of the table and move down that column until you reach the row that corresponds to the income variable. The same procedure can be employed to obtain the bivariate correlation between any two variables.

Since the variables on the side are the same as those across the top you will notice that on occasions a variable is correlated with itself. When this occurs a correlation of 1.00 is obtained: a variable will be perfectly correlated with itself. If you look down the diagonal from the top left-hand corner of the matrix you will see a series of 1.00 coefficients representing variables correlated with themselves. Above the diagonal is a triangle of coefficients. Below it is a mirror image of the same coefficients. In the top triangle the correlation of income (column) with gender (row) is –0.212. In the lower triangle the correlation of income (row) with gender (column) is –0.212. Whenever the variables across the top are the same as those on the side the same pattern will occur. In fact all that is required to represent the matrix is one of the triangles. The coefficients of 1.00 and the mirror triangle are redundant.

Given the way the variables are scored in Table 15.13 we can work out the substantive meaning of the coefficients. A positive relationship means that people who obtained a *high* score on one variable tended to obtain a *high* score on the other variable.

Table 15.13 Correlation matrix of seven variables

	No. of hrs worked last week	Occupational prestige	Age	Highest year of schooling	Father's highest year of schooling	Gender	Income
				Correlations			
No. of hrs worked last week	**1.000**	0.188**	−0.042	0.116**	−0.063	−0.108**	0.457**
Occupational prestige	0.188**	**1.000**	0.028	0.528**	0.256**	0.014	0.412**
Age	−0.042	0.028	**1.000**	−0.215**	−0.339**	0.075**	0.178**
Highest year of schooling	0.116**	0.528**	−0.215**	**1.000**	0.467**	0.002	0.375**
Father's highest year of schooling	−0.063	0.256**	−0.339**	0.467**	**1.000**	0.000	0.109**
Gender	−0.108**	0.014	0.075**	0.002	0.000	**1.000**	−0.212**
Income	0.457**	0.412**	0.178**	0.375**	0.109**	−0.212**	**1.000**

** Correlation is significant at the 0.01 level (2-tailed). Gender is coded 1 = male; 2 = female.

A negative relationship means that those who obtained a *high* score on one variable tended to obtain a *low* score on the other (p. 257). For each of the variables in Table 15.13 a high score means a high number of hours worked, high prestige, high education, high age and high income respectively. Gender is coded so that 1 = male and 2 = female. Thus the positive correlation between hours worked and income means that the more hours worked the higher the income; the negative correlation of −0.25 between age and years of schooling means that the older a person is the fewer years of schooling they obtained. The *negative* correlation between gender (where a low score of 1 = male) and income means that males are higher income earners than females. That is, those with a low score or code on the gender variable (males) tended to get higher scores on the income variable.

Correlation matrices do not have to be balanced with the same variables on the side as across the top. When they are different there will not be a set of 1.00 coefficients and the matrix cannot be divided into two triangles and there will be no redundant (repeated) coefficients. While the coefficients in Table 15.13 are Pearson's correlations, the same format can be employed to present any set of correlation coefficients whether they be gammas, Spearman's rho, Kendall's tau or whatever. A matrix is simply a convenient format for presenting a great deal of information. In the above example only the coefficients are presented, but additional information can also be included. Often significance levels are also included (normally represented by symbols such as * or **) to represent the level of statistical signifi-cance. The number of cases on which the correlations are based can also be included.

CHECKLIST FOR BIVARIATE ANALYSIS OF INTERVAL VARIABLES

1 What is the level of measurement of the independent and dependent variables?
2 Do you have a probability sample?
3 What type of analysis is appropriate?
    a Descriptive?
    b Inferential?
4 If the dependent variable is interval and the independent variable has a small number of categories how will results be displayed?
    a Table of means?
    b Tree diagram?
    c Graph?
        i If a graph is used which type of graph is most appropriate?
5 How will any relationship be summarised statistically?
    a Table of means?
    b Eta coefficient?
6 What type of inferential analysis will be used?
    a Tests of significance?
        i How many categories does the independent variable have?
        ii If only two, is the sample the right size for a T-test?
        iii If using a T-test, which sort of T-test will be used?

    iv Do the groups display equality of variance?

    v Are the samples (groups) independent?

    vi If more than two groups will you use an F-test?

    vii If using an F-test, is a Scheffé test also required?

  b Interval estimates of differences between means?

7 If both variables are interval level:

  a Will you undertake descriptive analysis?

  b Will you use a scatterplot to display the relationship?

  c Is the number of cases small enough to make the scatterplot readable?

  d Do the variables have a large number of categories to produce 'scatter'?

  e How do you wish to summarise the relationship between the variables?

    i Correlation?

    ii Is the relationship linear? Use Pearson's r if linear. Use eta if non-linear.

    iii Regression?

    iv Both regression and correlation?

8 Is inferential analysis appropriate?

  a Which type of inferential analysis is required?

    i Tests of significance? For r, b or both?

    ii Interval estimates? For r, b or both?

KEY CONCEPTS

Correlation matrix	Kendall's tau	Rank–order correlation	Slope
eta	Pearson's correlation	Regression coefficient	Spearman's rho
Explained variation	Post hoc comparison	Regression line	T-test
F-test	r	Scatterplot	
Intercept	r^2	Scheffé test	

FURTHER READING

Both Freeman, *Elementary Applied Statistics* (1965), Chapter 9 and Johnson, *Social Statistics Without Tears* (1977), pp. 100–13, provide exceptionally clear accounts of bivariate regression and r^2. Mueller, Schuessler and Costner in *Statistical Reasoning in Sociology* (1977), Chapter 9 and Blalock in Chapters 17 and 18 of *Social Statistics* (1972) give outlines which are more advanced but still clear.

    The outlines of regression, correlation and other bivariate techniques by Nie et al., in *SPSS: Statistical Package for the Social Sciences* (1975), Chapters 17 and 18 and Norusis *SPSSX: Introductory Statistics Guide* (1983), Chapters 6–9 are excellent. For a slightly more advanced treatment of regression see Chapters 1 and 2 of the paper 'Applied Regression: An Introduction' (1980) by Lewis-Beck.

    For a more thorough treatment of statistical inference Freeman (1965) provides a systematic introduction in section D of his book. All of Loether and McTavish's *Inferential Statistics for Sociologists* (1974) is worth reading but Chapter 8 is especially relevant. Johnson (1977), Chapter 12, and Mueller, Schuessler and Costner (1977), Chapters 14 and 15, cover similar material.

    The websites listed in Web Pointer 15.2 are worth visiting as the interactive simulations can help clarify many points outlined in this chapter.

Table 15.14 Guidelines for selecting correlation coefficients

Level of measurement of variables	'Shape' of variables	Appropriate methods	Appropriate descriptive summary statistics	Reference for formula computation	Appropriate inferential statistic
1 Nominal/Nominal	2 by 2	Cross-tabulations	i Phi ii Yule's Q III Lambda iv Goodman & Kruskal's tau	[a]93 [e]264 [e]182 90–3 [b]196, 179 [c]219–20 [e]184–5 [b]214–18 [c]194–7 [d]ch.7 [e]285–8 [a]94–7 [b]219–21 [c]196–206	chi square
2 Nominal/Nominal	3+ by 2+	Cross-tabulations	i Lambda ii Goodman & Kruskal's tau iii Cramers V	as above [b]197	chi square
3 Nominal/Ordinal	Nominal variable with 3+ categories	Cross-tabulations	i Theta ii Any statistics in 2 above	[d]ch.10	Mann–Whitney U-test (dichotomous nominal independent variable) K-sample median test Kruskal–Wallis
4 Nominal/interval	Nominal variable independent	a Cross-tabulations (if interval variable has only a few categories) b Comparison of means (esp. if interval variable has many categories)	i Eta (also called correlation ratio) ii Any statistics in 2 or 3 above but not very wise i Eta	[b]248–51 [e]233–41 [d]ch.11	F-test (one-way analysis of variance) chi square F-test (one-way analysis of variance)
5 Ordinal/Ordinal	Both with few categories	Cross-tabulations	i Gamma ii Kendall's tau b (square tables) iii Kendall's tau c (any shape table)	[a]97–9 [b]228–9 [c]207–22 [d]ch.8 [e]280–82 [b]224–30 [e]283 [b]230	Test for significance of gamma Test for significance of tau
6 Ordinal/Ordinal	One variable with many categories	Rank correlation	i Kendall's tau	[a]101–2 [b]230 [e]158–61	Test for significance of tau

Table 15.14 *continued*

Level of measurement of variables	'Shape' of variables	Appropriate methods	Appropriate descriptive summary statistics	Reference for formula computation	Appropriate inferential statistic
7 Ordinal/Ordinal	Both variables with many categories	Rank correlation	i Kendall's tau ii Spearman's rho	[a]100–101 [c]230–2 [e]152–6	as above Test for significance of rho
8 Ordinal/Interval	Both with few categories	a Cross-tabulations b Comparison of means (if dependent variable is interval)	i Eta ii Any statistics in 5 above i Eta	[b]248–51 [c]233–41 [d]ch.11 as above	F-test F-test
9 Ordinal/Interval	Ordinal with few categories Interval with many	a Comparison of means b Rank order correlation	i Eta i Kendall's tau	as above [a]101–2 [b]230 [c]158–61	F-test Test for significance of tau
10 Ordinal/Interval	Both with many categories	Rank correlation	i Kendall's tau ii Spearman's rho	as above [a]100–1 [b]230–2 [e]151–6	as above Test for significance of rho
11 Interval/Interval	Both variable with small number of categories	Cross-tabulations	i Pearson's r		Test for significance of r
12 Interval/Interval	At least one variable with many categories	Scatterplot	i Pearson's r ii Regression		

Reference key: [a]Freeman (1965)

[b]Loether and McTavish (1974) *Descriptive Statistics*

[c]Mueller et al. (1977)

[d]Johnson (1977)

[e]Cohen and Holliday (1982)

EXERCISES

1 Describe a research question (i.e. specify the dependent and independent variables) in which the comparison of means approach to analysis would be appropriate.

2 If you obtained the following figures for the mean annual income levels of three groups (based on random samples) what else would you find helpful before drawing conclusions?
Professional workers = $68 263; clerical = $43 261; manual workers = $31 036.

3 Under what circumstances and for what purposes would you use the following:
 a a T-test
 b an F-test
 c comparison of means
 d Scheffé test
 e eta

4 Below is a scatterplot of the relationship between number of years in the job (X) and income (Y) for people in a private enterprise industry (hypothetical data).

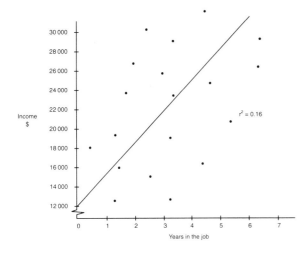

 a Describe the character of the relationship in this scatterplot.
 b What income would you predict for someone with two and three years on the job respectively?

5 The following regression equation applies to the same variables as in exercise 4 but for people in government employment (hypothetical data):
Y = 15 000 + 1000X; r = 0.56

 a What is the impact of years of education on income for government employees?
 b How accurately can we predict Y from X?
 c How much variation in income is explained by X?
 d Compare as thoroughly as you can the relationship between years on the job and income for the government employee sample and the private enterprise sample in exercise 4?

6 Draw two scatterplots. Draw the first plot so that the relationship is strong and negative but the impact of X on Y is relatively low. Draw the second plot so that the relationship is positive, the impact of X on Y quite high and in which X provides an accurate basis for predicting Y. Select whatever variables you feel are appropriate.

7 Go to the website:
www.stat.uiuc.edu/~stat100/java/guess/GCApplet.html
and generate four scatterplots. Indicate which correlation goes with each scatterplot. Check the answers. Repeat until you get four out of four answers correct.

8 Explain in your own words why it is valuable to report both a regression coefficient and a correlation coefficient.

9 Examine the regression equation below which represents the relationship between years of education of a person's father (X) and the number of years education they receive themselves (Y):
Y = 4 + 1.2X; r = 0.40.
Briefly explain:
 a The equation as a whole.
 b The meaning of each element.
 c The meaning of r.
 d If someone's father had thirteen years of education, how much education would you estimate they would have?

10 Imagine the comparable equation when X is mother's years of education:
Y = 4 + 1.5X; r = 0.22.
Compare this with the relationship in exercise 9.

11 In what sense is a regression line or a line of best fit similar to a mean?

12 a   You obtain a Pearson's r correlation of 0.34 in a random sample of 1500 cases. At the 95 per cent confidence level what would be the confidence interval for this correlation?

b   You obtain a regression coefficient of 1200 for the impact of years in the labour force on salary level (in dollars). The standard error of b (the regression coefficient) is 300. What does this mean?

13 Using the correlation matrix in Table 15.13, explain in simple English what the following coefficients mean:

a   −0.212 (column 6, row 7);
b   0.188 (column 2, row 1);
c   0.457 (column 1, row 7);
d   −0.215 (column 3, row 4);
e   −0.042 (column 3, row 1).

14 We have two variables: years of education (Y) and country of birth (X) which is coded 1 for native-born and 0 for overseas-born. Regression analysis produces an 'a' coefficient of 9.5 and a 'b' coefficient of 2.2. What do these figures tell you about the education levels of native-born and overseas-born people? How many years of education do native-born people have on average? How many years of education do overseas-born people have on average?

15 Examine the scores below for ten cases on two variables (X and Y).

a   Without calculating the correlation and regression statistics what would you expect the relationship between X and Y to be:
    i   positive or negative?
    ii   strong or weak?
    Now go to the website http://faculty. vassar.edu/~lowry/corr_stats.html and enter the following data in for ten cases (when asked how many units enter 10).
    Use the calculator on the web page to calculate r, r^2, slope the intercept and significance levels.

b   Explain what these statistics mean.

c   What would be the predicted score on Y for a person who obtained a score of 4 on X?

Case	1	2	3	4	5	6	7	8	9	10
X	10	7	8	9	6	3	4	4	2	1
Y	2	1	3	4	5	6	8	7	10	8

16

Elaborating bivariate relationships

Establishing relationships between two variables is only the beginning of analysis. Having identified a bivariate relationship the next set of questions to ask are:

1 Why does the relationship exist? What are the mechanisms and processes by which one variable is linked to another?
2 What is the nature of the relationship? Is it causal or non-causal?
3 How general is the relationship? Does it hold for most types of people or is it specific to certain subgroups?

This chapter outlines one survey-based approach to analysing survey data to answer these types of questions. This approach, which is a simple form of multivariate analysis, is known as *elaboration analysis*. This chapter will examine the logic behind this technique and apply the technique using summary statistics, tables and graphs. Related, but more powerful, techniques appropriate for interval-level variables are discussed in Chapter 17. Behind both sets of techniques lies the concept of statistical controls.

THE LOGIC OF STATISTICAL CONTROLS

Experimental controls

To understand the logic of elaboration analysis and statistical controls it is useful to review the logic of experimental design (Chapter 3 on research design). The basic experimental design focuses on two variables: the treatment (X) and the outcome (Y). To determine whether the treatment affects the outcome variable one group (the experimental group) is given the treatment while the control group is not. The design of the experiment should be such that any differences between the experimental group and the control group can be attributed to the effect of the treatment.

To ensure that this is the case, the two groups should be identical *before* the treatment. One way of achieving this is to match individuals in each group—for each person in the treatment group we select a similar person in the control group. Obviously we cannot get an identical person but we can match on particular attributes (e.g. age, gender etc).

An alternative and more powerful method of ensuring that the two groups are similar before the treatment is to *randomly allocate* individuals to one of the two groups. So long as the groups are of sufficient size, random allocation should automatically produce groups with comparable profiles on both known and unknown factors. From a statistical perspective random assignment to groups will make the groups identical for all intents and purposes and provides what Davis (1985) calls 'The all purpose spuriosity insurance of randomisation' (p. 35). We control for an infinite number of variables without specifying what any of them are (Campbell, 1989).

The strength of the experimental design, which

lies in its usefulness for drawing conclusions about causal processes, is based on two things:

1 the use of a control group (the group not exposed to the experimental treatment);
2 the assumption that, except for the key experimental variable, the two groups are identical.

Without a control group we cannot know for sure if any changes that the experimental group exhibits would have occurred without the treatment. Without ensuring that the groups are identical to begin with we cannot be sure that any differences between the groups after the treatment were due (in part at least) to pre-treatment differences.

Cross-sectional designs and statistical controls

Survey research is normally based on cross-sectional samples where groups are formed on the basis of *existing* differences rather than by creating groups and then *making* them different by means of an intervention.

In survey analysis these groups are compared with one another in terms of the dependent variable (see Chapters 14 and 15). Differences between the groups on the dependent variable might be taken to be due to the influence of their different group membership. Thus income differences (dependent variable) between males and females (independent variable) might lead to conclusions about the causal effect of gender on income. We might detect income differences and take this as evidence of discrimination against women. But such a conclusion is only warranted if the men and women we compare are *alike in all other relevant respects*. To the extent that they differ then any variation between them on the dependent variable (income) could be due to these other differences.

While experimental designs eliminate the influence of other variables, by matching or by random allocation to groups, survey designs do not provide this degree of control. Instead control must be introduced at the data *analysis* stage rather than at the data *collection* stage. This control is achieved by statistically controlling or removing the influence of *specified* other variables.

This removal involves comparing groups that are similar in other relevant ways. For example, with the gender and income example we would want to make sure that the men and women we compared were the same in terms of their level of work involvement. Clearly it would be inappropriate to compare a group of women where many worked part-time with a group of men who mainly worked full-time. We would need to ensure that we only compared men and women who had the same level of workforce participation: we would compare women who worked full-time with men who worked full-time and see if they had different levels of income. Then we would separately compare men and women who worked, say, 25–35 hours a week and so on. *Like must be compared with like.*

If the income differences persist when the possible influence of other variables is removed by limiting comparisons to those who are alike on relevant variables (hours worked, type of job, level of experience etc), then we have at least eliminated some alternative explanations for the gender difference in income. If the gender income differences persist among men and women with the same level of workforce participation then any remaining gender differences cannot be explained as being due to different levels of work involvement of men and women—the gender differences persist even when only full-time workers (or only part-time workers or whatever) are compared. Equally we would want to ensure that we compared men and women with similar types of jobs.

The question to answer is 'Do men and women have different income levels when they are *similar in other relevant respects*?'. The strongest evidence for gender discrimination comes when income differences persist amongst men and women who are *alike in all other respects*.

On the other hand, if there are no income differences when we compare similar men and women (e.g. same level of education, hours of work, and job type) then we know that these particular factors, and not gender *per se*, are responsible for the overall income differences between men and women. If we learn that the gender differences in income are the result of gender-based differences in hours of work and job type this provides clues about where to direct energies should we wish to narrow the gender differences in income. We would ask why women work fewer hours and identify policy initiatives to address this matter (e.g. more accessible child care). In other words, we need to analyse data to more fully understand what is behind statistical relationships. We need to 'expand' or elaborate on the factors behind our original bivariate relationships.

Multiple statistical controls

We would also want to control *simultaneously* for other variables so that their effects could be removed from being possible explanations for any differences between men and women. For example, we might think that income differences between men and women could be due to the cumulative effects of level of work involvement, types of jobs that men and women have, age differences, different amounts of workforce experience and different educational backgrounds. We would try therefore to remove the influence of these differences in any comparison of men and women. Thus we would want to divide our sample into many groups so that one group might be women who work full-time in professional jobs, have tertiary qualifications, are between the ages of 35 and 40 and have at least 14 years experience in the workforce. This group would be compared with a similar group of men. Another comparison might be similar to the above except that both men and women were employed in trade jobs. Many other pairs of groups would be compared. By controlling or removing the effects of these other variables we are able to answer the question 'When other things are equal does gender make any difference to income?'. If men and women still have different incomes when all other things are equal, we have evidence of discrimination: even when women have similar characteristics to men they still earn less.

Of course, it is not possible to control for every other relevant variable so the possibility always remains that any income difference between men and women that remains could be due to the influence of uncontrolled variables rather than of gender. If the income differences between men and women disappear when other male–female differences are controlled in the analysis we would argue that the initial, observed differences in income must be due to the variables we controlled. Or, to put it differently, we would say that the variables we had controlled *explained* the original relationship.

THE PURPOSE OF ELABORATION

Experimental designs allow us to focus on the causal impact of X on Y. We can isolate the effect of X on Y relatively unambiguously by eliminating the impact of other variables by using random allocation to groups.

However, while controlling for an infinite but unspecified set of variables via randomisation helps isolate the impact of the experimental variable it prevents us understanding the reasons *why* X affects Y. We can work out *how much* effect X has on Y but learn nothing about why X affects Y.

For example we know from the records that students in private schools (schools for which fees are charged) on average achieve higher marks than do students in government-funded schools. However, we suspect that these differences might be because different sorts of students go to private schools in the first place. Private school students may come from homes that provided more resources that assist better academic achievement, value education more and are academically more able. Imagine an experiment where we could randomly allocate students to attend private schools and government-funded schools. We would measure the academic performance of these randomly allocated students when they first go to their respective school. Since they were randomly allocated to public and private schools the students in the two types of schools should begin with similar academic abilities. At the completion of their schooling their academic ability could again be tested. Let us assume that the private school students performed substantially better than the government school students. We would be reasonably confident that these differences were produced by the school rather than by initial student differences.

While we may learn that private schools do indeed have an effect we learn little about *why* they have this effect. What is it about the private schools that produces better performance? Is it better teachers, superior resources, an environment that emphasises academic performance or what? All that we know is that private school students perform better academically.

In contrast, elaboration analysis enables us to refine our understanding of the means by which X affects Y—in this example elaboration analysis could help clarify *how* private schools affect academic achievement. In other words, elaboration analysis can help develop *explanations* of the links we discover between variables.

Elaboration analysis begins by focusing on a relationship between two variables and then asking the question: 'What might this relationship be due to?'. Is the relationship causal? Does X cause Y? Is the relationship direct or indirect? Is the relationship possibly due to selective factors (e.g. are more able students sent to private schools?) and so forth. Having identified a relationship between two variables the next step is to identify other variables that might account for the relationship and conduct the analysis to see if these other variables do explain the initial bivariate relationship. This is the purpose of elaboration analysis.

TYPES OF RELATIONSHIP BETWEEN THREE VARIABLES

Before outlining how to go about this it is useful to explore the different forms that a relationship between two variables can take when we add just one other variable into a bivariate model. The diagrams in Figure 16.1 all represent different ways of interpreting or explaining an initial correlation between X and Y.

Direct causal relationship—Figure 16.1a represents a direct causal relationship between just two variables X and Y. The arrow represents the direction of the cause and the link between X and Y is not mediated by any other variable.

Indirect causal relationship—Figure 16.1b introduces a third variable (Z) into the model. The causal link between X and Y is mediated by Z: the link between X and Y is causal but it is indirect. The Z variable in this type of model is called an *intervening* variable.

Spurious relationship—Figure 16.1c illustrates another possibility when working with just three variables. It indicates that there is no causal relationship between X and Y (no arrow that goes in one direction from X to Y). Rather it indicates that a third variable (Z) is causally linked to X *and* to Y. While X and Y might be correlated this does not mean that X *causes* Y. They might be correlated because they are both affected by the same common third factor. For example, the correlation between type of school attended (private or government) might not be because school type (X) affects achievement (Y) but because parental wealth affects the sort of school to which they send their children *and* because parental wealth also affects student achievement (because they can afford extra help, computers, books, study etc). In other words X and Y are correlated because both are *outcomes* of Z. Where the original relationship between X and Y is not causal but

due to a third variable in the way illustrated in model (c) the original relationship is said to be *spurious*. The Z variable is called an *extraneous* variable.

Direct and indirect causal relationship—the relationship between X and Y can be partly direct and partly indirect (see Figure 16.1d). For example, the relationship between gender and income may be partly due to straightforward gender discrimination (direct relationship) but partly because more females than males are part-time workers (indirect relationship).

Direct, indirect and spurious relationships—the simple bivariate relationship might consist of three elements (see Figure 16.1e). For example, the relationship between type of school and academic achievement might be partly direct (i.e. X→Y—private schools produce better achievement). It may be partly spurious (Z→X and Z→Y). For example, parents who place a great deal of value on education and educational achievement may send their children to private schools. While the schools may contribute to academic achievement the parental emphasis on education may, on its own, also contribute to their children's performance. Furthermore the relationship may be indirect (X→Z→Y). That is, private schools may further increase the parental emphasis on educational achievement which in turn promotes achievement.

Direct and spurious relationships—Figure 16.1f indicates this pattern. An example of this pattern is where attending private schools produces better academic performance but where some of the difference between the achievement levels of children in private and government schools is because of the resources of the families they come from: wealthier parents send their children to private schools *and* wealthier parents also provide resources that assist with performance.

Spurious and indirect—Figure 16.1g illustrates this pattern. An example of this pattern is where the relationship between school type and performance is attributable to these two types of relationships.

In summary there can be at least three elements that explain an initial bivariate relationship. The initial relationship may be because the relationship is:

- directly causal
- indirectly causal
- spurious
- some combination of the above.

(a) Direct causal relationship

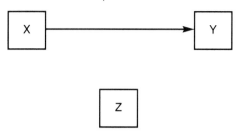

(b) Indirect causal relationship

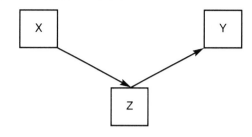

(c) Spurious (non-causal) relationship of X with Y

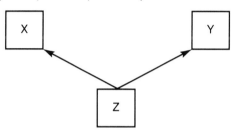

(d) Direct and indirect causal relationship

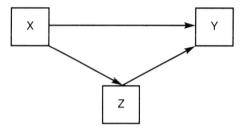

(e) Direct and indirect causal relationship and a spurious component

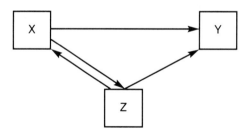

(f) Spurious (non-causal) and direct causal relationship of X with Y

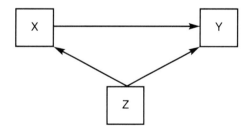

(g) Spurious (non-causal) and indirect causal relationship of X with Y

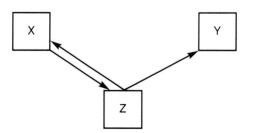

Figure 16.1   Types of relationships between three variables

STEPS IN ELABORATION ANALYSIS

The focus in elaboration analysis is the relationship between the initial two variables: X and Y. The purpose of elaboration analysis is to better understand *this* relationship—to elaborate on what lies behind the correlation of these two variables. There are several steps in this elaboration process.

1   Begin with the bivariate relationship between X and Y. This is called the *zero order* relationship.
2   Identify a variable for which to control. This is called the Z variable or the *test* variable. The test variable will be introduced on the basis of sound reasoning rather than just to see what happens. In the examples above the test variables were variously parental wealth, parental emphasis on education, hours worked and so forth. These were introduced because they were plausible—it was possible that they might help explain something of the zero order relationship. Avoid simply controlling for anything. Use the literature and commonsense reasoning to guide your selection of test variables (see Box 16.1).
3   While controlling for the test variable recompute the relationship between X and Y. This relationship between X and Y while controlling for one test variable is called a *first order partial relationship*. A first order partial relationship identifies how much of the original relationship between X and Y remains after the effect of one test variable (Z) has been removed.
4   Compare the first order partial relationship with the zero order relationship.

┌──┐
│ **BOX 16.1** *Selecting test variables*   │
│   │
│ 1   Must be selected from among the   │
│   variables in the data set.   │
│ 2   Must make sense theoretically.   │
│ 3   The test variable must be correlated at │
│   the zero-order level with both the X and Y │
│   variables.   │
│ 4   To assist, obtain a correlation matrix of │
│   all the plausible test variables with both │
│   the X and Y variables.   │
└──┘

5   Interpret the comparison. The discussion below describes how to interpret any differences between zero-order and first-order relationships.

Elaboration analysis can be achieved by using summary statistics or by using tables such as cross-tabulations or with graphs.

ELABORATION USING SUMMARY STATISTICS: PARTIAL CORRELATION

The logic and use of a partial correlation is best illustrated using Pearson's correlation. To use a partial version of Pearson's correlation requires that the variables are measured at the interval level or are at least dichotomous. Equivalent analyses for ordinal level variables can be conducted with other correlation coefficients such as gamma and Kendall's tau.[1]

The Pearson's correlation between just two variables as outlined in Chapter 15 is called a zero-order correlation. If we want to know whether this correlation between two variables is due to the influence of another variable (Z) we can simply recompute this correlation between X and Y after controlling for or removing any contribution of Z. The resulting correlation is called a *partial correlation*. This statistic indicates the relationship between X and Y but it is the amount of the zero order correlation remaining after the influence of Z has been removed or partialled out.

Interpreting partial correlation statistics

Spurious relationships
Table 16.1 provides different sets of zero-order and partial correlation coefficients for elaborating the relationship between school type and achievement. The analysis reported in Table 16.1 is testing whether students in private schools perform better simply because brighter children are sent to private schools. Three patterns are provided.

Relationship is partly spurious (Table 16.1a)—the test variable (Z) is said to *partly* explain the zero-order relationship when:

■   the partial correlation is lower than the zero-order relationship and
■   the partial correlation is significantly different from 0 and
■   the confidence intervals of the zero-order and partial coefficients do not overlap.

Table 16.1 Testing for a spurious relationship

The hypothesis being tested is that the relationship of X (school type) →Y (academic achievement) is spurious and due to Z (child's IQ).

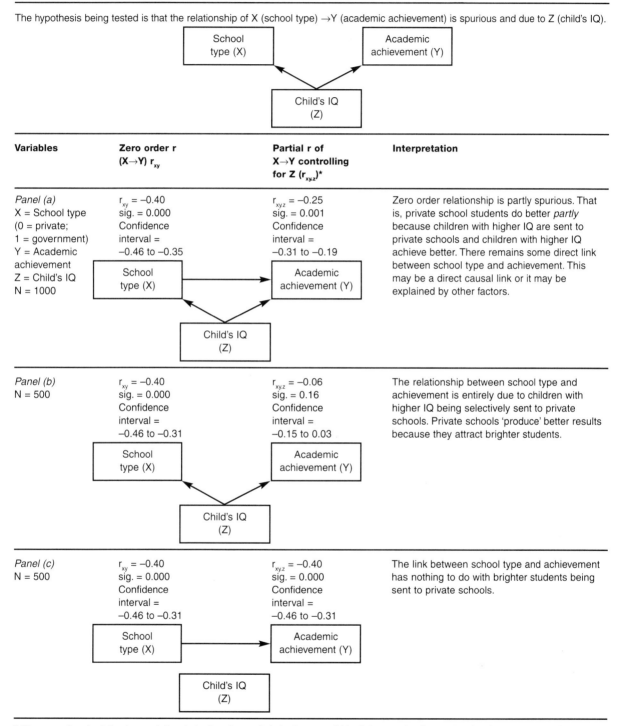

Variables	Zero order r (X→Y) r_{xy}	Partial r of X→Y controlling for Z $(r_{xy.z})$*	Interpretation
Panel (a) X = School type (0 = private; 1 = government) Y = Academic achievement Z = Child's IQ N = 1000	$r_{xy} = -0.40$ sig. = 0.000 Confidence interval = −0.46 to −0.35	$r_{xy.z} = -0.25$ sig. = 0.001 Confidence interval = −0.31 to −0.19	Zero order relationship is partly spurious. That is, private school students do better *partly* because children with higher IQ are sent to private schools and children with higher IQ achieve better. There remains some direct link between school type and achievement. This may be a direct causal link or it may be explained by other factors.
Panel (b) N = 500	$r_{xy} = -0.40$ sig. = 0.000 Confidence interval = −0.46 to −0.31	$r_{xy.z} = -0.06$ sig. = 0.16 Confidence interval = −0.15 to 0.03	The relationship between school type and achievement is entirely due to children with higher IQ being selectively sent to private schools. Private schools 'produce' better results because they attract brighter students.
Panel (c) N = 500	$r_{xy} = -0.40$ sig. = 0.000 Confidence interval = −0.46 to −0.31	$r_{xy.z} = -0.40$ sig. = 0.000 Confidence interval = −0.46 to −0.31	The link between school type and achievement has nothing to do with brighter students being sent to private schools.

* The conventional notation for correlations is to place the symbols for the two variables being correlated as a subscript after r and then to place the symbols for the variables being controlled in the subscript after a dot. Thus $r_{xy.z}$ means the correlation is between x and y controlling for z. The correlation r_{xy} indicates a zero order correlation between x and y since there is no indication of a variable being controlled.

We can tell that the initial relationship is partly *spurious* because:

■ a decline in the partial correlation means that the initial relationship was either spurious or indirectly causal and

■ given the particular variables it does not make sense to argue that the relationship is indirectly causal. To be indirectly causal we would have to argue that school type→IQ→achievement. Since IQ is meant to be a fixed attribute it makes no sense to argue that school type affects IQ. Therefore we should accept the interpretation that the initial bivariate relationship is (partly) spurious.

Zero-order relationship is entirely spurious (Table 16.1b)—the test variable *completely* explains the zero-order relationship when:

■ the partial correlation is lower than the zero-order relationship and

■ the partial correlation is *not* significantly different from 0 and

■ the confidence intervals of the zero-order and partial coefficients do not overlap.

Robust zero-order relationship (Table 16.1c)— where an initial relationship is not due to the test variable the relationship is said to be *robust*. That is, when the zero-order relationship is *replicated* as a partial correlation we know that the test variable does not explain the initial relationship. A robust relationship can be detected when:

■ the partial correlation is much the same as the zero-order correlation and

■ both the partial and zero-order coefficients are statistically significant and

■ the confidence intervals for both the partial and zero-order correlations overlap.

Indirect relationships

Table 16.2 provides correlations for a set of variables designed to test whether the zero-order relationship was causally indirect—in this case whether the link between gender and income is due to women working fewer paid hours per week than men. In this example there is no point repeating the discussion about whether a zero-order relationship is explained completely, partly or not at all (see above). The only difference between the examples in Tables 16.1

and 16.2 is that in panel (a) and (b) the initial relationship would be causally indirect rather than spurious.

The interpretation of a relationship as causally indirect rather than spurious is based on theory and commonsense (see Box 16.2). Given the variables in Table 16.2 it makes most sense to argue that X (gender)→Z (hours worked)→Y (income). For the relationship to be spurious we would need to argue that Z (hours worked) affected both X (gender) and Y (income). Since it makes no sense to say that hours worked somehow causes a person's gender it makes no sense to argue that the zero-order relationship is spurious.

Partial correlations can be computed for other correlation coefficients such as gamma and Kendall's tau and can be interpreted in exactly the same way as described above. Web Pointer 16.1 points to some sites or software for calculating partial correlations for a range of different correlation coefficients.

USING TABLES FOR ELABORATION ANALYSIS

Instead of using zero-order and partial correlation coefficients the same type of analysis can be undertaken using cross-tabulations. Before explaining how to do this it is important to note four key points:

1 Elaboration analysis focuses on the relationship between X and Y.
2 Test variables are introduced to see whether they change the relationship between X and Y.
3 The logic of elaboration analysis requires that we examine X and Y for people who are the same on the control variable.
4 When using tables in elaboration analysis we produce a separate cross-tabulation of X by Y for each category of the Z variable.

Spurious relationships

Suppose we find that young people who attend religious schools are more religious than those who attend secular government schools. Table 16.3 panel (a) provides figures that demonstrate such a relationship.

The zero-order table shows that students from religious schools are more likely to be religious than

Table 16.2   Testing for an indirect relationship

Hypothesis being tested is that the relationship of X (gender)→Y (income) is an indirect causal relationship and the zero order relationship is due to gender differences in Z (hours of paid work)

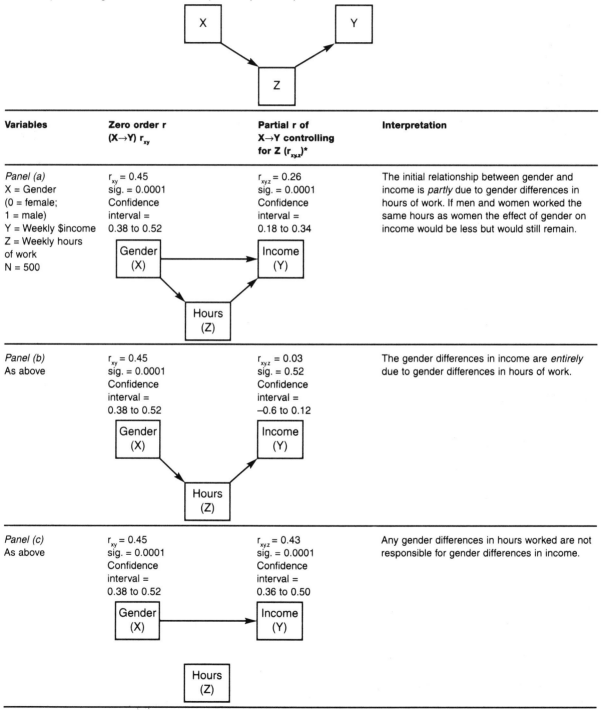

Variables	Zero order r (X→Y) r_{xy}	Partial r of X→Y controlling for Z ($r_{xy.z}$)*	Interpretation
Panel (a) X = Gender (0 = female; 1 = male) Y = Weekly \$income Z = Weekly hours of work N = 500	$r_{xy} = 0.45$ sig. = 0.0001 Confidence interval = 0.38 to 0.52	$r_{xy.z} = 0.26$ sig. = 0.0001 Confidence interval = 0.18 to 0.34	The initial relationship between gender and income is *partly* due to gender differences in hours of work. If men and women worked the same hours as women the effect of gender on income would be less but would still remain.
Panel (b) As above	$r_{xy} = 0.45$ sig. = 0.0001 Confidence interval = 0.38 to 0.52	$r_{xy.z} = 0.03$ sig. = 0.52 Confidence interval = −0.6 to 0.12	The gender differences in income are *entirely* due to gender differences in hours of work.
Panel (c) As above	$r_{xy} = 0.45$ sig. = 0.0001 Confidence interval = 0.38 to 0.52	$r_{xy.z} = 0.43$ sig. = 0.0001 Confidence interval = 0.36 to 0.50	Any gender differences in hours worked are not responsible for gender differences in income.

WEB POINTER 16.1   *Calculating partial correlations*

Interval-level variables

Partial Pearson's correlation SPSS	In SPSS partial Pearson's correlations can be computed using the CORRELATE procedure or the REGRESSION procedure and selecting the appropriate options
Simstat computes partial correlations and confidence intervals for the partial coefficients.	www.simstat.com/simstw.htm
Modstat	http://members.aol.com/rcknodt/pubpage.htm
Partial correlations can be computed from zero-order correlations using online calculators at:	http://faculty.vassar.edu/~lowry/par.html http://home.clara.net/sisa/correl.htm (read help correlation to learn how to use this useful calculator)

Ordinal variables

Partial Kendall's tau (rank order) Modstat	http://members.aol.com/rcknodt/pubpage.htm
Partial gamma SPSS computes partial gamma coefficients but only through syntax commands. The required syntax is:	CROSSTABS VARIABLES = *varx* (minvalue, maxvalue), *vary* (minvalue, maxvalue), *varz* (minvalue, maxvalue) /tables = *vary* BY *varx* By *varz* /statistics = gamma /format = notables.

Visit www.social-research.org to use these links and to check for updates and additions.

---

those from secular schools (52 per cent cf 29 per cent highly religious). How can we explain this? Is it because the religious schools effectively promote religion? Or are there selective factors? Do religious parents send their children to religious schools? Perhaps the parents promote their children's religiousness *and* send their children to religious schools. Perhaps religious schools have nothing to do with the religiousness of their students.

Let us test the proposition that students in religious schools are more religious because they have religious parents rather than because they attend a religious school. If this is the case we would expect that when we look just at students with religious parents there will be virtually no differences in religiousness between students attending religious schools and those attending secular schools. Make sure that you understand the logic of this before you read on.

To test this we conduct the original analysis separately for those with religious parents (and do the same for those with non-religious parents). Panel (b) of Table 16.3 reports just such analysis. These separate tables are called *conditional tables* (a separate table for each category or condition of the Z variable). Beneath the tables are correlation coefficients (Yule's Q) that summarise the relationship in each table. These coefficients for each subtable are called *conditional correlations.*

The top part of panel (b) provides the figures for the relationship between school type and religiousness just for those from religious homes. It shows that among students from religious families the type of schooling makes no difference to religiousness. Similarly among those from non-religious families going to a religious or secular school makes no difference (bottom section of Table 16.3, panel (b)). If they come from a non-religious family young

Table 16.3 Conditional tables showing relationship between student religiousness, school type and parental religiousness

Panel (a) Zero-order table of religiousness by type of school

			School type	
			Religious	Secular
Student religiousness	Low		48%	71%
	High		52%	29%
		N	800	800
			100%	100%

Zero-order Yule's Q			
	Yule's Q	Std error	Sig.
Student religiousness by gender	0.45	0.04	0.00

Panel (b) Conditional tables: Religiousness by type of school by parental religiousness

Parental religiousness			School type	
			Religious	Secular
Religious parents	Student religiousness	Low	35%	37%
		High	65%	63%
		N	600	200
			100%	100%
Non-religious parents	Student religiousness	Low	85%	82%
		High	15%	18%
		N	200	600
			100%	100%

Conditional correlations				
Parental religiousness		Yule's Q	Std error	Sig.
Religious	Student religiousness	0.04	0.08	0.61
Not religious	Student religiousness	−0.11	0.11	0.31

Type of school (X) ← Parental religiousness (Z) → Child's religiousness (Y)

The patterns of zero-order, first-order partials and conditionals and tables are the same when the test variable reflects a spurious relationship or an indirect causal relationship. Therefore further criteria must be used to identify which of the two interpretations fits best.

Draw diagrams of a spurious and of an indirect relationship. The direction of arrows is different for the two types of relationships. Which one makes most sense?

If the Z variable is to be treated as an intervening variable:

1 Z must be capable of being changed by X (fixed attributes such as age, sex and race clearly cannot be changed and therefore will not be intervening variables).

2 Z must occur in time after X and before Y.

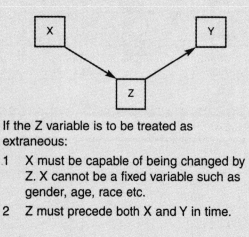

If the Z variable is to be treated as extraneous:

1 X must be capable of being changed by Z. X cannot be a fixed variable such as gender, age, race etc.

2 Z must precede both X and Y in time.

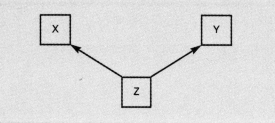

people are fairly non-religious regardless of the type of school they attend.

In other words, when we control for parental religiousness the relationship between school type and religiousness disappears. The zero-order relationship made it appear that school type affected religiousness simply because there is a preponderance of children from religious families in religious schools and a preponderence of those from non-religious families in secular schools.

Indirect causal relationships

Cross-tabulations can also be used to see whether an indirect causal relationship exists. If X and Y were related via Z we would expect to see the same pattern as in Table 16.3—that is a significant zero-order relationship and no significant relationship in each of the conditional tables. The only difference between a set of cross-tabulations that reflects a spurious zero order relationship and an indirect causal relationship is the nature of the variables.

Specification

When separate analysis is conducted within each category of the test variable (Z) there is always the possibility that a relationship between X and Y will be found in some categories of Z but not in others. That is, the relationship between X and Y might be specific to some subgroups (e.g. among males but not females; among young people but not older people).

For example, panel (a) of Table 16.4 presents a zero-order table that shows females are more in favour of equality for gays than are males (44 per cent cf 30 per cent). This is confirmed by the statistically significant zero-order gamma of −0.305. However, when age is controlled the gender difference in attitude to gays only exists among younger people. Among younger people 67 per cent of females favour gay equality compared to 43 per cent of males (conditional gamma = −0.446 sig. = 0.000). However, among older people males and females have similar views about gay equality with 22 per cent of females and 19 per cent of males favouring gay equality (conditional gamma = −0.10 sig. = 0.379). In other words any gender difference in attitudes to gay equality is specific to younger people. In this case the gender difference among young people

Table 16.4   Zero-order and conditional tables indicating a specification of the initial relationship

Panel (a) Zero-order table

Attitude to equality for gays by gender

	Gender	
	Male	Female
Approves of equality	30%	44%
Disapproves of gay equality	70%	56%
N	899	1138
	100%	100%

Zero-order gamma

	Gamma	Std error	Sig.
Attitude to gay equality by gender	0.305	0.043	0.000

```
┌──────────────┐          ┌──────────────────┐
│   Gender     │─────────▶│ Attitude to equality │
│    (X)       │          │  for gays (Y)     │
└──────────────┘          └──────────────────┘
```

Panel (b) Conditional tables

Attitude to equality for gays by gender by age group

		Gender	
AGE		Male	Female
Young	Approves of gay equality	43%	67%
	Disapproves of gay equality	57%	33%
	N	162	203
		100%	100%
Old	Approves of gay equality	19%	22%
	Disapproves of gay equality	81%	78%
	N	209	263
		100%	100%

Conditional gamma correlations

AGE		Gamma	Std error	Sig.
Young	Approval of gay equality by gender	0.446	0.087	0.000
Old	Approval of gay equality by gender	−0.100	0.114	0.379

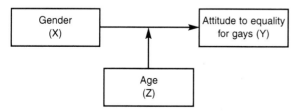

is because of the relatively high level of young females who favour equality for gays.

Another term that is given to the pattern where the relationship between X and Y differs according to the value of the control variable is *statistical interaction*. This means that the X variable does not have an effect on its own. But when it occurs in *combination* with particular other characteristics it has a special effect. In other words the effect of X and Y is partly dependent on additional characteristics of the person. It is when there is a particular 'brew' of characteristics that X affects Y. In this example it is not being female that leads to greater support for gay equality but being both young *and* female.

Replication

If a zero-order relationship persists after we control for particular Z variables the relationship is said to have been *replicated*. That is, if all the conditional coefficients or tables are much the same as the zero-order relationship/table we can be confident that the initial bivariate relationship is *not* due to the influence of the test variable. This variable can then be dropped from any model that seeks to explain the initial relationship (see Tables 16.1, 16.2 and 16.5).

Problems with conditional tables

While elaboration analysis that relies on separate analysis for each category of the control variable can be valuable it confronts a number of important problems.

First, it requires large samples. Since separate cross-tabulations are produced for each category of a control variable we can end up with very small numbers in each cell and column of the cross-tabulations. The more categories the Z variable has the more subgroups the sample has to be split into for analysis. Where gender is the control variable the initial sample is split two ways but if age was the control variable the sample could be split into many subgroups—with separate analysis for each age group.

One way to reduce the number of subgroups into which the sample needs to be split is to group the categories of the control variable. For example, rather than splitting the analysis of X with Y for 20-year-olds, 21-year-olds, 22-year-olds etc we could group ages into groups (e.g. 20–29; 30–39 etc or under 40 and over 40). However, the purpose of controlling is to restrict the cross-tabulation of X with Y to people who are the same on Z. If we group categories on the Z variable too broadly we fail to properly control for the control variable.

Second, the effect of breaking the sample into small subgroups for analysis is that the small sample sizes produce unstable results and make generalisation very difficult. The problem of numbers becomes much worse if we want to control for more than one variable at the same time (e.g. we want to make sure that the relationship between X and Y is examined only among people who are of the same sex and age. If age has just six age groups and gender has two this means that we would have to break the sample into twelve subgroups.

Third, when controlling for several variables a fair number of conditional tables and coefficients are produced. Not only does this take up a great deal of space in any report but these sets of tables and coefficients can be quite difficult to interpret and very difficult for readers to understand. One way to reduce this problem of multiple conditional tables is to use what is called a standardised table (Loether and McTavish, 1974a). This is a method of combining all the conditional tables into one. The standardised table is analogous to the partial correlation coefficient and has the effect of showing what the zero-order table would look like with the influence of the control variable removed.

GRAPHICAL METHODS OF ELABORATION ANALYSIS

Graphs can be used in elaboration analysis in much the same way as conditional tables can be. Line graphs are the most common graph but these are only appropriate when the X variable is at least ordinal. These graphs contain three core elements:

1   *The X-axis:* this is placed on the bottom of the graph and represents the values of the X variable.
2   *The Y-axis:* this is placed on the side of the table. The scale used for the Y variable can vary (see below). The ability to use different scales for the Y variable makes it possible to use nominal, ordinal or interval level Y variables in the graphs.
3   *The data lines in the graph:* a separate line will appear in the graph for each category of the Z variable. Each line represents the relationship

Table 16.5   Interpreting conditional relationships

Patterns of conditionals	Interpretation	Diagram
Conditional relationships are all less than zero order but are still statistically significant.	Relationship between X and Y is partly spurious or indirect.	Spurious X → Y, Z Indirect X → Z, Y
Conditional relationships are all less than zero order and are *not* statistically significant.	Relationship between X and Y is completely spurious or indirect.	Spurious X Y, Z Indirect X Y, Z
Relationship between X and Y varies according to category of Z.	Relationship is specific to certain subgroups. Interaction affects operating.	X → Y, Z
Conditional relationships are all similar to the zero-order relationship.	Replication. The zero-order relationship is *not* due to the control variable.	X → Y, Z

between X and Y for people belonging to a particular category of Z. Graphs should only be used when the Z variable has a small number of categories since a separate line is produced for each category of Z. Too many such lines can make graphs unreadable.

Line graphs

Regardless of the way in which the Y variable is represented in the graph the interpretation of line graphs in elaboration analysis is the same. Therefore, before illustrating the different ways of producing the graphs it is useful to show how to interpret line graphs for elaboration purposes. First, however, it is worth repeating two points made earlier in relation to tabular analysis.

1   There should be a zero order relationship to explain in the first place.[2]
2   The interpretation of graphs involves comparing the:
    a   zero–order relationship with the conditional or partial relationships;
    b   conditional relationships with one another.

The graphs in Figure 16.2 illustrate different explanations of the zero–order relationships.

Line graphs using different scales on the Y-axis

Line graphs can differ according to the way in which the Y-axis is scaled (refer to Chapter 13). These differences allow the construction of graphs regardless of whether the Y variable is measured at the nominal, ordinal or interval level.

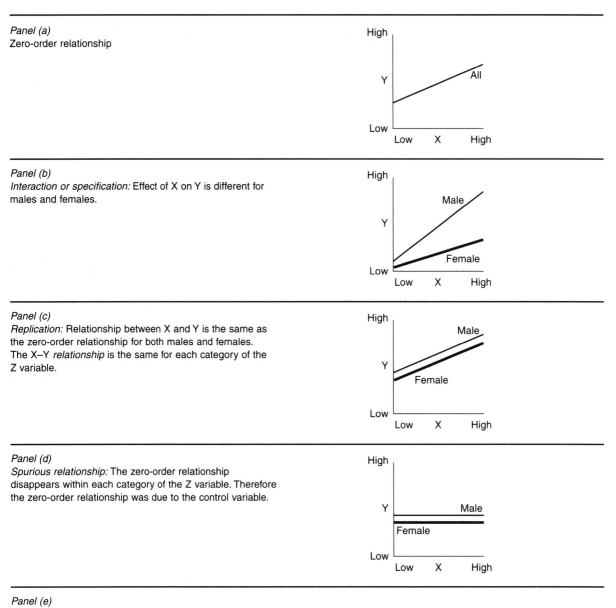

Panel (a)
Zero-order relationship

Panel (b)
Interaction or specification: Effect of X on Y is different for males and females.

Panel (c)
Replication: Relationship between X and Y is the same as the zero-order relationship for both males and females. The X–Y *relationship* is the same for each category of the Z variable.

Panel (d)
Spurious relationship: The zero-order relationship disappears within each category of the Z variable. Therefore the zero-order relationship was due to the control variable.

Panel (e)
Indirect causal relationship   Same pattern as spurious relationship

Figure 16.2 Graphs illustrating different effects of a test variable

Actual values of Y

If, for example, X was years of education and Y was annual income the scale of the Y-axis would be the units of the Y variable—dollars. The lines in the graph would represent the relationship between education and income in the same way that a regression line represents a relationship in a scatterplot. Each line would represent the relationship between education and income for each category of Z. In Figure 16.2b the lines would indicate that as education increases so does income earned. However this impact of education on income is greater for males than for females. This method is best suited to interval level Y variables but might be used for ordinal-level variables.

Mean on Y

The Y-axis could represent the mean on Y (refer to Chapter 13). Again the scale of the Y-axis would be the units of measurement of the Y variable—dollars. Thus the lines would be plotted by calculating the mean income of males with various years of eduction. The line for females would be plotted by calculating the equivalent female income means for different years of education. This approach is limited to interval-level Y variables. With ordinal-level Y variables the median can be used instead of the mean.

Per cent above (or below) a given value of Y

The scale of the Y-axis will be percentages—the percentage of people who were above a particular value of Y (e.g. percentage on the left–right scale of political position who scored above the midpoint of 5; refer also to Chapter 13). The graph is plotted by obtaining the per cent who scored above the specified point on Y for each category of X (e.g. for each age group). Where a third variable is introduced these values are plotted separately for each category of Z. This approach is useful for interval or ordinal variables.

Per cent in a particular category of Y

The graph is constructed by focusing on a particular category of the Y variable. The scale of the Y-axis is the percentage of people belonging to the specified category of Y (e.g. per cent approving of the legalisation of marijuana). The lines in the graph are plotted using the per cent in each category of X (e.g. age group) who approve of legalisation. Where a third variable is introduced these values are plotted separately for each category of Z. This approach is useful when the Y variable is nominal or ordinal.

Tree diagrams

Another form of graphic presentation that can be used in elaboration analysis is the tree diagram. This is mainly used when both the X and Z variables have only a small number of categories. The discussion below is restricted to comparing means of various subgroups. However other comparisons such as those discussed above (medians, per cent above a particular value of Y, per cent in a specific category of Y etc) could equally be used in this form of graphic presentation.

This form of presenting results involves:

1 Computing the mean (median etc) on Y separately for each category of X.

2 Comparing the means at the bivariate level in the second level of the diagram in Figure 16.3

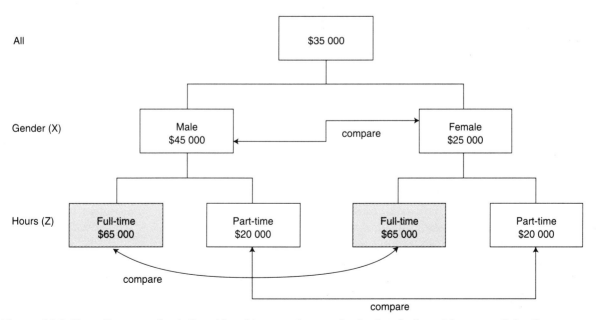

Figure 16.3 Tree diagram of relationship of income by gender by level of workforce participation (mean annual income)

(i.e. mean income for males and females). The difference between these means indicates a bivariate relationship.

3   Then, *within* each category of the X variable computing the mean of the dependent variable separately for each category of the Z variable.

4   Comparing the means between the categories of the X variable holding constant the category of the Z variable in the third level of the diagram in Figure 16.3 (i.e. compare male and female full-time workers and compare male and female part-timers).

5   Compare the pattern of relationships at level 2 and level 3 in Figure 16.3 and interpret these in the same way as with cross-tabulations and conditional tables (Table 16.5).

Figure 16.3 is a tree diagram of mean income by gender by level of workforce participation. The second row illustrates that males receive a higher average income than females. However this difference could be because more females than males are part-timers. If it was not for this difference the gender-based income differences may not exist. To test this proposition we must control for level of workforce participation. The third row of the diagram shows that men who work full-time have the same average income as women who work full-time. Similarly men who work part-time have the same average income as women who work part-time. If there were as many women as men who worked full-time it would appear that the overall gender differences in income would not exist. Therefore according to Figure 16.3 it is not gender *per se* that leads to income differences but the link between gender and level of workforce participation.

ELABORATION CHECKLIST

1   What is your independent variable (X) and your dependent variable (Y)?

2   What level of measurement is each variable?

3   Is there a bivariate relationship between these two variables?

4   If so what other variable(s) might explain the bivariate relationship? (That is, what test (Z) variable will you examine?)

5   Is this Z variable correlated with both the X and the Y variable at the bivariate level? (It needs to be for it to be able to explain the relationship between X and Y.)

6   How many categories does Z have? Does it need collapsing into fewer categories?

7   What method of controlling will be employed?

  a   If correlations are to be used will you use partial correlations or a set of conditional correlations?

  b   If tables are to be used will you use a standardised partial table or a set of conditional tables?

  c   If graphs are to be used what type of graphic format will you employ?

8   Do the first-order partial or conditional relationships differ from the zero-order relationship?

9   What is the significance level of the zero-order and first-order partial or conditional relationships?

10 Do the confidence intervals of the zero-order and first-order relationships overlap?

11 How can the differences between the zero-order and first-order patterns be interpreted? (See Tables 16.1, 16.2 and 16.5 for a summary.)

KEY CONCEPTS

Conditional relationship	Extraneous variable	Partial gamma	Test variable
Conditional table	First-order coefficient	Replication	Zero-order relationship
Control variable	Indirect causal effect	Robust relationship	Zero-order table
Controlling	Interaction	Specification	
Elaboration	Intervening variable	Spurious relationship	
	Partial correlation	Statistical control	

ENDNOTES

[1] See Loether and McTavish (1974a: 300) for the computation of partial correlation. The computation for partial gamma is also outlined by Loether and McTavish (1974a: 298). Partial Kendall's tau is outlined by Cohen and Holliday (1982: 171). See also Web Pointer 16.1.

[2] This need not apply in the case of specification where there might be no zero-order relationship but there may be very different conditional relationships (e.g. a positive and a negative) that cancel each other out to result in a non-existent zero-order relationship.

FURTHER READING

Without doubt Rosenberg's *The Logic of Survey Analysis* (1968) is the classic treatment of the elaboration model. It is packed with examples, is comprehensive and very clear. Another excellent discussion is in part II of Hirschi and Selvin's *Delinquency Research* (1967) where they illustrate the benefits of this approach and use it to highlight the shortcomings of much research.

For brief but very clear discussions see Johnson, *Social Statistics Without Tears* (1977); Chapter 7 or Chapter 8 of Loether and McTavish, *Descriptive Statistics for Sociologists* (1974).

Davis presents a more complex statistical treatment of the approach in *Elementary Survey Analysis* (1971) and

Marsh, *The Survey Method* (1982) and Hellevik, *Introduction to Causal Analysis* (1984) highlight the value of the approach when trying to establish causal links with survey data. Davis's paper 'The Logic of Causal Order' (1985) provides a superb and very readable discussion of the logic of control variables in causal models. Marsh's (1988) outline of some additional methods of controlling for third variables (in Chapters 14 and 15 on standardisation and median polishing) is also worth examining once you feel confident with the methods outlined in this chapter.

EXERCISES

1 a Briefly interpret the following set of tables.
   b Represent the relationship between these three variables diagrammatically.

Zero order

		Workforce participation	
		In	Out
Level of religiousness	Low	63%	42%
	High	37	58

First order; controlling for gender

		MALE		FEMALE	
		In workforce	Out of workforce	In workforce	Out of workforce
Level of religiousness	Low	63%	62%	43%	42%
	High	37	38	57	58

2 a Opposite is a zero-order table showing a relationship between social class and IQ scores. Examine the table, select a test variable and draw hypothetical first-order conditional tables illustrating that the test variable is an intervening variable.

		Class	
		Lower	Middle
IQ score	Low	60%	35%
	High	40	65

b Represent the relationship between the three variables diagrammatically.
3 We find a zero-order relationship between two variables (X and Y correlation = 0.60). Imagine we have a dichotomous test variable. What might the partial coefficient be if:
a The test variable is an intervening variable which completely accounts for the zero-order relationship?
b The zero-order relationship is partly spurious?
c The test variable is an intervening variable which partly accounts for the zero-order relationship?
e The test variable is irrelevant to the zero-order relationship?
4 Explain in your own words the purpose of elaboration analysis.
5 Explain in your own words the logic of controlling for third variables. In particular explain why, if the test variable is responsible for the zero-order relationship, the first-order relationships should be zero.

6 Below is a zero-order and two first-order conditional tables and coefficients. Examine them and select the correct statements from those which follow.
a The zero-order relationship was spurious.
b Regular visiting by women is affected by the quality of the relationship with their mother whereas this is not true for men.
c The zero-order correlation is largely due to the contribution of the correlation between visiting and the relationship with mother among women.
d Overall, people visit their mother more when the relationship is poor than when it is not.
e Among men a poor relationship does not make much difference to the frequency with which they visit their mother.
f Gender is an intervening variable.
g Gender specifies the zero-order relationship.

| | | Relationship with mother is | |
		Poor	Good
Visits mother	Often	29%	43%
	Moderately	25	23
	Infrequently	46	34
	N	274	295
Gamma = –0.25		Significance = 0.001	

Controlling for sex

| | | MALE | | FEMALE | |
| | | Relationship with mother is | | Relationship with mother is | |
		Poor	Good	Poor	Good
Visits mother	Often	31%	38%	26%	46%
	Moderately	30	26	20	21
	Infrequently	39	36	54	33
	N	142	131	132	164
	Gamma = –0.10 Significance = 0.46			Gamma = –0.38 Significance = 0.0004	

7 What is the difference between:
  a A zero-order and a first-order relationship?
  b Conditional correlations and partial correlations?
  c Specification and replication?
  d A spurious relationship and an indirect causal relationship?

8 Draw a graph that shows that:
  a there is an interaction effect between age (X) and social class (working, middle and upper) (Z) on conservatism (Y);
  b the relationship between age (X) and religiousness (Y) [the older the more religious] is due to gender (Z) [theory: women live longer and women are more religious thus making it appear that age is related to religiousness].

17

Multivariate analysis

This chapter deals with five quite sophisticated and related techniques for multivariate analysis of interval-level variables. The aim is to develop an awareness of the potential of these techniques, but you will not become an expert on the basis of the chapter, which gives the flavour of the techniques rather than being comprehensive. All the methods assume one dependent variable and two or more 'independent' variables. These techniques are all based on bivariate correlation and regression, so make sure you are clear about these techniques before reading further. They also make use of the notions of controlling and intervening variables discussed in Chapter 16.

The five multivariate techniques to be discussed are:

1 *Partial correlation*—this identifies which variables have the *strongest relationship* with the dependent variable when all other variables in the model are controlled.
2 *Partial regression*—indicates how much *impact* each variable in the model has independently of the others. It can also tell us which variable has the *greatest* impact.
3 *Multiple regression*—tells us how well a whole set of information jointly predicts values on the dependent variable.

4 *Multiple correlation*—indicates how well a model fits the data; how much variation in the dependent variable is explained by the model.
5 *Path analysis*—what are the direct and indirect paths by which a set of independent variables affect the dependent variable?

To illustrate these five techniques we will use an example for most of this chapter in which there is one dependent variable and four independent variables (see Table 17.1 and Figure 17.1).

Before outlining these statistical methods it is important to pause and note that the importance of these multivariate techniques lies not in their statistical sophistication but in their value for testing complex theoretical models. The potential of these techniques is realised when they are preceded by careful, theoretical reasoning. These techniques help us evaluate our models and encourage us to specify our model clearly but they do not create models out of thin air. Of course they can help refine models, but the validity of the coefficients we calculate is dependent on the correctness of the causal model. If the model does not make sense, any coefficient, no matter how impressive, is meaningless (Marsh, 1982: 79).

The sophistication of the techniques is no substitute for theoretical sophistication. The importance of

Table 17.1   Variable names

Variables	Abbreviation	Symbol	Scale
Independent variables			
Father's occupational prestige	FOCC	X_1	17–86: High score = high prestige
Respondent's number of years of education	EDUC	X_2	Years: range 0–20
Respondent's occupational prestige	ROCC	X_3	17–86: High score = high prestige
Number of hours of work	HOURS	X_4	Hours: range 2–89
Dependent variable			
Respondent's annual income	INC	X_5	Dollars

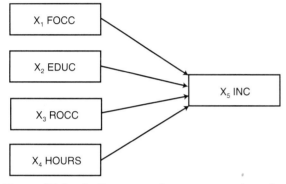

Figure 17.1   A diagrammatic representation of the variables in Table 17.1

the answers these techniques provide is a function of the questions we ask and the models we test, not the sophistication of the technique we apply. The value of these techniques is that we can ask the complex questions and propose complicated models and know that there are systematic ways of analysis to help answer them. Being able to test models that allow for multiple causes and multiple intervening variables enables us to take the notion of multiple causation of phenomena seriously and to escape analysis that reflects Durkheim's idea that each effect has only one cause. Enabled to unpack causal mechanisms, we can achieve a better understanding of causal processes that underlie simple correlations and do not have to rely on our stock of plausible, ad hoc explanations of these correlations. As such these multivariate techniques can be used (but do not by any means guarantee) to help develop explanations which in Weber's sense are adequate at the level of both cause and meaning.

INDIVIDUAL VARIABLES

Two of the procedures discussed in this chapter focus on the role of individual independent variables in explaining variation in the dependent variable. These two techniques, partial correlation and partial regression, will be discussed first and then followed by an outline of methods that examine the effect of a *set* of variables and that enable us to evaluate the worth of a whole model rather than just a single relationship.

Partial correlation

A correlation coefficient for interval data (r) indicates how strongly two variables are related. It tells us how accurately we can predict people's scores on one variable given a knowledge of their score on the other variable (see p. 256).

The partial correlation coefficient provides the same information except that the distorting effects of some other factors have been removed (partialled out). It is as if we have looked at r for the two variables X and Y among people who are identical on all the other independent variables. A partial r can be computed between each independent variable and the dependent variable, and these can be compared to see which variable enables the most accurate predictions of scores on the dependent variable (i.e. has the strongest relationship).

The following set of coefficients illustrates these points.

INC (X_5) with *FOCC (X_1)* controlling for EDUC (X_2), ROCC (X_3) and HOURS (X_4) = –0.02

i.e. $r_{51.234}$ = –0.02

INC (X_5) with *EDUC (X_2)* controlling for FOCC (X_1), ROCC (X_3) and HOURS (X_4) = 0.23

i.e. $r_{52.134}$ = 0.23

INC (X_5) with *ROCC (X_3)* controlling for FOCC (X_1),
EDUC (X_2) and HOURS (X_4) = 0.21

i.e. $r_{53.124} = 0.21$

INC (X_5) with *HOURS (X_4)* controlling for FOCC (X_1),
EDUC (X_2) and ROCC (X_3) = 0.32

i.e. $r_{54.123} = 0.32$

These same coefficients are provided in the second last column in the output from SPSS in Table 17.2.

Partial correlation coefficients will normally differ from zero-order correlations. Partial correlations reflect the relationship of two variables after the effects of all the other variables in the model have been removed. Notice how these partial correlations are summarised. An r with subscripts indicates that it is a partial correlation. The subscripts mean that it is a correlation of the two variables before the dot with the effects of those variables after the dot removed. These coefficients show which variable has the strongest 'pure' relationship with INC. Since HOURS has the strongest partial r (0.32), it is the best predictor of INC followed by EDUC (0.23), ROCC (0.21) and FOCC (–0.02).

Partial regression coefficients

Partial regression coefficients come in two forms: unstandardised and standardised. The characteristics

of these two forms of regression coefficients are summarised in Box 17.1.

A simple bivariate regression coefficient (symbolised as b) is an estimate of how much impact an independent variable has on the dependent variable. Specifically, for each unit change in the independent variable the score on the dependent variable will change by the number of units indicated by the regression coefficient (b). The b coefficient is measured in the same units as the dependent variable (see Chapter 15). Thus we saw in Chapter 15 that a b of 5200 for the relationship between dollars income (dependent) and years of tertiary education (independent) means that for each additional year of tertiary education we estimate that income will increase by $5200: the 'payoff' of a year of education is $5200.

However, when a variable such as education is linked with income we cannot be sure that the apparent impact is purely due to the impact of education. Education will be correlated with other variables that also affect income. Consequently we need to remove the effect of these other variables to identify the 'pure' effect of education. A partial regression coefficient indicates the effect of one independent variable on the dependent variable with the effect of the other specified contaminating variables removed.

The interpretation of the partial regression coefficient can be illustrated with the variables

Table 17.2 Partial correlation and regression coefficients from SPSS

		Coefficients[a]								
	Unstandardised coefficients		Standardised coefficients			95% confidence intervals for b		Correlations		Collinearity statistics
	b	Std error	Beta	t	Sig.	Lower bound	Upper bound	Zero-order	Partial	VIF
(Constant)	–$45 481	$5 817		–7.82	0.00	–$56 902	–$34 059			
Father's occupational prestige [X_1 = FOCC]	–$37	$83	–0.02	–0.44	0.66	–$199	$126	0.13	–0.02	1.17
R's number of years of education [X_2 = EDUC]	$2 717	$429	0.25	6.34	0.00	$1 875	$3 559	0.39	0.23	1.51
Hours worked in last week [X_4 = HOURS]	$625	$71	0.29	8.76	0.00	$485	$765	0.35	0.32	1.03
R's occupational prestige score [X_3 = ROCC]	$494	$86	0.22	5.74	0.00	$325	$663	0.40	0.21	1.45

[a] Dependent Variable: INC

WEB POINTER 17.1
Web-based software for multiple regression and multiple correlation

SIMSTAT is a very versatile package that can be downloaded for evaluation and purchased for a reasonable price (also special priced student edition). Has an excellent multiple regression routine.

www.simstat.com/

MODSTAT. Trial can be downloaded and program purchased cheaply. Has simple to use multiple regression module. Also has module for calculating multiple correlation for three variables by entering in three zero-order correlations.

http://members.aol.com/rcknodt/pubpage.htm

SISA. Free online data analysis. Computes partial and multiple correlation for three variables based on entering zero-order correlations between each of the three variables. Also computes significance and confidence intervals.

http://home.clara.net/sisa/

STATLETS 2.0 from statpoint. Free academic version can be downloaded or used freely online. Has a wide range of analysis and an excellent multiple regression module. Also includes built-in example data for examining effects of various options and learning about regression. Examples come with a statistics adviser option that explains the output. These two features are invaluable for learning about multiple regression.

www.statpoint.com/

WEBSTAT 2. Online analysis package that handles multiple regression well. Go to the site and select the webstat 2 option.

www.stat.sc.edu/webstat/

SPSS. Although this is not an online product it is widely used in educational and research institutions. It has an extremely comprehensive multiple regression module. The later versions of SPSS also provide an excellent 'results' coach which will take you step-by-step through your output explaining how to read it and what to watch out for.

To use this coach produce your output and then right click the mouse (windows users) on the table you want to interpret and choose results coach.

BOX 17.1 *Some characteristics of partial regression coefficients*

	Unstandardised	Standardised
1 Symbolised as	b or $b_{subscript}$	B, $B_{subscript}$, β or BETA
2 Units of measurement	Those of the Y variable*	Standard deviation of Y
3 Lower limit	0	0
4 Upper limit	Maximum value of the Y variable	1.0 (can range from −1.0 to +1.0)
5 Meaning of 0	Variable has no independent impact on Y	Variable has no independent impact on Y
6 Can have positive and negative signs	Both positive and negative are possible	Both positive and negative are possible
7 Can compare coefficients to determine the relative impact of each independent variable	No	Yes
8 Interpretation of coefficient	For each unit change in X the Y variable changes by b amount	When X changes by the amount of one standard deviation of X then Y changes by B amount of a standard deviation of Y.

* In multiple and partial regression analysis the Y variable is often given the symbol X and the highest subscript to indicate that it is the last variable in the model. Thus in Figure 17.1 the dependent variable is symbolised X_5 rather than Y.

---

outlined in Table 17.1. We will concentrate on the interpretation rather than the calculation of these coefficients and begin with *unstandardised partial regression coefficients*. Here b with subscripts are read as described earlier (p. 320). Often the subscripts are abbreviated so that only the number of the independent variable is given with the rest assumed.

Regression of INC (X_5) with FOCC (X_1) controlling for EDUC (X_2), ROCC (X_3) and HOURS (X_4) = −36.8
i.e. $b_{51.234}$ = −36.8 or b_1 = −36.8

Regression of INC (X_5) with EDUC (X_2) controlling for FOCC (X_1), ROCC (X_3) and HOURS (X_4) = 2717
i.e. $b_{52.134}$ = 2717 or b_2 = 2717

Regression of INC (X_5) with ROCC (X_3) controlling for FOCC (X_1), EDUC (X_2), HOURS (X_4) = 494
i.e. $b_{53.124}$ = 494 or b_3 = 494

Regression of INC (X_5) with HOURS (X_4) controlling for FOCC (X_1), EDUC (X_2) and ROCC (X_3) = 625
i.e. $b_{54.123}$ = 625 or b_4 = 625

Each of these coefficients indicates how much independent impact each variable has on INC. To say that b_2 = 2717 means that for each unit increase (year) in EDUC (X_2), INC will increase by $2717. This is independent of FOCC, ROCC and HOURS which might be correlated with EDUC. Thus if people have the same FOCC (i.e. class background) and ROCC (own occupational status) and work the same HOURS the person with the higher education will, on average, earn more at the rate predicted ($2717). The same interpretation applies to each of the other partial regression coefficients.

The information provided by these partial coefficients is useful but has one important limit. They cannot be compared with one another. Therefore they cannot be used to work out which factor has the greatest effect. This is because each of the independent variables is measured on a different scale. While one unit increase on EDUC leads to an independent increase of $2717 and one unit increase on ROCC (one unit of occupational prestige) leads to an independent increase of $494 on INC, we cannot talk of these units being of equivalent size. EDUC as a variable has a range of only twenty years while occupational prestige is scored on a scale of 17 to 86. One unit of education is not the same 'size' as a unit of occupational prestige.

To see which factor has the greatest independent impact we must standardise them. These *standardised partial regression coefficients* are called *beta coefficients* and are symbolised by B or ß with appropriate subscripts. Rather than exploring the formula for standardisation (see Johnson, 1977: 142) it is more important to focus on the interpretation of these standardised partial regression coefficients (betas).

The beta coefficients for independent variables in our model are listed in column 4 of Table 17.2. The b for EDUC was 2717. Standardised this is 0.25 and means that for each increase of the size of one standard deviation of EDUC (standard deviation of EDUC = 2.8 years) the INC will increase by 0.25 of a standard deviation of INC (standard deviation of INC = $30 593). Since 0.25 of the standard deviation of INC is $7648 ($30 593 × 0.25) then a beta of 0.25 means that for each standard deviation increase of EDUC (i.e. 2.8 years) INC will increase by $7648. Normally only the beta coefficients (rather than their converted dollar value) are given and are used to pinpoint which variables have the greatest effect. Since betas are standardised values we can compare the betas to assess the relative impact of different variables. Thus if one variable has a beta of 0.29, it has more effect than one with a beta of −0.02 or 0.22 or 0.25.

For our example the unstandardised (b) and standardised partial regression coefficients (beta) are provided in Table 17.2.

Whenever you want to compare the relative importance of independent variables you should use the beta (standardised) regression coefficients (B). In this example EDUC has the highest b but only the second higher beta. HOURS has a much lower b than EDUC but in terms of relative impact (beta) the two variables have a similar impact.

So far the discussion of regression coefficients has focused on these regression figures as descriptive statistics: they describe the patterns in the sample. However our interest normally extends beyond the sample. If we have a random sample we can estimate how likely these patterns are to hold in the population.

Significance levels are calculated for both the b and beta coefficients (column 6, Table 17.2). These test the null hypothesis that the coefficient is zero (i.e. the variable has no impact). Where the significance level is below the critical point (0.05 or 0.01) we can reject this null hypothesis of no impact. Where the significance is above 0.01 or 0.05 we will continue to accept that the variable probably has no impact in the population. In the example in Table 17.2 all the variables except FOCC have a significance level below 0.01 which means that in the population these variables are likely to have at least this level of impact. However FOCC has a significance of 0.66 which means that there is a 66 per cent probability that this b or beta coefficient is greater than zero simply because of sampling error. We would treat the impact of FOCC as being zero—of no consequence in affecting income.

Confidence levels are also computed for these individual b coefficients. Where these confidence intervals include zero (as it does with FOCC) it means there is a reasonable possibility that the b for FOCC is zero.

Regression for subgroups

Another very useful way of applying regression coefficients is to calculate them separately for different subgroups and then compare whether each variable has the same payoff for the different groups. This can be done with either unstandardised or standardised regression coefficients as long as the use of the unstandardised ones is confined to comparing the *same variable* across groups.

For example, we might calculate the coefficients separately for men and women (see Table 17.3).

According to these figures men get a greater 'payoff' than do women for each year of education ($3525 cf. $2400) and each extra point of occupational prestige ($650 cf. $535).

In summary, partial regression coefficients indicate how much independent impact or 'payoff' each independent variable has. When standardised we can tell which one has the greatest impact. Partial regression differs from partial correlation. Partial regression enables us to predict how much impact one variable has on another, while partial correlation enables us to assess the accuracy of those predictions.

Table 17.3 Partial regression coefficients for men and women

	Male			Female		
	b	B	Sig.	b	B	Sig.
FOCC X₁	−78	−0.03	ns	99	0.06	ns
EDUC X₂	3525	0.34	0.000	2400	0.23	0.000
ROCC X₃	600	0.28	0.000	530	0.13	0.000
HOURS X₄	730	0.32	0.000	550	0.27	0.000

MODELS

While analysis can focus on the impact of individual variables it is common also to examine the overall impact of a *set* of variables and consider their *joint* impact on the dependent variable. When examined as a set of variables we are evaluating the impact of a *model* rather than a variable. Two ways in which models are analysed and evaluated are with multiple correlation and multiple regression.

Multiple correlation

We have already seen the difference between regression coefficients and correlation coefficients for bivariate analysis (Chapter 15). Regression (b) enables the prediction of people's score on a dependent variable. Correlation (r) enables us to assess the accuracy of those predictions.

Multiple correlation enables us to do two main things:

1 evaluate the explanatory power of a model by assessing the joint effect of a set of variables;
2 assess how accurate our regression predictions from the model will be (see below).

The first role of assessing how well a model explains variation in the dependent variable is accomplished by looking at the R^2 coefficient (Table 17.4). This is the same as r^2 except that it reflects the explanatory power of a set of variables. R^2 is interpreted in the same way as the bivariate correlation coefficient (r^2). Like r^2 the R^2 value ranges from 0 to 1 and is always positive. The higher the R^2 the more powerful the model is. Table 17.4 (which reports the R^2 for our model) shows a R^2 of 0.29 which means that 29 per cent of the variation in income in the sample is due to differences in education, hours worked and the prestige of people's jobs.

Table 17.4 R^2 for model

	Model summary	
R	R square	Adjusted R square
0.53[a]	0.29	0.28

[a] Predictors: (Constant), ROCC (X3), FOCC (X1), EDUC (X2) and HOURS (X4)

This table also reports an *adjusted R^2* of 0.28. Since the size of R^2 can be affected by the number of independent variables in the model (even if many of the variables have no explanatory power) it is desirable to adjust for the number of variables. Since the adjusted R^2 makes this adjustment it is the preferable statistic to use.

Having obtained a R^2 value that summarises the explanatory power of the model in the sample, we need to work out whether a R^2 this large could have occurred due to sampling error. We need to work out whether the R^2 is likely to be greater than zero in the population. To determine this we use an F-test and its significance level. The significance of F tells us whether the R^2 is greater than zero because of sampling error. In Table 17.5 the significance value is very low which means that the R^2 this high (29 per cent) is not simply an aberration due to sampling error.

Multiple regression

The earlier discussion of partial regression focused on the impact of individual variables and the relative importance of each variable. Multiple regression provides a way of examining the joint impact of the whole set of variables.

Multiple regression works on the principle that

Table 17.5   Analysis of variance of model indicating significance of R^2

	Sum of squares	df	Mean square	F	Sig.
	ANOVA[b]				
Regression	184979136628	4	46244784157	68.72	**0.000**[a]
Residual	463626692003	689	672897956		
Total	648605828631	693			

[a] Predictors: (Constant), ROCC (X3), FOCC (X1), EDUC (X2) and HOURS (X4)
[b] Dependent Variable: INC

the more we know about a person the more accurately we can guess other attributes of that person. It makes use of the information provided by partial regression. To estimate someone's income I could use my knowledge of their EDUC. But if FOCC and ROCC and HOURS have unique effects additional to EDUC it would make sense to use this information as well to obtain a better estimate than that provided by EDUC alone.

To be statistical we can do this by simply extending the bivariate regression formula of $\hat{Y} = a + bX$ into

$$\hat{X}_5 = a + b_1X_1 + b_2X_2 + b_3X_3 + b_4X_4 \text{ etc.}$$

where each X represents a particular variable and each b represents the partial regression coefficient of the variable.

When standardised b coefficients are used, this equation changes slightly. The X values are transformed into standard scores (z scores) and the 'a' term is dropped as it is always zero. The standardised formula becomes:

$$\hat{Z}_5 = B_1z_1 + B_2z_2 + B_3z_3 + B_4z_4 \text{ etc.}$$

Since the unstandardised equation is normally used when making predictions the following discussion will use the unstandardised equation.

Using our example we can translate this formula into:

$$\text{Predicted INC} = a + b_1 \text{ (FOCC)} + b_2 \text{ (EDUC)} + b_3 \text{ (ROCC)} + b_4 \text{ (HOURS)}$$

The 'a' symbol in this equation is the *constant* figure in Table 17.2. This represents the income of a person who obtained a zero score on each of the four predictor variables. In this case this figure of −$45 481 makes no intuitive sense but that remains the starting point for any prediction.

To use the equation for prediction we simply substitute the a and b values from Table 17.2 into the equation and get:

$$\text{Predicted INC} = -45\,481 + -37(\text{FOCC}) + 2717(\text{EDUC}) + 494(\text{ROCC}) + 624(\text{HOURS})$$

For any particular person we can take their scores on each variable and insert them into the formula instead of the variable's name to predict that person's income. For example, we might have a person with these values:

FOCC = 50 (on a 17–86 scale); EDUC = 15(years); ROCC = 70 (on a 17–86 scale) and HOURS = 40 hours worked per week).

For this person we would get the equation:

$$\begin{aligned}\text{Predicted INC} &= -45\,481 + -37(50) + 2717(15) + \\ &\quad 494(70) + 624(40) \\ &= -45\,481 + -1850 + 40\,755 + 34\,580 \\ &\quad + 24\,960 \\ &= \$52\,964\end{aligned}$$

For sociologists who often want to make predictions about *groups* rather than individuals, multiple regression can be used in another productive way. Using the same basic procedure we can estimate the mean score for a group (e.g. the mean INC) rather than an individual's score. To do this we insert the group *mean* for each variable into regression equation and predict from these rather than individual scores.

For example, if we had the following group means for a whole country:

$$X_{\text{FOCC}} = 40, X_{\text{EDUC}} = 13, X_{\text{ROCC}} = 60 \text{ and } X_{\text{HOURS}} = 30$$

we could estimate the mean income for people in this particular country. Assuming that the earlier partial regression coefficients were representative we can put these group means into the equation with the result:

Predicted INC = −45 481 + −37(40) + 2717(13) +
494(60) + 624(30)
= −45 481 + −1480 + 35 321 + 29 640
+ 18 720
= $36 720

If we wished we could use this application of multiple regression in useful ways. We could calculate partial regression coefficients and group means separately for different subgroups (e.g. men and women) and make estimates of the X_{INC} for each subgroup (see Table 17.6).

Using the figures from columns 1 and 2 from Table 17.6 we can develop a separate regression equation and estimate mean incomes for men, and using columns 4 and 5 we can do the same for women. Columns 3 and 5 provide the calculations for each variable and the shaded cells provide the estimated average income for males and females given the typical attributes of males and females on these four predictor variables. The same calculations are provided below in the more conventional form of a regression equation.

Males:
Predicted INC = −46 695 + −78(40) + 3525(14) +
600(65) + 730(32)
= −46 695 + −3120 + 47 588 + 39 000
+ 23 360
= $60 133

Females:
Predicted INC = −43 253 + −99(40) + 2400(13) +
530(55) + 550(25)
= −43 253 + 3960 + 30 000 + 29 150
+ 13 750
= $33 607

The male and female income estimates vary for two reasons:

1 the group means differ—women have lower mean EDUC, lower status jobs and work fewer HOURS;

2 the payoff or impact (b) of these variables differs for the two groups. Women, for example, get less benefit in terms of income for each hour of work, for each year of education and for each unit of occupational prestige. Not only do females have less education, work fewer hours and have lower status jobs, they are rewarded less pro rata for what they have.

We could go further and demonstrate the disadvantage that women suffer. If women got the same income benefits for their FOCC, EDUC, ROCC and EDUC that men do, we could look at women's income compared with what they would earn under the benefits men get. To test this we can simply put the male b coefficients in the female equation to get:

Females:
Predicted X_{INC} = a + −78(40) + 3525(13) + 600(55) +
730(25)
= −46 695 + −3120 + 45 825 + 33 000
+ 18 250
= $47 260

This means that even given female lower means on FOCC, EDUC, ROCC and HOURS, women would earn $47 260 rather than $33 607 if they were rewarded at the same rate as men per ROCC prestige point, per FOCC prestige point, for each year of EDUC and per HOUR of work.

In summary, multiple regression can be used in a variety of ways. Apart from the use to which partial

Table 17.6 Subgroup means and b coefficients for males and females

	Males			Females		
Variables	Mean col 1	b col 2	Mean × b col 3	Mean col 4	b col 5	Mean × b col 5
X₁ FOCC	40	−78	−$3 120	40	99	$3 960
X₂ EDUC	14	3 525	$47 588	13	2 400	$30 000
X₃ ROCC	65	600	$39 000	55	530	$29 150
X₄ HOURS	32	730	$23 360	25	550	$13 750
a		−46 695	−$46 695		−43 253	−$43 253
	Predicted mean income		$60 133	Predicted mean income		$33 607

regression coefficients can be put, multiple regression can be used so that a set of variables is used to make predictions for particular individuals, whole groups or subgroups. These procedures can be applied to a wide variety of research problems.

Finally, the R^2 provides a way of evaluating how good the predictions we make will be. If R^2 is low then the predictions are likely to be subject to a lot of error. If the R^2 is high then the regressions and estimates made on the basis of regression coefficients are likely to be fairly close to the mark.

Cautions

Care needs to be taken when using multiple regression analysis. The technique is only sensitive to certain types of relationships between variables and is based on various statistical assumptions. It is beyond the scope of this book to discuss these matters in detail. They are dealt with in detail in Lewis-Beck (1980), Norusis (1985), Berry and Feldman (1985) and Schroeder, Sjoquist and Stephan (1986).

The most important of these limitations and assumptions include:

1 The form of regression described above is only sensitive to linear relationships between vari-

ables: it does not detect non-linear relationships.

2 It does not automatically detect interaction effects between independent variables.

3 It assumes that the variance in the dependent variable is constant for each value of the independent variable (technically called *homoskedasticity*). If this is not so, then regression results can be distorted.

4 It assumes that the independent variables are not highly correlated with one another. If they are highly intercorrelated the R^2 can be inflated and it is impossible to distinguish between the separate effects of the independent variables. High intercorrelations between independent variables is called *multicollinearity*. One way of detecting multicollinearity is to look at the zero-order correlations between each of the independent variables. Correlations over 0.70 in large samples are likely to reflect multicollinearity. Another way is to examine the VIN statistics (Table 17.2). Numbers that are above 10 for a variable indicate serious multi-colinearity.

5 Multiple regression assumes that variables are measured at the interval level. This can severely limit the range of situations in which it can be used. There are two solutions to this problem.

WEB POINTER 17.2 *Online, interactive demonstrations for multivariate analysis*

The examples and statistics advisers in STATLETS provide an excellent means for experimenting with regression analysis and seeing what effect different options and variables have.	www.sgcorp.com/statlets.htm
Online demo (with your data) of calculation of R^2. OK but not brilliant.	www3.sympatico.ca/mcomeau/webpublic/ javapage/reg/reg.htm
Online interactive analysis with online data sets.	www.math.montana.edu/jeff-bin/Rweb1.03/ buildModules.cgi
Online calculator for standardised regression coefficients (beta) and R^2. All you have to do is enter in the zero-order correlations (from a bivariate correlation matrix) and the program does the rest. Really simple.	
For two independent variables:	http://faculty.vassar.edu/~lowry/mult_r2.html
For four independent variables:	http://faculty.vassar.edu/~lowry/mult_r4.html

When an *independent* variable is not an interval-level variable *dummy regression* can be used (see below). When the *dependent* variable is nominal a different form of regression called *logistic regression* can be used (see Table 17.9).

MULTIPLE REGRESSION WITH NON-INTERVAL INDEPENDENT VARIABLES: DUMMY REGRESSION

Multiple regression can be used in situations when the dependent variable is interval but one or more independent variables are nominal or ordinal. We can, for example, use variables such as religious affiliation, country of birth, political preference as independent variables. This is possible by converting these nominal variables into a *series* of dummy variables—variables with just two categories coded 0 and 1. It is easiest to explain how this is done by using an example. Since the variables in the example used so far in this chapter are all interval we will use a different example in which the independent variables are non-interval.

Suppose we wanted to look at the effect of religious denomination on the frequency of attendance at religious services. We have two variables: number of times religious services are attended each year (ATTEND) and denomination (DENOM) with five categories:

1 Catholic;
2 Protestant;
3 Jewish;
4 non-Christian; and
5 no religion.

Since DENOM is a nominal variable we cannot do regression in the normal way. Instead we can 'trick' regression by breaking up the nominal variable into a number of dichotomous variables. Since dichotomous variables can be treated as interval variables) we can then quite legitimately perform a regression analysis. These variables which are called dummy variables are created by taking a category of the variable DENOM and creating a new dichotomous variable from that category. This task is easily accomplished by computer packages such as SPSS. When creating the dummy variable from a category the people from that category will be coded as 1 and everyone else as 0.

In this case we might end up with the following dummy variables:

1 CATH: 1 = Catholic, 0 = everyone else;
2 PROT: 1 = Protestant, 0 = everyone else;
3 JEW: 1 = Jewish, 0 = everyone else;
4 NONXIAN: 1 = other non-Christian, 0 = everyone else.

In this example there is no dummy variable for the 'no religion' category of the original variable. This is important. The number of dummy variables must always be one less than the number of categories of the original variable. This is necessary to avoid the technical problem with multiple regression—multicollinearity. The category for which we do not create a dummy variable becomes a baseline against which we compare regression coefficients for the other categories. This variable is called the *reference category*. As will be seen shortly, omitting a particular category does not stop us obtaining regression information for that category.

Using these dummy variables, our regression equation will be:

N of services attended = a +b_{cath}(CATH) + b_{prot}(PROT) + b_{jew}(JEW) + $b_{nonxian}$(NONXIAN)

Suppose we obtained the following unstandardised regression coefficients (b figures) from our analysis (see Table 17.8):

a =1; b_{cath} = 27; b_{prot} = 12; b_{jew} = 9; $b_{nonxian}$ = 22

we get the following:

N of services attended = 1 + 27(CATH) + 12(PROT) + 9(JEW) + 22(NONXIAN)

Using normal regression procedures we can predict how often, on average, Catholics attend religious services in a year. Since Catholic is coded as 1 and a Catholic will necessarily receive a code of 0 on each of the other dummy variables (Table 17.7) we can estimate that for Catholics:

N of services attended = 1 + 27(1) + 12(0) + 9(0) + 22(0)

Using the same approach, estimates can be made for every other group except the omitted group—those with no religion.

In dummy regression the estimate for the omitted category is obtained by using the intercept (a). In this

BOX 17.2 *Using dummy variables*

1 Dummy variables will always be coded 0 and 1.

2 For each dummy variable the substantive category will be coded 1 and everything else will be coded zero.

3 The number of dummy variables will equal one less than the number of categories of the original variable.

4 The values of the dummy variables can be directly compared even when not standardised.

case the intercept (a) is 1 so this means that those with no religious affiliation attend religious services, on average, once a year. Given that the intercept represents the regression estimate for the omitted category

it also means that the b figures for the groups represented by the dummy variables can be interpreted as being that much higher (or lower) than the omitted category. That is, the figures for Catholics, Protestants and others is the average attendance of these groups *relative to the attendance of the omitted category*. Thus, Catholics attend church on 27 more occasions per year than those with no religion; Protestants on 12 more occasions and so on.

Given that this type of interpretation is possible, it makes sense, when selecting the base category (the omitted category), to choose a category against which we want to compare other groups. Thus if the variable was country of birth and our main interest was to compare differences between native-born and those born in various overseas countries it would make sense to make native-born the base category and create dummy variables to represent various overseas birth places. A useful guideline, when using ordinal variables, is to use one of the extreme categories as the base category.

In the end however the choice of the base

Table 17.7 Constructing dummy variables and codes

| | | Dummy variable codes | | | |
Category on DENOM	Code on DENOM	CATH	PROT	JEW	NONXIAN
Catholic	1	1	0	0	0
Protestant	2	0	1	0	0
Jewish	3	0	0	1	0
Non-Christian	4	0	0	0	1
No religion	5	0	0	0	0

Table 17.8 SPSS regression output for analysis of dummy variables

Coefficients[a]

| | Unstandardised coefficients | | Standardised coefficients | | | 95% confidence interval for b | | Correlations | |
	b	Std error	Beta	t	Sig.	Lower bound	Upper bound	Zero-order	Partial
(Constant)	1	2		0.29	0.77	−3	5		
CATH	27	2	0.46	11.22	0.00	22	32	0.11	0.28
PROT	12	1	0.46	10.93	0.00	10	14	0.09	0.28
JEW	9	5	0.05	1.81	0.07	−1	20	−0.07	0.05
NONXIAN	22	4	0.16	5.53	0.00	14	30	0.00	0.14

[a] Dependent Variable: ATTEND

$R^2 = 0.09$; F for model = 36.2, sig. = 0.000

category makes no difference to the final estimates we obtain. Had we chosen Catholics as the baseline in the above example we would have obtained the same final estimates.

Dummy variables can be included in regression analysis together with interval-level independent variables and their interpretation remains essentially the same. If age was added to the above equation the figures would change and the interpretation of the figures would simply be that these are the effects of denominational membership with the effect of age controlled.

If more than one set of dummy variables is used in the one equation the value of 'a' will represent the value for the combination of omitted categories. If gender was added to the earlier equation with males being coded as 0 and females as 1, the value of 'a' would represent the attendance levels of males with no religious affiliation, the 'b' value for Catholics would be the attendance frequency of male Catholics relative to males without a religious affiliation and so on. Thus, in an equation with the following figures:

N of services attended = −1 + 27(CATH) + 12(PROT) + 9(JEW) + 22(NONXIAN) + 4(FEMALE)

males with no religious affiliation attend religious services on average minus once a year (a bit of statistical nonsense) and *male* Catholics attend 26 (27−1) times a year. Female Catholics attend, on average, 30 times a year (−1 + 27 + 4). Females with no religious affiliation attend three times a year on average (a + b (female) = −1 + 4).

In summary, by converting nominal and interval independent variables into a series of dichotomous or dummy variables coded 0 and 1 it is possible to extend the power of multiple regression to problems where not all the variables are measured at the interval level.

PATH ANALYSIS

Path analysis is a procedure for analysing and presenting results, which draws heavily on the techniques already outlined in this chapter. It is used for testing causal models and requires that we formulate a model using a pictorial causal flowgraph (Figure 17.2). The flowgraph is used as a way of presenting results and also helps us see what we are trying to say. It makes use of R^2, thus enabling us to

evaluate how good the model is, and by using beta coefficients (called path coefficients in path analysis) also enables us to specify how much effect each variable has. In addition, path analysis enables us to work out the *mechanisms* by which variables affect one another; it can pinpoint the extent to which a variable's effect is *direct* or *indirect*. As such, path analysis provides a lot of information about causal processes in an easily understandable way.

Using our earlier variables (INC, FOCC, ROCC, EDUC, HOURS) we can draw a path diagram (see Box 17.3). Learning how to develop and read these diagrams is the key to path analysis.

In a path diagram we must place the variables in a causal order. The variables we include, the order in which we place them and the causal arrows we draw are up to us. We will develop the model on the basis of sound theoretical reasoning. We could, of course, develop such a model even if we did not intend to use path analysis. These diagrams provide a useful way of specifying what our theory is and for keeping several ideas in the air at once. The point of path analysis is to provide one means of evaluating how well a set of data fits that model. The key point is that we must develop the model and do it before conducting any fancy statistical analysis. Statistical analysis will not create the model for us. Sophisticated statistics and analysis do not substitute for sound and careful theoretical reasoning: rather they rely on it. Marsh argues that (1982: 72):

> It is the model that stands between the researcher and unbridled empiricism in the attempt to draw causal inference, for it forces researchers into explicit theory making activity.

I have only drawn some of the possible arrows in this model. I have omitted those links that I expected would not be important. It is important to note that the paths by which many variables are expected to have an impact in this model are both direct and indirect. For example, EDUC is posited to have a direct impact and an indirect impact (EDUC → ROCC → INC and EDUC → ROCC → HOURS → INC).

Each path has a path coefficient. These are beta coefficients and indicate how much impact a variable has on various other variables. In Figure 17.3 the path diagram has been redrawn with path coefficients. For the sake of clarity some arrows have been enlarged roughly proportionate to the size of each

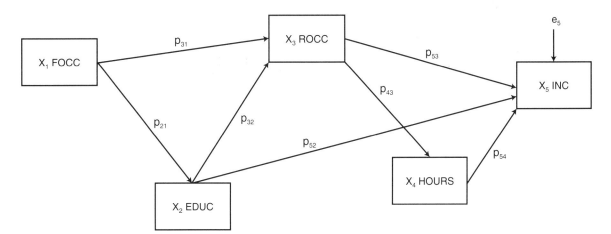

Figure 17.2   Path model without coefficients

BOX 17.3   *Drawing a path diagram*

1   Draw the model before doing the analysis.

2   Place the variables in causal order.

3   Place the dependent variable to the extreme right of the diagram.

4   Of the independent variables place the variables in the causal order being tested. The variable being treated as the initial cause is placed to the left of the diagram.

5   Name each variable as $X_{subscript}$ where the subscript is the number of the variable.

6   Place causal arrows between variables to indicate the expected causal links between variables. These paths can include direct paths (variable goes directly from one variable to another) or indirect (path goes via another variable) or both direct and indirect. All arrows should point from left to right only.

7   Each arrow is named with a p and a subscript. The subscript indicates the numbers of the two variables connected by the arrow. The number of the 'dependent' variable in the pair is placed first. Thus p_{52} in Figure 17.2 refers to an arrow from variable 2 (EDUC) to 5 (INC).

8   After the analysis the p will be replaced with a Beta value (a path coefficient).

9   An arrow pointing from nowhere in particular is directed to the dependent variable. The figure associated with this arrow indicates the amount of variance in the dependent variable that is *not* explained by the variables in the model. This figure is $1 - R^2$. The *lower* this figure the better the model.

---

path coefficient. To clarify the idea of the direct and indirect paths and the relative importance of each path, it is helpful to think of the arrows as water pipes of varying diameters depending on the size of the path coefficient (p_{32} is 'wider' than p_{31}). If you poured water in at, say, EDUC, by which path would the most get through? By looking at the diagram in this way we can track down by what mechanisms variables have their effect and evaluate the relative importance of each mechanism. This is extremely

helpful in developing a sophisticated understanding of causal processes.

In path analysis we can work out how much a variable affects another variable and compare this effect with the effects of other variables to work out which is the most important. Multiple regression enables us to examine and compare the *direct* effects of each independent variable. However, path analysis takes us one step beyond this point.

The effect of a variable is called the *total effect*. It

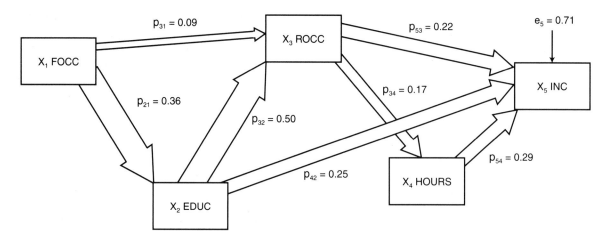

Figure 17.3   Path model with coefficients

consists of two different types of effects: *direct effect* and *indirect effect*. Using EDUC and INC as an example, the indirect effects are those where EDUC affects INC via some other variable (e.g. via ROCC) while the direct effects are unmediated effects. The total effect of EDUC on INC is the sum of these two sets of effects. The process of working out the extent to which an effect is direct or indirect and in establishing the importance of the various indirect paths is called *decomposition* and this is illustrated in Figure 17.4.

In path analysis these direct and indirect effects are calculated by using the path coefficients. Since these coefficients are standardised they can be compared directly with one another. Working out the importance of a direct effect between two variables is done simply by looking at the path coefficients. To assess the importance of any indirect effect or path just multiply the coefficients along the path. This is done separately for each indirect path. To get the total indirect effect between two variables simply add up the effect for each indirect path that joins those variables. To find the total causal effect (to use the water analogy, to find how much water would get through), simply add the direct and indirect coefficients together (see Figure 17.4).

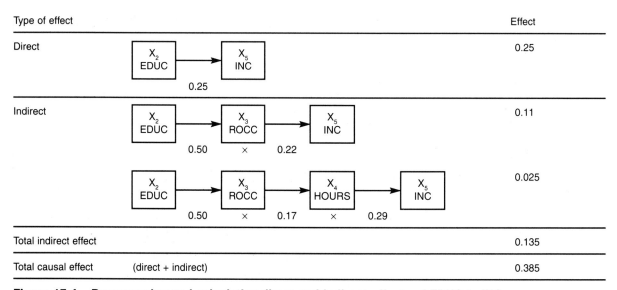

Figure 17.4   Decomposing and calculating direct and indirect effects of EDUC to INC

To interpret the various figures in Figure 17.4 refer back to the earlier outline of the meaning of beta coeffcents. By simply looking at the figures, it is easy to see that the direct path is the most important way in which EDUC affects income but that there is an additional effect via the effect of education on ROCC while the additional effect of the other path is negligible.

The final point to note about the model in Figure 17.3 is the error term (e_5). (Error terms are normally provided for all but the X_1 variable but I have omitted them in the figures here for the sake of simplicity.) As indicated earlier this is the amount of *unexplained* variance in INC. In this case it is 0.71 or 71 per cent (calculated by subtracting R^2 from 1). In social science research this amount of unexplained variance is not unusual but clearly there are other important factors that also contribute to variations in income. A fuller model would undoubtedly include additional variables such as gender, age, race and other factors that we know affect earning power.

It has only been possible to introduce the five related multivariate techniques covered in this chapter. Web Pointer 17.3 provides links to some excellent and accessible discussions of these methods which will take you further.

OTHER MULTIVARIATE METHODS

The five multivariate methods outlined in this chapter are all closely related. There are a number of other important multivariate techniques that are beyond the scope of this book. Each of these methods is appropriate for different purposes and makes different assumptions about the data to be

WEB POINTER 17.3 *Web-based reading material for multivariate analysis*	
Regression explained: Download a word file that provides a clear set of guidelines to assist with reading and interpreting regression output from SPSS.	www.spss.org/wwwroot/tips_and_summary_sheets_for_regr.htm
The STATLETS online manual explains how to interpret and use the various statistics that are routinely produced by most multiple regression statistical programs.	www.statlets.com/statletsmanual/sect6_2_4.htm
'The InStat Guide to Choosing and Interpreting Statistical Tests' provides an excellent and understandable guide to doing multiple regression—when to do it, how to do it, what to watch out for and how to read the results.	www.graphpad.com/instatman/instat3hh.htm
STATSOFT electronic textbook provides a reasonable online outline of multiple regression. Select the **linear regression** button to take you to an outline of multiple regression.	www.statsoft.com/textbook/stathome.html
WEBSTAT online text has an excellent easy to read chapter on multiple regression.	http://sbmconnect.tees.ac.uk/webstat/content%20pages/chapter9/chapter9unit24_Multiple_Regression.htm
Path analysis	www2.chass.ncsu.edu/garson/pa765/path.htm
Multiple regression	www2.chass.ncsu.edu/garson/pa765/regress.htm

analysed (see Table 17.9). A key factor that determines the use of these techniques is the nature of the variables.

MULTIVARIATE CHECKLIST

1 What is the level of measurement of the dependent variable? If not interval use another multivariate method.
2 What is the level of measurement of the independent variables?
   a If some independent variables are not interval can they be converted into a set of dummy variables?
   b If dummy variables are to be used what will your reference category be?
   c If not interval, or appropriate for dummy, variable analysis select another multivariate method.
3 What question do you want the analysis to answer? Does the question focus on individual independent variables?

a If yes, do you want to know about the strength of the relationship between the variable and the dependent variable independent of other variables (partial correlation)?
b Do you want to know about the independent impact of an independent variable (unstandardised or standardised partial regression)?
c Do you want to compare the relative importance of the independent variables (standardised partial regression, beta coefficients)?
4 Does the question relate to the joint effects of a set of independent variables?
   a If yes, do you want to evaluate the impact of the model as a whole (multiple correlation)?
   b Do you want to know how much variance in the dependent variable is explained by the model (multiple correlation)?
   c Do you want to make predictions for individuals or subgroups on the dependent

Table 17.9 Other multivariate methods

Method	Dependent variable	Independent variables	References
Discriminant analysis	Nominal	Interval	Silva and Stam (1995) Norusis (1985) www.statsoft.com/textbook/stathome.html (select discriminant analysis button) www2.chass.ncsu.edu/garson/pa765/discrim.htm www2.chass.ncsu.edu/garson/pa765/mda.htm
Logistic regression	Dichotomous	Interval or mixture of interval and non interval	Wright (1995) Hosmer and Lemeshow (1989) Gilbert (1993)
Multinomial logistic regression	Nominal or ordinal (categorical) with more than two categories	Interval or mixture of interval and non interval	Wright (1995) Hosmer and Lemeshow (1989) www2.chass.ncsu.edu/garson/pa765/logistic.htm#LL
Multiple analysis of variance (ANOVA)	Interval	Nominal or ordinal (categorical)	Weinfurt (1995) Norusis (1985) www.statsoft.com/textbook/stathome.html (select ANOVA/MANOVA button) www2.chass.ncsu.edu/garson/pa765/anova.htm
Log linear analysis	Nominal or ordinal (categorical)	Nominal or ordinal (categorical) or mixture of categorical and interval	Rogers (1995) Gilbert (1993) Norusis (1985) www.statsoft.com/textbook/stathome.html (select log linear button) www2.chass.ncsu.edu/garson/pa765/logit.htm

variable using the information gained from the set of independent variables (multiple regression)?

5   Do you want to learn about the mechanisms (direct and indirect) by which variables have an impact (path analysis)?

a   Do you want to examine the relative role of direct and indirect effects (decomposition)?

KEY CONCEPTS

Beta coefficient	Multiple R	Reference category	Standardised regression
Constant	Multiple regression	Significance level of b	coefficient
Dummy variable	Partial regression	(or B)	Total causal effect
Model	coefficient	Significance of model	Unstandardised partial
Multicollinearity	Path coefficient	Standardised partial	regression coefficient
Multiple cf. partial	Path model	regression coefficient	
Multiple correlation	R^2		

FURTHER READING

A very clear non-technical introduction to the multivariate techniques outlined in this chapter is given by Johnson in Chapter 8 of *Social Statistics Without Tears* (1977). Kerlinger provides a very good conceptual and non-statistical explanation of a range of multivariate techniques in *Behavioural Research: A Conceptual Approach* (1979), Chapters 4, 11–13. Loether McTavish's *Descriptive Statistics for Sociologists* (1974), Chapter 9 and Blalock in *Social Statistics* (1972), Chapter 19 give slightly more advanced outlines. Perhaps the best moderate level discussion are in Nie at al. in *SPSS: Statistical Package for the Social Sciences* (1975), pp. 301–5, 320–42, 383–97 and in Norusis in *SPSSX: Introductory Statistics Guide* (1983).

For advanced, statistical treatments of a fair range of multivariate techniques see Tabachnick and Fidell's *Using Multivariate Statistics* (1983) for a very well organised discussion which gives a great deal of practical advice. Kerlinger and Pedhazur present a very thorough discussion of multiple regression techniques in *Multiple Regression in Behavioural Research* (1973). An excellent set of books that deals with both the theoretical and practical aspects of multiple regression is published in the Sage series on Quantitative Applications in the Social Sciences (Berry and Feldman, 1985; Achen, 1982; Schroeder, Sjoquist and Stephan, 1986 and Lewis-Beck, 1980).

EXERCISES

1   In multivariate analysis, which statistics or techniques are used to:

a   work out which independent variable has the greatest independent impact?

b   see how well a set of independent variables jointly explains the variance in the dependent variable?

c   estimate the indirect effects of independent variables on dependent variables?

d   determine which independent variable has the strongest independent relationship with the dependent variable?

e   work out the joint impact of a set of independent variables?

f   estimate the independent impact of a variable?

2   Examine the path diagram below and explain what it means as fully as you can.

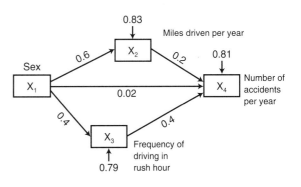

3 Examine the figures in the table below and answer the following questions:

a Which independent variable has the greatest independent impact on conservatism (the dependent variable)? (Give figures to support your answer.)

b What would be the predicted conservatism score of a 35-year-old black woman with ten years of education, who attended church 25 times a year? What would be the conservatism score for a comparable male? (*Note:* the coding for these variables is explained immediately beneath the regression results.)

c What does the minus sign in front of some of the b and B coefficients mean?

d How satisfied would you be with your explanation of conservatism given the above figures? Why?

e For what purpose would you use the b and B coefficients respectively?

f What do the significance figures associated with each variable tell you?

g What do the lower and upper bound figures of 0.15 and 0.24 associated with ATTEND tell you?

4 Examine the path model below and answer the questions which follow.

a By what paths does education affect prejudice?

b By which path does education have the most effect on prejudice?

Coefficients[a]

	Unstandardised coefficients		Standardised coefficients			95% confidence interval for b		Correlations
	b	Std error	Beta	t	Sig.	Lower bound	Upper bound	Partial
(Constant)	54.57	3.78		14.45	0.00	47.17	61.98	
ATTEND	0.20	0.02	0.22	7.95	0.00	0.15	0.24	0.21
EDUC	−0.49	0.22	−0.06	−2.23	0.03	−0.92	−0.06	−0.06
AGE	0.05	0.04	0.04	1.37	0.17	−0.02	0.12	0.04
FEMALE	−2.43	1.25	−0.05	−1.95	0.05	−4.88	0.01	−0.05
BLACK	−6.80	1.78	−0.10	−3.81	0.00	−10.30	−3.30	−0.10

[a] Dependent Variable: CONSERVATISM; CODES: Attend = 0–70 times a year; Educ = years of education; Age = coded in years; Female = 1; Male = 0; Black = 1; White = 0; Conservatism 0–100. 100 = most conservative.
$R^2 = 0.062$; F = 17.6; sig. = 0.000

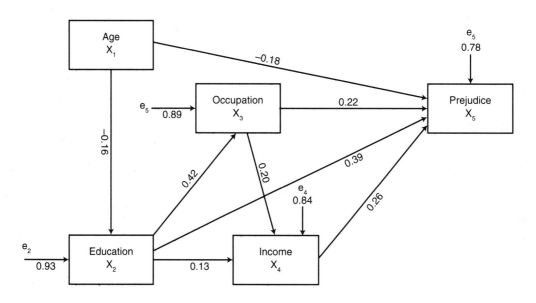

c Which variable has the greatest total effect on prejudice: education or age?

d How much variance in prejudice is explained by this path model?

e What is the single most important direct effect on prejudice?

5 Explain in your own words the differences between:

a multiple correlation and partial correlation;

b multiple correlation and multiple regression;

c partial correlation coefficients and partial regression coefficients;

d partial regression coefficients and beta coefficients;

e indirect effects and direct effects;

f path analysis and regression analysis.

6 Examine the following multiple regression equations (there is a separate one for men and women). The coefficients are not standardised.

WOMEN:

$$Y = 2.4 + 7.8X_1 + 11.2X_2 + 3.6X_3 + 0.04X_4$$
$$R^2 = 0.34$$

MEN:

$$Y = 4.3 + 3.5X_1 + 6.9X_2 + 2.5X_3 + 3.9X_4$$
$$R^2 = 0.46$$

a In which group does X_2 have the greatest independent effect: men or women?

b In which group are X_1, X_2, X_3 and X_4 together best at predicting Y?

c Among men, which variable is the best independent predictor of Y?

7 Explain the purpose and value of multivariate analysis.

8 What role does theory play in these complex multivariate statistical methods of analysis?

9 We initially have two variables: years of completed education (Y) and type of secondary school attended (X). Type of school attended has five categories: (1) government only, (2) Catholic only, (3) private (non-government and non-Catholic) only, (4) a combination of government and Catholic, and (5) a combination of government and private. To do regression analysis the type of schooling variable needs to be formed into a set of dummy variables. When this was done the following results were obtained:

Variable	b
Catholic education only (EdCATH)	1.01
Private school education only (EdPRIV)	1.61
Combination of government and Catholic schooling (EdGOVCAT)	1.61
Combination of government and private schooling (EdGOVPRV)	1.10
Constant	10.30

On the basis of these results answer the following questions:

a What is the omitted category?

b What is the average number of years of completed schooling of students who went only to government schools?

c Which type of schooling leads to the greatest number of years of completed education? Provide estimates for each type of schooling.

d On average, how many years do students who only attend Catholic schools complete?

10 If we add gender (coded 0 = male; 1 = female) to the above equation we obtain the following results:

Variable	b
EdCATH	1.04
EdPRIV	1.64
EdGOVCAT	1.60
EdGOVPRV	1.05
Gender	−0.46
Constant	10.06

a Given that all the variables are dummy or dichotomous variables what does the figure 10.06 for the constant represent?

b How many years of completed education would you estimate that males who attended Catholic schools only would have?

c Which groups of people would have more completed years of education than the above group?

d When the type of school attended is the same, who has the greatest number of years of completed schooling—males or females?

11 When age (coded in years) is added to the above equation, the following results are obtained:

Variable	b
EdCATH	0.97
EdPRIV	1.67
EdGOVCAT	1.32
EdGOVPRV	1.03
Gender	−0.44
Age	−0.04
Constant	11.70

a What does the figure 11.70 for the constant represent?

b Looking at the results for the above equation, which type of schooling results in the greatest number of years of completed schooling? How many years is that?

c Do older people tend to have more or less years of completed schooling than younger people when other things (gender and type of schooling) are taken into account?

d How many years of schooling would you predict the following would have?

  i 25-year-old male who exclusively attended a private school;

  ii a comparable female;

  iii a male who attended a combination of Catholic and government schooling;

  iv a male who attended only Catholic schools.

12 Using a standard multiple regression equation $Y = a + b_1(X_1) + b_2(X_2) + B3(X_3) + b_4(X_4)$ the following figures were obtained.

		BLACKS		WHITES	
Variable		b	Mean	b	Mean
X_1	FOCC	−196	39	−18.8	44
X_2	EDUC	1818	12.2	2664	13.3
X_3	ROCC	414	39	441	44
X_4	HOURS	270	40	639	42

Predicted variable: Dollars INCOME

a Estimate the average income of blacks and whites from these figures.

b What would be the predicted average income of blacks if they were 'rewarded' at the same rate as whites? How much worse off would whites be if they were 'rewarded' at the same rate as blacks.

18

Putting it into practice: a research example

As well as describing the various stages of research and techniques of data analysis it is helpful to see how these are applied. This chapter, which is based on a piece of research in which I was involved (de Vaus and McAllister, 1987), provides an example of various stages and decisions involved in the research process.

THE RESEARCH QUESTION

Throughout this book the importance of specifying the research question has been emphasised (see in particular Chapter 3). The study on which the example in this chapter is based arose out of the observation in the sociology of religion literature that on whatever measure you choose to look at, women seem to be more religious than men. While the *descriptive* data showing that women are typically more religious than men are available, no-one has tried to *explain* empirically why this is so (pp. 23–5). So our research question was: Why are women more religious than men? Does the gender difference have a sociological basis?

Having formulated the question the next step was to see what sorts of explanations other people had put forward in the literature (pp. 25–30). We were anxious to put our own research within a theoretical framework both so that the analysis would have direction and the results would have some significance for broader theoretical and sociological issues (refer to Chapter 2). We were able to detect some *ex post facto* explanations in the literature (pp. 12–13). These included explanations that emphasised the role of psychological processes and differences between men and women and those that interpreted the religious differences as the result of different sex role socialisation.

There were also hints of another type of sociological explanation. Rather than focusing on sex role socialisation, some people drew attention to the different roles and the different position occupied by men and women in society. We called this a *structural location* explanation. Reference to different aspects of structural location was detected in the literature: these included the different roles of men and women in *child rearing*, their different rates of *workforce participation* and different degrees of *focus on the family* among men and women. It is not possible here to go into the reasons why people suggested that these differences could account for religious differences between men and women. This is dealt with at some length in our original article.

But in essence the proposition was that if it was not for the fact that women have greater child-rearing responsibilities than men, are less likely to be involved in the workforce and have a greater family focus than men, then gender differences in religion would not exist. Presumably therefore, among men and women where these structural location differences are not evident there should be little evidence of gender differences in religious orientation.

Because of the data to which we had access (see below) we could not directly test the socialisation explanation, so we narrowed the focus of the research still further. We decided to concentrate on the extent to which structural location factors (child-rearing role, workforce participation and family focus) accounted for the greater religiousness of women. This process of progressively narrowing a research topic is typical in social research. We started with a broad topic but eventually narrowed down the topic to a defined and manageable question. The model that we ended up testing is represented diagrammatically in Figure 18.1.

HYPOTHESES

In order to test each of the three 'paths' in this model at least seven hypotheses can be developed:

1   The differences between the religious orientation of men and women will disappear once the effect of stage in the child-rearing cycle is removed.
2   Among men and women who have no children and those whose children are grown up there should be fewer religious differences than among men and women still in the active child-rearing stage.
3   Women in the workforce will be less religious than women out of the workforce.

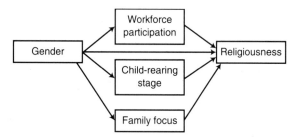

Figure 18.1   Theoretical model to test structural location theory

4   The religious orientation of women in the workforce will be more similar to males in the workforce than to females out of the workforce.
5   When the effects of gender differences in workforce participation are removed (controlled), gender differences in religious orientation will be reduced markedly.
6   Those who are focused more on the family than work will be more religious than those with less family focus.
7   When the effects of gender differences in family focus are removed, gender differences in religious orientation will be markedly reduced.

CLARIFYING AND OPERATIONALISING THE CONCEPTS

We were fortunate enough to have access to data from the 1983 Australian Values Study Survey (part of an international study conducted in over 25 countries worldwide) which provided a national probability sample for Australia (N = 1228) that had questions that enabled us to tap the main concepts required for this research. Rather than collecting our own data we were able to do a secondary analysis of these data (pp. 86–8). Had we been collecting the data we would have collected additional information and asked some of the questions differently but the advantages of a large, representative data set far outweighed these disadvantages.

The variables that were used in the study can be divided into three main groups: measures of the *dependent variable* (religion), measures of the *independent and intervening variables* (gender, workforce participation, stage in child-rearing cycle and family focus) and measures of *background variables* including age, country of birth, education, family income and occupation (p. 95).

Religion

Religion is a concept that can be divided into a number of dimensions. Glock and Stark (1965) have distinguished between public and private religious practice, belief, experience and knowledge. Others have added dimensions such as commitment and the salience of religion in people's lives. A number of questions regarding religion were included in the data set. On the basis of the distinctions made by others and on the basis of a correlation matrix of the various religious questions (pp. 187–8) we initially distinguished between four dimensions of religiousness and decided to look at gender differences on each of these dimensions. Other dimensions would have been included had the data been available but four dimensions were considered adequate for the purposes of the research. These were:

1 *Church attendance:* the question was 'Apart from weddings, funerals and baptisms, about how often do you attend religious services these days?'. The response categories were ordered in such a way that the variable was measured as a nine-category ordinal scale.

2 *Belief:* respondents were asked to indicate whether or not they believed in: a soul, devil, hell, heaven and sin. Each of the questions simply had yes/no answers.

3 *Commitment or salience:* two questions were used: 'How important is God in your life?' Respondents were asked where, on a scale of one to ten, they would place themselves. The second question asked 'Independently of whether you go to church or not, would you say you are a religious person, not a religious person, or a convinced atheist?'.

4 *Revelation or experience:* two questions were asked: 'Next, about being aware of, or influenced by, a presence or power, either God or something else—but different from your everyday self— have you been aware of such a presence or not?' and 'Have you ever felt as though you are very close to a powerful, spiritual force that seemed to lift you out of yourself?'. Both these questions were answered using an ordinal-based scale indicating the frequency with which they had such experiences.

Independent and intervening variables

A variable to measure stage in the child-rearing cycle was constructed from a number of variables in the data set. Using separate questions about marital status, number of members of the household, age of each child and whether or not the children had left home, we developed a composite variable using conditional transformations (pp. 169–70). This new variable consisted of four categories: single, married without children, married with children at home and married with all children having left home. Workforce participation was based on a single question which originally had nine categories. We collapsed it into five categories: working full-time, working part-time, unemployed, home duties and retired. Because of the small numbers involved we excluded students and those with some other employment status because their small numbers would create problems of statistical reliability (p. 164). Family focus was a scale constructed from four questions measuring the relationship between work and family values and was intended to reflect the degree of family focus. These questions asked how important it was to have a job that did not disrupt family life, did not interfere with the spouse's career, did not require having to move home and that the family thought was worthwhile. Each of these questions was answered with either a yes or a no answer. The composite variable had a range of 0 to 4 (consisting of four items each scored as either 0 or 1) with 4 indicating the highest level of family focus.

Background variables

To ensure that any observed effects of variables such as workforce participation were not contaminated by other background characteristics associated with workforce participation (e.g. age, living in cities, education etc) we introduced these variables so that their effect could be removed (controlled) in the analysis (pp. 297–9).

PREPARING THE VARIABLES FOR ANALYSIS

Having selected the variables we intended to use it was necessary to reduce the number of variables to a manageable number and to try to simplify the form in which they were presented so that the analysis and presentation of results could be simplified. The initial preparation of the independent and intervening variables was relatively straightforward and has been described above. It simply involved constructing composite variables or collapsing the categories of extant variables. Further modifications will be discussed shortly.

The preparation of the measures of religion involved a number of steps. Proper unidimensional scales were required to reduce the number of variables to be analysed (refer to Chapter 11): we had to ensure that the items in each scale belonged together, that each variable in each scale was scored in the same direction and we had to construct the scales so that the scoring or number of categories of one variable did not bias the overall scale. We also wanted to transform each scale so that they had the same upper and lower limits so that scores on each of the four dimensions of religiousness could be compared easily.

Producing the scales

The first task was to ensure that each item was *scored in the same direction* (pp. 168–9) both so that the scores on the scales could be compared and so that the items within each of the scales could be combined to form the scale in the first place. We first had to make a decision about what a high score was to mean (p. 168). We decided that all variables should be coded so that a high score indicated a religious response while a low score represented the less religious response. Because some of the selected items (the five belief questions and the religious person question) were originally coded so that a low code indicated a religious response, they had to be reverse coded.

The second step was to decide how to treat missing data (p. 176). Because missing data can lead to an unacceptable loss of cases, especially when constructing scales, we decided to substitute the mean of the variable for missing data. To do this we first had to obtain the mean of each variable and then recode the variable so that the missing data code was recoded to the mean. Thus, if the mean was 1.23 and missing data were coded as −1 then all people who had missing data on that variable would be recoded to have the valid code of 1.23 and would thus be included in the analysis. This approach to handling missing data is relatively straightforward and, because

it uses the mean, avoids biasing the results and eliminates problems caused by a loss of cases. It does however lead to a reduction in the size of correlation coefficients (p. 176).

The third step was to ensure that each of the items in the scale contributed equally to the final scale score. To adjust for variables with different numbers of categories, the scale scores were adjusted by dividing each person's score on each scale item by the standard deviation of that item (we obtained this when we calculated the mean of each item in the above step). In this way each item has an *equal weight* in the final scale (p. 192–3).

The fourth step was to see whether the now equally weighted items we had selected for each scale actually belonged together empirically. Was the scale *undimensional* and had the questions been answered *reliably*? We had earlier obtained a correlation matrix (p. 184) of all the religion variables, which gave us a rough idea that they would probably form a unidimensional scale: the items we had selected for the scales all correlated quite highly (0.45 or higher). But a reliability analysis is a more rigorous way of ensuring that each scale is unidimensional (item–total correlations). For each scale the alpha coefficient was well above 0.7 and no item–total correlation fell below 0.3 (see Table 18.1). Since the items met the criteria of a good scale we created a summated scale by simply adding together the already weighted scores for each item in the scale.

But since each of the scales had a different number of items, the final scores of each of the items varied considerably. The measure of church attendance ranged from 0.000 to 2.67, belief ranged from 8.53 (least religious) to 17.06 (most religious), commitment from 2.10 to 8.47 and revelation from 0.78 to 7.03. (The scores have these decimal places because the raw item scores in each scale have been

Table 18.1 Reliability statistics for the three religion scales

Belief		Commitment		Revelation	
Soul	0.57[a]	Importance of God	0.67	Experience 1	0.56
Devil	0.71	Religious person	0.67	Experience 2	0.56
Hell	0.72				
Heaven	0.67				
Sin	0.60				
Alpha	0.84		0.80		0.72

Note: [a] These are corrected item–total correlations. The total scale score against which they are correlated does not include the item in that total.

divided by the item's standard deviation.) To make scores on the scales comparable we decided to transform them so that each scale had a minimum of 0 (least religious) to 10 (most religious). This transformation was made using the formula described on p. 194 and resulted in four religion variables or scales ranging from 0 to 10.

Finally, because these scales potentially have many categories since there can be any number of possible scale scores between 0 and 10 (e.g. 5.54, 5.55 etc), it is desirable to have a collapsed version of the scale for cross-tabulation analysis (p. 247). Because the transformed scale was needed in its detailed form for interval-level analysis it was necessary to create collapsed versions of the scales in addition to the uncollapsed versions. To do this, frequency distributions of the transformed scales were obtained and, using the cumulative percentage column for each scale, the distribution of each scale was collapsed into thirds. Because the items had previously been recoded so that low scores indicated low levels of religiousness, the bottom third of each distribution was categorised as being non-religious, the middle third was moderately religious, the top third as being highly religious (pp. 165–6).

Preparing variables for regression analysis

Since we planned to use regression analysis we had to get variables in an appropriate form. This meant that all variables had to be either interval-level or dichotomous, but since most of our variables were not initially in this form we had to change their character. The workforce participation, family stage and family focus variables were each converted into sets of dummy variables. Workforce participation was a five-category variable (full-time, part-time, unemployed, home duties and retired). This variable can be represented by creating four dummy variables and omitting one category—full-time workers (pp. 328–30). Family stage was converted into three dummy variables with those who were single and childless being the omitted category, and family focus produced four dummy variables with the most focused being the omitted category.

The background variables also needed to be modified to make them appropriate for regression analysis. Country of birth and the occupation of the head of the household, which were measured at the nominal and ordinal level respectively, were recoded

to create two dichotomous variables coded 0 and 1. This necessarily led to a loss of information but was the simplest way of including these variables in the analysis. Education was originally measured in terms of the level achieved rather than as an interval level based on the number of years. One way of coping with this is to estimate the number of years of education that would normally be required to reach a certain highest level. Thus someone who had completed year 10 would normally have completed eleven years of schooling and thus their education code was recoded to reflect this. This can be done for each level of education, thus producing an approximation to an interval scale. A similar process can be applied to grouped numeric data. Family income was collected in income groups such as $0 to $1999, $2000 to $3999 and the like. To convert this to an interval scale in which income was coded in terms of thousands of dollars earned, the midpoint of each category can be used as an average of the income of people in that category. Thus the income category $2000 to $3999, that originally had a code of 2, was recoded to 3 to indicate that on average people in this category would earn $3000. Those in the income category of $15 000 to $19 999 would be recoded to a code of 17 to reflect an average income of $17 000. The selection of the midpoint of the category is based on the assumption that precise incomes of people in each category are evenly distributed through the category. The midpoint thus represents the average income of those in that category.

INITIAL ANALYSIS

The central aim of the project was to see if gender differences in religious orientation were open to a sociological explanation. The first step was to establish the extent to which there were gender differences in religion.

The first stage of most analyses is to obtain a picture of how the sample is distributed on each of the variables. Not only does this furnish a useful picture to guide the analysis, but it often provides crucial information that is required in later analyses. In this case these figures were helpful in part of the regression analyses. These results are summarised in Table 18.2.

The first decision to make was how to analyse the data to answer this question. The problem was

Table 18.2   Variables, definitions and means

Variable	Definition	Means Male	Female
Ascribed characteristics			
Age	Years	41.1	38.2
Australian born	1 = yes, 0 = no	0.77[a]	0.78
Lives in urban area	From a low of 0 to a high of 1.0	0.80	0.80
Socioeconomic status			
Education	Years	12.20	11.20
Head of household non-manual worker	1 = yes, 0 = no	0.44	0.41
Family income	$1000's	21.50	21.50
Life cycle stage			
Single		0.21	0.13
Married, no children		0.09	0.09
Married, children in home	1 = yes, 0 = no	0.45	0.58
Married, children not in home		0.25	0.20
Workforce participation			
Working, full-time		0.76	0.23
Working, part-time		0.03	0.22
Unemployed	1 = yes, 0 = no	0.05	0.04
Home duties		0.00	0.48
Retired		0.15	0.03
Family focus			
Very important		0.10	0.15
Fairly important		0.13	0.19
Indifferent	1 = yes, 0 = no	0.27	0.26
Fairly unimportant		0.31	0.27
Very unimportant		0.19	0.13

Note: [a] The figures in this table that are based on dichotomous variables (those coded 0 and 1) will be expressed in decimal points. These can be converted to the percentage of people in that category. Thus the figure of 0.77 for Australian-born males means that 77 per cent of the males in the sample were Australian born.

that only one of the four scales (belief) was, strictly speaking, an interval-level scale. Although the other scales had the appearance of being interval through the various transformations (and the transformations had assumed that they were measured at the interval level) they were in fact based on questions which were measured at only the ordinal level. Two points should be made at this stage. There is considerable disagreement about how scales such as these ought to be treated. While, strictly speaking, they are ordinal, the convention is to treat scales with many categories such as those in this study as being close enough to interval level to justify interval level statistics. While few people would be prepared to do this with single-item, Likert-style questions, the convention is that scales based on *summated* ordinal questions can safely be treated in this way. The reality is that in most cases the same patterns occur regardless of whether the

variable is treated as ordinal or interval (see Table 18.3). Given this, the argument is that interval-level analysis ought to be used since it opens up a whole range of more powerful and sophisticated techniques that allow us to control more readily for the effect of extraneous variables.

The data can be analysed in at least three different ways to see whether there are gender differences in religiousness.

Kendall's tau and Spearman's rho
On the assumption that the scales are ordinal, either Kendall's tau or Spearman's rho provide appropriate measures of correlation between religiousness and gender. They are appropriate because gender is a dichotomous variable and thus can be regarded as being at any level of measurement (p. 260), and the scales are at least ordinal level. Since gender is only

Table 18.3   Gender differences in religion using different methods of analysis

Method of analysis	Attendance	Belief	Commitment	Revelation
		Scale		
Kendall's tau[d]	0.10[a]**[c]	0.14	0.16**	0.12**
Spearman's rho[d]	0.11**	0.17**	0.18**	0.13**
Crosstabs[e]				
Male %[b]	26.3	26.0	23.2	20.8
Female %	35.3	35.8	38.1	30.0
Gamma	0.18**	0.25**	0.29**	0.23**
Comparing means[d]				
Male mean	3.2	5.2	6.2	1.8
Female mean	4.0	6.0	7.1	2.3
Difference (F–M)	0.8**	1.4**	0.9**	0.5**

Notes: [a] Positive coefficients mean women are more religious than men.

[b] % = Per cent high on scale

[c] ** significant at 0.001 level. Significance test of tau and rho are those designed for these measures, chi square is used for gamma, while F-tests are used for the comparison of means (pp. 277–8).

[d] Calculated using uncollapsed scales

[e] Based on trichotomised scales

dichotomous, Kendall's tau is probably more appropriate than Spearman's rho (p. 290), but the pattern of the results is the same regardless of which of the two coefficients is used (see Table 18.3): the statistically significant correlation means that gender differences exist on all the scales with women being more religious than men.

Cross-tabulations with gamma

While treating the scales of religiousness as ordinal, an alternative approach is to cross-tabulate the scales with gender and calculate gamma coefficients as measures of association (p. 258). Because cross-tabulation results become both unreliable and difficult to interpret if the variables have too many categories, it is necessary to collapse variables with too many values (p. 248). Accordingly, each of the scales was trichotomised as described earlier and yielded gamma coefficients that showed the same pattern of gender differences as described above (see Table 18.3).

Comparing means

If the scales are treated as interval-level variables it is appropriate to calculate the means of males and females on each other (pp. 272–6). When this was done (Table 18.3), the same pattern as described above occurred. In other words, regardless of which method was used, exactly the same pattern emerged:

women were consistently more religious than men. In all cases the differences were statistically significant: they are highly likely to reflect real patterns in the wider population from which the sample was drawn (pp. 276–7).

TESTING THE EXPLANATIONS

Since the above results show that there is something to explain we can proceed to the next stage of the analysis to test the hypotheses. Again we could adopt various methods, depending on the assumptions made about level of measurement. However, the same pattern of results was obtained regardless of whether we treated the scales as ordinal or interval.

Workforce participation: cross-tabulation analysis

One way of looking at the data was to treat the scales as ordinal and to do cross-tabulations of the collapsed scales by gender controlling for the effect of workforce participation. Zero- and first-order partial gammas were obtained (pp. 302–4, 304). According to our hypotheses, women who work will be less religious than those not in the workforce and women in the workforce will have levels of religiousness more similar to those of working men than of non-working women. Furthermore, when level of workforce participation is controlled, the gender differences in workforce participation should disappear or at least decline. That is, the zero-order correlation should be significant while the partial correlation will be statistically insignificant. Table 18.4 shows that each of these hypotheses is strongly supported.

That is, the relationship between gender and religion is virtually non-existent when level of workforce participation is controlled. On each of the scales there are significant zero-order relationships indicating that women are more religious than men. The partial gammas, from which the influence of different levels of workforce participation has been removed, show that without this effect there are next to no differences between the religiousness of men and women with comparable levels of workforce participation. This is reinforced by looking at the religiousness of men and women in the full-time workforce. There are almost no differences in the percentages of men and women who are highly religious: if anything, men are slightly more religious than women. The same picture emerges when we compare women who work full-time with those engaged in home duties full-time: working women are markedly less religious. All of these results support the three hypotheses relating to the effect of workforce participation on gender differences in the religiousness of people.

Workforce participation: multiple regression analysis

The difficulty with this cross-tabulation analysis is that we have not controlled for any other variables.

For example, we do not know whether the lower religiousness of working women relative to non-working women is because of differences in the age, education and social class profile of the two groups of women. We do not know whether the similarity of working women to men is because of the similarity of their age and education profiles. Ideally, if we are to assess the importance of variables such as workforce participation on gender differences, we should ensure that the comparisons made between the various groups of men and women are comparisons of men and women who are alike in all relevant respects (pp. 297–9).

It is very difficult to do this with cross-tabulation analysis. The more variables that are controlled at once, the more we confront problems with small sample sizes and statistical reliability. One way around this problem is to use analysis techniques that allow us to control for a whole set of background variables simultaneously without running into the problem of small sample sizes. Multiple regression is such a technique.

We therefore tested our hypotheses by using multiple regression. This enabled us to estimate the scores of people on each of the religious scales after the effects of other variables had been controlled. These scores are those we would expect if people were alike on all the variables that are controlled. Since our interest was in gender differences in religiousness, we did the analysis separately for men and women and then calculated the differences between the male and female estimates of religiosity under various controlled conditions.

Treating each of the scales as interval, our strategy was to estimate the mean score separately for

Table 18.4 Religious scales by gender controlling for workforce participation (cross-tabulation analysis)

Scale	Full-time		Home duties		Zero gamma	Partial gamma
	M	F	M	F		
	%	%	%	%		
Attendance	25[a]	21	100[c]	38	0.19**[b]	0.01
Belief	27	23	100	43	0.25**	0.05
Commitment	21	20	100	46*	0.29**	−0.02
Revelation	47	43	0	55*	−0.22**	−0.02

Notes: [a] These percentages represent the percentage *high* on these dimensions.

    [b] Positive gammas indicate that women on the whole were more religious than men.

    [c] Percentages in this column are based on an N of 1 and are therefore totally unreliable.

    ** Statistically significant at the 0.001 level

men and women according to their level of workforce participation whilst controlling for the background variables of age, whether Australian born (Aust), whether an urban resident (Urban), occupation of head of household (HHocc) and family income (Faminc). As previously described, a set of four dummy variables was created to reflect the five categories of workforce participation: part-time workers (WrkPT); the unemployed (WrkUEMP); those engaged full-time in home duties (WrkHD); and the retired (WrkRTD), with full-time workers being the omitted category.

This was done by using an equation of the following form:

Belief score = $a + b_1$(Age) + b_2(Aust)
   + b_3(Urban) + b_4(Educ) + b_5(HHocc) +
   b_6(Faminc) + b_7(WrkPT) + b_8(WrkUNEMP) +
   b_9(WrkHD) + b_{10}(WrkRTD)

Using the multiple regression procedure in SPSS we were able to calculate the unstandardised regression coefficients (b figures) for each variable (pp. 320–3). This procedure was run separately for men and for women, thus yielding separate b figures for men and women. Since the aim was to calculate the mean belief of men and women according to their level of workforce participation, we simply obtained the mean value for each of the variables (Age to Faminc) and multiplied the means by the b value of the appropriate variables. Using the mean of a group provides estimates for groups rather than individuals and is appropriate for a great deal of social science analysis (p. 323). Since workforce participation was broken down into a set of dummy variables and full-time workers were the excluded category (p. 328),

the mean belief score for full-time workers was obtained simply by summing the 'a' value with each of the 'b' values for each variable after they had been multiplied by the mean of the variable. For full-time workers the value of the other workforce participation variables necessarily was 0 (p. 328).

The estimate for those who worked part-time was obtained by giving the WrkPT variable the value of 1 and multiplying it by the b value for WrkPT and adding this figure to the estimate, gained for full-time workers (the omitted category). That is, the b value for WrkPT was simply added to the value obtained for full-time workers. This procedure is illustrated in Figure 18.2 and is worth working through carefully to understand how the regression estimates in the following tables were obtained. This procedure was repeated for each of the categories of workforce participation and for each of the scales. This provided us with separate estimates for men and women on each of the scales controlling for the relevant set of background variables. To see whether there were differences between the estimates for men and women in each of the workforce participation categories we simply subtracted the male estimate from the female estimate and obtained the values in Table 18.5. Positive values indicated that women had higher levels of religiousness.

Similar conclusions can be drawn from this table as from the cross-tabulation analysis. The bottom row (6) indicates the overall differences in the means of men and women regardless of their level of workforce participation. Thus on a 0 to 10 scale of church attendance there was a difference of 0.8 of a point in the average for males and females. The first row indicates the difference among men and women who

Figure 18.2   Calculating regression estimates for the belief scale

| Variable | Males | | Females | |
	b	Mean[d]	b	Mean
Age	−0.002[a]	41.1	−0.002	38.2
Aust'n	−0.287	0.77	−0.132	0.78
Urban	−0.373	0.80	0.37	0.80
Education	−0.073	12.1	−0.057	11.2
Occupation	0.357	0.44	0.12	0.41
Family income	−0.025	21.5	−0.02	21.5
Part-timers	0.31		0.71	
Unemployed	−0.59		0.80	
Home duties	*[c]		1.55	
Retired	−0.32		0.40	
	Constant (a) = 7.34		Constant (a) = 6.96	

Figure 18.2 *continued*

Equation for males
Belief score = 7.34 + −0.002(41.1) + −0.287(0.77) + −0.373(0.80) + −0.073(12.1) + 0.357(0.44) + −0.025(21.5) + 0.31(WrkPT) +
−0.59(WrkUNEMP) + 0.00(WrkHD) + −0.32(WrkRTD)
= 7.34 + −0.08 + −0.22 + −0.298 + −0.88 + 0.157 + −0.537 + 0.31(WrkPT) + −0.59(WrkUNEMP) + 0.00(WrkHD) +
−0.32(WrkRTD)

For male full-time workers (the omitted category) we estimate that:

Belief score = 7.34 + −0.002(41.1) + −0.287(0.77) + −0.373(0.80) + −0.073(12.1) + 0.357(0.44) + −0.025(21.5)
= 5.48

For the other categories of workforce participation we simply add the estimates for b coefficients for these groups to the estimate
obtained using the omitted category (full-time workers) and get the following:

Full-timers		= 5.48
Part-timers	5.48 + 0.31	= 5.79
Unemployed	5.48 + −0.59	= 4.89
Home duties	5.48 + 0.00	= 5.48
Retired	5.48 + −0.32	= 5.16

Equation for females
Belief score = 6.96 + −0.002(38.2) + −0.132(0.78) + 0.371(0.80) + −0.057(11.2) + 0.120(0.41) + −0.020(21.5) + 0.71(WrkPT) +
0.80(WrkUNEMP) + 1.55(WrkHD) + 0.58(WrkRTD)
= 6.96 + −0.076 + −0.103 + 0.297 + −0.638 + 0.049 + −0.43 + 0.71(WrkPT) + 0.80(WrkUNEMP) + 1.55(WrkHD) +
0.40(WrkRTD)

For female full-time workers (the omitted category) we estimate that:

Belief score = 6.96 + −0.002(38.2) + −0.132(0.78) + 0.371(0.80) + −0.057(11.2) + 0.120(0.41) + −0.020(21.5)
= 6.06

For the other categories of workforce participation we simply add the estimates for b coefficients for these groups and get the
following:

Full-timers		= 6.06
Part-timers	6.06 + 0.71	= 6.77
Unemployed	6.06 + 0.80	= 6.86
Home duties	6.06 + 1.55	= 7.61
Retired	6.06 + 0.40	= 6.46

To estimate the *differences* between the belief estimates of males and females in the various workforce participation categories we
simply subtract the male scores from the female scores.

	Female	Male	Difference
Full-timers	6.06	5.48	0.58
Part-timers	6.77	5.79	0.98
Unemployed	6.86	4.89	1.97
Home duties	7.61	5.79	*c
Retired	6.46	5.16	1.3

Notes: [a] The b values in this example are approximations only since at the time of writing I did not have access to the results from the weighted sample
that we used in our paper. They represent the *patterns* in the weighted sample but the precise figures are estimates only. They are used here
to illustrate the method of calculation rather than to provide precise figures.
[b] Since these workforce participation variables are dummy variables it is not their mean that is relevant for the calculation of regression
estimates. Instead the b coefficient would be multiplied by 1 to arrive at its contribution when we are trying to estimate the religious belief of
people in that category of workforce participation.
[c] Because of too few N it was not possible to calculate a figure for males involved in full-time home duties.
[d] These are the same as in Table 18.2.

work full-time. For each of the scales these values are very low and much lower than the overall men/women differences (see Table 18.3).

Another hypothesis developed to test the workforce participation argument was that women in the workforce will be less religious than those engaged in full-time home duties. Although the figures in Table 18.5 did not allow us to estimate this, the original regression estimates obtained from the analysis described above did. The means for women who worked full-time were lower on each of the scales than for women engaged in home duties. On all four scales, full-time female workers had an average score of 4.4 compared with 5.2 for those engaged in home duties—a difference of 0.8 points, which is much more than the average difference between men and women who worked full-time (0.2 points—see Table 18.5).

Stage in the family life cycle: multiple regression analysis

Because of the advantages of regression analysis and the fact that it yields a similar picture to the cross-tabulation analysis it is not necessary to report further results from the cross-tabulations.

To examine the stage in the family life cycle model we conducted a similar regression analysis to that described above. The only difference was that instead of using the four dummy variables for workforce participation we used three dummy variables for family stage with single people being the omitted category.

The results in Table 18.6 were obtained in this way. What they show is that stage in the family life cycle does not generally affect the extent of religious differences between men and women. The hypothesis that gender differences will be smaller among men and women who no longer have child-rearing responsibilities was not supported. The figures in row 3 represent those still rearing children and show that the gender differences are much the same for other people as for those whose children have left home. The extent of gender differences declines over the life course rather than being related to the presence or absence of children.

Table 18.5 Workforce participation and religious orientation: differences in regression estimates for men and women

Workforce participation		Church attendance	Belief	Scale Commitment	Revelation	(Mean)
Working full-time	(1)	−0.1	0.6	0.2	0.2	(0.2)
Working part-time	(2)	1.5	1.0	1.3	−0.5	(0.8)
Home duties	(3)	na	na	na	na	
Unemployed	(4)	1.2	2.0	1.8	1.2	(1.6)
Retired	(5)	−0.1	1.3	0.0	1.6	(0.7)
(Mean)	(6)	(0.8)	(1.4)	(0.9)	(0.5)	(0.9)

Notes: Positive values indicate that women are more religious than men.
All religious scales are scored 0 to 10.
The regression estimates were calculated by evaluating the regression estimates at the mean (see above).

Table 18.6 Stage in child-rearing cycle by religious orientation: differences in regression estimates for men and women

Family stage		Church attendance	Belief	Scale Commitment	Revelation	(Mean)
Single	(1)	1.5	2.0	0.8	0.8	(1.3)
Married, no children	(2)	0.6	1.2	0.3	0.9	(0.8)
Married, children in home	(3)	0.7	1.3	1.0	0.5	(0.9)
Married, children left home	(4)	0.1	0.6	0.5	−0.1	(0.3)
(Mean)	(5)	(0.8)	(0.9)	(0.9)	(0.5)	(0.8)

Family focus: multiple regression analysis

The same type of regression analysis was undertaken to examine the extent to which the different levels of family focus among men and women might account for their different levels of religiousness. Dummy variables were created for the family focus scale that had a range of 0 through 4. A comparison of the figures in Table 18.7 with those in Table 18.3, where no variables are controlled, shows a very similar pattern in both tables in relation to family focus. This means that the variables which have been controlled in Table 18.7 are not responsible for the gender differences observed in Table 18.3. The family focus hypothesis therefore was not supported.

So far our analysis, that was designed to test the extent to which gender differences in religious orientation are due to structural location factors, has shown that one structural location variable—workforce participation—is responsible for virtually all the gender differences. The other two were relatively unimportant.

Decomposing the gender gap

So far we have examined the initial (zero-order) gender gap and tested the extent to which each of the three structural location explanations, *on its own*, helps explain the gender differences. But each of these explanations is not entirely independent of the other. Workforce participation of women is tied to stage in the child-rearing cycle and the degree of family focus is linked to both workforce participation and child-rearing stage. To work out how important these factors are relative to each other (that is, independent of their joint relationship) it is desirable to look at the effect of each, controlling for the effect of the other variables. This also enables us to work out

which of the structural explanations has the greatest independent impact on religious orientation. We need a way of evaluating their relative importance.

In addition, the regression estimates in the three tables above do not provide us with one easy-to-interpret figure to estimate how much overall effect these variables have on gender differences. The zero-order and partial gammas reported earlier provided a simple way of comparing the uncontrolled relationship with that when the structural variables are controlled (p. 346). A similar thing can be accomplished with regression analysis. To do this we had to solve a *series* of regression equations. This was accomplished by obtaining a bivariate regression figure for the relationship between gender and a religious scale. This figure was the same as the difference between the mean for men and women on that scale (Table 18.3) and will not have the effects of any variables controlled.

Next the variables representing each of the *sets* of independent variables were entered into the regression equation in blocks. Thus all the ascribed characteristics (age, country of birth and urban residence) were entered as a block followed by the socioeconomic variables (education, occupation and family income). Then the set of dummy variables representing stage in the family life cycle were entered as a block followed by the labour force participation dummy variables and then the family focus variables. The order in which these blocks of variables were entered reflected our assumptions about causal order. We assumed that ascribed characteristics came before socioeconomic status, which precedes family stage which itself influences workforce participation and in turn affects the level of family focus.

This procedure can be illustrated with church attendance.

Table 18.7 Family focus and work by religious orientation: differences in regression estimates for men and women

Family focus		Church attendance	Belief	Scale Commitment	Revelation	(Mean)
Very unimportant	(1)	0.8	2.0	0.8	0.3	(1.0)
Fairly unimportant	(2)	0.9	1.1	0.8	0.5	(0.8)
Indifferent	(3)	0.6	0.9	0.2	0.0	(0.4)
Fairly important	(4)	0.8	1.4	0.9	0.4	(0.9)
Very important	(5)	0.4	1.8	0.8	0.5	(0.9)
(Mean)	(6)	(0.8)	(0.9)	(1.3)	(0.2)	(0.8)

Equation 1

The first regression equation involved only the gender and church attendance variables and produced a 'b' figure of 0.8 which represents 0.8 points on the 0 to 10 scale of church attendance. The value of 0.8 is the unstandardised regression coefficient for the zero-order relationship between gender and church attendance. Since gender was coded 0 for men and 1 for women, a positive value indicates that women are more regular attenders than men.

Equation 2

In the second equation we forced in the block of variables designed to measure ascribed characteristics. To ascertain the extent to which the original value of 0.8 was due to the effect of the ascribed characteristics we simply compared the 'b' coefficient for gender in the first equation with the 'b' coefficient for gender in the second. Any difference between the two represents the extent to which the original 'b' coefficient of 0.8 was due to the effect of ascribed characteristics. In this case the value of b for gender in the second equation was 0.8—exactly the same as in the first equation when the effects of ascribed characteristics were not included. This means that none of the original, overall relationship was due to differences in the ascribed characteristics of men and women in the sample. This is indicated by the value of 0 in column 1 row 4a of Table 18.8.

Equation 3

In this equation we added the block of variables designed to measure socioeconomic status in addition to those already entered in equations 1 and 2. We compared the 'b' coefficient for gender with that obtained in equation 2. Any change represents the effect of socioeconomic status on the original relationship between gender and church attendance with the effects of ascribed characteristics removed. In this case the 'b' value for gender was 0.9 which yields a difference value of −0.1 (0.8 − 0.9) as indicated in column 1 of Table 18.8. That is, if it were not for socioeconomic status differences between men and women in the sample, the initial gender difference would have been slightly greater.

Equation 4

Next we added the dummy variables for stage in the family life cycle to those added in the previous equation. Again the focus is on the b value for gender and how it changes from the previous value. In this case the b value for gender was 0.8, indicating that the effect of life-cycle stage to the overall relationship was only 0.1 points (0.9 from equation 3; 0.8 from equation 4).

Equation 5

Here we added the dummy variables for workforce participation as a block. Adding workforce participation variables to the explanation results in a drop from the previous 0.8 points difference (equation 4) to 0.3. This means that if it was not for the gender differences in workforce participation the original gender differences would have been only 0.3 points. Overall 0.5 of the gender difference remaining after equation 4 was due to gender differences in workforce participation (0.8 from equation 4; 0.3 from equation 5 = 0.5).

Equation 6

Finally we added the variables for family focus and found that the b value of 0.3 for gender was the same

Table 18.8   Decomposing the gender gap in religious orientation

		Church attendance	Belief	Commitment	Revelation
1	Total effect (lines 2 + 3)	0.8	1.4	0.9	0.5
2	Direct effect (lines 1 − 3)	0.3	0.7	0.4	0.1
3	Indirect effect (lines				
	4(a) + 4(b) + 4(c) + 4(d) + 4(e))	0.5	0.7	0.5	0.4
	(a) Ascribed characteristics	0.0	0.0	−0.1	0.0
	(b) Socioeconomic status	−0.1	−0.1	0.0	0.0
	(c) Life stage	0.1	0.1	0.1	0.0
	(d) Workforce participation	0.5	0.6	0.5	0.4
	(e) Family focus	0.0	0.1	0.0	0.0

as in the previous equation, indicating that once other variables were controlled, different levels of family focus did not contribute anything to the overall gender differences.

This procedure enabled us to work out how much the overall gender difference in church attendance is due to various sets of factors and how much remained after these effects were removed. The logic is akin to comparing zero-order correlations with first-, second- and third-order partial coefficients and interpreting the drop in the coefficient as being due to the effect of the variable that is being controlled. The remaining relationship is seen to be due to the direct effects of the original two variables (pp. 300–2). Using this procedure we can calculate how much of the original (total) effect is due to the influence of the control variables (indirect effect) and how much remains (direct effect).

The step-by-step procedure also enables us to work out how much of the indirect effect is due to the influence of the various control variables. All that we have to do is to compare the size of the co-efficients. The meanings of the terms total, direct and indirect effect are outlined on pp. 330–3 in the discussion of path analysis, although the method of arriving at the figures is different from the method described here.

In this case we can see that the bulk of the original total effect of gender on church attendance is indirect. Of the indirect effect, by far the most important factor was gender differences in workforce participation. Other variables had virtually no effect on the gender difference in church attendance.

Exactly the same sort of analysis was conducted for each of the other indices of religion. Since each of the scales had been converted to a scale ranging from 0 to 10 we were able to compare the effects of gender on each of the scales even though unstandardised coefficients were used. These results are presented in Table 18.8. For each of the four dimensions of religiousness at least half of the original gender gap disappeared once the effects of these structural location variables were removed (compare line 1 with line 2). On each of the scales workforce participation was responsible for the bulk of the initial effect (line 3d), while the other variables had virtually no effect.

DISCUSSION

There were many other things that we could have looked at. We could have conducted further analyses to locate the groups among which gender differences in religion are greatest (e.g. among which age groups, which denominations and so forth) but such analysis would have diverted us from our main goal. The analysis outlined above was directed to answering specific questions.

Once the results have been analysed and described it is useful to do a number of things.

Summarise relevant results

Having obtained results that bear directly on the original hypotheses it is valuable to briefly summarise the main findings insofar as they relate to hypotheses and theory. In this case three main points could be made.

1 Gender differences in religiousness exist across at least four dimensions of religious orientation.
2 A large amount of these differences can be accounted for in terms of gender differences in structural location.
3 Of the three structural location factors examined, only one was important—gender differences in levels of workforce participation. If it was not for the fact that women are less likely than men to be in the full-time workforce, then religious differences would be either non-existent or much less pronounced than they currently are.

Ex post facto *explanations for further examination*

The results will not always be quite what were anticipated. Some might be in accord with expectations while others might be more surprising. It is useful to suggest possible explanations for the observed patterns. In this case we have identified that workforce participation is an important explanatory variable, but it is not clear precisely *why* this is so. Some possible explanations might be offered that could be pursued in further research using appropriately collected data. It is possible that working *displaces* the need for religion: that it provides activities, interests, friendships, meaning and identity that some people otherwise might gain from religion. The greater religious similarity of working men and women might be due to *conformity* pressures in the workplace that reduce the religion of women to that of men. Alternatively the greater religiousness of women out of the workforce might be due to a greater sense of *deprivation* among those not participating in an activity that is valued by society thus encouraging a religious response as a way of relieving this feeling. Whatever the explanation might be, it is worthwhile speculating about some possibilities that other people might pursue in the future.

Implications

The results can have both theoretical and practical implications and these are worth spelling out briefly in the discussion section of a report.

In this case the results have implications for important sociological questions and *theories* in areas such as value formation, attitude change, gender differences and for secularisation theories. These should be spelt out in the final part of the paper.

Results can also have important *policy implications* and careful thought should be given to these. These results should be of direct relevance to church policy makers. Because of the increasing involvement of women in the workforce, the church can anticipate a decline of women in the church.

Finally, suggestions for *future research* that flow from the current research are always desirable. Is the basis of gender differences in religion applicable to other gender-based value differences (e.g. does it also account for political differences, differences in attitudes to war, sexual morality and the like)? Suggestions for more detailed research with a different design may be warranted. A longitudinal study of women who return to the workforce might help clarify whether it is workforce participation that actually produces religious change and, if so, clarify the processes and reasons. Suggestions for future research with a different research design, alternative data collection techniques and different types of sample are often appropriate.

SUMMARY

In this chapter I have shown how we have moved from a broad research topic to a much narrower and more manageable question that has been placed within a theoretical context. The concepts have been operationalised within the limits imposed by the available data. The number of variables have been reduced by creating reliable, undimensional, equal-weight scales all ranging from 0 through 10 to enable easy comparison across scales. Variables were modified by recoding, combining information from various questions and creating dummy variables to facilitate the later analysis.

A range of analysis techniques were employed. The first step was to obtain the distribution and summary statistics on all the final variables. A range of methods of bivariate analysis were employed on the basis of different assumptions about the level of measurement of the variables but all showed exactly the same pattern in the data. The same was done with the initial multivariate analysis in which the influence of other key variables was controlled. This showed that, regardless of the assumptions about whether the indices of religion were ordinal or interval, the same substantive patterns emerged. Because of this we felt confident in treating the scales as being appropriate for interval-level analysis and employed a variety of more complex multiple regression procedures.

The final point to make is that these more complex methods, while very helpful in helping us draw firmer conclusions because they enable us to control for the effects of many variables simultaneously, and to easily decompose the zero-order relationship into its component parts, are not indispensable. Analysis can be undertaken at many different levels. In this case similar substantive conclusions would have been drawn had we only done the first-order cross-tabulation analysis. The more complex procedures improve the analysis and our confidence in the final results and can help eliminate alternative explanations of the initial results. The aim should be to try to learn to use these more powerful methods. But in the meantime a lot can be accomplished with simpler methods and careful, systematic thinking.

EXERCISES

1 Explain what the figures in the two right-hand columns of Table 18.1 mean.

2 Based on Table 18.2, what percentage of women in the sample worked full-time?

3 Put each of the figures in column 1 of Table 18.3 into words.

4 What do the partial gammas in Table 18.4 tell you? Why are they not sufficient on their own to evaluate the extent to which workforce participation accounts for the relationship between gender and religiousness?

5 The figures below represent the regression estimates for church attendance for females using the same data and variables as used in Figure 18.2. Remember that church attendance has been converted to a score on a 0 to 10 scale and that the workforce participation variables are dummy variables.

Variable	b
Age	0.05
Australian	−0.79
Urban	−0.53
Education	0.18
Occupation	0.75
Family income	−0.02
Part-timers	1.63
Unemployed	1.25
Home duties	1.25
Retired	0.70
Constant	1.25

a Using the regression equation on p. 347 estimate the church attendance score for females in each of the five workforce participation categories.

b Explain, in simple English, what the coefficient 1.63 for part-timers means.

c Explain, in simple English, the meaning of the figure 1.25 for the constant.

6 Explain as clearly as you can why the figures in Table 18.6 mean that the greater overall religiousness of women is not due to their child-rearing responsibilities.

7 Examine Table 18.8 and answer the following questions:

a What does the figure 1.4 in the belief column represent?

b What does the figure 0.7 (direct effect) in the belief column mean?

c What does the figure 0.7 (indirect effect) in the belief column mean?

d Explain how the figures in the belief column support the view that workforce participation is the most important single reason for gender differences in religious belief.

Glossary

acquiescent response set: the tendency of some respondents to automatically agree with 'agree/disagree' questionnaire statements.

adjusted Cronbach's alpha: Cronbach's alpha if a particular item was omitted from the scale. Provides clues as to which items should be omitted from a scale.

adjusting for missing items: the procedure by which scale scores are adjusted to compensate for questions that a respondent has not answered. The adjustment is required to make the scores of respondents who have missed answering some questions comparable with those who have answered all questions.

adjusting scale length: the adjustment made to convert the lower and upper limits created by simply summing the scores of items to a lower and upper limit fixed by the data analyst. This adjustment is useful when comparing scales that would otherwise have different lower and upper limits.

arithmetic transformation: creating a new variable by performing an arithmetic operation on the values of one or more variables.

association: see correlation

asymmetric coefficient: a coefficient that takes on different values depending on which variable is regarded as the dependent variable. Examples are regression coefficients, and eta.

attitudes: what a person regards as desirable.

availability sample: a form of non-probability sampling in which the sample units are selected simply because they are available.

average: a general term that refers to statistics (mode, median and the mean) measuring central tendency or typicality. The choice of which average to use depends on the variable's level of measurement and distribution.

balanced response categories: a set of responses to a forced choice question in which the number of 'pro' responses is the same as the number of 'anti' responses.

ballot box stuffing: the practice in surveys where some respondents respond multiple times thus biasing responses. This is a particular problem in surveys such as some web surveys where no controls are established to monitor or control the number of responses from individuals.

beliefs: what a person regards as being true.

beta coefficient: a standardised regression coefficient that represents how many standard deviation units the dependent variable changes for each standard deviation unit change of the independent variable.

bias: where error tends to go in one direction more than another.

binary choice: a question in which a respondent is presented with only two alternative responses.

binomial test: a test of statistical significance of a single variable with just two categories. The test compares the sample distribution between the two categories and tests the null hypothesis that the sample split does not deviate from a 50/50 split or some other pre-specified split.

bivariate analysis: a general category of analysis in which two variables are analysed simultaneously in order to examine the relationship between the two variables.

branching: the technique in questionnaires where respondents are directed to go to particular modules or skip a set of questions depending on their response to a filtering or branching question.

CAPI: computer-assisted personal interviewing. This method of administering a questionnaire involves an interviewer conducting a face-to-face interview using a questionnaire that has been pre-programmed into a computer. Such packages usually build in skips, branching, automatic coding and the like.

case: the 'unit of analysis' about which information is collected. A survey must consist of at least two and normally far more cases. Cases are represented by rows in the variable by case data grid.

CASI: computer-assisted self interviewing. The method whereby a respondent is given access to a computer on which a questionnaire is programmed. The respondent self-administers the questionnaire. CASI is the electronic equivalent of the self-administered paper and pencil questionnaire.

CATI: computer-assisted telephone interviewing. This method of administering a questionnaire involves an interviewer conducting an interview over the telephone using a questionnaire that has been pre-programmed into a computer. Such packages usually build in skips, branching, automatic coding and the like and have smart sample tracking and call queuing systems.

census: the collection of data from *all* the population elements rather than from a subset (a sample).

central tendency measures: see average.

checklist format: a questionnaire item in which a respondent can select a number of the alternative responses. Normally each possible response is a binary choice. For analysis purposes each response is a separate binary variable.

closed question/forced choice question: a question format where all the responses are provided to the respondent who is asked simply to select or rank one or more of the alternatives.

cluster sampling: a form of probability sampling in which sample elements are concentrated in selected geographic areas (e.g. census collectors' districts, city blocks).

codebook: a listing of the contents of a data file that identifies the characteristics of each variable. It contains the variable's column location, name, codes, labels, the form of the data (e.g. numeric or alphanumeric) and its frequency distribution.

coding: the symbols used to represent categories of a variable (e.g. 1 = male; 2 = female). Although these symbols are usually numeric (numbers), alphanumeric (letters) characters may be used.

column percentage: the percentage in a cross-tabulation in which the cell frequency is converted to a percentage based on the number of cases in the column.

communality: a statistic used in exploratory factor analysis. It indicates the amount of variance in a variable that is explained by a combination of the extracted factors. It is obtained by squaring and summing the correlations between the factors and the variable. Communalities range from 0 to 1.

computer-assisted interviewing: (CAI) The use of computers to assist in conducting interviews. The most common form of CAI is to use pre-programmed questionnaires and administering the questionnaire either personally (CAPI), over the telephone (CATI) or allowing the respondent to self-administer the questionnaire (CASI). Self-administration may be conducted in a variety of ways including via email or the internet.

computer column: the location of the codes of a variable on a record in a data set. Each column can accommodate only one digit. Double digit codes (10–99) require two columns, three digit codes (100–999) require three columns and so forth. Knowing the column in which a variable is located on a record can be crucial in writing programs to analyse survey data. Computer columns are usually indicated in a codebook.

concept: general and abstract notion that is not directly measurable or observable. Concepts are the building blocks of theories but need to be operationalised before being used in empirical research.

conceptual proposition: a statement of a relationship between two concepts. Conceptual propositions may be *causal* (religiousness produces conservatism) or *non-causal* (religiousness is related to conservatism). They may be *directional* (the greater the religiousness the greater the conservatism) or *non-directional* (religiousness is related to conservatism).

conditional relationships: a relationship between two variables that varies depending on the presence of other conditions. For example, if the relationship between education and income is stronger among males than among females the relationship between education and income is conditional because it depends on a third factor (gender). This is also known as statistical interaction.

conditional table: a cross-tabulation between two variables within a category of a third variable. A separate conditional table of a relationship between two variables will be produced for each of the categories of a third (control) variable.

conditional transformation: creating a new variable in which the categories are based on the combination of particular conditions of two or more other variables. They take the general form: IF (VARA = n and VARB = n) then VARC = n.

confidence interval: the range of values between which the population parameter is estimated to lie. The confidence interval should be used in conjunction with the *confidence level*.

confidence level: indicates how *likely* it is that the population parameter will lie within the range specified by the confidence interval.

confidentialising data: the process by which data are altered so that no individual in the data set can be recognised. This is achieved in a variety of ways including reducing the level of detail in the variables in the data set. Confidentialising is required to meet the ethical requirements of confidentiality.

confidentiality: ensuring that no survey respondent will be identifiable. Confidentiality differs from anonymity in that in a confidential survey the researcher may know the identity of individual respondents but guarantees that no-one else will know the individual's responses or their identity. In an anonymous survey no-one knows the identity of respondents.

constant: in regression analysis the constant is the predicted value on the dependent variable when all other variables in the equation have the value of zero. It is the point at which the regression line crosses the Y-axis.

construct validity: the evaluation of the validity of a measure by comparing results using that measure with the results expected on the basis of theory. If the results do not conform to the theory it is usually assumed that the measure rather than the theory is at fault.

content validity: the assessment of validity based on whether the measure of the concept covers the concept's full meaning (e.g. does a test of mathematical skills cover the full range of mathematical operations?).

contingency question: a question which is asked of only some respondents depending on their answers to previous filter questions.

control variable: a variable, often called the Z variable or the test variable, that is held constant when exploring the nature of the relationship between other variables. By holding a variable constant we can ascertain the extent to which the control variable is responsible for the initial relationship.

controls/controlling: the process of removing the effect of control variables from the relationship between other variables.

correlation: co-variation of variables. Where values of one variable differ systematically by values of another variable, the variables are correlated or associated. Correlation does not prove causation.

correlation coefficient: an index of the extent to which two variables co-vary within the same sample (e.g. are differences in income linked to educational differences?). There are many different correlation coefficients (e.g. gamma, Pearson's r, Spearman's rho) and most range between 0 (the two variables do not co-vary) and 1 (the variables always vary together). Coefficients may have negative values.

correlation matrix: a grid in which each column and each row represents a variable. The intersection of each column and row contains a correlation coefficient of the column and row variables.

Cramer's V: a chi-square based correlation coefficient for nominal variables where at least one variable has more than two categories.

criterion validity: the evaluation of validity by comparing results based on new measures of a concept with those using established measures.

Cronbach's alpha: a measure of internal reliability used in the evaluation of Likert scales.

cross-sectional design: a study in which all observations are made at a single point of time. See also longitudinal design.

cross-tabulation: a table consisting of rows and columns. The columns represent the categories of one variable while the rows represent the categories of another variable. The intersection of a column and a row produces a cell which represents cases having the attributes of *both* that column and that row.

cumulative per cent: in a frequency distribution the cumulative percentage is the 'rolling' addition of the per cent of cases in each category of the variable. The first cumulative percentage will be the percentage of cases in the first category, the next cumulative percentage represents the percentage of cases in the first *and* second category and so forth. This percentage is usually based on the adjusted percentage and will sum to 100 per cent.

curvilinear relationship: a non-linear relationship. With two variables this may take the form of a U, an inverted U relationship or some other pattern where a straight line cannot adequately represent the nature of the relationship.

DBM: disk-by-mail is a form of CASI survey. It is a questionnaire administration method where a respondent is sent an electronic questionnaire in the form of a self-extracting file to complete on a computer. The file normally has the features of a CATI or CAPI survey with skips, automatic coding and a variety of audio and visual stimuli.

dead giveaway: a questionnaire item in which the extreme wording is such that the question will result in very little variation in responses.

decile: the nine levels that subdivide a frequency distribution into ten equal parts. Each decile contains 10 per cent of the cases of the distribution.

declared pre-test: a pilot test in which respondents are informed that the survey is a pilot test designed to evaluate the instrument. Respondent comments on questions are often invited.

deductive reasoning: the process whereby specific expectations or hypotheses are logically derived from more general principles.

dependent variable: the variable, frequently referred to as the Y variable, that is assumed to be the effect in a 'cause-effect' relationship.

descending the ladder of abstraction: abstract concepts require precise, concrete indicators before they can be measured in a survey. The steps in moving from the abstract to the concrete measures is called the *ladder of abstraction*.

descriptive statistic: statistics that summarise the characteristics of a sample as opposed to inferential statistics that are used to generalise to the population from which the sample is drawn.

dichotomise: to divide a distribution (sample) into two equal-sized groups.

dichotomous variables: a variable having only two categories.

directory listing sampling: using a directory (e.g. telephone directory, electoral roll, membership list etc) as a sampling frame.

distribution based recoding: recoding a distribution into equal-sized groups.

double-barrelled question: a single question that effectively asks two questions at once.

dummy regression: a form of regression where nominal variables are able to be used by transforming them into a *set* of dichotomous (dummy) variables which are appropriate for regression analysis.

dummy variable: a dummy variable is a dichotomous variable coded 1 to indicate the presence of a characteristic and 0 to indicate the absence of a characteristic. Used in regression where a non-interval-level variable has more than two categories.

dynamic questionnaire: a questionnaire in which the pathway through the questionnaire and the particular questions asked take into account the responses provided by the respondent earlier in the questionnaire. Computer-based questionnaires can build complex dynamic questionnaires that effectively tailor-build the questionnaire 'on the fly'.

eigenvalue: the eigenvalue is a statistic obtained in factor analysis and is a measure that attaches to factors. It indicates the amount of variance in the pool of original variables that the factor explains. The higher this value, the more variance the factor explains. To be retained, factors must have an eigenvalue greater than 1.

elaboration analysis: the analysis technique by which the nature of a bivariate relationship is explored by the introduction of control variables.

email survey: a survey in which questionnaires are distributed and returned via email. These can vary in sophistication from simple text-based questionnaires to HTML questionnaires and self-executing CASI questionnaires. A range of software packages are available to assist in the development, collection, coding and analysis of email surveys.

equal weight scales: a scale in which each item has the potential to contribute equally to scale scores. Each item will either have the same number of categories and distributions or will be adjusted to achieve comparability between items.

eta: a PRE-based measure of correlation that measures the strength of the relationship between an interval-level dependent variable and a nominal or ordinal independent variable. Ranging from 0 to 1 eta is an asymmetrical coefficient that is sensitive to non-linear relationships.

***ex post facto* theories:** a theory developed after data have been analysed to explain the patterns in the data. *Ex post facto* theories are usually consistent with the data but often are simply plausible rather than compelling since more than one *ex post facto* explanation is often consistent with the data.

exclusiveness: a characteristic of question response categories. For a question to represent a single variable no categories should be overlapping. One and only one response should be applicable to each respondent.

exhaustiveness: a characteristic of question response categories that requires that a response category is provided for all possible responses.

explained variance: the amount of variance in an interval-level dependent variable that is explained by one or more independent variables. The percentage of variance explained is summarised by PRE-based correlation coefficients such as eta^2, r^2 and R^2.

explanation: the attempt to account for variation in a dependent variable.

extraneous variable: the explanatory variable where a bivariate relationship is spurious. An extraneous variable will operate where two variables (X and Y) co-vary, not because they are causally related but because they are both outcomes of a third (extraneous) variable.

extremity of attitudes: refers to how far from the norm a particular attitude is. Extremity of an attitude should be distinguished from the intensity with which an attitude may be held.

factor: the (unmeasured) higher level variable that is thought to underlie a set of specific attitudes. Exploratory factor analysis seeks to identify such higher level variables or factors by examining patterned ways in which sets of items are answered. It is assumed that the underlying factor is causing the inter-correlations between a set of (related) attitude responses.

factor analysis: analysis that detects the more general dimensions (factors) underlying responses to a set of questions. It helps detect the structure of attitudes, reduces data and assists in scale development.

factor-based scales: scales in which the items are selected by factor analysing a set of items. The factor analysis identifies which items are suitable for the development of a unidimensional scale.

factor loading: a coefficient that indicates the extent to which a particular variable 'belongs' to an underlying factor. The higher the loading the more the variable is thought to belong to the factor.

factor scale: scales based on scores generated by factor analysis.

filter check: a method of checking and cleaning data. Where filter questions are used some respondents should not have answered particular questions. A filter check involves analysing the data to ensure that only eligible respondents have answered particular questions.

filter question: a question designed to divide respondents into those who need to answer a subsequent contingency question and those who should skip to a later question.

first-order coefficient: the correlation between the X and Y variable with the effect of one control variable removed.

frequency distribution: the display of the number of sample elements that belong to each category of a variable.

frequency table: a table in univariate analysis in which the number and percentage of cases in each category of the variable is displayed.

F-test: a statistical test for testing the null hypothesis of no difference between the mean of three or more groups.

Goodman and Kruskal's tau: an asymmetric PRE-based correlation coefficient for two nominal variables.

gratuitous qualifier: the use of a qualifier in a questionnaire item that effectively presents an argument for a particular response.

group means substitution: substituting missing values on a variable with the mean of the valid cases of that variable. Rather than using the mean for the whole sample the mean of a subgroup to which the respondent belongs (e.g. male and female) will be used.

harmonisation: the development of standardised questions to be used across different surveys.

HTML: Hypertext Markup Language. The formatting language used to create web pages. The language enables a range of formatting and dynamic features on web pages and web-based questionnaires.

hypothesis: a statement, logically derived from a theory, that states what one expects to find in the real world if the theory is correct.

idiographic: explanations that focus on a particular case and that seek to develop a complete understanding of the case.

imputation: the process of creating values for a case based on other information derived either from the case or from other cases in the data set.

inclusiveness: see exhaustiveness.

independent variable: frequently referred to as the X variable, it is the assumed *cause* in a 'cause-effect' relationship.

indicator: specific measure of a more abstract concept.

indirect relationship: a causal relationship between two variables that is mediated via a third, intervening variable.

inductive reasoning: the process, used in theory construction, whereby one uses specific observations to draw general conclusions consistent with the particular observations.

inferential statistics: a class of statistics which enables one to estimate whether sample results are likely to hold in the population. They can only be used with probability samples (see significance tests).

informed consent: the ethical requirement of research with human subjects that requires that a research participant's agreement to participate in the research is based on an accurate understanding of what the participation involves.

intensity of attitudes: the strength with which an attitude is held. Should be distinguished from the extremity of an attitude.

interaction: a statistical term to refer to data in which at least part of the effect of a variable is conditional on the presence of other characteristics.

intercept: the point at which the regression line crosses the Y-axis. The value of the Y variable in regression analysis when X = 0. See also constant.

internet server: a computer on the internet that gives other internet users access to material contained on the server. The server can also receive and store information from other internet users. A server is normally used to distribute internet surveys, dynamically administer the survey and receive responses from participants.

interquartile range: the range of values of a variable within which the middle 50 per cent of a distribution lies.

interval estimate: the range of values within which the population value is estimated to lie from the sample value. The interval estimate is calculated using the standard error of a distribution and will vary depending on the confidence level at which the estimate is required.

interval-level variable: a variable where the rank-ordered categories are separated by numerically equal distances.

intervening variable: see indirect relationship.

item-scale (item-total) correlation: the correlation between a scale item and the sum of all the scale items. This is often corrected by removing the particular item from the calculation of the sum of the scale. When developing Likert scales the item-scale correlations provide an indication of unidimensionality of the scale and each item should have a coefficient above 0.3.

Kendall's tau: a correlation coefficient for ranked ordinal data.

kurtosis: the extent to which the distribution of an interval-level variable is flat or peaked compared to a normal distribution.

leading question: a question in which the wording is likely to incline the respondent to give a particular response.

level of measurement: a characteristic of variables that fundamentally affects the type of analysis that can be applied to the variable. The level of measurement is determined by the nature of the categories of the variable and the relationship they have to each other. See also nominal-level variable, ordinal-level variable and interval-level variable.

Likert scale: a scaling method developed by Renis Likert which typically uses attitude statements using the standardised 'strongly agree, agree, disagree, and strongly disagree' format. Before individual items are formed into a scale, the scale must meet statistical requirements of reliability and unidimensionality.

linear relationship: a relationship between two ordinal or interval variables in which a change in one variable is related to a change in the other variable in a consistent direction. As one variable increases, the other increases or decreases at a consistent rate.

listwise deletion: a method of handling cases in analysis in which some variables have missing values. Listwise deletion involves dropping from the analysis any case that has missing values on any of the variables involved in the analysis. In multivariate analysis or the production of a correlation matrix listwise deletion results in a cumulative loss of cases. See also pairwise deletion.

logic checking: a method of cleaning data based on identifying illogical combinations or inconsistencies between answers to particular questions.

longitudinal design: a study in which data are collected from the same cases at two or more points of time.

marginals: in a cross-tabulation the marginals are the number or percentage of cases in a particular row or column. They are the equivalent of the figures obtained in a simple frequency distribution of a variable.

mean: an average for interval-level data that is computed by adding the values for all cases and dividing by the number of cases.

means substitution: substituting missing values on a variable with the mean of the valid cases of the whole sample of that variable. See also imputation.

measure of association: see correlation coefficient.

measure of dispersion: a class of statistic that indicates the extent to which cases in a sample differ from one another.

measurement error: error in accurately measuring a person's true value on a given variable.

median: an average, appropriate for ordinal or interval data where the median is the value of the middle case in a ranked set of cases.

missing cases values: where a case does not have a valid value on a particular variable the case is called a missing case (for that variable). Alternative terms are missing values or missing data.

missing data bias: where particular types of people or people with a particular type of true value on the variable do not respond to a question this may bias the overall pattern of responses and distort the analysis.

mode: an average, mainly used for nominal level variables, that reflects the most frequently observed value of a variable.

mode effect: the effect on responses produced by the particular method of questionnaire administration (e.g. face-to-face, telephone, internet, postal etc) or data collection.

model: a theoretical specification of the way in which a set of variables are proposed to be causally related.

multicollinearity: a problem encountered in multiple regression analysis where two or more predictor variables are highly correlated with one another so that it is impossible to disaggregate the unique effects of these variables. The effect of multicollinearity is to produce inflated and unreliable R^2 coefficients.

multilevel classification scheme: coding schemes in which coding and analysis can proceed at various levels of generality or detail. The higher levels of classification are broad categories while lower levels of the classification break each of the broad, higher level categories into more detailed categories.

multiple choice: question format in which respondents are provided with a set of alternative responses from which they are required to select one response.

multiple dichotomy coding: where respondents can select more than one response to a question, one way of coding all their answers is to treat each possible response as a separate variable and to give each of these variables two codes: one to indicate that this response was not selected and the other to indicate that it was selected.

multiple regression: regression analysis in which there is one dependent variable and two or more independent variables.

multiple response coding: a method of coding questions where respondents can provide more than one answer. It involves determining the maximum number of responses given by any respondent and creating that many variables. Each variable will have identical categories and codes to cover the range of responses to the question. Each respondent's responses will be coded to these variables. If a respondent provides only one response then only one variable will be used (they will receive missing value codes on the others). If a person provides three responses then three of the new variables will be used to encapsulate these responses.

multiple response questions: a question to which a respondent may provide more than one answer.

multistage sampling: a sample involving a series of sequential samples. For example, a sample of school children might be obtained by first obtaining a sample of cities, then of schools within the selected cities and then of children within the selected schools. This is a useful method of sampling where a sampling frame of the final sample elements is unavailable.

multivariate analysis: analysis in which the simultaneous relationships of three or more variables are examined.

negative kurtosis: a distribution of an interval-level variable that has a flatter profile than a normal distribution has negative kurtosis (platykurtic).

negative relationship: a relationship in which an increase in one variable tends to produce a decrease in the other variable.

negative skewness: a non-symmetrical distribution of an interval-level variable in which cases are clustered towards the high end of the distribution with a 'tail' of cases pointing to the low (negative) end of the distribution.

no harm to participants: an ethical principle in research involving human subjects that requires that participants are not in danger of any harm.

nominal definition: the theoretical definition of a concept. This is often an abstract definition that needs to be translated to a precise working definition before measures of the concept can be developed.

nominal-level variable: a variable in which the categories cannot be ranked or the intervals between categories quantified.

nomothetic: explanation that focuses on the impact of particular factors on a class of cases. Normally results in partial explanations.

non-probability sample: a form of sampling in which cases are selected on a basis *other than* the random selection criteria required by probability theory.

non-response bias: bias introduced into a sample by people who either refuse to participate in the study or to answer particular questions being systematically different from those who do respond.

***ntile/ntile* ranking:** placing cases into ranked categories according to where their score falls in an ordered set of scores. The number of ranked categories can be anything from two or more. Each category will contain the same percentage of cases. The number of categories depends on the percentage of cases to be placed in each category. Quartile ranking involves four categories each with 25 per cent of cases, decile ranking results in ten categories each with 10 per cent of cases, percentile ranking will have 100 categories each with one per cent of cases.

null hypothesis: a hypothesis that states that there is *no* relationship between two variables in the population from which the sample is drawn. A null hypothesis is used in statistical inference where we begin with the assumption of no relationship and seek, via tests of statistical significance, to *reject* it. If we can reject the null hypothesis we assume a real relationship in the population.

one-sample T-test: a statistical method to test the null hypothesis that the sample mean does not differ from a known population mean any more than would be expected by sampling error.

open-ended question: a question response format in which respondents formulate their own responses rather than selecting from a set of predetermined responses.

operational definition: where a concept has been translated into a set of indicators, the indicators and the decisions about how to classify individuals provide the operational definition of the concept. For example, we might use education, occupation and income to operationalise social class and then specify the specific criteria to classify people into particular social classes.

operationalisation: the process of translating abstract concepts into operational definitions.

ordinal-level variable: a variable in which the categories can be ranked but for which there is no meaningful numeric interval between categories.

pairwise deletion: a method of handling cases in analysis in which some variables have missing values. Pairwise deletion involves dropping from the analysis only cases that have missing values on any two variables being analysed at any given point. In a correlation matrix a case will be dropped when data has missing data on either of the two variables for which a given correlation is computed. However when another correlation is computed in the matrix each case will be re-evaluated for missing values on *those* two variables. Unlike listwise deletion, the pairwise method is a non-cumulative method of dropping cases.

PAPI: paper and pencil survey. The traditional method of administering questionnaires where either the respondent or the interviewer fills in answers on a paper questionnaire. PAPI interviews are to be distinguished from computer-assisted interviews or questionnaires.

partial correlation: the strength of a relationship between two variables in which the influence of at least one other variable has been removed (controlled).

partial gamma: a gamma correlation between two variables with the influence of a third or additional variable controlled.

path analysis: a form of multivariate analysis using multiple correlation and multiple regression which enables the analysis of direct and indirect relationships between the variables in the model. The relationships between the variables (paths) are represented diagrammatically and the importance of each path is represented by path coefficients (beta weights).

path coefficient: a standardised regression coefficient indicating the importance of a direct path between two variables in a path model with the influence of prior variables controlled.

Pearson's correlation: a symmetric measure of linear correlation between two interval-level variables that indicates the strength and direction of a relationship. When squared it has a PRE interpretation that indicates the percentage of variance in one variable explained by the other.

phi: a chi-square based correlation coefficient for two dichotomous variables.

piping: the importation of information supplied in earlier sections of a questionnaire into the wording and routing of later questions.

population: a precisely defined set of elements from which a sample is drawn.

positive kurtosis: a distribution of an interval-level variable that has a more peaked profile than a normal distribution has positive kurtosis (leptokurtic).

positive relationship: a relationship in which a change in one variable tends to produce a change in the other variable in the same direction.

positive skewness: a non-symmetrical distribution of an interval-level variable in which cases are clustered towards the low end of the distribution with a 'tail' of cases pointing to the high (positive) end of the distribution.

post hoc comparison: the pair-by-pair comparison of means of the dependent variable when the independent variable has three or more groups. The analysis identifies which pairs of means exhibit statistically significant differences in means. Particularly useful when an F-test indicates that there are differences between a set of means.

postcoding: coding questions after the collection of responses.

PRE measure: a type of correlation coefficient that indicates the proportion of variance in the dependent variable that is due to variation in the independent variable.

precoding: providing codes for question responses prior to the collection of data.

prestige bias: a form of bias introduced into question wording by connecting a particular response or attitude with a prestigious person.

pre-test/pilot test: testing the questionnaire or other aspects of methodology on a trial sample so that the instrument and procedures can be finetuned.

privacy: the ethical principle in research involving human subjects of respecting a person's right to privacy.

probability sample: a form of sampling in which some form of random selection is used to select sample elements. Accordingly, every element in the population has a known probability of being included in the final sample.

purposive sample: a form of non-probability sample in which elements are selected for their presumed typicality.

quartile: the three levels that subdivide a frequency distribution into four equal parts. Twenty-five per cent of cases fall below the first quartile.

question discrimination: the capacity of a question to distinguish between cases where real differences in the item exist. A question with good discrimination will be sensitive to real differences.

quintile: the four levels that subdivide a frequency distribution into five equal parts. Twenty per cent of cases fall below the first quintile.

quota sample: a form of non-probability sampling in which elements are selected to fill quotas of elements with particular characteristics. The quotas are established so as to reflect the population in relation to the quota characteristics.

R: the multiple correlation coefficient that indicates the linear correlation between a set of interval-level (or dichotomous) variables and an interval-level dependent variable.

R^2: the squared multiple correlation coefficient. Indicates the proportion of variance in the dependent variable due to the linear effect of a set of interval-level (or dichotomous) independent variables.

r^2: the squared Pearson's bivariate correlation. Indicates the proportion of variance in the dependent variable due to the linear effect of variations in the independent variable.

random allocation: the method used in experimental designs to allocate cases to experimental and control groups to ensure pre-treatment comparability. Controls for an infinite set of external variables. Must be distinguished from random *sampling*.

random sample: a form of probability sample in which all population units have a known probability of selection. Random sampling enables the estimation of the likelihood of sample results reflecting population patterns.

rank–order correlation: correlation coefficients for variables where precise numeric scores are unavailable and cases are ranked instead. The correlation is based on comparing the similarity of ranks of cases across the two variables but does not take account of the 'distance' between cases that true numeric scores would provide.

ranking format: the question format requiring that respondents rank–order a set of alternatives rather than select only one alternative.

rating scale: the question format requiring that objects, groups, individuals etc be rated on a numeric rating such as a score out of ten or on a feeling thermometer.

RDD sampling: a method of obtaining a sample of telephone numbers by which telephone numbers are randomly generated using a set of rules. Avoids the bias of relying on incomplete telephone directories.

recoding: altering the initial codes given to a variable. Changes are made to reorder categories of a variable and to combine a number of initial categories into a single, broader category.

record: the row of data in a data file containing the codes of a single case.

reference category: the omitted category in dummy regression against which the regression coefficients of the dummy variables are compared.

regression: a method for describing the relationship between two or more interval-level variables. It estimates the impact of one variable on another (i.e. how much does the dependent variable change for each unit change of the independent variable?), evaluates the relative impact of various independent variables (beta weights) and predicts the value of the dependent variable under various conditions.

regression coefficient: a coefficient used in regression analysis that estimates how much the dependent variable changes for each unit change of the independent variable.

regression line: a straight line representing the best linear summary of the relationship between two interval-level variables. Also called the line of best fit, the regression line is like a mean except that it summarises a relationship between two variables while the mean summarises the distribution on a single variable.

reliability: a measure of the consistency with which people give the same response on different occasions assuming no change in the characteristic being measured. A consistent but false response is still reliable.

replication: a technical term used in elaboration analysis which is used to describe the pattern whereby the zero-order relationship remains after control variables have been introduced. Also means duplicating a set of results by means of an identical study.

representative: the extent to which the characteristics of a sample match those of the population from which the sample is drawn. Representativeness is best achieved by probability sampling.

response rate: the percentage of a sample from which information is successfully obtained. Response rates are calculated differently depending on the method of questionnaire administration.

reverse coding: reversing the direction of coding of an ordinal or interval-level variable. Usually required when scaling a set of variables where all variables must be coded in the same direction.

robust relationship: a zero-order relationship that persists after controlling for various test variables (see also replication).

rotation: a stage in factor analysis designed to help identify more clearly which variables load on which factors.

row percentage: the percentage in a cross-tabulation in which the cell frequency is converted to a percentage based on the number of cases in the row.

sample: a subset of a population. The method of obtaining a sample affects the extent to which sample results can be extrapolated to the population.

sample heterogeneity/heterogeneity: the extent to which the sample varies on a given characteristic.

sampling error: the extent, reflected by the standard error statistic, to which the sample differs from the population.

sampling fraction: the proportion of the population represented by the sample. If the sample is 5 per cent of the population, the sampling fraction is one in twenty. Except with small populations, the sampling fraction is unimportant.

sampling frame: the complete list of elements of the population from which a sample will be drawn.

scale: a composite measure where the individual measures are designed to tap the same underlying concept. The individual measures should be both logically and empirically related.

scale of axis: the units of measurement used in a graph.

scatterplot: a graph showing the relationship between two interval-level variables. The datapoints represent cases with specific values on each of the two variables. The scatter of datapoints in a scatterplot can be summarised by a regression line and by r^2.

Scheffé test: a conservative post-hoc comparison statistical test for assessing the statistical significance of differences between pairs of means.

secondary analysis: the re-analysis of data often for a different purpose from that for which the data were originally collected.

significance level of b (or B): the test of statistical significance for a regression coefficient. Tests the null hypothesis that b (or B) = 0.

significance tests: significance tests assess the probability that a statistical result in a sample could be due to sampling error alone.

simple random sample: a form of probability sampling in which each population element is assigned a number and a set of numbers which are selected from a table of random numbers. Population elements matching the selected numbers constitute the sample.

skewness: the extent to which scores on an interval-level variable are concentrated at either end of the distribution.

slope: the slope of the regression line. This is the regression coefficient and is the best estimate of the impact of X on Y for a unit change in X.

social desirability response set: the tendency of people to answer a set of questions in a socially approved manner rather than in a way that truly reflects their own views.

Somer's d: a correlation coefficient for two ordinal variables. Has both symmetric and asymmetric forms and detects only linear relationships.

spamming: broadcasting uninvited emails.

Spearman's rho: a correlation coefficient for ranked data. Similar to Pearson's r but can be used for non-normal distributions and for ordinal variables where cases can be ranked.

specification: see conditional relationships.

spurious relationship: a relationship in which two variables co-vary and may therefore appear to be causally related but in fact co-vary because they are both consequences of a third, extraneous variable. See also extraneous variable.

standard deviation: a measure of dispersion appropriate for interval-level variables.

standard error: the standard error is the variability of a sample statistic. The size of the standard error is affected by sample size and the variance of individual variables. In a random sample we can be 95 per cent confident that the population parameter will be within ±2 standard error units of the sample statistic.

standard error of the binomial: the standard error of a percentage figure where the sample is classified into two groups.

standard error of the mean: this enables the estimation of the range within which the population mean is likely to lie.

standardised classification scheme: a predetermined coding scheme applied uniformly to open-ended data.

standardised partial regression coefficient: the regression coefficient of X on Y controlling for the influence of other variables in the regression model. The coefficient is expressed in standard deviation units which enables the comparison of coefficients based on variables with different scales of measurement.

standardised scale: a scale in which each person's score on each variable is expressed in terms of the number of standard deviation units from the mean thereby adjusting for items with a varying number of categories and different distributions.

standardised scores: see z-scores.

standardised variable: a variable where the individual scores are expressed as z-scores or the number of standard deviation units above or below the mean.

standardisation: the conversion of raw scores to z-scores.

statistical control: holding the values of a variable constant while examining the relationship between two other variables. This removes any effect that the controlled variable might have on the relationship between the two variables being examined.

statistical generalisation: generalisation from a sample to a population based on the probability that the sample results are likely to reflect a pattern in the population. Such generalisation requires a random sample. Should be distinguished from generalisation based on replication of repeated experiments.

statistical independence: where two variables do not co-vary.

stratified sample: a probability sampling method where a stratifying variable is used to minimise sampling error in respect to the stratifying variable. Having selected a stratifying variable the sampling frame is divided into groups according to the category of the stratifying variable to which cases belong. A system-atic sample is drawn from each subgroup thus ensuring that each category of the stratifying variable (strata) is represented in their correct proportion in the final sample.

structured data set: a variable by case data grid in which the same information is collected for each case so that each case has a value on each variable.

substantive recoding: combining categories of a variable based on the extent to which the categories of the variables have characteristics in common.

summated scale: a scale formed by adding together scores for each sample member across a number of related variables.

symmetric coefficient: a coefficient that has the same value regardless of which variable is regarded as the dependent variable.

symmetrical distribution: a distribution in which the shape of the distribution is the same on both sides of the midpoint of the distribution. Applies to interval-level variables.

systematic sample: a form of probability sampling in which a sampling fraction is established (e.g. one in twenty) and then every twentieth (or whatever) case is selected for the sample.

test variables: see control variables.

testable proposition: a conceptual proposition in which the concepts have been operationalised.

theory: a set of interrelated conceptual causal propositions.

theory construction/building: the process of developing explanations on the basis of data and observations (see also inductive reasoning).

theory testing: deducing predictions from a theory and testing these against empirical observations. If the predictions hold, the theory is supported, but if they do not hold, the theory is revised or rejected.

total causal effect: the causal effect of one variable on another that includes both direct and indirect effects. The total causal effect can be calculated using path models by summing the direct and indirect path effects.

trichotomising: dividing a distribution into three groups each with a similar number of cases. The first group will be the third of cases with the lowest scores on the variable, the second group will be the middle third of cases while the final group will be the third of the sample with the highest scores.

T-test: a statistical test applied to test the null hypothesis that the difference between the means of two groups is zero. There are various forms of the T-test depending on sample type and similarity of variance on the dependent variable in the two groups.

type I error: where we reject the null hypothesis where in fact it is true in the population (i.e. there really is no relationship in the population). The chance of a type I error is higher if we use a less demanding cut-off point (critical value) such as 0.05 instead of 0.01.

type II error: where we accept the null hypothesis of no relationship or difference where in fact it is incorrect in the population (i.e. there really is a relationship in the population). The chance of a type II error is higher if we use a demanding cut-off point (critical value) such as 0.01 instead of 0.05.

undeclared pre-test: a pilot test where respondents are unaware that the test is a pilot test.

unidimensional scale: a scale that taps one and only one concept.

unit of analysis: the element about which data are collected. In surveys the unit of analysis is frequently the individual respondent but it equally might be a whole family or household or some other unit. In such cases we collect data that relate specifically to this different unit of analysis (e.g. household size, total household income, education of head of household).

univariate analysis: the analysis of a single variable.

unstandardised partial regression coefficient: the regression coefficient of X on Y controlling for the influence of other variables in the regression model. The coefficient is expressed in the original units of each variable. Where these variables are measured in different units the coefficients cannot readily be compared.

unweighted factor-based scale: a scale in which the variables to be included in the scale are identified using factor analysis. Variables with a factor loading above a given value (e.g. 0.3) are selected for the scale and the variables are simply summed to form a summated scale.

URL: uniform resource locator. The address of an internet site or page.

valid per cent: the valid percentage is reported in frequency tables and is calculated by computing the percentage of cases in a category based on the number of cases with non-missing values.

valid range check: a procedure used to clean data. The check involves ensuring that no values of the variable are outside the range of valid and designated missing values for the variable. The check does not identify miscoding within the valid range but only detects miscodes outside of the range.

validity: whether an indicator measures the concept that we say it does.

variable: a characteristic that has two or more categories or values but where a case belongs to only one category.

variable by case data grid: the form of structured data on which survey research is based. Rows represent cases (e.g. individuals) while columns represent variables. The conjunction of any particular row and column will contain the value of a particular variable for a particular case.

variance: a measure of dispersion appropriate for interval-level variables.

variation ratio: a measure of dispersion appropriate for nominal-level variables.

voluntary participation: an ethical principle required of research involving human subjects that requires that individuals agree to participate and are in no way coerced to participate.

web page survey: a survey in which individuals gain access to the questionnaire at a particular URL.

weighted factor-based scale: a scale in which the variables to be included in the scale are identified using factor analysis. Variables selected for inclusion in the scale are weighted according to the factor loading calculated during the factor analysis and then summed. Thus scores of a variable with a factor loading of 0.5 would be multiplied by 0.5. The scores of a variable with a factor loading of 0.75 would be multiplied by 0.75. The resulting weighted scores are then summed for each individual to give a scale score.

weighting: the procedure by which the contribution of an element is adjusted. Weighting can apply to scale items so that some items contribute more than others to a final scale score. Weighting can also be used to adjust samples so that the sample characteristics resemble those of the population. Sample weighting results in some individuals counting as less than one case while others may count as more than one case.

Yule's Q: a PRE-based correlation coefficient for two dichotomous variables. It is the 2×2 case of gamma.

zero-order relationships: a relationship between two variables without controlling for the effects of additional variables.

zero-order table: a cross-tabulation between two variables in which no other variables have been controlled.

z-score: the difference between an individual's score and the mean score of a distribution expressed in standard deviation units.

Bibliography

Australian Bureau of Statistics (1997) *Australian Standard Offence Classification*, Catalogue No. 1234.0, Canberra: Australian Government Publishing Service

——(2000) *Household Use of Information Technology, Australia, 1999*, Catalogue No. 8146.0, Canberra: Australian Government Publishing Service

Achen, C.H. (1982) 'Interpreting and Using Regression' Sage University Paper series on Quantitative Applications in the Social Sciences, 07-029 Beverly Hills: Sage

Acton, G.J., Irvin, B.L. and Hopkins, B.A. (1991) 'Theory-Testing Research: Building the Science' *Advances in Nursing Science* 14, 1 (Sept) 52–61

Agresti, A. and Finlay, B. (1986) *Statistical Methods for the Social Sciences* (2nd edn) London: Collier Macmillan

Alwin, D.F. (1997) 'Feeling Thermometers Versus 7-Point Scales: Which Are Better?' *Sociological Methods & Research* 25, 3 (Feb) 318–40

Arleck, P.L. and Settle, R.B. (1995) *The Survey Research Handbook: Guidelines and Strategies for Conducting a Survey* New York: McGraw-Hill

Babbie, E. (1995) *The Practice of Social Research* (7th edn) Belmont: Wadsworth

Barnes, J.A. (1979) *Who Should Know What? Social Science, Privacy and Ethics* Cambridge: Cambridge University Press

Bateson, N. (1984) *Data Construction in Social Surveys* London: George Allen & Unwin

Baumrind, D. (1964) 'Some Thoughts on Ethics in Research: After Reading Milgram's "Behavioural Study of Obedience"' *American Psychologist* 19: 421–23

Bearden, W.O., Netemeyer, R.G. and Mobley, M.F. (1993) *Handbook of Marketing Scales: Multi-Item Measures for Marketing and Consumer Behavior Research* London: Sage

Beere, C.A. (1990) *Gender Roles: A Handbook of Tests and Measures* New York: Greenwood Press

Bell, C. and Encel, S. (eds) (1978) *Inside the Whale* Sydney: Pergamon

Bell, C. and Newby, H. (eds) (1977) *Doing Sociological Research* London: George Allen & Unwin

Belson, W.A. (1981) *The Design and Understanding of Survey Questions* Aldershot: Gower

Berger, P.L. (1974) 'Some Second Thoughts on Substantive Versus Functional Definitions of Religion' *Journal for the Scientific Study of Religion* 13: 125–33

Berry, W.D. and Feldman, S. (1985) 'Multiple Regression in Practice' Sage University Paper series on Quantitative Applications in the Social Sciences, 07-050, Beverly Hills: Sage

Biderman, A.D. and Drury, T. (eds) (1976) *Working Groups on Indicators of the Quality of Employment: Measuring Work Quality for Social Reporting* Beverly Hills: Sage

Blalock, H.M. (1972) *Social Statistics* (2nd edn) New York: McGraw-Hill

Blumer, H. (1934) 'Science Without Concepts' *American Journal of Sociology* 36, 515–33

——(1954) 'What is Wrong with Social Theory?' *American Sociological Review* 19: 3–10

——(1956) 'Sociological Analysis and the Variable' *American Sociological Review* 21: 683–90

Bogen, K. (1996) 'The Effect of Questionnaire Length on Response Rates—a Review of the Literature' US Census Bureau www.census.gov/srd/papers/pdf/kb9601.pdf

Bonjean, C., Hill, R.J. and McLemore, S.D. (1967) *Sociological Measurement: An Inventory of Scales and Indices* San Francisco: Chandler

Boruch, R.F. and Cecil, J.S. (1979) *Assuring the Confidentiality of Social Research Data* Philadelphia: University of Pennsylvania Press

Bourdieu, P. and Wacquant, L. (1992) *An Invitation to Reflexive Sociology* Chicago: University of Chicago Press

Bowling, A. (1997) *Measuring Health: A Review of Quality of Life Measurement Scales* (2nd edn) Buckingham: Philadelphia, Open University Press

Bradburn, N.M. (1992) 'Presidential Address: A Response to the Non-Response Problem' *Public Opinion Quarterly* 56: 391–7

Bradburn, N.M. and Sudman, S. (1979) *Improving Interview Method and Questionnaire Design* San Francisco: Jossey-Bass

Bradburn, N.M., Sudman, S. and Blair, E. (1978) 'Question Threat Response Bias' *Public Opinion Quarterly* 42: 221–34

Brodsky, S., O'Neal and Smitherton (1983) *Handbook of Scales for Research in Crime* New York: Plenum

Bruner, G.C. and Hensel, P.J. (1993) *Marketing Scales Handbook, a Compilation of Multi-Item Measures* Chicago: American Marketing Association

Bullen, P. and Onyx, J. (1998) 'Measuring Social Capital in Five Communities in NSW', Management Alternatives Pty Ltd www.mapl.com.au/A13.htm

Burke, P. (ed.) (1973) *A New Kind of History: From the Writings of Febvre* London: Routledge and Kegan Paul

Burgess, R.G. (ed.) (1986) *Key Variables in Social Investigation* Routledge: London

Campbell, D.T. (1989) 'Foreword', in Yin, R.K. (ed.), *Case Study Research: Design and Methods* (Revised Edition) Beverly Hills and London: Sage Publications

Campbell, D.T. and Stanley, J.C. (1963) *Experimental and Quasi-Experimental Designs for Research* Chicago: Rand McNally

Carmines, E.G. and Zeller, R.A. (1979) 'Reliability and Validity Assessment', Sage University Paper series on Quantitative Applications in the Social Sciences, 07-017, Beverly Hills: Sage

Carr-Hill, R.A. (1984) 'Radicalising Survey Methodology' *Quality and Quantity* 18, 3, 275–92

Chavetz, J. (1978) *A Primer on the Construction and Testing of Theories in Sociology* Itasca, Illinois: Peacock

Cho, H. and LaRose, R. (1999) 'Privacy Issues in Internet Surveys' *Social Science Computer Review* 17, 4, 421–34

Chun, K.T., Cobb, S. and French, J.P. (1975) *Measures for Psychological Assessment: A Guide to 3,000 Original Sources and Their Applications* Michigan: Institute for Social Research, University of Michigan

Church, A.H. (1993) 'Estimating the Effect of Incentives on Mail Survey Response Rates: A Meta-Analysis' *Public Opinion Quarterly* 57: 62–79

Cohen, J. (1988) *Statistical Power Analysis for the Behavioral Sciences* (2nd edn) New Jersey: Lawrence Erlbaum

Cohen, L. and Holliday, M. (1982) *Statistics for Social Scientists* London: Harper & Row

Comrey, A.L., Backer, T.E. and Glaser, E.M. (1973) *A Sourcebook for Mental Health Measures* Los Angeles: Human Interaction Research Institute

Converse, J.M. and Presser, S. (1986) 'Survey Questions: Handcrafting the Standardized Questionnaire', Sage University Paper series on Quantitative Applications in the Social Sciences, 07-063, Beverly Hills: Sage

Converse, P.E., Watson, J.D., Hoag, W.J. and McGee, W.H. III (eds) (1980) *American Social Attitudes Data Sourcebook 1947–1978* Cambridge: Harvard University Press

Cooper, H.M. (1985) 'Literature Searching Strategies of Integrative Research Reviewers', *American Psychologist*, 40, 11, 1267–69

——(1998) *Synthesizing Research: A Guide for Literature Reviews* (3rd edn) London: Sage Publications

Coulter, P.B. (1989) *Measuring Inequality: A Methodological Handbook* Boulder: Westview Press

Couper, M.P. (2000) 'Web Surveys: A Review of Issues and Approaches' *Public Opinion Quarterly* 64: 464–94

Craig, G., Corden, A. and Thornton, P. (2000) 'Safety in Social Research' *Social Research Update*, 29, www.soc.surrey.ac.uk/sru/SRU29.html

Crespi, I. (1998) 'Ethical Considerations When Establishing Survey Standards' *International Journal of Public Opinion Research* 10, 1, 75–82

Curtice, J. and Sparrow, N. (1997) 'How Accurate Are Traditional Quota Opinion Polls?' *Journal of the Market Research Society* 39, 3, 433–48

Dale, A., Arber, S. and Proctor, M. (1988) *Doing Secondary Analysis* London: Unwin Hyman

Davis, J.A. (1968) 'Tabular Presentation' in D.L. Sills (ed.) *International Encyclopaedia of the Social Sciences* 15, New York: Macmillan and Free Press

——(1971) *Elementary Survey Analysis* Englewood Cliffs: Prentice Hall

——(1985) 'The Logic of Causal Order' Sage University Paper series on Quantitative Applications in the Social Sciences, 07-055, Beverly Hills: Sage

de Leeuw, E. and Collins, M. (1997) 'Data Collection Methods and Survey Quality: An Overview' in L. Lyberg, P. Biemer and M. Collins (eds) *Survey Measurement and Process Quality* New York: Wiley, pp. 199–220 de Vaus, D.A. (2001) *Research Design in Social Research* London: Sage

de Vaus, D. and McAllister, I. (1987) 'Gender Differences in Religion: A Test of Structural Location Theory' *American Sociological Review* 52: 472–81

Denzin, N.K. (1978) *The Research Act* (2nd edn) New York: McGraw Hill

Diener, E. and Suh, E. (1997) 'Measuring Quality of Life: Economic, Social, and Subjective Indicators' *Social Indicators Research* 40, 1–2, 189–216

Dillman, D.A. (1978) *Mail and Telephone Surveys: The Total Design Method* New York: Wiley

——(2000) *Mail and Internet Surveys: The Total Design Method* New York: Wiley

Donsbach, W. (1997) 'Survey Research at the End of the Twentieth Century: Theses and Antitheses' *International Journal of Public Opinion Research* 9, 1, 17–28

Downey, R.G. and King, C.V. (1998) 'Missing Data in Likert Ratings: A Comparison of Replacement Methods' *Journal of General Psychology* 125, 2, 175–91

Dubin, R. (1969) *Theory Building* New York: Free Press

Dunn-Rankin, P. (1983) *Scaling Methods* Hillsdale: Erlbaum

Durkheim, E. (1970) *Suicide* London: Routledge and Kegan Paul

Edwards, A.L. (1957) *Techniques of Attitude Scale Construction* New York: Appleton-Century-Crofts

Ehrenberg, A.S.C. (1975) *Data Reduction: Analysing and Interpreting Statistical Data* London: Wiley

Fabozzi, F.J. and Greenfield, H.I. (1984) *The Handbook of Economic and Financial Measures* Homewood: Dow Jones-Irwin

Fadden, R.R. and Beauchamp, T.L. (1986) *A History and Theory of Informed Consent* New York: Oxford University Press

Ferneau, E.W. (1973) *Drug Abuse Research Instrument Inventory* Cambridge: Social Systems Analysis

Fielding, J. (1995) 'Coding and Managing Data' in Gilbert, N. (ed.) *Researching Social Life* London: Sage

Fink, A. (1995) *How to Sample in Surveys* Thousand Oaks: Sage

——(1998) *Conducting Research Literature Reviews: From Paper to the Internet* London: Sage

Fischer, J. and Corcoran, K.J. (1994a) *Measures for Clinical Practice: A Source Book. Volume 1—Couples, Families and Children* (2nd edn) New York: Free Press

——(1994b) *Measures for Clinical Practice: A Source Book. Volume 2—Adults* (2nd edn) New York: Free Press

Foddy, W.H. (1993) *Constructing Questions for Interviews and Questionnaires* Melbourne: Cambridge University Press

——(1996) 'The In-Depth Testing of Survey Questions: A Critical Appraisal of Methods' *Quality & Quantity* 30, 4, 361–70

Fowler, F.J. (1988) *Survey Research Methods* (rev. edn) Beverly Hills: Sage

Frankel, M.R. and Frankel, L.R. (1987) 'Fifty Years of Survey Sampling in the United States' *Public Opinion Quarterly* 51, 4, 127–S138

Freeman, L.C. (1965) *Elementary Applied Statistics* New York: Wiley

Fukuyama, F. (1995) *Trust: The Social Virtues and the Creation of Prosperity* New York: Free Press

Gallagher, J.J. and Anderson, C.W. (1999) 'Editorial: Designing, Implementing, and Reporting Research. The Significant Role of Literature Review' *Journal of Research in Science Teaching* 36, 6, 619–21

Gardiner, M.J. and Altman, D.G. (1989) *Statistics with Confidence: Confidence Intervals and Statistical Guidelines* London: British Medical Journal

Gilbert, G.N. (1993) *Analyzing Tabular Data: Loglinear and Logistic Models for Social Researchers* London: UCL Press

Glaser, B.G. (1978) *Theoretical Sensibility* Mill Valley: Sociological Press

Glaser, B.G. and Strauss, A.L. (1967) *The Discovery of Grounded Theory* Chicago: Aldine

Glock, C.Y. and Stark, R. (1965) *Religion and Society in Tension* Chicago: Rand McNally

Gowers, E. (1962) *The Complete Plain Words* (2nd edn) Ringwood: Penguin

Greeley, A. (1996) 'In Defence of Surveys' *Society* 36, 4, 26–29

Green, B.F. (1954) 'Attitude Measurement' in G. Londzey (ed.) (1984) *Handbook of Social Psychology* Cambridge: Addison-Wesley

Groves, R.M. and Kahn, R.L. (1979) *Surveys by Telephone: A National Comparison with Personal Interviews* New York: Academic Press

Guildford, J.P. (1965) *Fundamental Statistics in Psychology and Education* (4th edn) International student edition, New York: McGraw-Hill

Hak, T. (1997) 'Coding Effects in Comparative Research on Definitions of Health: A Qualitative Validation Study' *European Journal of Public Health* 7, 4 (Dec) 364–72

Halfpenny, P. (1982) *Positivism and Sociology: Explaining Social Life* London: Allen & Unwin

Hardy, M.A. 'Regression with Dummy Variables' Sage University Paper series on Quantitative Applications in the Social Sciences, 07-093, Beverly Hills: Sage

Hellevik, O. (1984) *Introduction to Causal Analysis* London: George Allen & Unwin

Henkel, R.E. (1976) 'Tests of Significance' Sage University Paper series on Quantitative Applications in the Social Sciences, 07-004, Beverly Hills: Sage

Henry, G.T. (1990) *Practical Sampling* Newbury Park: Sage

——(1995) *Graphing Data: Techniques for Display and Analysis* Thousand Oaks: Sage Publications

Hertel, B. (1976) 'Minimizing Error Variance Introduced by Missing Data Routines in Survey Analysis' *Sociological Methods and Research* 4: 459–74

Hilderbrand, D.K., Laing, J.D. and Rosenthal, H. (1977) 'Analysis of Ordinal Data' Sage University Paper series on Quantitative Applications in the Social Sciences, 07-008, Beverly Hills: Sage

Hirschi, T. and Selvin, H. (1967) *Delinquency Research: An Appraisal of Analytic Methods* New York: Free Press

Hoinville, G., Jowell, R. and associates (1978) *Survey Research Practice* London: Heinemann

Homan, R. (1991) *The Ethics of Social Research* London: Longman

Homans, G. (1967) *The Nature of Social Science* New York: Harcourt Brace Jovanovich

Hosmer, D.W. and Lemeshow, S. (1989) *Applied Logistic Regression* New York: Wiley

Hox, J.J. (1991) 'The Effect of Interviewer and Respondent Characteristics on the Quality of Survey Data: A Multilevel Model' in P. Blemer, R. Graves and L. Lyberg (eds) *Measurement Errors in Surveys* New York: Wiley, pp. 439–61

Hox, J.J. and de Leeuw, E. (1994) 'A Comparison of Nonresponse in Mail, Telephone and Face-to-Face Surveys: Applying Multilevel Modeling to Meta-Analysis' *Quality and Quantity* 28: pp. 329–44

Huck, S.W. and Sandler, H.M. (1979) *Rival Hypotheses: Alternative Interpretations of Data Based Conclusions* New York: Harper & Row

Huff, D. (1954) *How to Lie With Statistics* London: Gollancz

Hyman, H. (1972) *Secondary Analysis of Sample Surveys* New York: Wiley

Johnson, A.G. (1977) *Social Statistics Without Tears* New York: McGraw-Hill

Johnson, O.G. (1976) *Tests and Measurements in Child Development: Handbook II,* San Francisco: Jossey-Bass

Kalton, G. (1983) 'Introduction to Survey Sampling' Sage University Paper series on Quantitative Applications in the Social Sciences, 07-035, Beverly Hills: Sage

——(1993) 'Sampling Considerations in Research on HIV Risk and Illness' in Ostrow, D.G. and Kessler, R.C. (eds) *Methodological Issues in Aids Behavioral Research. Aids Prevention and Mental Health* New York: Plenum

——(2000) 'Developments in Survey Research in the Past 25 Years' *Survey Methodology* 26, 1, 3–10

Kalton, G. and Anderson, D.W. (1986) 'Sampling Rare Populations' *Journal of the Royal Statistical Society Series A* 149, 1, 65-82

Kane, R. and Kane, R. (1981) *Assessing the Elderly: A Practical Guide to Measurement* Lexington: Lexington Books

Kaye, B.K. and Johnson, T.J. (1999) 'Research Methodology: Taming the Cyber Frontier-Techniques for Improving Online Surveys' *Social Science Computer Review*, 17, 3, 323–37

Kerlinger, F.N. (1979) *Behavioural Research: A Conceptual Approach* Chapter 4, New York: Holt, Rinehart & Winston, pp. 11–13

Kerlinger, F.N. and Pedhazur, E.J. (1973) *Multiple Regression in Behavioural Research* New York: Holt, Rinehart & Winston

Kiecolt, K.J. and Nathan, L. (1985) 'Secondary Analysis of Survey Data' Sage University Paper series on Quantitative Applications in the Social Sciences, 07-053, Beverly Hills: Sage

Kim, J. and Mueller, C.W. (1978a) 'Introduction to Factor Analysis: What it is and How to Do it' Sage University Paper series on Quantitative Applications in the Social Sciences, 07-013, Beverly Hills: Sage

——(1978b) 'Factor Analysis: Statistical Methods and Practical Issues' Sage University Paper series on Quantitative Applications in the Social Sciences, 07-0414, Beverly Hills: Sage

Kimmel, A. J. (1988) *Ethics and Values in Applied Social Research* Applied Social Research Methods Series, Vol 12. Beverly Hills: Sage

——(1996) *Ethical Issues in Behavioral Research: A Survey* Cambridge: Blackwell

Kish, L. (1949) 'A Procedure for Objective Respondent Selection Within a Household' *Journal of the American Statistical Association* 44: 380–87

——(1965) *Survey Sampling* New York: Wiley

Knapp, J. (1972) *An Omnibus of Measures Related to School-Based Attitudes* Princeton: Educational Testing Centre

Kuhn, T.S. (1964) *The Structure of Scientific Revolutions* Chicago: University of Chicago Press

Labovitz, S. (1970) 'The Nonutility of Significance Tests: The Significance of Tests of Significance Reconsidered' *Pacific Sociological Review* 13: 141–48

Larsen, R.J., Diener, E. and Emmons, R.A. (1985) 'An Evaluation of Subjective Well-Being Measures' *Social Indicators Research* 17, 1, 1–17

Larson, J.S. (1996) 'The World Health Organization's Definition of Health: Social Versus Spiritual Health' *Social Indicators Research* 38, 2, 181–92

Lavrakas, Paul (1993) *Telephone Survey Methods: Sampling Selection and Supervision* (2nd edn) Beverly Hills: Sage

Lazarsfeld, P.F., Pasanella, A. and Rosenberg, M. (eds) (1955) *The Language of Social Research* Glencoe: Free Press

——(eds) (1972) *Continuities in the Language of Social Research* New York: Free Press

Lester, D. (1997) 'Operationalizing "Modernization" A Response to Stack's Comments' *Archives of Suicide Research* 3, 2, 137–38

Lewis-Beck, M.S. (1980) 'Applied Regression: An Introduction' Sage University Paper series on Quantitative

Applications in the Social Sciences, 07-022, Beverly Hills: Sage

Lewontin, R.C. (1996) 'In Defense of Science' *Society* 33, 4(222) 29–30

Liebetrau, A.M. (1983) 'Measures of Association' Sage University Paper series on Quantitative Applications in the Social Sciences, 07-032, Beverly Hills: Sage

Locke, L.F., Spirduso, W.W. and Silverman, S.J. (1999) *Proposals That Work: A Guide for Planning Dissertations and Grant Proposals* (4th edn) London: Sage Publications

Loether, H.J. and McTavish, D.G. (1974a) *Descriptive Statistics for Sociologists* Boston: Allyn & Bacon

——(1974b) *Inferential Statistics for Sociologists* Boston: Allyn & Bacon

Lyberg, L., Biemer, P. and Collins, M. (eds) (1997) *Survey Measurement and Process Quality* New York: Wiley

McDowell, I. and Newell, C. (1996) *Measuring Health: A Guide to Rating Scales and Questionnaires* (2nd edn) New York: Oxford University Press

McIver, J.P. and Carmines, E.G. (1981) 'Unidimensional Scaling' Sage University Paper series on Quantitative Applications in the Social Sciences, 07-024, Beverly Hills: Sage

McQuiston, C.M. and Campbell, J.C. (1997) 'Theoretical Substruction: A Guide for Theory Testing Research' *Nursing Science Quarterly* 10, 3 117–23

Madge, J. (1965) *The Tools of Social Science* New York: Doubleday Anchor

Maisel, R. and Hodges Persell, C. (1996) *How Sampling Works* Thousand Oaks: Pine Forge Press

Mangen, D.J. and Peterson, W. (1984) *Research Instruments in Social Gerontology* Minneapolis: University of Minnesota

Market Research Society (1983) 'The Guide to Good Coding Practice' Brighton: Market Research Society

Marsh, C. (1982) *The Survey Method: The Contribution of Surveys to Sociological Explanation* London: George Allen & Unwin

——(1988) *Exploring Data: An Introduction to Data Analysis for Social Sciences* Cambridge: Polity

Marsh, C. and Scarbrough, E. (1990) 'Testing Nine Hypotheses About Quota Sampling' *Journal of the Market Research Society* 32, 4, 485–506

Martin, E., McDuffee, D. and Presser, S. (1981) *Sourcebook of Harris National Surveys: Repeated Questions 1963–1976* Chapel Hill: Institute for Research in Social Science, University of North Carolina Press

Menard, S. (1991) 'Longitudinal Research' Sage University Paper series on Quantitative Applications in the Social Sciences, 07-076, Beverly Hills: Sage

Merton, R.K. (1968) *Social Theory and Social Structure* (2nd edn) New York: Free Press

Meuller, D.J. (1986) *Measuring Social Attitudes: A Handbook for Researchers and Practitioners* New York: Teachers College Press

Milgram, S. (1964) 'Issues in the Study of Obedience: A Reply to Baumrind' *American Psychologist* 19: 848–52

Mill, J.S. (1879) *A System of Logic* (10th edn) London: Longmans Green

Miller, D.C. (1991) *Handbook of Research Design and Social Measurement* (5th edn) Newbury Park: Sage

Miller, W.E., Miller, A.H. and Schneider, E.J. (1980) *American National Election Studies Data Sourcebook 1951–1978* Cambridge: Harvard University Press

Mills, C.W. (1959) *The Sociological Imagination* New York: Harper & Row

Misztral, B. (1996) *Trust in Modern Societies: The Search for the Bases of Social Order* Cambridge: Polity Press

Montgomery, A.C. and Crittenden, K.S. (1977) 'Improving Coding Reliability for Open-Ended Questions' *Public Opinion Quarterly* 41, 2, 235–43

Moser, C. and Kalton, G. (1971) *Survey Methods in Social Investigation* (2nd edn) London: Heinemann

Mueller, J.H., Schuessler, K.F. and Costner, H.L. (1977) *Statistical Reasoning in Sociology* (3rd edn) Boston: Houghton Mifflin

National Opinion Research Center (1990) *General Social Surveys 1972–1990: Cumulative Codebook* Chicago: NORC

Nie, N.H., Hull, C., Jenkins, J., Steinbrenner, K. and Bent, D. (1975) *SPSS; Statistical Package for the Social Sciences* (2nd edn) New York: McGraw-Hill

Norusis, M.J. (1983) *SPSSX: Introductory Statistics Guide* New York: McGraw-Hill

——(1985) *SPSSX: Advanced Statistics Guide* New York: McGraw-Hill

Oppenheim, A.N. (1968) *Questionnaire Design and Attitude Measurement* London: Heinemann

Ornstein, M. (1998) 'Pretesting and Data Collection' *Current Sociology* 46, 4, 49–73

Orwin, R.G. (1994) 'Evaluating Coding Decisions' in Cooper, H. and Hedges, L.V. (eds) *The Handbook of Research Synthesis* New York: Russell Sage Foundation

Oxford (1979) *Oxford Dictionary of Quotations* (3rd edn) Oxford: Oxford University Press

Pandey, M.D. and Nathwani, J.S. (1996) 'Measurement of Socio-Economic Inequality Using the Life-Quality Index' *Social Indicators Research* 39, 2 (Oct) 187–202

Parmenter, T.R. (1994) 'Quality of Life as a Concept and Measurable Entity' *Social Indicators Research* 33, 1–3, 9–46

Parsons, T. (1949) 'The Social Structure of the Family' in R.N. Ashen (ed.) *The Family; Its Function and Destiny* New York: Harper

Payne, S. (1951) *The Art of Asking Questions* Princeton: Princeton University Press

Plake, B.S. and Impara, J.C. (eds) (2001) *The Fourteenth Mental Measurements Yearbook* Lincoln: Buros Institute

Presser, S. and Blair, J. (1994) 'Survey Pretesting: Do Different Methods Produce Different Results?' *Sociological Methodology* 24, 73–104

Presser, S. and Schuman, H. (1980) 'The Measurement of the Middle Position' *Public Opinion Quarterly* 44: 70–85

Procter, M. (1995) 'Measuring Attitudes' in Gilbert, N. (ed.) *Researching Social Life* London: Sage

Putnam, R. (1993) *Making Democracy Work: Civic Traditions in Modern Italy* Princeton: Princeton University Press

Raphael, D., Renwick, R. and Brown, I. (1996) 'Quality of Life Indicators and Health: Current Status and Emerging Conceptions' *Social Indicators Research* 39, 1, 65–88

Reynolds, H.T. (1977) 'Analysis of Nominal Data' Sage University Paper series on Quantitative Applications in the Social Sciences, 07-007, Beverly Hills: Sage

Reynolds, N., Diamantopoulos, A. and Schlegelmilch, B. (1993) 'Pretesting in Questionnaire Design: A Review of the Literature and Suggestions for Further Research' *Journal of the Market Research Society* 35, 2, 171–82

Reynolds, P.D. (1979) *Ethical Dilemmas and Social Science Research* San Francisco: Jossey-Bass

Ritzer, George (ed.) (1974) *Social Realities: Dynamic Perspectives* Boston: Allyn & Bacon

Robinson, J.P., Athanasiou, R. and Head, K.B. (1969) *Measures of Occupational Attitudes and Occupational Characteristics* Ann Arbor: Institute for Social Research, University of Michigan

Robinson, J.P., Rusk, J. and Head, K. (1968) *Measures of Political Attitudes* Ann Arbor: Institute for Social Research, University of Michigan

Robinson, J.P., Shaver, P.R. and Wrightsman, L.S. (eds) (1991) *Measures of Personality and Social Psychological Attitudes* Academic Press: San Diego

Rogers, W. (1995) 'Analysis of Cross-Classified Data' in Grimm, L.G. and Yarnold, P.R. (eds) *Reading and Understanding Multivariate Statistics* Washington: American Psychological Association

Rose, G. (1982) *Deciphering Sociological Research* London: Macmillan

Rosenberg, M. (1968) *The Logic of Survey Analysis* New York: Basic Books

Rossi, P.H., Wright, J.D. and Anderson, A.B. (eds) (1983) *Handbook of Survey Research* Academic Press, New York

Runciman, W.G. (ed.) (1978) *Weber* Cambridge: Cambridge University Press

Schaefer, D.R. and Dillman, D.A. (1998) 'Development of a Standard E-mail Methodology: Results of an Experiment' *Public Opinion Quarterly*, 62, 3 (Fall), 378–97

Schmid, C.F. (1983) *Statistical Graphics*, New York: Wiley

Schmid, C.F. and Schmid, S.E. (1979) *Handbook of Graphic Presentation* (2nd edn) New York: Wiley

Schreiber, E.M. (1976) 'Dirty Data in Britain and the USA: The Reliability of "Invariant" Characteristics Reported in Surveys' *Public Opinion Quarterly* 39: 493–506

Schroeder, L.D., Sjoquist, D.L. and Stephan, P.E. (1986) 'Understanding Regression Analysis: An Introductory Guide' Sage University Paper series on Quantitative Applications in the Social Sciences, 07-057, Beverly Hills: Sage

Schuman, H. and Presser, S. (1981) *Questions and Answers in Attitude Surveys* New York: Academic Press

Schwarz, N., Hippler, H.J., Deutsch, B. and Strack, F. (1985) 'Response Scales: Effects of Category Range on Reported Behavior and Comparative Judgments' *Public Opinion Quarterly* 49, 3, 388–95

Seiber, J.E. (ed.) (1982) *The Ethics of Social Research: Surveys and Experiments* New York: Springer-Verlag

——(1992) *Planning Ethically Responsible Research: A Guide for Students and Internal Review Boards* Beverly Hills: Sage

Selvin, H. (1957) 'A Critique of Tests of Significance in Survey Research' *American Sociological Review* 22: 519–27

Shaw, M.E. and Wright, J.M. (1967) *Scales for the Measurement of Attitudes* New York: McGraw-Hill

Silva, P.D. and Stam, A. (1995) 'Discriminant Analysis' in Grimm, L.G. and Yarnold, P.R. (eds) *Reading and Understanding Multivariate Statistics* Washington: American Psychological Association

Singer, E. (1993) 'Informed Consent and Survey Response: A Summary of the Empirical Literature' *Journal of Official Statistics* 9, 2, 361–75

Singer, E. and Presser, S. (1989) *Survey Research Methods: A Reader* Chicago: University of Chicago Press

Singer, E., von Thurn, D.R. and Miller, E.R. (1995) 'Confidentiality Assurances and Response: A Quantitative Review of the Experimental Literature' *Public Opinion Quarterly* 59, 1, 66–77

Smith, T.W. (1989) 'The Hidden 25 Percent: An Analysis of Nonresponse in the 1980 General Social Survey' in E. Singer and S. Presser (eds) (1989) *Survey Research Methods: A Reader* Chicago: University of Chicago Press

Smith, T.W. (1995) 'Trends in Non-Response Rates' *International Journal of Public Opinion Research* 7: 157–71

Spector, P.E. (1981) 'Research Designs' Sage University paper series on Quantitative Applications in the Social Sciences, 07-023, Beverly Hills: Sage

——(1992) *Summated Rating Scale Construction: An Introduction* Newbury Park: Sage

Steeh, C.G. (1981) 'Trends in Non-Response Rates 1952–1979' *Public Opinion Quarterly* 45: 40–57

Stinchcombe, A. (1968) *Constructing Social Theories* New York: Harcourt, Brace Jovanovich

Stone, W. (2001) 'Measuring Social Capital' *Research Paper 24* Melbourne: Australian Institute of Family Studies

Stouffer, S.A. (1950) 'Some Observations on Study Design' *American Journal of Sociology* 55: 355–61

Strauss, A. (1978) *Negotiations: Varieties, Contexts, Processes and Social Order* San Francisco: Jossey-Bass

Strauss, A. and Corbin, J. (1994) 'Grounded Theory Methodology: An Overview', in Denzin, N. and Lincoln, Y. (eds) *Handbook of Qualitative Research* Thousand Oaks: Sage Publications

Strauss, M. (1969) *Family Measurement Techniques* Minneapolis: University of Minnesota Press

Strunk, W. Jr and White, E.G. (1972) *The Elements of Style* (2nd edn) New York: Macmillan

Sudman, S. (1976) *Applied Sampling* New York: Academic Press

Sudman, S. (1983) 'Applied Sampling', in Rossi, P.H., Wright, J.D. and Anderson, A.B. (eds) *Handbook of Survey Research* New York: Academic Press

Sudman, S. and Blair, E. (1999) 'Sampling in the Twenty-first Century' *Journal of the Academy of Marketing Science* 27, 2, 269–77

Sudman, S. and Bradburn, N.M. (1982) *Asking Questions: A Practical Guide to Questionnaire Design* San Francisco: Jossey-Bass

Tabachnick, B.G. and Fidell, L.S. (1983) *Using Multivariate Statistics* New York: Harper & Row

Touliatos, J., Perlmutter, B.F. and Strauss, M.A. (eds) (1990) *Handbook of Family Measurement Techniques* Newbury Park: Sage

Tufte, E.R. (1983) *The Visual Display of Quantitative Information* Cheshire: Graphics

Turner, C.F. and Martin, E. (eds) (1984) *Surveying Subjective Phenomena* (2 vols) New York: Russell Sage Foundation

van der Zouwen, J. and de Leeuw, E. (1990) 'The Relationship between Mode of Administration and Quality of Data in Survey Research' *Bulletin de Methodologie Sociologique* 29: 3–14

Wallace, W.L. (1971) *The Logic of Science in Sociology* Chicago: Aldine

Warwick, D.P. and Lininger, C.A. (1975) *The Sample Survey: Theory and Practice* New York: McGraw-Hill

Weinfurt, K.P. (1995) 'Multivariate Analysis of Variance' in Grimm, L.G. and Yarnold, P.R. (eds) *Reading and Understanding Multivariate Statistics* Washington: American Psychological Association

Willer, D. and Willer, J. (1974) *Systematic Empiricism: a Critique of Pseudo-science* Englewood Cliffs: Prentice Hall

Winter, I. (2000) 'Towards a Theorised Understanding of Social Capital' *Working Paper 21* Melbourne: Australian Institute of Family Studies

Wright, R.E. (1995) 'Logistic Regression' in Grimm, L.G. and Yarnold, P.R. (eds) *Reading and Understanding Multivariate Statistics* Washington: American Psychological Association.

Zeller, R.A. and Carmines, E.G. (1980) *Measurement in the Social Sciences* Cambridge: Cambridge University Press

Index